THE UNITING STATES

THE UNITING STATES

The Story of Statehood for the Fifty United States
Volume 1: Alabama to Kentucky

☆☆☆

Edited by
Benjamin F. Shearer

GREENWOOD PRESS
Westport, Connecticut • London

Library of Congress Cataloging-in-Publication Data

The uniting states: the story of statehood for the fifty United States/edited by
  Benjamin F. Shearer.
     p. cm.
   Includes bibliographical references and index.
    ISBN 0-313-33105-7 (v. 1 : alk. paper) — ISBN 0-313-33106-5 (v. 2 : alk. paper) —
   ISBN 0-313-33107-3 (v. 3 : alk. paper) — ISBN 0-313-32703-3 (set : alk. paper)
    1. Statehood (American politics). 2. U.S. states. I. Shearer, Benjamin F.
JK2408.U65 2004
320.473'049–dc22   2004042474

British Library Cataloguing in Publication Data is available.

Library of Congress Catalog Card Number: 2004042474
ISBN: 0-313-32703-3 (set)
      0-313-33105-7 (Vol. I)
      0-313-33106-5 (Vol. II)
      0-313-33107-3 (Vol. III)

First published in 2004

Greenwood Press, 88 Post Road West, Westport, CT 06881
An imprint of Greenwood Publishing Group, Inc.
www.greenwood.com

Printed in the United States of America

JUN 0 5 2005

Contents

List of Maps

Maps

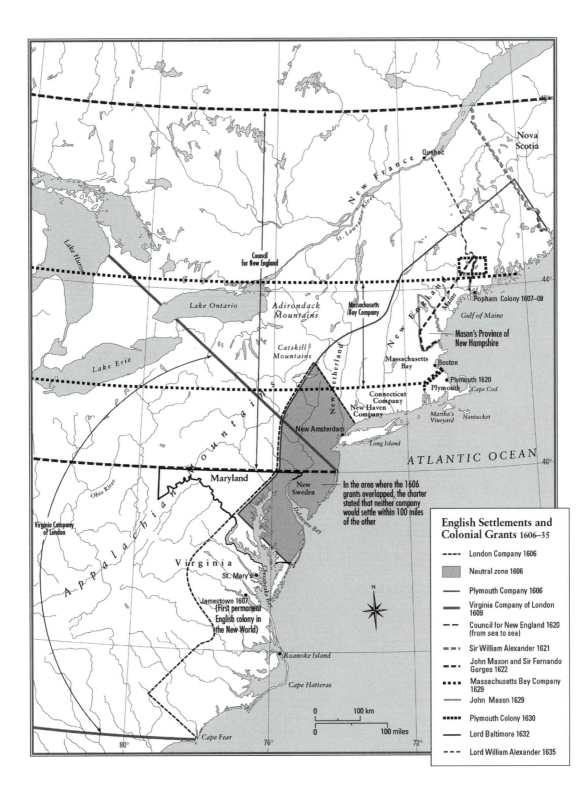

Quebec

Nova Scotia

Lake Huron

Lake Ontario

Lake Erie

St. Lawrence River

New France

Council for New England

Adirondack Mountains

Catskill Mountains

New Netherland

Massachusetts Bay Company

New England

Maine

Popham Colony 1607–08

Gulf of Maine

Mason's Province of New Hampshire

Massachusetts Bay

Boston

Plymouth 1620

Plymouth

Cape Cod

Connecticut Company

New Haven Company

Martha's Vineyard

Nantucket

New Amsterdam

Long Island

ATLANTIC OCEAN

Ohio River

Maryland

New Sweden

In the area where the 1606 grants overlapped, the charter stated that neither company would settle within 100 miles of the other

Appalachian Mountains

Virginia Company of London

Virginia

St. Mary's

Delaware Bay

Chesapeake Bay

Jamestown 1607 (First permanent English colony in the New World)

Roanoke Island

Cape Hatteras

N

0   100 km
0   100 miles

Cape Fear

80°   76°   72°

40°

44°

English Settlements and Colonial Grants 1606–35

- - - - London Company 1606

▓ Neutral zone 1606

—— Plymouth Company 1606

━━━ Virginia Company of London 1609

- - - Council for New England 1620 (from sea to sea)

-·-·- Sir William Alexander 1621

- - - John Mason and Sir Fernando Gorges 1622

····· Massachusetts Bay Company 1629

—— John Mason 1629

····· Plymouth Colony 1630

—— Lord Baltimore 1632

- - - Lord William Alexander 1635

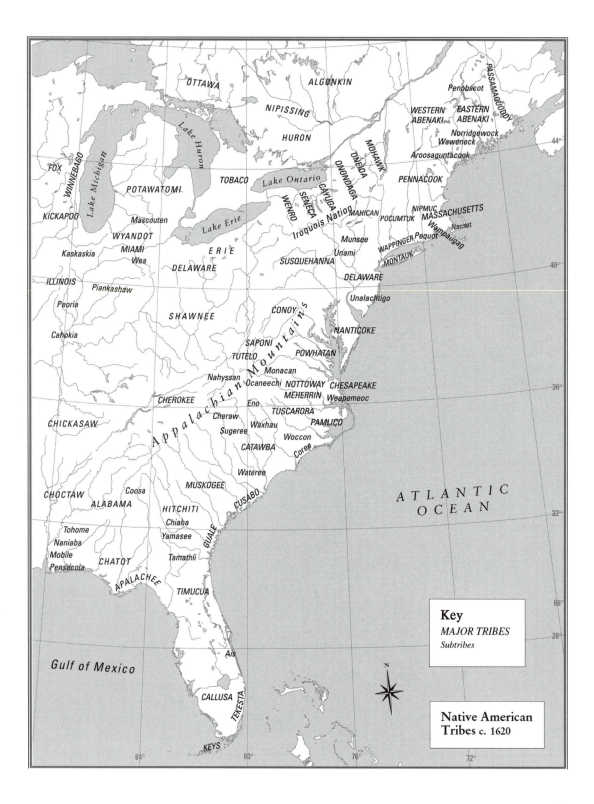

Key

MAJOR TRIBES

Subtribes

Native American Tribes c. 1620

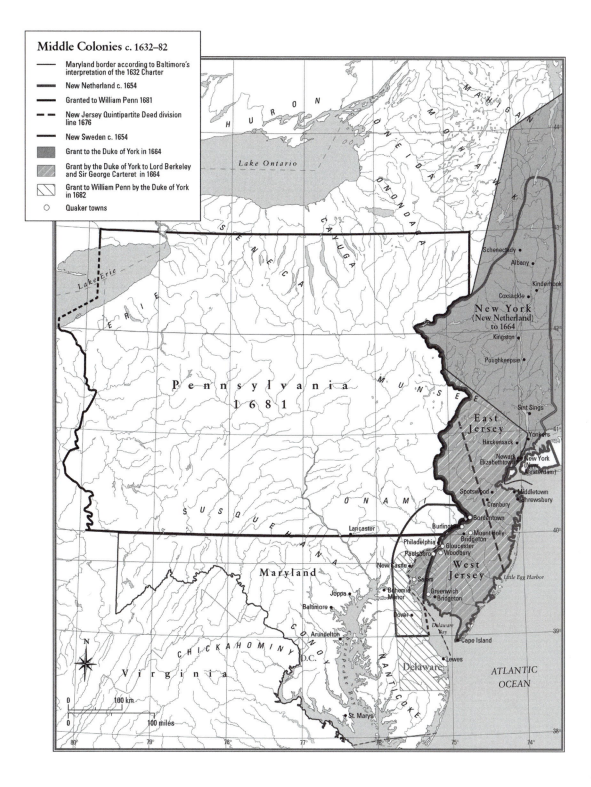

Middle Colonies c. 1632–82

——— Maryland border according to Baltimore's interpretation of the 1632 Charter

━━━ New Netherland c. 1654

━━━ Granted to William Penn 1681

▬ ▬ ▬ New Jersey Quintipartite Deed division line 1676

━━━ New Sweden c. 1654

▨ Grant to the Duke of York in 1664

▨ Grant by the Duke of York to Lord Berkeley and Sir George Carteret in 1664

▨ Grant to William Penn by the Duke of York in 1682

○ Quaker towns

HURON

MICHIGAN

MOHAWK

Lake Ontario

S E N E C A

O N E I D A

O N O N D A G A

C A Y U G A

E R I E

Lake Erie

Schenectady •
Albany •
Kinderhook •
Coxsackle •

New York
(New Netherland)
to 1664

Kingston •

Poughkeepsie •

M U N S E E

P e n n s y l v a n i a
1681

Sint Sings •

East
Jersey

Hackensack •   Yonkers

Newark ○ New York
Elizabethtown •   (New Amsterdam)

Spotswood •   Middletown
                   Shrewsbury
Cranbury •

S U S Q U E H A N A

O N A M I

Lancaster •

Bordentown ○

Burlington ○   Mount Holly ○
              Bridgeton ○
Philadelphia ● Gloucester ○
Paulsboro ○ Woodbury ○

New Castle ●   **West**
              Jersey
         Salem ○   Little Egg Harbor

Maryland

Joppa •   Bohemia
              Manor •   Greenwich ○
Baltimore •   Bridgeton •

Dover •

Arundelton •   Delaware
              Bay

D.C.   Cape Island ●

C O N O Y

C H I C K A H O M I N Y

N A N T I C O K E

Delaware   Lewes •

V i r g i n i a   **ATLANTIC**
                                       OCEAN

Chesapeake Bay

0 ___ 100 km
0 ___ 100 miles

St. Marys •

N

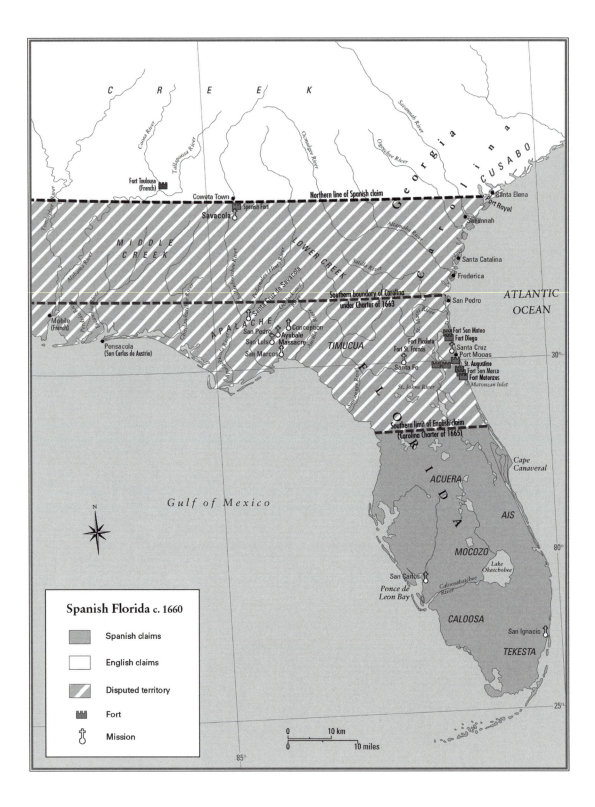

Spanish Florida c. 1660

Spanish claims

English claims

Disputed territory

Fort

Mission

C R E E K

Coosa River

Tallapoosa River

Fort Toulouse (French)

Coweta Town

Spanish Fort

Savacola

MIDDLE CREEK

Alabama River

Tombigbee River

Escambia River

Mobile (French)

Pensacola (San Carlos de Austria)

APALACHE

Santa Cruz de Savacola

San Pedro

Ayubale

Concepcion

San Luis

Massacre

San Marcos

Ochlockonee River

Flint River

Chattahoochee River

LOWER CREEK

Satilla River

Altamaha River

Ocmulgee River

Oconee River

Ogeechee River

Savannah River

Georgia

Carolina

CUSABO

Santa Elena

Port Royal

Savannah

Santa Catalina

Frederica

San Pedro

Southern boundary of Carolina under Charter of 1663

Northern line of Spanish claim

ATLANTIC OCEAN

TIMUCUA

Santa Fe

Fort Picolata

Fort St. Francis

Suwannee River

St. Johns River

Fort San Mateo

Fort Diego

Santa Cruz

Port Mooas

St. Augustine

Fort San Marco

Fort Matanzas

Matanzan Inlet

30°

Southern limit of English claim (Carolina Charter of 1665)

FLORIDA

ACUERA

Cape Canaveral

AIS

MOCOZO

Lake Okeechobee

80°

Gulf of Mexico

San Carlos

Ponce de Leon Bay

Caloosahatchee River

CALOOSA

San Ignacio

TEKESTA

25°

N

85°

| 0 | 10 km |
| 0 | 10 miles |

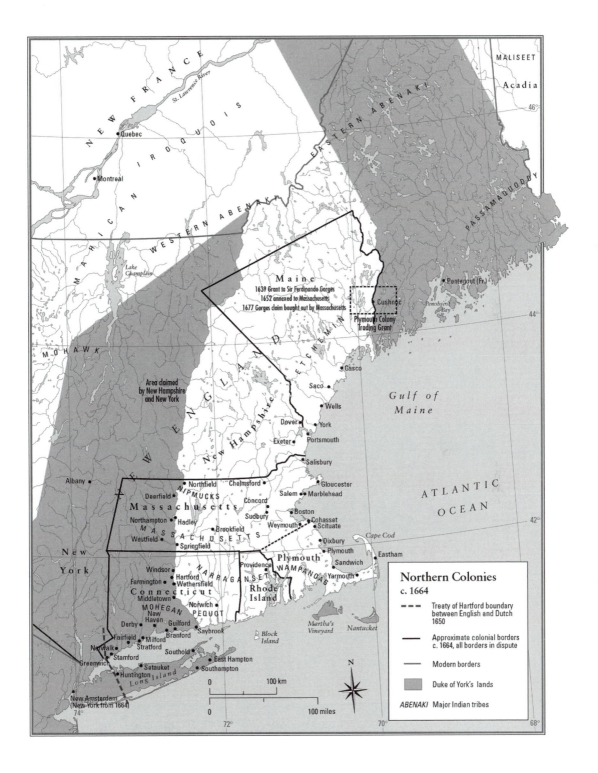

MALISEET

Acadia

NEW FRANCE

St. Lawrence River

Quebec

IROQUOIS

Montreal

EASTERN ABENAKI

46°

PASSAMAQUODDY

WESTERN ABENAKI

AMERICAN

MOHAWK

Lake Champlain

Maine
1639 Grant to Sir Ferdinando Gorges
1652 annexed to Massachusetts
1677 Gorges claim bought out by Massachusetts

Cushnoc

Plymouth Colony
Trading Grant

Pentagoet (Fr.)

Penobscot
Bay

44°

ETCHEMIN

NEW

ENGLAND

Gasco

Saco

Wells

Gulf of
Maine

Area claimed
by New Hampshire
and New York

New Hampshire

Dover

Exeter

York

Portsmouth

Salisbury

Albany

Northfield

Chelmsford

Gloucester

ATLANTIC

OCEAN

42°

Deerfield

NIPMUCKS

Concord

Salem Marblehead

Massachusetts

Northampton Hadley

Sudbury

Boston

MASS-
ACHUSETTS

Brookfield

Weymouth

Cohasset
Scituate

Westfield

Springfield

Dixbury

Plymouth

Cape Cod

Eastham

New
York

Windsor

Providence

Plymouth

Sandwich

WAMPANOAG

Yarmouth

Hartford

NARRAGANSETT

Farmington Wethersfield

Connecticut

Rhode
Island

Middletown

MOHEGAN

Norwich

New
Haven

PEQUOT

Derby

Guilford

Martha's
Vineyard

Nantucket

Fairfield

Branford

Milford

Saybrook

Block
Island

Stratford

Southold

Norwalk

Stamford

East Hampton

Greenwich

Setauket

Southampton

Huntington

Long Island

New Amsterdam
(New York from 1664)

74°

72°

70°

68°

N

0   100 km

0   100 miles

Northern Colonies
c. 1664

- - - Treaty of Hartford boundary
between English and Dutch
1650

——— Approximate colonial borders
c. 1664, all borders in dispute

——— Modern borders

▨ Duke of York's lands

ABENAKI Major Indian tribes

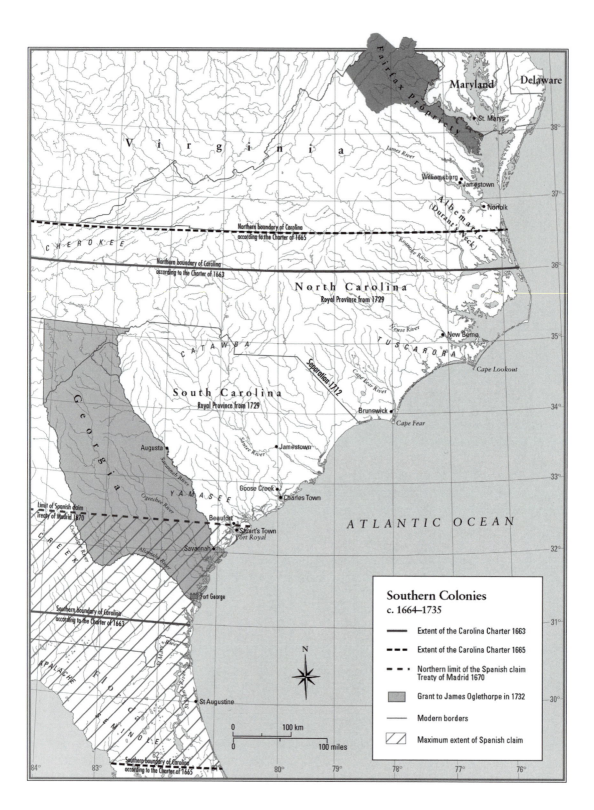

Fairfax Proprietary

Maryland   Delaware

● St. Marys

V i r g i n i a

James River

Williamsburg ● ● Jamestown

A l b e m a r l e
(Durant's Neck)

● Norfolk

Roanoke River

CHEROKEE

Northern boundary of Carolina
according to the Charter of 1665

Northern boundary of Carolina
according to the Charter of 1663

North Carolina
Royal Province from 1729

Neuse River   ● New Berne

C A T A W B A

T U S C A R O R A

Cape Lookout

Separation 1712

Cape Fear River

South Carolina
Royal Province from 1729

Brunswick ●

● Cape Fear

G e o r g i a   Y A M A S E E

Savannah River

Augusta ●

Santee River   ● Jamestown

Goose Creek ●

Ogeechee River   ● Charles Town

Limit of Spanish claim
Treaty of Madrid 1670

Beaufort ●

C R E E K   *Altamaha River*   ● Stuart's Town
                                  Fort Royal

Savannah ●

ATLANTIC OCEAN

Ocmulgee River   ● Fort George

Southern boundary of Carolina
according to the Charter of 1663

A P A L A C H E

R I O   *St. Marys River*

Suwannee River

● St. Augustine

N

S E M I N O L E

0   100 km

0   100 miles

Southern boundary of Carolina
according to the Charter of 1665

Southern Colonies
c. 1664–1735

——————   Extent of the Carolina Charter 1663

– – – – –   Extent of the Carolina Charter 1665

– — – —   Northern limit of the Spanish claim
            Treaty of Madrid 1670

▨   Grant to James Oglethorpe in 1732

————   Modern borders

▨   Maximum extent of Spanish claim

38°
37°
36°
35°
34°
33°
32°
31°
30°

84°   83°   82°   80°   79°   78°   77°   76°

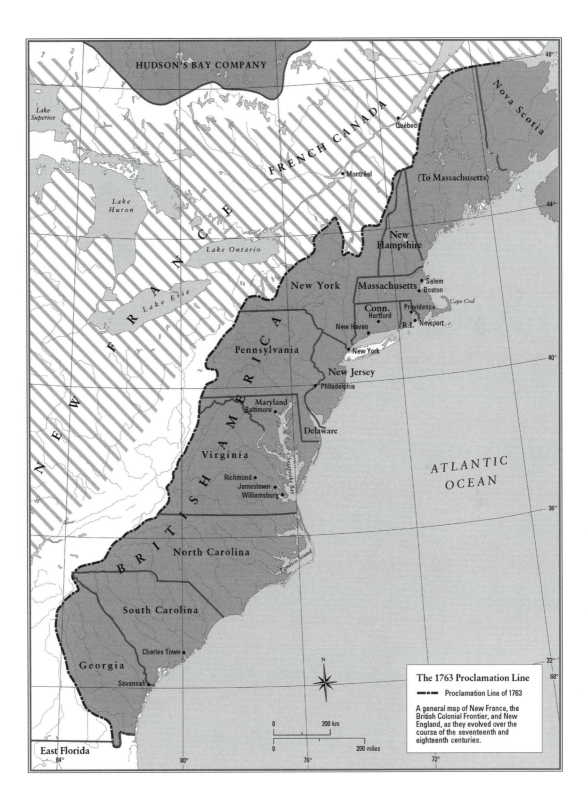

HUDSON'S BAY COMPANY

Lake Superior

Lake Huron

N E W

FRENCH CANADA

Lake Ontario

F R A N C E

Lake Erie

Québec

Montréal

Nova Scotia

(To Massachusetts)

New Hampshire

New York

Massachusetts
Salem
Boston

Conn.
Hartford
Providence
R.I.
Newport
Cape Cod

New Haven

Pennsylvania

New York

New Jersey

Philadelphia

Maryland
Baltimore

Delaware

Virginia

Richmond
Jamestown
Williamsburg

Chesapeake Bay

ATLANTIC OCEAN

B R I T I S H   A M E R I C A

North Carolina

Pamlico Sound

South Carolina

Charles Town

Georgia

Savannah

East Florida

84°   80°   76°   72°

48°

44°

40°

36°

32°
68°

N

0   200 km

0   200 miles

The 1763 Proclamation Line

- - - - Proclamation Line of 1763

A general map of New France, the British Colonial Frontier, and New England, as they evolved over the course of the seventeenth and eighteenth centuries.

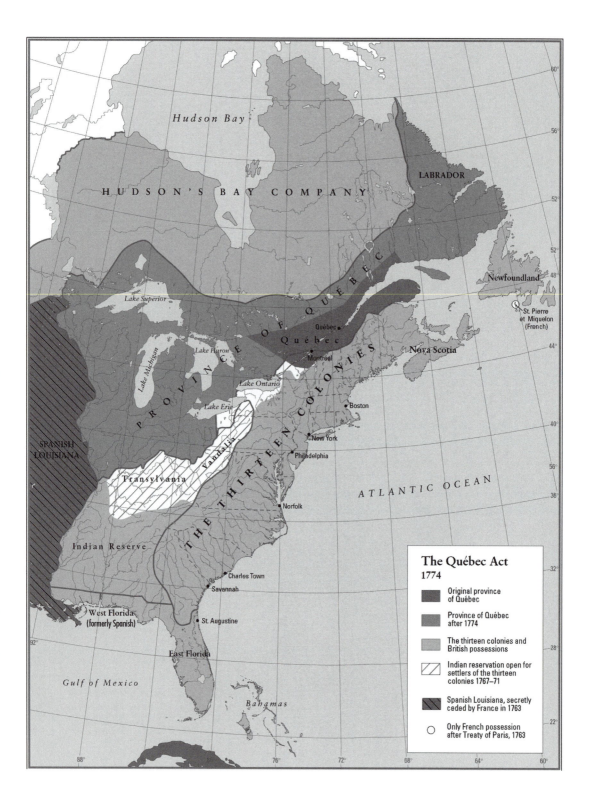

Hudson Bay

HUDSON'S BAY COMPANY

LABRADOR

Newfoundland

St. Pierre
et Miquelon
(French)

Lake Superior

PROVINCE OF QUÉBEC

Québec
Québec

Lake Huron

Montréal

Nova Scotia

Lake Michigan

Lake Ontario

Lake Erie

Boston

THE THIRTEEN COLONIES

New York

Vandalia

Philadelphia

SPANISH
LOUISIANA

Transylvania

ATLANTIC OCEAN

Norfolk

Indian Reserve

Charles Town

Savannah

West Florida
(formerly Spanish)

St. Augustine

East Florida

Gulf of Mexico

Bahamas

The Québec Act
1774

- Original province of Québec
- Province of Québec after 1774
- The thirteen colonies and British possessions
- Indian reservation open for settlers of the thirteen colonies 1767–71
- Spanish Louisiana, secretly ceded by France in 1763
- ○ Only French possession after Treaty of Paris, 1763

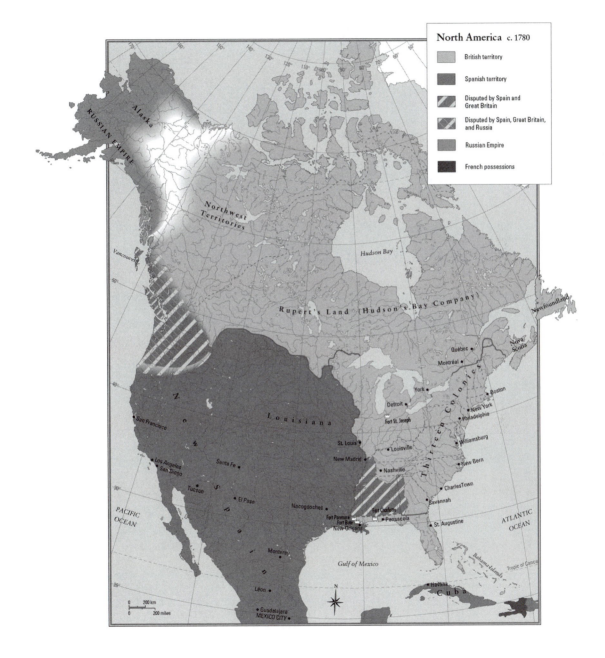

North America c. 1780

- British territory
- Spanish territory
- Disputed by Spain and Great Britain
- Disputed by Spain, Great Britain, and Russia
- Russian Empire
- French possessions

RUSSIAN EMPIRE

Alaska

Northwest Territories

Vancouver

Hudson Bay

Rupert's Land (Hudson's Bay Company)

Newfoundland

Nova Scotia

Québec

Montréal

York

Boston

Detroit

New York

Philadelphia

San Francisco

Louisiana

Thirteen Colonies

Williamsburg

Los Angeles
San Diego

Santa Fe

St. Louis

New Madrid

Louisville

New Bern

Tucson

Nashville

CharlesTown

El Paso

Nacogdoches

Fort Panmure
Fort Bute
New Orleans

Fort Charlotte

Pensacola

Savannah

St. Augustine

ATLANTIC OCEAN

PACIFIC OCEAN

New Spain

Monterey

Gulf of Mexico

Bahama Islands

Tropic of Cancer

Havana

Cuba

Léon

Guadalajara
MEXICO CITY

0   200 km
0   200 miles

N

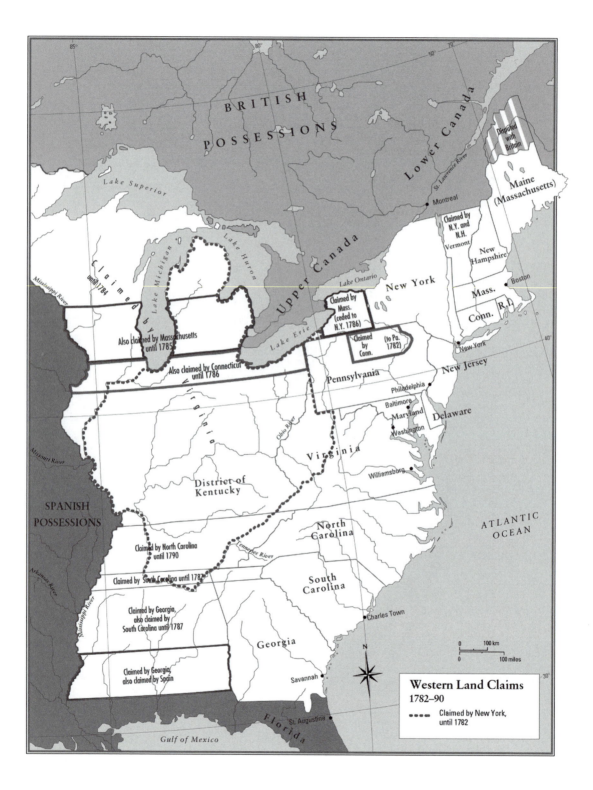

BRITISH
POSSESSIONS

Lower Canada

Lake Superior

Claimed
until 1784

Also claimed by Massachusetts
until 1785

Also claimed by Connecticut
until 1786

Lake Michigan

Lake Huron

Upper Canada

Lake Erie

Lake Ontario

Montreal

St. Lawrence River

Disputed
with
Britain

Maine
(Massachusetts)

Claimed by
N.Y. and
N.H.

Vermont

New
Hampshire

Boston

New York

Mass.

Conn.

R.I.

Claimed by
Mass.
(ceded to
N.Y. 1786)

Claimed
by
Conn.

(to Pa.
1782)

New York

New Jersey

Pennsylvania

Philadelphia

Baltimore

Maryland

Washington

Delaware

Mississippi River

Missouri River

Virginia

Ohio River

Virginia

Williamsburg

District of
Kentucky

SPANISH
POSSESSIONS

ATLANTIC
OCEAN

Arkansas River

Mississippi River

Claimed by North Carolina
until 1790

Claimed by South Carolina until 1787

Claimed by Georgia,
also claimed by
South Carolina until 1787

Claimed by Georgia,
also claimed by Spain

Tennessee River

North
Carolina

South
Carolina

Charles Town

Georgia

Savannah

N

Florida

St. Augustine

Gulf of Mexico

0   100 km
0   100 miles

Western Land Claims
1782–90

- - - - Claimed by New York,
until 1782

xxii

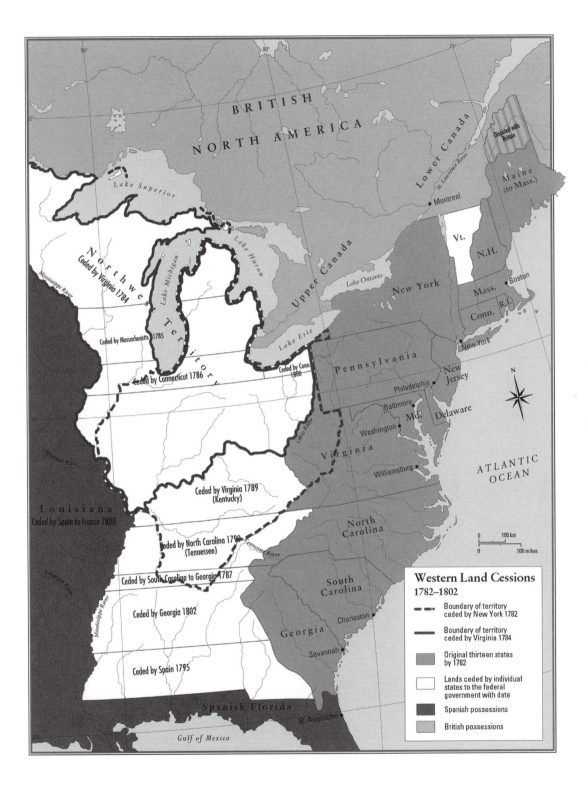

Western Land Cessions
1782–1802

- – – – Boundary of territory ceded by New York 1782
- ——— Boundary of territory ceded by Virginia 1784
- Original thirteen states by 1782
- Lands ceded by individual states to the federal government with date
- Spanish possessions
- British possessions

BRITISH NORTH AMERICA

Lower Canada

Disputed with Britain

Maine (to Mass.)

Lake Superior

Montreal

St. Lawrence River

Northwest Territory
Ceded by Virginia 1784

Mississippi River

Lake Michigan

Lake Huron

Upper Canada

Lake Ontario

Vt.

N.H.

New York

Mass.

Boston

Ceded by Massachusetts 1785

Conn.

R.I.

Ceded by Connecticut 1786

Lake Erie

Ceded by Conn. 1800

New York

Pennsylvania

New Jersey

Philadelphia

Baltimore

Ohio River

Missouri River

Louisiana
Ceded by Spain to France 1800

Ceded by Virginia 1789
(Kentucky)

Washington

Md.

Delaware

Virginia

Williamsburg

ATLANTIC OCEAN

Ceded by North Carolina 1790
(Tennessee)

Tennessee River

North Carolina

Arkansas River

Mississippi River

Ceded by South Carolina to Georgia 1787

Ceded by Georgia 1802

South Carolina

Charleston

Georgia

Savannah

Ceded by Spain 1795

Spanish Florida

St. Augustine

Gulf of Mexico

0   100 km
0   100 miles

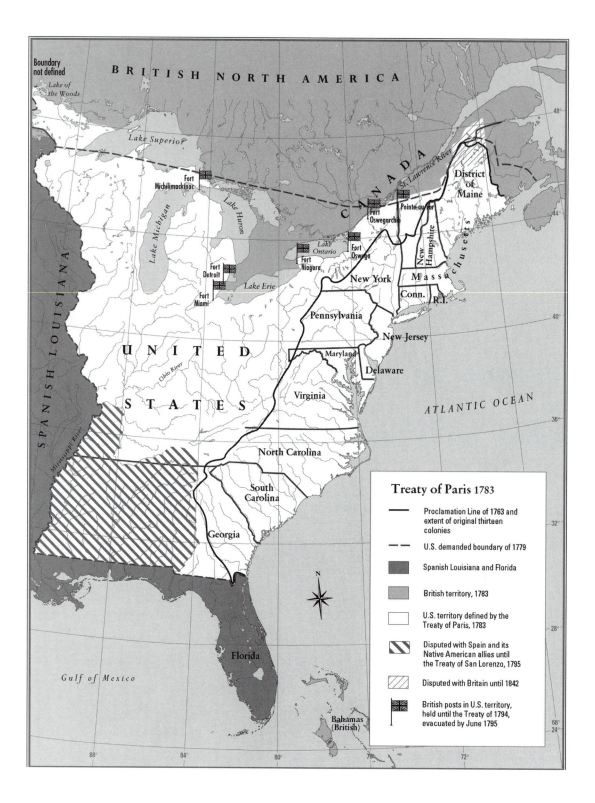

Boundary not defined

BRITISH NORTH AMERICA

Lake of the Woods

Lake Superior

CANADA

Fort Michilimackinac

Lake Michigan

Lake Huron

Fort Detroit

Lake Erie

Fort Miami

Lake Ontario

Fort Niagara

Fort Oswego

Fort Oswegarchie

Pointe-au-for

St. Lawrence River

District of Maine

New Hampshire

Massachusetts

New York

Conn.

R.I.

Pennsylvania

New Jersey

Maryland

Delaware

Virginia

Ohio River

UNITED STATES

North Carolina

South Carolina

Georgia

SPANISH LOUISIANA

Mississippi River

Florida

Gulf of Mexico

ATLANTIC OCEAN

Bahamas (British)

N

Treaty of Paris 1783

— Proclamation Line of 1763 and extent of original thirteen colonies

- - - U.S. demanded boundary of 1779

Spanish Louisiana and Florida

British territory, 1783

U.S. territory defined by the Treaty of Paris, 1783

Disputed with Spain and its Native American allies until the Treaty of San Lorenzo, 1795

Disputed with Britain until 1842

British posts in U.S. territory, held until the Treaty of 1794, evacuated by June 1795

xxiv

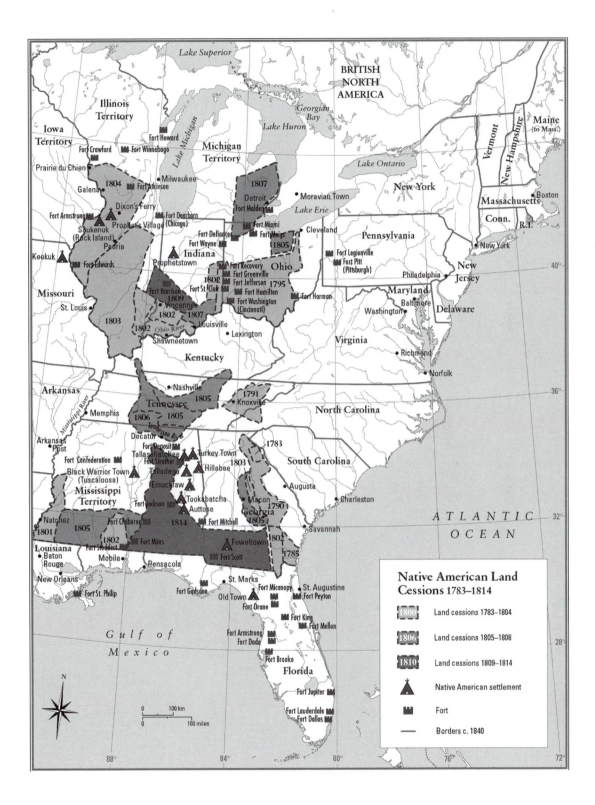

Native American Land Cessions 1783–1814

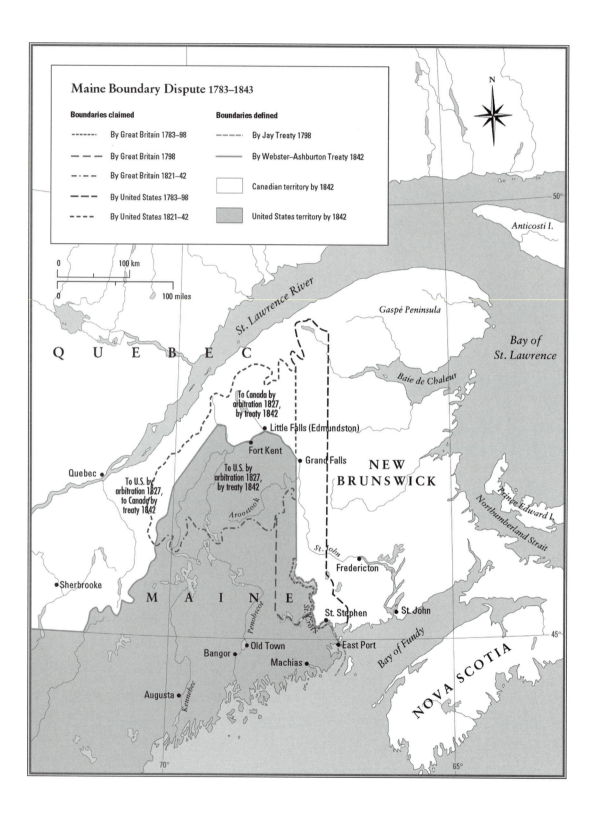

Maine Boundary Dispute 1783–1843

Boundaries claimed

- – – – – – By Great Britain 1783–98
- – – – – By Great Britain 1798
- –·–·– By Great Britain 1821–42
- – – – By United States 1783–98
- ······· By United States 1821–42

Boundaries defined

- – – – – By Jay Treaty 1798
- ——— By Webster–Ashburton Treaty 1842
- Canadian territory by 1842
- United States territory by 1842

N

50°

Anticosti I.

0   100 km

0   100 miles

St. Lawrence River

Gaspé Peninsula

Bay of
St. Lawrence

Q   U   E   B   E   C

Baie de Chaleur

To Canada by
arbitration 1827,
by treaty 1842

Little Falls (Edmundston)

Fort Kent

Grand Falls

NEW
BRUNSWICK

Quebec

To U.S. by
arbitration 1827,
to Canada by
treaty 1842

To U.S. by
arbitration 1827,
by treaty 1842

Aroostook

Prince Edward I.

Northumberland Strait

Sherbrooke

St. John

Fredericton

M   A   I   N   E

Penobscot

St. Croix

St. Stephen

St. John

45°

Bangor

Old Town

East Port

Machias

Bay of Fundy

N   O   V   A   S   C   O   T   I   A

Augusta

Kennebec

70°

65°

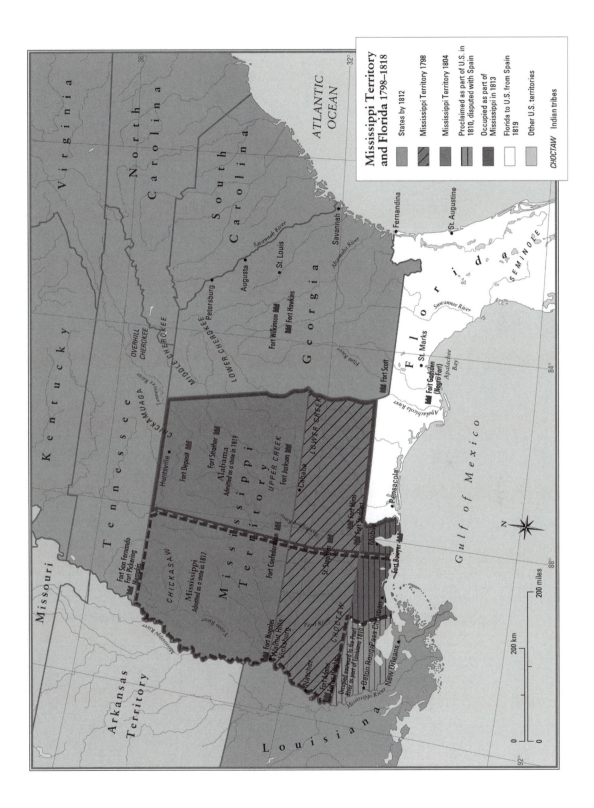

Mississippi Territory and Florida 1798–1818

States by 1812
Mississippi Territory 1798
Mississippi Territory 1804
Proclaimed as part of U.S. in 1810, disputed with Spain
Occupied as part of Mississippi in 1813
Florida to U.S. from Spain 1819
Other U.S. territories

CHOCTAW Indian tribes

Rupert's Land (Hudson's Bay Company)

BRITISH NORTH AMERICA

Oregon
Country

Jointly administered
by Great Britain and
the United States;
also claimed by Spain

Lake of the Woods

Illinois Territory

Lake Superior

Lake Michigan

Manuel's Fort

Fort Mandan

Fort Manuel

Fort aux Cedres
(Loisels Post)

Fort Snelling
(St. Anthony)

Fort Howard

Fort Dearborn
(Chicago)

District of
Louisiana

Fort Lisa

Fort Madison

Fort Armstrong

Fort Clark
(Peoria)

Ohio

Fort Osage
(Clark)

Fort Bellefontaine

St. Louis

UNITED STATES

Colorado River

N

Potosi

Kaskaskia

Louisville

Kentucky

Santa Fe

New Madrid

Tennessee

Nashville

Fort Smith

Fort Pickering

Louisiana Purchase and
Border Settlements 1803–19

Red River

MEXICO

Mississippi
Territory

Louisiana Purchase 1803,
natural border of Louisiana,
drainage of the Mississippi

Territory of Louisiana from
1805–12, then Missouri Territory

U.S.–British Treaty line of 1818,
the 49th Parallel

Adams–Onis Treaty line of 1819

Red River Basin ceded by
Great Britain to U.S. in 1818

Area ceded by U.S. to Great
Britain 1818

Spanish territory

Nacogdoches

Sabine River

Fort Adams

Florida

Pensacola

San Antonio

New Orleans

0   200 km
0   200 miles

Gulf of Mexico

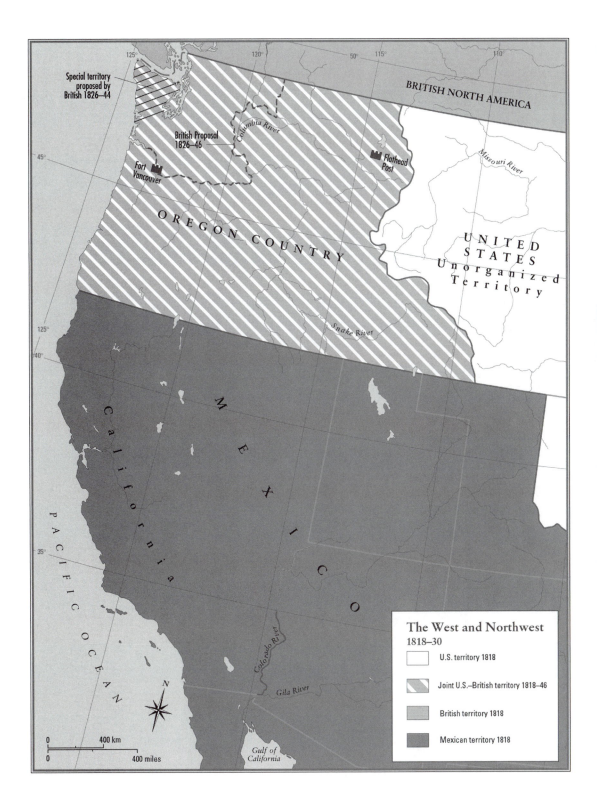

Special territory
proposed by
British 1826–44

British Proposal
1826–46

Fort
Vancouver

Columbia River

Flathead
Post

BRITISH NORTH AMERICA

Missouri River

UNITED
STATES
Unorganized
Territory

OREGON COUNTRY

Snake River

MEXICO

California

PACIFIC OCEAN

Colorado River

Gila River

N

Gulf of
California

0   400 km
0   400 miles

125°   120°   50°   115°   110°

45°

125°

40°

35°

The West and Northwest
1818–30

U.S. territory 1818

Joint U.S.–British territory 1818–46

British territory 1818

Mexican territory 1818

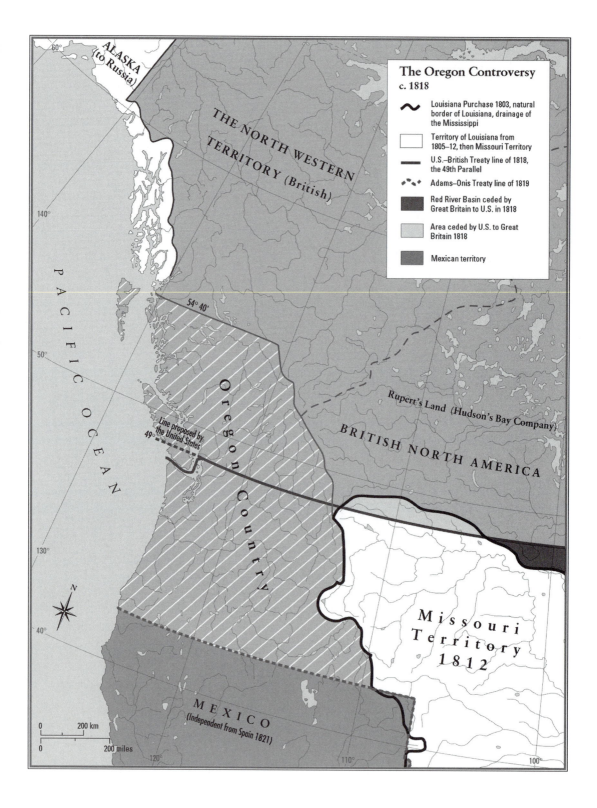

The Oregon Controversy
c. 1818

~ Louisiana Purchase 1803, natural border of Louisiana, drainage of the Mississippi

☐ Territory of Louisiana from 1805–12, then Missouri Territory

▬ U.S.–British Treaty line of 1818, the 49th Parallel

◆·◆·◆ Adams–Onis Treaty line of 1819

■ Red River Basin ceded by Great Britain to U.S. in 1818

☐ Area ceded by U.S. to Great Britain 1818

■ Mexican territory

ALASKA (to Russia)

THE NORTH WESTERN TERRITORY (British)

PACIFIC OCEAN

54° 40'

Oregon Country

Rupert's Land (Hudson's Bay Company)

BRITISH NORTH AMERICA

Line proposed by the United States
49°

Missouri Territory 1812

MEXICO
(Independent from Spain 1821)

0   200 km
0   200 miles

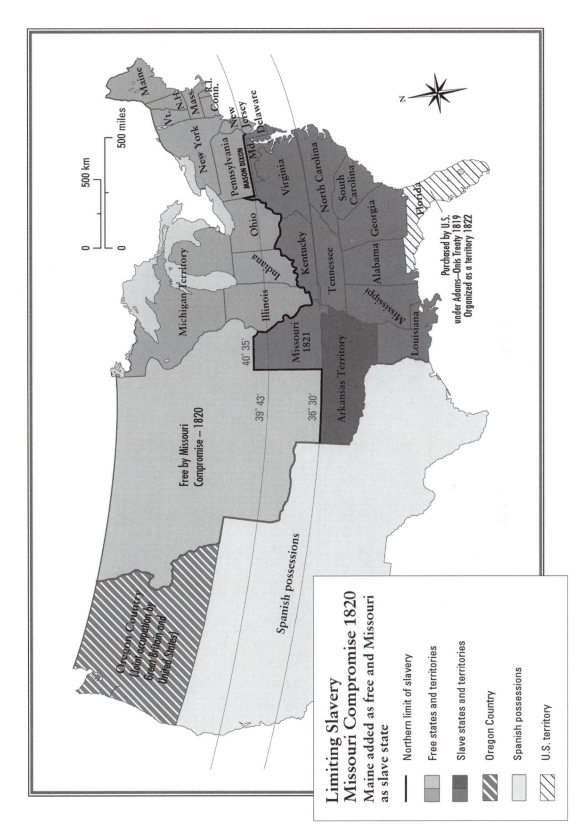

Limiting Slavery
Missouri Compromise 1820
Maine added as free and Missouri as slave state

— Northern limit of slavery
Free states and territories
Slave states and territories
Oregon Country
Spanish possessions
U.S. territory

Maine
Vt.
N.H.
Mass.
R.I.
Conn.
New York
New Jersey
Delaware
Pennsylvania
MASON DIXON
Md.
Virginia
North Carolina
South Carolina
Georgia
Alabama
Mississippi
Louisiana
Florida
Purchased by U.S. under Adams–Onis Treaty 1819 Organized as a territory 1822
Ohio
Indiana
Illinois
Kentucky
Tennessee
Michigan Territory
Missouri 1821
Arkansas Territory
40° 35'
39° 43'
36° 30'
Free by Missouri Compromise – 1820
Spanish possessions
Oregon Country (Joint occupation by Great Britain and United States)

N

0   500 miles
0   500 km

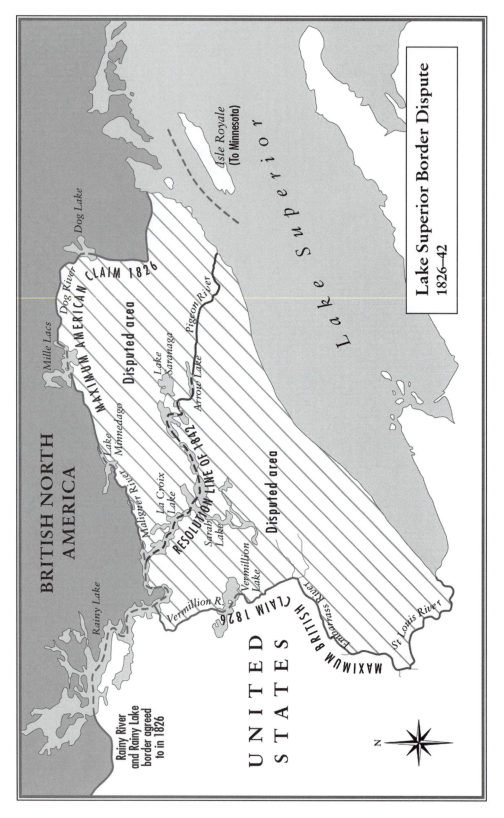

Lake Superior Border Dispute
1826–42

BRITISH NORTH
AMERICA

UNITED
STATES

Lake Superior

Isle Royale
(To Minnesota)

Dog Lake

Dog River

MAXIMUM AMERICAN CLAIM 1826

Disputed area

Pigeon River

Lake Saranaga

Arrow Lake

Mille Lacs

Lake Minnedago

La Croix Lake

Maligner River

RESOLUTION LINE OF 1842

Sarah Lake

Vermillion Lake

Vermillion R.

Rainy Lake

Disputed area

MAXIMUM BRITISH CLAIM 1826

Embarrass River

St Louis River

Rainy River and Rainy Lake border agreed to in 1826

N

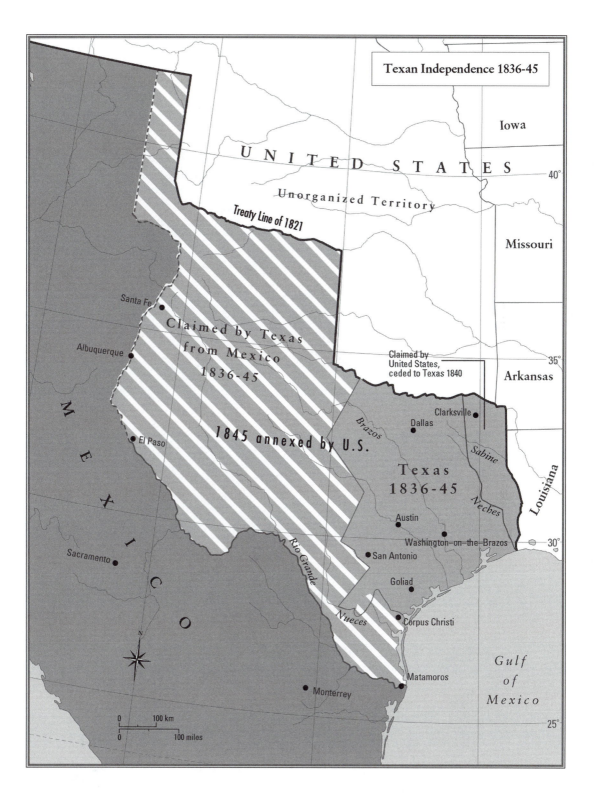

Texan Independence 1836-45

Iowa

UNITED STATES

Unorganized Territory

40°

Treaty Line of 1821

Missouri

Santa Fe

Claimed by Texas
from Mexico
1836-45

Claimed by
United States,
ceded to Texas 1840

35°

Arkansas

Albuquerque

Clarksville

1845 annexed by U.S.

Dallas

Brazos

M
E
X
I
C
O

El Paso

Sabine

Texas
1836-45

Louisiana

Neches

Austin

Sacramento

Rio Grande

Washington-on-the-Brazos

30°

San Antonio

Goliad

Nueces

Corpus Christi

Gulf

Matamoros

of

Monterrey

Mexico

25°

0   100 km

0   100 miles

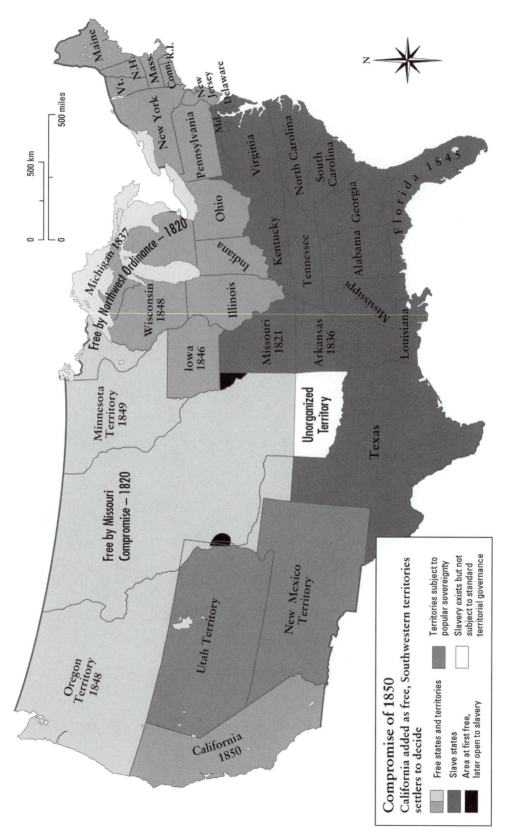

Compromise of 1850
California added as free, Southwestern territories settlers to decide

Legend:
- Free states and territories
- Slave states
- Area at first free, later open to slavery
- Territories subject to popular sovereignty
- Slavery exists but not subject to standard territorial governance

Maine
Vt.
N.H.
Mass.
Conn. R.I.
New York
New Jersey
Delaware
Pennsylvania
Md.
Virginia
North Carolina
South Carolina
Florida 1845
Ohio
Kentucky
Tennessee
Alabama
Georgia
Indiana
Illinois
Mississippi
Missouri 1821
Arkansas 1836
Louisiana
Michigan 1837
Free by Northwest Ordinance – 1820
Wisconsin 1848
Iowa 1846
Minnesota Territory 1849
Unorganized Territory
Texas
Free by Missouri Compromise – 1820
Oregon Territory 1848
Utah Territory
New Mexico Territory
California 1850

500 miles
500 km
0

N

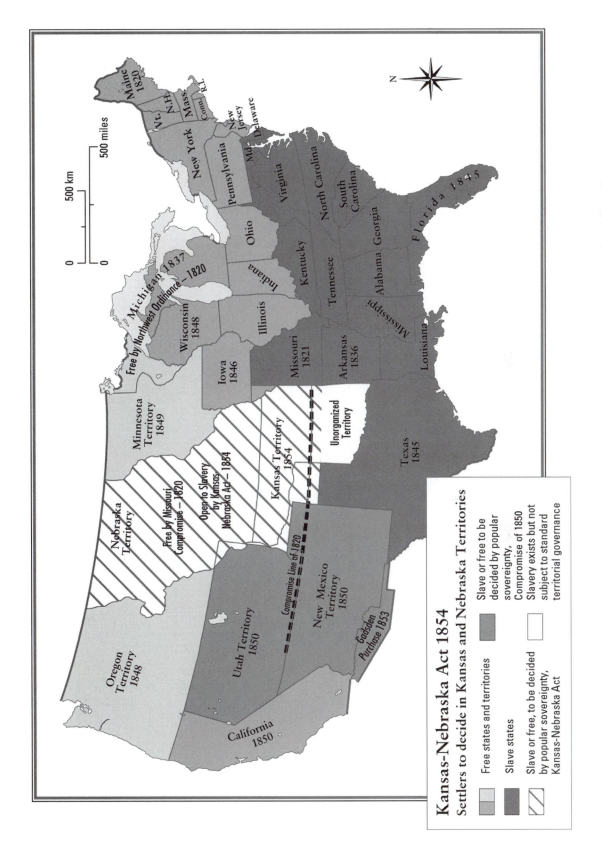

Kansas-Nebraska Act 1854
Settlers to decide in Kansas and Nebraska Territories

Free states and territories

Slave states

Slave or free, to be decided
by popular sovereignty,
Kansas-Nebraska Act

Slave or free to be
decided by popular
sovereignty,
Compromise of 1850

Slavery exists but not
subject to standard
territorial governance

Maine 1820
Vt.
N.H.
Mass.
Conn. R.I.
New York
New Jersey
Pennsylvania
Md.
Delaware
Virginia
North Carolina
South Carolina
Florida 1845
Alabama
Georgia
Mississippi
Louisiana
Ohio
Indiana
Kentucky
Tennessee
Illinois
Michigan 1837
Free by Northwest Ordinance – 1820
Wisconsin 1848
Iowa 1846
Missouri 1821
Arkansas 1836
Texas 1845
Unorganized Territory
Minnesota Territory 1849
Nebraska Territory
Free by Missouri Compromise – 1820
Open to Slavery by Kansas-Nebraska Act – 1854
Kansas Territory 1854
Compromise Line of 1820
New Mexico Territory 1850
Gadsden Purchase 1853
Utah Territory 1850
Oregon Territory 1848
California 1850

N

500 miles

500 km

0

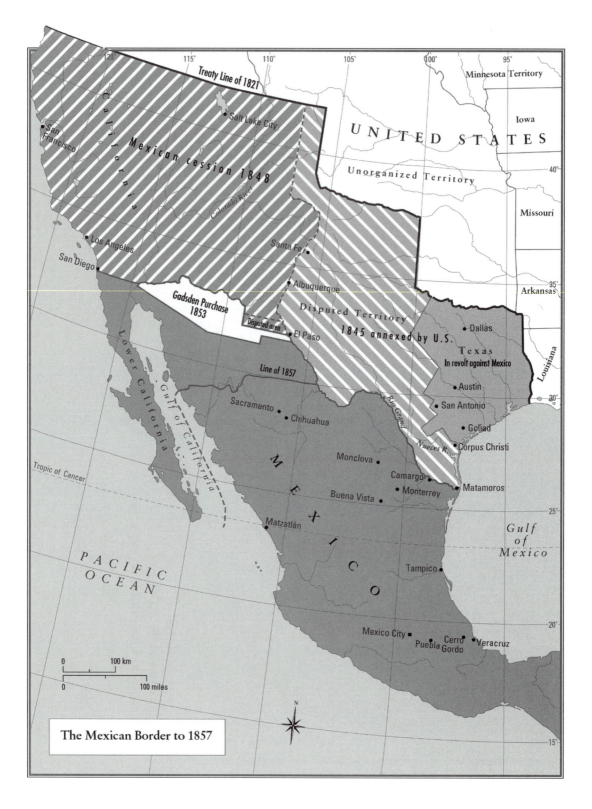

The Mexican Border to 1857

Treaty Line of 1821

UNITED STATES

Minnesota Territory

Iowa

Missouri

Arkansas

Louisiana

Unorganized Territory

Mexican Cession 1848

California

Salt Lake City

San Francisco

Los Angeles

San Diego

Santa Fe

Albuquerque

Gadsden Purchase 1853

Disputed area

El Paso

Line of 1857

Disputed Territory 1845 annexed by U.S.

Dallas

Texas
In revolt against Mexico

Austin

San Antonio

Goliad

Corpus Christi

Nueces R.

Lower California

Gulf of California

Colorado River

Sacramento

Chihuahua

Monclova

Buena Vista

M E X I C O

Rio Grande

Camargo

Monterrey

Matamoros

Matzatlán

Tropic of Cancer

Tampico

PACIFIC OCEAN

Gulf of Mexico

Mexico City

Puebla

Cerro Gordo

Veracruz

0   100 km

0   100 miles

N

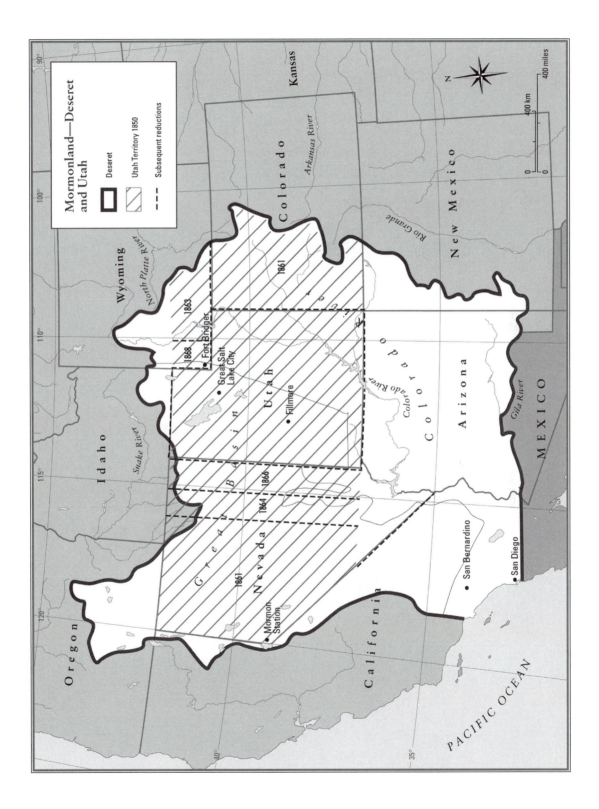

Mormonland—Deseret
and Utah

☐ Deseret

▨ Utah Territory 1850

-- Subsequent reductions

1775

MINNESOTA
MICHIGAN
WISCONSIN
VT.
N.H.
NEW YORK
MASSACHUSETTS
CONN.
R.I.
IOWA
PA.
NEW JERSEY
DELAWARE
ILLINOIS INDIANA OHIO
Proclamation Line of 1763
MD.
VIR.
VIRGINIA
KANSAS MISSOURI
KENTUCKY
NORTH CAROLINA
OKLAHOMA
TENNESSEE
ARKANSAS
SOUTH CAROLINA
MISSISSIPPI
ALABAMA
GEORGIA
TEXAS
LOUISIANA
FLORIDA

United States Territorial Growth
1775–1960

◼ Thirteen Colonies

◼ British Territories

◻ Spanish Territories

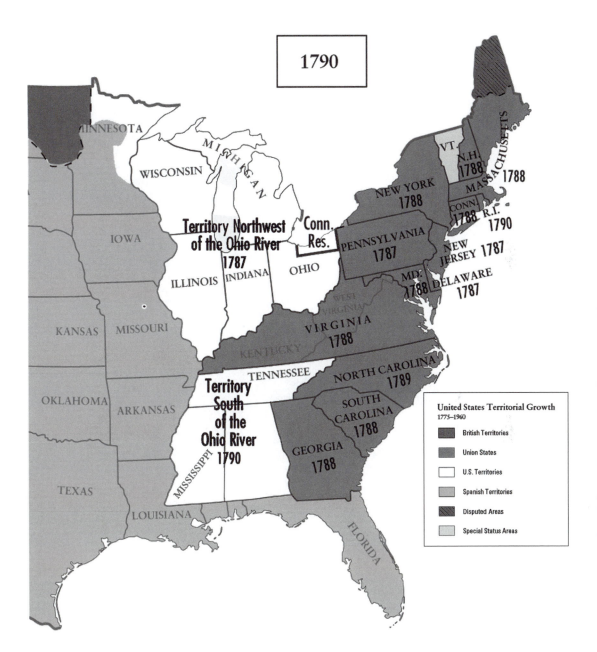

1790

MINNESOTA

WISCONSIN

M I C H I G A N

IOWA

Territory Northwest of the Ohio River 1787

Conn. Res.

ILLINOIS   INDIANA   OHIO

VT.

N.H. 1788

MASSACHUSETTS 1788

NEW YORK 1788

CONN. 1788   R.I. 1790

PENNSYLVANIA 1787

NEW JERSEY 1787

MD. 1788   DELAWARE 1787

WEST VIRGINIA

KANSAS   MISSOURI

VIRGINIA 1788

KENTUCKY

OKLAHOMA   ARKANSAS

Territory South of the Ohio River 1790

TENNESSEE

NORTH CAROLINA 1789

SOUTH CAROLINA 1788

TEXAS

MISSISSIPPI

GEORGIA 1788

LOUISIANA

FLORIDA

United States Territorial Growth
1775–1960

British Territories

Union States

U.S. Territories

Spanish Territories

Disputed Areas

Special Status Areas

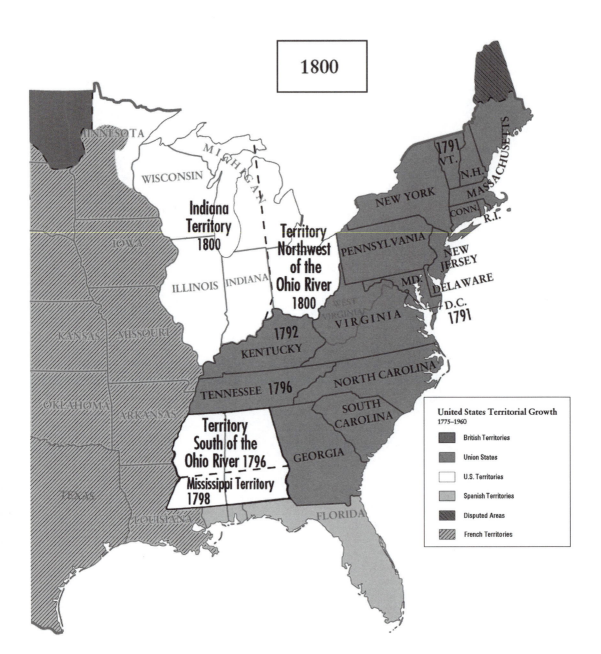

1800

MINNESOTA

WISCONSIN

MICHIGAN

Indiana
Territory
1800

IOWA

ILLINOIS   INDIANA

KANSAS   MISSOURI

Territory
Northwest
of the
Ohio River
1800

WEST
VIRGINIA   VIRGINIA

1792
KENTUCKY

TENNESSEE   1796

NORTH CAROLINA

OKLAHOMA   ARKANSAS

Territory
South of the
Ohio River 1796

Mississippi Territory
1798

SOUTH
CAROLINA

GEORGIA

TEXAS

LOUISIANA

FLORIDA

1791
VT.

N.H.

NEW YORK

MASSACHUSETTS

CONN.

R.I.

PENNSYLVANIA

NEW
JERSEY

MD.

DELAWARE

D.C.
1791

United States Territorial Growth
1775–1960

- British Territories
- Union States
- U.S. Territories
- Spanish Territories
- Disputed Areas
- French Territories

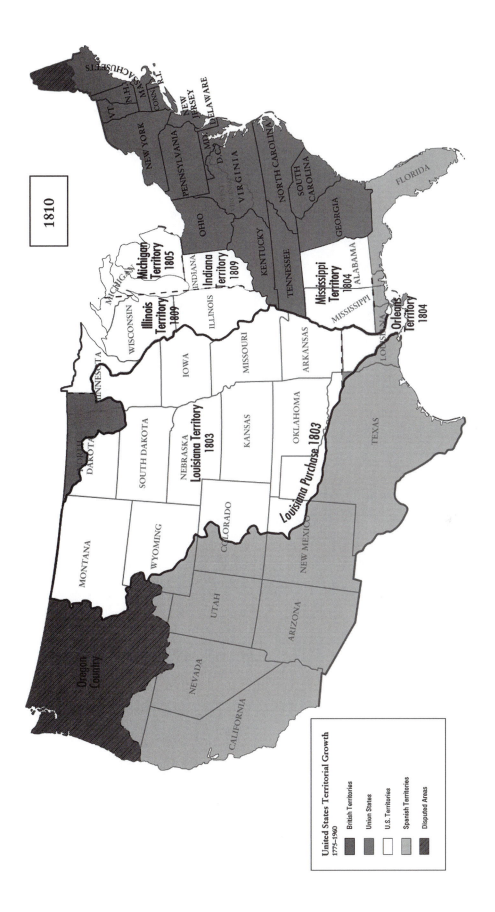

1810

United States Territorial Growth
1775–1960

British Territories
Union States
U.S. Territories
Spanish Territories
Disputed Areas

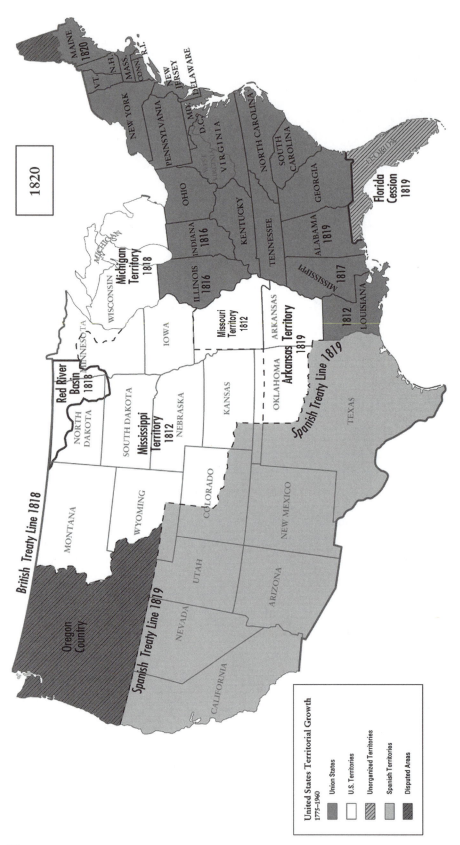

United States Territorial Growth
1775–1960

Union States
U.S. Territories
Unorganized Territories
Spanish Territories
Disputed Areas

1820

MAINE 1820
VT. N.H. MASS. CONN. R.I.
NEW YORK
PENNSYLVANIA
NEW JERSEY
DELAWARE
MD.
D.C.
VIRGINIA
WEST VIRGINIA
OHIO
NORTH CAROLINA
SOUTH CAROLINA
GEORGIA
KENTUCKY
TENNESSEE
ALABAMA 1819
GEORGIA
Florida Cession 1819
INDIANA 1816
ILLINOIS 1816
MISSISSIPPI 1817
Michigan Territory 1818
MICHIGAN
WISCONSIN
MINNESOTA
IOWA
Missouri Territory 1812
ARKANSAS
Arkansas Territory 1819
LOUISIANA 1812
Red River Basin 1818
NORTH DAKOTA
SOUTH DAKOTA
NEBRASKA
Mississippi Territory 1812
KANSAS
OKLAHOMA
Spanish Treaty Line 1819
TEXAS
British Treaty Line 1818
MONTANA
WYOMING
COLORADO
NEW MEXICO
Spanish Treaty Line 1819
Oregon Country
UTAH
NEVADA
ARIZONA
CALIFORNIA

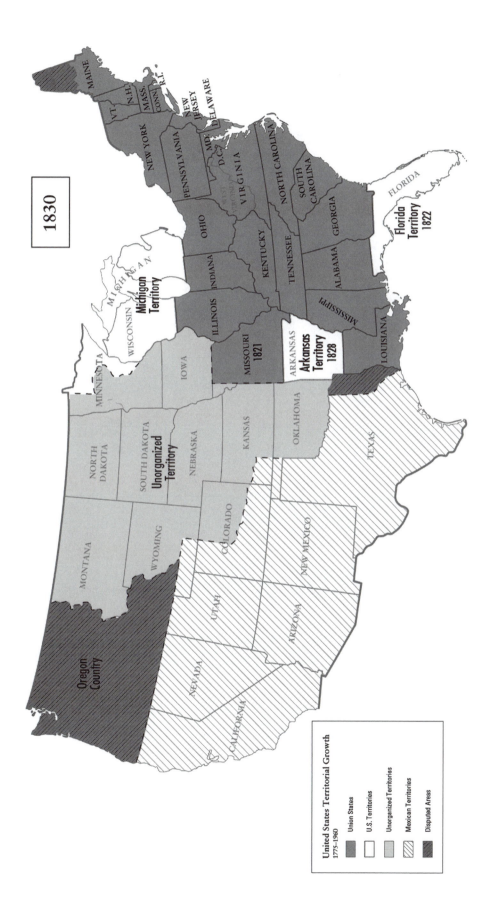

1830

United States Territorial Growth
1775–1960

Union States
U.S. Territories
Unorganized Territories
Mexican Territories
Disputed Areas

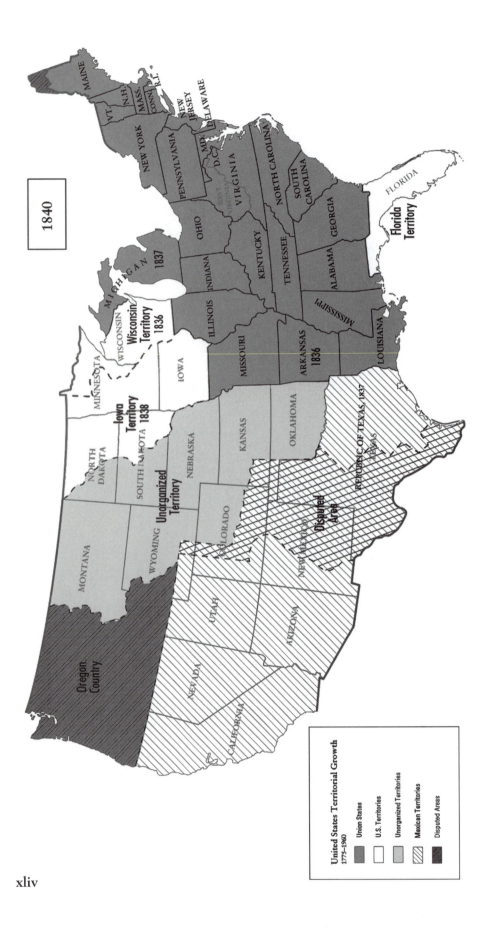

1840

MAINE

VT.

N.H.

MASS.

CONN.

R.I.

NEW YORK

NEW JERSEY

DELAWARE

PENNSYLVANIA

MD.

D.C.

WEST VIRGINIA

VIRGINIA

NORTH CAROLINA

SOUTH CAROLINA

FLORIDA

OHIO

KENTUCKY

TENNESSEE

GEORGIA

Florida Territory

MICHIGAN 1837

INDIANA

ALABAMA

WISCONSIN

Wisconsin Territory 1836

ILLINOIS

MISSISSIPPI

MINNESOTA

IOWA

MISSOURI

ARKANSAS 1836

LOUISIANA

Iowa Territory 1838

NORTH DAKOTA

SOUTH DAKOTA

Unorganized Territory

NEBRASKA

KANSAS

OKLAHOMA

REPUBLIC OF TEXAS, 1837

TEXAS

Disputed Area

MONTANA

WYOMING

COLORADO

NEW MEXICO

Oregon Country

UTAH

ARIZONA

NEVADA

CALIFORNIA

United States Territorial Growth
1775–1960

Union States

U.S. Territories

Unorganized Territories

Mexican Territories

Disputed Areas

xliv

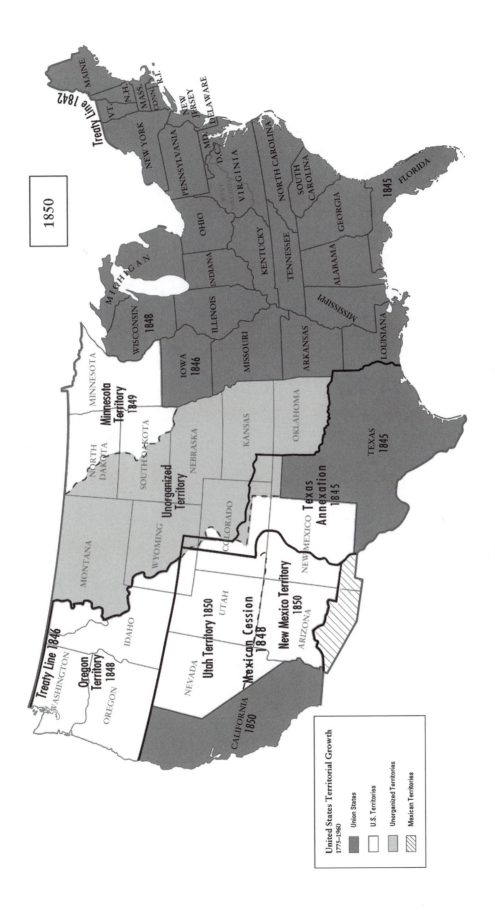

1850

United States Territorial Growth
1775–1960

Union States
U.S. Territories
Unorganized Territories
Mexican Territories

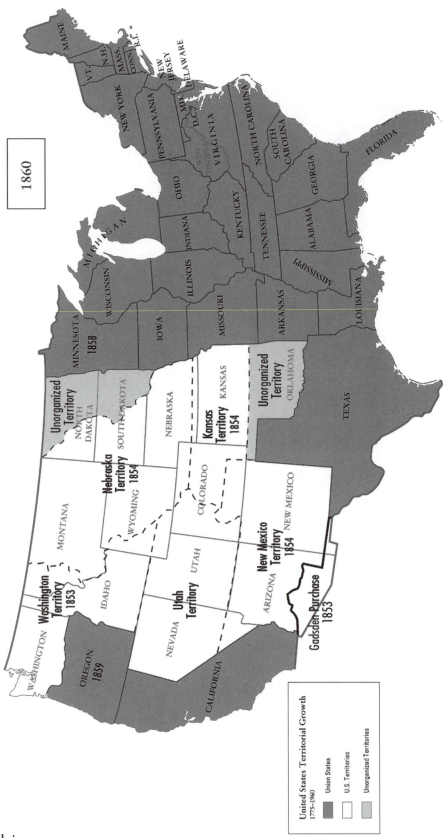

1860

MAINE

VT.

N.H.

MASS.

CONN.

R.I.

NEW YORK

NEW JERSEY

DELAWARE

PENNSYLVANIA

MD.

D.C.?

WEST VIRGINIA

VIRGINIA

NORTH CAROLINA

SOUTH CAROLINA

GEORGIA

FLORIDA

OHIO

KENTUCKY

TENNESSEE

ALABAMA

MISSISSIPPI

LOUISIANA

ARKANSAS

MICHIGAN

INDIANA

ILLINOIS

WISCONSIN

IOWA

MISSOURI

MINNESOTA
1858

Unorganized
Territory
NORTH DAKOTA

SOUTH DAKOTA

NEBRASKA

Kansas
Territory
1854

KANSAS

Unorganized
Territory

OKLAHOMA

TEXAS

Nebraska
Territory 1854

WYOMING

COLORADO

New Mexico
Territory
1854

NEW MEXICO

Godsden Purchase
1853

ARIZONA

MONTANA

Utah
Territory
UTAH

Washington
Territory
1853

IDAHO

NEVADA

WASHINGTON

OREGON
1859

CALIFORNIA

United States Territorial Growth
1775–1960

Union States

U.S. Territories

Unorganized Territories

xlvi

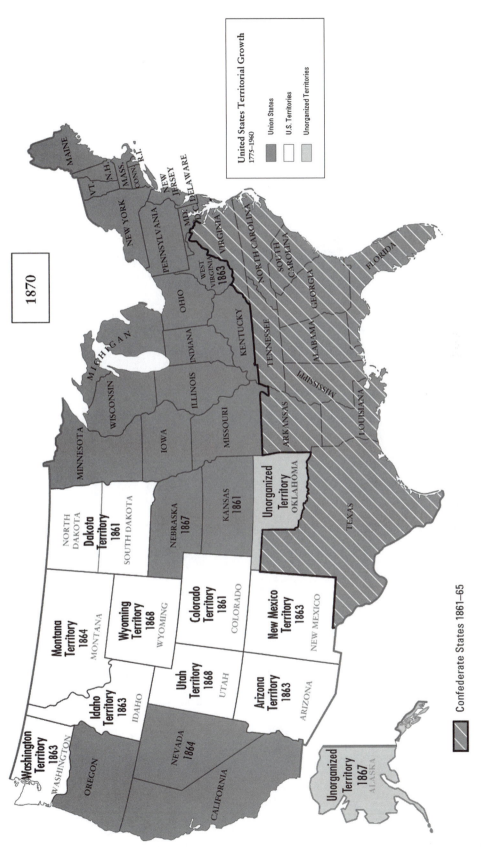

United States Territorial Growth
1775–1960

Union States
U.S. Territories
Unorganized Territories

1870

MAINE
N.H.
VT.
MASS.
CONN.
R.I.
NEW YORK
NEW JERSEY
PENNSYLVANIA
MD.
DEL.
DELAWARE
WEST VIRGINIA 1863
VIRGINIA
NORTH CAROLINA
SOUTH CAROLINA
GEORGIA
FLORIDA
ALABAMA
MISSISSIPPI
LOUISIANA
TENNESSEE
KENTUCKY
OHIO
INDIANA
ILLINOIS
MISSOURI
ARKANSAS
IOWA
WISCONSIN
MICHIGAN
MINNESOTA

NORTH DAKOTA
Dakota Territory 1861
SOUTH DAKOTA

NEBRASKA 1867

KANSAS 1861

Unorganized Territory OKLAHOMA

TEXAS

Montana Territory 1864
MONTANA

Wyoming Territory 1868
WYOMING

Colorado Territory 1861
COLORADO

New Mexico Territory 1863
NEW MEXICO

Washington Territory 1863
WASHINGTON

Idaho Territory 1863
IDAHO

Utah Territory 1868
UTAH

Arizona Territory 1863
ARIZONA

NEVADA 1864

OREGON

CALIFORNIA

Unorganized Territory 1867
ALASKA

Confederate States 1861–65

xlvii

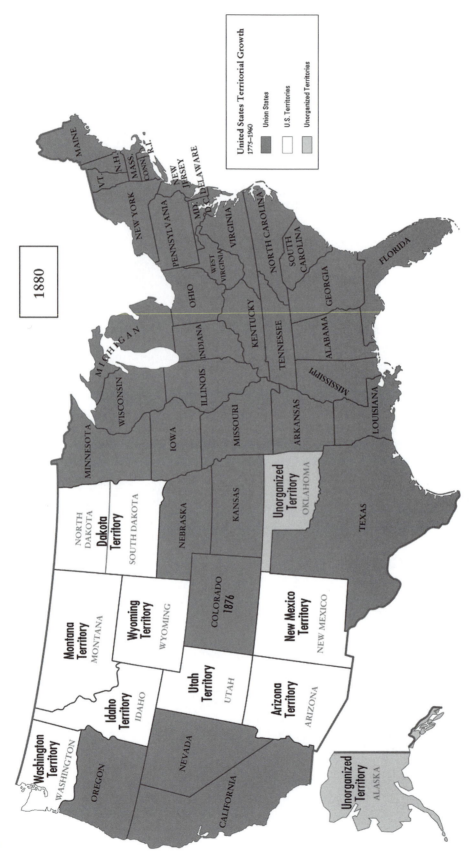

United States Territorial Growth
1775–1960

- Union States
- U.S. Territories
- Unorganized Territories

1880

MAINE
VT.
N.H.
MASS.
CONN.
R.I.
NEW YORK
NEW JERSEY
DELAWARE
MD.
D.C.
PENNSYLVANIA
WEST VIRGINIA
VIRGINIA
OHIO
NORTH CAROLINA
SOUTH CAROLINA
GEORGIA
FLORIDA
MICHIGAN
INDIANA
KENTUCKY
TENNESSEE
ALABAMA
WISCONSIN
ILLINOIS
MISSISSIPPI
MINNESOTA
IOWA
MISSOURI
ARKANSAS
LOUISIANA
NORTH DAKOTA
Dakota Territory
SOUTH DAKOTA
NEBRASKA
KANSAS
Unorganized Territory
OKLAHOMA
TEXAS
Montana Territory
MONTANA
Wyoming Territory
WYOMING
COLORADO 1876
New Mexico Territory
NEW MEXICO
Idaho Territory
IDAHO
Utah Territory
UTAH
Arizona Territory
ARIZONA
Washington Territory
WASHINGTON
OREGON
NEVADA
CALIFORNIA
Unorganized Territory
ALASKA

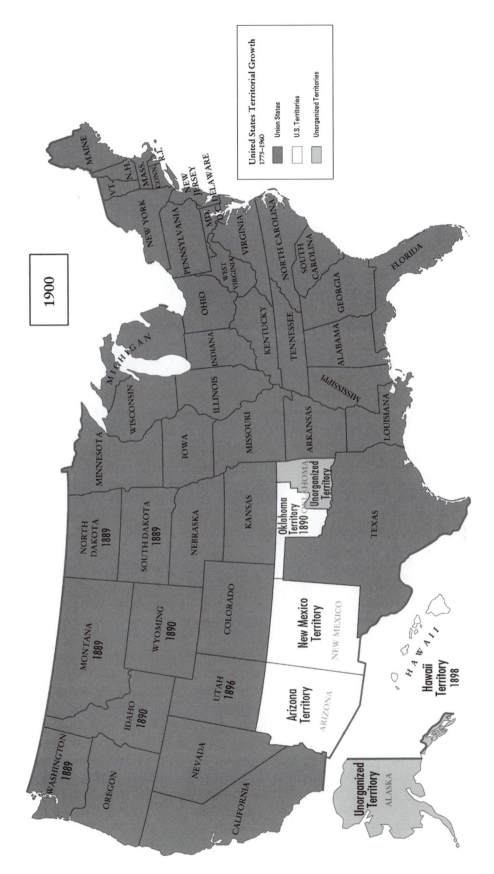

1900

United States Territorial Growth
1775–1960

- Union States
- U.S. Territories
- Unorganized Territories

United States Territorial Growth
1775–1960

Union States

U.S. Territories

1920

1

United States Territorial Growth
1775–1960

Union States

1960

1959

ALASKA
1959

HAWAII
1959

☆☆☆

E PLURIBUS UNUM

The Uniting of the States of America

Benjamin F. Shearer

BRITISH COLONIZATION OF NORTH AMERICA

In one of the great ironies of history, the British colonization of North America, from which proceeded the greatest capitalist power of the late twentieth century, began in the failure of two joint-stock companies. For only £12 and 10 shillings, investors could buy a share in the promise of America. On April 10, 1606, James I, king of England, Scotland, and Ireland, chartered two companies "to make habitacion, plantacion, and to deduce a colonie of sondrie of our people into that parte of America commonly called Virginia and other parts and territories in America either appertaining unto us or which are not nowe actuallie possessed by anie Christian prince or people."

While the king hoped such a noble enterprise would result in the "propagating of Christian religion to suche people as yet live in darknesse and miserable ignorance of the true knowledge and worshippe of God and may in tyme bring the infidels and salvages living in those parts to humane civilitie and to a settled and quiet govermente," he also had earthly concerns. Each colony was given the power to govern its internal matters through a council of thirteen. Another council of thirteen, "our Counsell of Virginia," appointed by the monarch would manage and direct matters concerning the government and the new colonies. In exchange for granting permission to dig and mine for precious metals, even "on the backside of the same Colonies," the crown would receive yearly "the fifte parte onlie of all the same goulde and silver and the fifteenth parte of all the same copper soe to be gotten or had."

The promise of protection of the colonies by the Crown and the duty-free shipment of necessities from the realm to America were important inducements to investors as well as to the opportunity for future growth. The charter gave to the colonists themselves, however, the most important and enduring benefit:

> Alsoe wee doe, for us, our heires and successors, declare by theise presentes that all and everie the parsons being our subjects which shall dwell and inhabit within everie and anie of the saide severall Colonies and plantacions and everie of theire children which shall happen to be borne within the limits and precincts of the said severall Colonies and plantacions shall have and enjoy all liberties, franchises and immunities within anie of our other dominions to all intents and purposes as if they had been abiding and borne within this our realme of Englande or anie other of our saide dominions.[1]

The companies had claim to land between the 34th and 41st northern parallels. The Virginia Company of Plymouth planted a settlement on the Sagadahoc River in 1607 that lasted one cold Maine winter. In 1620, the company gave up its rights to the newly formed Council for New England, which had a new charter giving it proprietary rights, including the rights of governing and fishing, to the land between the 40th and 48th parallels from the Atlantic to the Pacific. At first, the Virginia Company of London fared better; it successfully established a settlement at Jamestown in 1607. A new charter in 1609 led to the selling of more company stock. By 1618, reforms were undertaken to strengthen the company, but internal squabbling, debt, poor returns, and a 1622 Indian attack that killed more than three hundred settlers ended any bright prospects for the company's future. The king dissolved the company in 1624, and its nebulously defined land reverted to the Crown as a royal colony.

Financial ruin and the difficulties of life in the New World did not dampen the allure of America to those who sought higher ideals. The Pilgrims who established a settlement at Plymouth, Massachusetts, in December 1620 had been headed for Virginia in search of religious freedom and true separation from the Church of England. When they realized that they had landed outside Virginia's boundaries, they agreed among themselves to provide their own government, immortalized in the Mayflower Compact, and elected John Carver as their governor. One of the first acts of their government was to arrange a peace treaty with neighboring Indian tribes. On March 4, 1629, the Massachusetts Bay Company was formed by royal charter with Puritans in control. Governor John Winthrop and other leaders blended the trading company into a commonwealth, using the charter's right to govern. The Plymouth Colony was eventually subsumed into the Colony of Massachusetts.

In 1632, George Calvert, Lord Baltimore, a friend of Charles I, asked for and posthumously received a royal charter for 10 million acres on Chesapeake Bay. The area was to be named Maryland after Queen Henrietta Maria and was to be governed by the Calvert family. The Calverts were Catholics and, therefore, proponents in England of religious freedom, but their colony permitted people of all denominations to settle within its boundaries. Twelve years later, radical separatist Roger Williams, who had been kicked out of Massachusetts for his religious beliefs, managed to obtain a charter for his own colony from Parliament. In 1663, Rhode Island received a royal charter that allowed religious freedom.

With the beheading of Charles I in 1649 and Oliver Cromwell's Puritan governments in power from 1649 to 1658, the development of new colonies was slowed even as the population in the existing colonies increased. When Charles II was restored to the throne in 1660, England began to take more notice of her colonies. Navigation Acts were passed in 1660 and 1663 and frequently thereafter to enhance revenues to England by restricting shipping to other countries and the use of foreign vessels. The 1660s became a period of rapid colonial growth.

Connecticut received a royal charter in 1662, which incorporated the Colony of New Haven as well as the other territory that Thomas Hooker had claimed when he and his followers left Massachusetts in 1636 looking for more land to settle. On March 24, 1663, a group of proprietors received a royal charter that included the eastern boundaries of what are now North Carolina, South Carolina, and Georgia, all the way to the Pacific Ocean. The proprietors remained in control of this territory until 1729, when they surrendered their claims and a royal charter created North Carolina and South Carolina, each with a governor and council appointed by the king and assemblies elected by landowners. In 1664 the Dutch surrendered New Amsterdam at the mouth of the Hudson River to the English upon the arrival of English commissioners and ships. Charles II had given his brother, the Duke of York, the Dutch colonies before he even owned them. When the duke became King James II in 1685, New York, as New Amsterdam was now named, became a royal colony. The Duke of York had, however, been kind to his friends John, Lord Berkeley, and Sir James Carteret. Shortly after receiving the colonial grant from his brother, the duke gave his friends the property rights to what is now New Jersey. In 1674, Berkeley and Carteret divided their property into east and west, and Quakers purchased both pieces. New Jersey was reunited in 1702 as a royal colony based on the fact that the duke had given his friends only property rights in the colony, not the property itself.

Pennsylvania was the final colony to be chartered in the seventeenth century. In 1681, Charles II gave William Penn a royal charter in payment of a debt the king owed Penn's father. Penn then bought what is now Delaware from the Duke of York and added it to the colony of Pennsylvania. Thus, as the eighteenth century dawned, the British colonies in America were firmly established. Colonial charters left many of the colonies with extensive land claims that would be sorted out later. The land claims of the Indians would also have to be determined later. Slavery had crept into southern plantations as an answer to the lack of labor needed to produce valuable crops like tobacco and, later, cotton. On the international scene, King William's War, which lasted from

1689 until 1697, left French claims in the New World intact. The French began to fortify their claims to a territory that stretched from New Orleans to Quebec.

The last colonial charter was granted by George II in 1732 to a group led by General James Oglethorpe, who founded a colony named Georgia after the king. The charter was to remain in effect for twenty-one years. As a trustee for Georgia, Oglethorpe wanted to start a place where debtors could get a second chance. In 1752, Oglethorpe's idealistic experiment ended, and Georgia reverted back to the Crown. From the outset of the new century, however, British colonial lands were defined by wars rather than by royal charters.

WARS RESHAPE EUROPE'S COLONIAL POSSESSIONS

In 1713, the Treaty of Utrecht ended the twelve-year-long Queen Anne's War by giving Great Britain Newfoundland and Nova Scotia. During that war, the French had shown their ability to ally with Indian tribes who acted as their mercenaries in attacking British territory and citizens. King George's War, which lasted from 1740 to 1747, did not affect colonial boundaries; in Europe, France and Spain were allied against Britain and Austria. But the Seven Years' War (1756–1763), known as the French and Indian War in the colonies, had a profound effect on colonial boundaries. Spain and France were again pitted against Britain. In North America, immigration was pushing the frontier ever westward, as settlers of the Ohio Company, with a land grant based on Virginia's claims, attempted to settle in territory claimed by France. The First Treaty of Paris in 1763 recognized Britain's victory over France and Spain by awarding Britain New France, essentially the Mississippi Valley, Eastern Louisiana, and Florida. The French were left with the Caribbean islands of Martinique and Guadeloupe, and the Spanish, with Cuba and the Philippines.

British victory did not, however, settle the Indian question. On October 7, 1763, George III issued an order creating the Proclamation Line of 1763. Settlers were forbidden to cross west of a line that ran down the backbone of the Appalachians. Settlers already there, in what was then acknowledged as Indian Country, were to remove themselves. Although unhappy with the Proclamation Line, colonists pressing the western frontier were not greatly affected by this unenforceable royal proclamation. In May 1763, the great Indian leader Pontiac began a rebellion against the unceasing encroachment of European settlers on Indian land by destroying most of the British fortifications in the West. Peace was not achieved with Pontiac until July 1766.

AN INDEPENDENT UNITED STATES LOOKS WESTWARD

On July 4, 1776, the colonies declared their independence from Britain. Delaware, which had been given its own legislature by William Penn in 1701, also declared its own independence from both Britain and Pennsylvania, thereby becoming the thirteenth colony. As the Revolutionary War progressed, Congress was not only managing the war effort but also looking beyond war to the future of what its members hoped would be their new independent nation. On October 10, 1780, a year before the war ended with General Cornwallis's surrender at Yorktown, Virginia, Congress concerned itself with public lands by passing the following resolution:

> Resolved, that the unappropriated lands that may be ceded or relinquished to the United States, by any particular States, pursuant to the recommendation of Congress on the 6th day of September last, shall be disposed of for the common benefit of the United States, and be settled and formed into distinct republican States, which shall become members of the Federal Union, and shall have the same rights of sovereignty, freedom and independence, as the other states.[2]

The Articles of Confederation, which Congress adopted toward the end of 1777, were finally ratified on March 1, 1781. In that year, New York became the first state to cede to the federal government its rather weak claims to western lands. Signed on September 3, 1781, the Treaty of Paris ended the Revolutionary War and created an independent nation whose new borders straddled the Mississippi River rather than the Appalachian Mountain chain. Britain would no longer have a southern border with the United States, because Spain reaped the benefit of alliance with France in the war and repossessed the Floridas.

Congress took the steps necessary to begin the sale of public lands by passing a land ordinance on May 20, 1785. This landmark legislation provided for surveyors and geographers to lay out townships in thirty-six numbered subdivisions of one square mile each. No land could be sold for less than $1 an acre, and lot sixteen of every township was set aside for public schools. On July 13, 1787, Congress passed the Northwest Ordinance, which set the pattern for the admission of future states to the Union. After Congress organized a territory with a governor, a secretary, and a court of three judges, a general assembly would be elected when there were "five thousand free male inhabitants of full age" in the district. When the territory's population reached "sixty thousand free inhabitants," the territory could be admitted to the Union if it had developed a republican constitution and government in conformity with the law. Provision was also made to permit the entry of territories into statehood if the number of free inhabitants was less than sixty thousand and it was in the interest of the nation.

The ordinance set up a temporary government for the territory northwest of the Ohio River, out of which not less than three nor more than five states were to be formed. The five states of Ohio, Indiana, Illinois, Michigan, and Wisconsin would eventually be carved out of the Northwest Territory. Most significantly, the ordinance dealt with the two primary issues that would shape the debate on westward expansion. One article of the ordinance addressed the issue of Indian rights, declaring that

> the utmost good faith shall always be observed towards the Indians; their lands and property shall never be taken from them without their consent; and, in their property, rights, and liberty, they shall never be invaded or disturbed, unless in just and lawful wars authorized by congress; but laws founded in justice and humanity, shall from time to time be made for preventing wrongs being done them, and for preserving peace and friendship with them.

Article 6 of the ordinance foreshadowed political compromises that would follow as later states came into the Union.

> There shall be neither slavery nor involuntary servitude in the said territory, otherwise than in the punishment of crimes whereof the party shall have been duly convicted: *Provided, always,* That any person escaping into the same, from whom labor or service is lawfully claimed in any one of the original States, such fugitive may be lawfully reclaimed and conveyed to the person claiming his or her labor or service as aforesaid.[3]

Thus, though slavery would not be extended into the five states of the Northwest Territory, fugitive slaves and indentured servants would find no haven in them.

The states continued to cede their western land claims to the federal government or to other states. Virginia ceded its western claims, except for Kentucky, in 1784. Massachusetts followed in 1785, and Connecticut, in 1786. In 1787 South Carolina ceded its claims to north and south Georgia to Georgia, and three years later North Carolina gave up its claim to the future state of Tennessee. In 1791 Vermont separated from New York, and in 1792 Virginia gave up its claim to Kentucky. Pennsylvania, Vermont, Delaware, Rhode Island, New Hampshire, Maryland, and New Jersey had no western claims. The issue of western land claims of the states finally came to an end in 1802, when Georgia ceded its claims to the national government with the proviso that the Cherokee Indians be removed from its land.

THE NEWLY CONSTITUTED UNITED STATES

The Constitution that was sent to the thirteen states for ratification in 1787 was a series of compromises for the sake of national unity. The Great Compromise created a Senate based on state representation and a House based on representation of the people. This decision necessitated that a census be taken at regular intervals, because the population for representation and direct taxation was defined "by adding to the whole Number of free Persons, including those bound to Service for a Term of Years, and excluding Indians not taxed, three fifths of all other Persons." The Constitution also prohibited Congress from passing laws that would inhibit "the Migration or Importation of such Persons as any of the States now shall think proper to admit" until 1808, but it did allow that a tax of not more than $10 could be levied per person imported.[4]

The United States, now with a strong but debt-laden federal government, was growing rapidly. The 1790 census counted a total population of 3,893,874, of whom 694,207 were slaves. Representative Thomas Scott of Pennsylvania laid out the pro-growth position when he addressed the House of Representatives on July 13, 1789, in support of a western land office. Noting that the government had already earned nearly $5 million through western land sales, he believed "this treasure, which we possess, has done thus much towards extinguishing a debt bearing hard upon every part of the Union." Furthermore, he said, "a due observance of the treaties heretofore entered into with Indian tribes, must be enforced; if the country is settled by a lawless banditti, they will keep the nation in a perpetual brawl with the savages." Scott told his colleagues that settlers were already there in the West; they were not going to come back to the East, and more were in line to go. They needed government, and he exhorted the lawmakers to accept the inevitable.

> Remember, ye sages of my country, an historic truth recorded for your instruction, that empire has been slowly, but invariably, moving from East to West; emigration has uniformly receded in that direction, from the time that our common parents quitted the garden of Eden, till the present hour; nor doubt but it will continue to pursue that course, as long as there are lands to be inhabited.[5]

Article IV, Section 3 of the Constitution provided that "new States may be admitted by the Congress into this Union." Congress was also given the "Power to dispose of and make all needful Rules and Regulations respecting the Territory or other Property belonging to the United States." The admission of new states was, therefore, inexorably intertwined from the start with political discussion, debate, and hegemony.

PRESIDENT WASHINGTON DEFINES THE ISSUES OF NATIONAL EXPANSION

The security of settlers in the western lands depended on some resolution of the Indian question as well as on formalizing the new nation's boundaries with the European countries, whose colonies shared North America with the United States. Indian hostilities were a continuing issue. George Washington told Congress in his 1790 message that he had been forced to call out the militia because "certain banditti of Indians from the Northwest of Ohio," along with "some of the tribes dwelling on and near the Wabash," had "renewed their violences with fresh alacrity and greater effect," including the sacrifice of lives. These "aggravated provocations" made it essential for the aggressors to understand that the government "is not less capable of punishing their crimes than it is disposed to respect their rights and reward their attachments."[6]

In his 1791 message to Congress, Washington announced that some provisional treaties with friendly tribes had been concluded but that offensive operations conducted "as consistently as possible with the dictates of humanity" had been required to deal with others. Most importantly, however, Washington set out two goals to avoid future hostility, since the government desired to pursue a peaceful Indian policy; these goals were "to advance the happiness of the Indians and to attach them firmly to the United States." To reach these twin goals, these objectives would be necessary:

That they should experience the benefits of an impartial dispensation of justice.

That the mode of alienating their lands, the main source of discontent and war, should be so defined and regulated as to obviate imposition and as far as may be practicable controversy concerning the reality and extent of the alienations which are made.

That commerce with them should be promoted under regulations tending to secure an equitable deportment toward them, and that such rational experiments should be made for imparting to them the blessings of civilization as may from time to time suit their condition.

That the Executive of the United States should be enabled to employ the means to which the Indians have been long accustomed for uniting their immediate interests with the preservation of peace.

And that efficacious provision should be made for inflicting adequate penalties upon all those who, by violating their rights, shall infringe the treaties and endanger the peace of the Union.[7]

Washington thus provided the framework for the later development of Indian policy, but note that, in his last message to Congress, he was still dealing with Indian issues. Washington's presidency, nevertheless, also saw the admission of three new states, all born out of territory claimed by the original states. Vermont, which had claimed its independence from New York in January 1777 after numerous battles over land titles made famous by Ethan Allen and his Green Mountain Boys, joined the Union as the fourteenth state in 1791. As an independent entity, Vermont's entry into the Union was relatively simple compared with that of Kentucky, the fifteenth state. Kentucky needed both the permission of Congress and of its parent, Virginia, to create a new state. Before this separation could occur, Virginia had to secure its claim to the land from both its original inhabitants and land speculators. After seven years and ten constitutional conventions, Kentucky became the first western state in 1792. It was also the first new slave state, which, paired with Vermont, maintained the North-South balance in the Senate. Like Kentucky, Tennessee had to be freed from its indifferent parent, North Carolina, and Native American problems had to be settled. The people of Tennessee believed that a secure future on the frontier could only be achieved as a state joined to the Union, and in 1796 that ideal was realized.

The admission of new states beyond the Appalachians set precedents for the growth of the nation as envisioned by Washington and his party, the Federalists. Another notable success of Washington's administration, from the government point of view, was the successful routing of the Northwest Indians by General "Mad" Anthony Wayne, which resulted in the Treaty of Greenville. This 1795 treaty opened most of Ohio to legal settlement. In that same year, the U.S. minister to Great Britain, Charles Pinckney, secured from Spain a southern boundary at the 31st parallel that ran from southern Georgia to the Mississippi River. In addition, the Treaty of San Lorenzo, also known as Pinckney's Treaty, gave the United States perpetual free navigation on the Mississippi and the right to deposit goods in the Spanish port of New Orleans, both of which were vital for internal commerce. In 1800 Spain secretly ceded Louisiana to France in the Treaty of San Ildefonso, but on December 23, 1803, Louisiana was transferred to the United States after the Jefferson administration purchased it from France.

PRESIDENT JEFFERSON TAKES THE BOUNDARY OF THE UNITED STATES TO THE MISSISSIPPI

Interference with American commerce at New Orleans led to President Thomas Jefferson's effort to buy the city from France. When American ministers put forth the question to Napoleon's government, they were surprised to find all of Louisiana for sale. Napoleon, in need of funds, had his eye on Europe, not America. The United States paid $15 million for over 800,000 square miles of territory, out of which would be carved the states of Louisiana, Arkansas, Missouri, Iowa, Nebraska, South Dakota, and parts of seven other western states. Thus by 1803, when Ohio became the first state from the Northwest Territory, the young United States had admitted seventeen states and owned the entire Mississippi River Valley, having acquired the lands of the Kaskaskia Indians, which ran along the Mississippi from the mouth of the Illinois River up to the Ohio River. Jefferson told Congress that

> whilst the property and sovereignty of the Mississippi and its waters secure an independent outlet for the produce of the Western States and an uncontrolled navigation through their whole course, free from collision with other powers and the dangers to our peace from that source, the fertility of the country,

its climate and extent, promise in due season important aids to our Treasury, an ample provision for our posterity, and a wide spread for the blessings of freedom and equal laws.

He asked Congress to act quickly to occupy the new territory and set up a temporary government so that it could be incorporated into the Union. He also asked Congress to confirm "to the Indian inhabitants their occupancy and self-government, establishing friendly and commercial relations with them." Jefferson also noted that the geography of the new territory would need to be ascertained.[8] Only nine years later, Louisiana became the eighteenth state of the Union and the first from the Louisiana Purchase.

The population of the United States continued to expand rapidly in the early nineteenth century, owing in part to the ongoing effort to push the Indians out of settled lands through treaties with various tribes. Jefferson told Congress at the end of his last term as president in 1808 that "with our Indian neighbors the public peace has been steadily maintained. Some instances of individual wrong have, as at other times, taken place, but in no wise implicating the will of the nation."[9] The total population of the United States rose from 5,084,912 in 1800 to 6,807,786 in 1810. By 1820, there were 10,037,323 Americans. Even though Congress took the first opportunity given to it by the Constitution to restrict the importation of slaves in 1808, the number of slaves also increased from 887,612 in 1800 to 1,130,781 in 1810, and to 1,529,012 in 1820. The number of states likewise expanded. Indiana joined the Union in 1816, and Mississippi, in 1817, with Illinois admitted in 1818 and Alabama, in 1819. With the admission of these four states, Indiana and Illinois as free states and Mississippi and Alabama as slave states, the political balance between North and South continued to be maintained in the U.S. Senate.

FEDERAL LAND POLICY AND FURTHER BOUNDARY SETTLEMENTS

Federal land policy promoted the settlement of new territories. In 1796, Congress provided for the sale of land parcels of one square mile (640 acres) for $2.00 per acre. Purchasers had one year to pay for their claim. Four years later, the Harrison Land Act permitted sales of 320-acre plots at the same price per acre, but with four years of credit available to buyers. And in 1804, 160-acre plots were put up for sale at only $1.64 an acre. With the 1820 land act, 80-acre plots could be purchased for $1.25 an acre, but credit was no longer available. The public lands had been surveyed, and buyers received clear titles to their land. Large land development companies had been formed that purchased vast tracts of public land and resold parcels to settlers at a profit, but cheaper land in smaller parcels made direct purchases by the settlers themselves possible.

The first years of the nineteenth century also saw the uncertain boundaries of the United States begin to take shape. While the 1814 Treaty of Ghent that ended the War of 1812 settled nothing, three years later the United States and Great Britain agreed in the Rush-Bagot Treaty to demilitarize the Great Lakes. Then in 1818, the two nations agreed further to a U.S.-Canadian border at 49° latitude from Lake of the Woods to the crest of the Rockies. They also agreed to joint occupation of the Oregon country. With U.S.-British land issues in the north settled for the time being, it remained to settle disputes with Spain on lands to the south and west. Agreement between the United States and Spain was reached in 1819; the United States would take possession of Florida for the payment of $5 million in U.S. claims against Spain. A southwestern boundary following the Sabine, Red, and Arkansas rivers to the Rockies and then to the 42nd parallel to the Pacific was further agreed on, thus leaving Spain no claim to the Pacific Northwest. In return, the United States gave up its claim to the Texas Gulf Coast, which had been part of the Louisiana Purchase. The Adams-Onís Treaty was ratified in 1821, the year Mexico's independence from Spain gave the United States a new southern neighbor.

THE MISSOURI COMPROMISE

In 1820 there were twenty-two states in the Union, evenly divided between slave and free states. Missouri's petition for admission as a slave state in 1819 promised to upset this delicate balance. In a series of compromises, Maine, separated from Massachusetts, was admitted to the Union as a free state in 1820. Missouri was admitted in 1821 with a constitution that did not outlaw slavery and a promise that the rights of citizens would not be denied by its constitution, a promise necessitated by the desire of Missouri to forbid the immigration of free blacks. In addition, Congress prohibited slavery in the old Louisiana Purchase territory above 36°30', with the exception of the state of Missouri. This decision drew the line between slave states and free states at Missouri's southern border all the way west to Mexican territory. It would be fifteen years before another state was admitted to the Union. The expansion of slavery would continue only slightly abated, and Native Americans would continue to feel the push of a population headed westward with the opening of new territories and states.

OPENING MORE LAND FOR SETTLERS:
THE INDIAN REMOVALS

James Monroe opened his second presidential term in 1821 with some sober reflection on the American relationship with the Indians.

The care of the Indian tribes within our limits has long been an essential part of our system, but, unfortunately, it has not been executed in a manner to accomplish all the objects intended by it. We have treated them as independent nations, without their having any substantial pretensions to that rank. The distinction has flattered their pride, retarded their improvement, and in many instances paved the way to their destruction. The progress of our settlements westward, supported as they are by a dense population, has constantly driven them back, with almost the total sacrifice of the lands which they have been compelled to abandon. They have claims on the magnanimity and, I may add, on the justice of this nation which we must all feel. We should become their real benefactors; we should perform the office of their Great Father, the endearing title which they emphatically give to the Chief Magistrate of our Union. Their sovereignty over vast territories should cease, in lieu of which the right of soil should be secured to each individual and his posterity in competent portions; and for the territory thus ceded by each tribe some reasonable equivalent should be granted, to be vested in permanent funds for the support of civil government over them and for the education of their children, for their instruction in the arts of husbandry, and to provide sustenance for them until they could provide it for themselves.[10]

On January 27, 1825, as Monroe was about to leave office, he sent Secretary of War John C. Calhoun's plan to remove the remaining Indians to "a sufficient tract of country west of the State of Missouri and Territory of Arkansas, in order to establish permanent settlements in that quarter of the tribes which are proposed to be moved," as well as a War Department report on the status of the Indians in the United States, to Congress. The report summarized numbers, locations, and conditions of the various tribes. In total, it found there were 129,266 Indians in the states and territories (California, New Mexico, and Texas were still Mexican provinces). These Indians had land claims totaling 77,402,318 acres.[11]

Monroe and Calhoun's plan, which Andrew Jackson brought to fruition, recalled the principles laid down by Washington. The Indians would be given the Great Plains, not thought to be of tremendous value to European settlers. Congress was to give the War Department power to negotiate, the Senate was to ratify the treaties, eastern Indians were to be moved where there was some assurance of peace with western tribes, and the eastern tribes were to give their land to the United States. Treaties with western Indians were made in 1825, and laws were passed within the next five years in regard to Indian colonization policy. Between 1825 and 1841, the Indian frontier generally followed the western borders of Louisiana, Arkansas, and Missouri, went east almost to Illinois on Missouri's northern border, and included most of what would be Iowa and southern Wisconsin. In 1832 the Bureau of Indian Affairs was created in the War Department. Also in that year, the Supreme Court decided *Johnson v. MacIntosh*, which settled the issue of Indian land ownership. The court ruled that the Indians had occupancy rights but no ownership rights to their land.

In 1835, President Andrew Jackson's message to Congress summed up the status of the Indians as follows:

> The plan of removing the aboriginal people who yet remain within the settled portions of the United States to the country west of the Mississippi River approaches its consummation. It was adopted on the most mature consideration of the condition of this race, and ought to be persisted in till the object is accomplished, and prosecuted with as much vigor as a just regard to their circumstances will permit, and as fast as their consent can be obtained. All preceding experiments for the improvement of the Indians have failed. It seems now to be an established fact that they can not live in contact with a civilized community and prosper.

He went on to note that "the pledge of the United States has been given by Congress that the country destined for the residence of this people shall be forever 'secured and guaranteed to them.'" Jackson hoped that the federal policy, when brought to fruition, would secure for the Indians "prosperity and improvement, and a large portion of the moral debt we owe them will then be paid."[12] By 1840, the Indians were for the most part moved to their "secured" lands away from settlers.

THE 1830s AND 1840s: POPULATION GROWTH, NEW STATES, NEW BOUNDARIES, AND NEW TERRITORIES

Two new states entered the Union during the 1830s. Arkansas, a slave state, was admitted in 1836, and Michigan, a free state, was admitted the next year. The political balance in the Senate was maintained in accordance with the Missouri Compromise of 1820. The 1840s, however, were truly momentous years in the growth of the United States. The decade saw the population increase from 16,987,946 to 23,054,152, of which 3,200,600 were slaves, and the extension and definition of American territory from North to South and East to West.

Maine's northern border, long in dispute with England, was finally drawn in the Webster-Ashburton Treaty of 1842. The Republic of Texas, independent from Mexico since 1836, was annexed in 1845 at its own behest. Texas at that time did not yet have its Rio Grande border. Florida also attained statehood in 1845 as a slave state. Statehood for the free states of Iowa in 1846 and Wisconsin in 1848 continued to maintain balance in the Senate between slave and free states. The Oregon Territory, still jointly occupied by Britain and the United States, was finally divided in 1846 by mutual agreement. The Buchanan-Pakenham Treaty extended the border between Canada and the United States along the 49th parallel, which had been agreed as the boundary in 1818. With the border settled, Oregon Territory could now be organized for the future states of Washington, Oregon, and Idaho. Parcels of Montana and Wyoming were also part of the territory.

War with Mexico, precipitated in part by the annexation of Texas whose independence as a republic was not recognized by Mexico, concluded with the Treaty of Guadalupe Hidalgo in 1848. Texas received south and west Texas and its Rio Grande border with Mexico. The United States took possession of what would become the states of California, Nevada, New Mexico, most of Colorado and Arizona, the Oklahoma panhandle, and the southwestern corners of Kansas and Wyoming. In just the sixty years since George Washington took office as president of a nation that comprised the thirteen former colonies hugging the Atlantic coast, the territory of the United States stretched from sea to sea. President James K. Polk, an avid expansionist who believed that enlarging the limits of the Union was "to extend the dominions of peace over additional territories and increasing millions," proudly summed up the four years of his presidency in his December 1849 message to Congress.

> Within less than four years the annexation of Texas to the Union has been consummated; all conflicting title to the Oregon Territory south of the forty-ninth degree of north latitude, being all that was insisted on by any of my predecessors, has been adjusted, and New Mexico and Upper California have been acquired by treaty. The area of these several Territories...contains 1,193,061 square miles, or 763,559,040 acres; while the area of the remaining twenty-nine States and the territory not yet organized into States east of the Rocky Mountains contains 2,059,513 square miles or 1,318,126,061 acres. These estimates show that the territories recently acquired, and over which our exclusive jurisdiction and dominion have been extended, constitute a country more than half as large as all that which was held by the United States before their acquisition.... The Mississippi, so lately the frontier of our country, is now only its center. With the addition of the late acquisitions, the United States are now estimated to be nearly as large as the whole of Europe.[13]

THE COMPROMISE OF 1850: SLAVERY VERSUS FREE LABOR, SOUTH VERSUS NORTH

New territory meant new states. By 1849, California was ready to join the Union as a free state. New Mexico, then a huge territory spreading from Texas to California, drafted a constitution free of slavery in 1850. The delicate balance in the Senate was again in grave danger of being upset, and no one was more upset than the ailing senator from South Carolina, John C. Calhoun. In his last speech to the Senate on March 4, 1850, which was read for him by Senator Mason, Calhoun outlined the history of southern discontents against the North and offered a solution to the growing political crisis.

One of the causes is, undoubtedly, to be traced to the long-continued agitation of the slave question on the part of the North, and the many aggressions they have made on the rights of the South during the time…. There is another, lying back of it, with which this is intimately connected, that may be regarded as the great and primary cause. That is to be found in the fact that the equilibrium between the two sections in the Government, as it stood when the constitution was ratified and the Government put in action, has been destroyed.

As a result, the North, with its greater population, was running every department of government, and the South had been closed out of new territories. He cited the Northwest Ordinance's prohibition of slavery as the first transgression and the Missouri Compromise as another in a long string of evidence of northern domination. "To sum up the whole, the United States, since they declared their independence, have acquired 2,373,046 square miles of territory, from which the North will have excluded the South, if she should succeed in monopolizing the newly acquired territories, from about three-fourths of the whole, leaving to the South but one-fourth." In addition, Calhoun said that the revenues and disbursements of the government favored the North at the South's expense. All in all, he declared, "What was once a constitutional Federal Republic is now converted, in reality, into one as absolute as that of the Autocrat of Russia, and as despotic in its tendency as any absolute Government that ever existed."

While there were many things that united the states, "the relation between the two races in the southern section" was, Calhoun allowed, a source of absolute opposition and hostility. He discerned three gradations of abolitionists. The most ardent found slavery a sin. Next were those who thought slavery a crime. The rest thought slavery a blot on the nation. Southerners thought differently. "On the contrary, the southern section regards the relation as one which cannot be destroyed without subjecting the two races to the greatest calamity, and the section to poverty, desolation, and wretchedness; and accordingly they feel bound by every consideration of interest and safety, to defend it." Calhoun believed the solution to sectional strife was simple because the South wanted only "justice, simple justice." Justice would have to come from the transgressor, not the transgressed. "The responsibility of saving the Union rests on the North, and not the South," Calhoun stated. The North had "only to will it to accomplish it." Give the South an equal right to expand into the new territories, cease the agitation of the slavery question, faithfully keep the fugitive slave laws, and amend the Constitution to "restore to the South in substance the power she possessed of protecting herself, before the equilibrium between the sections was destroyed by action of this Government." California would become, Calhoun concluded, "the test question."[14]

Calhoun did not live to see how the test question was finally answered in September 1850. Senator Henry Clay of Kentucky patched together the compromise that promised to keep the Union together. California would enter the Union as a free state, but New Mexico would not be admitted for another sixty-two years. Instead, the New Mexico Territory was divided with the creation of Utah Territory. Slavery was not prohibited in either territory. Texas gave up its claims to New Mexico Territory and other lands beyond the Rio Grande, thus attaining its modern boundary. In return, the federal government assumed $10 million of Republic of Texas debt. The slave trade was abolished in the nation's capital, and the fugitive slave laws were enhanced.

HOMESTEADING AND THE END TO POLITICAL COMPROMISE

Political compromises that seemed to give something to everyone but the Indians proved in the end to give no one anything. The compromises begged the issues of slavery and growing sectionalism. As the United States made its final purchase for $10 million of contiguous land from Mexico in 1853—45,000 square miles of what became southern Arizona—the government promoted expansion, and new territories were being organized. The 1862 Homestead Act gave heads of households 160 free acres of public western land for the promise of improving it in five years. The Kansas-Nebraska Act, signed by President Franklin Pierce in May 1854, again avoided the slavery issue by organizing the two territories out of Indian lands on the same basis that was employed in the New Mexico and Utah territories, namely, that the government would let the citizens of the territories decide whether they would be slave or free. This new tack effectively ended the Missouri Compromise by permitting slavery, if the citizens wanted it, above the 36°30' line. Avoidance dressed as political nicety satisfied no group. As Calhoun had feared, the South was being shut out of westward expansion. The free states of Minnesota and Oregon were admitted to the Union in 1858 and 1859, respectively.

In 1857 Chief Justice Roger B. Taney blew the lid off all the congressional compromises that tiptoed around slavery for the sake of the Union. Writing for the majority in its decision on the Dred Scott case, Taney declared that Congress did not have the constitutional authority to expand or prohibit slavery. That authority rested in the realm of the courts. Furthermore, Taney wrote that the federal government did not have the power to free slaves or to make freed slaves citizens. Taney's decision would leave Congress completely out of the slavery debate. There would be no more political deals. Shortly after Kansas entered the Union in January 1861—following bloody skirmishes that were precursors to what was about to happen nationally—soldiers rather than politicians would settle the slavery issue.

THE CIVIL WAR STATES OF WEST VIRGINIA AND NEVADA AND THE LEGAL END OF SLAVERY

The Civil War did not inhibit the admission of new states to the Union. In the cases of West Virginia and Nevada, it accelerated it. The western counties of Virginia split from the state when Virginia seceded from the Union in 1861. This action provided the North with the opportunity to reclaim Confederate land quickly. West Virginia was hastily admitted to the Union in 1863 with a constitution revised by Congress that allowed for the eventual emancipation of slaves. Nevada became the thirty-sixth state in 1864 under somewhat less dramatic, but still unusual, circumstances. Emergency provisions were employed to admit Nevada, which lacked the required population for statehood, to assure the needed votes for the emancipation of slaves. On December 18, 1865, the Thirteenth Amendment outlawing slavery in the United States was ratified. Thus ended the legal issue of slavery after nearly a century of compromises, but there would be no foreseeable solution to the human issue of race.

ALASKA

As Congress and President Andrew Johnson tossed back and forth the scenarios for Reconstruction that promised to reunite the nation in 1867, Nebraska entered the Union, and Secretary of State William Seward negotiated a purchase of land too good to be true. For a mere $7.2 million, Russia agreed to cede the vast wilderness of Alaska, which many contemporaries thought worthless, to the United States. Alaska, twice the size of Texas, increased U.S. territory by 20 percent. Alaska brought with it more Native Americans. The convention between Russia and the United States permitted those who wished to remain Russian citizens three years to return to Russia. Those who wished to stay in Alaska, however, "with exception of the uncivilized native tribes, shall be admitted to the enjoyment of all the rights, advantages, and immunities of citizens of the United States, and shall be maintained and protected in the free enjoyment of their liberty, property, and religion. The uncivilized tribes will be subject to such laws and regulations as the United States may from time to time adopt in regard to the aboriginal tribes of that country."[15]

FEDERAL INDIAN POLICY SHIFTS AS THE WEST OPENS

By the middle of the nineteenth century, the Indians living on the Plains found themselves wedged between expanding European populations from both coasts. Agriculture was moving west, mining was moving east, and railroads would be the vehicle to unite them. There were around 83,000 northern Plains Indians, including the Santee, the Yankton, the Oglala, the Teton, the Sioux, the northern Cheyenne, the Arapahoe, and the Crow. In Colorado, the Southwest, and the central Rockies, southern Cheyenne, Arapahoe, Navajo, and Apache numbered about 65,000. The Five Civilized Tribes removed earlier from the Southeast—Cherokee, Choctaw, Chickasaw, Creeks, and Seminoles—shared the southern Plains with the Comanche, Kiowa, and Pawnee tribes. They numbered about 75,000.[16] Since the 1850s, the federal government had pursued a policy of containing and limiting Indian lands. The Civil War provided the opportunity, just as the Kansas-Nebraska Act had, further to limit Indian claims as some southern tribes were accused of Confederate sympathies. After the war and amidst a series of Indian revolts, the government attempted to make treaties with the tribes that would limit them to an Indian territory in the future state of Oklahoma. The development of reservations in that territory went on for almost twenty years. The federal promises made over the years had proved worthless as Indians' lands were constantly limited and the Indians themselves were forced to accept smaller parcels in changing locations.

In 1871 Congress passed legislation that took away nationhood status from all the Indian tribes. This action meant no more treaties. Congress would now be able to make decisions in Indian internal affairs and impose federal laws on them. After another series of Indian uprisings in the 1870s, in the midst of which Colorado became the thirty-eighth state in 1876 (the centennial year of the Declaration of Independence), the movement to reform federal Indian policy came to fruition. The 1887 Dawes Act, also known as the Indian Homestead Act, authorized the president of the United States to allot reservation lands suitable for agricultural or grazing purposes to the Indians living on them in accordance to this formula:

> To each head of a family, one-quarter section; to each single person over eighteen years of age, one-eighth of a section; To each orphan child under eighteen years of age, one eighth of a section; and To each other single person under eighteen years now living, or who may be born prior to the date of the order of the President directing an allotment of the lands embraced in any reservation, one-sixteenth of a section.

Not only could Indians living on reservations obtain individual lands, but Indians who had no reservation or were living independently of them could also receive the same allotments on any unappropriated federal land by applying to the local land office, where they would not be charged the traditional land office fees. Such allotted lands would be held in trust for twenty-five years, after which time the Indians would receive clear title to it. Most significantly, once lands were allotted and patents to the land received,

> each and every member of the respective bands or tribes of Indians to whom allotments have been made shall have the benefit of and be subject to the laws, both civil and criminal, of the State or Territory in which they may reside; and no Territory shall pass or enforce any law denying any such Indian within its jurisdiction the equal protection of the law. And every Indian born within the territorial limits of the United States to whom allotments shall have been

made under the provisions of this act, or under any law or treaty, and every Indian born within the territorial limits of the United States who has voluntarily taken up, within said limits, his residence separate and apart from any tribe of Indians therein, and has adopted the habits of civilized life, is hereby declared to be a citizen of the United States.[17]

The Dawes Act promised American citizenship to the Indians, who were considered members of foreign nations only a few years previously, if they became "civilized" farmers, but it also gave the federal government the opportunity to buy up Indian land after allotments were made. The land purchased was to be used solely for new settlers' homesteads in tracts no larger than 160 acres, and the money paid by the government for the land was to be maintained in the U.S. Treasury at three-cent-per-annum interest for the benefit of the tribes selling the land. The act specifically excluded the Five Civilized Tribes as well as the Osage, Miamies, Peorias, and Sauks and Foxes who dwelt in Indian Territory, the Seneca reservations in New York, and some land in Nebraska adjoining the Sioux Nation.

As Indian policy continued to develop along these new lines, the West was quickly being added to the Union. North Dakota, South Dakota, Montana, and Washington became states in 1889. One year later, Idaho and Wyoming attained statehood. Utah's admission was delayed until 1896 owing to a number of issues, among them the Mormon acceptance of polygamy. Meanwhile, the Dawes Commission established in 1893 brought the Five Civilized Tribes into the Dawes Indian policy reform, and, by the end of the century, they, as well as other tribes, had given up their claims.

Oklahoma, which had once been Indian Territory, became both an organized territory in 1890 and Indian Territory. In 1898, the Curtis Act abolished tribal courts and required allotments for the Five Civilized Tribes. On March 3, 1901, the Indians in Oklahoma became U.S. citizens by act of Congress, and on November 16, 1907, Oklahoma became the forty-sixth state. Thus ended the long and sordid saga of the Native Americans from the Southeast, the old Northwest, and the Plains, who were promised their own land in Indian Territory for perpetuity.

TWENTIETH-CENTURY DEVELOPMENTS

The twentieth century opened with 74,607,225 Americans living in defined U.S. territory from coast to coast. The nation had also added to its possessions beyond the lower forty-five states. Alaska was slow to develop, not receiving a local government until 1884. Nine years later, Canada and the United States settled an Alaskan boundary dispute. In 1912, when Arizona and New Mexico completed the mosaic of forty-eight states, Alaska was finally organized by Congress as a territory. Homesteading had been extended there in 1903. As early as 1916, Alaska petitioned for statehood, but such would not become a reality until 1959.

The United States and Great Britain had vied for hegemony in Hawaii in the 1870s. In 1893, a group of pro-American revolutionaries overthrew the Hawaiian monarchy and set up a republic the next year, hoping to be admitted as a state. Instead, Hawaii was annexed to the United States in 1898 and a territorial government established in 1900. Hawaii would have a fifty-nine-year wait for statehood.

The resolution of the Spanish-American War in 1898 left the United States with the former Spanish possessions of Cuba, the Philippines, Guam, and Puerto Rico. A Cuban government was set up in 1902, but the United States intervened between 1903 and 1909. Congress overcame President Herbert Hoover's veto to grant the Philippines independence in 1933. A 1950 Organic Act made Guam an unincorporated, organized territory of the United States and made its inhabitants U.S. citizens. Puerto Rico became and remains a commonwealth associated with the United States. Puerto Ricans are U.S. citizens.

There were still more issues to be settled on the mainland. The Dawes Act did not end the Indian question. A U.S. Indian Service report looked back on this period.

> Until comparatively recently the policy of the Federal Government has been to convert the Indian to the conventional land owning white farmer. The first step consisted in an attempt to break up tribal assets into individual allotments, to terminate historical tribal governments, and to suppress Indian customs and tribal laws. As a result some tribal governments had virtually disintegrated or had lost a great deal of their original vigor and importance. Broken treaties and promises, and harsh to cruel treatment naturally caused many Indians to feel varying degrees of hostility to the white race. The suspicion was ingrained that any new policy which might be started by the government was motivated by a desire to aid the whites and hurt the Indians. Since Indians were denied their natural way of life, the government had to establish the odious ration system which sapped initiative and resourcefulness. Many of the Indians become dependent upon government aid as consequence. A tradition of need for assistance therefore has been developed among many who have experienced long periods of dependency on rations or other government assistance as well as unemployment or partial employment.[18]

On June 2, 1924, all native-born Indians became U.S. citizens in recognition of Indian volunteers during World War I. This new law did not impair their rights to Indian or tribal property. Ten years later, Congress completely reversed federal Indian policy. The Wheeler-Howard Act, also called the Indian Reorganization Act, was passed on June 18, 1934. It effectively repealed the Dawes Act, declaring that "hereafter no land of any Indian reservation, created or set apart by treaty or agreement with the Indians, Act of Congress, Executive order, purchase, or otherwise, shall be allotted in severalty to any Indian."

Existing "periods of trust" and any restrictions of the sale of Indian lands were indefinitely extended. The secretary of the interior was authorized "to restore to tribal ownership the remaining surplus lands of any Indian reservation heretofore opened, or authorized to be opened, to sale." The secretary was authorized further to acquire lands for Indians, proclaim new Indian reservations, and issue charters of incorporation to those tribes in which at lease one-third of the adult Indians so requested them. Loan funds were authorized to promote economic development of the incorporated tribes and the education of Indian high school and college students. All tribes, whether on reservations or not, were given the right to organize themselves with constitutions and bylaws and to ratify them through the majority vote of the adults in the tribe. With the approval of the interior secretary, the constitutions would go into force, and Indian tribes would, for the first time since being pushed off their lands, begin to experience "certain rights of home rule." Native customs were now to be appreciated and promoted rather than eradicated. In 1936, the elemental provisions of the Reorganization Act were extended to the Territory of Alaska and the state of Oklahoma, which had been excluded from the 1934 law.[19]

By 1935, homesteading was ended, and public lands were no longer up for sale except in Alaska. The settlement of the lower forty-eight states was complete. In 1947, the U.S. Indian Service noted that "195 tribes, bands, and communities, or groups thereof" were operating under the Indian Reorganization Act, excluding the Indian tribes in Oklahoma and Alaska who were automatically placed under the amended act. In spite of some obstacles, tribal self-government, based on the principle that "people who are most active in the making of their government will in the long run do most to perfect it," had taken "a long step forward." Furthermore, "the gradual increase in self-government among the Indians during the last decade has contributed much toward overcoming historical bitterness and mistrust felt by some Indian groups against the United States." Tribal councils were generally managing their resources well, developing good environmental policies, adding social services, and adopting their own law and order codes.[20]

Whatever good was accomplished in the government's effort to promote Indian self-government and the restoration of Indian cultural values was undone when Congress again reversed Indian policy in 1953. House Concurrent Resolution 108 recommended legislation to terminate the trust relationships between tribes in Texas, California, Florida, and New York, as well as some other particular tribes. Private trustees rather than the government would watch over these "terminated" tribes' assets, thus relieving the federal government of any responsibility. Public Law 83-280 came into force in 1953. It allowed some states, whether or not those states had any such interest, to assume legal jurisdiction over Indian reservations, following the resolve of Congress to get the federal government out of Indian affairs. Many tribes correctly viewed this law, which was amended in 1968 to require the assent of affected Indians before implementing it, as a danger to their own sovereignty. The chairman of

9. From Revolution to Reconstruction, "Jefferson's Eighth State of the Nation Address, November 8, 1808," http://odur.let.rug.nl.

10. The Avalon Project at Yale Law School, "Second Inaugural Address of James Monroe," Monday, March 5, 1821, www.yale.edu.

11. *American State Papers*, Senate, 18th Cong., 2nd Sess., p. 543, www.loc.gov.

12. *A Compilation of the Messages and Papers of the Presidents*, vol. 3 (New York: Bureau of National Literature, Inc., 1897), 3: 1390–1391.

13. Ibid., 5: 2230; 6: 2483–2484.

14. *Congressional Globe*, March 4, 1850.

15. Commager, *Documents of American History*, pp. 492–493.

16. Frederick Merk, *History of the Westward Movement* (New York: Alfred A. Knopf, 1978), p. 419.

17. Commager, *Documents of American History*, pp. 574–575.

18. Theodore H. Haas, *Ten Years of Tribal Government Under I.R.A.* (Washington, DC: Department of the Interior, United States Indian Service, 1947), p. 7, http://thorpe.ou.edu.

19. 25 USCA §1.

20. Haas, *Ten Years of Tribal Government*, p. 16.

21. Menominee Nation, "Chairman—Statement to Senate Committee, May 6, 1998," www.menominee.nsn.us.

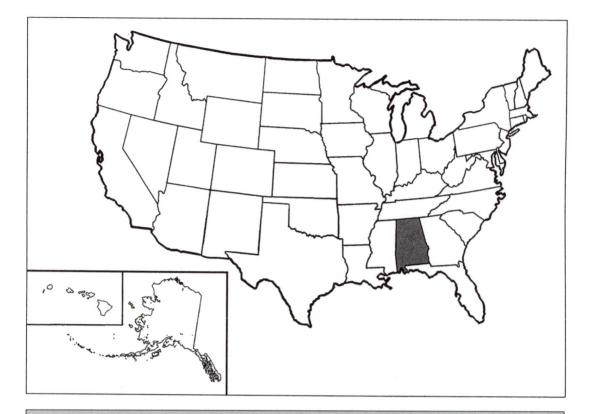

Alabama

Territorial Development:

- Great Britain ceded future Alabamian territory on September 3, 1783, with the Treaty of Paris; incorporated into the United States as part of Georgia
- The United States passed the Northwest Ordinance: territorial claims inherited from colonial charters ceded to the public domain, July 13, 1787
- Future Alabamian territory reorganized as part of the Mississippi Territory, 1798
- Alabama organized as a U.S. territory, March 3, 1817
- The United States obtained future lands of the state of Alabama from Spain through the Adams-Onís Treaty, February 22, 1819
- Alabama admitted into the Union as the twenty-second state, December 14, 1819

Territorial Capitals:

- St. Stephens, 1817–1819
- Huntsville, 1819

State Capitals:

- Cahaba, 1819–1826
- Tuscaloosa, 1826–1846
- Montgomery, 1846–present

Origin of State Name: It is possible that the state name comes from the Indian tribe that settled near the Alabama River or that it is taken from a Choctaw Indian word meaning "thicket clearer" or "vegetation gatherer."

First Governor: William Wyatt Bibb
Governmental Organization: Bicameral
Population at Statehood: 144,317
Geographical Size: 50,744 square miles

THE STATE OF ALABAMA

Admitted to the Union as a State: December 14, 1819

Harriet E. Amos Doss

INTRODUCTION

In the westward migration after the War of 1812, "Alabama fever" lured settlers to the southwestern lands lying between Georgia on the east and the Mississippi River on the west. Initially the eastern part of Mississippi Territory, Alabama eventually experienced such tremendous population growth that within two years after Mississippi achieved statehood, Alabama followed suit. Development toward statehood indeed proceeded at a brisk pace after the War of 1812, as four new states joined the Union in rapid succession, alternating between free and slave status: Indiana (1816), Mississippi (1817), Illinois (1818), and Alabama (1819).

After the war, countless Americans decided to start their lives over in a new place farther west. Many Southerners moved to the Northwest Territory through Kentucky via the Ohio River to pioneer settlements in Indiana and Illinois. After the Erie Canal opened in 1825, New Englanders and residents of the Middle Atlantic States joined them. Southerners predominated in the Southwest, as they opened or expanded the Cotton Kingdom. Leaving exhausted soils in the south Atlantic region, they flocked to the virgin soil of the Gulf Plains, which eventually became Mississippi and Alabama. Before 1812, some southern frontier farmers cultivated cotton in the Natchez District along the Mississippi River and in Madison County on the Great Bend of the Tennessee River.

American military victories against the Indian tribes in the Southwest in the War of 1812 opened huge tracts of land that planters and farmers from the Upper South found particularly attractive. Some powerful tribes still retained control of key areas, so settlers proceeded with considerable risk to such isolated settlements as those on the lower Tombigbee and Alabama rivers. American military occupation of Mobile in 1813 offered those settlers on the Alabama and Tombigbee rivers, and others in central Alabama, critically desired access to the sea.[1]

ALABAMA UNDER FRENCH, BRITISH, AND SPANISH RULE

Access to the sea had long assumed priority for residents of the lands that became Alabama, whether successive French, British, or Spanish rulers set the terms of navigation for rivers that flowed into the Gulf of Mexico. Since the French had founded Mobile in 1702 as the first capital of Louisiana, residents had sustained themselves by trade with Native Americans and export trade with foreign countries via the Alabama and Tombigbee rivers, which formed the Mobile River flowing into Mobile Bay and finally the Gulf of Mexico. The French built Fort Tombecbe in 1736 on the Tombigbee River for protection and trade. It served as a depot for the army and a post for trade with the Choctaws.[2]

This economic pattern continued when the British claimed the area as a result of their victory over the French in the French and Indian War, arranged by the Treaty of Paris of 1763. The British signed a treaty with the Choctaw nation at the Indian Congress in Mobile in 1765 when Great Britain received what is now Washington County "south of the Choctaw boundary line running south from Hatchipki Bluff on the Tombigbee River to the Bucktunna River." This Choctaw cession for the Tombigbee settlements provided the beginning of Alabama, as it gave the British government land to grant to settlers, who then became permanent residents. These early settlers included Loyalist refugees of the American Revolution, planters of French descent, and "Indian Country-men" from the Atlantic seaboard colonies who migrated to the frontier to seek their fortunes or "to escape the law."[3] The economy in the area continued to focus on Indian trade and export trade when the Spanish occupied Mobile in 1780 during the American Revolution and gained title to British West Florida in the Treaty of Paris of 1783.

For the remaining areas that became Mississippi Territory, and later, Alabama Territory, boundaries with Louisiana and East and West Florida complicated land claims. Under the French, the eastern boundary of Louisiana had been the Perdido River. In 1763, when England received Florida from Spain, the territory was divided into East and West Florida, with a western boundary of the Mississippi River. When Spain regained the Floridas in 1783, the boundaries remained the same as under England.[4]

In 1784, Spain closed the lower Mississippi to all ships but its own. This policy, while not strictly enforced, worried western settlers who needed navigation rights to the lower Mississippi. As more Americans settled in Spanish territories, Spanish officials maintained amicable relations with Native Americans, especially the Creeks, for possible aid in resisting any American attack. To protect Americans from Indian attacks in the spring of 1789, Vincente Folch, the Spanish commandant at Mobile, ordered construction of a fort at the head of navigation on the Tombigbee River. Fort San Esteban, as it was called in Spanish for Governor Esteban Miro, translated in English to Fort St. Stephens. This fort provided vital defense for settlers in the Tombigbee-Tensaw District against Indian attacks. The first structure of the fort, hastily constructed of oak, eventually rotted. In 1795, a new Spanish commander replaced it with a fort built of cypress on a new site in the vicinity, which served its purpose until evacuated by the Spanish in 1799.[5]

When Spain made peace with revolutionary France and faced possible war with Great Britain, Spain then fostered good relations with the United States as a protection against attacks on its territories. In 1795, the U.S. diplomat Thomas Pinckney negotiated a treaty with Spain to secure navigation rights of the Mississippi. According to Pinckney's Treaty, or the Treaty of San Lorenzo, Spain accepted the 31st parallel as the southern boundary of the United States. The treaty recognized the mutual right of citizens of Spain and the United States to navigate the entire length of the Mississippi River as well as the right of U.S. citizens to deposit goods at New Orleans prior to shipment overseas. The place for deposit of goods might be changed after three years.

Westerners enjoyed the opportunity to deposit goods at New Orleans for transfer to ocean-going ships without paying Spanish duties. When Spain later attempted to withdraw the right of deposit, the United States intensified its efforts to acquire New Orleans. In the secret Treaty of San Ildefonso of 1800, Spain ceded Louisiana to France. Thomas Jefferson learned of the cession of Louisiana to France shortly after he assumed the presidency. He instructed the American minister to France to try to purchase New Orleans, only to discover that France wished to sell all of Louisiana. The treaty of cession in 1803 contained vague boundary provisions, which the United States later resolved while exercising its right of navigation on the Mississippi River and settling its territory, which had doubled in size.[6]

At the time of the Louisiana Purchase, the Mississippi River had served as the boundary between West Florida and Louisiana, except for New Orleans. When France had settled the Gulf Coast, however, the eastern boundary of Louisiana extended to the Perdido River. After the cession of Louisiana, the United States claimed that the Perdido River was the eastern boundary of that portion of Louisiana located south of the 31st parallel.[7]

ALABAMA AS PART OF MISSISSIPPI TERRITORY

With navigation opened on the lower Mississippi River, Americans settled in such numbers on the eastern side of the river that Congress passed and the president approved the Enabling Act for Mississippi Territory on April 7, 1798. The new territory encompassed land west of the Chattahoochie River, north of the 31st parallel, and south of the cession of South Carolina to the United States. Georgia asserted claim to much of the territory, but Congress provided for ways for the state to relinquish its claim and receive compensation from the sale of public lands. The president received authority to establish a government in the Mississippi Territory "in all respects similar to that now exercised in the territory northwest of the Ohio, excepting and excluding the last article" of the Northwest Ordinance adopted July 13, 1787. The last article forbade slavery in the Northwest Territory, but this prohibition did not apply to the Mississippi Territory, where slavery was an established institution.

With the advice and consent of the Senate, the president had the authority "to appoint all necessary officers" of the Mississippi Territory who would receive the same compensation for their services as for similar officers in the Northwest Territory. While the Mississippi Territory constituted one district for government purposes, Congress might at its discretion later divide the Territory into two districts with separate territorial governments. The people of the Mississippi Territory received promise of "the rights, privileges, and advantages granted to the people" of the Northwest Territory in 1787. The act also made it illegal to import or bring into the Mississippi Territory slaves from foreign countries without financial penalty. Finally, the act appropriated $10,000 to facilitate the president's carrying out its terms.[8]

Within Mississippi Territory, settlers in its western sector along the Mississippi River secured the most attention from territorial and federal officials, as they composed the most populous group. But settlers in the eastern part of the territory that eventually became Alabama, those residing near St. Stephens along the Tombigbee and Tensaw rivers, reminded authorities frequently of their concerns. Hundreds of miles from the Mississippi River and isolated from the seat of territorial government, they agitated for attention and services. Their great distance and small numbers initially secured them limited response, but eventually their population growth and proximity to new territorial acquisitions brought them increased attention in the Mississippi Territory.

The governors of the territory faced numerous challenges in providing executive leadership that would satisfy both the settlers and the authorities in Washington. In practical terms, the territory essentially held colonial status in the nation. Federal officials alone had the authority and funds necessary to redress residents' basic complaints. The governor's constitutional power permitted him to handle routine administration of business. Federal officials appointed territorial officers, set land policy, financed defense of the territory, and managed diplomacy with the Indians and Spaniards. Given these parameters, governors faced tough challenges no matter what choices they made.

President John Adams's appointee as the first governor, Winthrop Sargent, proved controversial even in confirmation, as the Senate barely approved his appointment by a vote of eleven to ten. Sargent, a native of Massachusetts, came to the post in the Mississippi Territory following ten years as secretary of the Northwest Territory.[9] As Secretary of State Timothy Pickering informed Sargent of his selection as governor, "It is at this time peculiarly important that a man of energy, of application to business, and a *military* character be charged with this new government." Pickering, recognizing that Sargent had ten years' experience as secretary of the Northwest Territory, thought that he would "with great facility organize the new government, the whole course of proceeding being perfectly familiar to him." Furthermore, Pickering observed of Sargent, "He is a man of education, fair character, and an experienced and brave military officer."[10] Some residents of Mississippi Territory agreed that Sargent was "a man of integrity, of courage, and of fair ability"; but, they complained, "he was a Puritan of the Puritans, narrow-minded, illiberal, and of strong prejudices.... He was ascetic...cold, austere and suspicious" in temperament, which did nothing to endear him to Mississippians.[11]

The president's other initial appointees were John Steele of Virginia as secretary, and as judges, Peter Bryan Bruin of Mississippi Territory, Daniel Tilton of New Hampshire, and William McGuire of Virginia. Bruin was the only appointee with firsthand knowledge of Mississippi Territory. Governor Sargent reached Natchez in August 1798 and Judges Tilton and McGuire came the next year. Secretary Steele arrived in poor health and never regained his health enough to perform his duties.

Of necessity, Sargent issued executive orders that some of his critics considered more arbitrary and oppressive than Spanish decrees. He also established a probate court to administer estates, take bonds and security, and "care for orphans." McGuire, the chief justice, had the most knowledge of the law, but he did not arrive in the territory until the summer of 1799. While settlers repeatedly requested a code of laws, Governor Sargent proceeded with Judges Bruin and Tilton to adopt a code of laws based on that of the Northwest Territory. Settlers then found fault with the code and the process of its creation and issuance.[12] By late spring 1799, opponents of Governor Sargent in the Natchez District sent memorials, petitions, and grand jury presentments to Congress detailing their grievances.[13]

Not to be ignored, settlers in the Tombigbee-Tensaw District sent their petitions to Congress as well. John Caller and his neighbors, on the Tombigbee and Tensaw rivers in what became south Alabama, requested clarification of their land titles. Some claimed land on the rivers under British titles, most claimed "by virtue of Spanish Grants, obtained since the Cession of the Floridas to Spain, and some [held] by settlement and occupancy." Clashes in British and Spanish titles could lead to much litigation unless settlers could be granted some means of resolution by established regulations. These petitioners recognized that they were "differently circumstanced from their fellow citizens of the Territory residing on the Mississippi, with respect to Commercial and Marine relations." Lacking free navigation of the Tombigbee or Tensaw rivers and free access to the ports of Mobile and Pensacola, they felt particularly disadvantaged as they depended on ocean trade with the United States, the West Indies, and Europe to sell their surplus produce. Furthermore, they urgently needed free navigation to protect themselves from extortion practiced "by foreign Adventurers and Traders residing near, and coming among them." Settlers also complained against Indian traders "on their way to and from the posts or places of Trade" who were "guilty of every species of theft violence and out-rage...." The Tombigbee-Tensaw settlers requested Congress to require Indian traders "to reside and deal within the settlements."

These Tombigbee-Tensaw District residents even suggested that Congress enlarge their territory by purchasing from the Choctaw and Creek nations the lands that lay between the two rivers. They argued, "This acquisition of Territory will unite the Settlements of Tombigby [sic] and Tensaw; will admit an increase of population, will add to the stability and safety of the settlements, and we apprehend will pertain to the advantage of the United States."

As more and more residents settled in Mississippi Territory, Congress extended them second-grade territorial government status on May 10, 1800, which permitted a two-house legislature. Qualified male voters could choose members of the lower house, while the president appointed councillors for the upper house. The two older and larger counties in the territory, Adams and Pickering, were initially entitled to four representatives to the General Assembly, while the Tensaw and Tombigbee settlements were entitled to one.[14]

These settlements on the Tombigbee and Alabama rivers became the nucleus of the new Washington County established by proclamation of Governor Sargent on June 4, 1800. Washington County, which ultimately became the first county in Alabama, encompassed an area four times larger than the two previously established counties in Mississippi Territory. According to the 1800 census, the county, exclusive of Indians, had 1,250 residents, including 454 slaves. McIntosh's Bluff, chosen by Governor Sargent on the recommendation of Secretary Steele, served as the first county seat. John McGrew won the vote there in August 1800 for the district's first representative to the General Assembly of Mississippi Territory, and the residents thus secured legislative representation. They also got judicial services when Governor Sargent appointed justices of the county courts, a treasurer, a sheriff, and other officers.[15]

For old and new residents of Mississippi Territory, clarification of land claims carried tremendous importance. On April 24, 1802, Georgia ceded to the United States its colonial claim to lands south of Tennessee between the Mississippi and Chattahoochie rivers, opening thousands of new acres. Under the agreement between Georgia and the United States, people who had been settlers on October 27, 1795, in the Georgia cession received promise of confirmation of grants prior to that day by the British or Spanish governments. Additional clarification came when the Choctaw cession of 1765, confirmed to the United States by the Treaty of Fort Confederation on October 2, 1802, marked the old Choctaw Boundary Line. The Choctaws surrendered that part of

Washington County north of the boundary line in the treaty they signed at Mount Dexter in the Choctaw Country on November 16, 1805. Disputes dating back to the American Revolutionary War remained, however, between Spain and Britain over the boundary between East and West Florida. The contested area fell between the 31st parallel of latitude running east and west just north of Mobile and the line at 32°28' latitude between the Mississippi River and the Georgia border known as the "Yazoo Strip." Not only did Spain and the United States dispute this strip, but the southeastern Indians—the Creeks, the Choctaws, and the Chickasaws—also occupied it in an effort to counter whites' invasion.[16]

To resolve this extremely complex situation, Congress passed an act on March 3, 1803, that confirmed landownership of settlers holding British or Spanish grants who had title to that specific property on October 27, 1795. Claims could be validated in four categories: ones based on British patents, on Spanish warrants of survey, on occupancy, and on right of preemption. Those with claims in the first three categories had only to pay small fees for surveying and registration. Claimants on the basis of preemption, however, had to pay the United States $2 per acre to secure ownership of the claim. President Thomas Jefferson appointed Ephraim Kirby of Connecticut and Robert Carter Nicholas of Kentucky as land title commissioners to work with the Land Register of Washington County to ascertain rights of people claiming land in Mississippi Territory east of Pearl River. They arrived in the Tombigbee settlements in January 1804 and set up office for the Land Board on the premises of the U.S. military post, Fort Stoddert.[17]

In the Washington District, Kirby found seven American families on the Chickasawhay, near Pascagoula, and about two hundred American families on the Mobile and Tombigbee rivers from the 31-north latitude line to the mouth of the Sintee-bogue, or Snake Creek, a northern boundary between the United States and the Choctaw nation. Fifty to sixty of these families made their homes in the Tensaw settlement on the eastern side of the Mobile River. "This section of the United States has long afforded an assylum [*sic*] to those who prefer voluntary exile to the punishments ordained by law for heinous offenses," Kirby maintained. He judged most of the inhabitants "illiterate, wild and savage, of depraved morals, unworthy of public confidence or private esteem; litigious, disunited, and knowing each other, universally distrustful of each other."

The oldest inhabitants of the area were French settlers who had come prior to the Treaty of Paris of 1763 and had remained under successive changes of government since then. These settlers of French heritage Kirby considered "generally peaceable, honest, well disposed citizens." Settlers with the next-longest residence in the area emigrated from the Carolinas or Georgia where they were, according to Kirby, "proscribed for treasonable practices during the revolution." They, he contended, exhibited hostility "to all law and to every government." Another group who emigrated from the Carolinas and

Georgia came as "fugitives from justice." Still others, Kirby believed, moved from those same states as poor people to the Tombigbee-Tensaw settlements "to avoid the demands of creditors, or to gain a precarious subsistence in a wilderness."[18]

Land commissioners carefully adhered to the land claim requirements set by the act of 1803 and the Georgia cession policy. No matter what their findings based on the evidence submitted by the claimants, some applicants protested to Congress that landholders had already had to pay for two surveys of their lands to satisfy the British and Spanish governments. They asked to have the American public bear the cost of final surveys. As they contended, their area became valuable to the United States "wholly due to the exertions of Your Petitioners, who colonized this Country and reclaimed it from a state of nature, often at the hazard of life itself; and by privations and sacrifizes [sic] unknown to the parent States, have now brought it to a state of high improvement, capable of affording comfort to a great accession of population...."

While commissioners decided cases of existing landholders, other purchasers sought to acquire newly surveyed lands. The U.S. government had pledged Georgia in 1802 to pay $1.25 million in proceeds from the sale of lands in its cession, so new land offices had to open for business in Mississippi Territory to honor that pledge. One office in Adams County handled lands west of the Pearl River, and one in Washington County handled lands east of the Pearl River. Residents complained about delays in surveys required for parcels to be listed for sale. In a memorial to Congress from the Territorial Legislature in January 1807, residents observed that more than three years had elapsed since the surveyor of lands south of the state of Tennessee had arrived in Mississippi Territory to survey lands set for public sale. But the surveys, and consequently the sales, fell behind schedule. Rather than patronize government land offices, newcomers were compelled to buy from individuals at premium prices. The situation clearly irked the memorialists identified as "a people inhabiting an out post of our beloved Country, and exposed on the One hand to the rapacity of a faithless neighbor and on the other to the inroads of the ferocious Savage."[19]

As new lands opened to settlers, Americans increased efforts to befriend their Indian neighbors. In 1802, Governor William C.C. Claiborne, who succeeded Winthrop Sargent, established U.S. trading houses for the Indian tribes in Mississippi. The trading house for the Chickasaws opened near Fort Pickens. In what later became Alabama, the Choctaw trading house opened on the Tombigbee River. Shipments of trade goods for the Choctaw house came south by the Mississippi River to New Orleans and then via Mobile up the Tombigbee River when the Spanish authorities granted clearance.[20]

While these trading houses opened in places that required navigation through Spanish territory, American officials augmented their efforts to get close to the Indian leaders whom the Spanish had previously befriended. When Governor Claiborne feared attack by the Choctaws in the spring of 1803, James Wilkinson, the U.S. military commander, concluded that the Choctaws would not attack

American settlers "unless they are stimulated by a strong hand" and promises of support. Neither proved forthcoming at that time. In a few months, the U.S. commissioners and the chiefs ratified the Indian boundary near St. Stephens on the Tombigbee.[21]

Major land cessions opened large parcels of Alabama to new settlement. Georgia ceded its claim in 1802; Choctaws ceded land in the Tensaw basin in 1805; and Chickasaws and Cherokees ceded land in the Huntsville area in 1805 and 1806, respectively. Land surveys followed the system set by the Land Ordinance of 1785. They established townships of thirty-six square miles surveyed off two east-west lines, the Huntsville Base Line and the St. Stephens Base Line, and two north-south lines, the St. Stephens Meridian and the Huntsville Meridian.

Land sales proceeded under terms of the Land Law of 1800, as amended by the Land Act of 1804 that permitted settlers to buy as few as 160 acres and pay in four installments. Land was first auctioned to the highest bidder. Unsold land was then offered at $2 per acre, or $1.64 if payment was made in cash. Generous credit arrangements allowed poor farmers to purchase land, but they also encouraged speculation that contributed to the Panic of 1819. Public land offices opened in St. Stephens in 1803 and in Huntsville in 1811.

Eager to occupy still more land, white settlers engaged the Indians in battles that took many lives but eventually gave them what they desired. Creeks sought arms from the Spanish in Pensacola, but the Spanish gave them no guns. Instead they contributed only gunpowder and some supplies. On their way back to Alabama in July 1813, an American militia group led by Colonel James Caller of Washington County attacked the Creeks and won the first round at Burnt Corn Creek, but the Indians regrouped, attacked, and defeated Caller's men. As the Indians came to believe that all whites should be slain, settlers moved their families into hastily constructed "forts" for their protection in the ongoing Indian war.

A massacre of monumental significance to the Alabama frontier occurred at one of these palisaded forts built around Sam Mims's house on Tensaw Lake off the Alabama River. Major Daniel Beasley, a Mississippi attorney who secured his commission through politics, commanded the militia at Fort Mims. He lacked military training, Indian warfare experience, and common sense. Despite warnings from Brigadier General Ferdinand L. Claiborne of the Mississippi territorial militia that his position was quite exposed, Beasley did not take any further defensive measures. When scouting reports came from several sources that Indians in war paint were hiding near Fort Mims, Beasley did not believe them. He even refused to believe a man who rode on horseback to the front gate and shouted a specific warning. At noon on August 30, 1813, the Creeks rushed the fort, where stockade doors could not be shut because sand had drifted against them. Creeks killed some 250 men, women, and children, while the attackers lost some 100 of their number. The Fort Mims Massacre spread alarm among whites throughout the frontier.

This danger to the remote part of Mississippi Territory brought new military attention from the United States. When Creeks assembled at their holy ground on a high bank of the Alabama River, prophets distributed potions that they claimed would kill whites who entered the site of religious rituals. Nevertheless, the militia army of General Ferdinand L. Claiborne of Mississippi Territory prevailed, decimating the Indians on December 23, 1813.[22]

By the end of 1813 both Generals Claiborne and Andrew Jackson of Tennessee faced problems with expiring enlistments of their militiamen and were encountering difficulty in securing new recruits when they heard rumors of limited rations. Jackson persisted, for he knew that the Indians were gathering at a major fort inside a bend of the Tallapoosa River called Tohepeka, or Horseshoe Bend. After securing reinforcements from American forces and friendly Creeks under William McIntosh, Jackson's forces attacked the hostile Creeks at Horseshoe Bend on March 27, 1814. Sam Houston, a twenty-one-year-old Tennessee militiaman, recalled, "Arrows, and spears, and balls were flying; swords and tomahawks were gleaming in the sun; and the whole Peninsula rang with the yell of the savage, and the groans of the dying." Indeed, hundreds of Indians became casualties and few escaped. At the battle of Horseshoe Bend, American forces destroyed Creek power in Alabama.[23]

From Horseshoe Bend, Jackson's men marched to the site of old Fort Toulouse and constructed a stockade he called Fort Jackson. There, defeated Indians came to surrender personally to him. On August 9, 1814, Creek chiefs signed the Treaty of Fort Jackson, by which they gave up lands that covered almost half of Alabama.[24] (Then Jackson's volunteers marched toward the defenses of New Orleans.)

During the War of 1812 and the Creek wars, the United States acquired another extremely valuable addition: the port and hinterland of Mobile, vitally needed for access to the sea by Alabama. Mobile, located in the disputed territory between the Perdido and Mississippi rivers, was placed into a U.S. Customs district in 1804. Spain protested this action and refused to surrender West Florida to the United States on the grounds that West Florida was not part of Louisiana. In 1810, after planters with large landholdings in the western part of West Florida declared their independence from Spain, President James Madison issued a proclamation that annexed parts of the province between the Mississippi and Pearl rivers and along the Gulf Coast to the Perdido River. Even though the town of Mobile was included in this proclamation of annexation, Spain maintained the garrison there.[25]

Some Americans in the Tombigbee settlements plotted to take hostile action against Mobile and Pensacola, as they remained in Spanish hands. Those who emigrated from Kentucky and West Tennessee via New Orleans complained of delays and expenses exacted on goods shipped to them. Many balked at the duties levied daily by Spanish authorities on exports and imports into the settlement, which hurt their chance for prosperity. Some expressed disappointment that their expectations, based on the president's statement to representatives from Tennessee in Congress, had not materialized regarding free navigation of the Tombigbee and Alabama rivers. "Designing demagogues," as the U.S. military commander at Fort Stoddert labeled them, remained ready at all times to foment popular discontent and fan the embers of sedition. Spanish authorities ordered troops from Pensacola to reinforce Mobile and solicited Choctaws and Creeks to provide further protection. Governor David Holmes of Mississippi Territory and Judge Harry Toulmin, Mississippi Territory judge for the Washington County District, repeatedly advised the reported conspirators that people in illegal combinations put themselves, their fortunes, and their reputations at risk. Panic gripped residents of Mobile in the fall of 1810 as rumors circulated of an army on its way there from Baton Rouge. No such army appeared, but Spanish troops defeated a small party of American attackers near Mobile.

When the U.S. Congress passed its Act to Enlarge the Boundaries of the Mississippi Territory on May 14, 1812, the territory expanded to include land lying east of Pearl River, west of the Perdido River, and south of the thirty-first degree of north latitude. On August 1, Governor David Holmes issued the Proclamation Organizing Mobile County for the newly annexed lands. Laws of Mississippi Territory and pertinent acts of Congress then had force in Mobile County.[26]

The Spanish occupation finally ended during the War of 1812. Since the Spanish allowed British naval vessels to rendezvous in Mobile and other Gulf ports in their possession, the American government decided to occupy Mobile in order to stop this indirect Spanish aid to the British. In February 1813, Madison ordered Major General James Wilkinson, the commander at New Orleans, to take possession of Mobile. Wilkinson moved effectively in mid-April to cut off the land and sea communications from the Spanish garrison in Fort Charlotte (formerly Fort Conde). He informed the commander of the garrison that he was simply relieving the forces occupying a post considered within the legitimate boundaries of the United States. The Spanish forces were out of provisions and surrendered the fort without bloodshed. As Spanish civilians departed along with the troops, Americans moved into the town, situated in the only territory that the United States acquired as a result of the war. Thus, the United States effectively annexed West Florida by military force, while it obtained East Florida by diplomacy in the Adams-Onís Treaty signed in 1819 and consummated in 1821.

Americans soon provided government for the town of Mobile. Under the provisions of an act of the Mississippi Territorial Legislature passed in January 1814, the white male landholders, freeholders, and householders within the town elected seven commissioners and a town treasurer, collector, and assessor. These new officers translated their resolutions into French and posted copies in English and French in public places, for French, rather than Spanish, was the predominant language besides English in early American Mobile.[27]

As Mobile made the transition from its colonial and foreign history into its American future as part of Alabama, the U.S. commander at Fort Charlotte, Captain George P. Peters, penned this assessment in 1816 of the town and its residents:

> The Town of Mobile was built *under the guns and protection of the Fort*, and consists chiefly of old buildings, one story high, of frames of wood filled in with *Spanish Moss*—The inhabitants (with a few exceptions) are a mixture consisting of the Creoles, (principally couloured) and emigrants from England, Scotland, Ireland, and different parts of the United States who are governed entirely by personal interest; and exhibit very little of what may be termed *National feeling*— As however Mobile must eventually become the grand commercial depot for all the fertile Country on the Tombigby and Alabama Rivers, the necessary increase of population must in a short time produce an alteration for the better in the character of the inhabitants.

Shortly thereafter, Mobilians petitioned Congress to demolish Fort Charlotte, and in 1818, John C. Calhoun, secretary of war, recommended the demolition and sale of land attached to the fort, which was no longer needed for defense.[28]

DIVISION OF MISSISSIPPI TERRITORY AND STATEHOOD FOR MISSISSIPPI

After the War of 1812, the movement for statehood assumed new importance for Mississippi Territory. Since 1803, the major consideration had been whether to seek admission for the entire territory or to divide it before requesting statehood. Prior to the War of 1812, residents of the Tombigbee District had championed separation. After 1815, as the population grew in the eastern sector faster than in the western sector, many easterners changed their views. Those in the Natchez District had favored unified admission until treaties of cession with the Creeks in 1814 and the Choctaws, Chickasaws, and Cherokees in 1816 more than doubled the land available for sale in the eastern half of the territory. Some Natchez politicos came to have reservations about admission of the entire territory. Thus, between 1812 and 1816, the western and eastern sections of the territory reversed their views about the way to seek statehood.[29]

Inadequate population had, of course, held up admission of Mississippi Territory before 1816. Other factors had also complicated the movement toward statehood. While the population remained relatively small, many feared their tax base would be inadequate to cover public expenses. Others believed all land controversies should be resolved before statehood. Disunity among Mississippians provided an excuse for denial of statehood to several eastern congressmen who opposed admitting any new states.[30]

Territorial division had a long history, for residents of the Tombigbee District had petitioned Congress as early as 1803 to divide their territory so their interests would be addressed appropriately. At that time they estimated the population of their Washington District on the Mobile, Tombecbe, and Alabama rivers in excess of three thousand, many of whom had recently migrated from Georgia and other parts of the United States. They were subject to the laws of Mississippi Territory, "which are enacted at the distance of nearly three hundred miles from us, all of which distance is a howling wilderness with its usual inhabitants of Savages and beasts of prey." Their district had "people different in their manners and customs, different in their interests" from those in the Natchez District. They asked for a separate government. Again, in 1809, they requested Congress to grant them a separate government. This time inhabitants east of the Pearl River held a meeting to draft the petition, which they requested Judge Harry Toulmin to transmit directly to the Speaker of the House of Representatives to present to the House. They maintained "that the remoteness of their situation, and the total dissimilarity of their channels of Trade, give the people of the Mobile and its adjacent waters, no common interest with those of the Mississippi." A wilderness of two to three hundred miles between settlements east and west of the Pearl River, they said, "deprives us of every thing but a merely nominal representation in Congress." This petition, like others, made it no further than referral to a select committee.[31]

Major, albeit unsuccessful, efforts at statehood began in 1810 when Mississippi Territory's delegate to Congress, George Poindexter, advocated immediate admission of the whole territory. When he failed in that attempt, he changed strategy in November 1811 to seek admission of the southern half of the Mississippi Territory and the whole of West Florida, which the United States was in the process of acquiring from Spain. This proposal failed as well. Poindexter only succeeded in securing Georgia's agreement to divide the Mississippi Territory, should Congress deem it expedient.

A more serious campaign for statehood began in 1815 under the direction of Poindexter's successor, Dr. William Lattimore. In February 1815, Lattimore introduced "an enabling act that would authorize the territory to proceed with the writing of a constitution." While Congress began its debates on this proposal, residents of the territory sent a flood of memorials with varied messages about seeking admission as a unified territory. Opponents of territorial division met in October 1815 at John Ford's on the Pearl River to draft a petition for "indestructible" admission. Representatives at the Pearl River convention drafted Judge Harry Toulmin to proceed to Washington to present their petition and to confer with Lattimore. When cooperation between the two proved impossible, Toulmin eventually turned to Representative Israel Pickens of North Carolina for aid.

Contradictory messages from residents of Mississippi Territory indeed gave Lattimore no clear direction, so he opted on his own for division. He calculated that a majority of the Senate, then controlled by Southerners, preferred territorial division, as it would eventually give the South four senators rather than two.

Lattimore, himself a westerner in the territory, thus introduced a resolution to permit "the western half of the territory to call a constitutional convention." Eastern congressmen opposed this bill, for they feared losing power to the western states. Finally, in early 1817, Congress agreed to two bills that more nearly met the goal of Lattimore than Pickens and Toulmin. On March 1, 1817, President Madison signed the Enabling Act that provided for "the admission of the western section as the state of Mississippi and for the reorganization of the eastern part as the Alabama Territory." Another act compromised the wishes of the easterners who favored the Pearl River and westerners who pushed for the Tombigbee River in setting a division between Mississippi and the prospective Alabama Territory. The dividing line proceeded north from the Gulf of Mexico to the northwestern corner of Washington County and thence directly to where Bear Creek emptied into the Tennessee River. This arrangement put the Mobile District, the Tombigbee settlements, and Madison County in the Alabama Territory, while it left the Pascagoula and Pearl River settlements and the old Natchez District in the new state of Mississippi.[32]

CREATION OF ALABAMA TERRITORY

"Alabama fever" drew thousands of migrants to the eastern part of Mississippi Territory following the Creek war. So many came that they might have held the balance of power in Mississippi had the territory not been divided for statehood. Politicians considered several division lines. One, which followed the example of Tennessee, advocated an east-west line of division. John Williams Walker wrote Charles Tait in January 1817 supporting the east-west division "with a view of preventing as far as might be, any collision of interests between the upper and lower country." This concern about dividing the Tennessee Valley and north Alabama from the Tombigbee Valley and south Alabama focused on the sectionalism that bedeviled Alabama because its two major regions depended on two different river-trade systems for their livelihoods. Once north Alabama politicians realized that the rapidly increasing population in the Tennessee Valley would enable the area to control the new territory, they halted objections to a north-south dividing line. That division was the way Georgia senator Charles Tait, and future Alabama resident, advocated the separation of Mississippi Territory in 1817.[33]

The Broad River group of politicians from Georgia exercised tremendous influence in Alabama's economic and political development from pre-territory through early statehood periods. William Harris Crawford, their most prominent figure, served first as a senator from Georgia, then as secretary of war, and later secretary of the treasury under President James Monroe. Crawford made his home in the Broad River area of Georgia, where a number of closely connected Virginia families had immigrated after the American Revolution.

Some of their sons, including Leroy Pope and John Williams Walker, purchased land in the Huntsville region in the land sales of 1809 and moved their families to Alabama in 1810. While serving Georgia in the Senate, Crawford also represented the interests of his friends in Madison County. When he moved into the cabinet, he came to depend on two other Broad River men, U.S. senators Charles Tait and William Wyatt Bibb of Georgia. Tait introduced in the U.S. Senate the crucial bills Alabama needed: one enabling Mississippi to form a state government, and another establishing Alabama as a territory. Crawford influenced sales of land in what became Alabama for the benefit of his friends in Georgia. He located the first land office for the sale of Indian cession lands in Milledgeville, Georgia, a convenient place for Georgians but inconvenient for poor squatters in Alabama who had to travel to place bids for their lands. Crawford helped his friend Alexander Pope secure the position of register of the land office.

Crawford remained a Georgian, but many of his friends relocated to Alabama. Tait and Bibb purchased land and moved to south Alabama. William Wyatt Bibb and his brother Thomas, Leroy Pope, and John Williams Walker, who married Leroy Pope's daughter Matilda, formed the "Georgia faction" (later called the Royal party or identified with the Broad River of Georgia). For over a decade, the group dominated Alabama politics.

In Milledgeville, friends of the Georgia faction purchased lands from the Creek cession when they were first auctioned on August 4, 1817. The next year, when a land office opened in Conecuh County, small farmers purchased land at better prices, and squatters frequently managed to secure title to their homesteads. By 1819, another office operated in the new state capital at Cahaba.[34] Land continued to sell at a brisk pace in the land office at Huntsville. John Read documented more applicants than tracts available for sale along the Tennessee River. "There appears to prevail something like a land mania," he reported in April 1818.[35]

Opposition to the Georgia faction evolved from democratic politicians who spoke for the interests of yeomen farmers, by far the largest element of the frontier population. One who shaped his public service by championing the common man was Gabriel Moore, a native North Carolinian, who migrated in 1810 to Huntsville in Madison County, then the most populous county in the eastern part of Mississippi Territory. The young attorney immediately entered public service with his appointment in 1810 as tax assessor and collector for Madison County. His duties included supervising the census for Madison County that helped to determine the apportionment of representatives for the Mississippi Territorial Assembly.

Moore built his political career with appeals to the small farmers who populated Madison County and with attacks on that area's Broad River faction, whose members often resided in the county seat of Huntsville. This champion of the people owned almost five hundred acres of land and four slaves in 1815, property holdings that placed him closer to the typical pioneer settler of the county than the business elite of the town. An affluent attorney as well as small planter, Moore, observed a contemporary, was "a skillful electioneer [who] courted the lower stratum of society." He appealed to the common man by delivering stump speeches in which he declared that he came not from the "Royal Party," but from the poor. Moore represented Madison County in the Mississippi Territorial Assembly from 1811 to 1817, and he served as its speaker from 1815 to 1817. When Alabama became a separate territory in 1817, Moore continued to represent the county in the assembly and served as speaker during its first session in January and February 1818.[36] Moore consistently championed the interest of farmers whose pressing worries often centered on land debt relief. These people, who had purchased public lands on credit, found it impossible due to the Creek wars and Panic of 1819 to make their installment payments on schedule.

Senator Tait from Georgia introduced the legislation because of his keen interest in Alabama, for he planned to make his new home there. John Williams Walker, one of the Broad River group who moved to Alabama in 1810, corresponded regularly with Tait to inform him about political developments in Alabama. Tait took particular interest in the news, for his son, James Asbury Tait, had relocated his family to land he had purchased in south Alabama, and the senior Tait planned to join him there at the end of the congressional term.[37] From his ties of politics and kinship, Senator Charles Tait shepherded two vital bills through Congress, one enabling Mississippi to organize a state government and another establishing the Territory of Alabama.

Senator Tait, who was a member of the committee that had been assigned the bill to establish a separate territorial government for the eastern part of the Mississippi Territory, reported a bill on February 4, 1817. This bill was reported as amended on February 5, and on February 19 the Committee of the Whole considered it. It was then reported with an additional amendment. It was read the third time and passed on February 21, then sent to the House. In the House, members had to choose from several options whether Congress should enable Mississippi to enter the Union as a whole or after division. The Senate bill to enable people in the western part of the territory to organize a state then advanced to its third reading and soon passed. The act was approved March 1, 1817. Then the Senate bill to establish Alabama Territory was quickly advanced to its third reading and passed on March 3, 1817.[38]

The Enabling Act establishing Alabama Territory took effect at Mississippi's admission to the Union on December 10, 1817. It established the new Alabama Territory as that part of Mississippi Territory within these boundaries: beginning where the thirty-first degree of north latitude intersects the Perdido River, east to the western boundary of Georgia, then along that line to the southern boundary of Tennessee, west along that line to the Tennessee River, up the Tennessee River to the mouth of Bear Creek, then by direct line to the northwest corner of Washington County, then due south to the Gulf of Mexico, then east to the Perdido River, and up the river to the beginning.[39]

In accord with the Ordinance of 1787 all territories prior to Alabama Territory had progressed through two stages of supervised development, with the first stage operating under a presidentially appointed governor, secretary, and three judges, and the second stage adding a representative assembly and appointed legislative council for the residents when their numbers warranted it. Alabama Territory marked a departure from this pattern, for it bypassed the first stage and acquired representation, a second-stage feature, from the outset. The president of the United States received the power to appoint a governor, secretary, and an additional judge to make a total of three. In addition, he would select three names from a list of six nominated by the Territorial Legislature to appoint as legislative councillors to serve in the upper house. The legislature would elect its own territorial delegate to Congress.

President Monroe appointed as governor William Wyatt Bibb, former Georgia senator and a close friend of William Harris Crawford, former Georgia senator and now his secretary of the treasury. He appointed John W. Walker from Huntsville as secretary, but he declined the position due to ill health. Henry Hitchcock of Washington County served as secretary. The judges included one new appointee and two continuing ones. Continuing in service were Judge Harry Toulmin, whose appointment was confirmed on November 20, 1804, for the Tombigbee District, and Judge Obadiah Jones, who was appointed March 6, 1810, for Madison County. The other judge for Alabama Territory was initially Stevenson Archer of Maryland, whose commission was dated March 6, 1817. Jones resigned in 1819 and was succeeded by John Williams Walker, who resigned within a year of his March 2, 1819, appointment and returned to Maryland.[40] Elected representatives and members of the Legislative Council of Mississippi Territory who served from counties now in Alabama Territory would serve in the new Territorial Assembly until their terms expired or Congress provided otherwise.[41]

The Enabling Act established that St. Stephens would serve as the seat of government for Alabama Territory until its legislature provided otherwise. Whatever balance remained in the treasury of the Mississippi Territory when it formed a state government was to be divided between the new state and territory on the basis of amounts paid in by counties lying in the bounds of the state and territory.[42]

TERRITORIAL GOVERNMENT FOR ALABAMA TERRITORY

First Territorial Legislature at St. Stephens (January 1818)

Owing to Alabama's rapid population growth, only two sessions of its territorial legislature met, both in 1818, before statehood. Territorial governor William Wyatt Bibb, appointed by President James Monroe, called the first Territorial Legislature to convene on January 19, 1818, at St. Stephens. The first session operated with holdover members of the Mississippi Territorial Legislature who had represented the Alabama region. At the Douglas Hotel, where the legislature rented meeting rooms, only twelve members of the House and one member of the Senate initially assembled for the session. Madison County representatives played a major part in the proceedings. On the day appointed for the meeting of the Legislative Council, James Titus of Huntsville in Madison County, "being the only member" present, ran the upper house. He, as its president, appointed a secretary and a doorkeeper, called roll, made motions, voted on bills and resolutions, and moved adjournment. Four representatives from Madison County led the House. They were Clement C. Clay, Hugh McVay, Gabriel Moore, and John Williams Walker.[43] Moore served as speaker of the House of Representatives.

This first session handled a number of basic organizational matters. Members divided the territory into three judicial circuits for the three territorial judges. The assembly created thirteen new counties, mostly in the upper Alabama and Tombigbee River valleys or in the Tennessee Valley. Members nominated six men for the president of the United States to select from for appointments to three council positions. And they elected John Crowell as the first Alabama Territory delegate to Congress.[44]

Governor Bibb advised the members of the Territorial Legislature: "[T]he period cannot be distant, when the haunts of the savage will become the dwelling place of civilized man, and the forests of the wilderness be converted into fruitful fields." To facilitate that process, the governor encouraged legislators to provide for schools and the means of education for their population; to develop roads, ferries, and bridges to encourage more immigration into the territory; to establish a commission to locate the best route for a road from the Tennessee River to the Tuscaloosa Falls of the Warrior River.[45] In the matter of internal improvements, the Alabama Territorial Assembly sent a memorial to Congress seeking aid to remove obstructions at Muscle Shoals in the Tennessee River, the navigation of which, they noted, was important not just to Alabama but also to Tennessee, Georgia, and Mississippi.[46]

In a rapidly developing area, banking and usury laws, controversial as they might be, influenced economic opportunity. John J. Walker took the lead in presenting pro-creditor legislation to the assembly. Walker supported repeal of the Mississippi Territory Act Against Usury, which allowed any interest rate agreed to in writing by both parties. He introduced a bill dealing with the charter of the renamed Huntsville Planters and Merchants Bank. Had his bill become law, it would have committed the Alabama Territory to accept the bank's notes and allowed the bank to expand by establishing new branches. Breaking with Walker on this banking issue, Governor Bibb vetoed the bill. He feared that bank directors in Huntsville would wield disproportionate power over the commerce of Alabama. Walker's bill also alienated him from average settlers in Alabama, who harbored suspicions of banks and their directors as agents of the rich. He later submitted another bill, basically a name change, for the Planters and Merchants Bank in Huntsville that did pass and secure the governor's approval. The Territorial Legislature also enacted a bill to establish the Tombecbe Bank in St. Stephens, which would be led by Israel Pickens, then an associate of the Georgia faction. As a member of the Georgia faction, Walker clearly represented the interests of creditors in using his political power to protect his own interests at the expense of his constituents. Democratic groups in Alabama frowned upon pro-creditor legislation as private banks and public credit became important political issues.[47]

The first Territorial Legislature took other less controversial actions. The legislature expanded the militia, with the territorial government supplying provisions for the men. It provided for a territorial census, chartered a school, approved two divorces, and authorized the manumission of three slaves.

The legislature also took a significant step for future political and economic development during the first session in its appointment of a commission to choose a site for the state capital and report to the next session of the legislature. Location of the capital would boost economic development and land values, so both the Alabama-Cahaba River and Tombigbee-Warrior River groups competed for it. Representatives from the Tennessee Valley could not secure the location of the capital so far north, but they held powerful swing votes sought by the other two factions. By the next session of the legislature in November, capital site selection became a major political issue.[48]

Second Territorial Legislature at St. Stephens (November 1818)

When the Territorial Legislature assembled for its second session in November 1818, Alabama's population had exceeded the number required for admission to the Union. John Williams Walker, speaker of the House, prepared the petition for Alabama statehood and sent it to Senator Tait, who presented it to the upper house of Congress. With a newly completed census, the legislature began to apportion representation so Congress could use its calculations to allocate delegates to a state constitutional convention. Members also created two new counties. And, as they anticipated a constitutional convention, they passed a law authorizing its expenses.[49]

Apportionment provided the key to allocation of power. Representatives from north Alabama advocated counting only whites for representation, rather than using the federal ratio that included counting each slave as three-fifths of a person. If only whites were counted, Madison County could claim twice as many representatives as any other county. Representatives from south Alabama failed to get enough support for use of the federal ratio, but they passed an amendment locating the permanent capital in the southern part of the territory at Cahaba, a site preferred by Governor Bibb. While Cahaba was laid out and a capitol building constructed, Huntsville would serve as the temporary capital. These legislative decisions dashed any hopes that

St. Stephens would become the capital of Alabama. Tuscaloosa, the place favored by the legislative commission, also lost its opportunity to serve as the capital at this time.[50]

THE ALABAMA CONSTITUTIONAL CONVENTION

Huntsville, the temporary capital of Alabama Territory, hosted not only the scheduled constitutional convention on July 5, but also the surprise visit of the president of the United States on June 1. The town of approximately 1,000, which was county seat of Madison County with its 16,500 residents, had a new courthouse, numerous brick commercial and residential buildings, a market house, a bank with authorized capital of $500,000, several taverns and hotels, a theater, a library, a weekly newspaper, a Masonic lodge, and a busy U.S. Land Office. Near midday on June 1, 1819, three men on horseback rode into Huntsville and strolled into the Huntsville Inn. These unexpected visitors were none other than President James Monroe and his two young aides, Samuel L. Gouverneur, his private secretary, and James Monroe, his military aide. Local citizens rose to the occasion by giving the president a public dinner the next day. The president's party joined more than one hundred of the most respectable citizens of Madison County at a sumptuous banquet, certainly the grandest event ever in Alabama Territory. Leroy Pope presided at the dinner, assisted by Clement C. Clay and Henry Minor.[51]

As the *Alabama Republican* reported, after dinner the guests drank toasts, "accompanied by the discharge of cannon, and appropriate songs." Many of the toasts proved routine for public dinners of the era, but two had special timeliness. As Missouri was seeking statehood when Alabama was doing the same, both as slave states, one toast highlighted the states' rights concern: "The people of the territories west of the Mississippi—when their numbers entitle them, may they be admitted into the union, with no other restrictions, than those prescribed by the Constitution." Prompt admission for Alabama might enable the state's congressmen to vote on Missouri's statehood. President Monroe eloquently toasted: "The Territory of Alabama—may her speedy admission into the Union advance her happiness, and augment the national strength and prosperity."[52]

About one month after President Monroe left Huntsville, delegates elected to the Constitutional Convention assembled there to write a constitution for Alabama, which, according to the Enabling Act, "shall be republican." The Enabling Act also made certain generous offers of federal public land to the state on condition of receiving certain promises in return from the state. The U.S. government set aside the sixteenth section of land in each township for public schools. Five percent of money from the sale of public land was set aside for internal improvements. A grant made in 1818 of one section of land at Cahaba for the site of a capitol was enlarged to 1,620 acres, and two full townships were granted to Alabama Territory for a "seminary of learning," rather than the one given by Congress in 1818. In return, the Constitutional Convention was required to pass an ordinance forever disclaiming "all right and title to the…unappropriated lands lying within the said Territory." The state also had to pledge not to tax land sold by the federal government within the state for five years after the sale.[53]

The forty-four delegates to the Constitutional Convention included twenty-eight from north Alabama and sixteen from south Alabama, thus representing population concentrations at the time. Despite differences in views on some issues, they unanimously chose John W. Walker as president of the convention. John Campbell served as the secretary. Among the delegates were at least eighteen attorneys, four physicians, two ministers, one surveyor, one merchant, and four planters or farmers. They decided early in their deliberations to turn over the process of writing a draft constitution to a Committee of Fifteen: Chairman Clement Comer Clay; John M. Taylor and Henry Chambers of Madison County; Israel Pickens and Henry Hitchcock of Washington; John Murphy and John Watkins of Monroe; Thomas Bibb and Beverly Hughes of Limestone; William R. King of Dallas; Arthur F. Hopkins of Lawrence; Reuben Saffold of Clarke; John D. Bibb of Montgomery; Richard Ellis of Franklin; and George Phillips of Shelby County.[54]

On July 13, Clay reported the original draft of the constitution. The document in its original (and final form) contained a preamble and six articles dealing with a declaration of rights, separation of powers, the legislature, the executive, the judiciary, and general provisions. These general provisions dealt with education, banks, slavery, the amendment process, and a schedule for implementation. Notable features of the draft constitution were requirements that a voter be a white male who was a member of the militia (unless exempt by law from military service), that the federal ratio serve as the basis of apportionment in the legislature, that annual elections for and annual sessions of the legislature be held, and that a governor elected by the people carry veto power and some appointive power.

The article on the legislature provided suffrage for white male citizens at least twenty-one years old who were residents of the state for at least one year and of the district for three months. The Committee of the Whole eliminated the militia service requirement in the original draft, so the Alabama constitution contained no qualification based on property holding, tax paying, or militia service. Kentucky had no additional qualifications beyond the basic ones retained by Alabama. Thus, Alabama and Kentucky alone among the southern states had universal white manhood suffrage in 1819.

The Committee of Fifteen proposed use of the federal ratio of counting five slaves as three white men for representation in the state legislature. This proposal followed what was then included in the Georgia constitution, which may account for its inclusion in the draft for Alabama, owing to the Georgia influence on its representatives. But the Committee of the Whole voted against the federal ratio, just as delegates had two years earlier in Mississippi. So

Alabama, like Mississippi, adopted white population as the basis for representation in the state legislature. Because of expected rapid growth and population shifts in the new state, provisions were made for frequent censuses and subsequent reapportionment.

The legislative article of the draft constitution contained provisions regarding the state capital. The Enabling Act had granted land at Cahaba for a capital, but north Alabamians wanted the site further north. South Alabamians thought Cahaba was satisfactory. The Committee of Fifteen drafted a compromise that was essentially adopted by the convention and included in the constitution. The agreement provided that the first legislature would meet in Huntsville, but subsequent sessions would meet in Cahaba until 1825. At that time a permanent capital, perhaps Cahaba, would be chosen by the legislature. This arrangement meant that north and south Alabama had more time to contest for the capital of the state.

The report by the Committee of Fifteen on the executive department provided for popular election of the governor for a term of two years. This provision resembled that of the new southern and western states. The governor had no property-holding requirement. He had to be at least thirty years old, a resident of the state for four years before the election, and a native of the United States. The governor might serve two terms in succession. The Committee of the Whole placed limits on the governor's appointive powers, removing the power to appoint (with the advise and consent of the Senate) inferior judges and militia officers above quartermaster general. The original draft made no provision for a lieutenant governor. Instead, the president of the Senate and then the speaker of the House followed in line of succession to the governor. Other executive officers, all of whom were elected by joint ballot of both houses of the legislature, were the secretary of state, state treasurer, and comptroller of public accounts.

The original draft of the judiciary article made provisions for a supreme court, circuit courts, and such inferior courts as established by the legislature. Joint ballots of the legislature were to elect judges of the circuit and supreme courts. The governor was originally charged with appointing inferior judges, but the Constitutional Convention removed that power from him and stipulated election by joint ballot of the legislature. While life tenure for judges was originally recommended, an amendment from the floor succeeded in limiting their terms to six years. Even though by this time Georgia and Indiana had provided for popular election of inferior judges, delegates to the Alabama Constitutional Convention in 1819 thought that popular election would undermine independence of the judiciary.

Unusual constitutional stipulations regarding the establishment of banks reflected serious concerns of the delegates in a time of rampant land speculation and financial panic. Only the year before the convention, land near Cahaba had sold for $150 an acre. As the Panic of 1819 gripped the nation, banks that had accepted land as collateral collapsed. Delegates wanted to prevent a recurrence of such situations in Alabama, so they placed numerous restrictions on state banks. The legislature might establish only one bank and only one branch at any one session and this action required a two-thirds vote. A bank might open for business only when it had on hand half of the minimum capital of $100,000. The state would hold reservation for two-fifths of the capital stock of the bank and a similar proportion of control of the bank. Any bank that suspended specie payments would have to pay holders of its notes 12 percent interest, unless the legislature, after investigation, approved of its course.

The original draft constitution also contained unusual provisions regarding slavery that ultimately became part of the constitution of 1819. These provisions resembled the constitutions of Mississippi, Georgia, and Kentucky, which the Committee of Fifteen had consulted in detail. The constitution protected both the institution of slavery and the rights of slaves. The legislature had the power to pass laws setting the permissible conditions for manumission, but it might not free a slave without the consent of his or her owner. As long as Alabama had slavery, the legislature could not stop immigrants from bringing their slaves with them to the state. Slaves guilty of high crimes in other states could, however, be excluded from Alabama. Protections for slaves were incorporated into the constitution. The legislature had the power to pass laws "to oblige the owners of slaves to treat them with humanity, to provide for them necessary food and clothing, to abstain from all injuries to them extending to life and limb." Slaves had the right to trial by jury for all crimes above that of petty larceny.

The Committee of Fifteen did not provide for calling a convention to change the constitution, but it did provide a complex process for amending it. The section, as ultimately adopted, was one of the first in the nation to grant the people direct participation in the amending process. It required the legislature to submit a proposed amendment to the voters at the next general election and then vote again as a legislature to approve it.

Delegates did not submit the Alabama constitution of 1819 to the people for ratification. Neither the *Journal* nor contemporary newspapers indicated that they ever considered such a plan. None of the original southern states and none of the new ones had submitted constitutions to the people for ratification.

The Alabama constitution of 1819 reflected elements of the frontier as well as of the aristocracy that had developed in the new state. The frontier tended to place all people on the same level, regardless of property or social position. Although much of the state remained in the frontier stage in 1819, settlements in the Tennessee, Alabama, and lower Tombigbee valleys had an established aristocratic element that operated on the basis of plantation slavery. Representatives from this group, largely immigrants from Georgia, Virginia, the Carolinas, and Tennessee, led the convention and its Committee of Fifteen, who wrote the original draft of the constitution. Representatives from the frontier counties amended the constitution, making it into an even more democratic document than originally proposed. On August 2, 1819, all forty-four members of the convention in Huntsville signed the constitution and directed that an official copy of the document be made under the direction of President John J. Walker and "transmitted to the Congress of the United States."[55]

While the members of the Alabama Legislature waited to hear of the official admission of their state to the Union, they held a session of the state legislature in Huntsville from October 25 to December 17, 1819. They clearly proceeded on the assumption that admission would be quick and routine, for they passed a series of acts that established basic functions of the new state government: regulating the proceedings in the courts of law and equity, organizing and disciplining the militia, regulating patrols, regulating elections and establishing certain precincts and counties, and so on.[56]

No doubt they felt the urgency to get on with public business, as some areas had major gaps in service. For instance, in the Northern Judicial District of Alabama Territory, courts had been suspended for more than seven months when David Moore and others wrote Secretary of State John Quincy Adams of their judicial problems. Their appointed territorial judge, John W. Walker, had not received his commission, so he could not hold court. Six counties in the district had missed the first term of court and might miss the second term as well. Creditors lacked the ability to enforce payment of debts. The district reportedly had no public goal (jail). Three people had lately been confined on charges of murder; two of them had escaped. The third one remained in custody because volunteers took turns guarding him. People in north Alabama pleaded for a commission to be delivered to Judge Walker so he could meet the set schedule for court sessions.[57]

STATEHOOD

Congress accepted the constitution of Alabama by passing a resolution of admission on December 3, 1819. President James Monroe signed the resolution on December 14, 1819, and that day Alabama became a state. The resolution proclaimed the Alabama constitution to be "republican, and in conformity to the principles of the articles of compact between the original states and the people and states in the territory northwest of the river Ohio…so far as the same have been extended to the said territory by the articles of agreement between the United States and the state of Georgia."[58]

CONCLUSION

After nearly two decades as part of Mississippi Territory and less than two years as Alabama Territory, Alabama finally achieved statehood. Foreign and Native American control of lands that became Alabama had once inhibited American settlement. Since the French had founded Mobile in 1702, successive colonial rulers, whether French, British, or Spanish, had maintained interest in the area's river system and lone seaport for purposes both of defense and trade. After the United States gained rights to navigation on the lower Mississippi River, Congress created the Mississippi Territory in 1798. In this huge territory, scattered settlements on the Mississippi River at Natchez and on the Tombigbee and Tensaw rivers in south Alabama struggled to confront dangers of the frontier, barriers to foreign trade, and dissatisfaction with government.

Lands that became part of Alabama came together in a series of cessions from Georgia, from Spain, and from the Choctaw, Cherokee, Creek, and Chickasaw nations, with each cession sparking a flurry of new settlement. When settlement along the great bend of the Tennessee River led to the establishment of Madison County in 1808 and American annexation of Mobile in 1812 led to the practical acquisition of West Florida, Alabama settlers petitioned more insistently for attention in Mississippi Territory. As settlers poured into Alabama following the American victories in the War of 1812 and the Creek wars, the eastern portion of Mississippi Territory grew faster than the western part. From the western area of Mississippi Territory, Congress admitted the state of Mississippi to the Union in 1817 and created Alabama Territory from the remaining eastern lands. A very fast-growing area, Alabama began its brief territorial life with the second stage of territorial operations, as it had both the presidentially appointed territorial officers and an elected representative assembly. In the midst of debates over the admission of new slave states in March 1819, Congress passed the Enabling Act for Alabama Territory to write a state constitution, which delegates did in July and August 1819. So confident were they of impending admission to the Union that they held the first meeting of their state legislature from October to December 1819. During that time, Congress approved the resolution of admission. President Monroe signed the resolution, and on December 14, 1819, Alabama joined the Union.

NOTES

1. Don E. Fehrenbacher, *The Era of Expansion, 1800–1848* (New York: John Wiley and Sons, 1969), p. 47; and Malcolm Rohrbough, *The Trans-Appalachian Frontier: People, Societies, and Institutions, 1775–1850* (Belmont, CA: Wadsworth Publishing Company, 1990), pp. 153–156.

2. See Jacqueline Anderson Matte, *The History of Washington County, First County in Alabama* (Chatom, AL: Washington County Historical Society, 1982), p. 5.

3. Ibid., pp. 5–6.

4. Harriet E. Amos, *Cotton City: Urban Development in Antebellum Mobile* (Tuscaloosa: University of Alabama Press, 1985), pp. 11, 12.

5. Matte, *History of Washington County*, pp. 8–9, 14.

6. Joe Gray Taylor, *Louisiana: A History* (New York: W. W. Norton and Company, 1984), pp. 39–45.

7. Amos, *Cotton City*, p. 12.

8. Francis Newton Thorpe, ed., *The Federal and State Constitutions, Colonial Charters, and Other Organic Laws of the States, Territories, and Colonies Now or Heretofore forming the United States of America*, 7 vols. (Washington, D.C.: Government Printing Office, 1909), 4:2025–2027.

9. Robert V. Haynes, "The Formation of the Territory," in Richard Aubrey McLemore, ed., *A History of Mississippi*, 2 vols. (Hattiesburg: University and College Press of Mississippi, 1973), 1:178–179, 185–186.

10. Clarence Edwin Carter, ed., *The Territorial Papers of the United States*, Vol. 5, *The Territory of Mississippi, 1798–1817* (Washington, D.C.: U.S. Government Printing Office, 1937), pp. 27, 31.

11. Robert Lowry and William H. McCardle, *A History of Mississippi, With a New Introduction and Index by Thomas W. Henderson* (Jackson, MI: R. H. Henry and Co., 1891; reprint, Spartanburg, SC: The Reprint Company Publishers, 1978), p. 165.

12. Haynes, "Formation of the Territory," pp. 180–182.

13. Regarding complaints from the Natchez District in 1799, see Carter, *Territorial Papers*, 5:71–76, 78–82, 83–89.

14. Ibid., pp. 69–70, 95–98.

15. Matte, *History of Washington County*, pp. 22–24.

16. Ibid., p. 8; and Carter, *Territorial Papers*, 5:142–146. For the text of "A Treaty of Limits between the United States of America and the Choctaw Nation of Indians," see Charles J. Kappler, comp. and ed., *Indian Treaties 1778–1883* (New York: Interland Publishing, 1972), pp. 87–88.

17. Matte, *History of Washington County*, pp. 25–26; and Carter, *Territorial Papers*, 5:192–205, 292–295, 313.

18. Ephraim Kirby to President Thomas Jefferson, May 1, 1804, in Carter, *Territorial Papers*, 5:322–324. Kirby was responding to a series of questions posed by Jefferson.

19. Carter, *Territorial Papers*, 5:191, 192–205, 313, 497–507; see also pp. 292–295, 479–482.

20. Lowry and McCardle, p. 188; Carter, *Territorial Papers*, 5:175–176, 176–177, 217, 236–238.

21. Carter, *Territorial Papers*, 5:176–177, 217, 236–238.

22. Leah Rawls Atkins, "Part One: From Early Times to the End of the Civil War," in William Warren Rogers et al., *Alabama: The History of a Deep South State* (Tuscaloosa and London: University of Alabama Press, 1994), pp. 44, 48–49, 50–52. See also H. S. Halbert and T. H. Ball, *The Creek War of 1813 and 1814*, Frank L. Owsley Jr., ed. (Tuscaloosa: University of Alabama Press, 1969), pp. 241–265.

23. Atkins, *Alabama*, pp. 52–53. Atkins quotes from Donald Day and Harry Herbert Ullom, eds., *The Autobiography of Sam Houston* (Norman: University of Oklahoma Press, 1954), pp. 11–12.

24. Ibid., p. 53. For the text of "Articles of agreement and capitulation, made and concluded this ninth day of August, one thousand eight hundred and fourteen, between major general Andrew Jackson, on behalf of the President of the United States of

America, and the chiefs, deputies, and warriors of the Creek Nation," see Kappler, *Indian Treaties*, pp. 107–110.

25. Amos, *Cotton City*, p. 12.

26. Carter, *Territorial Papers*, 6:79–82, 84–90, 98, 104–105, 113–119, 128–131, 149–151, 152–159, 173–175, 305–306.

27. Amos, *Cotton City*, pp. 12, 13.

28. Peters citation in Carter, *Territorial Papers*, 28:124; see also 28:27, 288.

29. Robert Y. Haynes, "The Road to Statehood," in McLemore, *A History of Mississippi*, p. 242. For the text of the treaties, see Kappler, *Indian Treaties*, pp. 107–110, 125–126, 133–134, 135–137.

30. Haynes, "Road to Statehood," pp. 242–243.

31. Carter, *Territorial Papers*, 5:290–292 (quotations on p. 290), 732–737 (quotations on 733); and Haynes, "Road to Statehood," p. 243.

32. Haynes, "Road to Statehood," pp. 244, 245–246.

33. Atkins, *Alabama*, pp. 62–63. The quotation comes from John Williams Walker to Charles Tait, January 18, 1817, Tait Family Papers, Alabama Department of Archives and History, Montgomery, Alabama.

34. Ibid., pp. 61, 62. Cahaba was originally spelled Cahawba, a Choctaw word meaning "water above."

35. Carter, *Territorial Papers*, 18:300.

36. Harriet E. Amos Doss, "Gabriel Moore," in Samuel L. Webb and Margaret E. Armbrester, eds., *Alabama Governors: A Political History of the State* (Tuscaloosa and London: University of Alabama Press, 2001), pp. 24–25.

37. Atkins, *Alabama*, p. 61.

38. Carter, *Territorial Papers*, 18:39, n. 92.

39. *The Code of Alabama Adopted by Act of the Legislature of Alabama; Approved August 17, 1923...*, James J. Mayfield, comp., 4 vols. (Atlanta: Foote and Davies Co., 1923), 1:29.

40. Carter, *Territorial Papers*, 18:54, nn. 39–41; 56, n. 46; 256; 278. The next occurrence of the omission of the first stage came for the Territory of Wisconsin in 1836.

41. Ibid., pp. 53–57.

42. "An Act Establishing the Alabama Territory, March 3, 1817," in Carter, *Territorial Papers*, 18:56.

43. Malcolm C. McMillan, *Constitutional Development in Alabama, 1798–1901: A Study in Politics, the Negro, and Sectionalism* (Chapel Hill: University of North Carolina Press, 1955; reprint, Spartanburg, SC: The Reprint Company, Publishers, 1978), pp. 24–25; and *Journal of the Legislative Council of the Alabama Territory; at the First Session of the First General assembly, in the Forty Third Year of American Independence* (St. Stephens: Thomas Eastin, 1818), p. 3.

44. McMillan, *Constitutional Development*, pp. 24–25.

45. *Journal of the Legislative Council of the Alabama Territory; at the First Session* (1818), pp. 7–11.

46. Carter, *Territorial Papers*, 18:249. The memorial was dated February 12, 1818.

47. Atkins, *Alabama*, pp. 64–65; and *Acts Passed at the First Session of the First General Assembly, of the Alabama Territory, in the Forty Second Year of American Independence* (St. Stephens: Thomas Eastin, 1818), pp. 62–76, 86–88, 105–107.

48. Atkins, *Alabama*, p. 65.

49. McMillan, *Constitutional Development*, p. 26; and Atkins, *Alabama*, pp. 65–66.

50. Atkins, *Alabama*, p. 66.

51. Chriss H. Doss, "Alabama Territory's Surprise Presidential Visit: James Monroe in Huntsville, 1819," unpublished paper presented to the Alabama Historical Association in Auburn, Alabama, April 22, 1995, copy in possession of the author.

52. Ibid., and *Alabama Republican* (Huntsville), June 5, 1819. Carter, *Territorial Papers*, vol. 18, includes the first paragraph only of the newspaper account.

53. McMillan, *Constitutional Development*, pp. 28–29; and Thorpe, *Federal and State Constitutions*, 1:92–95.

54. Unless otherwise noted, discussion of convention issues is taken from McMillan, *Constitutional Development*, pp. 31–46.

55. Ibid., p. 45; and *Journal of the Constitutional Convention of the Alabama Territory begun July 5, 1819* (Huntsville: John Boardman, 1819).

56. *Acts of the General Assembly of the State of Alabama, Passed at Its First Session...* (Huntsville: John Boardman, 1820).

57. David Moore and others to Secretary of State John Quincy Adams, May 28, 1819, in Carter, *Territorial Papers*, 18:636.

58. Carter, *Territorial Papers*, 18:753–755. When word was received of Monroe's approval, the credentials of Alabama's first congressmen (both serving at large) were presented: John Crowell, representative, and John W. Walker, senator.

BIBLIOGRAPHY

Abernethy, Thomas Perkins. *The Formative Period in Alabama*. With an introduction by David T. Morgan. Tuscaloosa: University of Alabama Press, 1990.

Amos, Harriet E. *Cotton City: Urban Development in Antebellum Mobile*. Tuscaloosa: University of Alabama Press, 1985.

Brantley, William H., Jr. *Three Capitals: A Book about the First Three Capitals of Alabama: St. Stephens, Huntsville & Cahawba*. Tuscaloosa and London: University of Alabama Press, 1947.

Dupre, Daniel S. *Transforming the Cotton Frontier: Madison County, Alabama, 1800–1840*. Baton Rouge and London: Louisiana State University Press, 1997.

Matte, Jacqueline Anderson. *The History of Washington County, First County in Alabama*. Chatom, AL: Washington County Historical Society, 1982.

McMillan, Malcom C. *Constitutional Development in Alabama, 1798-1901: A Study in Politics, the Negro, and Sectionalism*. Chapel Hill: University of North Carolina Press, 1955. Reprint ed., Spartanburg, SC: The Reprint Company, Publishers, 1978.

Rogers, William Warren, Robert David Ward, Leah R. Atkins, and Wayne Flynt. *Alabama: The History of a Deep South State*. Tuscaloosa and London: University of Alabama Press, 1994.

Southerland, Henry De Leon, Jr., and Jerry Elijah Brown. *The Federal Road through Georgia, the Creek Nation, and Alabama, 1806–1836* . Tuscaloosa and London: University of Alabama Press, 1989.

Thornton, J. Mills, III. *Politics and Power in a Slave Society: Alabama, 1800–1860* . Baton Rouge and London: Louisiana State University Press, 1978.

Webb, Samuel L., and Margaret E. Armbrester, eds. *Alabama Governors: A Political History of the State*. Tuscaloosa and London: University of Alabama Press, 2001.

Alaska

Territorial Development:

- Alaska purchased from Russia, October 18, 1867
- Alaska organized as a U.S. territory, August 24, 1912
- Alaska admitted into the Union as the forty-ninth state, January 3, 1959

Territorial Capitals:

- Sitka, 1867–1900
- Juneau, 1900–1959

State Capitals:

- Juneau, 1959–present

Origin of State Name: "Aláxsxaq" is an Aleutian word meaning "the object toward which the action of the sea is directed."

First Governor: William A. Egan
Governmental Organization: Bicameral
Population at Statehood: 223,866
Geographical Size: 571,951 square miles

THE STATE OF ALASKA

Admitted to the Union as a State: January 3, 1959

William S. Hanable

INTRODUCTION

Physical Geography

Alaska is a maritime province, surrounded on the north, west, and south sides by oceans and on its eastern border by all but impenetrable mountain barriers backed by the vast, sparsely populated interior of Canada, a foreign nation. For all practical purposes, this situation has given Alaska the character of an island for nearly all the time it spent on the path to statehood. Of all the jurisdictions that are now states, it has shared that "islandness" only with the Hawaiian Islands. This geographic characteristic had a significant influence on when and how both Alaska and Hawaii achieved statehood. Unlike Hawaii, which lies on shipping routes to other Pacific destinations, and despite the hopes of eighteenth- and nineteenth-century explorers seeking a northwest passage, Alaska leads to nowhere.

Human Geography

Scholars of antiquity think Alaska's first human inhabitants were hunters from the Asian landmass. They crossed to Alaska between 10,000 and 20,000 years ago over a land bridge connecting Asia and North America. The "bridge" appeared some 25,000 or 30,000 years ago as the world's oceans subsided when glaciers expanding over much of the earth absorbed their waters. More recent immigrants to Alaska arrived by other routes. Some came via coastal waters, others by following the rivers and glaciers that pierced the mountains bordering the state on the east, and a relative few by sailing east across the North Pacific.

Since their arrival in Alaska, humans have depended on the region's waters for economic survival, protection, and transportation. Sea mammals and fish became centerpieces of Native culture. Natives living along the northern and western coasts of Alaska focused on hunting whales, walrus, and seals. Natives living in interior Alaska and along its southern coastline depended on the native salmon, which spawned in Alaska's streams, migrated to the oceans in Alaska's rivers, grew to maturity in the oceans washing Alaska's shores, and returned along the same routes to deposit their eggs and die. When Europeans and Americans of European heritage (Euro-Americans) arrived in Alaska, they too relied on Alaska's maritime resources.

Non-natives filtered into Alaska only gradually, and then only in small numbers. Russians were the first to arrive as they pursued fur-bearing sea mammals. The first permanent Russian settlement in Alaska dates either from 1776 at Unalaska or from 1784 at Kodiak Island. From that time until the sale of Russian interests in Alaska to the United States in 1867, the Russian population in the area never exceeded eight hundred, with most of that number located in Sitka, the Russian American headquarters.

Alaska's history is also connected with the sea through many of its more than 3,000 rivers. They have historically provided access to the interior of the vast state, which at 586,412 square miles is one-fifth the size of the contiguous United States (known to Alaskans as "Outside," "Down Below," or the "Lower Forty-Eight"). That access is as fundamental as the life cycle of the salmon, a critical element of the Alaskan diet and economy. Without the rivers, western exploration of Alaska's interior, exploitation of its fur resources, and extraction of its minerals would have been impossible.

Human use of the sea and river connection began when prehistoric hunters crossed the Bering Sea land bridge to follow game through the river corridors. All of Alaska's inhabitants found some measure of protection in its waters. For centuries, Native societies grew with only minimal interference from alien cultures. Remote and isolated by unexplored seas, they were among the last of North America's aboriginal inhabitants to suffer from contact with Euro-Americans. Before that time, what we now know as Alaska did not exist as a political idea or have geographic definition.

The original inhabitants of Alaska conceived of the region that later became a single historical entity as a series of cultural territories interconnected by traditions of warfare and trade. These traditions were as complex as any political or geographic concepts developed within the past three hundred years. Definition of today's Alaska did not begin until the eighteenth century, when Euro-Americans arrived on the northwestern coast of North America. That definition was not completed until the twentieth century. As the Euro-Americans created a modern definition of Alaska, they relied on ocean barriers to define its northern and western boundaries and mountain ranges to shape its eastern borders. The rough shape of today's political entity, the state of Alaska, was established by treaties of 1824–1825 between Russia and Great Britain, on the one hand, and between Russia and the United States, on the other.

Social and Economic Geography

Until recent times, both the Natives and the Euro-Americans in Alaska, living where waterways allowed them to bypass tall mountain ranges and swamplike prairies of muskeg and tundra, used Alaska's coastal waters and rivers for transportation. Air travel, available for only a fraction of the period of human presence in Alaska, transformed the territory by enabling Alaskans to leap over the old barriers and to decrease their dependence on water transportation. Until human use of that third entity in the triumvirate of earth, sea, and air became routine, oceans and rivers were the principal means of transportation in what is now Alaska.

Transportation, indeed, has been the key to Alaska's economy. Although it has always been resource rich, exploitation of its many resources often faltered because of the absence or expense of transportation from resource areas to market. Even after Seattle became the principal entrepôt, or intermediate trade center, for Alaska during the Klondike Gold Rush, distances between the contiguous U.S. principal port serving Alaska and Alaskan destinations remained staggering. Point Barrow, the most northerly, lay over 3,000 miles north on the shortest shipping route, whereas more southerly Alaskan communities such as Valdez and Juneau were 2,180 and 1,100 sea miles distant, respectively.[1]

Only extremely high value resources such as gold, copper, and oil, or ones that could be shipped rapidly and in bulk, such as fish, have been successfully developed. Early on, mining, gold, fish, and furs became the four pillars of the Alaskan economy. Because there was little capital in Alaska, ownership of these industries concentrated outside the region. The result was that outside interests, anxious to protect their investments and maintain their profits, usually opposed any kind of self-rule for Alaska such as territorial or state status. Specific examples of this were the San Francisco–based Alaska Commercial Company, which dominated the fur trade for many years; the salmon fishing and canning industry, based both in San Francisco and Seattle; and the Alaska Syndicate, a creature of the New York–based Guggenheim financial empire, which dominated Alaskan copper mining and shipping and owned gold dredges in Alaska in the late nineteenth and early twentieth centuries.[2]

Although fisheries remained a continuing economic activity, subject only to periodic rises and falls in fish stocks, the fur trade dwindled in the first half of the twentieth century, and mining shut down almost completely as mining machinery and miners were requisitioned for World War II. The war, however, caused government input into the Alaskan economy to boom as airfields, coastal defense fortifications, and support facilities were created to protect the large territory. After the end of World War II, military response to the Cold War kept government money flowing into Alaska. Fisheries continued to be an important segment of the economy, and tourism in Alaska, which had begun in the latter part of the nineteenth century, increased as Lower Forty-Eight families and European and Japanese travelers spent significant amounts of their disposable income on Alaskan travel.

BECOMING A TERRITORY

As Alaska's social and economic situation evolved, so too did its government. The Russian government had chosen to administer Alaska through the agency of a quasi-public corporation, the Russian-American Company. The United States chose to send first soldiers, then sailors, and finally civil administrators to govern Alaska. Notably, the treaty of purchase by which the United States acquired Russian interests in Alaska differed in significant ways from treaties negotiated with France, Spain, and Mexico, resulting in territorial acquisitions. In those instances, the treaties clearly stated, "the inhabitants of the ceded territories should be incorporated into the Union." In the Alaska treaty, the language stated only that the civilized inhabitants of the region should have the rights and privileges of citizens of the United States.[3]

Major General Henry W. Halleck developed plans for the initial dispatch of U.S. Army troops to Alaska. Halleck had been de facto chief of staff to Abraham Lincoln in the latter's role as commander in chief of federal armies during the Civil War. In 1867, he was commanding general of the U.S. Army's Military Division of the Pacific. In that capacity, he proposed immediately sending infantry companies to Sitka, Cook Inlet, Kodiak, and Unalaska. Additional companies destined for Norton Sound, Bristol Bay, and the Yukon should, he said, follow in 1868.[4]

An assumption that organization of a civil territorial government would come quickly after transfer ceremonies accompanied Halleck's recommendation for assignment of military forces to Alaska. In a May 22, 1867, letter to Assistant Adjutant General E. D. Townsend in Washington, D.C., Halleck anticipated extension of the general laws of the United States to Alaska.[5] He recommended that when they did so, civil authorities should pay particular attention to Indian affairs, and he strongly urged that:

> should our Indian system, with its treaties, annuities, agents, frauds, and peculations, be introduced there [Alaska], Indian wars must inevitably follow, and instead of a few companies for its military occupation, as many regiments will be called for, with the resulting expenditure of many millions of dollars. More than 70 years experience on this [the Pacific] coast has satisfied me that the introduction of the Indian bureau system into the Pacific States and Territories has had a most pernicious effect, both upon the settlers and the Indians.[6]

Word came back from Washington that until federal authorities established civil government in Alaska, Halleck or his designee would govern Alaska as a military district. Because communications were expected to be better between San Francisco and Alaska, the army's Department of California, rather than the geographically closer Department of the Columbia in Oregon, was to over-see the new district. "Better communications," in this instance, turned out to be sporadic visits by the U.S. Army's Quartermaster Corps ship *Newbern* and a sometimes-monthly mail steamer between the California port and the newly acquired American possession.[7]

Accompanied by several newly appointed civilian officials, Brevet Major General Jefferson C. Davis, colonel of the Twenty-third Infantry and command-ing officer of the new Military District of Alaska, arrived with his troops aboard the *John L. Stephens*, which reached Sitka on October 9, 1867. Brigadier General Lovell H. Rousseau, President Andrew Johnson's designated represen-tation at the formal transfer ceremonies held at Sitka on October 18, arrived on that day aboard the USS *Ossipee*. Also present at the ceremony were Sitka's new $12-a-year postmaster, John M. Kinkead, and freshly appointed Collector of Customs William S. Dodge.[8]

One infantry company and one artillery company, just over 250 military personnel altogether, had arrived at the former Russian capital. With winter looming, the troops remained at Sitka until the following spring. Then, supple-mented by fresh troops from the western United States, they scattered. One detachment remained to garrison Sitka, one went to Wrangell, one to Tongass Island south of Wrangell, and others scattered to Kenai, Kodiak, and St. Paul Island. The last two were only small trading posts, though St. Paul Island was the site of the profitable annual fur seal harvests. In 1870, the outlying posts closed. The remaining troops concentrated at Sitka as a prelude to total army withdrawal from Alaska in 1877.[9]

General Davis became a significant figure in Alaskan political history because he announced, without much basis in fact, that the general laws of the United States had been extended to Alaska because of the treaty of purchase. In his first public announcement, General Order No. 1 of the Military District of Alaska, October 29, 1867, he proclaimed, "[T]he laws of Congress of general application to all other Territories of the United States will be enforced." Congress, however, repudiated this assumption within the year by only extending a few American laws to Alaska.[10]

The army units operated on instructions to maintain order and suppress illegal liquor trafficking. The units were ill-suited to their task, had insuffi-cient authority to complete it in any case, and were generally unsuccessful. The most significant action of the army during its "administration" of Alaska between 1867 and 1877 was erratic sponsorship of a civilian attempt to organize a municipal government. When the citizens of Sitka formed a provisional government to manage local affairs, the army's commanding officer at first encouraged the effort. A few years later, economic decline led many of Sitka's government officials to depart; the resulting lack of interest in government by civilians led to gradual military encroachment into the civil government's affairs and the end of this first exercise in self-government.[11]

Congress regarded Alaska as "Indian Country," and the first formal extension of American law to Alaska came with the Customs Act of July 27, 1868 (15 Stat. L. 240). The act extended customs, commerce, and navigation laws of the United States to Alaska and assigned the secretary of the treasury oversight of the fur trade. It also reserved the regulation of the fur seal trade to Congress and prohibited the killing of fur seals. Also in the year 1868, statehood for Alaska was first mentioned publicly. William Henry Seward, who as secretary of state had negotiated the purchase of Alaska, gave a speech at Sitka in August of 1869 in which he forecast that in time Congress would provide territorial government for Alaska and full self-government eventually, "ultimately as a state or many states."[12]

In early 1869, Congress debated whether to provide a civil government for Alaska but decided against doing so at that time. The principal reasons given were the expense, in relation to the small number of white American citizens in the area, and the potential that any kind of civil government in Alaska might have for interfering with management of the fur seal trade, by then an exclusive franchise of the California-based Alaska Commercial Company.[13]

Only a customs collector and his deputies at Wrangell represented American authority in Alaska and Kodiak from the time the army withdrew in mid-1877 until early 1879. At that time, an American warship, the USS *Alaska*, sailed into Sitka harbor with instructions to protect life and property in the face of an anticipated uprising by the Tlingit Indians in Sitka. The uprising, if it ever was planned, was discouraged. The USS *Jamestown* shortly replaced the *Alaska*. Several other navy ships would follow in the ensuing years. The last of these was the USS *Pinta*, which arrived in 1884, the last year of naval administration, and stayed until 1897 to support the ensuing civil government.

Navy "administration" of Alaska differed little from that accomplished by the army, except that there were beneficial effects from not having drunken soldiers from the pervasively present garrisons at Sitka, Wrangell, and Kodiak rambling about in those communities. Although sailors also got into trouble, they could be kept aboard ship when necessary and were perceived to have had less detrimental influences on the Native peoples than the army garrisons. As their army predecessors had, navy officers tried without success to encourage local self-government.

Perhaps the most significant navy-related incidents during the 1879 to 1884 period were controlling the gold rush to Juneau and opening of the Chilkoot Trail (the shortest route from tidewater to interior gold fields) to white prospectors. The navy also provided substantial aid in the establishment of Alaska's first boarding school, which eventually became the Sheldon Jackson School (now Sheldon Jackson College).

The captain of the *Pinta*, however, exercised authority as the senior government official in Alaska for only a few months. Soon after his ship's arrival at Sitka, a newly appointed governor of the District of Alaska replaced him in that capacity. Congress had earlier been reluctant to provide for any form of civil government. The needs of a still small but expanding white population, resulting from gold strikes at various points, helped to overcome this resistance.

THE DISTRICT OF ALASKA

Agitation in 1880 at the new gold mining camp of Juneau, first known as Harrisburg, was the stimulus for the Organic Act. Customs Collector M. D. Ball and navy officers were disputing an unofficial land survey made by Ball, with the result that Sitkans taking Ball's side urged him to go to Washington with a view to getting civil authority established in Alaska. At the same time, they petitioned Secretary of Treasury John Sherman for the same purpose. When Ball got to Washington, he found Henry W. Elliott testifying before Congress on conditions in the Pribilof Islands, where the Alaska Commercial Company held a monopoly over the fur seal harvests.

Discussion of the Alaska issue in Washington in 1880 did not result in any Alaskan legislation. It did set the stage for further discussion about government for the far northwest area in the following year. Once again, a dispute between a naval officer and miners over land issues triggered a trip to Washington. In this instance, a miners' meeting with delegates from Sitka, Wrangell, and Juneau assembled in Juneau for Alaska's first territorial meeting. This appears to have been the first approximation of a "statewide" political meeting in Alaska, although delegates to it came only from a few locations in one geographic area of the territory.

The convention took place on August 16, 1881, with delegates arriving on the mail steamer to join those from Juneau. Fifteen were seated, and the group elected W. B. Robertson Jr., owner of some Juneau gold claims, as its president and Presbyterian missionary S. Hall Young of Wrangell as its secretary. The participants developed a plan calling for elections to be held on September 5, 1881. Suffrage was extended to "all civilized male persons over 21 years of age, residents of Alaska at the time, and citizens of the United States, or who have declared their intentions to become such, or may declare it in writing before the judges of election on the day thereof."[14]

The August convention further developed a "Memorial of the people of Southeastern Alaska to the President and the Congress of the United States." It reminded Washington officials that Alaska had been under the American flag for fourteen years without civil government. That absence, those assembled said, deprived Alaskans of their rights as citizens and held back development of Alaska's natural resources. They requested that Congress receive their delegate as the legal representative of the Territory of Alaska.[15]

Two hundred and ninety-four members of the electorate participated in delegate selection on September 5. A majority of the voters chose Ball to go to Washington as the representative of "the Territory of Alaska." Ball took with him a mandate to ask for legislation establishing Alaska as a territory and to ask for the privilege of representing Alaska to Congress. He arrived at the capital for the opening session of the Forty-seventh Congress on December 5, 1881, to present his credentials. In the ensuing discussion, Congress questioned whether those electing Ball had constituted more than 25 percent of potential Alaskan voters. It also worried about the expense of maintaining any kind of civil government in a huge territory inhabited by a population of "civilized" persons estimated at from 400 to 1,500, finally determining that Alaska was an "unorganized" territory and thus its residents had no right to representation in Congress.[16]

Although congressional discussions in 1881 and 1882 did not produce an immediate civil government for Alaska, they did pave the way. Senate Bill 153, which took effect in 1884, has been labeled by one of the foremost historians of this period of Alaskan politics as "evolved from a composite of honest intentions, ignorance, stupidity, indifference, and quasi-expediency."[17]

The District of Alaska, authorized by the Organic Act of 1884 (23 Stat. L. 24), was a civil and judicial district. A district, as opposed to a territory, was not a new concept, though it was a rarely exercised designation. In 1804, after the Louisiana Purchase, Congress had chosen to designate the southern part of Louisiana as the Territory of Louisiana. For the northern part of that area, Congress chose the nomenclature "District of Louisiana" and assigned its management to territorial officials in Indiana.[18]

The 1884 Organic Act creating the District of Alaska provided for a presidentially appointed governor, a district attorney, a district judge, and four subordinate judicial officials known as commissioners, as well as a district marshal and four deputy marshals. The commissioners and deputy marshals were located at Sitka, Wrangell, Juneau, and Unalaska. Simultaneously, the Organic Act extended the laws of Oregon and federal mining laws to Alaska. It also authorized the establishment of schools and created a land district but authorized no taxes to pay for schools and did not extend existing land laws to Alaska. The Organic Act also expressly prohibited the formation of a legislative assembly in the new district or the dispatch of a delegate from the district to Congress.

The seat of government, which had been established at Sitka in 1884, was moved by act of Congress to Juneau on June 6, 1900. Most government officials moved to Juneau within a short time, but Governor John G. Brady, a twenty-two-year resident of Sitka, refused to move. The governor's office did not move to Juneau until President Roosevelt removed Brady from office, for other reasons, in late 1906. One early occupant of the governor's office noted that at Juneau he was closer to Eastport, Maine, than to the farthest reaches of the area he oversaw. At best, a governor was able to make an annual trip to southcentral Alaska and the Aleutian Islands and occasional forays around southeast Alaska on visiting government vessels. Several governors appointed between 1884 and 1912, when Congress granted territorial status to Alaska, spent a substantial part of each year not in Alaska but in the nation's capital, where they believed their lobbying efforts were more beneficial for the territory.

District government was not a success. All but one of the new officials were appointed from outside Alaska on the recommendation of senators, congressmen, and governors from existing states. Alaskan resident John G. Brady of Sitka, appointed a commissioner, was the sole exception, due to the influence of Presbyterian missionary Sheldon Jackson. As a student of the period has said, "The incoming government…found its relations with the former de facto government of the Treasury and Navy decidedly strained, because the Organic Act gave the former all the responsibility for good order and left in the possession of the latter what instruments existed for maintaining it." Frustrated, many of the new appointees chose to take up their offices in Washington and left Alaska to run itself.[19]

THE TERRITORY OF ALASKA

District government continued to be generally unsatisfactory, and dissatisfaction with it grew as the mining and fishing industries in Alaska grew. In 1888, a report of the House Committee on Territories outlined the deficiencies of the Organic Act of 1884. That act, said the report, failed to fulfill the commitments made in the purchase treaty of Alaska and was even more repugnant because it "stopped far short of a full observation of the Treaty stipulations…[and] set up a form of civil government wholly devoid of the vital principle of representation, as well as of the essential privilege of local legislation."[20]

By the late 1890s, agitation from Alaska for the traditional territorial form of government was causing Congress to give the matter serious consideration. That consideration became urgent when the Klondike Gold Rush of 1898 and a subsequent rush to the Nome gold fields in 1900 drew thousands of gold seekers to the far north. For the next several years, Congress responded to the needs of Alaska by tinkering with the powers of the district government. It provided transportation and homestead acts in 1898, a criminal code in 1899, and a civil code in 1900. Twelve years of increasingly heated debate about territorial status and even statehood followed.

The U.S. Supreme Court played a key role in Alaska's future when, in 1905, it made legal distinctions among the possessions of the United States that were not yet territories. Alaska joined other areas on the mainland of North America as "incorporated," with its citizens afforded constitutional rights. The noncontiguous areas of Hawaii, Puerto Rico, and the Philippines were regarded as "unincorporated," and not so entitled. The Alaska purchase treaty, said the court, made clear the intention to grant American citizenship to residents of Alaska and to incorporate Alaska into the United States.[21]

The years of struggle for territorial status came to fruition in 1912 but were preceded by an intermediate step in which the District of Alaska was authorized to send a nonvoting delegate to Congress. An Alaska-wide election chose Frank H. Waskey, a Nome miner, as the district's first official representative to Congress, reflecting a shift in population from southeast to interior Alaska. Waskey and District Governor Wilfred B. Hoggatt immediately clashed, as would Waskey's successors and Hoggatt, when asked by President Theodore Roosevelt to outline Alaska's needs. Waskey's report focused on the specific needs of miners and on the general need for a territorial government. Hoggatt's report focused on improving the mechanisms of district government while suggesting that territorial government would be premature.[22]

Alaska's progress toward territorial status took a detour when William Howard Taft became president. Taft, who had been chair of the commission overseeing the Philippines, announced in 1909 that he favored a similar arrangement for Alaska. He thought that Alaska's population was too sparse to support a territorial government. Taft changed his mind, however, after hearing a report on Alaska from Secretary of the Interior Walter I. Fisher, who recommended territorial status after visiting the northern district in 1911.[23]

With the president's support coupled with considerable interest among senators and representatives, particularly those from the West, and with special interests such as coal, transportation, and fisheries placated by limitations on the power of the proposed territorial legislature, Congress finally passed the Territorial Organic Act for Alaska on August 24, 1912. The act granted territorial status, extended the Constitution and laws of the United States to the territory, and provided for a territorial legislature with limited powers. Congress reserved to itself jurisdiction over Alaskan fisheries, game, and lands. The long-sought territorial legislative body was to consist of a Senate and a House, with eight members in the former and sixteen members in the latter. Two senators and four representatives were to be elected from each of Alaska's four judicial districts. There was no provision for election of the territory's chief executive officer, so Alaska's governors remained presidential appointees and Alaska continued to send only a single, voteless delegate to Congress.[24]

After Alaska finally achieved territorial status, there were continuing efforts to obtain additional powers for the territorial legislature, but few met with success. It was obvious that statehood was the route to full enfranchisement of Alaska's residents. However, it was also obvious that the road to statehood would be a long one. Even its advocates recognized that without more residents and a broader tax base, the territory could not sustain the costs of statehood.

On March 30, 1916, the forty-ninth anniversary of the transfer of Alaska from Russia to Alaska, James V. Wickersham, then serving as Alaska's delegate to Congress, introduced the first Alaska statehood measure in Congress. Acknowledged even by Wickersham to be without hope of passage, the bill was referred to committee and died there. In the following years, statehood for Alaska was discussed frequently, but little came of the discussions. Proposals for smaller states to be carved out of the larger Alaska also failed to come to fruition. What the proposals illustrated, among other things, was the lack of a sense of community among various parts of the state. This was particularly true of southeast Alaska vis-à-vis the rest of Alaska. The panhandle region retained a sense of being the political center of the territory and locus of its former capital (Sitka) and present capital (Juneau), while fearing that the expanding population and economy of southcentral and interior Alaska would eventually take that status away. Despite these fears, a 1935 federal planning board could report there were only seven communities in Alaska with populations greater than one thousand, and in the entire territory—586,000-plus square miles in size—there were only 2,500 miles of public roads, the length considered necessary to serve thirty-six square miles in the continental United States.[25]

With the onset of World War II came hundreds of thousands of service personnel and thousands of civilian workers who built, maintained, and operated airfields, highways, and ports as well as conducting combat operations. The territory's military population numbered approximately 750 in 1940 but peaked at 152,000 on July 1, 1943. Construction employment, estimated at 1,255 workers in 1940, exploded to over 10,000 in 1941.[26]

In the midst of the war, Anthony J. Dimond, who had become the territorial delegate to Congress in 1933, prevailed upon Senators William L. Langer of North Dakota and Pat McCarran of Nevada to submit the first Alaska statehood bill since 1916. The promoted bill, which was not only based on home rule but also made a prerequisite of postwar economic development in Alaska, went nowhere. However, it did spark interest in the issue. A companion bill introduced in the House of Representatives by Delegate Dimond fared no better.[27]

Robert B. Atwood, owner and publisher of the *Anchorage Daily Times*, observed that until reading an Associated Press dispatch about the Langer-McCarran bill, he had not given the statehood issue any thought. Since Atwood later became a leading advocate of statehood, this one incident may have made the bill worthwhile.[28]

Statehood for Alaska was only considered seriously again after the end of World War II. Many military men and women and civilian workers who had served in Alaska during the conflict chose to return to begin their postwar lives. The 1947 onset of what is now known as the Cold War then brought many active-duty service personnel to Alaska when the air force built a chain of early warning radar stations, fighter-interceptor bases, and bomber staging bases in Alaska. The territory's military population, which had dropped to

19,000 in 1946, rose to 25,000 in 1947 and soared to 50,000 in 1953. It held at that level for four years before beginning to decline in 1956 and finally leveling off at 34,000 in 1959.[29]

Thousands of civilian workers who built the air bases and support facilities accompanied the military population. Radar stations, thought necessary to defend the United States from an over-the-Pole attack by the Soviet Union, were also constructed and staffed. Once again, many military personnel chose to remain in Alaska when they left the service, as did many of the civilian workers brought north for military construction. Most of these new Alaskans chose to live in the southcentral and interior regions of the territory, further shifting the political balance away from southeast Alaska.

Ernest Gruening, who had been Alaska's governor since 1939, took up the statehood cause in the midst of World War II. Unable to find funding for a study of the pros and cons of statehood, he encouraged Evangeline Atwood, wife of newspaper publisher Robert Atwood, to found the Alaska Statehood Association to give her an individual identity. Chapters soon sprouted forth not only in Anchorage, but also in Fairbanks, Juneau, Ketchikan, Sitka, Wrangell, Palmer, Valdez, Kodiak, and Seward. The association soon had 350 members and, with membership fees at $5 each, was able to contract with George Sundborg to prepare the report Gruening desired.[30]

Sundborg, a Gruening friend employed by the Bonneville Power Administration in Oregon, had just written *Opportunity in Alaska*. Published by the Macmillan Company in 1945 with a preface by Governor Ernest Gruening, the book extolled the opportunities to be found in Alaska and detailed the extensive infrastructure of the territory. The year 1945 was also the time when federal attitudes about statehood changed. Previous administrations had opposed home rule for Alaska, but with the ending of the war in the summer of 1945, Acting Secretary of the Interior Abe Fortas announced that statehood for Alaska was now a part of the department's policy. However, members of the House Committee on Territories, visiting Alaska about this time to gather information, could not agree on when Alaska should seek admission as a state. They also expressed concern about the territory's inadequate tax system. Largely because of opposition by the liquor, mining, and salmon industries, reformers had heretofore had no success in revising an archaic tax structure. Despite these legislative reservations, in his January 1946 State of the Union speech, President Harry S. Truman included the recommendation that Alaska and Hawaii be admitted as states.[31]

When casting ballots in the general election in October 1946, Alaskans had the opportunity to express their preferences on statehood in a referendum. They voted for statehood by 9,630 to 6,822, with only 23 percent of eligible voters turning out. All regions but the remote northwestern judicial division favored statehood. Sundborg's report, financed by the Alaska Statehood Association and elaborating on the advantages of statehood, had just received wide distribution.

With a majority of Alaskans and the federal government now seeming to support the concept of statehood, a new status for Alaska seemed within reach. Major issues remained to be resolved, however. These included determining how to finance a state government, devising a formula for transfer of public lands to a new state, and allaying the concerns of the many special interest groups potentially affected by a state government. There were no easy answers to any of these questions, and a series of statehood bills introduced in the following years failed to resolve them. This impasse began to be solved in 1949, when the reasoned arguments of leaders such as Gruening and E. L. "Bob" Bartlett, the territorial delegate to Congress, were supplemented with widespread popular support.

The 1949 Territorial Legislature took a major step toward statehood by instituting a rational tax system and by creating an official Alaska Statehood Committee. Intended to be a bipartisan group, the committee was to be staffed by a researcher who would provide information necessary to support a constitutional convention and aid in the transition from territory to state. The committee met for the first time in the summer of 1949. Its efforts were supplemented by a national committee of distinguished Americans, including Eleanor Roosevelt, Pearl Buck, and General Douglas MacArthur, recruited by Gruening to support statehood. These efforts resulted in a serious hearing for an Alaska statehood bill in the U.S. House of Representatives. The discussion quickly revealed that to be successful, an Alaskan bill would have to be paired with a statehood for Hawaii bill. Alaska was expected to send Democrats to Congress, whereas Hawaii could be expected to elect Republicans. However, even if they were paired, statehood for both territories was opposed by many on the grounds of noncontiguity (which might set a precedent for statehood by other noncontiguous areas), racial issues, and disproportionate Senate representation.[32]

Statehood bills introduced during the next few years also faltered, but statehood advocates were encouraged when Truman's competitor in the 1952 presidential contest, Dwight D. Eisenhower, also came out in favor of statehood status for Alaska and Hawaii. Not to be outdone, the Democrats included a plank in their platform urging statehood for Alaska and Hawaii.[33]

In 1953, Senator Hugh Butler, chair of the Senate Interior and Insular Affairs Committee, traveled to Alaska to hold hearings on a statehood bill. Butler specifically asked that people who had testified before Congress in the past not appear. He wanted, he said, to hear "the reaction of the little people, not just a few aspiring politicians who want to be Senators and Representatives." Butler's hearings began what Alaskan historian Claus-M. Naske has called "the populist phase of the Alaska statehood movement." He drew in people who had come to Alaska during and after World War II and who, while aware of the movement, had not participated actively. "Little Men for Statehood" clubs sprang up. Of the 140 people who testified before Butler, fewer than twenty opposed statehood.[34]

Butler left Alaska saying that prospects for Alaska statehood had been improved. But he would later initially say that he was more convinced than ever that statehood for Alaska was premature and then reverse course again and favor statehood for Alaska. In Alaska, "Operation Statehood" grew out of the Little Men for Statehood clubs. With broader support, the statehood issue became a matter of demanding a right, not pleading with Congress for a favor. Statehood advocates marked a milestone on March 11, 1954, when the U.S. Senate approved Alaskan and Hawaiian statehood bills. These came to nothing, however, blocked by political considerations in the House of Representatives and stymied by presidential concerns about the effect of statehood on possibly needed military land withdrawals in Alaska.[35]

In the midst of this discussion of the pros and cons of Alaska statehood, B. Frank Heintzleman, the territorial governor from 1953 to 1957, introduced the idea of partitioning Alaska. The area containing the bulk of the population and the larger population centers was, in this concept, to be admitted as a state. The remaining fragments of northern and western Alaska, to be known as "Frontier Alaska" or "Alaska Outpost" were to remain a territory until their development justified incorporation into the State of Alaska. Opponents quickly arose to dispute this scheme, but President Eisenhower said that he might modify his opposition to Alaskan statehood since the partition proposal would address military needs. A. L. Miller (R–Nebraska), chair of the House Interior and Insular Affairs Committee, pointed out that although partition might facilitate statehood for a portion of Alaska, any resulting new state would never be able to annex the regions left behind.[36]

In addition to concerns about the impact of Alaskan statehood on political balances in Washington, D.C., economic and environmental considerations also raised some opposition. Fish traps, for example, were illegal in all forty-eight states, but not in Alaska, where the federal government managed fisheries. The traps, which were weirs into which migrating salmon swam, were a remarkably efficient and economical way to fill the millions of cans of salmon exported from Alaska each year. Most Alaskans hated the traps because of their purported adverse impact on the fisheries resource and because profits generated by the traps went mostly to companies based outside Alaska. Those companies, in turn, feared and fought any development such as statehood that might endanger their earnings. There were also environmental concerns about the impact of statehood, as most active statehood advocates supported unchecked economic development and were skeptical about the environmentalists' motives. As a statehood opponent who later became the state's fifth governor would say, the "statehooders" were either "would-be political plum pickers... who had their sights set on higher office" or "advocates of aggressive, no-holds-barred growth."[37]

A constitutional convention became the next major milestone on Alaska's path to statehood. First suggested in 1948, the idea had been brought up several times since. In June 1954, Representative A. L. Miller, chairman of the House Interior and Insular Affairs Committee, suggested that such an action might persuade the House Rules Committee to release statehood bills it was holding.[38]

Alaskans eagerly seized upon the idea of a constitutional convention. In March of 1955, the Territorial Legislature authorized a constitutional convention and appropriated $300,000 for its expenses. Alaskans were to elect fifty-five delegates to the convention, based upon twenty-two election districts. The Public Administration Service, an arm of the Council of State Governments, received a contract to support the convention.[39]

Territorial Governor B. Frank Heintzleman opened the convention shortly after 10 A.M. on November 8, 1955, in an old gymnasium on the University of Alaska campus outside Fairbanks. Fifty-three of the fifty-five elected delegates were present: thirteen from Anchorage, eleven from Fairbanks, seven from Juneau, and the balance from eighteen smaller communities. According to one analysis of the attending delegates,

> a majority were Democrats. Six were women; 13 were lawyers; the rest represented a wide variety of occupations. Their ages ranged from 29 to the early eighties, with most in the 40- to 60-age bracket. Four were members of the Alaska Statehood Committee, created by the Territorial Legislature in 1949 to work for statehood.... There was one Native delegate, Frank Peratrovich, a Tlingit Indian leader. Nearly half of the delegates had served in the Territorial Legislature at one time or another; nine of them, all Democrats, had served in the 1955 legislature, which had appropriated $300,000 to pay for [the constitutional convention].[40]

E. L. "Bob" Bartlett, the Territory of Alaska's delegate to Congress, made an opening statement to the convention attendees. Bartlett, as would many of the convention's speakers, made reference to the national Constitutional Convention of 1787. However, the focus of his speech was the prospective state's natural resource policy. He predicted that a state of Alaska would be entitled to select vast acreages from unreserved federal land and warned that the costs of managing such lands were far beyond those that had faced the new state of Arizona in 1912. Land management had become much more complicated. When selected, Alaska's lands, like its fisheries, could be the source of unimagined wealth. The history of land disposition in other new states had often been that inexperienced or corrupt officials sold public lands at bargain-basement prices to special interests. Moreover, the experience of territorial days showed that revenues derived from resource development such as mining and fishing had seldom remained in Alaska, while greed promoting unchecked exploitation had doomed the resources to exhaustion. Alaskans also needed to fear the possibility that large corporations would lock up huge areas of Alaska. They would open them only when their development suited the corporations' needs, without regard to the needs of the new state's residents. The new state capital was likely to be the scene of lobbying far more intense than anything Alaskans had encountered before. The convention participants, said Bartlett, were starting with a clean slate and enormous responsibilities.[41]

Ernest Gruening, who had been governor of Alaska Territory from 1939 to 1953, provided the convention's keynote address on the day following Bartlett's presentation. In a stirring address, Gruening compared Alaska's grievances against the federal government with those of the American colonists against King George III. Alaskans were, he said, taxed without representation, obliged to give military service to a country that did not accord them full rights of citizenship, and subjected to discriminatory legislation. The ex-governor then went on to trace examples of these injustices as they related to control of Alaskan affairs by outside interests. Rampant colonialism was, he charged, preventing the fullest development of Alaska's resources in the interests of its citizens. The convention was but the first step in a hard struggle to end that colonialism.[42]

George Lehleitner, a New Orleans businessman promoting the "Tennessee Plan," was invited in January 1956 to address the Constitutional Convention after it convened on the University of Alaska campus outside Fairbanks. The Tennessee Plan, so called because it had been used as a device when Tennessee was seeking admission to the Union, called for a would-be state to elect senators and representatives as delegates to Congress without waiting for an enabling act. It presumed that the moral force generated by the presence of freely elected delegates at its door would encourage Congress to grant statehood.

Lehleitner, speaking on January 23, 1956, advised the assembled Alaskans that merely drafting an excellent constitution would not guarantee statehood. He pointed to Hawaii, which had prepared a constitution six years earlier and still awaited statehood while the document "gathered dust in the Hawaiian Archives Building." Anti-statehood Southerners, Lehleitner said, held eleven out of sixteen key committee chairmanships in the U.S. House of Representatives and seven out of twelve in the U.S. Senate. In the Democrat-controlled Congress, both the chairman of the critically important Rules Committee and the Speaker of the House were anti-statehood. These statehood opponents, he predicted, would not be appeased even if, once admitted, Alaska and Hawaii elected all-Democratic slates to Congress. Their concern was that any new seats in Congress, regardless of the party affiliation of the occupants, would weaken the South's dominance of the House and the Senate.

Continuing his analysis of the obstacles facing Alaskan statehood, Lehleitner cited the fact that senators and representatives had much less time to research issues than did their early-twentieth-century predecessors. Thus, they probably knew less about Alaska and Hawaii than their predecessors of 1912 had known about Arizona when considering bringing that territory into the Union as a state. Issues of reapportionment also came into play, as congressmen from other sparsely populated regions had to calculate the odds of future loss of

House seats to an expanding Alaskan population. Lehleitner's prescription for overcoming these obstacles was to adopt the Tennessee Plan, a strategy that had served not only the Volunteer State, but also Michigan, Iowa, Oregon, Kansas, Minnesota, and California.[43]

The Constitutional Convention generated excitement throughout Alaska. Daily radio reports and newspaper coverage kept Alaskans informed. Key issues were the location of the new state's capital and rural representation in the state legislature. The capital location issue was ultimately postponed by designating Juneau as the state capital in a "transitional measure," rather than as a permanent part of the constitution. This opened the way for later consideration of the questions. A unicameral legislature was considered, but the proposition faltered. Its opponents feared that a single-house legislative body would have its members elected solely based on population, thus giving overwhelming influence to urban areas such as Anchorage, Fairbanks, and Juneau.

Over the 1955 Christmas holidays, the convention recessed and its committees held hearings around the state. They reported good attendance at their sessions, although bad weather kept some audiences to a minimum. The public was well disposed, they said, toward a bicameral legislature with seats in one house apportioned on the basis of population and seats in the other apportioned on the basis of geography.[44]

When finished, the proposed constitution called for a powerful executive and a bicameral legislature consisting of a senate with twenty members elected for four-year terms and a house with forty members serving two-year terms. The number of executive departments in state government could never exceed twenty. Overall, the projected structure for the executive branch of government seemed a reaction to the powerless territorial governors and the days when more than fifty federal agencies had a hand in administering the public affairs of Alaskans. The judicial branch of government was to consist of a supreme court, a superior court, and such additional courts as the legislature might establish, with judges to be named by a gubernatorially appointed judicial council. Local government was structured in boroughs, the equivalent of counties, but contemplated to be vastly larger than most counties in the Lower Forty-Eight, and in cities of various classes of sophistication. Areas of the state not included within boroughs or cities were designated as the "unorganized borough," to be administered by the state.[45]

The constitution writers appended three ordinances to the basic document. The first provided for its ratification at the state primary election to be held on April 24, 1956. The second asked for voter approval of an Alaskan version of the Tennessee Plan. Concurrent with approval of the plan, the electorate was to select delegates to Congress. The third ordinance outlawed fish traps, which were thought both to be unfair competition for fishermen using boats and to be ruining the piscine resource.[46]

Alaskans approved the proposed constitution, the Alaska version of the Tennessee Plan, and abolition of fish traps by large majorities. Democratic candidates Ernest Gruening, William Egan, and Ralph J. Rivers won spots as delegates to Congress over their three Republican rivals.

At the end of 1956, Alaska's Tennessee Plan delegates arrived in Washington, D.C., to be greeted by Alaska Territory's delegate to Congress, E. L. "Bob" Bartlett. On January 14, 1957, the U.S. Senate agreed to hear a memorial from the Alaska Constitutional Convention. The memorial asked Congress to seat its representatives and to admit Alaska to the Union. Congress did neither, but the publicity gave Gruening, Egan, and Rivers the opportunity to lobby for statehood. January also saw appointment of a new territorial governor, Mike Stepovich. Unlike his predecessor, who was a career federal employee reluctant to take a position contrary to that of the Eisenhower administration, Stepovich became an ardent supporter of statehood.

January 1957 also saw the introduction of several statehood bills for Alaska and Hawaii in Congress, with newly appointed Secretary of the Interior Fred Seaton, himself a statehood supporter, announcing that the administration would oppose neither if its concerns about military land withdrawals in Alaska were accommodated. Senate and House hearings on the Alaska statehood bills were held in March. Administration concerns were alleviated by a provision in the 276-million-acre area north of the Yukon River, the president could make special national security withdrawals in which the federal government would have exclusive executive, legislative, and judicial authority. Other accommodations were also built into the statehood bill, such as a restriction on charging nonresident commercial fishermen higher fees than resident fishermen.

Legislative maneuvering delayed congressional consideration of the Alaska Statehood Act until mid-1958, although in his January 1958 State of the Union message President Eisenhower for the first time unequivocally recommended statehood for Alaska. Subsequently, Congress went back and forth on whether Alaska and Hawaii should be admitted separately or at the same time. In addition to the issue of noncontiguity, some congressmen charged that admission of the two non-mainland territories would open the door to communism, according to one, "to Bridges [head of the communist-dominated International Longshoremen's and Warehousemen's Union], to Honolulu and Juneau…into our Congress."[47]

Congress's conservative Southerners had been chronic opponents of Alaska statehood bills, for they feared that representatives of a new, Democratically inclined state with a large nonwhite population might help to loosen their stranglehold on civil rights legislation. They seldom admitted the real reason for their concern. Senator John Stennis of Mississippi, who led senatorial opposition to statehood, invoked the unfairness of giving two seats in the Senate to what he estimated to be the mere 1,500 square miles of developed Alaska and, like some of his Dixie colleagues, asserted that Alaska remained undeveloped because of the extreme climatic conditions. He echoed

Senator Clyde R. Hoey of North Carolina, who said, "[T]hey [the resources of Alaska] have not been developed because people do not want to stay there in the extremes of climate which are found there." An unusually frank Dixiecrat spoke the unpleasant truth when he said: "I'm sorry, but a group of us are committed to oppose the admission of any states whose senators are not likely to support our stand on cloture. The merits of the statehood won't play any part in our decision."[48] Ultimately, an alliance of liberal Democrats and moderate Republicans able to force passage of the 1957 civil rights bill made this concern moot, and most Southern senators acquiesced in the matter of statehood for Alaska.[49]

In the House of Representatives, Howard Smith of Nevada proved to be a chief obstacle. He feared that admission of Alaska and Hawaii would foretell admission of Puerto Rico, Taiwan, and the Philippines, creating a situation in which "offshore" senators would upset the balance of power in the U.S. Senate. Smith was bypassed in May 1958, when Representative Wayne Aspinall brought the Alaska Statehood Act to the floor of the House of Representatives as a privileged matter, admission of states being one of the few legislative actions falling into that category. Once on the floor, the bill triggered heated debate. Most significantly, a successful amendment reduced the future state's land entitlement from 180 million to 102.55 million acres. When a final roll call was held, the Alaska Statehood Act passed in the House of Representatives by a vote of 210-166.[50]

When the House bill went to the Senate, that body was considering its own statehood legislation for Alaska and Hawaii. Fearing that the differences between the House bill and the proposed Senate legislation might send the matter to a conference committee from which it might never emerge, statehood advocates urged Senate leaders to consider the House bill. They acquiesced, and on June 30, 1958, after opponents tried variously to scuttle or weaken the bill, the Alaska Statehood Act passed the U.S. Senate. President Eisenhower signed the bill on July 7, 1958, and Alaska had finally achieved statehood.[51]

The Alaska Statehood Act (72 Stat. 339) accepted the constitution proposed by Alaska. It also defined the state as consisting of the lands then included in the Territory of Alaska. Further significant provisions of the act entitled the state to select 400,000 acres from vacant National Forest lands and 102.55 million acres of vacant public lands within twenty-five years of admission into the Union. It was important that these grants of land included mineral rights. Equally important, lands to which Alaska Natives held title or to which they might be entitled were excluded from state selection, as were lands previously reserved by the federal government. The act made provision for the special national defense withdrawals desired by the administration. Admission to the Union was additionally contingent upon approval of that proposition by the people of Alaska in a general or special election.[52]

Alaskan voters approved their territory's admission to the Union as a state in a special election held on August 26, 1958. They voted 40,452 to 8,010 for immediate admission of Alaska as a state; 40,421 to 7,766 to accept the Alaska Statehood Act's definition of the new state's boundaries; and 40,739 to 7,500 to accept other provisions of the act. On the morning of January 3, 1959, President Eisenhower interrupted a vacation at his Gettysburg, Pennsylvania, farm and traveled by helicopter back to Washington to sign a proclamation admitting Alaska as the forty-ninth state. William Egan in Juneau took the oath of office as Alaska's first state governor a few minutes later.[53]

EPILOGUE

Even in 1959, Alaskan communities in roadless areas were isolated both physically and intellectually. Even many communities located along Alaska's one thousand miles or so of roadway could be reached by surface transportation only in summer months. Expensive air taxis and bush airlines flying weekly schedules in antiquated equipment provided the only year-round links to the outside world. Few of these communities had telephone service. They depended instead on high-frequency point-to-point radio for long-distance communication. Broadcast radio (except for the Armed Forces Radio Network beamed to remote radar sites and receivable by nearby villages) was available only by shortwave radio except in the vicinities of Anchorage, Fairbanks, and Juneau. Television, dependent on taped programs flown in from Seattle, was also available only in the larger cities. The communities had small, stable populations. Community leadership tended to be white, middle-aged or older, and drawn from active or retired professionals such as teachers, government officials, and medical personnel.

In the years following 1959, this environment changed dramatically. Alaska's population increased from 226,000 to 550,000. Revolutionary new communications technologies coupled with new oil revenues flowed into the state. The latter allowed the application of the new technologies, such as satellite and relayed microwave communications, to Native and non-Native settlements throughout Alaska. Almost concurrently, the Alaska Native Claims Settlement Act of 1971 brought increasing sophistication (in a Western sense) and surplus wealth to Native communities, ushering in a somewhat drawn-out process of resolving conflicting state and Native land claims.

Government agencies and their employees also changed dramatically in the decade following 1959. At the state level, Alaska's small population could support limited government and, in the words of one opponent of statehood, "Alaska went from being a broke territory to being a broke state." The state's situation changed in 1969, however, when a tremendous oil field was discovered on state-selected lands bordering the Arctic coast. Once a pipeline was built to carry that oil to a year-round port at Valdez, oil revenues began to flow into state coffers at the rate of millions of dollars a day. State and local governments and government services expanded dramatically.

In 1959 at the federal level, a coordinating superintendent, supported by a few rangers and a single historian at Sitka National Monument, supervised National Park Service operations in Alaska. These included the monument at Sitka and huge natural areas at Mount McKinley National Park and Katmai National Monument. Millions of acres of other federal lands held by agencies such as the Bureau of Land Management and Forest Service were attended to only on a part-time basis by agency land managers as crises arose. Passage of the Alaska Native Land Claims Act of 1971 revolutionized this picture. Hordes of federal planners poured into Alaska to identify lands that should be reserved to the federal government or transferred to Native or state ownership. The subsequent Alaska National Interest Lands Conservation Act of 1981 formalized most of the planners' recommendations after years of controversy and struggle among the federal government, the state, and the Native corporations created by the 1971 land claims act.

Although "man-on-the-street" interviews might show that the average Alaskan thinks that his or her annual dividend from the Permanent Fund—an endowment set up to protect surplus oil revenues—is the most important outcome of statehood for Alaska, in fact, that distinction should go to statehood's having given Alaskans at large a strong voice in the classification and distribution of public lands in Alaska.

CONCLUSION

Alaska waited for nearly a century to become a state. No U.S. possession has waited longer, even though Alaska represents a landmass 20 percent that of the Lower Forty-Eight states. Although early critics thought the 1867 purchase of an icebox from Russia for $7.2 million was folly, time slowly proved them wrong. Alaska was ruled as a military district first by the army, from 1867 until 1877, and then by the navy from 1879 to 1884, when the District of Alaska was organized. District status created no local government, but it did give Alaska presidentially appointed district officers, the laws of Oregon, and federal mining laws. Following the Klondike gold rush in 1898 and the Nome rush in 1900, the population began to increase, and mining, gold, furs, and fish remained the economic mainstays of the district, but corporations outside of Alaska reaped the economic benefits of Alaska's resources. With increased population and dissatisfaction with district government, such as it was, Alaska achieved territorial status in 1912. In 1916, the first request for Alaska statehood was introduced into Congress, but it was not until thirty years later that President Truman supported statehood for Alaska and Hawaii. Alaska finally proved its strategic value during World War II, proving it again during the

Cold War that followed. President Eisenhower supported statehood for Alaska once possible federal land needs were recognized, and he signed the bill making Alaska the forty-ninth state into law in 1959. Ten years later, the mammoth Alaska oil find ended Alaska's history as a tiny population living in an economic backwater.

NOTES

1. George Sundborg, *Opportunity in Alaska* (New York: Macmillan Company, 1941), p. 279.

2. U.S. Department of the Interior, *The Problem of Alaskan Development* (Washington, DC: U.S. Department of the Interior, April 1940), p. 1; George W. Rogers, *Alaska in Transition: The Southeast Region* (Baltimore: Johns Hopkins Press, 1960), pp. 162–165.

3. Max Farrand, "Territory and District," *American Historical Review* 5 (4) (July 1900): 678.

4. Lyman L. Woodman, *Duty Station Northwest: The U.S. Army in Alaska and Western Canada, 1867–1987*, vol. 1, *1867–1917* (Anchorage: Alaska Historical Society, 1996), p. 1.

5. Bobby D. Lain, "North of Fifty-Three: Army, Treasury Department, and Navy Administration of Alaska, 1867–1884," Ph.D. diss., University of Texas at Austin, May 1974, University Microfilms, pp. 26, 74, 889.

6. Ibid., p. 2.

7. Ibid., p. 4.

8. Ibid., pp. 8, 14.

9. Ibid., pp. 14, 23, 77.

10. Ibid., p. 48.

11. Ibid., p. 61.

12. Reported in the San Francisco newspaper *Alaska Times*, August 6, 1869, and quoted in Jeanette Paddock Nichols, *Alaska: A History of Its Administration, Exploitation, and Industrial Development During Its First Half Century Under the Rule of the United States* (Cleveland: Arthur H. Clark Company, 1924), p. 44.

13. "Civil Government for Alaska Debate," in Ronald Lautaret, *Alaskan Historical Documents Since 1867* (Jefferson, NC: McFarland & Company, Inc., Publishers, 1989), pp. 19–23, extracted from *Congressional Globe*, 40th Cong., 3rd Sess., June 13, 1869, pp. 341–343.

14. R. N. DeArmond, *The Founding of Juneau* (Juneau: Gastineau Channel Centennial Association, 1967), p. 120.

15. Ibid., p. 121.

16. Ibid., pp. 121–122; Nichols, *Alaska*, pp. 66–68.

17. Nichols, *Alaska*, p. 72.

18. Farrand, "Territory and District," pp. 677–678.

19. Nichols, *Alaska*, pp. 84–85.

20. House Report 1318, 50th Cong., 2nd Sess., quoted in Nichols, *Alaska*, p. 122.

21. See Nichols, *Alaska*, pp. 249–251, for a fuller discussion.

22. "Needs of Alaska," the combined reports of Waskey and Hogatt reproduced in Lautaret, *Alaskan Historical Documents*, pp. 53–60.

23. Nichols, *Alaska*, pp. 330, 381.

24. "A Territorial Organic Act for Alaska: An Act to Create a legislative assembly in the Territory of Alaska, to Confer Legislative Power Thereon, and for Other Purposes," 37 *Statutes at Large* 518.

25. National Resources Committee Findings, cited in Claus-M. Naske, *A History of Alaska Statehood* (New York: University Press of America, 1985), p. 77. This is an updated and expanded edition of Naske's *An Interpretative History of Alaska Statehood* (Anchorage: Alaska Northwest Publishing Company, 1973).

26. Claus-M. Naske, "Some Attention, Little Action: Vacillating Federal Efforts to Provide Territorial Alaska with an Economic Base," *Western Historical Quarterly* 26 (1) (Spring 1995): 46.

27. Ernest Gruening, *The State of Alaska* (New York: Random House, 1954, 1968), p. 464.

28. Naske, *A History of Alaska Statehood*, p. 83.

29. Ernest Gruening, *Many Battles* (New York: Liverwright, 1973), pp. 362–365; George W. Rogers, *The Future of Alaska: Economic Consequences of Statehood* (Baltimore: Johns Hopkins Press, 1962), p. 95.

30. Ernest Gruening, *Message of the Governor of Alaska to the Sixteenth Legislative Assembly* (Juneau: Territory of Alaska, January 27, 1943), p. 8; Naske, *A History of Alaska Statehood*, p. 95.

31. Naske, *A History of Alaska Statehood*, p. 98; Claus-M. Naske, "Governor Ernest Gruening, the Federal Government, and the Economic Development of Alaska," *Pacific Historian* 28 (4) (Winter 1984): 13; Naske, "Some Attention: Little Action," p. 58.

32. Naske, *A History of Alaska Statehood*, pp. 129–130, 133–134, 136.

33. Ibid., p. 167.

34. Quoted in ibid., p. 175.

35. Ibid., pp. 184–185.

36. Claus-M. Naske, "Little Men Demand Statehood," *Journal of the West* 13 (4) (October 1974): 45–46.

37. John Whitehead, "The Governor Who Opposed Statehood: The Legacy of Jay Hammond," *Alaska History* 7 (2) (Fall 1992): 15–16, 23.

38. Naske, *A History of Alaska Statehood*, pp. 206–207.

39. Ibid., p. 210.

40. Gerald E. Bowkett, "The Alaska Constitutional Convention," *Alaska Journal: History and Arts of the North Quarterly* 6 (3) (Winter 1976): 154.

41. "Meeting the Challenge," Delegate E. L. Bartlett, November 8, 1955, in *Alaska Constitutional Convention, Part 6* (Juneau: Alaska Legislative Council, 1965), n.p.

42. "Let Us End American Colonialism," Ernest Gruening, November 9, 1955, in *Alaska Constitutional Convention.*

43. "Address by George H. Lehleitner (Private Citizen), New Orleans, Louisiana, January 23, 1956," in *Alaska Constitutional Convention.*

44. Bowkett, "The Alaska Constitutional Convention," pp. 156–157.

45. Appendix 4, "The Constitution of the State of Alaska," in *Alaska Constitutional Convention.*

46. "Ordinance No. 1, Ratification of Constitution," 51; "Ordinance No. 2, Alaska-Tennessee Plan," 52; and "Ordinance No. 3, Abolition of Fish Traps," 54, in Appendix 4, Constitution of the State of Alaska, in *Alaska Constitutional Convention.*

47. Naske, *A History of Alaska Statehood*, p. 263.
48. Gruening, *The State of Alaska*, pp. 477–480.
49. Naske, *A History of Alaska Statehood*, p. 257.
50. Ibid., p. 268.
51. Ibid., pp. 270–271.
52. Alaska Statehood Act, July 7, 1958, 72 Stat. 339, Public Law 85-508.
53. Gerald E. Bowkett, "The Day Alaska Became a State," *Alaska Journal* 14 (1) (Winter 1984): 13–14; R. N. DeArmond, *Alaska: 1867–1959* (Anchorage: Alaska Historical Commission, 1981), p. 13.

BIBLIOGRAPHY

Alaska Legislative Council. *Alaska Constitutional Convention, Parts 1–6.* Juneau: Alaska Legislative Council, 1965.

Bowkett, Gerald E. "The Alaska Constitutional Convention." *Alaska Journal: History and Arts of the North Quarterly* 6 (3) (Winter 1976): 154–160.

Gruening, Ernest. *The State of Alaska.* New York: Random House, 1954.

———. *Many Battles.* New York: Liverwright, 1973.

Lain, Bobby D. "North of Fifty-Three: Army, Treasury Department, and Navy Administration of Alaska, 1867–1884." Ph.D. diss., University of Texas at Austin, May 1974, University Microfilms.

Lautaret, Ronald. *Alaskan Historical Documents Since 1867.* Jefferson, NC: McFarland & Company, Inc., Publishers, 1989.

Naske, Claus-M. *A History of Alaska Statehood.* New York: University Press of America, 1985.

———. "President Harry S. Truman and the West." *Journal of the West* 34 (2) (April 1995): 49–57.

Nichols, Jeanette Paddock. *Alaska: A History of Its Administration, Exploitation, and Industrial Development During Its First Half Century Under the Rule of the United States.* Cleveland: Arthur H. Clark Company, 1924.

Whitehead, John. "The Governor Who Opposed Statehood: The Legacy of Jay Hammond." *Alaska History* 7 (2) (Fall 1992): 14–28.

Woodman, Lyman S. *Duty Station Northwest: The U.S. Army in Alaska and Western Canada, 1867–1987. Vol. 1, 1867–1917.* Anchorage: Alaska Historical Society, 1996.

THE STATE OF ARIZONA

Admitted to the Union as a State: February 14, 1912

Valerie L. Adams

INTRODUCTION

In the mid-nineteenth century, Arizona was an arid land, devoid of rich farmlands and covered with either desert or cumbersome mountains. Upon traveling through the area in 1863, travel writer John Ross Browne wrote a book about Arizona, titled *Adventures in the Apache Country*, in which he wrote, "I believe Arizona to be a territory wonderfully rich in minerals, but subject to greater drawbacks than any of our territorial possessions."[1] Perhaps he was right. Despite a vibrant mining economy, Arizona had a long haul to prove itself worthy of statehood. After becoming a territory in its own right in 1863, Arizona had to wait another forty-nine years before becoming a state.

Admittance for Arizona into the Union was framed by national party politics. Both the Republicans and Democrats worried over how it might affect the balance of power in Congress. Their concerns were such that the 1889 omnibus bill that admitted Montana, Washington, South Dakota, and North Dakota was a pure compromise between the parties. Montana and North Dakota were expected to be Democratic, whereas Washington and South Dakota were expected to be Republican. It was in this vein that a proposal for joint admittance of Arizona and New Mexico as one state with New Mexico emerged in Congress in 1903. Arizona had tried for statehood nearly every congressional session since 1890 but had been denied because the requests were premature for the developing territory and because it had a long tradition of Democratic politics. The jointure proposal intended to use Republican-dominated New Mexico to dilute the heavy Democratic population of Arizona. Likewise, to strengthen New Mexico's bid for statehood, merging with Arizona's more

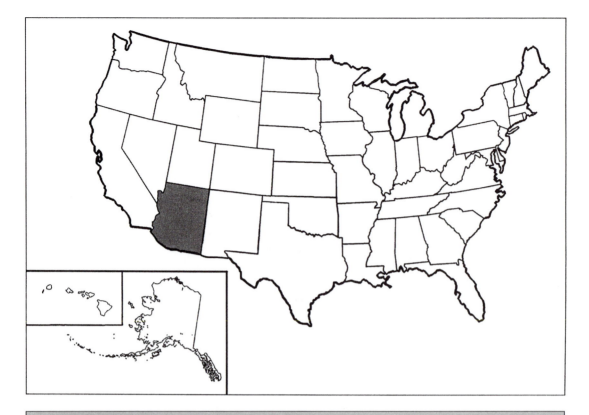

Arizona

Territorial Development:

- Mexico ceded future Arizonan territory to the United States with the Treaty of Guadalupe Hidalgo, February 2, 1848
- The United States obtained more land containing future Arizonan territory from Mexico through the Gadsden Purchase, April 25, 1854
- Arizona organized as a U.S. territory, February 24, 1863
- Arizona admitted into the Union as the forty-eighth state, February 14, 1912

Territorial Capitals:

- Fort Whipple, 1863–1864
- Prescott, 1864–1867
- Tucson, 1867–1877
- Prescott, 1877–1889
- Phoenix, 1889–1912

State Capitals:

- Phoenix 1912–present

Origin of State Name: From the Indian "Arizonac," meaning "little spring" or "young spring." This refers to springs located in what is now Mexican territory.

First Governor: George W.P. Hunt
Governmental Organization: Bicameral
Population at Statehood: 204,354 (1910)
Geographical Size: 113,635 square miles

Anglo-Saxon population was supposed to dilute the Hispanic population of New Mexico. Despite having sought statehood for over a decade, Arizonans vigilantly fought against jointure, preferring to remain a territory rather than unite with New Mexico. There was a heavy racist undertone to Arizona's resistance to jointure, as well as worries over increased taxes from taking on New Mexico's debt. Successful in defeating jointure, Arizona finally got its own Enabling Act in 1910.

A state constitutional convention met for two months in 1910 and was gripped by state political rivalries and Progressive politics. The nation was in the middle of what historians would later call the Progressive Era. Business regulation, social justice, and increased democracy were the banners of the day. Consumers and farmers cried out for increased business regulation, which would protect them from the huge monopolies and trusts. Labor unions, women, and blacks all fought for more rights and protections. And states began enacting direct legislation measures such as the direct primary, referendum, initiative, and recall to enlarge democracy. The delegates at the convention had the daunting task of producing a constitution that both reflected the Progressive ideals many delegates held dear but was also conservative enough to appeal to President William Taft and the largely Republican Congress. In the end, the delegates turned out what historian Mark Pry called "a masterwork of political accommodation by the Democratic party of Arizona."[2]

Unfortunately, although Congress approved Arizona's constitution, President Taft vetoed it because it allowed for the recall of judges. Taft held the judiciary dear; a judge himself, he would go on from the presidency to serve on the U.S. Supreme Court, a position in which he was much more comfortable than the presidency. New Mexico had also submitted its proposed constitution for approval at the same time. New Mexico's constitution did not contain the recall, and it nudged out Arizona to become the forty-seventh state. For Arizona to achieve statehood, it had to remove the recall of judges from its constitution. The people agreed to do so, and Taft signed into law the state of Arizona on February 14, 1912. Sixty-two years after having attained territorial status as part of New Mexico Territory, Arizona finally achieved its goal. The last contiguous state to be admitted, Arizona had the distinction of being the "Baby State" until Alaska and Hawaii were both admitted in 1959.

TERRITORIAL GOVERNMENT

The land that was to become the Arizona Territory was once held by Mexico and had been obtained by the United States after the Mexican-American War of 1846–1848. Left unorganized after that war, the people fought for a territorial government to no avail. In 1850, Congress organized the Territory of New Mexico, which included Arizona. The first government survey of northern Arizona was not done until 1852. The territory was enlarged in 1853 by the Gadsden Purchase, which secured 29,670 square miles of land from Mexico south of the Gila River. This desert land was sought after because it would allow building a transcontinental railroad without having to blast through the mountains of northern Arizona. Attempting again to attain independence from New Mexico, territorial residents met in Tucson to petition Congress for division of the territory in 1856. They elected Nathan B. Cook as delegate. Consumed by sectional politics, Congress ignored the request and Cook was never seated. Arizona residents tried again in 1857, 1858, and 1859, but each time Congress refused to seat the delegate. In 1860, Arizonans changed tactics and drew up a territorial constitution to create a provisional government until Congress granted it independence from New Mexico. That same year, the western half of the territory was named Arizona County by the New Mexican territorial government. After the 1860 census revealed that Arizona County had only 6,482 persons, Congress again refused to organize a territory with such a small population.

With the outbreak of the Civil War in 1861, it seemed likely that the cry from Arizona would continue to be ignored. Frustrated, an appeal went out to the Confederacy. President Jefferson Davis replied to that appeal with a proclamation, and Confederate Lieutenant Colonel John Baylor took possession of Mesilla and declared Arizona to be a territory in August. Granville Oury, seeking official recognition, was immediately sent to the Confederate Congress in Richmond as the Arizona delegate. Although he was not seated, in January 1862 the Confederate Congress passed a statute creating the Arizona Territory and formally seated Marcus H. McWillie, the second delegate sent by Arizona. Meanwhile, back in Washington, D.C., Congress took swift action and reintroduced a bill in March 1862 to create a territorial government in Arizona. By April 1862, the Confederates had fled the area and the territory was back in Union hands. Perhaps feeling that the pressure was now off, Congress did not actually pass the Arizona Territorial Bill until February 20, 1863. President Lincoln signed it into law four days later.[3]

Lincoln appointed John Gurley of Ohio to be the first governor. Before he could even pack, Gurley died on August 18. John Goodwin of Maine was named as his replacement on August 21. Richard C. McCormick of New York was appointed secretary of state, William F. Turner was the chief justice, and Charles Poston was made Indian agent. It was an admirable group of respectable and remarkably capable men being called on to settle a territory as challenging as Arizona.

Although Tucson was the only community of any size and the obvious choice for the capital, the troupe settled in northwestern Arizona, near Fort Whipple. Tucson had frankly been too eager to join the Confederate states and lost the prize of territorial seat. There was also great interest in protecting the newly discovered mineral deposits in the Bradshaw Mountains of northern Arizona. Fort Whipple had been established in essence to protect those mines. After staying a while at the fort, the members of government established a capital on the banks of nearby Granite Creek.

The town they settled was first called Granite, then Goodwin City, before finally being named Prescott, upon the suggestion of Secretary McCormick, who happened to have with him what he considered an outstanding history of Mexico authored by William Prescott.[4] In his 1916 history of Arizona, state politician turned historian James McClintock praised the territory's first capital for being "a distinctly American town from the very start and at no time in its history has it had any considerable number of Mexicans within its population."[5] Of course, this stands to reason. Prescott was truly created by the men charged with establishing a territorial government. Given that they were all Easterners, the town took on a distinctly Yankee personality. As McClintock rightly observed, there was no Santa Fe or Tucson influence on the town. Its architecture, culture, and residents were all very Anglo-American.

Moving quickly, Governor Goodwin proclaimed civil law in the territory and created three judicial districts, at Tucson, La Paz, and Prescott. The First Legislature, meeting in September 1864, partitioned the territory into four large counties. Yavapai County was the largest, and Prescott was made the county seat. The other counties included Mohave, Yuma, and Pima. Legislation creating a university was also issued, and a civil code was adopted. Since creating an infrastructure was vital for economic development, establishing toll roads became a priority for the early legislatures. Finally, organizing the seat of government itself was accomplished with Prescott being divided into an organized township. Looking back, local historians Kitty Jo Parker Nelson and Gail Gardner remarked that it was "astonishing to discover how well prepared were the members of the Governor's party for their job of organizing a government and building a city in such land as Arizona of the 1860s."[6]

In March 1865, Governor Goodwin replaced Charles Poston as delegate to Congress and Richard McCormick was appointed as the third governor. Goodwin never did return to Arizona, retiring from his position as delegate to a law practice in New York. McCormick, however, made a name for himself in Arizona, establishing both the *Arizona Miner* newspaper in Prescott and the *Arizona Citizen* in Tucson. McCormick was loved and hated, but he did work for improving the territory's schools, infrastructure, and economy. He went on to become a delegate himself in 1869, the first of three terms. However, his election to the delegate seat came only after he made a deal with Pima County legislators to move the territorial capital to Tucson. Residents of Prescott did not let it go without a fight.

Soon after it was founded, Prescott was enjoying a vibrant economy based on the territorial government, supplying Fort Whipple and serving the various mining communities. The town supported hotels, restaurants, banks, general merchants, and a slew of saloons. However, Prescott was still far away from the more densely populated areas of the territory in the south. In 1867, the Fourth Territorial Legislature voted 5-4 to move the capital to Tucson. The Prescott *Weekly Miner* immediately labeled the McCormick deal a scandal. Unhappy about the move, especially since its economy was being dealt a severe blow, Prescott lobbied hard for the capital to return. In 1877, the Ninth Legislature witnessed bids for the capital seat from Prescott, Phoenix, Florence, and, of course, Tucson. Enough votes were cast to send the capital back to Prescott, where business once again boomed. Although Pima County legislators tried to bribe the Thirteenth Territorial Legislature in 1885 to move the capital back to Tucson, it stayed in Prescott until permanently moving to Phoenix in 1889.[7]

The move to Phoenix occurred during the session of the Fifteenth Legislature. According to state historian Marshall Trimble, the delegates of Maricopa County, where the relatively new town of Phoenix was located, used a bit of trickery to win the vote. Knowing that the vote would be close, the Maricopa delegates needed to ensure that a Yavapai County delegate would miss the crucial vote. Making a deal with "Kissin' Jenny," a lady of the evening who worked in Prescott, the Maricopa delegates saw to it that their fellow legislator was delayed. This fellow wore a glass eye, and after visiting with Ms. Jenny, he took his eye out and fell asleep. Jenny took the eye and swallowed it. When he awoke and found his eye missing, he refused to go out in public, and she was unwilling and unable to give the eye back. The plan worked, he missed the vote, and the capital was moved to Phoenix.[8]

Shenanigans such as related in the story above were not terribly uncommon in Arizona politics. Since presidents appointed territorial governors, they did not always have the best interests of the Arizonans at heart, especially since no president was from Arizona. Long-term residents of the territory often proved to be the better governors. Congressional delegates, on the other hand, were elected by the territorial residents and represented the majority voice of the people. Territorial delegates did not have a vote in the House, but they served an important function in introducing statehood bills and in educating eastern politicians about the territory. Given that Arizona spent over forty years as a territory, it had many able and many not-so-able governors and delegates.

After McCormick left the governor's house, Anson P.K. Safford replaced him. Hiram Stephens of Tucson defeated McCormick in 1875 for the delegate seat. In 1877, John P. Hoyt became governor, but he only served a year, after which John C. Frémont was appointed in 1878. John G. Campbell of Prescott won the delegate seat in 1879, and John Irwin became governor in 1880. In 1881, the first Confederate delegate, Granville Oury, was seated as delegate from Arizona. Frederick Tritle was appointed governor the following year. In 1885, before leaving office, Tritle approved legislation that created the University of Arizona in Tucson. C. Meyer Zulick succeeded him later that year, the first Democrat appointed governor and good friend of President Grover Cleveland. Curtis C. Bean was elected delegate in 1885. In 1887, Democrat Marcus A. Smith of Tombstone was seated as delegate and became one of the loudest advocates for statehood.

In 1889, Lewis Wolfley, a Yavapai County mining man, was appointed governor, but he was despised by many because he held up plans for a constitutional convention and was replaced only a year later by John Irwin, appointed for the second time. Republican and Prescott businessman Nathan O. Murphy, who had been serving as acting governor, was officially appointed in 1892 but was replaced by Louis C. Hughes, a Democrat, in 1893, when Grover Cleveland assumed the presidency for the second time. In 1895, Nathan Murphy re-placed Marcus Smith as territorial delegate. Embroiled in controversy, Cleveland removed Hughes from office, replacing him with Benjamin Franklin. The year 1897 saw Marcus Smith regain his seat as delegate and Myron McCord appointed as governor. When war broke out with Spain, McCord stepped down to fight in Cuba and Nathan Murphy took his place, serving as governor for a second time. In a contentious election, Democrat John F. Wilson won the territorial seat in 1899, only to lose it in 1901 to the admired Marcus Smith. Murphy resigned as governor in 1902 and was replaced by Alexander O. Brodie, who had served with Theodore Roosevelt in the Rough Riders. John Wilson became delegate in 1903. Joseph M. Kibbey, former judge on the Arizona supreme court, was appointed governor in 1905 as the delegate seat once more went back to Marcus Smith. In 1909, Richard E. Sloan was appointed as last territorial governor while Republican Ralph H. Cameron replaced Marcus Smith as the last territorial delegate.[9]

For any territory to be admitted into the Union, it had to prove that it had a large enough population and sufficient taxable wealth to be financially solvent. For Arizona, that meant convincing politicians in Washington, D.C., that the lack of big cities and heavy industry did not preclude the territory from being economically prosperous. Arizona had a large mining industry and lucrative lumber and agricultural industries. Although the population was still small in 1890, at 59,620 non-Indian residents, it was a dramatic increase from the 4,573 non-Indian residents counted in the first census in 1864. However, Easterners who controlled Congress viewed the small mining towns that dotted the landscape not as centers of industry but as centers of loose morals and rampant corruption, populated by far too many saloons and not enough schools and churches. This image hurt Arizona, but until the Wild West was tamed, the stereotyping was often deserved.

Part of that taming involved ending the Indian wars. The federal government devoted its time in the second half of the nineteenth century to placing the Native Americans on reservations. In Arizona, most of the Native Americans had been moved to reservations by the mid-1870s. Shortly after becoming a territory, Colonel Kit Carson had led an attack on Navajos in Canyon de Chelly, which resulted in the surrender of 12,000 Navajos in the ensuing months and an end to their strength in the area. General George Crook assumed command of the military in Arizona in 1871 and was ordered to stop the Indian raids on Arizona communities and to curb the frequency of stagecoach holdups. Chiricahua Apache chief Cochise negotiated a peace treaty with the army in 1872, but war with the other Apache tribes continued up to 1886, when Geronimo surrendered to the U.S. cavalry. Once Arizona seemed safe from Indian raids, the railroads came quickly, which helped propel the mining, lumber, and winter agriculture industries. The Southern Pacific Railroad had the territory linked to a transcontinental line by 1881.

The perception that corruption ran rampant in Arizona was not helped in 1885 when the Thirteenth Legislature doubled the territory's debt and overspent by $45,000. Some of the legislators' actions were scandalous; others were simply unlucky. For example, the legislature appropriated a sizable sum to build a bridge over the Gila River at Florence, but within two years the river had cut another channel and left the bridge with no river. After coming before a grand jury in October 1885, the legislature was officially condemned for its extravagances. Dubbed the "Thieving Thirteenth" or the "Bloody Thirteenth," this Republican-controlled legislature hurt both Arizona's image and the state Republican Party, and from that point on, it was viewed by many as corrupt and loyal to special interests.[10]

If one considers the immoral mining towns, the problems with the Indians, and the inept legislatures and also adds the fact that train and stagecoach robberies and gunfights were common headlines, it is easy to understand why Arizona found itself with an image problem. The infamous gunfight at the O.K. Corral in 1881, celebrated in folklore and Hollywood, was only one of many very real scenes in the territory in the 1880s and 1890s. And it is fair to say that many Arizonans enjoyed gambling and drinking. For example, in the summer of 1900, Prescott suffered a devastating fire. Four and a half blocks of buildings were completely destroyed, including twenty-five saloons. But amid the chaos, patrons still managed to haul the bar from one of the saloons, a few roulette tables, and several kegs of whiskey onto the courthouse plaza, where they continued to drink and gamble while the fire burned.[11]

Arizona historian Leo Banks explained that in the late 1800s and early 1900s, "panning Arizona was the thing to do, almost a national sport for newspapers on both coasts and some in between." An 1895 cartoon from the *Los Angeles Times*, for example, mocked Arizona's pure and industrious image as depicted on the official territorial seal by representing the territory instead as a mustached, longhaired, gunslinging bandit with a pistol in one hand and a knife dripping with blood in the other. More often than not, men who had never been out West and, in the words of Banks, "couldn't find Arizona with a lantern," often penned the slanderous articles and editorials that were printed about the territory.[12] Although these stories represented only a small part of life in Arizona, having little other evidence to the contrary, eastern politicians were inclined to concur with public opinion: Arizona was a lawless land. Against such odds, the proponents for statehood began their uphill struggle.

DEBATE OVER STATEHOOD

Arizona wanted statehood for a number of reasons. Self-preservation was one of them. Believing that territories were never intended to remain subservient forever but rather mature into states, Arizonans viewed statehood as a natural progression in self-government and self-preservation. It was their right. After the United States gained territories overseas from the Spanish-American War in 1898, statehood was especially desirable. There was little difference in status or in the rights extended to Arizonans as compared to the Filipinos. In a racist era, being on equal footing with the newly acquired possession of the Philippines was not something for which Arizonans wished to settle.

Economic development and prosperity were other reasons for wanting statehood. Given that the territory had no voting member in Congress to represent its interests, it was beholden to eastern politicians, who often viewed Arizona as an arid wasteland. It was also believed that with greater control over its destiny, Arizona could prosper. Territorial governor Nathan Murphy explained this in 1890: "With statehood a greater degree of confidence in the stability of our institutions and the reliability of our values would be obtained. Our natural resources would be more rapidly developed and our wealth proportionately increased with the right to tax ourselves for public and internal improvements, which is now denied us by Congressional limitation."[13] The territory was ready for independence.

When congressional delegate Richard McCormick had unsuccessfully made a plea for Arizona statehood in 1872, the request was premature. However, the major economic industries of cattle, copper, citrus, and cotton had proved the worth of the territory by the late 1880s. With this in mind, William Springer, a Democrat from Illinois, introduced an omnibus statehood bill for Idaho and Arizona in the House of Representatives in January 1889.[14] It got no further than the House Committee on the Territories, but Governor Zulick took up the call in his annual message to the legislature that same year. "For more than a quarter of a century the people of Arizona have been deprived of all voice in the government which they help by their taxes to maintain," he told the people. Recalling history, he went on to explain that a territorial government was never meant to be permanent and that "[w]hen a territory had sufficient population and taxable property to be able to stand independent of the parent government, it was the custom to admit it upon an equality with the original thirteen states."[15] Zulick was clear that he thought that the time had come for Arizona and that the territory ought to petition Congress for an enabling act. The next year, in 1890, both the Democratic and Republican parties included statehood in their campaign platforms. The battle for statehood had begun.

Arizona congressional delegate Marcus Smith introduced a statehood bill later in 1889, but, like the Springer bill, it never got out of committee. Believing that their chances might improve in Congress if a constitution was attached to the bill, Richard Sloan of Pinal County introduced a bill to the Territorial Legislature that called for a constitutional convention. Both parties agreed this was a good idea and passed the bill. However, soon after Governor Zulick signed the bill, he was replaced by Governor Wolfley, who thought Arizona was not ready for a constitutional convention. Wolfley blocked the bill by refusing to call an election for delegates. Luckily, Wolfley's tenure as governor was short. As McClintock explained, Wolfley "was hardly fit for the trials and irritations of his office…. He wrote altogether too many letters to the Secretary of the Interior concerning the administration of Arizona affairs, and finally was removed from office."[16]

John Irwin, who fully supported statehood, replaced Wolfley in 1890. The next year, J. V. Vickers of Cochise County introduced a similar bill calling for a constitutional convention and it passed again with bipartisan support. Irwin signed it into law, called for elections, and the convention was held in Phoenix during the fall of 1891.[17]

After considerable debates over Mormons, Hispanics, and the economy, the delegates adjourned after less than a month. The final draft of the constitution dealt mostly with economic issues like taxes and business regulations, but rather radical ideas had been discussed. For instance, women suffragists had been given the floor on two afternoons of the convention and it seemed as if many delegates were intrigued by the argument that the female vote would "offset the ignorant Mexican vote."[18] Although full suffrage was not granted, the constitution did allow women to vote in school board elections.[19] The large Mormon population was another hotly debated issue. Republicans wished to limit Mormons' rights by including a test oath, similar to the one Idaho had recently included in its constitution. Democrats were not keen on stifling civil rights. In the end, the test oath was not included.

The constitution was ratified in a December vote. With the new constitution in hand, delegate Marcus Smith introduced a statehood bill in early 1892. It was denied on the basis that seeking statehood was premature for the territory since it was underdeveloped, not "Americanized" enough, and not Republican enough. The balance of power in the Congress was of significant concern to Washington politicians, and voting for Arizona statehood was seen as voting for two Democratic senators and a House representative. This attitude held on throughout Arizona's quest for statehood.

Smith tried again in 1893 but was again denied. Part of the problem was that many viewed the constitution that was attached to the statehood bills as a Democratic document, since the majority of the delegates to the convention had been Democrats. After 1893 it was decided, therefore, to drop the constitution from the statehood bills submitted to Congress. When an Enabling Act was passed, Arizonans would have to call for a new constitutional convention.

Arizona's chances did not improve in 1896. Although the national Democratic Party endorsed statehood for Arizona, Oklahoma, and New Mexico, the Republican Party did not. Given that Republicans controlled the House, Senate, and White House after the 1896 election and that Arizona voted Democratic in its local elections, Congress was not in any mood to help the statehood process along. Furthermore, silver was a hot issue. Western states and territories favored free silver, that is, the free and unlimited coinage of silver. Since many of the western states and territories had interests in the mining industries, it stood to reason that they would favor more coinage of silver. Free silver also meant easy money for developing local economies. However, politicians who favored the gold standard controlled Congress and they were not eager to approve statehood to any territory whose senators might favor silver. Eastern politicians thus looked at western territories with suspicion and hostility.

Despite the odds, Marcus Smith put in another statehood bill in 1897, but it quickly died. With the outbreak of the Spanish-American War in the spring of 1898, the issue of statehood was put on hold. The war, however, only strengthened Arizonans' insistence for statehood. Arizona had volunteered many good men for the war, including Yavapai County sheriff William "Bucky" O'Neill, who gave his life on San Juan Hill in Cuba serving with Teddy Roosevelt's Rough Riders. In addition, Arizonans now questioned their status in light of the growing American empire after the war. Arizonans were pioneer men who helped settle the West and adhered to American principles, yet they were not voting citizens. Were they to have the same status as the people of Puerto Rico or the Philippines? Surely not. Governor Murphy made a plea in 1899 to Washington: "By their patriotism and valor, by their thrift and ability, by their loyalty to the republic, fealty to national principles and every consideration of true Americanism, the citizens of Arizona have earned and are entitled to statehood and the inestimable privilege of self-government."[20] Three bills were introduced in 1899 by inspired supporters. Two were put forward by Arizona delegate John Wilson, and one by Senator Clarence Clark of Wyoming. All three languished in committee.

Statehood was continually denied in 1892–1900 for a number of reasons. First, the statehood issue was caught up in national politics. Even when the Democrats did have congressional control in 1893–1895, Arizona's allegiance to "free silver" frustrated its chances at statehood, since President Cleveland was trying to repeal the Sherman Silver Purchase Act to bolster the economy. Second, Arizona never enjoyed much support from eastern politicians, who viewed the territory as arid and underpopulated. For example, the 1891 constitution asked for Congress to grant Arizona more land because so much of it was unusable, yet in the next breath, supporters of statehood bills claimed that the territory was rich in agriculture, mining, and lumbering. The evidence that Arizona was an economic oasis with a sufficient population was not yet convincing to Congress by 1900. The road toward statehood still stretched a long way for the territory.

In 1902, things started to look up. Both national parties had endorsed the idea of statehood for Arizona in 1900. President William McKinley even visited the territory in 1901, although he made only vague promises to help the process along. More encouraging was that the 1902 omnibus bill to admit Arizona, New Mexico, and Oklahoma finally got out of committee and was passed by the House.[21] However, when the bill got to the Senate, the same set of objections that had been made for the previous ten years was repeated. The reasons Republicans gave for denying Arizona statehood were a familiar refrain by now: the population was not large enough to support a financially solvent government, the territory did not boast industrial centers like those of the East, and the land seemed too arid to be fruitful. Freshman senator Albert Beveridge of Indiana was chair of the Senate Committee on the Territories. The Republican delayed the bill by calling for subcommittee hearings.

After quickly touring the territories in question, the subcommittee concluded that Arizona and New Mexico were not ready for statehood but that Oklahoma should go forward. Delegate Marcus Smith was livid. He accused the subcommittee, which had only visited three Arizona towns—Phoenix, Tucson, and the mining town of Bisbee—of trying to prove that Arizona had a significant Spanish-speaking population like its neighbor to the east. Being tainted as "too Hispanic," Arizona's application for statehood was to be once more denied. As Beveridge himself stated, Arizona was still seen as nothing more than simply a "mining camp." But party politics formed the real objection for Beveridge. Convinced that statehood would mean two Democrats to the Senate, he accused the statehood bill of being "gerrymandered so shamefully that if the Republicans were to carry the State by ten thousand, she would still send two Democratic senators to Washington."[22]

Fellow Republican Matthew Quay of Pennsylvania disagreed with Beveridge and fought for the admission of all three territories. Quay and Beveridge went at it. Beveridge accused Quay of being interested in statehood for Arizona and New Mexico only because he wished to help a fellow Pennsylvanian with a railroad project in that area. Whether the allegation was true or not, Quay did take Beveridge on in the Senate. Beveridge, however, was determined to defeat the bill and held a filibuster that dragged into 1903. With the congressional session nearing an end, the filibuster threatened to deny vital appropriations as well as treaty ratifications, and Quay was forced to back down. The statehood bill was defeated, and Arizona remained a territory.[23]

What was striking about the omnibus bill of 1902 was that the House members of the Committee on the Territories recognized the issue of citizenship in light of the American empire. "The comparison," wrote the committee members, "is not an inviting one when the newcomers to the national fold, the Hawaiian, the Puerto Rican, and the Filipino are placed side by side as to political rights with the pioneers of American civilization in the great West."[24] However, there were still the issues of the sparse population and political loyalties. While the omnibus bill was being debated on the House floor, Jesse Overstreet, a Republican from Indiana, introduced an amendment that would admit Arizona and New Mexico jointly under the new name Montezuma. The reasoning behind this was to make congressional representation more reflective of the small population—assigning only two senators instead of four. Overstreet's amendment was defeated, but the idea of jointure would catch on.[25] Once the bill was in the Senate, Governor Murphy wrote to

Beveridge assuring him that Arizona was a stronghold of Republicanism. He explained that as a territory, businesses and corporations had stayed out of local politics, thus the frequent Democratic victories, but as a state, those industries would become active in state politics and be reliably Republican.[26] Murphy's and other Arizonans' attempts to sway the senator were in vain. Even though Quay had fought a good fight, statehood had to wait.

Ironically, at the start of the Twenty-second Territorial Legislature in January 1903, there was no push for legislation because it was believed that Arizona was on the eve of becoming a state.[27] Unfortunately, statehood was still nine years away. The next stop on the road toward statehood for Arizona was a bitter struggle over joint statehood with New Mexico, a confrontation that lasted three years. First introduced by Overstreet in 1902, the idea was embraced by many Republicans, including Senator Beveridge and President Roosevelt.

In 1904, the House passed a bill that proposed Arizona and New Mexico enter the Union as one state. Democrats felt that the time for statehood had come for all of the continental territories. Some Republicans agreed. Offering jointure was a compromise of sorts, allowing statehood for all, but theoretically reducing the chances Democrats would take all of the congressional seats. However, historian Mark Pry has suggested that jointure was actually intended to block the admittance of Arizona and New Mexico altogether. By offering the proposition of jointure, something that Arizonans were sure to hate, Republicans like Beveridge hoped that the territories would remain territories. Other Republicans, like Joseph Foraker of Ohio, who favored individual statehood, worked quickly to block the jointure bill from passing in the Senate.

In early 1905, the bill was changed to admit the merger of the Oklahoma and Indian Territories as one state, which was believed to be reliably Democratic, and to admit New Mexico, which was likely to vote Republican, and to leave Arizona a territory. Arizona was happy to be left a territory rather than be admitted as one state with New Mexico, but Arizonans were also frustrated that the issue of statehood was clearly embroiled in national politics. The Senate bill went back to the House, where it was rejected. The bill was sent to conference with the House and Senate, but with only one week left in the session, the bill died in conference.[28]

In May 1905, Arizonans acted quickly to establish the bipartisan Anti-Joint Statehood League. The bill had died in conference, but it was sure to be revived again at the next session. As Governor Kibbey explained it, the anti-joint statehood movement was not a political movement but rather something uniquely Arizonan. Despite the efforts of the Anti-Joint Statehood League to educate Washington against jointure, the House had another joint-statehood bill introduced when it reconvened that fall. Afterward, in his annual address to Congress in December, President Roosevelt also endorsed joint statehood. This was too much for Arizona Republicans, who called the joint-statehood bill "dictatorial" and openly criticized Roosevelt in mass meetings throughout the territory.[29] With Roosevelt's support, the bill passed the House in early 1906 when it then encountered some opposition from the Senate. However, floor management of the bill was given to freshman senator Charles Dick of Ohio, instead of Beveridge. Unable to stop the bill, opponents of the bill finally settled on an amendment introduced by Foraker that said Arizona and New Mexico would be joined together only upon the approval of the people in separate territorial referendums. Before the Senate voted on the bill with the Foraker amendment, Nathan Scott, a Republican from West Virginia, introduced an amendment that removed Arizona and New Mexico altogether, but left Oklahoma. The Senate passed that bill, omitting Arizona and New Mexico, but the House again refused to pass it with amendments. It seemed to many that putting the question to a popular vote was a fair way of settling the issue. The bill was finally passed with the Foraker amendment on June 16, 1906. The people would decide their own fate in a referendum slated for November.[30]

Not willing to let this latest move spell defeat, Beveridge continued his campaign as agitator. He pleaded to President Roosevelt that the territorial governor, Joseph Kibbey, ought to be fired. Kibbey's vocal opposition to jointure was proof enough for Beveridge that he was abusing his position, particularly since Roosevelt had appointed him and Roosevelt publicly supported jointure. Beveridge expressed to Roosevelt that he had it on good authority that Kibbey was going to use his position to ensure the vote went against jointure, even if fraud was necessary. Not willing to stand for voting fraud of any kind, Roosevelt took action to ensure the Arizona election was fair. He did not, to Beveridge's disgust, fire Kibbey. The president maintained that Kibbey was free to have whatever opinions he liked, as long as he did not abuse the office of governor.[31]

Anti-jointure advocates dug in their heals that summer, campaigning hard against the merger, and it seemed as if the entire nation was watching. Michael G. Cunniff, a progressive Democrat and mining man from Crown King, wrote that the debate over jointure was "a national drama." But, he added, the topic stirred the most passion from Arizonans. While he traveled through New Mexico, he asked its residents their opinions on joint statehood. Most preferred single statehood but believed that was unattainable, so joint statehood would have to do. In Arizona, when asked the same question, Cunniff got speeches, not simply "We don't want it." He recalled:

> They shot forth reasons. They told stories. They made parables. Lawyers over-whelmed me with arguments, doctors analyzed the situation, storekeepers de-tained me to tell me all about it, conductors hung over rear seats of cars to discuss it; mining men, business men, teachers, editors, Democrats, Republicans, Prohibitionists, were all in the same mood.[32]

While New Mexicans were willing to settle for a half loaf instead of no bread at all, Arizonans preferred to remain a territory forever rather than unite with New Mexico.

Why was New Mexico so loathsome to the people of Arizona? The answers are many. There was an ugly racist undertone to Arizonans' dislike of New Mexico. Despite having a Hispanic population of its own, Arizona viewed New Mexico as too Hispanic. An editorial cartoon that ran on the front page of the *Washington Post* in 1906 at the height of the debate captured the perception well. It portrayed Arizona as a white maiden and New Mexico as a Hispanic suitor, fitted with guitar and sombrero, chasing her up a ladder to her second-floor room. The fair maiden was using an ax to chop down the ladder.[33] To be fair, not every New Mexican was eager to be absorbed by the Anglo-Americans of Arizona. As the governor of New Mexico explained, "The new State would be an unnatural and an unwilling alliance. It would be the coercion of two populations which are unlike in character and ambition, and largely in occupation."[34] The difference in occupation was of grave concern to Arizonans. Arizona had worked hard to improve its industry and become financially solvent. New Mexico, on the other hand, had a large debt and was primarily an agricultural society. Arizonans feared that their taxes would increase dramatically with the absorption of New Mexico's debt. Furthermore, Arizona railroad and mining men loathed the idea of joining an agricultural population that had historically presented them with nothing but opposition. Ultimately, however, the thought of uniting with a territory whose culture, religion, customs, and heritage were so different from Arizona's was more than any of the residents could bear.

The vote was held on November 6 and, to no one's surprise, Arizona voted 3,141 for jointure and 16,265 against.[35] The 59 percent voter turnout and the reelection of anti-jointure delegate Marcus Smith by the biggest margin for any delegate since 1888 were proof that few supported having anything but their own state.

The statehood issue was dead, and there was little progress in the ensuing two years. No enabling acts were put forth. Everyone seemed tired of the contentious issue, but new circumstances changed that climate and encouraged Arizonans to try again. Oklahoma was finally admitted to the Union in November 1907, leaving only Arizona and New Mexico in the spotlight. Then Arizona elected a Republican, Ralph Cameron, as congressional delegate in 1908. After Cameron's election, President Roosevelt dropped his commitment to jointure and asked that statehood be granted "without delay" to Arizona in his annual address to Congress in December 1908, making statehood part of the national platform.[36]

Cameron campaigned on the issue: only a Republican could bring statehood to Arizona. It stood to reason. Republicans held all of the territorial offices in 1908, Republicans controlled Congress, and by 1909 the new president, Taft, was a Republican, and the GOP went on record supporting separate statehood for Arizona. The time was right to try again. Unfortunately, Beveridge still stood against statehood for the territory, and he was able to block the first enabling acts issued. Those were his last victories. By 1909, no longer a junior senator, Beveridge was consumed with his own reform agenda and reelection. He also realized that further interference would anger President Taft, since he had endorsed the idea of separate statehood for Arizona in his 1909 annual message. In fact, Taft had taken Beveridge aside and strongly suggested he back off.

When the last bill to admit Arizona and New Mexico as separate states passed the House in 1910, Beveridge made a feeble attempt to delay it in the Senate, but the bill passed and Taft signed it in June. Arizona erupted in celebration. However, the Enabling Act did have one important provision. Statehood was contingent upon both Congress and the president approving the state constitution. Caution was the word as Taft called for a simple and conservative document. But in an era of reform and with a state constitutional convention dominated by Progressive thinkers, simple and conservative was not a foregone conclusion.[37]

STATE POLITICAL PARTIES VIE FOR STATEHOOD

Interestingly, in the forty-nine years as an organized territory, Arizona only had three Democratic governors (Zulick, Hughes, and Franklin), and only five Democratic delegates to Congress (Stevens, Campbell, Oury, Smith, and Wilson), but it was the national Republican Party that continually blocked statehood for fear the state would send all Democrats to Washington. Of course, those GOP concerns were most likely valid. Presidents appointed governors, and Johnson and Cleveland were the only Democrats to serve in the White House during Arizona's tenure as a territory. Delegates, who were voted by the people, were more representative of the local political climate. Although there were only five Democrats to serve in that office, Democrats served all but four years between 1875 and 1909. Had Arizona become a state prior to 1912, its senators would most likely have been Democrats. As it was, in 1912 the Arizona legislature sent Democrats Marcus Smith and Henry Ashurst as their first senators.[38]

Despite the obvious conflicts between parties at the national level, state politics enjoyed a long period of bipartisanship with regard to the statehood question. Just as the majority consensus before 1863 was to become a territory separate from New Mexico, everyone in Arizona wanted the territory to become a state. There was a bid for statehood in 1872, but the process became serious in 1890. That year both major parties included statehood in their campaign platforms.[39] With the exception of the time during each of the constitutional conventions, the two parties cooperated on statehood issues.

Bipartisanship was in everyone's best interest, but at both constitutional conventions, Democrats held the majority. This did cause conflict. For example, of the twenty-two delegates to the 1891 Constitutional Convention, seventeen were Democrats. In protest, all but one of the Republican delegates stayed away the first day of the convention. One never showed up at all, but the others attended diligently after their brief dissent. However, the Democratic majority ensured a constitution that reflected the party's attitudes, which in turn prolonged the attainment of statehood. When the territory sought statehood on the basis of that constitution, the Republicans in Congress denied Arizona in part because of party politics: the proposed state constitution was viewed as a Democratic document.

One issue in particular that highlights this divide was the question of a test oath for Mormons. The Democrats, although not advocates for the Mormons per se, did defend their rights. Idaho had just been granted statehood with a state constitution that included a test oath for Mormons, an oath that denounced polygamy and promised allegiance to American values. Arizona Republicans argued that Mormons did not value the essence of American individualism to vote freely and that the Mormon Church influenced bloc voting among its followers. Republicans feared that that practice might lead to a Mormon majority in state politics. Furthermore, they were convinced that Congress would deny Arizona statehood if it did not include a test oath of its own. Democrats stayed fast as defenders of civil liberties and insisted that no oath be included. The Democrats won the battle, but the Republicans were correct in thinking admission into the Union would be denied.[40]

Differences between the two major parties did not really arise again until 1909, when the Republican Ralph Cameron had won the delegate seat on the premise that only a Republican could secure statehood. With all the major offices controlled by Republicans, it seemed that bipartisanship was no longer necessary. Although that may have held true at the national level, state Democrats were inclined to disagree. Bipartisanship was completely shattered after the passage of the enabling act. Both parties claimed victory, with the Republicans crediting Taft, and the Democrats giving credit to their Senate supporter, Joseph Bailey of Texas. Regardless of who got credit, state Democrats had their revenge in the state election for delegates. Realizing that they might have overplayed their hand and that they were outnumbered at the polls, the Republicans requested that the delegates be divided evenly between Democrats and Republicans. Denied that request, the parties campaigned hard against each other, and when the people went to the ballot box on September 12, they elected forty-one Democrats to only eleven Republicans.[41]

The campaign was long and marked by many interesting events. When the Enabling Act was signed and Taft cautioned for a conservative constitution, state politicians had to balance between that call from Washington and pressures from reform groups within the state. To achieve statehood, it was clear that the constitution had to appeal to the Republicans in Washington. However, it was also the age of progressivism and prohibitionists, women's suffragists, and labor unionists, all of whom had pressing agendas. In addition, there was a strong appeal for the installment of direct legislation: the initiative, referendum, and recall. Commonplace today, these measures to broaden the scope of democracy were seen by many as radical reform. The Republicans ran a campaign that avoided direct legislation altogether. The Democrats supported direct legislation and also vaguely promised labor reforms and increased corporate regulation. However, most Democratic Party leaders were not as passionate about the cause of direct legislation as the rank-and-file Democrats were. Marcus Smith feared that support of such reform measures would simply antagonize Congress and ruin any chance Arizona had at statehood. One notable exception to party leaders' apprehension was Gila County's Legislative Council representative and future governor, George Hunt, who was a loud supporter of most Progressive reforms. But most of his colleagues realized that a more conservative document produced at the constitutional convention increased their chances at statehood. Had it not been for the emergence of a third party during the delegate campaign, state Democrats would have likely sided more with the Republicans.

Believing that they had much to gain from influencing the final constitution, Arizona labor unions, particularly the mine unions, worked to form a third party. "The working class, if it only utilizes it, has the power to make this constitution to its own liking, and if it is properly drafted, our economic struggles of the future will be greatly simplified and our opportunities of bettering our conditions rendered much easier," the Bisbee representative of the Western Federation of Miners claimed.[42] Urging unionists to convene in Phoenix for their own convention, the Labor Party in Arizona was born in July. Its platform reflected the platforms of earlier radical groups like the Knights of Labor and the Populist Party. The Labor Party called for direct legislation, an eight-hour workday, a ban on child and women's labor, an end to convict labor, the establishment of a state industrial commission with inspectors, an employers' liability act, conditions making it easier to organize and strike, and, for good measure, women's suffrage.[43] The Democrats felt that they could not ignore the demands of the Labor Party. Fearful that the Labor Party would take votes and delegates away from them, the Democrats took on as their own many of the Labor Party's platform issues, thus pushing the divide between Republican and Democrat even further.

Republicans responded to this increased spirit of reform badly. First, they accused the Democrats of risking the chance for statehood with their radical reforms. Many did not see the need for direct legislation, since they viewed republicanism as the people speaking via their representatives. Republican governor Richard Sloan was vocally against it, believing that the initiative was the equivalent of minority rule and that the threat of recall destroyed "the manly independence" that public officials needed. The Republican newspaper, *Arizona Republican*, called direct legislation "socialist doctrines."[44] Not all Republicans felt this strongly, but most did and there were few exceptions.[45] But as the election results clearly demonstrated, most Arizonans sided with the Progressive thinkers of the day and voted overwhelmingly for the Democrats. So, for the second time, the Democrats held a significant majority at the constitutional convention and faced a considerable challenge in producing a constitution that stayed true to their convictions but was not offensive to conservative politicians back in Washington.

TWO STATE CONSTITUTIONS

Before the Enabling Act of 1910 was passed and the state delegates met for the constitutional convention, Arizonans had come together once before in 1891 to write a constitution. As mentioned earlier, both parties wanted to achieve statehood and felt that their chances might improve if they attached a constitution to the bills submitted to Congress requesting statehood. After the delegates were elected, they met in Phoenix that spring and wrote Arizona's first constitution.

The drafters of the constitution aimed to demonstrate to Congress that Arizona was ready for statehood and to provide the foundation for a state government. The constitution had to embody proof to the nation that the territory was mature and developed, not a lawless frontier, and that the territory was "Americanized" enough for admittance.

Issues over the Mormons consumed the debates at the first constitutional convention. Republicans had generally feared that Mormons might gain a balance of power and had wished to include a test oath, similar to the one Idaho had included in its constitution. In the end, the oath was not included.

In a similar vein, just as delegates had tried to discriminate against Mormons, they discriminated against the Hispanic population. Unwilling to outlaw gambling as a measure to improve its image as "civilized," the delegates were, however, willing to ban lotteries in the constitution. This was in part due to racist politics. Lotteries were a popular sport of the Hispanics, but not of much interest to the rest of the population. Banning lotteries and not gambling was meant as a strike against the Hispanics in an attempt to appear more "Americanized."

The constitution that had been drafted at the 1891 convention embodied numerous statements that had prevented its acceptance by Washington. For example, as a response to the excesses of the Thirteenth Legislature, the previous constitution had prohibited state legislatures from approving public debt on behalf of private enterprises, but it largely left the state government out of the affairs of individuals and corporations in regard to water rights. Congress viewed many of the provisions in this constitution as proofs that the territory was not mature enough for statehood. For example, one provision asked Congress for more federal lands, since Arizona did not have much fertile soil. Furthermore, other provisions called for state aid to railroads, claimed all rivers to be state property, and established silver as legal currency. These were measures that were not acceptable to Congress. However, to Arizonans, that constitution had cemented universal support for statehood.[46]

By 1910, the issues that plagued the 1891 convention were no longer factors. As Arizona's population grew, the Mormon population became diluted and Mormons did not prove to be the voting threat Republicans had earlier perceived. Hispanics and immigration in general had become a national issue, not just a state problem. Arizona's agriculture, mines, and lumbering had proved the economic vitality of the state. On the eve of the convention, Governor Kibbey observed that "the territory is in better condition financially today than at any previous period."[47]

George Hunt, who had led the charge for Progressive reform during the elections, was elected president of the convention, which convened in October. His appointments to the various chairs of committees reflected his Progressive spirit and predetermined that the convention was to be controlled by men who shared his views. Furthermore, Oklahoma and Oregon had both recently adopted relatively progressive constitutions and many of the Arizona delegates intended to follow their lead.

The vice president of the convention was a Democrat, Morris Goldwater. Goldwater had a good sense of humor and was liked by many. His nephew, the future senator Barry Goldwater, said of his uncle, "When Morris Goldwater was vice president of the Arizona Constitutional Convention, he told the delegates that for a small sum he would insert 'applause' or 'laughter' in the record after their remarks." This was not a bad offer, considering there was little to laugh at during the convention. Democrats and Republicans had to work out a document that would pass muster in Washington. The process was not easy, and it took two months.

As one might imagine after the contentious election campaign, direct legislation became the most significant issue debated at the convention. It was also the most symbolic and the one issue that would secure the veto for statehood from President Taft. Other issues that were debated included suffrage, prohibition, labor issues, business regulation, the economy, and the logistics of public office.

The delegates did not extend the full right to vote to women or enact prohibition, but both issues were discussed at length. In 1903, Arizonan Frances Lillian Munds (who preferred to go by the name Frances Willard Munds, undoubtedly after the suffrage and temperance leader Frances Willard), worked hard to see a suffrage bill pass in both Arizona houses. Disappointingly, Governor Brodie vetoed the bill.[48] As chair of the Arizona Equal Suffrage Association in 1910, Munds wrote to President Hunt during the convention, proposing that the First Legislature call a referendum on the issue of suffrage. The delegates denied the request. Temperance leaders tried for a similar proposal, but they too were denied. One of the major concerns with allowing prohibition or suffrage to be written into the constitution was that it would stall ratification. Mr. Cunningham of Cochise County voiced a typical thought during the debates when he expressed concern that "if we write into that document the question of prohibition [then] it will endanger the approval of this constitution, and I do not wish to encumber the constitution by any such measures."

Prohibition and suffrage were both defeated, with a vote of 33-15 and 30-19, respectively.[49] However, in spite of the delegates' apprehension about these issues, the people saw to it after statehood that Arizona set an example for Progressive reform. The First State Legislature gave women the vote, and Arizonans sent Frances Willard Munds to the Arizona Senate in 1914, the same year Arizona adopted prohibition. By 1915, Arizona was one of only five states to have adopted all three of the major Progressive reforms: prohibition, full women's suffrage, and direct legislation.[50]

Labor issues were also discussed at length, a reflection of the influence the Labor Party had during the campaign. Labor sympathizers tried to discriminate against Mexican labor. They argued that the inability to speak English was dangerous, and they wanted a clause that forbade non-English-speaking persons from working, particularly in the mines. During the debates, Mr. Connelly of Cochise County claimed that an accident in a smelter in Douglas "was caused by some man who did not speak English in starting the mill, and not being able to stop it, or to understand what orders were given to him." Opponents of the measure argued passionately that such a clause would literally shut down the mines. Mr. Lynch of Graham County explained the ugly truth: Mexicans were willing to do work Anglo-Americans were not. He said:

> I would say in the town of Morenci the conditions are that probably 90 percent of the men who work underground are Mexicans and Italians. They are under the control of shift bosses who also speak Mexican as well as English. Their whole work is conducted by American people, but the work is done by the Mexicans. There is a great deal of work that no white man will do. I seriously believe this is too drastic, as it means absolutely shutting down the mines of Metcalf and Morenci, and the ruin of the county....

Furthermore, not only would the mines close, but the men who had been working in the territory for generations and were citizens would be unable to find work in the only trade they knew. In the end, the measure was not included.

Laborites also tried to include the right to strike and boycott in the constitution, but failed. Nor was their argument for a clause against the use of court injunctions against strikers included. However, labor did have a few victories, seeing the inclusion of an eight-hour workday, an employers' liability law, and a workmen's compulsory compensation law. Children under the age of sixteen were forbidden to work in the mines or in any other hazardous occupations. In addition, the office of mine inspector was created, and blacklisting was made illegal.

Corporations were discussed thoroughly. Delegates from the more agricultural counties fought hard for the inclusion of a few provisions for corporate regulations, particularly over the railroads. The result was that a corporation commission was established to oversee the proper conduct of all public service corporations, banks, and any other corporation that issued public stock. However, other economic interests and water rights, by and large, went unchallenged.

Finally, the constitution had all the expected inclusions, including the acknowledgment of the national Constitution and allowing for three branches of government. Legislators had to be twenty-five years old and have resided in the county for three years. They were to be paid $7 a day and receive 20 cents a mile for travel costs. The governor had a salary of $4,000 per year. A few other notable inclusions dealt with minorities and schools. Reflecting that the issues with Mormons were now securely in the past, the constitution called for universal religious toleration. However, the delegates felt compelled to add that polygamous marriages were prohibited, in case the Mormons had any ideas to the contrary. Liquor sales to the Indians were forbidden. A state Board of Education was created; public schools were to be maintained and teaching conducted in English. And although mine workers were not required to be English speakers, any officeholder of the state had to be able to read, write, speak, and understand the English language. It seemed that by 1910, Arizona had become sufficiently "Americanized."[51] With the constitution complete, it was now up to Congress and President Taft.

FEDERAL APPROVAL

The final constitution included direct legislation. That meant recall and, furthermore, the recall of all public officials. In theory, the people of Arizona could use recall to remove a judge from the bench. This was something that President Taft absolutely would not tolerate. As already noted, Taft was a judge himself and held the judiciary dear. Arizona Democrats were determined to see their constitution ratified, however, and they argued to the people that should Arizona vote against ratification, Washington would see that as a vote against statehood. Arizona Republicans, by contrast, were fearful that a vote to ratify the constitution would only serve to antagonize an already hostile Congress. The people listened to the Democrats and ratified the constitution by a large margin on February 9, 1911.[52]

Congress was set to act on both Arizona's constitution and New Mexico's constitution. The New Mexican constitution sailed through Congress. Arizona had a more difficult row to hoe. After some debate, Congress finally approved the constitution on the condition that at the time of the first state elections, Arizona remove the recall of the judiciary from its constitution. When the paperwork went to the Oval Office for Taft's signature, he vetoed it. "If I sign this," wrote Taft, "I do not see how I can escape responsibility for the judicial recall of the Arizona constitution." Since congressional approval was based on the wisdom of the Arizona voters' removing the recall, he believed that the voters would repudiate it. Taft explained in no uncertain terms how he felt:

> This provision of the Arizona constitution, in its application to county and State judges, seems to me so pernicious in its effect, so destructive of independence in the judiciary, so likely to subject the rights of the individual to the possible tyranny of a popular majority, and, therefore, to be so injurious to the cause of free government, that I must disapprove a constitution containing it.[53]

Arizona had to amend its ways or forever be a territory on Taft's watch.

After Taft's veto, the Florence newspaper *Arizona Blade-Tribune* printed a poem that captured the sentiment across the state:

> You may think you've knocked us out
> With your little veto clous [*sic*/clout]
>   Billy Taft, Billy Taft
> But must think us awful tame
> If at that we'd quit the game
> And in bondage still remain
>   Billy Taft, Billy Taft
> We are made of sterner stuff
> And we will surely call your bluff
>   Billy Taft, Billy Taft
> We will tolerate your gall
> And surrender our recall
> Till safe within the statehood stall
>   Billy Taft, Billy Taft
> Then we'll fairly drive you daft
> With the ring of our horselaugh
>   Billy Taft, Billy Taft
> As we joyfully re-install
> By the vote of one and all
> That ever-glorious recall
>   Billy Taft, Billy Taft.[54]

As the poem suggests, the voters of Arizona agreed to a bill that was passed by the House and Senate requiring that judicial recall be exempted from the constitution. After the bill was voted on in Arizona in December 1911, Congress again approved the constitution, and it was ready for Taft on February 12. However, that day was Lincoln's birthday and the thirteenth was considered unlucky, so Arizona became the "Valentine State" when Taft signed the bill on February 14, 1912. Only seven months later, true to the words of the poem above, the voters approved a constitutional amendment reinstituting the recall.

SUMMARY

Both national parties, after fighting over statehood for decades, offered congratulations to the newest state in their 1912 platforms. The Democrats said: "We welcome Arizona and New Mexico to the sisterhood of States, and heartily congratulate them upon their auspicious beginnings of great and glorious careers." The Republicans made similar remarks: "We congratulate the people of Arizona and New Mexico upon the admission of those States, thus merging in the Union in the final and enduring form the last remaining portion of our continental territory."[55] The territories acquired by the United States through the 1848 treaty ending the Mexican-American War had all finally reached maturity.

After only a year of statehood, Arizona was enjoying great prosperity. The *Bisbee Daily Review* reported that "Arizona is in the heyday of its prosperity, and its people have every reason to be happy and contented. In the mining industry of Arizona we find the greatest recent expansion and prosperity and this satisfactory condition is reflected all over the state."[56] Governor Hunt reported in his first inaugural address that Arizona was Progressive and Democrat and the state moved forward with its Progressive agenda. Arizona outlawed gambling in 1907 and had become a "dry" state by 1914. Its image as an arid, poor, lawless, immoral territory was now securely in its past.

The road to statehood was a long one. Arizona had been part of the New Mexico Territory that was established in 1850 before becoming its own territory in 1863. It had petitioned Congress countless times for statehood since the 1870s. Opponents of statehood questioned whether Arizona was sufficiently developed and whether its Mormon population might control the balance of power. As Arizona's population grew, it demonstrated that it was an economically viable territory and had sufficiently absorbed the Mormon population. Yet statehood was still denied. Republicans in Washington, D.C., never believed Arizona's mining towns, winter agriculture, and lumber industry could match the industrial centers of the East. Arizona saw this attitude as part of an eastern conspiracy. Politicians in the East feared that statehood for the western territories would undermine their power. In the end, Arizona never had the full support of eastern politicians. Leaders like Matthew Quay and Joseph Foraker were rare, and for decades the Arizona statehood movement became a casualty of national party politics.

When statehood seemed possible through a merger with the New Mexico Territory, Arizonans fought against it. Picking territory over statehood, the battle against jointure played out as a national drama. Three years after jointure was first introduced in 1903, the people of Arizona defeated it. The Enabling Act of 1910 gave the territory a chance at statehood, providing that the people wrote a state constitution that Congress and President Taft approved. Caught in the Progressive spirit of the day, Arizonans wrote and ratified a constitution that included the recall of judges. As expected by many, President Taft vetoed the bill and Arizona remained a territory until its constitution was void of judiciary recall. Agreeing to pacify the president, Arizonans removed the measure and achieved statehood in February 1912.

NOTES

1. Quoted in James McClintock, *Arizona: Prehistoric-Aboriginal, Pioneer-Modern* (Chicago: S. J. Clarke Publishing, 1916), p. 323.

2. Mark Pry, "Arizona and the Politics of Statehood, 1889–1912" (Ph.D. diss., Arizona State University, 1995), p. 278.

3. Ellen Lloyd Trover, ed., *Chronology and Documentary Handbook of the State of Arizona* (New York: Oceana Publications, 1972), pp. 3–7; B. Sacks, M.D., *Be It Enacted: The Creation of the Territory of Arizona* (Phoenix: Arizona Historical Foundation, 1964), pp. 62–80.

4. Marshall Trimble, *Arizona: A Cavalcade of History* (Tucson: Treasure Chest Publications, 1989), pp. 195–196.

5. McClintock, *Arizona: Prehistoric-Aboriginal*, pp. 321–322.

6. Kitty Jo Parker Nelson and Gail Gardner, "Prescott's First Century, 1864–1964," *Arizoniana: The Journal of Arizona History* 4 (4) (Winter 1963): 5.

7. Ibid., pp. 6, 31.

8. Trimble, *Arizona: A Cavalcade*, pp. 203–204.

9. Trover, *Chronology and Documentary Handbook*, pp. 8–18; McClintock, *Arizona: Prehistoric-Aboriginal*, pp. 336–339, 376.

10. Pry, "Arizona and the Politics of Statehood," p. 33; McClintock, *Arizona: Prehistoric-Aboriginal*, pp. 333–334; Nelson and Gardner, "Prescott's First Century," pp. 31–32.

11. Nelson and Gardner, "Prescott's First Century," p. 10.

12. Leo W. Banks, "Newspapers Poke Fun at Arizona Territory," *Arizona Highways* (July 2003).

13. *Report of the Acting Governor of Arizona* (Washington, DC: Government Printing Office, 1890), quoted in Pry, "Arizona and the Politics of Statehood," p. 33.

14. Pry, "Arizona and the Politics of Statehood," p. 28.

15. George Kelly, ed., *Legislative History: Arizona, 1864–1912* (Phoenix: Manufacturing Stationers, 1926), p. 144.

16. McClintock, *Arizona: Prehistoric-Aboriginal*, pp. 340–341.

17. Kelly, *Legislative History*, pp. 153–156; Pry, "Arizona and the Politics of Statehood," pp. 28–30.

18. *Arizona Gazette*, 25 September 1891, quoted in Pry, "Arizona and the Politics of Statehood," p. 42.

19. *Constitution for the State of Arizona, as adopted by the Constitutional Convention, Friday, October 2nd, 1891* (Phoenix: Herald Book and Job Print, 1891), Article 10, 21.

20. Kelly, *Legislative History*, p. 192.

21. The omnibus bill was created because by the spring of 1902, the House Committee on the Territories had eight statehood bills for Arizona, New Mexico, Oklahoma, and the Indian Territory. See *Congressional Record*, 57th Cong., 1st Sess., pp. 95, 2338, 2814, 3533, 5137 (omnibus bill H.R. 12543).

22. Beveridge quoted in Rufus Kay Wyllys, *Arizona: The History of a Frontier State* (Phoenix: Hobson and Herr, 1950), p. 298.

23. Pry, "Arizona and the Politics of Statehood," p. 80.

24. House Committee on the Territories, *Admission of Certain Territories into the Union*, 57th Cong., 1st Sess., 1 April 1902, H.R. 1309, quoted in Pry, "Arizona and the Politics of Statehood," p. 82.

25. *Congressional Record*, 57th Cong., 1st Sess., pp. 5224, 5226, see Pry, "Arizona and the Politics of Statehood," p. 84.

26. Pry, "Arizona and the Politics of Statehood," p. 87.

27. Kelly, *Legislative History*, p. 221.

28. *Congressional Record*, 58th Cong., 3rd Sess., see Pry, "Arizona and the Politics of Statehood," p. 146.

29. *Arizona Journal-Miner*, December 7, 1905, found in Pry, "Arizona and the Politics of Statehood," p. 157; Trover, *Chronology and Documentary Handbook*, p. 17.

30. *Congressional Record*, 59th Cong., 1st Sess., see Pry, "Arizona and the Politics of Statehood," pp. 164–175.

31. Pry, "Arizona and the Politics of Statehood," pp. 177–178.

32. M. G. Cunniff, "The Last of the Territories," Trover, *Chronology and Documentary Handbook*, pp. 89–90. Cunniff would later go on to become the president of the first state Senate. See *Who's Who in Arizona*, vol. 1 (Jo Conners, Publishing, 1913).

33. *Washington Post*, January 24, 1906, quoted in Pry, "Arizona and the Politics of Statehood," p. 162.

34. Governor Miguel A. Otero of New Mexico, quoted in Wyllys, *Arizona: The History*, p. 301.

35. New Mexico voted 26,195 for jointure and 14,735 against. Kelly, *Legislative History*, p. 248.

36. Roosevelt quoted in Wyllys, *Arizona: The History*, pp. 303–304; Pry, "Arizona and the Politics of Statehood," p. 225.

37. Pry, "Arizona and the Politics of Statehood," pp. 220–227.

38. Direct election of senators was still a year away with the 1913 ratification of the Seventeenth Amendment.

39. For Republican Party platform, see *Phoenix Herald*, August 29, 1890. For the Democratic Party platform, see *Arizona Gazette*, October 10, 1890.

40. *Phoenix Herald*, March 28, 1891, found in Pry, "Arizona and the Politics of Statehood," pp. 35–38.

41. Pry, "Arizona and the Politics of Statehood," pp. 226, 251.

42. *Arizona Gazette*, July 6, 1910, quoted in Pry, "Arizona and the Politics of Statehood," p. 234.

43. *Arizona Democrat*, July 12 and 13, 1910, found in Pry, "Arizona and the Politics of Statehood," p. 234.

44. *Arizona Republican*, August 17, 1910, found in Pry, "Arizona and the Politics of Statehood," p. 236.

45. Editor of the Republican newspaper *Arizona Gazette*, Charles Akers, called upon his party to take up the call for direct legislation. When the Republican Party refused, his paper endorsed the Democrats in the delegate elections. Pry, "Arizona and the Politics of Statehood," p. 237.

46. See *Constitution for the State of Arizona, 1891*.

47. Kelly, *Legislative History*, p. 261.

48. *Who's Who in Arizona* (1913), pp. 606–608.

49. Pry, "Arizona and the Politics of Statehood," pp. 266–267; Trimble, *Arizona: A Cavalcade*, p. 207.

50. The other four states were Washington, Oregon, Idaho, and Colorado.

51. All information on the constitution taken from John S. Goff, ed., *The Records of the Arizona Constitutional Convention of 1910* (Phoenix: The Supreme Court of Arizona, n.d.).

52. The election results were 12,534 votes for ratification and 3,920 votes against. Election Records, Series 2, Box A-3, RG 2, Secretary of State, Arizona State Archives, Arizona Department of Library, Archives, and Public Records, Phoenix.

53. William Howard Taft, "Veto on Arizona Statehood," August 15, 1911, in Trover, *Chronology and Documentary Handbook*, p. 106.

54. *Arizona Blade-Tribune*, August 19, 1911.

55. Platforms quoted in Wyllys, p. 313.

56. McClintock, *Arizona: Prehistoric-Aboriginal*, p. 111.

BIBLIOGRAPHY

Banks, Leo W. "Newspapers Poke Fun at Arizona Territory." *Arizona Highways* (July 2003).

Constitution for the State of Arizona, as adopted by the Constitutional Convention, Friday, October 2nd, 1891. Phoenix: Herald Book and Job Print, 1891.

Geoff, John S., ed. *The Records of the Arizona Constitutional Convention of 1910*. Phoenix: The Supreme Court of Arizona, n.d.

Kelly, George, ed. *Legislative History: Arizona 1864–1912* . Phoenix: Manufacturing Stationers, 1926.

McClintock, James. *Arizona: Prehistoric-Aboriginal, Pioneer-Modern*. Chicago: S. J. Clarke Publishing, 1916.

Nelson, Kitty Jo Parker, and Gail Gardner. "Prescott's First Century, 1864–1964." *Arizoniana: The Journal of Arizona History* 4 (4) (Winter 1963).

Pry, Mark. "Arizona and the Politics of Statehood, 1889–1912." Ph.D. diss., Arizona State University, 1995.

Sacks, B., M.D. *Be It Enacted: The Creation of the Territory of Arizona*. Phoenix: Arizona Historical Foundation, 1964.

Trimble, Marshall. *Arizona: A Cavalcade of History*. Tucson: Treasure Chest Publications, 1989.

Trover, Ellen Lloyd, ed. *Chronology and Documentary Handbook of the State of Arizona*. New York: Oceana Publications, 1972.

Who's Who in Arizona. Vol. 1. Jo Conners Publishing, 1913.

Wyllys, Rufus Kay. *Arizona: The History of a Frontier State*. Phoenix: Hobson and Herr, 1950.

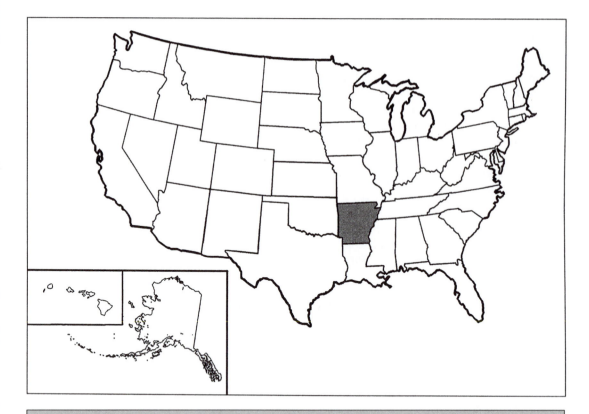

Arkansas

Territorial Development:

- The United States obtained lands containing the future Arkansas Territory from France through the Louisiana Purchase, April 30, 1803
- Future territory of Arkansas organized as a part of the Missouri Territory, 1812
- Arkansas reorganized as a U.S. territory, March 2, 1819
- Arkansas admitted into the Union as the twenty-fifth state, June 15, 1836

Territorial Capitals:

- Arkansas Post, 1819–1821
- Little Rock, 1821–1836

State Capitals:

- Little Rock, 1836–present

Origin of State Name: "Arkansas" is another form of the word "Kansas" (a Sioux tribe), but its pronunciation was altered to the French style, according to a statute from 1881.

First Governor: James S. Conway
Governmental Organization: Bicameral
Population at Statehood: 97,574
Geographical Size: 52,068 square miles

THE STATE OF ARKANSAS

Admitted to the Union as a State: June 15, 1836

William D. Baker

INTRODUCTION

By the time Arkansas achieved statehood in 1836, no new states had been allowed to join the Union for fifteen years. Missouri's entrance into the Union in 1821 had unleashed a firestorm of dissension and controversy over the spread of slavery. The Compromise of 1820 had been intended to calm the situation and settle the slavery issue for good. However, Arkansas' transition from sleepy French outpost to U.S. territory to statehood would rekindle that debate, and free-state interests would only acquiesce to Arkansas' statehood as a precondition for Michigan's entry as a free state. Arkansas' journey to statehood would be a tortuous one, replete with noble intentions, political corruption and intrigue, and factional infighting. During the territorial interregnum, dueling and violence between political officeholders was common, and many members of the ruling elite were related to one another.

As the nineteenth century began, the region that would become Arkansas was a portion of Louisiana, first claimed and sparsely settled by the French but ceded to the Spanish following the Treaty of Paris in 1763. Although France briefly reacquired the territory through the Treaty of San Ildefonso prior to the Louisiana Purchase in 1803, probably no more than five hundred Europeans, most of them French nationals, were living in Arkansas as the new century dawned, most in the vicinity of Arkansas Post, near the mouth of the Arkansas River. The area's population grew slowly over the decades that followed, spurred in part by congressional land grants between the Arkansas and St. Francis rivers awarded to veterans of the War of 1812.[1]

By the terms of the Northwest Ordinance of 1787, new territories would be required to proceed through three stages of territorial government before statehood would be possible. In the first stage, Congress would appoint a governor, a secretary, and three federal judges to oversee the territory until the population had reached 5,000, at which point the territory could elect a legislature and send a nonvoting delegate to Congress. Only upon realizing a population of 60,000 could a territory write a constitution and petition Congress for admission as a state. Based on these principles, Congress organized these new territories in 1804, dividing Louisiana at the 33rd parallel, Arkansas' current southern border, and establishing the Territory of Orleans to the south, with New Orleans as its capital. The less-populous northern portion of the Louisiana Purchase, attached initially to the Territory of Indiana as the District of Louisiana, was established as the Territory of Louisiana in 1805, with St. Louis as its capital. The District of Arkansas, established in the southern portion of the new territory a year later, marked the first official use of that name by the U.S. government.[2]

As the populations of the territories to its north and south grew, Arkansas' political status changed as well. With the admission of the Territory of Orleans into the Union as the state of Louisiana, the Territory of Louisiana was redesignated the Missouri Territory in 1812. The District of Arkansas became Arkansas County in 1813, with its county seat at Arkansas Post, and as Arkansas' population grew, new counties were created, including Lawrence in 1815 and Clark, Hempstead, and Pulaski in 1818. Finally, in 1818 Missouri Territory petitioned Congress for statehood but requested a southern border at 36°30', omitting the five counties in what is today Arkansas. However, settlers in northeastern Lawrence County reacted angrily to their pending eviction from Missouri and appealed to St. Louis. As a result, the final border would eventually run along the 36th parallel from the border with the Tennessee River west to the St. Francis River, where it then turned north to 36°30' before turning west once again, accounting for the famous Missouri boot heel.[3]

Bitter over years of perceived neglect by St. Louis and by their exclusion from Missouri's bid for statehood, Arkansans based primarily at Arkansas Post petitioned Congress to form a new territory from the five counties Missouri no longer wanted. Furthermore, the petition requested that the proposed new territory be allowed to elect a legislature immediately, thereby skipping the first stage of territorial development as required by the Northwest Ordinance. Although Congress began consideration of the issue in January 1819, Arkansas' territorial status was soon overshadowed by more pressing concerns over federalism, sectionalism, and slavery unleashed by the Missouri Crisis. As northern and southern interests battled in Congress over whether to admit Missouri as a slave or free state, Arkansas' territorial ambitions were affected as well. In February 1819, Representative John W. Taylor of New York unsuccessfully attempted to amend the Arkansas bill to prohibit slavery in the new territory, and a provision to free the children of slaves once they were twenty-one was defeated only when Speaker of the House Henry Clay cast his own vote to break a tie. Ultimately, however, the bill passed the House on February 22 and the Senate on March 1, and was signed by President Monroe on March 2, 1819, establishing the Territory of Arkansas with slavery intact. The following year, the Missouri Compromise would establish the Missouri-Arkansas border as the division between slave and free territory throughout the remainder of the Louisiana Purchase.[4]

TERRITORIAL GOVERNMENT

Prior to its acquisition by the United States, government in the territory that would become Arkansas was limited primarily to the area in and around Arkansas Post. Even under the territorial governments of Indiana, Louisiana, and Missouri, public officials paid relatively little attention to the few mostly French inhabitants of the sparsely populated region. However, as more and more Americans began settling in the region following the War of 1812, Washington began to allow the residents of Arkansas greater opportunities for self-governance and autonomy. While successive presidential administrations placed experienced and proven political and military figures in charge of the new territory, the political opportunities available in Arkansas also proved an irresistible temptation to ambitious politicians from more established states to the east. Over the course of the 1820s and 1830s, competition and conflict over political offices, patronage, land, and personal honor led to intense political and personal rivalries, the establishment of political factions and the beginnings of the first party organizations, and considerable violence as well.

Arkansas Territory officially came into existence on July 4, 1819, with its capital at Arkansas Post. The Monroe administration named General James Miller, a New Hampshire native and a hero of the battle of Lundy's Lane during the War of 1812, as the territory's first governor. He was to be assisted by twenty-two-year-old Robert Crittenden, a member of a prominent Kentucky political family and younger brother of U.S. senator John J. Crittenden, as territorial secretary. In addition, three federal judges—Andrew Scott, Charles Jouett, and Robert P. Letcher, all native Virginians—were appointed to serve as a superior court and interim legislature. Miller, however, did not arrive at Arkansas Post until December, and in his absence Crittenden, serving as acting governor, maneuvered to establish himself as a political force in his own right in the fledgling territory. Calling the superior court judges into legislative session in late July, the acting governor oversaw the establishment of a legal code based on that of Missouri, the appropriation of $4,816.87 to finance the new territorial government through January 1, 1821, the division of the territory into two judicial circuits, and the creation of several administrative and judicial offices, which Crittenden himself proceeded to fill. The judges were therefore in the position of enforcing legislation that they had enacted while providing the governor with both legislative and executive responsibilities. Having appropriated the monies to pay their salaries, Jouett and Letcher thereupon left Arkansas, never to return.[5]

The powers of the territorial governor exercised by Crittenden in Miller's absence were considerable. Under Section 3 of the legislation establishing the Arkansas Territory, the governor, appointed by the president for a three-year term with an annual salary of $2,000, would serve as commander in chief of the territorial militia and could grant pardons, appoint all officers not otherwise provided for in the enabling legislation, and convene the Territorial Legislature into extraordinary sessions. The governor was also to serve as federal superintendent of Indian affairs, a position carrying an additional annual salary of $1,500. The Territorial Legislature often chafed under the executive control of territorial governors. In 1828 the legislators accused then Governor Izard of attempting to exercise dictatorial powers in chiding them for straying from his agenda during a special legislative session. In 1831 the legislators petitioned Congress to remove then Governor Pope, whom they accused of being "totally irresponsible to those he governs."[6]

In October, Crittenden declared that Arkansas was now prepared to enter the second stage of territorial government. He called for elections the following month to seat a five-member Territorial Council and a nine-member House, and to select a delegate to the U.S. House of Representatives who would serve as the primary liaison between the territory and Washington. James Woodson Bates, a Virginian whose brother was territorial secretary in the Missouri Territory, was the first to be elected to this important and influential position in 1819. Given the frequent absences of Arkansas' first two territorial governors, Miller and Pope, Crittenden would wield enormous political influence for more than a decade. The following month, the newly arrived William Woodruff would publish the first edition of the *Arkansas Gazette* on November 20, which soon became the official publisher of U.S. laws in the territory.[7]

On his arrival at Arkansas Post, Governor Miller attempted to wrest political control of the territory from the upstart Crittenden. He accused the territorial secretary of having inappropriately called elections to fill the Territorial Council, despite the fact that the Missouri territorial law on which Arkansas law was based required presidential appointments to that body. Crittenden and the legislature maintained, however, that an 1816 amendment to the Missouri law allowing such elections applied to Arkansas as well. The Territorial Assembly, called by the governor into its first tumultuous session in February 1820, soon split into Miller and Crittenden factions. Later that year, two new counties were created and a bill was approved to move the territorial capital to the more centrally located Little Rock, where Miller, Crittenden and House Speaker Joseph Hardin owned real estate. Although other territorial officials subsequently relocated to Little Rock, where Crittenden and Chester Ashley established a law practice, Miller refused to do so and settled in nearby Crystal

Hill instead. The legislature first met in the new capital in October 1821, by which time the federal census reported 12,579 whites and 1,617 slaves in the territory's nine counties. On April 11, 1820, President Monroe signed legislation recognizing the territorial elections and officially elevating Arkansas to the status of a second-grade territory.[8]

New territorial elections were held on August 6, 1821, with one council member and one House member elected from each of the territory's nine counties. Turnover was high, with no sitting council members reelected and only two House members returning from the previous session. Bates was narrowly reelected as a delegate to Congress, defeating Matthew Lyon, a former New Hampshire Republican who had been jailed by the Federalists under the Sedition Act in the late eighteenth century, by just sixty-one votes. Although Lyon alleged voting irregularities, Crittenden refused to allow a recount. Both chambers initially had standing committees on elections, ways and means, and memorials, with new committees on the judiciary, the militia, rules, printing, auditing, divorce and alimony, and seminary lands established later. From 1820 through 1831, House and council salaries were set at $4 a day while in session, with the council president and speaker of the House entitled to $5 per day, in addition to one day's pay for each twenty-five miles of travel necessary to reach the capital. Travel reimbursements were discontinued in 1829, but in 1831 legislators were granted a $30 expense allowance. Legislative sessions varied in length from ten to forty-eight days during the 1820s, while as many as eighty and as few as twenty-one pieces of legislation were signed into law during various sessions.[9]

The politics of territorial Arkansas were often violent, and duels, fistfights, and vendettas were common among its political elites. Although the Territorial Assembly passed legislation outlawing dueling and prohibiting participants from holding public office, the practice continued unabated and violations were seldom prosecuted. "Party spirit among us has run high," Territorial Delegate Ambrose Sevier explained to Secretary of State Henry Clay in 1829, "and not infrequently these political disputes ended in bloodshed." Arkansas' most coveted electoral prize, with the potential to influence federal policy and direct federal patronage, was that of the nonvoting delegate to Congress. James Woodson Bates, a Crittenden ally, was narrowly elected to the seat in 1819, defeating Stephen F. Austin, who would later shift his ambitions to Texas politics. In the 1823 election, Crittenden withdrew his support for Bates and backed thirty-year-old Henry Conway, a Tennessean who had also served in the War of 1812. Conway won handily, Crittenden having urged his major opponents to drop out of the race, and defeated Bates to win reelection with 80 percent of the vote in 1825, in part by touting his success in forcing the Quapaw Indians to cede their Arkansas landholdings. Over time, Conway and his extended family would develop their own political machine, known alternately as "the Family" or "the Dynasty," that would develop close ties to the Jackson wing of the Democratic Party, come to rival and eventually eclipse that of Crittenden's, and dominate Arkansas politics until the Civil War.[10]

Crittenden and Conway had had a falling out by 1827, however, and Conway ran for reelection with the support of a new political faction, including William Woodruff, the influential publisher of the *Arkansas Gazette*, and Chester Ashley, a prominent Little Rock attorney and land speculator. In the bitter election that followed, Conway's opponent, Crittenden candidate Robert Oden, publicly accused Conway of having misused $600 in public funds for political purposes, charges corroborated by Crittenden himself. Although Oden was easily defeated by a margin of 2,427 to 856, Conway subsequently published an open letter in the pro-Dynasty *Arkansas Gazette* accusing Crittenden of having manufactured the charges in an effort to influence the election. Crittenden responded to this attack by challenging Conway to a duel. On October 29, 1827, Crittenden mortally wounded Conway in a duel on the eastern bank of the Mississippi River. Conway died of his wound eleven days later, and three-term territorial House member Ambrose Sevier, Conway's twenty-six-year-old cousin, was elected to succeed the late delegate later that year. This episode received national attention and tarnished Crittenden's reputation for years to come, while firmly establishing in the popular imagination Arkansas' image as a wild and lawless region.[11]

Governor Miller, whose health was poor and whose wife had remained in New Hampshire, never cared for Arkansas' frontier conditions and was frequently absent from the state. Although he was reappointed governor in 1823, Miller resigned his office in December 1824 to take a position as collector in the federal customs house in Salem, Massachusetts, to be replaced by George Izard, a Pennsylvanian with little knowledge of Arkansas who had been disappointed in his hopes for a diplomatic post. Although Izard adeptly negotiated the transfer of Quapaw and Cherokee lands to territorial control, he was otherwise ineffective and clashed frequently with Crittenden and the legislature before his death in 1828. Crittenden lobbied the John Quincy Adams administration to replace Izard as governor, but Sevier was able to block Crittenden's confirmation in the Senate. Convinced by Sevier that Crittenden was too controversial, the incoming Jackson administration turned instead to John Pope, a former U.S. senator from Kentucky, while Crittenden was replaced as secretary with William Savin Fulton of Alabama, who had served in the military with the president in Florida.[12]

Pope, a native Virginian who had lost his right arm in a cornstalk-cutter accident as a child, over the course of his six-year tenure finally brought some stability and leadership to Arkansas' territorial government and oversaw the construction of the first state capitol. In 1831, Congress had authorized the territorial government to sell ten sections of public land to raise funds for the construction of public buildings in Arkansas. Crittenden, now a private citizen, offered to exchange his Little Rock home for use as the state capitol in return for the ten sections, and a bill to that effect passed the legislature.

Despite heavy opposition, however, Pope vetoed the legislation and sold the federal lands for over $31,000; later that year, Crittenden's home sold for less than $7,000. When finally completed, the new state capitol building, still extant and now known as the Old State House, cost $123,379, well over the initial budget. Nevertheless, Pope's administration was undermined by backbiting from his secretary, William Savin Fulton, who was secretly critical of the governor and his policies in his correspondence with his patron, President Jackson. In 1835, Jackson replaced Pope with Fulton and selected Lewis Randolph, a grandson of Thomas Jefferson, as secretary.[13]

KEY TERRITORIAL PLAYERS

Competition for political power in territorial Arkansas reflected the profound changes in political values and expectations underway in the United States during the first decades of the nineteenth century. The political ideal during the revolutionary period had been the Republican officeholder, an educated, wealthy, and disinterested elite imbued with the classical virtues of the Roman Republic. Early political leaders such as Washington, Adams, and Jefferson had exemplified this ideal, sacrificing personal interests to take up the distasteful burden of civil office for the greater good of the commonwealth. By the time Arkansas was establishing its first territorial government, however, this ideal was changing. In the more egalitarian Jacksonian era, ambitious Democratic officeholders were more likely to see politics as an avenue toward personal economic enrichment and enhanced social status. As the historian S. Charles Bolton has noted, "Arkansas Territory represented the possibility of advancement, not only for settlers who wanted fertile and inexpensive land but also for aspiring politicians who wanted offices and the influences that came with them."[14]

A number of key players dominated Arkansas' territorial period and played influential, often antagonistic, roles in the transition to statehood. The state's first territorial governor, James Miller, was a native of New Hampshire who had established himself as a hero during the War of 1812 as a brigadier general. More important, Miller was destitute and his home state's congressional delegation arranged for his appointment in part to improve his financial situation. However, Miller's lack of enthusiasm for his new position, health issues—his concerns over a physical "[c]onstitution...impaired by privation and exposure to the inclement seasons of the North during the late war," which precluded travel during the "warm and unhealthy season of the South"—and a side trip to Pittsburgh to collect arms and ammunition for the territorial militia delayed the governor's arrival in Arkansas until December.[15]

Although honest and capable in civil administration and Indian affairs, Miller never developed close ties to Arkansas and managed to avoid much of the political infighting that consumed so many of his contemporaries in territorial government. Not long after his arrival in Arkansas, the governor wrote Secretary of War John C. Calhoun to inquire as to a return to military service. His letters to his wife in New Hampshire on frontier culture and society were not complimentary, and his health took a turn for the worse during Arkansas' hot, humid, and mosquito-infested summer of 1820. Anxious to avoid another Arkansas summer, Miller requested a leave of absence from President Monroe, and in April 1821 he left the state, not to return until November. He left the state again in June 1823, never to return. He finally tendered his resignation in December 1824, having actually been in the territory less than half the period of his tenure.[16]

What Miller lacked in drive and ambition was more than made up for by the first territorial secretary, twenty-two-year-old Robert Crittenden. Given Miller's frequent absences and lack of interest in matters Arkansan, Crittenden, who had commanded a volunteer company during the Seminole War and was admitted to the Kentucky bar at the age of twenty-one, dominated territorial politics for much of the decade that followed, employing his intelligence and political skills to establish Arkansas' first political machine. Unlike Miller, Crittenden was not opposed to bending or even breaking the rules to reward supporters and enhance his own political power. Among Crittenden's political allies were James Woodson Bates; Henry W. Conway, a member of a prominent family from Greene County, Tennessee; and Conway's uncle, William Rector, the surveyor general of Illinois, Missouri, and Arkansas. Other members of Conway's extended family included James Sevier Conway, who would later serve as the first governor of the state of Arkansas, and Ambrose Hundley Sevier, who would serve as Arkansas' territorial delegate and one of its first U.S. senators.[17]

Crittenden's fall from political power came almost as rapidly as his ascent. When the Monroe administration passed over Crittenden and appointed George Izard territorial governor following Miller's resignation, Crittenden arranged to be away from Little Rock when the new governor arrived. Izard, a member of a politically prominent South Carolina family who had served as a major general during the War of 1812, disapproved of Crittenden's poor administrative skills and political activities but had little taste for Arkansas politics himself. Nevertheless, Izard did report on Crittenden's activities to his superiors in Washington, and he began to lobby for the political support of other politically prominent Arkansans, including Henry Conway, Ambrose Sevier, and Chester Ashley. Crittenden's reputation never fully recovered from the scandal surrounding Conway's death. He was passed over once again for the position of territorial governor following Izard's death in 1828 and was replaced as territorial secretary the following year. Following his return to private life, Crittenden maintained influence in the legislature but became implicated in a widely reported land scandal involving fraudulent Spanish land grants known as the Bowie Claims. After receiving just 34 percent of the vote in a failed comeback bid for Sevier's territorial delegate position in 1833,

Crittenden, now identified with the Whig Party, spent the remainder of his life lobbying his brother in the U.S. Senate for political and financial assistance. Crittenden died of an apparent heart attack the following year in Vicksburg, Mississippi, at the age of thirty-seven.[18]

Following Conway's death, his politically savvy cousin, Ambrose Sevier, whose great-uncle John Sevier had been a popular Indian fighter and Tennessee governor, would emerge as one of the leading figures of the Dynasty. Admitting to Secretary of State Henry Clay his "unconquerable hatred for Mr. Crittenden," Sevier helped to engineer the political downfall of his cousin's murderer through his close ties with the Jackson administration and its supporters in Congress. As Jackson's man in Arkansas, Sevier enjoyed considerable influence and prestige in parceling out federal patronage, and steering lucrative positions to relatives and other political supporters. Over the course of his career in territorial politics, Sevier won five delegate elections, the last unopposed, establishing an impressive record of achievements in Washington, including the donation law that provided 320 acres to landowners displaced by the Cherokee Treaty of 1828. By the mid-1830s, Sevier's cousin, James Sevier Conway, was using his federal surveyor position as a launching pad for a state gubernatorial bid. Another cousin, Whorton Rector, was a federal Indian agent, his brother William was a federal marshal, and his father-in-law was a federal judge, leading Sevier to wonder to the president if "the people of Arkansas will consider that there is too much monopoly in the offices by my relatives and intimate friends" and whether this might "injure the cause in Arkansas."[19]

John Pope of Kentucky, selected by the Jackson administration to succeed the late George Izard as territorial governor in 1828, was a brother-in-law of President John Quincy Adams who had nevertheless supported Andrew Jackson in the election of 1828, in part due to his loathing of Henry Clay. Described as a genial and relaxed politician, Pope nevertheless tangled incessantly with Crittenden supporters in the Territorial Legislature and was criticized for publicly stating that his role in Arkansas was akin to that of an overseer on a plantation. Following his veto of the legislature's bill to trade ten sections of federal land in return for Crittenden's Little Rock home to use as the state capitol, Pope became the subject of persistent criticism on the part of the pro-Crittenden newspaper, the *Arkansas Advocate*. Although he actively cultivated the support of the Dynasty through patronage, Pope's leadership style provoked dissension even among members of his own party. Territorial Secretary William Fulton publicly criticized Pope for overspending on the new state capitol without legislative approval, while *Arkansas Gazette* editor William Woodruff—whom Pope referred to as a "little toad of an editor"—was angered that the governor had steered a state publishing contract to a rival printer, apparently in retaliation for the *Gazette's* failure to sufficiently defend the Pope administration against criticism levied by the *Arkansas Advocate*. By the time the Jackson administration replaced Pope with Fulton in 1835, the outgoing governor had blamed his political enemies for his difficulties, lamenting that "[t]his appetite for spoil and plunder is the main spring of the machinery that is working against me."[20]

THE DEBATE OVER STATEHOOD

By the early 1830s, those competing for political power and influence in the Arkansas Territory grew more and more interested in the prospect of statehood. Robert Crittenden and his followers, increasingly concerned over the growing dominance of the Dynasty over territorial affairs, saw a chance for a shift in the balance of political power through the opportunities for new state and federal elective offices, political patronage, and access to land that would follow statehood. Those in Ambrose Sevier's Dynasty, however, had prospered through their close relationship with the Jackson administration and saw little advantage in changing the status quo. Many were concerned that, given the territory's small population, minimal economic output, and meager revenues, Arkansas was simply unprepared for the responsibilities of statehood. Furthermore, the national implications of allowing another slave state to join the Union threatened to upset the fragile equilibrium established through the Missouri Compromise of 1820.

The 1830 federal census revealed a total non-Indian population in Arkansas of just over 30,000, still short of the 40,000 Congress now required for consideration for statehood; in its next session, Congress would increase the requirement to 50,000. Nevertheless, in the years that followed, interest in statehood grew, encouraged in part by two of the state's major newspapers, William Woodruff's pro-Dynasty *Arkansas Gazette* and the pro-Crittenden *Arkansas Advocate*, now under the editorial control of Charles Bertrand. Bertrand wrote in March 1830 that statehood would terminate Arkansas' "Territorial vassalage" and was "the only means of sundering our shackles and giving us the rights and rank to which we are entitled." Furthermore, reports that Washington was considering relocating the Chickasaw Indians west raised new fears among white settlers in western Arkansas. The political divisions over the statehood issue were apparent. Given the Dynasty's dominance over territorial politics and close ties to the Jackson administration, Crittenden and his allies likely felt that his best hope of returning to high office would only come through statehood. Sevier and the Dynasty, on the other hand, much preferred the territorial status quo.[21]

This political issue first emerged in the U.S. delegate election of 1831, in which Ambrose Sevier defended his seat against Benjamin Desha, the candidate of the Crittenden faction. Although Desha favored statehood once Arkansas' population was sufficient and Congress had requested the drafting of a state constitution, Sevier was more ambivalent, fearing that Arkansas did not as yet have the financial means to support a state government. According to one estimate, statehood would entail $15,000 for a constitutional convention, $10,000 to redeem territorial currency, and $26,000 for public buildings, while $20,000 in federal salaries for public officeholders would become a state responsibility as well. Noting that the state had not yet achieved the population necessary for statehood, Sevier believed that "we are pursuing our true interest by remaining as we are" and that he was "disposed to oppose" statehood until Arkansas had the population and financial resources "to support a State Government." Nevertheless, Sevier promised not to move on the statehood issue without consulting his constituents, and although he easily won reelection, the issue does not seem to have played a major role for most voters in the campaign. Nor did it when Sevier won reelection again, this time over Crittenden himself, in 1833.[22]

However, despite his misgivings and personal pledge not to pursue statehood without consulting his voters, on December 17, 1833, Sevier requested that the U.S. House Committee on Territories pass a resolution inviting Arkansas to begin work on a proposed state constitution and to seek admission as a state. Facing criticism from Arkansas' major newspapers for abandoning his pledge, Sevier explained his change of heart in a letter published in the *Arkansas Gazette* in January 1834, noting that Michigan would soon be a candidate for statehood itself. Given that since the Missouri Compromise, new slave and free states had been paired together in joining the Union so as to preserve the balance in the Senate, Sevier explained that he feared Michigan might enter in tandem with Florida, forcing Arkansas to wait as long as twenty-five years until Wisconsin was ready for admission. Sevier also expressed concern that growing anti-slavery sentiment in Congress might lead eventually to a repeal of the Missouri Compromise, which would threaten the interests of Arkansas' slaveholders. With Jacksonian Democrats in control of the White House and the U.S. House of Representatives, Sevier may have also believed that the interests of both Arkansas and the Dynasty might be best served by taking advantage of the current favorable political environment before a new administration entered office. Finally, Sevier and the Dynasty were actively promoting the presidential and vice-presidential prospects of Richard M. Johnson of Kentucky, the brother of Benjamin Johnson, territorial judge and Sevier's father-in-law, and may have hoped that Arkansas' electoral votes would provide the margin of Johnson's victory. Before Congress had acted, and concerned that Michigan might be admitted on its own, leaving Arkansas to the mercies of the free-state interests, Sevier urged Arkansans to follow Michigan's lead and elect delegates to a constitutional convention without formal congressional authorization.[23]

As Arkansas considered statehood, the slavery issue that had lain dormant in Congress since 1820 reemerged, with potentially catastrophic ramifications for the future state. Although the debate over the issue consumed both Congress and territorial Arkansas, the fact that Michigan was simultaneously applying for admission as a free state bolstered Arkansas' case. Together, the admission of both states would leave the balance of power between slave and free states in the Senate unchanged.

TERRITORIAL POLITICS

Politics in territorial Arkansas were largely personal and parochial, with few issues of ideology or national concern dividing the pro-Jackson Dynasty and Crittenden's Whig supporters. Most political conflict, fueled through newspapers such as William Woodruff's pro-Dynasty *Arkansas Gazette* and Albert Pike's pro-Crittenden *Arkansas Advocate*, centered on issues of character, ability, and ethics of members of the competing political factions. Southern concepts of honor were paramount, and political figures often reacted to perceived slights and insults with violence, invective, and challenges to duel. Several prominent political figures, including Henry Conway and William F. Pope, the governor's nephew, had their lives cut short as a result of political violence. When Crittenden supporters William Cummins and Absalom Fowler refused challenges to duel from Robert W. Johnson after a failed attempt to impeach Johnson's father, a territorial judge and Sevier's uncle, Johnson attacked Cummins in the street with a walking cane and published handbills accusing Fowler of being a coward. The younger Johnson would later serve as a U.S. senator from Arkansas. Prior to his death in a duel with Superior Court Judge Andrew Scott, fellow jurist John Selden wrote his wife that he would gladly face death rather than a "life in disgrace" following "a host of injuries & insults heaped upon me."[24]

The prevalence of dueling and matters of personal honor may perhaps be attributed to the generally young age of several of the prominent political figures in territorial Arkansas. As a newly developing territory, ambitious and well-connected young men from more established states to the east flocked to Arkansas with the intention of acquiring power, influence, and wealth. Although the territory's first governors—Miller, Izard, and Pope—were older and more seasoned, other political figures were younger and more aggressive in their pursuit of power and concern for matters of personal honor. In 1827, Crittenden was thirty, Conway was thirty-four, Oden was twenty-nine, Woodruff was thirty-two, and Sevier was just twenty-six. The youth and violence common among the governing classes in Arkansas reflected the demographics of the territory as a whole. In 1840, 47 percent of the white male citizens of Arkansas were in their twenties.[25]

What political issues there were in Arkansas in the 1820s and 1830s often revolved around landownership and speculation as well, primarily over how to acquire and distribute federal lands in the territory. The decision to move the capital from Arkansas Post to Little Rock in 1819 was driven in part by the fact that Crittenden, Conway, and House Speaker Joseph Hardin, among others, had all acquired speculative property holdings in the new community through questionable deals involving federal land claims. These claims had been designed to compensate property owners who had suffered damages associated with the devastating New Madrid earthquakes of 1811–1812. Although Miller also owned property in Little Rock, he favored placement of the capital in nearby Cadron, where the governor was building a home. Even more egregious was the political infighting and corruption surrounding the Bowie Claims, in which several prominent political figures, including Crittenden, Ashley, and John J. Bowie, the brother of Texas legend Jim Bowie, forged Spanish land grant documents in an attempt to acquire 50,000 acres of federal lands in Arkansas beginning in 1827. Finally, when Congress pledged ten sections of federal land to finance the construction of a new state capitol building in Little Rock, the *Arkansas Advocate* and pro-Crittenden forces in the legislature rallied to trade the 6,400 acres in return for Crittenden's home, a potential windfall for the former territorial secretary that was forestalled only by Governor Pope's veto. Territorial politicians also delighted in immortalizing themselves through the creation of eponymous counties, including Miller County in 1820; Izard, Crittenden, Conway, and Sevier counties in 1825; and Pope County in 1829.[26]

Other opportunities for land speculation were afforded by federal and territorial efforts to dispossess local Indians of their holdings in the 1810s and 1820s. Arkansas' original Indian inhabitants were forced to forfeit much of their land prior to Arkansas' establishment as a territory. Under the terms of an 1808 treaty, the Osage gave up their hunting rights in most of northwestern Arkansas and would give up what remained of their territory and relocate to Oklahoma in 1825. This removal made possible federal relocations of Cherokee and Choctaw tribes to western Arkansas in the 1800s and 1810s. Sporadic violence among the Cherokee, Choctaw, and Osage would continue through the early 1820s, leading to the establishment of a federal garrison at Fort Smith in 1817 to keep the peace. The Quapaw, in contrast, were forced to forfeit ownership of more than 30 million acres of land in southeastern Arkansas through an 1818 treaty, making available to white settlement some of the most fertile agricultural land in the region. Although the Quapaw ostensibly retained ownership of 2 million acres of Arkansas land under that treaty, further cessions resulted in their complete removal to Oklahoma as well by the early 1830s.[27]

Maintaining that the continued presence of the Quapaw, Cherokee, and Choctaw in the territory inhibited white settlement, the legislature later petitioned the Adams administration to have all Indians in Arkansas moved to the west, away from white settlements. In 1825, the territorial government petitioned Congress to donate 320 acres apiece to three thousand settlers "driven into the forest, without food, and almost without raiment," supposedly dispossessed of their lands in southwest Arkansas as a result of the Choctaw Treaty of 1825. As a result of the Cherokee Treaty of 1828, Arkansas acquired Cherokee lands east of a line extending from Fort Smith to the southwest corner of Missouri, while losing a large portion of Lovely County in the northwest section of Arkansas to what would become Indian territory in present-day Oklahoma. To compensate the three hundred families who would lose their territory to the Cherokee, Congress allowed each family to claim 320 acres of federal land elsewhere in Arkansas. The *Arkansas Gazette* reported that between four hundred and six hundred such claims would be filed, testament to the rampant abuse inspired by the prospect of free land in the territory. In 1829, 1831, and 1833, the legislature went even further, petitioning Washington to grant 160 acres to any white who would settle within twenty-four miles of the Cherokee or Choctaw territories. Arkansas' territorial government also lobbied Washington for reductions in federal land prices, land grants to finance public buildings and institutions, preemption privileges, the appointment of a federal surveyor general, and the authority for settlers to use federal lands and to purchase one's improvements.[28]

Transportation issues were also major concerns in territorial Arkansas. It was widely believed that improved transportation networks would facilitate new settlement and economic development. Toward that end, the territorial government lobbied Washington beginning in 1823 for construction and improvement of the Military Road connecting Little Rock and Memphis, as well as other roads to connect the territory's major population centers. Sevier's success as Arkansas' territorial delegate between 1829 and 1835 was based in large part on his prowess in petitioning Congress for improvements to water transportation, including federal funds to clear obstructions on the Arkansas, White, Ouachita, St. Francis, and Red rivers. Efforts to acquire federal funds to build levees and to construct a canal between Bayou Bartholomew and the Mississippi River, however, proved less successful.[29]

Issues of federal patronage also drove territorial politics. Robert Henry, a Kentucky attorney hopeful of being appointed to a federal judgeship in Arkansas, wrote his brother in 1819 that, if successful, he would thereby "have it greatly in my power to serve my friends" and that "we could do almost as we pleased...and thus acquire standing & consequence in the Country." During Miller's prolonged absences from the state, territorial secretary Robert Crittenden filled many territorial positions with friends and family members in building his own political machine, as did the Dynasty that eventually eclipsed him. In attempting to ingratiate himself with the Dynasty, Governor Pope himself wrote that "I have given all the offices and jobs to the friends of Col. Sevier ever since we have been identified in the party struggles of the country."[30]

As Arkansas' population grew and its economy developed, issues of political sectionalism began to emerge. King Cotton, slavery, and plantation agriculture in the southern and eastern portions of the territory, known as the Delta, fostered the development of a planter class akin to those of the lowlands of Kentucky, North Carolina, and Virginia, and the Deep South states of Mississippi, Alabama, and Georgia. The sparsely populated highlands of the northern and western regions, unsuited to large-scale slavery and plantation agriculture, encouraged the development of yeoman agriculture and emigration from Upper South regions of Kentucky, Tennessee, and North Carolina. By the early 1830s, the white population in northwestern Arkansas was larger than the white population in the Delta, and slaves outnumbered whites in several southeastern counties. Increasing tensions between these two regions would manifest themselves during legislative proceedings over a constitutional convention, with lowland politicians demanding "additional representation equal to three-fifths of their slave population," while upland interests demanded representation by districts without regard to population. As Albert Pike noted in his *Arkansas Advocate*, "It is plain from the contests in the last legislature, that the South of Arkansas has been placed in decided opposition to the North. There are two great divisions in this Territory—and there will be two in the future state. One of these, the South, is in a minority as to numbers." Sectional differences between northwestern and southeastern interests would continue through statehood and remain to the present day.[31]

DEVELOPMENT OF THE STATE CONSTITUTION

At the time Arkansas' first constitution was drafted, two distinct constitutional traditions competed for influence in the United States. The Whig tradition, based on the experiences of the seventeenth-century anti-monarchical English Whig movement, assumed the existence of a relatively homogeneous polity acting for the common good and emphasized legislative dominance and direct popular control of government. Whigs tended to view the executive with distrust and as a potential source of tyranny, and most state constitutions of the revolutionary period severely restricted executive power through legislative selection, brief terms, and limited veto authority. All other political offices, including the judiciary, Whigs felt, should be subject to frequent elections, thereby guaranteeing as much direct popular control of government as possible.[32]

The Federalist tradition, however, owing its intellectual foundations to James Madison, Alexander Hamilton, and other Founding Fathers, is most clearly reflected in the U.S. Constitution of 1787. Recognizing the great size and diversity of the nation, Madison posited a much larger and more heterogeneous polity than did the Whig tradition. Tyranny, Madison believed, was more likely to result from the influence on public policy of an irrational and uninformed public than from the executive branch. To prevent such a "tyranny of the majority," individual and group interests should be balanced so that "ambition [might] be made to counteract ambition," thereby ensuring that no single faction might seize control of government. Elite dominance, the protection of private property rights, and limitations on the electorate's direct influence on government would be ensured through large electoral districts, limitations on the franchise, indirect senatorial elections, long tenures of office, staggered terms, and an electoral college for the selection of the president. Both the Whig and Federalist constitutional philosophies were present in the crafting of Arkansas' first constitution.[33]

An 1835 census showed that Arkansas' population had increased to over 52,000, enough to finally qualify for statehood. Large majorities voted in favor of statehood in a nonbinding referendum that August. Two months later, the Territorial Assembly appointed a joint committee, chaired by Absalom Fowler of Pulaski County, to consider the issue. Although thirteen of the territory's sixteen counties participating in the referendum had supported statehood, not everyone was enamored of the idea. Delegate James F. Walker of Hempstead County, the author of the statehood legislative committee's minority report, was concerned that Arkansas was already too deeply in debt to take on the responsibilities of statehood and that the legislature would be forced to raise taxes to provide services currently provided by Washington. Walker also feared that the removal of federal troops would embolden hostile Indians and that the federal road construction appropriations would be lost as well. Most important, Walker believed that the "constitution in hand" strategy—developing a state constitution and submitting it to Washington without express enabling legislation from Congress—might be illegal or unconstitutional. Fulton also opposed the "constitution in hand" approach, fearing that acting without expressed congressional assent or the approval of his patron, President Jackson, bordered on revolution.[34]

Nevertheless, a majority of the members of the committee favored the movement toward statehood. They believed that the territory's burgeoning population and wealth warranted that status, and they attempted to counter the arguments against statehood put forth by Walker and Fulton. Voting representation in Congress, statehood advocates maintained, would lead to greater, not fewer, defense expenditures in Arkansas, while interstate road building was a national defense issue and would, therefore, still be fully funded by Congress. Furthermore, the increased settlement and the attendant sales of public lands that would accompany statehood would more than make up for any lost federal funding through increased revenues into the state's coffers. Most significant, the committee's majority felt that statehood would confer new legitimacy and respectability on the state, helping to counter the reputation Arkansas had acquired nationally as a lawless and backward hinterland.[35]

The Territorial Legislature overwhelmingly approved the committee's majority report by a vote of 29-2. Without prior approval from Congress, they passed legislation on November 16, 1835, calling for the election of forty-two delegates the following month to a constitutional convention to be convened in Little Rock in January 1836. Governor Fulton opposed the bill, but he allowed it to become law without his signature. However, debate over how to allocate delegates to the convention presaged the emergence of a growing geographic and cultural division within the state, a division that would persist through the nineteenth and twentieth centuries. Interests from the more mountainous northern and western regions of the territory favored allocating one delegate for every five hundred free white males, with each county guaranteed at least one delegate. Southern and eastern interests, however, with less than half of the territory's total population but more than two-thirds of its slaves, favored counting slaves as three-fifths of a white person for allocation purposes. Without including slaves, they argued, Arkansas' population would fall short of Congress's statehood threshold. After three weeks of debate, a compromise measure authored by House member David Walker, a Whig from Washington County, called for the election of fifty-two delegates, twenty-seven from northern and western Arkansas and twenty-five from the southern and eastern regions of the state. Once again, Fulton allowed the bill to become law without his signature, although he requested an opinion on the convention's legality from U.S. Attorney General Benjamin Butler. Butler responded favorably, noting that while Arkansas had no right to form a state government without Congress's consent, the territory was within its rights to petition Congress for statehood by presenting it with a proposed constitution.[36]

The constitutional convention convened in Little Rock on January 4, 1836. John Wilson of Clark County was elected president in a compromise between delegates from the mountain and plantation counties. Nevertheless, Clark's committee appointments ensured that pro-slavery delegates were in charge of most major issues. On the following day, all but one of the delegates—James F. Walker, the lone dissenter on the Territorial Legislature's Statehood Committee—voted in favor of a resolution to draft a state constitution to be submitted to Congress in a petition for statehood. Eleven standing committees and various other specialized committees were appointed to draft different sections of the constitution, and reports from the executive, judicial, and declaration of rights committees were returned in less than a week. Over the three and a half weeks that followed, the convention crafted a fairly brief 9,000-word state constitution closely reflecting the federalist values of the U.S. Constitution, somewhat surprising given the growing support for Jacksonian direct democracy then sweeping the nation.[37]

A Declaration of Rights consisting of twenty-four sections clearly reflected the social compact theory of the U.S. Constitution. It established that the political authority of the state was based on popular sovereignty and included protections for freedom of speech, religion, and petition, due process guarantees, and the right to keep and bear arms for white men. The declaration's debt to John Locke and Thomas Jefferson was evident in its assertion that the people retain "an unqualified right to alter, reform, or abolish their government, in such manner as they may think proper," while the limited government philosophies of the *Federalist Papers* and the Bill of Rights were reflected in its concluding statement that "everything in this article is excepted out of the general powers of the government and shall forever remain inviolate."[38]

The most controversial and contentious topic addressed at the constitutional convention concerned legislative apportionment. Once again, northern and western interests favored apportionment based solely on the number of free white males, while delegates from southern and eastern Arkansas held out for some sort of district representation based on total population without regard to race. The Legislative Committee's report to the convention favored planter interests. It called for a Senate with no fewer than nineteen and no more than thirty-three members, with nineteen senators elected from seven districts at least until 1840. Such an allocation would favor southern and eastern interests by a margin of nine to eight, with two Senate seats accorded to Pulaski, the most populous county and one with strong political and cultural ties to southern and eastern Arkansas. The House would include no fewer than fifty and no more than one hundred members, with twenty-five seats in the north and west, twenty-one in the south and east, and four in central Arkansas. Each county was guaranteed at least one House seat. Apportionment would be determined based on the number of free white males in a district, and redistricting would be necessary every four years after 1840 to maintain equal district sizes. Nevertheless, a minority report from the Legislative Committee more favorable to northern and western interests took issue with the plan, insisting on nine northern and western Senate seats, seven for the south and west, and one for central Arkansas, with no guarantee that each county have one representative.[39]

With no consensus in favor of either plan, Absalom Fowler of Pulaski County successfully moved to have the matter referred once again to a Select Committee, with Fowler as chairman, to craft a compromise. On January 25, the Select Committee presented to the full convention a plan for a bicameral General Assembly to be elected through universal white male suffrage. The Senate would have no fewer than seventeen and no more than thirty-three members, each representing 1,500 free white males. The House would have between fifty-four and one hundred members, each representing five hundred free white males and with at least one House member per county. Eight of the seventeen senators would be from southern and eastern regions, eight from the north and west, and one from central Arkansas. Following an 1838 enumeration, Senate districts would be periodically redrawn to ensure equal numbers of free white males. In the House, twenty-four representatives would be allocated to the south and east while twenty-six would represent the north and west, with four representatives from the central portion of the state. Every four years beginning in 1838, House districts would be redrawn based on the free white male population, with each county guaranteed at least one seat. While northern and western interests had been successful in ensuring that the legislature would be apportioned based on the free white male population and that legislative districts would be periodically adjusted, southern and eastern interests could rest assured that their counties would be guaranteed at least one House seat per county, regardless of the size of that county's white population. The full convention approved the select committee report by a margin of 28-22.[40]

With the most divisive issue settled, the remaining elements of the constitution quickly fell into place. Poll taxes were prohibited except to raise funds for counties. There were no property requirements to vote or hold office, but legislators and executive officials were required to acknowledge a belief in "the being of a God" to be eligible to serve in government or to testify in court.

Legislative terms were set at two years for House members and four years for senators. The legislature would be empowered to pass legislation, override gubernatorial vetoes with a majority vote, impeach the governor, and propose constitutional amendments through a two-thirds vote in two successive legislative sessions. The General Assembly would also have the authority to elect a secretary of state, treasurer, auditor, supreme court justices, circuit court judges, the attorney general, and the state's two U.S. senators. A judicial article vested judicial authority in a state supreme court, circuit courts, chancery courts, and justices of the peace, with circuit judges and supreme court justices selected by the General Assembly for four-year and eight-year terms, respectively. No legislative or other salaries were established.[41]

The proposed constitution established a fairly powerful executive with a long term as well. The governor would be popularly elected to a four-year term but constitutionally prohibited from serving more than eight years out of any twelve. He was to be commander in chief of the state's militia, could recommend measures to the legislature, fill executive and judicial vacancies, grant pardons, and veto bills, and he was responsible for seeing that the laws were faithfully executed. Although the governor's veto power and length of tenure aroused considerable debate, attempts to limit the term of the office to two years and to require vetoes to be overridden by a three-fifths rather than a simple majority failed. The governor would be subject to impeachment by the legislature and would have no authority to appoint judicial officials except to fill vacancies arising during periods in which the legislature was not in session. Although the auditor and treasurer had been appointed by the territorial governor, these positions were removed from gubernatorial control under the new constitution, establishing the Jacksonian plural executive as a check on executive power that would become common throughout the South and many other states. Interestingly, the governor, whose salary would be set by the legislature, was also constitutionally required to reside in the state's capital city, perhaps reflecting continuing disgruntlement concerning Miller's frequent absences from the seat of government and refusal to establish residence in Little Rock.[42]

Finally, an omnibus article within the constitution addressed a wide array of topics. The General Assembly was charged with promoting the intellectual, scientific, and agricultural development of the state. Rules on taxation were established, and the legislature was granted the authority to charter two state banks. A number of provisions addressed the issue of slavery as well. The legislature was authorized to prevent the introduction of slaves into the state who had committed crimes elsewhere, and fair and humane treatment as well as due process rights for slaves accused or convicted of crimes was guaranteed. The right of the legislature to regulate slave traders was recognized, as was the right of immigrants to bring their slaves into the state. However, another provision prohibiting the General Assembly from emancipating slaves without the consent of their owners would later provoke considerable debate in the U.S. Congress and would nearly scuttle Arkansas' progress toward statehood.[43]

On January 30, 1836, the Constitutional Convention completed work on the proposed constitution. Of the fifty-two delegates in attendance, all but two, Nathan Ross of Mississippi County and David Walker of Washington County, signed the finished document. Having completed their proposed constitution in less than a month, the convention selected Charles F. Nowland of Independence County to convey the document to Washington for presentation to Congress. Nowland left Little Rock on February 5, but he took a circuitous route to avoid bad weather and did not arrive in Washington until March 8, whereupon the constitution was presented to Jackson's secretary of state, John Forsyth. No popular referendum was envisioned. The constitution would take effect immediately upon congressional granting of statehood. Meanwhile, five thousand copies of the constitution were printed and distributed throughout the state, while William Woodruff's *Arkansas Gazette* published a special edition including the complete text of the document on February 4. A copy of the *Arkansas Gazette* imprint of the constitution would arrive in Washington on March 1, a week before Nowland's arrival with the official document, ensuring that both opponents and supporters of Arkansas' bid for statehood would have ample time to prepare for the bitter legislative battle to follow.[44]

FEDERAL APPROVAL OF STATEHOOD

Arkansas' bid for statehood arrived in Washington amid some of the most contentious political infighting in the nation's history. Whigs and anti-Jackson Democrats were understandably hesitant about allowing two new pro-Jackson states, Michigan and Arkansas, to bring their electoral votes into the Union just over a year before the next presidential election, in which Jackson's handpicked successor, Martin Van Buren, would be a candidate. Northern interests were opposed to the admission of yet another slave state and concerned that the anti-emancipation provision in Arkansas' proposed constitution seemed to preclude the possibility of ever abolishing that peculiar institution. Others were concerned that both Arkansas and Michigan had drafted constitutions and presented petitions for statehood without any formal invitation from Congress itself, seemingly violating precedent and constitutional protocol. Finally, a boundary dispute between Michigan and Ohio threatened to hold up Arkansas' progress toward statehood as well.[45]

To navigate these legislative and political minefields, pro-statehood forces chose to tie Arkansas' and Michigan's statehood prospects together in one legislative package. According to Senator Thomas Hart Benton of Missouri, "the fate of one is the fate of the other." The loyalties of pro-Jackson Democrats would be called upon for support, while the precedent of the Missouri Compromise would be invoked to counter those who opposed the admission of an Arkansas with guarantees for slaveholders. The Arkansas and Michigan constitutions were submitted concurrently in both the House and the Senate, but while the House Committee on Territories reported a bill to admit Arkansas, it was bottled up in the Committee of the Whole and never made it to the floor. In the Senate, however, to demonstrate a united front in support of both Arkansas' and Michigan's statehood bids, it was decided that Pennsylvania senator James Buchanan would sponsor the Arkansas bill, while the pro-slavery Benton would handle the Michigan bill.[46]

On March 14, Buchanan moved that a Select Senate Committee be convened to consider the Arkansas constitution. The five-member committee selected included Benton as a member and Buchanan as its chair. Just eight days later, on March 22, the committee reported out a favorable recommendation that Arkansas be admitted as a state, followed by a Benton motion that the Arkansas and Michigan bills be considered by the full Senate under a special order of business. The motion carried by a vote of 21-18, and it was agreed that the bills would be considered on March 29.

Senate opposition to Arkansas' statehood came primarily from Vermont senator Benjamin Swift, who was concerned that under the constitutional provision that the "General Assembly should have no power to pass laws for the emancipation of slaves without consent of the owners," slavery would essentially be perpetual and immune from future legislative restrictions. Others, including Vermont senator Samuel Prentiss and Louisiana senator Alexander Porter, were also irked that Michigan and Arkansas had disregarded constitutional niceties by drafting their constitutions without prior congressional consent. Once floor debate began, however, Senate opposition centered primarily on Michigan's admission, a subject of contentious debate for five days with several motions to table the measure and adjourn. Finally, the Senate narrowly voted to admit Michigan by a vote of 24-17 on April 2, after which opposition to Arkansas' statehood lost momentum.[47]

Following the Michigan vote, Buchanan immediately brought up the Arkansas bill and explained the importance of submitting it to the House concurrently with the Michigan bill. With the support of such Senate stalwarts as John C. Calhoun of South Carolina, Thomas Ewing of Ohio, and Benton of Missouri, Buchanan addressed those concerned about slavery in Arkansas. He maintained that the Missouri Compromise had clearly settled the geographical extent of slavery in the Louisiana Purchase territories and that the constitutional protections guaranteed slaves in Arkansas were more liberal than those of any other southern state. Benton countered the objections of those opposed to the methods by which Arkansas and Michigan had submitted themselves for statehood, noting that the citizens of those territories were simply making use of their First Amendment rights to petition Congress. On April 4, after just two days of debate, the Senate overwhelmingly approved Arkansas' bid for statehood by a margin of 31-6.[48]

The Senate's Arkansas and Michigan statehood bills were read in the House on April 27, where they were to face considerable opposition from the fiercely anti-slavery former president, John Quincy Adams of Massachusetts, as well as William Slade of Vermont, both of whom objected to Arkansas' admission to the Union on slavery grounds. Arkansas' House delegate, Ambrose Sevier, failed to have the House consider the Michigan and Arkansas bills as a special order of business on May 3, but on June 6 a special order to consider the bills on June 8 passed by a margin of 138-57. The size of the majority vote presaged a favorable outcome for the two territories.[49]

Although the Michigan statehood bill had precedence on the House calendar, given that it had passed the Senate first, when debate began on June 8, Representative Henry A. Wise of Virginia moved that consideration of the Michigan bill be postponed until June 13 to allow the Arkansas bill to be considered first. Wise, who was handling the Arkansas bill in the House, was apparently concerned that should the Michigan bill pass first, anti-slavery forces might then reject Arkansas' bid. By postponing the Michigan vote, that territory's statehood prospects were essentially being held hostage to those of Arkansas', a tactic that would arouse considerable resentment among anti-slavery representatives and force Wise to modify his motion to allow for both bills to be considered simultaneously. Nevertheless, when debate began on June 9, the Michigan bill was taken up first.[50]

In considering the Michigan and Arkansas bills, the House met as a Committee of the Whole, in which the entire House acts as a committee in considering special legislation. Any decisions must then be reported to the floor of the House for action by the House itself. Those opposed to the Michigan and Arkansas statehood measures attempted to stymie the legislation through frequent quorum calls, the failure of which would force the House to adjourn. Statehood supporters, however, were committed to keeping the House in session long enough to consider all proposed amendments and until the Committee of the Whole had successfully reported both bills in their entirety to the full House for consideration. Through such tactics, Whig opponents to the statehood bills time and again forced the Committee of the Whole to dissolve for lack of a quorum, forcing the House back into regular session. Attempts to adjourn the House itself, however, were always turned back as the Jacksonian Democrats successfully gathered enough members to maintain a quorum, whose members would then vote to return to the Committee of the Whole to consider the legislation at hand. Finally, by midnight on June 9, the Committee of the Whole passed the Michigan bill and took up the matter of Arkansas statehood.[51]

On the morning of June 10, Arkansas faced the greatest threat to its statehood hopes. Representative Adams proposed an amendment providing that approval of Arkansas' constitution would in no way signify congressional assent to the provision prohibiting emancipation of slaves without owner consent. Although Adams denied that his amendment was designed to thwart Arkansas' admission or to halt the spread of slavery, other supporters were less equivocal about their motives. "It is the duty of the members of the House at least to say: we wash our hands of the unclean thing," Massachusetts Representative Caleb Cushing noted. Nevertheless, Adams's proposed amendment provoked a firestorm of opposition from northern and southern legislators alike, who maintained that the amendment violated the Missouri Compromise and would force the legislation back to the Senate for concurrence. Such an outcome would likely doom Arkansas' statehood chances, given that the Senate planned to adjourn by July 4. Southern and Jacksonian interests ultimately prevailed, however, as the Adams amendment was defeated by a margin of 32-98. A subsequent amendment, proposed by Representative Slade of Vermont, to force Arkansas to convene a new constitutional convention to remove the offending anti-emancipation provision and to guarantee that nonwhites entering Arkansas following statehood would not be subject to slavery, was also rejected. After twenty-five hours of continuous debate, the Arkansas and Michigan bills were favorably reported from the Committee of the Whole and placed on the House calendar for June 10.[52]

When the full House convened once again on June 13 to consider the two statehood bills, still under the special order proposed by Sevier one week earlier, opposition to the admission of Arkansas and Michigan to the Union was largely pro forma. The Michigan bill was considered first and passed easily by a vote of 153-45. When the Arkansas bill was brought up, Representative Adams attempted one last time to add to the Arkansas bill the same emancipation amendment that had been defeated in the Committee of the Whole, but his measure failed for a second time and the vote was called. The Arkansas bill passed by a margin of 143-50, prompting Representative Henry Connor of North Carolina to note that the "House had been delivered of twins."[53]

In a supplementary act passed that same month, Congress laid out the conditions under which Arkansas would be admitted to the Union. One section in every township would be dedicated to public schools. Twelve salt springs and adjoining lands would be granted to the state and 5 percent of proceeds from the sale of public lands would be dedicated to road building and canal construction. Five sections of land would be awarded to the state for the construction of public buildings in Little Rock, and two townships would be dedicated to financing the establishment of institutions of higher learning. Arkansas' request that the federal government transfer ownership of the hot springs and surrounding lands, in what is today Hot Springs, was rejected.[54]

Two days after its House passage, President Andrew Jackson signed the Arkansas statehood bill into law on June 15, 1836, Arkansas' official birthday. Although Arkansas and Michigan were to enter the Union simultaneously, Michigan's lingering border dispute with Ohio would hold up Michigan's formal admission until September. On July 4, 1836, a twenty-fifth star was added to the American flag to represent the new state of Arkansas. State elections were held in Arkansas for the first time the following month to choose the members of the first state legislature and the state's first governor, James S. Conway of the Dynasty, who would be inaugurated on September 13. The state legislature also selected two U.S. senators, Ambrose Sevier and William Savin Fulton, who had been on opposite sides of the statehood debate over the previous year.[55]

SUMMARY

Arkansas' transition from territory to statehood took place during one of the most tumultuous periods in American history. The paternalistic and elite politics of the Federalists were gradually replaced by the expansion of white male suffrage, the development of mass-based political parties, and the increasingly egalitarian political values of the Jacksonian era. As the opportunities afforded by the Louisiana Purchase beckoned ambitious and well-connected men and women westward, Arkansas' Native American and French populations soon found themselves overwhelmed and often displaced by these new arrivals. The establishment of the Arkansas Territory in 1819 initiated a scramble for political power and patronage that led to the development of Arkansas' first political divisions and more than a decade of conflict between the pro-Jackson Dynasty and Robert Crittenden's Whig faction.

Territorial politics in Arkansas were typically violent, driven by loyalties to patrons and family ties, and more than occasionally corrupt and self-serving. Rivals such as Crittenden and the Sevier-Conway-Johnson-Rector Dynasty struggled with one another over control of political patronage, opportunities to acquire federal and Native American lands, and avenues of personal political advancement. As statehood beckoned and the Crittenden political machine collapsed in the early 1830s, new political divisions began to emerge based on divergent agricultural, economic, and cultural development in the northwestern and southeastern portions of Arkansas. Finally, Arkansas' movement toward and petition for statehood in 1835 and 1836 illustrated the extent to which these new regional divisions had come to dominate territorial politics, while the debate in Congress over Arkansas' admission to the Union provided further evidence that the nation remained deeply divided over the issue of slavery, despite the Missouri Compromise of 1820.

NOTES

1. S. Charles Bolton et al., *Arkansas Becomes a State* (Little Rock: Center for Arkansas Studies, 1985), p. 7.

2. Ibid., p. 9; S. Charles Bolton, *Arkansas, 1800–1860: Remote and Restless* (Fayetteville, AR: The University of Arkansas Press, 1998), p. 24.

3. Bolton, *Arkansas, 1800–1860*, pp. 10–12, 25.

4. Bolton et al., *Arkansas Becomes a State*, pp. 9–11; Bolton, *Arkansas, 1800–1860*, p. 25; Jeannie M. Whayne et al., *Arkansas: A Narrative History* (Fayetteville: University of Arkansas Press, 2002), pp. 93–94.

5. Bolton et al., *Arkansas Becomes a State*, p. 15; Jerry E. Hinshaw, *Call the Roll: The First One Hundred Fifty Years of the Arkansas Legislature* (Little Rock: Department of Arkansas Heritage, 1986), p. 3; Whayne et al., *Arkansas: A Narrative History*, p. 95.

6. Cal Ledbetter Jr., "The Office of Governor in Arkansas History," *Arkansas Historical Quarterly* 37 (1978): 48–50.

7. Bolton, *Arkansas, 1800–1860*, pp. 26–28; Hinshaw, *Call the Roll*, p. 6; S. Charles Bolton, *Territorial Ambition: Land and Society in Arkansas, 1800–1840* (Fayetteville: University of Arkansas Press, 1993), p. 105. The *Arkansas Gazette* was the oldest newspaper west of the Mississippi River when it ceased publication in 1991.

8. Bolton et al., *Arkansas Becomes a State*, pp. 15–18; Bolton, *Territorial Ambition*, pp. 105–110; Hinshaw, *Call the Roll*, p. 7; Whayne et al., *Arkansas: A Narrative History*, pp. 95–96.

9. Hinshaw, *Call the Roll*, pp. 8–9.

10. Bolton, *Arkansas, 1800–1860*, pp. 28–29; Bolton, *Territorial Ambition*, pp. 105–106; Lonnie J. White, "The Arkansas Territorial Election of 1823," *Arkansas Historical Quarterly* 18 (1959): 325–326.

11. Bolton, *Arkansas, 1800–1860*, pp. 30–31; Bolton, *Territorial Ambition*, p. 106; Lonnie J. White, "The Election of 1827 and the Conway-Crittenden Duel," *Arkansas Historical Quarterly* 19 (1960): 295–301.

12. Bolton et al., *Arkansas Becomes a State*, p. 18. Miller plays a minor role in "The Custom House," the prologue to Nathaniel Hawthorne's 1850 novel, *The Scarlet Letter*.

13. Bolton et al., *Arkansas Becomes a State*, p. 18.

14. Bolton, *Arkansas, 1800–1860*, pp. 3–24.

15. Ibid., p. 27.

16. Ibid., pp. 27–28.

17. Ibid., p. 29; Bolton, *Territorial Ambition*, p. 110. A third Conway brother, Elias, would be elected governor in 1852.

18. Bolton, *Arkansas, 1800–1860*, pp. 31, 40; Bolton, *Territorial Ambition*, p. 107; Lonnie J. White, "A Letter from Robert Crittenden to John J. Crittenden," *Arkansas Historical Quarterly* 21 (1962): 17–25.

19. Bolton, *Arkansas, 1800–1860*, pp. 30–32; Bolton, *Territorial Ambition*, pp. 104–107; Marie Cash, "Arkansas Achieves Statehood," *Arkansas Historical Quarterly* 2 (1943): 293.

20. Bolton, *Arkansas, 1800–1860*, p. 32; Lonnie J. White, "The Fall of Governor John Pope," *Arkansas Historical Quarterly* 23 (1964): 83–84.

21. Bolton, *Territorial Ambition*, pp. 117–118.

22. Hinshaw, *Call the Roll*, pp. 14–16; Bolton, *Arkansas, 1800–1860*, pp. 44–45; Cash, "Arkansas Achieves Statehood," pp. 293–294.

23. Bolton et al., *Arkansas Becomes a State*, pp. 39–40; Bolton, *Arkansas, 1800–1860*, p. 45; Cash, "Arkansas Achieves Statehood," pp. 294–295; Bill J. Scroggs, "Arkansas Statehood: A Study in State and National Political Schism," *Arkansas Historical Quarterly* 20 (1961): 234.

24. Bolton, *Territorial Ambition*, pp. 108–109; White, "Arkansas Territorial Politics, 1824–1827," p. 17.

25. Bolton, *Territorial Ambition*, pp. 108–109; Bolton, *Arkansas, 1800–1860*, p. 35; Scroggs, "Arkansas Statehood," p. 230.

26. Bolton, *Arkansas, 1800–1860*, pp. 35–40; Whayne et al., *Arkansas: A Narrative History*, pp. 96–97; Marie Cash, "Arkansas in Territorial Days," *Arkansas Historical Quarterly* 1 (1942): 231–233.

27. Whayne et al., *Arkansas: A Narrative History*, pp. 98–101; Jack Lane, "Federal-Quapaw Relations, 1800–1833," *Arkansas Historical Quarterly* 19 (1960): 64–65.

28. Bolton, *Arkansas, 1800–1860*, pp. 40–42; Bolton, *Territorial Ambition*, p. 114; Whayne et al., *Arkansas: A Narrative History*, pp. 97–98.

29. Bolton, *Arkansas, 1800–1860*, pp. 42–43.

30. Ibid., pp. 28–32.

31. Ibid., p. 46; Scroggs, "Arkansas Statehood," pp. 231–232, 240.

32. Cal Ledbetter Jr., "The Constitution of 1836: A New Perspective," *Arkansas Historical Quarterly* 39 (1982): 216–217. The anti-Jackson movement of the 1830s that coalesced into the Whig Party chose the name in part as a protest against what adherents saw as Jackson's increasingly tyrannical policies, as exemplified in the Bank War of 1832 and the Nullification Crisis of 1832–1833.

33. Ibid., p. 217. Quotes are from Madison's *Federalist 51*.

34. Bolton et al., *Arkansas Becomes a State*, pp. 43–45; Whayne et al., *Arkansas: A Narrative History*, pp. 105–106; Cash, "Arkansas Achieves Statehood," pp. 297–298.

35. Bolton et al., *Arkansas Becomes a State*, pp. 45–46.

36. Hinshaw, *Call the Roll*, pp. 16–17; Cash, "Arkansas Achieves Statehood," p. 299; Scroggs, "Arkansas Statehood," pp. 238–239; Ledbetter, "Constitution of 1836," pp. 226–229.

37. Bolton et al., *Arkansas Becomes a State*, pp. 46–47; Ledbetter, "Office of Governor," pp. 51–52; Ledbetter, "Constitution of 1836," pp. 230–231.

38. Ledbetter, "Constitution of 1836," p. 231.

39. Ibid., pp. 235–237.

40. Ibid., pp. 235–239.

41. Bolton et al., *Arkansas Becomes a State*, pp. 47–48; Hinshaw, *Call the Roll*, p. 17; Whayne et al., *Arkansas: A Narrative History*, p. 107; Ledbetter, "Constitution of 1836," pp. 231–232.

42. Bolton et al., *Arkansas Becomes a State*, p. 47; Ledbetter, "Office of Governor," pp. 51–53; Ledbetter, "Constitution of 1836," pp. 235–239.

43. Bolton et al., *Arkansas Becomes a State*, p. 48; Ledbetter, "Constitution of 1836," p. 233.

44. Bolton et al., *Arkansas Becomes a State*, pp. 50–51; Hinshaw, *Call the Roll*, p. 17; Cash, "Arkansas Achieves Statehood," p. 304. Once adopted, the 1836 constitution would serve with only minimal amendments until Arkansas seceded from the Union in 1861. Nevertheless, Arkansas' 1861 and 1864 constitutions made only minor modifications to the 1836 original.

45. Bolton et al., *Arkansas Becomes a State*, p. 51.

46. Ibid., pp. 51–53; Scroggs, "Arkansas Statehood," pp. 242–243.

47. Bolton et al., *Arkansas Becomes a State*, p. 53.

48. Ibid., p. 53; Ledbetter, "Constitution of 1836," p. 243.

49. Bolton et al., *Arkansas Becomes a State*, p. 54; Scroggs, "Arkansas Statehood," p. 243.

50. Bolton et al., *Arkansas Becomes a State*, p. 54.

51. Ibid., pp. 54–55.

52. Ibid., p. 55.
53. Ibid., p. 57.
54. Ibid., p. 58.
55. Ibid., pp. 57–58.

BIBLIOGRAPHY

Bolton, S. Charles. *Territorial Ambition: Land and Society in Arkansas, 1800–1840* . Fayetteville: University of Arkansas Press, 1993.

———. *Arkansas, 1800–1860: Remote and Restless* . Fayetteville: University of Arkansas Press, 1998.

———, Cal Ledbetter Jr., and Gerald T. Hanson. *Arkansas Becomes a State*. Little Rock: Center for Arkansas Studies, 1985.

Cash, Marie. "Arkansas in Territorial Days." *Arkansas Historical Quarterly* 1 (1942): 223–234.

———. "Arkansas Achieves Statehood." *Arkansas Historical Quarterly* 2 (1943): 292–308.

Hinshaw, Jerry E. *Call the Roll: The First One Hundred Fifty Years of the Arkansas Legislature*. Little Rock: Department of Arkansas Heritage, 1986.

Lane, Jack. "Federal-Quapaw Relations, 1800–1833." *Arkansas Historical Quarterly* 19 (1960): 61–74.

Ledbetter, Cal, Jr. "The Office of Governor in Arkansas History." *Arkansas Historical Quarterly* 27 (1978): 44–73.

———. "The Constitution of 1836: A New Perspective." *Arkansas Historical Quarterly* 41 (1982): 215–252.

Scroggs, Jack B. "Arkansas Statehood: A Study in State and National Political Schism." *Arkansas Historical Quarterly* 20 (1961): 227–244.

Whayne, Jeannie M., Thomas A. DeBlack, George Sabo III, and Morris S. Arnold. *Arkansas: A Narrative History*. Fayetteville: University of Arkansas Press, 2002.

White, Lonnie J. "The Arkansas Territorial Election of 1823." *Arkansas Historical Quarterly* 28 (1959): 325–337.

———. "The Election of 1827 and the Conway-Crittenden Duel." *Arkansas Historical Quarterly* 19 (1960): 203–313.

———. "Arkansas Territorial Politics, 1824–1827." *Arkansas Historical Quarterly* 20 (1961): 17–38.

———, ed. "A Letter from Robert Crittenden to John J. Crittenden." *Arkansas Historical Quarterly* 21 (1962): 16–25.

———. "The Fall of Governor John Pope." *Arkansas Historical Quarterly* 23 (1964): 74–84.

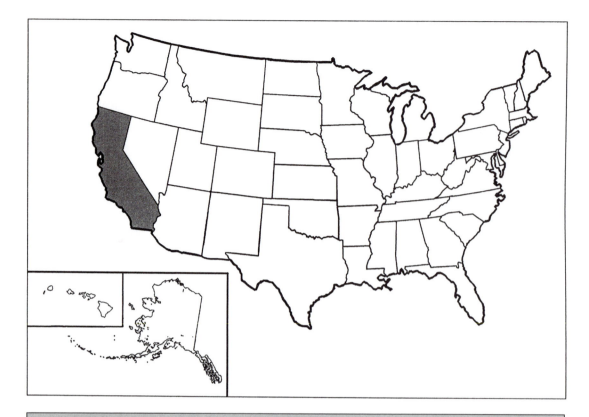

California

Territorial Development:

- California rebels loyal to the United States proclaimed the California Republic on June 14, 1846; the flag of the republic was lowered and the American flag raised in the same year, when the United States declared war on Mexico
- Mexico ceded land containing the future state of California to the United States with the Treaty of Guadalupe Hidalgo, February 2, 1848
- California was admitted into the Union as the thirty-first state, September 9, 1850

State Capitals:

- San Jose, 1850–1851
- Vallejo, 1851–1853
- Benicia, 1853–1854
- Sacramento, 1854–present

Origin of State Name: In *Las Sergas de Esplandián*, written by Garcia Ordóñez de Montalvo in the sixteenth century, California is an island filled with gold.

First Governor: James S. Conway
Governmental Organization: Bicameral
Population at Statehood: 92,597
Geographical Size: 155,959 square miles

In California's case, the larger international and domestic conflicts that accelerated and affected the admission of California were omitted from the state's official representation. The Mexican-American War, slavery, the complicated history of federal and state relations with the various Native American tribes, and contrary legal precedents on the path to statehood are not represented on the seal. Nor is the debate on who might properly claim citizenship represented there. Yet each of these factors in California's admission and the terms of its constitution speak profoundly to the fierce and significant debates of the era. It had been unclear what legal precedent would be used to admit California to the Union. Would California be required to follow the immediately preceding state, Wisconsin, and be forced to wait until Congress authorized the Wisconsin convention, in accord with the legal precedent established by the Northwest Ordinance of 1787? Or might California claim that the pattern set by the four states that had preceded Wisconsin to statehood and had not waited for Congress to act invalidated the Northwest Ordinance's dictates?

Although California's admission occurred within a breathtakingly short amount of time compared to many other states, both the informal and formal entry of the state into the Union was surrounded by fierce contests over the expansion of slavery. In 1846, the United States launched a war on Mexico, rooted in the desire of a number of Mexican citizens of American descent to expand slavery into the region against the wishes of the Mexican government. That war opened a window for a number of ambitious men in California to claim the territory as their own. When the war ended in California in January 1847 and the peace treaty with Mexico, the Treaty of Guadalupe Hidalgo, was signed in 1848, California joined Texas and the future Arizona and New Mexico as American spoils.[2] On May 31, Colonel Richard B. Mason was made governor and commander in chief of U.S. forces in California.[3]

If California's constitution made a pronouncement on slavery that contravened the general understanding in Congress that territory to the south of the 36°30' parallel could be slave states, there still was a fundamental question to be answered. Could California's renegade constitution be thrown out by Congress as illegitimate and the state forced to undergo the process of waiting for congressional approval before calling another constitutional convention, as many southern congressmen hoped? The Treaty of Guadalupe Hidalgo provided that the state would be admitted as soon as it had the requisite population, but prior practice suggested that the state's bid for admission could be derailed if the population counted for admission was racially suspect and thus unworthy of citizenship. Both at the state and federal level, there were clear debates over the import of the character of the state's population. In California those conflicts took the form of debates over who was entitled to citizenship. In Congress, the debate was transformed into a battle over whether the votes of Mexicans and foreigners counted in making the state eligible for drafting a constitution, submitting it to Congress, and admission, or whether their very presence and participation in the constitution's drafting, approval, and submission made it illegitimate. Who would constitute the body politic in California was a crucial question, a question that would influence the larger question of whether slavery would be permitted to expand or be condemned to a slow death through a denial of new soil for the land-intensive cotton that was its mainstay.[4] How that question was resolved in 1850 not only united California to the United States, but it also, temporarily, contributed to a uniting of the states, via Congress's compromise bill of 1850.

THE DEVELOPMENT OF CALIFORNIA:
THE FAST TRACK FROM MEXICAN TERRITORY
TO AMERICAN STATE

The Spanish long ignored the territory that would become the state of California, establishing their first mission only in 1697, followed by their second in 1700. A prolonged stretch of history transpired before the threat of Russian settlement motivated Jose de Galvez in 1768 to launch an expedition aimed at securing the California coast, which would result in the sending of padres and presidio soldiers. Soon thereafter, Joaquin de Serra and other Franciscans joined with soldiers to found missions in the territory, aimed at the conversion of Native Americans to Christianity. Spain's grip was shaken loose in 1821 when Mexico declared independence. Free of Spain's grasp, Mexico began secularizing the missions and, like Texas, invited settlers from the United States to become citizens. A number of notable Californians, including Abel Stearns, a Yankee trader who arrived in California in 1829 and became a Mexican citizen, responded, adapting themselves to Mexican culture and accumulating land grants as the spouses of prominent Spanish families' daughters. On the whole, the state was marginally developed, with little significant commercial activity other than the hide and tallow trade that Richard Henry Dana, a Harvard student who authored *Two Years Before the Mast*, one of the most widely read accounts of the future state's potential, witnessed on his visit.[5]

California, a Mexican territory dotted with presidios and missions, had inherited a system of governance that placed high emphasis on producing converts rather than developing the engines of capitalism. The hide and tallow trade and extensive ranchos granted to important individuals rather than a system of private property dominated. Americans eyeing the territory saw more. They saw an opening to the Pacific trade that had lured the original colonists to what became America, land that could be developed in private hands even before gold was discovered.[6] Interest in commerce and whaling in the Pacific had led the American government to offer money for California in 1837. Failing a financial transaction, talk of war to win the territory began long before war actually took place. In a peculiarly embarrassing 1842 incident, Commodore Thomas Catesby Jones demanded the surrender of Monterey's port and district only to discover his mistake, namely, that there was no war, a day later.[7]

Nonetheless, California invited the attention of Americans who were intent on joining it to the Union, and when war finally broke out with Mexico, they staged the Bear Flag Revolt under the leadership of the American explorer John C. Frémont and William B. Ide. Frémont was the son-in-law of Missouri Senator Thomas Hart Benton, whose encouragement he enjoyed. Frémont was an advocate of America's manifest destiny to spread its empire to the edge of the continent and beyond and was a popular figure at the time of his military expedition. His wife, Jessie Hart Benton, had authored a number of gripping and popular accounts of his earlier western expeditions. The Savannah-born progeny of a French father and a Virginia mother, Frémont was raised in Charleston, South Carolina, dropped out of college because of an illicit love affair, and after a stint as a schoolteacher, began a career of expeditions and military surveys eventually as a member of the Corps of Topographical Engineers.[8] Frémont would rally other Americans to defeat the Mexican government at its capital in Monterey and then set out to capture northern California's main defender, Mexican military leader Mariano Guadalupe Vallejo in Sonoma, the most significant Californian outside of California's then governor, Pio Pico. Among his companions on the trip to arrest Vallejo were Robert Semple and Thomas Larkin, who would later play pivotal roles in calling for a state constitutional convention and serve in the body that drafted the state constitution. Vallejo was arrested, a Bear Flag was erected in Sonoma to signify the victory, and in July 1846, Commodore Sloat declared California a free territory of the United States.[9] A provisional government was established.

California never endured a territorial phase, as would have been expected had California followed the confusing path of its immediate predecessor, Wisconsin, admitted in 1848, and the legal precedent established by the Northwest Ordinance of 1787. Although the established precedent had been for states to petition for admission only after Congress authorized a constitutional convention, in practice, all of the four states preceding Wisconsin's admission had violated that precedent and Wisconsin's observance of procedure was ironically a clear anomaly.[10] Congress adjourned after the Treaty of Guadalupe Hidalgo was signed, providing for the state's entry when it reached the normal population of 60,000, and efforts to pass a bill providing for a territorial government failed. On July 19, 1848, a bill to provide California, Oregon, and New Mexico with territorial governments with the courts deciding the slavery question was introduced and passed the Senate on July 26, but the House tabled it and Congress adjourned. An Oregon bill excluding slavery passed both houses, but California was left without a civil government.[11] Gold was discovered, and in December 1848, Congress resumed discussion of California's admission after receiving a presidential message conveying the likelihood that the state would soon apply for admission.[12]

Before the issue of territorial government could be resumed the next year, pressures in California had led to a successful constitutional convention and a request for admission as a state. On August 3, 1849, the provisional governor instructed a number of individuals to meet to draft a constitution, and they began their work at Colton Hall in Monterey, the capital of Spanish and then Mexican California. They began meeting on September 1. And within the next year, California had been formally admitted to the United States as a free state in the contentious Compromise of 1850, the last example of Congress's ability to keep the nation from fragmenting under the impact of the slave question.

THE POLITICS OF STATEHOOD

A number of factors pressed Californians to make their bid for statehood early. Most important were the immediate problems of regulating an economy run amok due to the discovery of gold and controlling the ethnic conflict and lawlessness that discovery inspired. More visionary actors, however, were also convinced that early action was the best way to help secure the state federal benefits that would build the infrastructure necessary to guarantee the state a preeminent place in the Pacific empire. The state's geographical location at the intersection of Latin America and Asia promised it. Representing these influences, the delegates to the California Constitutional Convention convened at Colton Hall in Monterey on September 1, 1849, to fashion a constitution that placed the state within the larger American political tradition and answered the immediate needs of the state.

Gold, Ethnic Conflict, and Lawlessness

The discovery of gold in January 1848 quickly swelled the population of California. The ensuing lawlessness precipitated by squatters promoted a search for order, and as argonauts from all over the world—Peru, China, Chile, France, Germany, and Africa—joined American immigrants, often bachelors, the desire for statehood intensified. Peter H. Burnett, an Oregonian, advocate of swift statehood, and later the first governor of California, recounted that an estimated two-thirds of Oregon's population emptied out into California in the summer and fall of 1848. Booming communities emerged in the "tented city" of San Francisco, which included Little Chile, Little China, and discernible French and German settlements. But these new settlements were not without their problems. The Hounds in San Francisco, a group composed of native-born Americans, many from a disbanded New York regiment, employed vigilantism to chase the foreigners from California (hence, their name, as in "to hound out"). "Race antipathy and rioting" against the Hispanic community marred the early years of the future state's life.[13] Walter Colton, the *alcalde* or chief judge and administrator at Monterey and the man whose name graced the building in which the constitutional convention was held, noted that Americans were as bad as the native population in California in upholding order: "Many of them appear to have left their good principles on the other side of the Cape Horn, or over the Rocky Mountains. They slide into gambling, drinking, and cheating, as easily as a frog into its native pond."[14]

Homicide and political instability were common features of gold rush life. In 1848, Pio Pico returned to reclaim the governorship, and "fears and rumors of revolt continued."[15]

Unrest in San Francisco and a general fear of political instability made it certain that efforts to achieve order would reach their boiling point when Congress failed to act. In December 1848, San Francisco and San Jose hosted meetings that recommended that delegates be elected for a March 5, 1849, convention establishing a provisional government, but the time for the meeting came and went. Then, on March 22, 1849, the *Alta*, the San Francisco newspaper, published a public communication signed by a number of delegates, including future constitutional convention representatives W. M. Steuart, Myron Norton, and Francis J. Lippitt, calling for a convention on the first Monday of August 1849 in Monterey, should no territorial government have been provided by then. Soon thereafter, on June 2, 1849, an *Alta* editorial declared the lack of a territorial government "A Legal Outrage," labeling it taxation without representation. On June 3, acting governor Bennett Riley issued the command for a state constitutional convention.

Unaware of Riley's action, a number of prominent men held a June 12 meeting in San Francisco that called for a convention. Headed by future governor Peter H. Burnett, the meeting was addressed by Thomas Butler King of Georgia and future convention member and first state senator William Gwin. The meeting participants resolved that Congress's failure to provide a government gave them "the undoubted right to organize a government for their own protection," and they elected delegates for a constitutional convention to present the case to Congress. The sense of urgency only increased with the July 14 attack on San Francisco's Chileans by the Hounds.[16]

The desire to develop the state's trade potential and the lack of opportunities for creating and protecting private property without provisions for state revenue further provided clear reasons for California's inhabitants to seek statehood. Statehood would allow the government to collect revenues, facilitate trade by erecting lighthouses along the Pacific Coast, regulate Indian affairs, evaluate land claims, and survey land. Indeed, regulating Indian affairs not only involved the protection of American settlers and maintaining the peace by preventing raids on Mexico, but it also involved negotiating treaties with Indians claiming title to the land. Bringing land into the public domain would ensure the extension of American democracy by giving American "citizens an opportunity of procuring a permanent right of property in the soil,"[17] and these citizens or potential citizens would themselves reduce the cost of defending the territory of California, the newest state. Such settlers, owing their property to the American government, would form "a home population—to defend her. Settlers are the natural and cheap defence [sic] of new countries; but settlers, to defend a country, must have a stake in it—an interest in the soil."[18]

Political Parties and the Delegates to the Constitutional Convention

Intriguingly, state political parties were not very prominent in the move for statehood. Despite the fact that the Democrats held a convention once the constitution was ready, there was no meeting of the opposing party. Robert Semple, a dentist by trade but also the printer of one of California's first newspapers, the *Monterey Californian*, would be among those most prominent in calling for statehood.[19] Although the Democrats met early on to call for statehood, the actual process was bipartisan, perhaps reflecting the fact that the bid for statehood emerged so early in the history of California.[20]

The delegates to the California Constitutional Convention had to accomplish two important objectives. First, they had to establish the basic framework within which California would be incorporated into the larger American body politic. Second, they had to guarantee that business as usual would continue. This meant assuring that the system of laws and general agreements made under the periods of Spanish (1769–1821) and Mexican rule (1821–1848) would not unravel into disorder even as they established obstacles to Anglo-American pursuits until a more suitable system for the Americans could be found.

In framing the state's relationship to the nation, the constitutional convention's delegates willfully pulled from the tried-and-true documents of the past, both national and state. The fact that they did was unremarkable, as many had had experience in other states and many state constitutions copied each other.[21] But as they framed the constitution, they brought to bear on California's constitution concerns forged in the debates over the proper scope of state and federal power, both past and present. These concerns spanned the spectrum from how wide the circle of "we, the people" should be to the admission of slavery into the state. In addition, because California was one of the most populous Mexican states and because the war claiming California had been waged with the rhetoric of bringing democracy to the people, the very place of both Mexicans and Native Americans was a source of intense debate. This debate was reconciled in 1849 very idealistically in comparison to the actual operation of California laws soon thereafter.

Colton Hall greeted the representatives of California's ten districts: Los Angeles, San Francisco, Sacramento, the Pueblo de San Jose, Monterey, Sonoma, San Joaquin, San Diego, San Luis Obispo, and Santa Barbara. Three men represented the old order. General Mariano Vallejo was considered one of the most important Californios, whose arrest in Sonoma signaled the American takeover of the state. Pablo de la Guerra, who commanded both English and Spanish languages fluently, was the *alcalde* of Santa Barbara during the American invasion and an American prisoner in 1847. José Carillo was a laborer and a lifelong resident of California, elected to represent Los Angeles. Ten districts were to elect thirty-seven delegates. Instead forty-eight were elected, including sixteen from slave states, ten from free states, and eleven native Californians, with more from mining districts and San Francisco where the greatest population was concentrated. Eight were native Californians and four were foreign born. "Fourteen were lawyers, twelve farmers, seven merchants," and the rest "engineers, bankers, physicians, and printers." Among the Americans, Thomas Larkin, Stephen Foster, Abel Stearns, and Robert Baylor Semple had arrived before the takeover.[22]

The Californios themselves were an interesting lot. Most, but not all, had been favorably inclined toward American assumption of control over California, including Vallejo. The vast majority of the state's constitutional convention members would defend the rights of the poor to representation, but that by no means meant that they were representative of the common class. None echoed the claim that they were men of "elegant leisure" like member Benjamin F. Moore, but there were a considerable number of men of wealth, obtained honorably and otherwise. Thomas Larkin had left Massachusetts like Abel Stearns and became the owner of a general store in Monterey, the state's "capital and chief port," as well as the American consul there. Stearns arrived in California in 1829 with an interest in the South America and China trade, settled in Los Angeles where he married Arcadia, the daughter of Juan Bandini, and acquired a large land grant in the San Joaquin Valley. This vast grant did not stop Stearns from engaging in smuggling. John Sutter, a failure in business like Larkin, had deserted his family in Switzerland to avoid debtor's jail when his dry goods store failed. Two other constitutional convention members—the business partners, Benjamin S. Lippincott and John McDougal—shared the distinction of being San Francisco town lot owners and gamblers.[23] John Frémont, John Marsh, Thomas Larkin, and Lansford W. Hastings were constitutional convention members who had played prominent roles in encouraging Americans' interest in California. Hastings, born in Ohio and a lawyer by trade, authored *The Emigrant's Guide to Oregon and California* (1845), having entered California with one of the last parties to arrive in the state that year.[24]

THE CALIFORNIA CONSTITUTION

California's constitutional convention delegates had a difficult task before them. Ultimately, however, they created a document that established the general principles under which the new state would be able to regulate civic and military affairs. It protected the poor, integrated the state's ethnic and racial minorities according to the dominant racial theories of the era and treaty obligations, expanded the rights of women, and avoided the contentious problem of including a religiously diverse population by not extending its boundaries.

California's constitution can be seen at least on the surface as a combination of the tidy adoption of the principles undergirding American political thought as expressed in the U.S. Constitution, in the Declaration of Independence, and in various provisions for the establishment of county governments. The first article of the California constitution essentially copied the U.S. Constitution's Bill of Rights. In this article, California's constitution reaffirmed the national commitment to inalienable rights, including life, liberty, property, and the pursuit of happiness. It also rooted power "in the people" and provided for amendments. Freedoms of speech, press, and assembly were guaranteed. Basic justice was effected through guaranteed trial by jury in criminal and libel cases, a pledge to honor habeas corpus in times of peace, and prohibitions on unreasonable bail and detention, warrantless searches and seizures, cruel and unusual punishment, double jeopardy, self-incrimination, and the violation of due process and eminent domain.

Religious freedom was guaranteed, although the opening of the constitution allowed for qualifications on such freedom if it endangered public morals, peace, or safety.[25] Article 1, Section 4, guaranteed Californians freedom of religion "forever" and declared that "no person shall be rendered incompetent to be a witness on account of his opinion on matters of religious belief." Furthermore, the succeeding articles proceeded to lay out the state's government along the U.S. Constitution's principle of separation of powers and representative bodies including a senate and assembly.[26] Paralleling the executive power of the president, the state's governor possessed the power to veto the state legislature's bills, and like the president, the governor was subject to impeachment. The constitution also shared with America's founding documents a concern for the equal rule of law and the desire to avoid standing armies, which was embedded in the Declaration of Independence.

Business as usual was established by Article 12, Section 16, guaranteeing contracts already in force. Voter intimidation was proscribed by Article 2, Sections 2 through 5. Arrests were not permitted during elections unless for "treason, felony, or breach of peace," and no person was required to serve in the militia on election days unless in war or emergency. Ballots rather than voice voting were guaranteed under Article 2, Section 6, although legislative votes continued the practice of *viva voce* voting. The legislature was granted the right to establish substate governments immediately. The basic framework and rights of corporations were also created, and guidelines for banks were established. The governor was styled commander in chief, executor of the laws, appointer to vacancies, and pardoner. More completely than the federal constitution, the California constitution called for the appointment of a comptroller treasurer, attorney general, and surveyor general. Education was provided for in Article 9. And the state was exhorted via the legislature to "encourage by all suitable means, the promotion of intellectual, scientific, moral and agricultural improvement." Amendments were permitted under Article 10.

California sought, like other states of the era, to attract settlers, whether native or foreign born. Foreigners who "bec[a]me bona fide residents of the state" were guaranteed "the same rights in respect to the possession, enjoyment, and inheritance of property, as native born citizens." No exception to this rule was made for Asian immigrants, perhaps because the question of their citizenship, entangled with that of other minorities, was still off in the distant horizon. At the same time, the state ensured the consistent representation of those who settled in California by requiring a census in 1852 and 1855 and then decennially, in combination with the federal census for the legislature.

Protecting the Poor

The interplay of larger political developments, including the arrival of Jacksonian democracy, the fierce and increasingly uncontainable debate over the expansion of slavery, continuing strains over foreign relations, including those with Native Americans, and the desire to boost the state's population in competition with other states are all in evidence beneath the text of the constitution.

Conflicts over who would be entitled to the benefits and expected to bear the burdens of citizenship were stamped all over the constitution and were a core site of contention in the constitutional debate. Such conflicts arose from a variety of sources, including the fact that California was wrested from a competing power with its own notions of citizenship and that representatives of this old order were invited to participate in the framing of the constitution. By 1849, there was a consensus that the state should empower the people and that the patrician politics of representative democracy should be abandoned. This break was a historic one, symbolized by the ascendancy of Jacksonian democracy, but it confirmed the larger truth that in America, the forty-shilling freehold adopted from England to limit the electorate to the wealthy had failed to act as a bar on the admission of many to the status of citizens. Land in the New World had been easy to obtain. Article 1, Sections 14 and 15, represented the more populist elements of the American experiment, insisting that representation be accorded by population and that debtors' prisons, the poor man's bane, were illegal.

The Debate over Ethnic and Racial Inclusion

Settling who would be within the circle of "we, the people," however, was only one part of the delegates' perceived responsibilities. The delegates understood that the body politic would be constantly reconstituted over time, and they took measures to create a community that reflected their vision of a proper state and barred those they deemed unworthy as citizens. Conflicts over the admission and status of Chinese laborers, which would become synonymous with the state's history, were not then an issue. The convention was noticeably silent on this question. The Chinese were too small a community until 1851 to arouse enmity.[27] By contrast, however, a concern with defining the status of Mexican, Native, and African Americans in the body politic was abundantly clear.

California's attachment to being a free state did not mean that it accorded much value to equality among the races. Although Article 1, Section 18, dramatically pronounced that slavery and involuntary servitude would "[n]ever be tolerated" in California, the constitutional convention was punctuated with haggling over what the relative status of Mexicans, Indians, and African Americans would be in the new polity. Article 2 established clearly that racially based citizenship was to be imported into California in most matters. For white males over twenty-one years old, who were not "idiot[s]," "insane," or criminals, political participation was very easy to attain. The constitution specified that all "white male citizen[s] of the United States, and every white male citizen of Mexico" over twenty-one years of age and resident in the state for six months who so elected to be a citizen could participate in state elections. A mere thirty days' residence was required for participation in county and district elections. Those desirous of serving in the state senate or assembly needed to be citizens and inhabitants of the state one year, and of the county and district represented for six months. Gubernatorial candidates and candidates for lieutenant governor were required to be citizens and state residents for at least two years and over twenty-five years old.

Native American Inclusion

Settling Native Americans' place in the new polity was a little more difficult. Competing American and Spanish conceptions of the political capacity of Native Americans and the American experience made policy in this arena unclear. Both groups, however, had manifested a belief that Native Americans could assimilate, even if the United States had never adopted a consistent policy on Native American citizenship and would not do so until the Dawes Act of 1924 granted Native Americans citizenship. On the one hand, the American constitutional precedent treated Native Americans as outside of the pale of citizenship. Native Americans were consistently described in the federal constitution and in court decisions as "Indians not taxed," a descriptor that highlighted a refusal to accept their contributions to and ability to call upon the federal government. On the other hand, the Supreme Court had decided that Native Americans were domestic dependent nations rather than foreign nations, and were thus wards of the United States Government. Spanish attitudes further complicated the picture. While some Spaniards insisted that the Native Americans were *gente sin razón*, or people without reason, others believed that the Native Americans were capable of religious salvation and reason. Thus, the duty of the missionaries was to guide their wards to salvation and ultimately turn power over to them. That is not to say that distinctions did not exist. Indians were seen as excessive drinkers and pagans and were prohibited from gaining social status by provisions like exclusion from horseback riding. And the *gente de razón* were often ideal in theory rather than practice. The latter view of Indian salvation and assimilability dominated formal policy throughout the Spanish experiment. Ultimately, Article 2, Section 1, of the California constitution struck a compromise recognizing the ambiguous status of Native Americans since the adoption of the federal Constitution and set forth that the legislature could "by a two thirds concurrent vote" admit Indians and their descendants to suffrage in "special cases." It did so, however, only after various phrasings that reflected this confused state of affairs.[28]

On September 26, 1849, de la Guerra interjected with his own substitution for the suffrage clause. He agreed with the provisions for admitting white male citizens of Mexico and the United States, but he wanted inserted "Indians, Negroes, and descendants of Negroes excepted," with a proviso that "this section shall not be construed to prevent the legislature from admitting in as Indians to the election franchise, as they may in [the] future deem capable thereof." Soon thereafter, Delegate Halleck moved to introduce into the suffrage clause a statement to the effect that citizens would include "every citizen of Mexico (Indians not taxed as owners of real estate and negroes excepted)." Delegate Charles T. Botts, a Virginia-born attorney representing Monterey, elaborated on this property disqualification, emphasizing that Indians' real estate was not taxed. Botts withdrew the motion, and the provision for white male suffrage passed on October 1.

African Americans: Anti-slavery but Exclusionary

The state's position on the inclusion of African Americans was equally complex. Article 1, Section 18, did dramatically pronounce that slavery and involuntary servitude would "[n]ever be tolerated" in California, making California a free state. Intriguingly Southerners did not object to this, because it was believed in California that the southern part of the state was suited to cattle and viticulture, but not slavery, and that the South, recognizing this, would demand another state below the 36°30' line only as a stalling device because the creation of two states would lead to the admission of two free states.[29]

That, however, did not mean that Californians were calling for equality with African Americans. African Americans were specifically precluded from citizenship by the constitution with the reference to whiteness being a qualification for citizenship in the article on suffrage. Furthermore, the refusal to incorporate into the constitution what was in effect a statewide racial restrictive covenant bothered some delegates, who kept trying to frame a section that would clearly prohibit either African Americans or African Americans and their descendants from migrating to the state. Opposition to African American migration was rooted in the fear that slaves would be used in the mines, providing their owners an unfair advantage. As it turned out, when it became clear that slave owners could not maintain the "peculiar institution"—by which slavery was known—in California, they stopped importing Africans.[30] At one point, Section 39 contained the words "as will effectively prohibit free persons of color from immigrating to and settling in the state" and proposals to strike, enlarge, and keep this prohibition flew back and forth. In response to a request for striking the words, another delegate countered that the clause should stay with a provision for admitting those African Americans who had exercised the rights of citizenship in another state but should prevent slave owners from coming to California "for the purpose of setting" their slaves free.

Unable to resolve the issue, delegates met the next day to consider framing the section so as to prohibit free persons of color from emigrating to and settling in the state and prevent slave owners from coming to California to free their slaves. That attempt failed, and a new effort to extend the ban to former slaves including mulattos was similarly rejected. Delegates M. M. McCarver, a Kentucky native and farmer representing Sacramento, and O. M. Wozencroft, an Ohio-born physician representing San Joaquin, stood on the side of restriction. But two New Yorkers, Delegate Edward Gilbert, a printer representing San Francisco, and Delegate Kimball H. Dimmick, a lawyer representing San Jose, challenged the principle. Gilbert tried to argue that the treaty with Mexico required a continued recognition of Africans as citizens. Dimmick pointed out that the trend of the time seemed to favor freedom. Granting African Americans the right to settle and become citizens was nothing more than extending them the same privileges granted to the other races that came from foreign lands. In addition, Dimmick asserted that African Americans were in fact better citizens since they were "better acquainted with [American] habits and customs."[31] Nonetheless, the debate suggests the limits of equality considered by the convention and the general agreement of both Mexican and American delegates that the migration of African Americans was to be discouraged, even as they clashed on the question of admitting Native Americans to citizenship.

Mexican Americans: A Partial Involvement

Regardless of the privileging of Mexicans of Spanish blood, the claim that conquering California would bring democracy to its inhabitants, and the publication of the text of the constitution in both English and Spanish, the proceedings of the California Constitutional Convention represented, at best, limited Spanish influences. A clerk and interpreter were appointed to allow the Spanish-speaking members to participate at the request of General Vallejo, but when Delegate Carillo wanted to fire the clerk and interpreter for incompetence and insolence, they were absent and a Los Angeles representative had to interpret for him. No copies of the preliminary articles and sections were made available in writing before a decision on their incorporation was made. Vallejo tried several times to get consideration of adopting a code of laws rather than general principles. Less sanguinely, Spanish delegates tried to introduce considerations of the caste system with its elaborate hierarchy of color and corresponding privilege into the constitution and failed.

The Rights of Women

Although the constitution focused on the rights of males and imported the American model, in one significant respect it stood in the advance guard of developing notions of citizenship and acknowledged Mexican influence. Article 11, Section 14, pronounced that wives' real and personal property acquired prior to or after marriage would be "her separate property." This statement flew in the face of the established practice of *femme couvert*, imported from British common law, which held that upon marriage women lost their political identity in that of their husbands, although it said nothing about their right to testify on their own behalf after marriage or to sue in courts of law.[32] However, its revolutionary impact was probably dulled by the fact that, usually, property returned to the fathers or brothers of such women.

The Boundary Debate

Religious diversity in the form of a boundary dispute presented the last potential wrinkle in the delegates' efforts. A debate pursued over extending California's eastern boundary into what constituted Mormon territory. Delegates rejected this move, insisting that the territory encompassed by moving the state's boundary east, past the natural boundaries of the Sierra Nevada, would give the state much useless territory. It also violated the principle of representation, since the Mormons were not present at the convention or consulted prior to it. With this issue decided, the delegates provided California with the boundaries it would keep into the twenty-first century.[33]

Content with the constitution, Californians ratified it and sent it to Congress. Many of the state's constitutional convention members went on to serve as prominent members in the state's political institutions. Pablo de la Guerra became a member of the state senate. John McDougal, the town lot owner and gambler, became a California governor. William McKendree Gwin joined John Frémont as one of the state's first two U.S. senators. And Pacificus Ord served as district attorney for the United States in California.[34]

FEDERAL APPROVAL OF THE CONSTITUTION: THE DEBATE IN CONGRESS AND PRESIDENTIAL ACTION

Californians had to wait almost a year before their petition for admission was approved. Although the president forewarned Congress that the petition was arriving and he urged Congress to accept the new state, debate soon erupted. Was California's bid to become a state a violation of formal and informal legal precedents? Given the agreed upon senatorial rules of debate regarding slavery, would the admission of California even be legal? Did the character of the state's population and state constitutional convention delegates and electors disqualify California from admission? The boundary question was also revisited, with a twist. One southern congressman proclaimed that admitting a state so large would distort the balance of power in Congress. Ultimately, however, the prospect of losing gold revenue to England stirred Congress to accept the state's bid, leaving only the president to approve admission.

Formal and Informal Legal Precedents

California's constitution was adopted at the encouragement of the state's civil governor, General Bennett Riley on June 3, 1849. The electorate that chose the state's constitutional convention delegates included Mexicans, a group that offended some representatives, and recent residents, which is to say, many foreigners. At the convention, delegates chose to prohibit slavery from the state even though Southerners presumed that the Missouri Compromise guaranteed them the right to bring slaves into the territory below the 36°30' parallel. Opponents argued that the president and his cabinet had illegally tried to hasten the admission of California by violating precedent. The state had not passed through the territorial phase, and its constitution offered a declaration on slavery. The sending of northern-born Georgia congressman Thomas Butler King, who had traveled to the mining districts to encourage the constitution's adoption as a representative of the president's wishes, was viewed as a violation. Southerners also launched their own missive, declaring the effort to push through California statehood as taxation without representation, since they had also furnished troops for the Mexican-American War that brought California into the American fold and paid the funds required to support the war. Southerners insisted that since the territories had been "purchased by the common blood and treasury of the whole people" they were "the common property of the people," which they would enjoy "in spite of the North" and by "ARMED OCCUPATION" if necessary.

Despite the speed with which California's constitution was adopted, it would become embroiled in the larger debate over the fate of slavery in the United States. Although the president supported the state's admission and presented the issue to Congress in a message, Congress stalled. The very speed of admission presumed in the state seal cloaked serious reservations as to how the constitution had been adopted and with what motives in mind. These questions assumed great importance in both houses because the admission of the new state could potentially tip the balance toward the free-soil states and away from the balance of power engineered after the Missouri Compromise of 1820. This tension had its roots in the founding era of the American republic and its key sinews: the Constitution and the Northwest Ordinance of 1787.

The Constitution and the Northwest Ordinance

The U.S. Constitution's vacillation on slavery, a delicate compromise between the southern and northern interests of the 1780s to unite the thirteen colonies into a viable political unit, sowed the seeds of the later trouble that would plague the Union as the foreign threat represented by British, French, and Spanish interests receded. The French threat diminished when the Revolutionary War's costs encouraged the French to part with their North American territory in the Louisiana Purchase of 1803. The British threat ended with the War of 1812 and the nation's claims to the future state of Oregon in 1846. The Spanish received a pounding in Florida in the second decade of the nineteenth century and lost their grip on their Mexican colony in 1821.[35]

The U.S. Constitution recognized slavery in its concession to the South that for purposes of representation in the House, slaves would count as three-fifths of a person and that fugitive slaves, as property protected under the constitution, should be returned. It struck a blow against slavery, however, in its provision that the slave trade would be abolished after 1808. The Northwest Ordinance, which prohibited slavery in the new territories, further pointed in the direction of the abolition of slavery, and it set forth the basic rules under which states would be admitted, providing that states with 60,000 inhabitants would receive an enabling act from Congress to establish a state constitutional convention after working through a territorial phase. When Southerners agreed to the Constitution and the Northwest Ordinance, they made concessions they believed would protect the future prospects of slavery.[36]

The Missouri Compromise of 1820 and the Gag Rule

The invention of the cotton gin aided in expanding the territory in which the institution of slavery could thrive. Cotton, a soil-depleting crop, needed newer, more fertile land. That development, in turn, fueled abolitionism in the North and then began to threaten the balance of power in Congress. This had become a major issue by 1820, when Missouri applied for admission. After a fierce debate, it was agreed to admit Missouri as a slave state and balance it with Maine as a free state. Thereafter, it was agreed, slavery would be allowed to exist in those territories south of the 36°30' parallel, but prohibited north of it. The compromise survived into the 1830s, and gag legislation in Congress was used to effectively suppress the introduction of petitions from Northerners calling for the abolition of slavery. In addition, between 1830 and 1848, four of the five states admitted to statehood ignored the pattern laid down in the Northwest Ordinance, calling their own constitutional conventions and petitioning for admission without an enabling act from Congress.

The introduction of the gag rule overshadowed broader developments in the 1830s that would force the issue of slave versus free states to a head. That same decade witnessed the intensification of efforts by American citizens who had moved to the Mexican territory of Texas and abided by the Mexican government's rules to gain land and other privileges to overthrow the Mexican government. These Americans were upset at the Mexican government's opposition to slavery, which prevented them from bringing their property into the state. Within a decade, these interests had convinced the American government to wage war on the Mexican government under the pretext of defending its soldiers. The Mexican-American War, in turn, was used by enterprising individuals who had settled in California to stage the Bear Flag Revolt.

By 1848, when the war had concluded, the American government had disgorged from Mexico a vast swath of territory including Texas and the future states of Arizona, New Mexico, Utah, and California. That acquisition of territory reopened the debate over free-soil versus slave states with intensity and brought into the American fold new members whose citizenship was the subject of deep controversy. Moreover, the North had a 10-15 vote majority in the Senate, and it was presumed that the census would tip the scales in favor of the North in the House. Much of this growth was due to immigration. Similar but not completely sectionally based divisions marked the two major political parties of the era, the Whigs and the Democrats. Whigs opposed war and Democrats favored it. According to Whigs, acquiring California and New Mexico would extend American influence too far, bring in more "undesirable" populations, raise the slavery issue, and thereby potentially destroy the Union. Democrats argued that Mexico had provoked the war and that it was necessary to acquire New Mexico and California. Reflecting this tension between North and South and Whigs and Democrats, Northerners and Whigs had attempted to pass the Wilmot Proviso prohibiting new slave territory but failed to get the bill passed in the Senate, ironically because of a Massachusetts senator's filibuster.[37]

The Slavery Debate

Throughout the debate over California's admission, Southerners asserted that free-soil interests were at work promoting California's bid for statehood, while Northerners argued that Southerners were obstructing it. There was speculation that Representative Thomas Butler King, a Georgia Whig who had helped the state adopt the constitution barring slavery, was hoping that the boundary would come up for debate in Congress and allow for a solution that permitted slavery in the southern part of the state.[38] On the other hand, Representative Frederick Stanton of Tennessee, a southern Democrat, asserted that the events leading up to California's adoption of a constitution constituted nothing less than a "crime against the Constitution of the land—against the rights of one half of the sovereign States of this Confederacy, and against the integrity and the very existence of the Union itself." That refrain was heard later when Stanton insisted that the Wilmot Proviso established an inequality of "rights of the citizens of the several States of the Union" in violation of Article 4, Section 2, that "citizens of each State are entitled to all the privileges and immunities of citizens in the several states." Representative Henry Washington Hilliard, an Alabama Whig, insisted that admitting California would upset the balance of power in the nation and "transfer the sceptre of political power at once and forever into the hands of the enemies of our institutions.... Today we hold a balance in the Senate of the United States, but the entrance of another non-slaveholding State into the Union would turn that balance against us.... The time is come when the slaveholding States must throw up barriers against all future aggressions." Wisconsin Democratic representative James Duane Doty and Brown of Mississippi called for an investigation of the role of the former president and cabinet members in California's seemingly precocious demand for entry. Intriguingly, Senator Stephen Arnold Douglas, an Illinois Democrat, agreed, charging "that two Administrations...have by fraud, by military force, by improper coercion, destroyed the free exercise of the elective franchise, coerced a people to form a constitution for themselves."

Northerners discounted the possibility of slavery being transported to the territories, noting that a succession of Mexican laws barred the institution, including a treaty with Great Britain, Guerrero's decree of 1829, a confirmatory act of 1837, and the 1843 Mexican constitution. Missouri senator Thomas Hart Benton opposed lumping the issues together and argued that "the admission of a new State in to the Union is a mere question of constitutional authority. Congress has written authority for the admission of States, and in some cases the duty becomes obligatory upon Congress to admit a new State. That is the case in every instance in which the Government of the United States is under obligation or compact."

The sectional division was equally apparent among the triumvirate of congressional leaders most highly regarded during their day. Of the trio, the two Whigs, Senator Henry Clay from Kentucky and Senator Daniel Webster from

Massachusetts, stood in favor of the state's admission. Clay called for the separate consideration of the issue and noted that several states had previously been admitted without congressional authorization of their constitutional conventions. Unable to secure that, Clay issued the famous compromise bill allowing for California's admission with suitable boundaries and no interference on the new state's right to determine the fate of slavery. Demands for the abolition of the District of Columbia slave trade were rejected and the provisions for the return of fugitive slaves were tightened. Webster, sworn to oppose slavery since 1837, called for the admission of the new state of California, insisting that its existence as a free state was determined by the law of nature, by its mountainous ranges being unsuited to the expansion of the institution. The opposition of South Carolina Democratic senator John Caldwell Calhoun, a Yale graduate, engineer of Texas's annexation, and former secretary of state, was silenced by his death on April 1, 1850.

The situation was complicated by the desire to lump the question of California's admission together with that of every other slavery-tainted debate. An escalating mountain of petitions, at first predominantly from citizens of New York, and then from throughout the country, placed the slavery issue squarely with the admission issue. Connecticut, Delaware, Illinois, Indiana, Kentucky, Maine, Massachusetts, Michigan, New Hampshire, New Jersey, Ohio, Pennsylvania, Rhode Island, Vermont, and Wisconsin similarly sent petitions. These petitions typically sought four things: right to trial by jury for fugitive slaves; the prohibition of slavery and the slave trade from the nation's capital, or barring that, the removal of the seat of government from Washington, D.C.; the admission of no new slave states; and, sometimes, an expressed clause prohibiting slavery in the constitutions of any new states before they could be admitted to the Union. Few were as extreme as that introduced in the Senate on March 25, 1850, by Whig senator William Henry Seward of New York. He presented a document crafted by Albany electors and citizens asking that any bill passed relating to fugitive slaves contain the scriptural clause: "Thou shalt not deliver unto his master the servant which is escaped from his master unto thee. He shall dwell with thee, even among you, in that place which he shall choose in one of thy gates where it liketh him best; thou shalt not oppress him." A few, gradually increasing in number, directly called for the admission of California. That they were recorded at all, represented the tremendous difficulty both houses were having in enforcing the gag and parliamentary rules to dissipate sectional tensions. An angry Thomas Butler King argued in the Senate that these petitions represented a new and dangerous trend, "a great change" in which the few who opposed the rule had been replaced by more and that as a consequence "the Senate of the United States w[ould] no longer endeavor to put down this excitement."

While debating the admission of California, Congress engaged in a parallel debate over who should be entitled to federal incentives in the form of homestead land in Oregon. This debate revealed the depth of the conflict over who would be recognized as the appropriate settlers and citizens of the new territories.

The Character of California's Delegates and Voters

Southerners also attempted to block the state's admission by assailing the character of the constitutional convention's delegates, California's voters, and California's population as unworthy. Take, for example, the objections of Senator Jeremiah Clemens, a Democrat from Alabama, who lambasted the hasty application of California for statehood. Clemens proclaimed:

> [N]o territorial government was ever established in California. The people who framed its constitution were not *inhabitants*, in the legal meaning of the word. They were composed of Indians, Mexicans, and a wild band of adventurers from every quarter of the globe, allured, by a lust of gold, to the shores of the Pacific, many of them without a permanent residence anywhere, and four-fifths of them without the remotest intention of remaining in the country whose organic law they undertook to establish.

Similarly, Representative Albert G. Brown, Democrat of Mississippi, denounced the convention, noting that "the whole heterogeneous mass of Mexican, and foreign adventurers, and interlopers voted" and that foreigners served in the constitutional convention. Such participation, he believed, contravened Congress's prerogative as the only legitimate grantor of citizenship. Alabama Democratic representative S. W. Inge lambasted the permission of adventurers "from every quarter of the globe" to elect delegates who defined "boundaries enclosing an area out of which half a dozen states might be carved." Virginia Democratic representative James Alexander Seddon noted that California was populated by "the most heterogeneous composition—Mexicans, Indians, Chinese, Otaheiteans, adventurers, and gold hunters from all the nations of the earth—of every language, complexion, and race," intent not on settling but on finding wealth to transport back home, having "no ties to the country, no families nor settlements," and thus not entitled to organize into a separate, sovereign political community. Other Southerners exploited reports that California was in anarchy with the sections "arrayed against" each other. Reflecting the sectional conflict, Douglas retorted that foreign taxpayers reduced the burden on mass of citizens.

This predisposition toward questioning the character of a state's population before admission and withholding benefits from states with potentially free black populations was not unique to California, as illustrated in a parallel debate over the granting of public lands in Oregon. In Oregon, white American settlers had favored the inclusion of half-breed—half-Indian, half-white—adults as potential recipients of the public land's bounty. Such half-breeds often were the conduits through which trade in new regions was opened up. After some debate in Congress, it was agreed that half-breeds might be included, but a furor arose when a number of members tried to ensure that the same rights be extended to free blacks and foreigners. The ultimate result of the debate was that foreigners were permitted to receive public bounties, but free blacks, although citizens, were denied the benefits of citizenship.

The furor started when a New York Whig representative, William Augustus Sackett, insisted that "the Legislature of Oregon had no power to exclude any portion, be they white or black, of the citizens of the country." When Ohio Free-Soiler representative Joshua Reed Giddings teasingly insisted that blacks were superior to whites, Louisiana Whig representative Charles Magill Conrad retorted that "morally, physically, intellectually, and by the institutions of the country, the negro race now are, and are destined to be, a very inferior race" and that it was "highly unjust that the people of the Pacific Coast should attempt to exclude free blacks from that portion of the country" since "we allowed Europeans, Chinese, Pacific Islanders, and people from all parts of the world, to come and settle upon these lands." Given that California and Oregon had been "acquired by the common resources of this country," the state "should be left open to" Southerners and their slaves "in common with the older states." Representative Thomas H. Bayly, a Democrat from Virginia, insisted that the Northwest Ordinance of 1787 established the entire Northwest Territory as an asylum for free people of color.

Conrad was answered by Maryland Whig representative Alexander Evans, who insisted that there was no prohibition on migration, just the receipt of bounties, which might be abused by slave states to get rid of their superannuated or weak slaves, and that such bounties had not been "earned" by African Americans. Reflecting another strain of thought, Missouri Democrat representative James Stephen Green countered that awarding property to African Americans would elevate them to the position of whites and lead to race mixing. Richard Coulter of Pennsylvania, a former representative, appeared to add that half-breeds should be covered, but he insisted that the granting of public domain property to blacks would violate the God-ordained separation of the races and allow slave states a safety valve to cast off "their worthless, worn out, and decrepit slaves." Coulter defined democracy in the specifically racial terms that characterized the nation before Reconstruction affirmed the citizenship of African Americans. He insisted that "if this continent is destined to be the home of free democracy and the legitimate inheritance of the Anglo-Saxon blood—the only relief is obtained, by a total separation of domicile between the two races." An angry Sackett retorted, "Let all be served alike," equal in reason and justice. African Americans were also entitled to benefits "if they suffered the toils, the hardships, the privation of life in the wilderness" to "cultivate the lands of Oregon."

California's Boundaries

The debate over the status of slavery in the California constitution was merely one of a number of assaults made by Southerners on the state's admission that dealt with its boundaries. As the slavery issue seemed to be a losing ground, Southerners, including Louisiana Democratic senator Pierre Soulé, began arguing that the "monstrous" size of the state, which placed it in contact with an even larger Pacific empire, was a threat to democracy since it would allow California to influence congressional affairs disproportionately and affect the "commerce of the East." Soulé's efforts to convince Eastern representatives of the mistake of admitting a challenger to their Atlantic empire failed, and California's boundaries were preserved as defined in its constitution.

The Gold Factor

By early April, the debate had shifted slightly. Congressmen argued that the admission of California "is almost absolutely certain." Action was further encouraged by reports in May that California bullion was being sent to England for coinage because of the lack of a mint, something that only Congress could provide. The lack of a mint meant that spending in the States was being subverted. Efforts to exploit divisions in California to preserve opportunities for the expansion of slavery, such as Soulé's proposal that a territory of Southern California be established, failed.

Congressional and Presidential Approvals

On September 7, the House passed the compromise bill, 150-56. The compromise was finally adopted on September 9, 1850.[39] Not surprisingly, all the House opponents were Southerners.

The acquisition and admission of California straddled seven administrations, most of which had actively pushed for the purchase or capture of the territory, and the administration that received California's constitution wholeheartedly backed the state's administration. Andrew Jackson, who served between 1829 and 1837, had made the first unsuccessful offer for California. Jackson's successor, Martin Van Buren, who served until his 1841 defeat by William Henry Harrison, failed to act decisively, and the acquisition of California stalled temporarily. Van Buren opposed expansion, including the annexation of Texas. Harrison's early death in office left John Tyler in charge, but not until expansionist president James K. Polk took office in 1845 and later took serious action. Polk, a friend of Jackson's and former Speaker of the House, tried first to buy California and New Mexico. Rebuffed by the Mexican government, Polk sent troops to disputed territory on the Texas-Mexico border, precipitating the Mexican-American War. Polk presided over the war's conclusion, but he died before the state was admitted to the American fold, as did his successor, Zachary Taylor, who, however, managed to introduce and support California's admission. It was left to Taylor's successor, Millard Fillmore, to preside over the actual debate on California's admission in Congress, and although not direct, Fillmore's advancement of Webster pointed to the eventual announcement he made favoring California's admission. Eleven days after the compromise was adopted, Fillmore approved it.

SUMMARY

A California delegation was appointed on September 11, 1850, and the Senate received California senators John Frémont and William McKendree Gwin, who was the Tennessee-born son of an Indian fighter and Methodist teacher, with training in law and medicine, and a stint as Mississippi's congressman. News of admission reached the state on October 18. Although delayed and subject to much controversy, the state's admission was surprisingly quick in comparison to the other territories acquired as a result of the Mexican-American War. The state entered with its original boundaries and with the prohibition of slavery intact. The controversy over the composition of the state's citizenry was not enough to bar it from statehood, in contrast to New Mexico, where, some have argued, admission was delayed for sixty-six years because the population was more proportionally Mexican than in California or Texas.[40]

California's admission, wedged between the May 1848 and 1858 admissions of Wisconsin and then Minnesota, occurred as the two dominant parties of the era were losing their ability to avoid the slavery question. The debate over California's admission in 1850 suggested that the agreement of the nation's political parties to avoid the issue of slavery was still holding the states together, but later conflicts would dash hopes of reconciliation. The United States would witness a trend in which the Democratic Party came to hold sway in one section and the representation of both Democrats and Whigs would ultimately give way to the sectionally based Republican Party, in the North. Within a few years of the state's admission, bleeding Kansas would be torn apart by rival citizens seeking to establish a government in line with their sentiments on slavery. The Supreme Court would make the Dred Scott decision, making it clear that the Court did not believe that passing through free territory made a slave free and that the federal Constitution did not intend for African Americans to be treated as "equal" when it came to basic issues such as citizenship. John Brown would launch his raid, Lincoln would win the presidency as the representative of a new, anti-slavery Republican Party, and the Civil War would break out.

Although the war would settle the question of African Americans' formal admission to citizenship, Californians would turn after the war to exclude their Chinese population and make significant inroads on the rights of native and foreign born to hold land. Indeed, all nonwhite citizens witnessed a gradual erasure of their rights as citizens, which was not reversed until the mid-twentieth century. In 1850, the California legislature adopted its Act for the

Government and Protection of the Indians, which provided under Articles 6 and 14 that Native Americans could not testify against whites and that if convicted, they could be granted a bond by a white person and then compelled to work until discharged, an early form of the much-despised vagrancy laws of the post-Reconstruction South.[41]

NOTES

1. *Journal of the Convention Assembled to Frame a Constitution for the State of California* (1849), in the California State Archives.

2. The biographical data on the California State Constitutional Convention members and basic background draw extensively from Hubert Howe Bancroft's *History of California, Volumes 1–7* (Santa Barbara: Wallace Hebberd, 1966–1970; San Francisco: The History Company, 1886). Additional biographical data come from the *California Blue Book* (Sacramento: State Printing Office, 1907); John Ross Browne, *Report of the Debates of the Convention of California* (Washington: J. T. Towers, 1850), available at: www.memory.loc.gov; and Rockwell D. Hunt, *California's Stately Hall of Fame* (Stockton, CA: College of the Pacific, 1950).

3. Bancroft, *History of California*, vol. 5, p. 583.

4. For the axiom that slavery had to expand in order to survive, see Eric Foner, *Free Soil, Free Labor, Free Men: The Ideology of the Republican Party Before the Civil War* (New York: Oxford University Press, 1970), p. 116.

5. See Richard Henry Dana's *Two Years Before the Mast and Twenty-Four Years After*, ed. Charles W. Eliot (New York: P. F. Collier & Son, 1909–1914; available: www.Bartleby.com, 2001); Bancroft, *History of California*, vol. 3, p. 413; Kevin Starr, *Americans and the California Dream, 1850–1915* (New York: Oxford University Press, 1973), p. 39.

6. On Pacific Coast trade, particularly with China, see *Congressional Globe*, 31st Cong., 1st Sess., pp. 70–71. All references to the *Congressional Globe* come from the same session and will hereafter be referred to as CG; references to pages in the appendix will be denoted with CGA and unless otherwise noted, citations refer to 1850.

7. Walton Bean and James J. Rawls, *California: An Interpretive History*, 6th ed. (New York: McGraw-Hill, 1993), pp. 68–69; Hunt, *California's Stately Hall*, p. 216.

8. Bean and Rawls, *California*, p. 72; Richard B. Rice, William A. Bullough, and Richard J. Orsi, *Elusive Eden: A New History of California* (New York: Alfred A. Knopf, 1988), p. 102; Bancroft, *History of California*, vol. 4, pp. 434–435; Hunt, *California's Stately Hall*, pp. 175–180.

9. Bancroft, *History of California*, vol. 6, p. 257; Genaro M. Padilla, *My History, Not Yours: The Formation of Mexican American Autobiography* (Madison: University of Wisconsin Press, 1993), p. 43.

10. Gordon Morris Bakken, *Rocky Mountain Constitution Making, 1850–1912* (Westport, CT: Greenwood Press, 1987), p. 5.

11. On the lack of a civil government, see CG, p. 71 and CGA, p. 106.

12. Bancroft, *History of California*, vol. 5, p. 599.

13. This description draws on Peter H. Burnett, *Recollections and Opinions of an Old Pioneer* (D. Appleton and Company, 1880; reprint, New York: Da Capo Press,

1969), p. 254; and quoted material from Bancroft, *History of California*, vol. 6, pp. 33, 39, 42–44, 117, 124, 184, 186, 222. On the Hounds, see Rice et al., *Elusive Eden*, p. 199.

14. Walter Colton, *Three Years in California* (Stanford, CA: Stanford University Press, 1949), p. 234.

15. On the banality of homicide, see Starr, *Americans*, pp. 55–56; on the fears of revolt, see the quote from Bancroft, *History of California*, vol. 5, p. 585.

16. Burnett, *Recollections*, pp. 319, 322–323, 339.

17. See CGA, pp. 21–23 (1849); see the contrasting description of the "wild," unrooted Sioux Indians in CGA, p. 25 (1849).

18. This comment was made in reference to New Mexico, see CG, p. 165.

19. Rice et al., *Elusive Eden*, p. 107; Bancroft, *History of California*, vol. 4, p. 586, and vol. 5, pp. 110, 715.

20. See the *California Blue Book or State Roster* (Sacramento: State Printing Office, 1907), p. 661.

21. Browne, *Report of the Debates*, p. 31.

22. On Vallejo, see Padilla, *My History*, p. 54; Rice et al., *Elusive Eden*, pp. 107, 111; Bancroft, *History of California*, vol. 5, pp. 113, 124, 757–759 on de la Guerra, see ibid., vol. 6, p. 258; Hunt, *California's Stately Hall*, pp. 228–230; for the numbers, see Bancroft, *History of California*, vol. 6, pp. 282, 288; Bean and Rawls, *California*, p. 97; and Rice et al., *Elusive Eden*, p. 192.

23. Bancroft, *History of California*, vol. 4, p. 650.

24. Bean and Rawls, *California*, p. 65; Starr, *Americans*, p. 15; Bancroft, *History of California*, vol. 3, pp. 778–779.

25. Browne, *Report of the Debates*, p. 30.

26. See Article 4, Section 1. The California constitution discussion rests on the *Journal of the Convention Assembled to Frame a Constitution for the State of California* (1849), and the *Constitution of the State of California* (1849), both in the California State Archives, and Browne, *Report of the Debates*.

27. Bancroft, *History of California*, vol. 6, p. 223; on the 1852 version of the Foreign Miners Tax as being directed at the Chinese, see Rice et al., *Elusive Eden*, p. 204.

28. For Indians not taxed, see Browne, *Report of the Debates*, pp. 69–70, 305–306; U.S. Constitution, Article 1, Section 2. For the political ideology, see Douglas Monroy, "The Creation and Re-Creation of Californio Society," in Ramón Gutiérrez and Richard J. Orsi, eds., *Contested Eden: California Before the Gold Rush* (Berkeley: University of California Press, 1998), pp. 190–192; and Douglas Monroy, *Thrown Among Strangers: The Making of Mexican Culture in Frontier California* (Berkeley: University of California Press, 1990), pp. 78, 136–140.

29. Bancroft, *History of California*, vol. 6, pp. 282, 290; Browne, *Report of the Debates*, p. 449.

30. Bancroft, *History of California*, vol. 6, p. 313.

31. The quote on Section 39 is from the *Journal of the Convention*; the other quotes are from Browne, *Report of the Debates*, pp. 48–49, 62–63, 140–142.

32. Rice et al., *Elusive Eden*, p. 193; Ray McDevitt, ed., *Courthouses of California: An Illustrated History* (San Francisco: California Historical Society; Berkeley: Heyday Books, 2001), p. 7.

33. Browne, *Report of the Debates*, p. 446.

34. Padilla, *My History*, p. 15; Bancroft, *History of California*, vol. 3, p. 769, and vol. 6, pp. 285–286.

35. On Louisiana, the War of 1812, Florida, Mexican independence, and Oregon, see Thomas G. Patterson, J. Garry Clifford, and Kenneth J. Hagan, eds., *American Foreign Policy: A History to 1914*, 3rd ed. (Lexington, MA: D. C. Heath and Company, 1988), pp. 60, 65–77, 93, and 105.

36. Unless otherwise noted, the discussion, quotes, and identification of speakers rely on the *Congressional Globe*. Biographical data for congressmen and the presidents come from the *Biographical Directory of the United States Congress, 1774–Present*, available: www.bioguide.congress.gov, and Frank Freidel and Hugh S. Sidey (contributor), *The Presidents of the United States of America*, available: www.whitehouse.gov/history/presidents.

37. See Bancroft, *History of California*, vol. 5, pp. 255, 596–597.

38. Ibid., vol. 6, pp. 279–283.

39. Rice et al., *Elusive Eden*, p. 194.

40. On Gwin, see Hunt, *California's Stately Hall*, pp. 249–252. The arrival of the news and final events are recounted in Bancroft, vol. 6, pp. 343, 345, 347–348; on New Mexico, see Padilla, *My History*, pp. 43, 51.

41. Michael F. Holt, *The Political Crisis of the 1850s*, 1st ed. (New York: Norton, 1983), documents the breakdown of the two-party system. On the state of Native Americans, see Monroy, *Thrown Among Strangers*, pp. 185–186.

BIBLIOGRAPHY

Bancroft, Hubert Howe. *History of California*. 7 vols. Santa Barbara: Wallace Hebberd, 1966–1970; San Francisco: The History Company, 1886.

Bean, Walton, and James J. Rawls. *California: An Interpretive History*. 6th ed. New York: McGraw-Hill, 1993.

Gutiérrez, Ramón, and Richard J. Orsi. *California Before the Gold Rush*. Berkeley: University of California Press, 1998.

Hunt, Rockwell D. *California's Stately Hall of Fame*. Stockton, CA: College of the Pacific, 1950.

Monroy, Douglas. *Thrown Among Strangers: The Making of Mexican Culture in Frontier California*. Berkeley: University of California Press, 1990.

Rice, Richard B., William A. Bullough, and Richard J. Orsi. *Elusive Eden: A New History of California*. New York: Alfred A. Knopf, 1988.

Starr, Kevin. *Americans and the California Dream, 1850–1915*. New York: Oxford University Press, 1973.

THE STATE OF COLORADO

Admitted to the Union as a State: August 1, 1876

William Virden

INTRODUCTION

Nine years elapsed between 1867, the year of Nebraska's admittance as the thirty-seventh state, and 1876, the year Colorado became the thirty-eighth. As a requirement for admission, Nebraska had adopted, at least in name, the idea of black suffrage that the Radical Republican Congress had demanded. Colorado, however, was divided in 1867, not only over the issue of Negro suffrage but also over the necessity for statehood. Isolated along the Front Range of the Rocky Mountains, Colorado faced a declining population, stagnating commerce, and an unresolved Indian war. Most people in Colorado Territory felt that the financial, economic, and military assistance that territorial status provided far outweighed the potential benefits and increased costs of statehood. In 1867, Colorado had not sufficiently matured, either politically or economically, to gain admission into the Union. By 1876, however, conditions had changed significantly.

Colorado Territory experienced rapid growth and development during the 1870s. Beginning with the arrival of the Denver Pacific and the Kansas and Pacific railroads in 1870, Colorado's connections to both the East and the West improved steadily. At the same time, new mineral strikes prompted a second wave of immigration to the region. Republican since its early days, Colorado Territory started to feel the effects of the Panic of 1873 in mid-decade, and residents began to turn to Democratic candidates who offered alternative solutions. A Republican Party, fractured over support for President Ulysses S. Grant's gubernatorial appointees and split over the choice of a capital city, failed to respond effectively. What had begun in 1861 as a solid

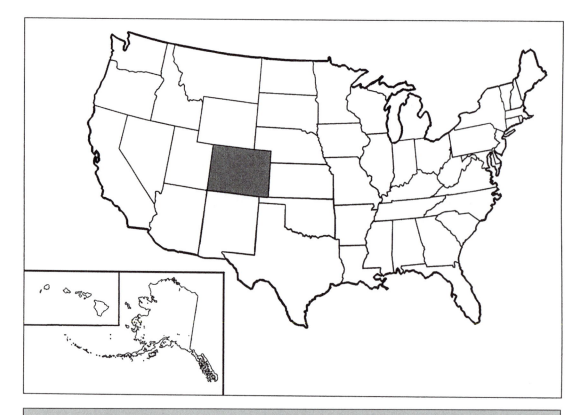

Colorado

Territorial Development:

- The United States obtained lands containing future Coloradan territory from France through the Louisiana Purchase, April 30, 1803
- The United States obtained more lands containing future Coloradan territory through the annexation of Texas, December 29, 1845
- The United States obtained more lands containing future Coloradan territory from Mexico through the Treaty of Guadalupe Hidalgo, February 2, 1848
- Colorado organized as a U.S. territory, February 28, 1861
- Colorado admitted into the Union as the thirty-eighth state, August 1, 1876

Territorial Capitals:

- Colorado City, 1861–1862
- Golden, 1862–1867
- Denver, 1867–1876

State Capitals:

- Denver, 1876–present

Origin of State Name: "Colorado" comes from a Spanish word for red, in reference to the color of the Colorado River.

First Governor: John L. Routt
Governmental Organization: Bicameral
Population at Statehood: 194,327
Geographical Size: 103,718 square miles

Republican region was, in 1874, in danger of becoming a Democratic outpost in the Trans-Mississippi West. As the national election of 1876 approached, Republicans, locally and nationally, scrambled to maintain their hold on power. In August 1876, Colorado became the thirty-eighth state. Its admission brought three important Republican electoral votes to the Electoral College that fall. Colorado's three votes insured that Samuel Tilden, winner of the popular vote in the national election, would not become the first Democrat to be elected president since Buchanan twenty years earlier. In 1876, Republicans managed to retain the presidency, and Coloradans achieved statehood. One would not have occurred without the other.

TERRITORIAL GOVERNMENT

Colorado's road to statehood began with the discovery of gold along Dry Creek in the summer of 1858. News of finding "color" in the Pikes Peak Country spread rapidly through the economically embattled towns in the Missouri River Valley and along the Kansas frontier. A rush to the Rockies began that fall, paused during the winter, and restarted in the spring of 1859. The movement to create a governing authority that would establish law and order, affirm title to the land, and provide military protection for the mining camps in the mountains and the supply centers at the base of the foothills emerged during the early stages of settlement. Efforts that began in 1858 provided a strange mixture of conflicting entities of dubious legal authority. Advocates of local control resisted efforts to create territorial government. Supporters of a territory defeated early attempts at statehood. Only the exigencies of secession and civil war resolved the conflict and brought established and recognized government to the area known as Pikes Peak Country.

Frontier Beginnings, Frontier Solutions

The Pikes Peak gold rush owed its beginnings to William Green Russell, a Georgia prospector. Russell possessed both prospecting and mining experience. He lived in the gold region of northern Georgia and had twice traveled to the California gold fields. Through correspondence with Cherokee prospectors and miners who had traveled to California along the Cherokee Trail, a route that followed the Arkansas River to the base of the Rocky Mountains and then turned north and followed the foothills into Wyoming, he learned of previous discoveries of small amounts of gold in the rivers and streams emerging from the Rockies. In 1858, William Green Russell, his brothers Levi and Oliver, and several others formed a party to prospect for gold in Pikes Peak Country. They left Georgia in February, traveled to Indian territory, joined a party of Cherokees with the same intent, and proceeded west along the Santa Fe Trail to present-day Colorado. Upon their arrival in June 1858, their numbers approximated one hundred men.[1] The group began its efforts at the intersection of Cherry Creek and the South Platte River, the location of present-day Denver. For nearly three weeks, the men stood knee-deep in freezing water, searching for the elusive "color" that would justify their long journey. By the Fourth of July, most had become discouraged and had returned home. William Green Russell and twelve others continued their efforts along Dry Creek, eight miles upriver from their original location. There, on July 5, 1858, in an area of sand and gravel, they found gold in its free form that yielded the equivalent of $10 a day per man.[2]

During that same summer, another group had set out for the Pikes Peak region in search of possible riches. Originating in Lawrence, Kansas, these people had little luck in the area of Pikes Peak and were in southern Colorado at Fort Garland in the San Luis Valley when they heard news of the Russell party's success. They moved quickly north to the banks of Cherry Creek and enjoyed limited success in their panning efforts. Their results, though not as lucrative, were sufficient to warrant remaining in the area to seek out more financially rewarding sites.

John Cantrell, a trader from Fort Laramie, visited the Russell party at Dry Creek in July, did some of his own prospecting, and returned to his home in Kansas City. There, he spread the word of gold strikes in the Pikes Peak Country. A ready audience greeted the news with enthusiasm.

The Panic of 1857 had not been kind to the frontier towns along the valley of the Missouri River. The Kansas-Nebraska Act (1854) had organized the region, and the typical settlement pattern of individual and family groups followed by town boomers emerged. Speculation led to overexpansion and overextension of credit. By 1857, the fragile economy collapsed and forced many along the Missouri River into bankruptcy. Few prospects existed for recovery. News of the gold discovery in Pikes Peak Country revived the excitement of the California gold rush, offered the immediate opportunity to regain what had been lost, and presented the chance to get rich quickly in the bargain. Parties left for Cherry Creek and the Rocky Mountains as soon as they could gather themselves and their belongings. They headed west on horseback, on foot, and in wagons and carriages, clutching their hastily packed worldly possessions, hopes for easy riches soaring. When they left the Missouri River, they were not heading into unknown territory.

The goal of the expectant millionaires in 1858 was commonly called "Pikes Peak Country." It had been named for Lieutenant Zebulon Pike, who led his famous expedition to the region in 1806. President Thomas Jefferson sent Pike and his group to explore the southern regions of the Louisiana Purchase at about the same time that Lewis and Clark were conducting their more famous "Voyage of Discovery" further north. Pike's men named the tallest peak they encountered after their leader, and it became a landmark for others who followed. In 1820, Major Stephen H. Long conducted his scientific expedition along the Platte and Arkansas rivers. His party named the most prominent peak in the northern area after their leader, but, on the whole, Long was not impressed with what he saw. In the report of his expedition, he often referred to the "inhospitable deserts of the Platte."[3] Both the American Fur Company and the Rocky Mountain Fur Company sent trappers and traders throughout the region during the 1830s and 1840s. Bent's Old Fort, located on the northern bank of the Arkansas River approximately seventy-five miles east of present-day Pueblo, was a welcome and popular stop along the Santa Fe Trail and the center of a booming international trade from 1835 to 1849. The end of the war with Mexico in 1848 brought the area officially into the United States as part of the Mexican cession. Most who traveled here, however, believed as Major Long had, that the area was "unfit for cultivation and of course uninhabitable by a people dependent upon agriculture for their subsistence."[4]

In 1858, when Russell and his party discovered gold on Dry Creek, they were officially in Arapahoe County, Kansas. In reality, the area that would become Colorado was part of four different territories of the United States, none of which had established effective governmental authority or had acquired title to the land. To the west of the Continental Divide was Utah Territory. East of the Continental Divide and south of the Arkansas River lay New Mexico Territory. North of the Arkansas River and east of the Continental Divide, northeastern Colorado was divided between Kansas Territory, south of forty degrees north latitude, and Nebraska Territory north of that same line. Present-day Boulder was in Nebraska, Denver in Kansas, Pueblo in New Mexico, and Vail and Aspen in Utah. In August 1855, the Kansas Territorial Legislature created Arapahoe County and extended it all the way to the Rocky Mountains, but it remained a paper entity only. The officials of Arapahoe County occupied neither office nor territory. Legal title to the land remained with the Ute, Arapahoe, and Cheyenne nations according to the Treaty of Fort Laramie (1851). The discovery of gold in the Pikes Peak Country, then, began a rush to a known, but not well thought of, area over which multiple authorities claimed jurisdiction, and in which existed no established, recognized legal entities. The rush to the Rockies was much different than the California gold rush of 1849.

When the forty-niners arrived in California, the area was already organized as the Bear Flag Republic. It possessed governmental officers, working institutions, and a long history of Spanish settlement and governmental control. Such was not the case in the Pikes Peak Country. The Spanish Empire had originally claimed the entire region, but effective control never extended northward beyond Santa Fe. For most of its existence prior to 1858, the area that would become Colorado served as a buffer zone among competing empires and Native American tribes. After the successful Mexican Revolution in 1821, the Mexican government attempted to thwart the westward march of the United States through the establishment of agricultural settlements and the awarding of land grants. They were only nominally successful in the southernmost portion of today's San Luis Valley, and then not until 1853. In 1858, prospectors arrived in an area without effective legal control. Distances to the nearest established legal authorities were immense—seven hundred miles to Lawrence and four hundred miles to either Salt Lake City or Santa Fe. Routes to any of these locations passed directly through the lands of increasingly restless Native American tribes. Lacking the established and familiar institutions and authorities that provided law, order, justice, and protection, the Pikes Peak Country was truly a frontier region. The resolution of its immediate needs called for frontier solutions. The small group of prospectors that remained at the confluence of Cherry Creek and the South Platte River in the fall of 1858 began to create the authorities and institutions they felt necessary to protect themselves and their property.

EARLY GOVERNMENT

The news of gold strikes along Cherry Creek reached the Missouri River towns in late summer. Those hoping to get a jump on their competition left immediately. By the end of October 1858, some two hundred adventurers were prospecting the streams and canyons along the Front Range from Cherry Creek in the north to the Arkansas River in the south.[5] The rapid approach of winter shifted their activities from panning for gold to planning for an anticipated rush of argonauts in the spring.

In the first week of November 1858, the Russell group founded Auraria City on the west bank of Cherry Creek. They elected town officers and chose A. J. Smith as their delegate to the Kansas Territorial Legislature. At the same time, voters selected Hiram P. Graham to represent the interests of the Pikes Peak region in the U.S. Congress. Thirty-five votes elected both men to their positions.[6]

The Lawrence party had earlier established the town of St. Charles on the east bank of Cherry Creek. By November, most of their members had returned to Kansas to regroup and resupply. In mid-November, William Larimer, an experienced town promoter, arrived at the head of a combined group from Leavenworth and Lecompton, Kansas. Members of this party carried with them credentials as officers of Arapahoe County.[7] Larimer convinced the few remaining members of the St. Charles Town Company to join his efforts. He assumed the St. Charles town site and renamed it Denver City. Both town companies platted the land, fixed prices for town lots, and established the beginnings of legal authority and government in the region. As 1859 began, they could only sit and wait for the spring to bring the thaw, the anticipated onslaught from the east, and positive results from their representatives in Lawrence and Washington, D.C.

A. J. Smith arrived in Lawrence in January 1859. The Kansas Territorial Legislature accepted his credentials and seated him as the representative from Arapahoe County. However, word of the gold strikes prompted further action in the legislature. On February 7, 1859, in anticipation of a great influx of both people and income, the Kansas Territorial Legislature abolished Arapahoe

County and created five smaller counties in its place. The legislature went so far as to appoint county officers for each of the new entities. A. J. Smith retained his seat as the representative from Pikes Peak Country.[8]

Hiram Graham, traveling at his own expense, arrived in Washington, D.C., in January 1859. Although not officially recognized as a delegate from a territory, he was accorded unofficial recognition as the spokesman for the Pikes Peak Country. Prior to his arrival, Representative Schyler Colfax of Illinois had introduced a bill to organize the "Territory of Colona" in the Pikes Peak region.[9] While the bill was read twice and ordered printed, it died in the House Committee on Territories. Graham then turned to the Senate for assistance, gaining the support of Senator James Green of Missouri, the chairman of the Senate Committee on Territories. Senator Green introduced a petition requesting his colleagues to organize a new territory carved from western Kansas, southwestern Nebraska, and southeastern Utah. This petition was referred to the Senate Committee on Territories; there, as in the House, no action was taken. Determined to achieve his goal, Graham turned again to the House for assistance.

Graham succeeded in winning support for a new territory from Representative Alexander Stephens of Georgia, the chairman of the House Committee on Territories. Stephens introduced a bill to establish "a temporary government for the Territory of Jefferson."[10] Attempts to change the name to "Osage" were thwarted, and the entire effort ended on February 16, 1859, when the House tabled the bill along with bills for the creation of Arizona and Dakota territories.[11] Graham's failure resulted from forces over which he had no control.

By 1859, the debate over slavery in the territories had divided the Congress and hindered any progress toward the creation of new territorial entities. Both the leadership and the desire that earlier had led to compromises in 1820 and 1850 were gone from the Congress. The congressional session ended in March with no further action concerning territorial organization. Activity in the Pikes Peak region, however, began to increase as spring arrived.

As the ground sprang to life, so did the residents at the foot of the Rockies. On March 28, 1859, in an election that saw 774 ballots cast, voters chose officers for Arapahoe County. Unknown to them, the county no longer existed and these men were denied their offices. This failure, coupled with the inaction in Washington, D.C., led to local efforts to establish government. On April 7, 1859, in Fountain City (present-day Pueblo) residents unanimously declared themselves in favor of a new state. A mass meeting in Auraria and Denver City four days later called for a convention to meet on April 15 to "take into consideration the propriety of organizing a new State or Territory."[12] At that meeting, thirty delegates unanimously declared that a convention should be held on the first Monday in June, 1859, that delegates to the convention were to be elected on the second Monday of May, 1859, and that the "discussions of this convention shall have but one object, viz: the formation of a new and independent State of Jefferson."[13] On May 7, members of the convention published "An Address to the Citizens," which listed six reasons for the immediate creation of the state of Jefferson. Those reasons included the great distances between themselves and established governments; the unreasonable time required for correspondence or communication; the fact that mining, the principal endeavor of the region, was so different from agriculture, the principal industry of Kansas, Nebraska, New Mexico, and Utah; that the areas were "incompatible"; the price of labor in the two industries was so different "that no laws that apply to one will apply to the other"; representation in any of the other territorial legislatures would be nominal and leave the area "at the mercy of men who know nothing of our wants, cannot realize our situation, and will use their positions only to enrich themselves at our expense"; and that the distance between the settlements in the region and the established territorial courts rendered law and order ineffective.[14] These arguments formed the basis of all claims for both territorial status and statehood and would not vary substantially for the next eighteen years. The election of delegates was held on Monday, May 9, and thirty-two of the fifty elected delegates met in the Denver House in Denver City on June 6.[15] As had occurred previously in Washington, D.C., outside events interrupted progress toward the creation of government in the region.

During the winter and spring of 1859 three important gold strikes occurred independently of each other. George Jackson, an experienced prospector and veteran of the California gold fields, had followed Clear Creek into the hills and had discovered substantial color at the confluence of Chicago Creek and Clear Creek (present-day Idaho Springs). In April, John Gregory, an experienced Georgia prospector, had followed the north fork of Clear Creek into the hills and discovered the first lode gold, or gold in combination with another mineral, usually quartz, in Colorado. The third important event occurred in Boulder Canyon, forty miles north of Denver City. Six men from Nebraska had followed Boulder Creek into the canyon and had found substantial gold deposits at a place they named "Gold Hill." Distances between settlements, poor communication, and the desire for secrecy had suppressed news of the strikes, but by June 1859, the word was out. The delegates at the Denver House determined that it would be wiser to "adjourn to a time when there could, and doubtless would, be a larger number of delegates in attendance."[16] The convention elected officers, established committees, and adjourned until August.

The anticipated rush to the Pikes Peak Country began in the spring of 1859. News of the Gregory and Jackson finds not only provided an additional impetus but also led to the notion that gold was easily found and extracted. Written guides to the Rockies appeared throughout the departure points in the East, most compiled by people who had never been west of the Mississippi or Missouri rivers. Prospecting, however, was hard, dirty, backbreaking work that required not only some knowledge of geology but also the stamina to work long hours in freezing water, shoveling tons of dirt in the hope of obtaining ounces of gold. The vast majority of the emigrants in 1859 were, however, "men who lacked energy, industry and no means...."[17] As a result, large numbers of initially enthusiastic arrivals quickly found nothing but disillusionment and left the region. Termed "Go-Backs," they formed an unanticipated outmigration that kept the population numbers low. This, in turn, affected the support for early statehood. In growing numbers, men who initially had advocated the creation of a state now felt that the population was insufficient to support a state organization. The call for territorial status rather than statehood became increasingly louder.

On Monday, August 1, 1859, the regional convention reconvened in the Denver House. This time 166 delegates representing forty-five precincts arrived to discuss the future. Their numbers were too large for the building, so the convention moved to Auraria City and a more sizable hall. The convention also changed officers, as those previously elected no longer represented the increased sentiment for a territory. On Wednesday, August 3, the Committee on Statehood reported. The majority favored the formation of a state government. The minority, fourteen of the forty-five committee members, felt that the population over the summer had reached only 15,000 and believed that it would shrink as low as 6,000 with the onset of winter. Under those conditions, the minority felt a state government to be both "impolitic and unwise." They called for the convention to memorialize the U.S. Congress to create a territory and to set a date for the election of a delegate to Congress, then adjourn. The next day, delegate Henry Allen from Auraria City offered a compromise suggesting that the convention prepare both a constitution for statehood and a memorial to Congress requesting the creation of a territory. Both would be submitted to a vote of the people on the first Monday of September for approval or rejection. The resolution was adopted *viva voce*.[18]

The constitution created for the state of Jefferson was standard for its era and patterned after the U.S. Constitution. It did call for an enlarged new state that would have included half of current Wyoming and parts of eastern Utah and western Kansas. In addition, all laws in force in the region were to remain valid until they could be reviewed in the new state's General Assembly. The convention then drew up a memorial to Congress for territorial status and adjourned.[19]

On September 7, 1859, voters in the Pikes Peak Country went to the polls to choose between "For statehood" and "For Territory." They rejected the state idea 2,007 to 1,649. The light turnout surprised state supporters, especially the low number of votes recorded in the mining districts.[20] On September 24, a mass meeting in Auraria-Denver City called for a provisional government to serve until a legal territory was created. On October 3, one week prior to convening a constitutional convention for the provisional government, voters elected Beverly D. Williams their delegate to Congress.[21] On the same day, the mountain settlements, demonstrating their independence, elected a full slate of officers for nonexistent Arapahoe County, Kansas. William N. Byers, publisher and editor of *The Rocky Mountain News*, summarized the political situation in an editorial on October 6:

> Here we go, a regular triple-headed government machine.... We hang on the outskirts of Kansas.... We have just elected a delegate to the United States Congress from the "Territory of Jefferson" and ere long we will have in full blast a provisional government.... One man claims he lives in Arapahoe county, whilst his neighbor asserts that he is in Montana, where one man acknowledges Kansas law and another says he is on Indian land where no law can reach.

On October 24, Pikes Peakers went to the polls yet again. They approved the provisional constitution, elected legislators for the provisional government, and chose Robert W. Steele as the governor of Jefferson Territory.[22] The Provisional Legislature convened on November 7 and conducted the necessary business to establish the agencies and institutions of government before adjourning for the holidays. They reconvened in January for two days to adopt civil and criminal codes. Although these men acted in great earnestness and with laudable goals, from the very beginning Jefferson Territory and its representatives confronted opposition from all sides.

On November 8, 1859, approximately three hundred settlers loyal to Kansas chose Captain Richard A. Sopris as their delegate to the Kansas Territorial Legislature from Arapahoe County. Kansas legislators recognized him and he took his seat as an official representative.[23] When the Jefferson assembly levied a poll tax of $1 and an occupational tax on all but mining and agricultural professions, 650 miners in the Clear Creek mining districts signed a petition and refused to pay the tax.[24] Miners preferred the grassroots, local government that had emerged during the California gold rush.

Mining districts were formally organized institutions that had developed in California a decade before the discovery of gold at Dry Creek. Miners in each area wrote their own constitutions that delineated boundaries, established offices, regulated the size of claims, and established procedures for settling disputes. Miners approved the constitutions and elected officers at mass meetings. They often determined punishments for serious offenses as well. Agricultural settlers along the South Platte and Arkansas rivers adopted a similar form of local government they called "Claim Clubs." They drew their models from the experiences of farmers in Wisconsin and Iowa who had established effective claim club institutions as they settled those areas. Charters for town companies usually protected property and governed the sale of town lots, while "people's courts"—mass meetings of town residents—provided justice in criminal cases. Most prospectors and farmers preferred local government to the larger, more sluggish, and generally less effective territorial institutions. As a result, support for Jefferson Territory was concentrated in the more urban Auraria-Denver City area.

Throughout 1860, Jefferson Territory struggled to become effective. The U.S. Congress ignored it, as did mining districts and claim clubs. Town companies validated their business transactions in Kansas Territory. Governor Steele, the

Provisional Assembly, and the rest of Jefferson Territory's officers had no valid legal claim to jurisdiction and no authority to levy taxes, adjudicate disputes, or deal with Indian problems. As a result, Jefferson Territory became progressively weaker and increasingly irrelevant. In September 1860, miners in Mount Vernon Canyon west of Denver City created the sovereign Mount Vernon District and pledged loyalty only unto themselves. On October 1, citizens of Denver City overwhelmingly approved the creation of the separate "People's Government of the City of Denver."[25] Delegates in Central City met on October 24 and created Idaho Territory. At the end of 1860, the area that would become Colorado was a slumgullion of conflicting jurisdictions and competing authorities. Only local, grassroots efforts offered any semblance of law and order, and that was rough and ready at best. The region required action at the national level to settle the conflicts, establish official institutions, and obtain title to the land. However, events at the national level focused on larger issues that both divided the nation and hindered progress toward legitimate government in the Pikes Peak Country.

The first session of the Thirty-sixth Congress convened on Monday, December 5, 1859. It was an inauspicious time to discuss territorial matters, as Virginia had hanged John Brown the previous Friday. Differences over slavery, its extension into the territories, and the rise of the Nativist movement known as the Know-Nothings, had prevented any one party from gaining a majority in the House of Representatives. A prolonged contest over the organization of the House held up most of the business for nearly two months. On February 1, the members elected William Pennington of New Jersey, a Republican, as Speaker, and business began to move forward once again. During the delay, B. D. Williams had been hard at work building support for the creation of a legitimate Jefferson Territory. He presented a memorial from Governor Steele and the Jefferson legislature requesting either the creation of a new territory or the recognition of the existing Jefferson Territory as legitimate.[26] Two weeks later, President Buchanan received eight identical memorials from citizens in the Pikes Peak region requesting "the extinguishment of Indian title, a survey and sale of public lands, the establishment of an assay office, and the creation of a territorial government."[27] Further, the memorials requested that the president issue a proclamation creating a territory if, by July 1, 1860, the population had reached 30,000 and an Enabling Act had not been passed. If the population achieved 150,000 persons, then the memorials requested that the president create a state.[28] These memorials were the products of S. W. Beall, whom the city of Denver had employed in December 1859 to advance its interests in the nation's capital. Beall and Williams worked together in their attempts to gain official status for the region.

Several bills were introduced into the Congress during this first session to form a territory in the Pikes Peak Country. Senator James Green of Missouri, chairman of the Senate Committee on Territories, reported Senate Bill No. 366 favorably out of committee. It was read and printed, but no further action was taken. Representative Galusha Grow, chairman of the House Committee on Territories, reported a bill to create the Territory of Idaho in the Pikes Peak region. It, too, was read and referred to the committee. In the spring of 1860, there were five bills before the House that would have created territories. Representative Grow chose the Idaho bill as a test. As expected, the debate centered on slavery and its extension west. When Representative John Bingham of Ohio introduced a bill to repeal New Mexico Territory's recognition of slavery, southern members blocked all further action on territorial questions.[29] Although Representative Grow managed to introduce a second "Idaho Bill," it was blocked, as had been the first. All activity on territorial questions was tabled until after the November election and the opening of the second session of the Thirty-sixth Congress. In June, the members did, however, manage to allot $35,000 to arrange a meeting with the Arapahoe and Cheyenne nations to negotiate a treaty resolving the question of land title. The council was held at Big Timbers (present-day Lamar) on the Arkansas River. In the Treaty of 1861, the Arapahoe and Cheyenne ceded their lands to the United States, except for a triangular-shaped reservation that lay between Big Sandy Creek and the Arkansas River.[30]

When the Thirty-sixth Congress opened its second session on December 3, 1860, the country was in crisis. The election of Abraham Lincoln had spurred the Georgia and South Carolina legislatures to call for secession conventions. Discussions on territorial matters in the House of Representatives were postponed eight times between December 18 and February 4 as members attempted to elect a Speaker and deal with secession fever. By the end of January, the pattern of secession was clear. It became imperative for Republicans to attach to the Union those areas that remained loyal. Though extra-legal, Jefferson Territory was one of those areas.

On January 30, 1861, the Senate took up Senate Bill No. 366, which had been tabled the previous April. The boundaries of the territory were reduced to Colorado's current borders, and the name of the territory was changed from Jefferson to Idaho, which supposedly meant "Gem of the Mountains." On February 4, the Senate amended the name once again from Idaho to Colorado at B. D. Williams's request.[31] It passed the Senate without roll call. By that time, six states had seceded from the Union.

Representative Grow introduced discussion of Senate Bill No. 366 in the House after receiving memorials from both the Kansas and Nebraska Territorial Legislatures supporting the cause of the Pikes Peak Country. The insertion of an amendment allowed the supreme court in the territory the authority to determine cases involving title to slaves, and the bill passed the House, 90-44. The Senate concurred on February 26, and President Buchanan signed into law the act that finally created a legitimate government in the region.[32] The Territory of Colorado emerged from three years of confusing and contradictory authority as a result of a divided nation and the threat of war. Those conditions would dominate and disrupt Colorado Territory's first years and present overwhelming obstacles in the early years on the road to statehood.

COLORADO TERRITORY

Abraham Lincoln appointed William Gilpin the first governor of Colorado Territory. Gilpin arrived in difficult times economically, politically, and militarily. Lack of population, poor communications, unreliable connections to the East, and troublesome Native Americans would mark not only Gilpin's term in office but also the terms of the six men who followed him as governor. Colorado's tenure as a territory was extended at first because of its isolated and exposed position. Not until 1876, when the Republican Party became desperate to retain its hold on the presidency, did Colorado emerge as a full-fledged member of the Union. The fifteen years between 1861 and 1876 saw great improvement in industry and technology, triumph and disaster on the battlefield, and conflict and compromise in politics.

William Gilpin was a good choice as the first governor of Colorado Territory. He was an experienced explorer and military commander. He had accompanied John C. Frémont's 1843 expedition to the area, commanded troops in the war with Mexico, and fought Indians along the Santa Fe Trail. He was a loyal Union man and a staunch Republican. Upon his arrival in May 1861, he toured the mining camps and settlements under his care, winning the support of Coloradans along the way. He gracefully accepted Robert Steele's ceremonial transfer of power from the illegitimate Jefferson Territory and was inaugurated on July 8, 1861. One of his first official acts was to order a census, which revealed the total inhabitants of Colorado Territory, excluding Native Americans, at 25,331. Two days after his inauguration, Governor Gilpin announced the organization of the territory into judicial and representative districts and called for a general election to choose Colorado's delegate to Congress.[33] Voters chose Hiram Bennett by two to one over their previous "unofficial" representative, B. D. Williams. The total votes cast, 9,597, indicated the outflow of population as prospectors, miners, and farmers returned to their points of origin to take up arms for the Union or the Confederacy.[34]

Gilpin faced three immediate problems: the internal threat from Confederate sympathizers, the external threat from Confederate troops in Texas and Arkansas, and the growing threat from increasingly agitated Native American tribes on the eastern Plains. The first difficulty mostly resolved itself. Union men outnumbered Confederate sympathizers three to one in the territory. Most left to join their compatriots in the southern cause. Other than minor banditry in the early stages of the war, the Confederates who remained in Colorado occupied themselves with their professions and mounted no serious opposition. A greater threat emerged from Confederate armies located to the south and west.

In the summer and fall of 1861, the only federal troops in the territory were small garrisons stationed at Fort Garland far to the south of Denver in the San Luis Valley, and Fort Lyon on the eastern edge of the Territory along the Santa Fe Trail. After the Union disaster at Bull Run on July 29, 1861, the idea that the Civil War would be short and easily won evaporated in both the East and the West. In addition, Governor Gilpin feared that the Union loss had emboldened the Confederate forces he saw surrounding him. He requested federal troops and military supplies, but Secretary of War Simon denied both. As a result, Gilpin began to raise volunteer regiments to defend the territory.[35]

Recruiting volunteers proved relatively easy through the summer, and the First Regiment of Colorado Volunteers arrived at Camp Weld outside of Denver in the fall. Colonel John P. Slough commanded the First Colorado with Samuel Tappan as his second in command and Methodist minister John Chivington third in line.[36] At Camp Weld they followed the normal, repetitive, and tiresome routine of garrison troops in training. As they were "good-sized, stout and hardy" boys, they found plenty of time during off-duty hours to cause trouble. In part, their raids on local farms, stores, and saloons resulted from the failure of the territorial government to pay them for four months.[37]

Paying the soldiers and their creditors proved more difficult than recruiting them. Construction costs for Camp Weld totaled $40,000.[38] Costs of supplies and equipment for the regiment mounted daily, and the governor had no way to raise the funds to meet the expenses. The Territorial Legislature did not meet until October, so there was no system of taxation in place. County governments, though designated in the fall, had to be formed, established, and functioning to assist. Governor Gilpin chose to resolve the matter himself and began to issue drafts on the U.S. Treasury, signed by him as "Governor of the Territory" and payable "on sight."[39] The sum total of drafts issued that fall amounted to $375,000. Gilpin, however, had no legal authority to issue the drafts. Coloradans at first accepted the drafts as payment, but as word spread that the secretary of the treasury refused to honor Gilpin's actions, the credibility of the governor and his "paper" sank rapidly. In desperation, Governor Gilpin left for Washington, D.C., in December in an attempt to resolve the issue. At the same time, the Confederacy began an invasion of New Mexico that threatened Colorado, its citizens, and the gold fields.

Major Henry H. Sibley, in command of nearly three thousand Confederate troops, left Texas and invaded the Rio Grande Valley in New Mexico. The goal was to capture Santa Fe and move north into Colorado. The intent was not only to capture the gold fields for the Confederacy but also to separate California from the Union and open it to Confederate domination. Major victories in the West might also bring the international recognition that the Confederacy needed to help win the war.[40] Opposing Sibley on the Union side stood Colonel Edward Canby and his troops at Fort Union north of Santa Fe. On February 21, 1862, Sibley and Canby met at Valverde, New Mexico, in the first Civil War battle in the West. Sibley won and next took both Albuquerque and Santa Fe. At that point, the First Colorado was ordered to New Mexico to assist Canby. The regiment left Camp Weld and arrived at Fort Union after a forced march of four hundred miles in just thirteen days. The First Colorado, combined with Canby's troops, met and defeated Sibley at Glorieta Pass on March 26–28. In the battle, Major John Chivington distinguished himself. He and about one-fourth of the Union force took advantage of a narrow trail around the pass that allowed them to outflank and encircle Sibley's main group in the canyon. Chivington and his men were able to destroy Sibley's supplies. Chivington burned nearly one hundred wagons and killed five hundred to six hundred horses and mules. With the loss of his reserve materiel and his transportation, Sibley was forced to withdraw. Canby, fearful that Sibley would attempt to capture the supplies at Fort Union, ordered the First Colorado back to the post. He did not pursue Sibley. Outraged at Canby's action, Colonel Slough, commander of the First Colorado, resigned. Major Chivington, the hero of Glorieta Pass, was the unanimous choice to replace him. Glorieta Pass marked the end of the Confederate military threat in the West and brought John Chivington enormous popularity in Colorado.[41] Although the First Colorado bolstered Chivington's military and political ambitions, it could not save William Gilpin.

While Governor Gilpin traveled to Washington, D.C., officials were choosing his replacement. Gilpin was successful in convincing the secretary of the treasury to honor his drafts, but stringent conditions were imposed that included both itemized and attested statements of charges. Those who met the conditions were paid. Those who could not, never received their money. Gilpin, however, could not save his job. In April 1862, Abraham Lincoln appointed John Evans of Illinois as the second governor of Colorado Territory.

John Evans was a wealthy and influential Republican. A medical doctor, he had founded the Illinois Medical Society and had been instrumental in establishing quarantine laws to prevent the spread of cholera. He founded the Illinois Republican Party and was a friend of Abraham Lincoln. He was also one of the founders of Northwestern University. Evanston, Illinois, was named in his honor. Investments in railroad stocks had brought him great wealth and political influence. Prior to 1862, he had never traveled west of the Mississippi River.[42]

Evans arrived in Colorado in May 1862. Of the three immediate problems that had confronted William Gilpin, only one remained, the increasingly hostile Arapahoe and Cheyenne nations. The necessities of the Civil War had drawn troops out of Colorado to Kansas and Missouri and reduced the population in general. In Minnesota, the Great Sioux War of 1862 fostered increased belligerence among the Plains tribes and initiated increased activity in their purchase of both horses and guns. Residents of Colorado feared the unification of the Plains tribes and a repeat of the Minnesota bloodshed. Governor Evans, who was also the ex-officio superintendent of Indian affairs in Colorado, attempted a two-pronged approach: preparation for the defense of the territory combined with negotiation with the Native Americans to avoid hostilities. Neither worked well.

The Legislative Assembly, Colorado's lower house, authorized the creation of county militias in July, but recruitment was sluggish. A second Colorado volunteer regiment had been formed in 1862, and there were few reliable, qualified men remaining. County governments were not fully operational, while others only existed on paper. County militias were not the answer.

The first hostilities in Colorado occurred in March 1863, in Larimer County along the Cache La Poudre River. Indians ran off stock and took guns and ammunition, but they did not kill settlers. Raids of this nature continued throughout the summer and fall along the South Platte River, affirming residents' and officials' fears that the Plains tribes were gathering the supplies necessary for a larger, more concentrated attack. In September 1863, Evans, acting in his role as Indian superintendent, attempted a meeting with leaders of the Plains tribes, but none bothered to come to the meeting. The Utes of western Colorado did attend a meeting and negotiated a treaty opening the San Luis Valley to settlement.[43]

In April 1864, detachments of the First Colorado encountered a large band of Cheyenne near the head of the Smoky Hill River in eastern Colorado, another smaller group at the mouth of Kiowa Creek near present-day Fort Morgan, and a band of three hundred Cheyenne on Cedar Creek in Logan County. All indications pointed toward the massing of men and materiel.[44] In June, the murder and mutilation of Nathan Hungate and his family south of Denver sent waves of panic throughout the territory. In response, Governor Evans issued the following proclamation:

> Patriotic citizens of Colorado:
> I again implore you to organize for defense of your homes and families against the merciless savages.... Any man who kills a hostile Indian is a patriot; but there are Indians who are friendly and to kill one of those will involve us in greater difficulty. It is important therefore to fight only the hostile, and no one has been or will be restrained from this.[45]

For their protection, Evans then ordered all friendly Indians to one of four federal forts in the area: Fort Laramie (Wyoming), Fort Larned (Kansas), Fort Lyon (southern Colorado), or Camp Collins (northern Colorado). Again, he met with little response. The lack of compliance with his order convinced Evans that the rumors of the Great Sioux War repeating on the Plains were true, so he authorized "all citizens of Colorado...to go in pursuit of all hostile Indians...and to hold to their own private use and benefit, all property of said Indians that they may capture."[46] That summer, President Lincoln authorized formation of the Third Colorado for one hundred days for the sole purpose of fighting Indians. Recruitment began immediately and was completed in September 1864.

In late September, Major Edward Wynkoop, commander of Fort Lyon, brought Black Kettle, a Cheyenne chief, and several others to Denver to meet with Governor Evans and Colonel John Chivington, now commander of the Colorado Military District. Evans was very ill at the time. Evans instructed Black Kettle to report to Fort Lyon. This he did with his followers in late October, joining a band of Arapahoe under Left Hand on the reservation along

Big Sandy Creek. The camp comprised a village of six hundred to seven hundred men, women, and children. "Feeling that they had complied with the Governor's directions, these Indians considered themselves secure from attack."[47]

In mid-November, events moved toward a tragic conclusion. Chivington was under some pressure to act. General Samuel Curtis, Chivington's immediate superior in Kansas, had recently instructed him that the Indians were to suffer more before peace could be made. In addition, Chivington's political aspirations began to dim as the luster of his victory at Glorieta Pass dulled through inactivity. The Colorado Third had seen no action. Known derisively as the "Bloodless Third" and the "Hundred Dazers" they were ridiculed throughout the territory. Governor Evans left for Washington, D.C., in early November to promote statehood for Colorado personally. After his departure, Colonel Chivington moved the Colorado Third east to Bijou Creek. From there they moved south to Fort Lyon, arriving on November 23. Major Wynkoop, considered a friend of the Cheyenne and Arapahoe, had been removed earlier. On the evening of November 28, Chivington marched his men forty miles north to the Indian encampment. At dawn on the November 29, they attacked the sleeping camp. One troop stampeded the horse herd, another cut off the escape routes. The fighting lasted until noon. Ten soldiers died and over one hundred Native Americans, mostly women and children, were killed. Native American women were raped and mutilated, while children were shot for sport.[48] Initial accounts of Sand Creek related that it was a great battle and a greater victory for Chivington and his troops, who were celebrated in Denver as heroes.[49] Chivington regained the luster of hero and the Colorado Third lost its bloodless reputation.

Disturbing accounts of the massacre began to emerge as early as January 1865. The U.S. Congress ordered an investigation, and hearings were held. By midsummer 1865, a negative reaction had set in that ruined the political aspirations of John Chivington and John Evans. The report of the investigation condemned Chivington but could not sentence him, as he had retired from service. Lincoln removed Evans, even though it was evident from the testimony of all parties that he had known nothing of Chivington's plans when he left for Washington, D.C.[50] Sand Creek also buried the statehood movement in 1865 and began five years of open warfare on the High Plains that interrupted transportation and communication, stymied growth and development, and witnessed great loss of life and property on both sides. Only in 1869, with the battle at Summit Springs near present-day Sterling, were the Cheyenne and Arapahoe finally defeated and removed to the Indian territory. Sand Creek and the Indian wars combined with national politics kept Colorado in territorial status for another twelve years.

FIRST ATTEMPTS AT STATEHOOD

The year 1864 was difficult for Republicans. The Civil War was entering its third year with no real sign of victory. Abraham Lincoln faced a stiff challenge from General George McClellan. A Republican victory in November was not a sure thing. Needing to increase their support in Congress and in the Electoral College, Republicans in Washington, D.C., introduced Enabling Acts for Colorado, Nebraska, and Nevada. The act for Colorado called for a constitutional convention to be held on the first Monday in July 1864, with an election to approve the document on the second Tuesday in October.[51] The convention opened on July 4 in Golden and immediately adjourned to Denver. Delegates favoring statehood dominated the proceedings and rapidly constructed a document that was patterned after the nation's Constitution with adjustments made for the state. They did, however, understand their political and economic situation well. With a low population and without extensive taxable property, the framers felt they needed to keep state salaries low. This would also work to diffuse the greatest opposition argument to statehood in 1864, that increased taxes would accompany statehood. The pro-statehood atmosphere was so potent at the convention that Republicans chose a full slate of candidates for state offices and decided to hold an election for state officials at the same time as the ratification election. D. T. Towne was named the candidate for governor and Colonel John Chivington stood for Congress. It was understood that the Republican Party leaders, John Evans and Henry Teller, would be the first senators.[52] Beyond the convention hall, however, serious opposition to statehood emerged.

Democrats led the anti-state movement. Though smaller in numbers, they conducted a vocal and effective campaign claiming that the statehood movement was merely an office seeker's scheme. In addition, they made two very pertinent points: Statehood would raise taxes to unreasonable levels to support the necessary institutions, and the federal government's conscription law would apply to Colorado's male citizens. In addition, Hispanic voters in the southern counties stood solidly against statehood, as they feared loss of federal protection for their rights in an Anglo-dominated state. Statehood advocates countered that direct representation in the House and Senate would advance Colorado's interests and prevent Colorado's exploitation. When the ballots had been cast and counted, statehood lost, by 1,520 to 4,672.[53] A defeat of nearly three to one usually means the end of an issue, but not so with Colorado statehood.

In the spring of 1865, a call for a new convention emerged. Both Republican and Democratic parties and the previously anti-state committee supported this second effort. Evans, Chivington, Teller, and Jerome Chaffee, the leaders of the Republican Party, kept their distance. As the Enabling Act passed in 1864 had specified only one election, no legal authority existed for a second attempt at statehood. Delegates at a new constitutional convention adopted essentially the same constitution as had previously been created, although salaries were increased. An election requesting approval for black suffrage accompanied the ratification of the second constitution. Outside the southern counties, there appeared to be little opposition to this second effort. The vote was close, 3,025 in favor and 2,870 against. Statehood had achieved a 155-vote majority. Black suffrage failed.[54]

An election for state offices followed on November 14, naming Republicans William Gilpin as governor and George Chilcott as congressman. The state legislature met on December 18, 1865, and elected Jerome B. Chaffee and John Evans to the U.S. Senate. Chilcott, Chaffee, and Evans then proceeded to Washington, D.C., to present their credentials and obtain acceptance of the new state's actions.

President Andrew Johnson refused to recognize the "State of Colorado" as he felt that the activities in Colorado in 1865 had not conformed to the Enabling Act of 1864. He sent the matter back to Congress.[55] Senator Stewart of Nevada then introduced a bill to recognize both the 1865 constitution and the election that approved it, and to admit Colorado as a state on that basis. The bill passed Congress and was sent to President Johnson for his signature. In the summer of 1865, Johnson and the Congress were already at odds over plans for and control of Reconstruction. The power struggle for supremacy at the federal level had begun over methods of and plans for bringing the secessionist states back into the fold. Johnson vetoed the Colorado bill on May 15, 1866. In his message to Congress explaining the veto, he listed lack of population and the fact that the 155-vote majority in 1865 did not outweigh the three-to-one defeat in 1864. The difficulties of Reconstruction and the struggle between the executive and legislative branches at the time were hinted at in the final paragraph:

> The condition of the Union at the present moment is calculated to inspire caution in regard to the admission of new States. Eleven of the old States have been for some time, and still remain unrepresented in Congress. It is a common interest of all the States, as well those represented as unrepresented, that the integrity and harmony of the Union should be restored as completely as possible, so that all of those who are expected to bear the burdens of the federal government shall be consulted concerning the admission of new States: and that in the meantime no new State should be prematurely and unnecessarily admitted.[56]

The Senate, which would shortly override the president's veto of the Civil Rights Bill, chose not to override his veto of Colorado statehood.

As the second session of the Thirty-ninth Congress opened, the contest between Congress and the president increased in intensity. Radical Republicans—those who favored black suffrage, adoption of civil rights, and acceptance of congressional requirements as the necessities for readmittance of the former Confederate states—needed to increase their numbers in the Congress to assure their ability to challenge presidential vetoes. On December 10, 1866, as a result of a petition from citizens of Colorado, a bill was introduced to admit Colorado as a state.[57] Congress passed the measure on January 16, 1867, and President Johnson, for the third time, vetoed Colorado's statehood.

He saw no substantial difference between this bill and the last one he had vetoed in 1866. In addition, he mentioned that Coloradans had rejected black suffrage, whereas the Congress required acceptance of black suffrage for the admittance of former Confederate states; that the official Legislative Assembly of Colorado Territory had voted against statehood; and that the population figures in the region continued to remain very low.[58] A similar bill admitting Nebraska to statehood was passed over the president's veto after a special session of the Nebraska Territorial Legislature allowed black suffrage.[59] The Colorado Legislative Assembly failed to accomplish the task, and the statehood bill failed the two-thirds majority.

In the Fortieth Congress, national and local politics combined to subvert Colorado statehood. At the federal level, the Radical Republicans had achieved their necessary strength in the election of 1866 and no longer needed additional support to enact their agenda. In Colorado, the struggle over statehood had divided the Republican Party. The "Denver Crowd," under the leadership of John Evans and Jerome Chaffee, supported statehood and Denver as the capital city, while the "Golden Crowd," under Henry M. Teller, opposed Colorado becoming a state and favored Golden as the capital of the territory. The breach had grown since 1864 to the point that Teller had gone to Washington, D.C., in 1866 to voice his opposition directly to congressional representatives.[60] In addition, the statehood movement claimed the election not only of state officers but also congressional representatives, while the territorial government continued to operate as the legitimate administration. Several attempts were made to obtain the Legislative Assembly's approval of statehood; all but one failed. The latter passed only because it contained a provision to extend Colorado's borders far enough into Wyoming to incorporate the Union Pacific Railroad into Colorado's boundaries.[61] Bills were introduced into every session of Congress between 1867 and 1873, but they received little attention as there was no compelling national or local issue that could override Colorado's principal obstacle to admittance: lack of population.

In Colorado, the movement opposing statehood gained momentum between 1867 and 1873. One indication of its strength was the election of Henry Teller as chairman of the Republican Party. In 1868, Teller went to Washington, D.C., again to counter the pro-state activities of Evans and Chaffee. He arrived too late to testify and, instead, submitted a memorial to Congress outlining the arguments and commenting on the pro-staters' claim that Colorado was a growing area with a population of 75,000 to 100,000. To the contrary, Teller proved a population of only about 30,000 and was so confident in his anti-state position that he challenged Congress to submit statehood to a vote of the people of Colorado Territory.[62] A mass meeting of citizens in Golden memorialized Congress in support of Teller's argument. Senator Roscoe Conkling adopted Teller's position and insisted upon a vote of the citizens of Colorado Territory before any consideration of admission.[63] This move effectively killed the statehood movement in the 1860s in Colorado and in the Congress.

TERRITORIAL GOVERNMENT, 1865–1876

Between 1865 and 1876, Colorado experienced tremendous change. Five men served as territorial governors over the eleven-year period, but only the last, John L. Routt, achieved success both in producing economic prosperity and in winning personal popularity. Colorado experienced the boom and bust of a developing economy in its last decade as a territory. The boom times brought business, industry, and increased population. The busts, especially the Panic of 1873, threatened the stability of Colorado's economy and the supremacy of the Republican Party. In the end, as it had in the 1860s, the national politics involved in Reconstruction opened the door for Colorado statehood.

Pennsylvanian Alexander Cummings replaced the popular John Evans in October 1865 and became Colorado's third territorial governor in four years. He arrived under suspect circumstances. When the Civil War began, he was appointed as a special purchasing agent for the War Department and was responsible for a $2 million budget. His purchases resulted in poorly made or out-of-date equipment arriving in the field, and after an investigation, he was removed. In 1864, Lincoln appointed him superintendent of troops of African descent for the state of Arkansas, and Andrew Johnson promoted him to the rank of brigadier general.[64] He arrived in the middle of the drive for statehood that consumed the state and split the Republican Party. Cummings did not support statehood because the proposed state constitution denied black suffrage; however, most Coloradans felt it was actually because it would cut short his term in office.[65] Controversy surrounded him again when the 1866 election for territorial delegate was contested. George Chilcott, the pro-statehood candidate, appeared to have defeated Alexander C. Hunt, who opposed statehood. The Territorial Board of Canvassers declared Chilcott the victor, but Cummings declared that Hunt had won. The House Committee on Elections finally declared Chilcott the winner and recognized him as the territorial delegate for Colorado.[66] After Coloradans submitted petitions for his removal from office, Cummings resigned to become collector of internal revenue for the Fourth District of Pennsylvania.

Alexander C. Hunt, originally of Illinois, replaced Cummings as the fourth territorial governor. He had been successful in the California gold fields, lost his fortune in the Panic of 1857, and had come to Colorado in the rush of 1859. He served as judge for the grassroots Vigilante Committee of the territory and assisted in establishing law and order in those early days. When Colorado became a territory, Lincoln appointed him marshal of the territory. He also served as superintendent of Indian affairs and as territorial treasurer. He was the same A. C. Hunt who lost the contested election of 1866 to George Chilcott. His good relations with the Ute tribes on the Western Slope allowed not only the negotiation of a favorable treaty in 1868 but also the rescue of Senator Schyler Colfax, Illinois governor Bross, and prominent Denver officials from a party of Arapahos.[67] President Grant removed the locally popular Hunt from office and replaced him with a personal friend in June 1869.

Edward Moody McCook had originally come to Colorado in 1859 as a prospector in Gregory Gulch. He moved to Central City in Gilpin County, practiced law, and was one of its wealthiest citizens when the Civil War began. He returned to his home state of Ohio and served honorably during the war. He achieved both the rank of brigadier general and the friendship of Ulysses S. Grant. After the war, he served as minister to Hawaii before Grant appointed him territorial governor of Colorado. McCook's four years as the fifth governor were bumpy, to say the least.[68]

The years 1869 to 1873 saw great economic progress and development in Colorado Territory. In June 1870, the Denver Pacific Railroad connected the area to the Union Pacific at Cheyenne. The Kansas and Pacific arrived in Denver two months later and provided a southern link to Kansas City and St. Louis. The year 1870 also saw the beginning of the Denver and Rio Grande Western Railroad that its founder, William Jackson Palmer, intended to build to Mexico City. At the same time, agricultural efforts began on the eastern Plains. Both Union Colony, which would become present-day Greeley, and the Chicago-Colorado Colony, which would become present-day Longmont, established successful agricultural enterprises in 1870. The success of these two efforts proved that Colorado was not the "Great American Desert," as Major Stephen Long had thought fifty years earlier. Mining activity improved as Professor Nathaniel Hill introduced new methods that allowed lode gold to be separated more easily and quickly from its combination with quartz. Numerous gold strikes in the San Juan Mountains of southwestern Colorado ignited yet another rush to Colorado. Railroads, agriculture, and mining combined to increase Colorado's population and cause the creation of six new counties in 1874. Unfortunately, Governor McCook did not benefit from this activity. Instead, his administration was linked to graft and corruption in dealing with the Utes. He had appointed his brother-in-law, James B. Thompson, as special agent to the Utes. Together, they made a $22,000 profit on a cattle sale to their wards. Although a federal investigation cleared him of any wrongdoing, the people of Colorado demanded McCook's removal so vehemently that President Grant replaced him in April of 1873.[69]

Samuel Hitt Elbert's appointment as Colorado's sixth territorial governor was welcomed in the territory. He had served as territorial secretary under John Evans and had married Evans's daughter, Josephine. Conflict with Alexander Cummings led to Elbert's removal, but he was elected to the Territorial Legislature in 1868 and became the chairman of the Colorado Republican Party in 1872. Elbert believed that irrigation was the key to agricultural success in the West. He called the first Western Irrigation Conference in October 1873 to promote the development of irrigation and canal systems. One of his first acts as governor was to host President Grant's visit to Colorado in 1873. He oversaw the negotiation of the Brunot Treaty of 1873 with the Utes that opened the San Juans to mining and settlement. He was a popular governor, yet Grant removed him because Elbert's enemies in Washington, D.C., had whispered that he was responsible not only for splitting the Republican Party but was also involved in suspect railroad and land speculation.[70]

Edward M. McCook returned as governor in June 1874. Insect plagues, the Panic of 1873, and party division marked Governor McCook's second term. Rocky Mountain locusts invaded Colorado in 1874 and 1875. Colorado farm losses were estimated at $4 million.[71] Gold discoveries in the Black Hills drew population away from Colorado, and at the same time, the economic effects of the Panic of 1873 began to be felt in the territory. Railroad construction halted for lack of funds. Real estate values plummeted as farms and businesses failed and the population diminished. Economic hard times gave rise to political hard times as well.

Republicans in Colorado split over support of Governor McCook. Some felt that turning away from McCook meant the rejection of President Grant. Others saw McCook as a "carpetbagger" and an example of the graft and corruption of the Grant administration. The split in the Republican faithful allowed the election of Thomas Patterson, a Democrat, to the office of territorial delegate in 1874. The election sent shock waves through the party and the administration, had a direct effect on Colorado statehood, and resulted in the removal of McCook for the second time.

John L. Routt replaced McCook as the last territorial governor in 1875. Born in Kentucky, he grew to adulthood in Illinois and served in town and county government until the Civil War, in which he served gallantly. After the war, his organizational talents gained him county offices and appointments as U.S. marshall and assistant postmaster general. It was his honesty and exceptional administrative skills that won him the appointment to Colorado.[72] Routt's principal focus as territorial governor was to meet the terms of an Enabling Act passed in 1874 that offered Colorado yet another chance at statehood.

STATEHOOD ACHIEVED

Governor Routt and the Colorado Republican Party faced an uphill battle for statehood in 1874. Eastern newspapers and politicians still felt that Colorado's population was insufficient for admission. After fifteen years of Republican domination, the breach in Republican Party ranks threatened that Colorado would become a Democratic state and undermine Republican power nationally. In the end, the rise of the Democratic Party nationally and in Colorado provided the compelling motive for Colorado's admission in 1876.

President Ulysses S. Grant favored Colorado statehood. His message to Congress in 1873 contained a recommendation for the passage of an Enabling Act for the admission of Colorado as a state.[73] Congress resisted, however, as the controversy surrounding the turnstile appointments and replacements of

Governors McCook and Elbert had created instability in Colorado's political situation. Jerome Chaffee, now Colorado's territorial delegate to the Congress, was successful in introducing an enabling bill in the House of Representatives in December 1873 as well as several petitions supporting statehood from Colorado Territory. He succeeded in gaining the bill's passage in the House, but it ran into trouble in the Senate. In August 1874, it was tabled. The volatility of Colorado's politics and its poor condition economically caused senators to be wary of Colorado's future.[74] In September 1874, Thomas Patterson, a Democrat, was elected territorial delegate. Republican senators feared that this was a portent of the future and that Colorado would emerge as a bastion of the Democratic Party in the elections of 1876. Patterson arrived in Washington, D.C., in January 1875. He immediately formed an alliance with the outgoing delegate, Republican Jerome Chaffee, in which each would attempt to gain support from his party for Colorado statehood. Patterson faced the more difficult task. The presidential election of 1876 looked to be a close race. Democrats feared that the admission of Colorado, Republican since 1860, would hurt their chances of winning. Patterson offered his election as proof that Democrats could win the state and that it would deliver three Democratic electoral votes in 1876.[75] The Patterson-Chaffee alliance worked. The bill passed the House with a five-vote margin. Eleven Democrats voted in favor of the bill. Chaffee exerted considerable skill and influence as well, using his long association with Republicans in Congress to convince them of a Republican victory in 1876. Final passage occurred on the final day of the First Session of the Forty-third Congress.[76]

The Enabling Act for Colorado statehood called for the election of delegates to a constitutional convention in October and for a meeting of the delegates to occur in December. Thirty-nine delegates convened in Denver that winter to frame a state constitution. Their overriding goal was to create a document that would be acceptable to the majority of Colorado voters and result, finally, in statehood. In this effort they generally set partisanship aside, as demonstrated in the message of the president of the convention, Joseph C. Wilson, "No act of mine shall be tainted with the slightest semblance of partisanship or sectional spirit. Here I know no party, but the entire people; no section but the entire Territory."[77] The convention continued until March 15, 1876, a session of eighty-six days. Much of the work was routine in nature. Colorado's convention utilized the recently revised Illinois constitution (1870) as a model and produced a document that established the executive, legislative, and judicial branches typical of states with bicameral legislatures. It also incorporated the basic Bill of Rights as they appear in the U.S. Constitution. There were, however, four issues that provided some controversy at the meeting: religion, railroad regulation, women's suffrage, and water rights.

Regarding religion, seven petitions from Colorado citizens requesting the recognition of God in the constitution were presented. The general trend among states after 1840 was to include such recognition; however, Colorado's delegates seemed to follow the lead of the framers of the U.S. Constitution and chose a compromise. The preamble to the Colorado constitution acknowledges a "Supreme Ruler of the Universe."[78] A second religious issue, that of public support for parochial schools, was not compromised. Article 9, Section 7, of the constitution prohibits any public entity from appropriating, paying from public funds, or donating land, money, or property to any church or for any sectarian purpose. Finally, the delegates managed the problem of taxing religious property through Article 10, Section 5, which allowed that property used for exclusively religious purposes would be exempt from taxation.

Railroad regulation proved more difficult to manage. The Society of the Patrons of Husbandry, known commonly as the Grange, had emerged in the 1870s as the voice of agricultural interests in the United States. One of its principal tenets called for state regulation of railroads and the rates they charged. The Panic of 1873, a national depression caused by the overexpansion of railroads, had hit Colorado hard by 1876. Railroads were not held in great favor. There existed great sympathy for inserting a version of the "Granger Laws," acts limiting railroad rates, into the constitution. At the same time, Colorado needed to be able to attract business and industry. Strict controls in the constitution would have limiting effects on growth. The compromise can be found in Article 15 of the Colorado constitution. It forbade consolidation of parallel or competing rail lines, unreasonable discrimination in establishing rates, and the creation of corporations by special law. That same article also gave the General Assembly the power to annul any corporate charter, declared all railways public roads, and designated all railroad companies as common carriers.

The Colorado convention proved both cautious and conservative concerning women's suffrage. Fearing that granting women's suffrage would alienate too many middle-of-the-road voters, the delegates chose to allow women to vote in school elections and to hold office in school districts. They further allowed the General Assembly to enact laws that granted women's suffrage at any time in the future without constitutional amendment.[79]

In the last controversial issue, the delegates dealt with Colorado's aridity. They incorporated practices that had emerged in mining districts and farming communities since 1860 into the constitution. Article 16, Sections 5 and 6, established the state's right to control water supplies within its borders and enumerated the doctrine of prior appropriation: "[T]he right to divert the unappropriated waters of any natural stream to beneficial uses shall never be denied. Priority of appropriation shall give the better right as between those using water for the same purpose." This doctrine at once ended the time-honored practice of Riparian Water Law that had served farmers east of the Mississippi River well and provided the foundation for water diversion, storage, and use throughout the West.

Finally, the delegates adopted a "Schedule" that set the dates for the approval of the constitution and the election of state officers. Sections 19 and 20 of the schedule allowed the General Assembly to choose the electors for the Electoral College in the election of 1876 and the public to choose the electors after 1876.

The legislature was to appoint the electors in an unprinted bill, without committee hearings, with one day of debate, and without the governor's approval.[80] The date for approval of the constitution was set for July 1, 1876, when Coloradans in an almost four to one majority (15,443 in favor, 4,062 against) adopted the work of the convention.[81] As presidential approval was assured, July 4, 1876, was cause for widespread celebration. The Board of Canvassers validated the vote on July 24, and on August 1, 1876, President Ulysses S. Grant issued the proclamation that made Colorado the thirty-eighth state. The addition of Colorado was felt immediately in the disputed national election of 1876.

Coloradans went to the polls on October 3, 1876, to elect their first state government. John L. Routt, the last territorial governor, became the first state governor. Republicans elected fifty of the seventy-five members of the General Assembly and held majorities in both houses. The first state legislature convened on November 1, 1876, in Denver. On November 7, the General Assembly elected three Republican presidential electors. Each of these men, in turn, cast their ballots in December 1876 for the Republican candidate, Rutherford B. Hayes.[82] The Electoral College reported 184 electoral votes for Democrat Samuel Tilden, the winner of the popular vote, and 165 electoral votes for the Republican Hayes, with twenty votes not cast because of disputed election returns. Because Colorado's three electoral votes had been added with its admission, a majority consisted of 185 electoral votes. Neither Tilden nor Hayes had achieved a majority. The national election was eventually decided after a joint congressional committee composed of five senators, five representatives, and five justices of the Supreme Court determined to whom the disputed returns should be allocated. Initially, the committee was balanced with seven Republicans, seven Democrats, and one Independent. However, the Independent member resigned to take another position. He was replaced with a Republican. The committee then voted according to party lines and awarded all twenty electoral votes to Hayes, giving him 185 and a majority. Congress accepted this action on March 2 after a series of agreements, known generally as the Compromise of 1877, had been negotiated. Historians mark the removal of federal troops from the South, one of the agreements in the compromise, as the end of the Reconstruction Era. Because Colorado's admission added three electoral votes, Samuel Tilden, whose total in the Electoral College would have brought him the presidency before Colorado's admission, lost, and Republicans retained their hold on the presidency. Chaffee had been right, and Patterson wrong. Colorado returned to its Republican roots in 1876, entered the Union as the Centennial State, and proved to be the deciding factor in the most disputed election of the nineteenth century.

SUMMARY

Colorado passed its territorial incubation amid the turbulence of the Civil War and Reconstruction. All the elements under national consideration appeared in Colorado during its apprenticeship. Black suffrage, the conflicts between the president and Congress, Native American removal and resettlement, railroad construction, and economic growth all played significant roles in the many attempts Coloradans made to become a state in the fifteen years between 1861 and 1876. Republican national politics drove statehood attempts in 1864, 1866, and 1874, but there existed a grassroots impulse for statehood from the very beginning of settlement in Pikes Peak Country. Unwilling to comply with national directives for admission, suffering the stigma of Sand Creek, and divided politically in 1866, Colorado Territory paused to gain its strength and secure its position along the Front Range of the Rocky Mountains before once again attempting statehood.

As economic conditions improved in the territory and as population grew in the 1870s, renewed efforts emerged to enter the Union. By 1874, Colorado had sufficiently matured economically to support state government and had adequately developed politically to meet the needs of national politicians who were seeking additional Republican support in Congress and in the Electoral College. Local and national agendas finally matched in 1876, and Colorado emerged as the thirty-eighth state. It was a momentous year. The nation celebrated its centennial in July, welcomed a new state in August, and conducted one of the most controversial elections in its history in November. It would be another sixteen years, until 1889, before any more stars would be added to the flag. When that occurred, both North and South Dakota entered the Union.

NOTES

1. LeRoy R. Hafen, *Colorado and Its People: A Narrative and Topical History of the Centennial State*, 2 vols. (New York: Lewis Historical Publishing Company, 1948) vol. 1, p. 145; Carl Ubbelohde, Maxine Benson, and Duane Smith, *A Colorado History*, 8th ed. (Boulder, CO: Pruett Publishing, 2001), p. 58.

2. Jerome C. Smiley et al., *Semi-Centennial History of the State of Colorado*, 2 vols. (New York: Lewis Publishing Company, 1913), vol. 1, p. 294.

3. Edwin James, *Account of an Expedition From Pittsburgh to the Rocky Mountains...Under Command of Major S. H. Long of the U.S. Topographical Engineers*, vols. 14–17 of Reuben Gold Thwaites, ed., *Early Western Travels, 1748–1846* (New York: AMS Press, 1966), vol. 15, pp. 223, 248–251, 261.

4. Ibid., vol. 17, p. 147.

5. Smiley, *Semi-Centennial History*, vol. 1, p. 296.

6. Ovando J. Hollister, *The Mines of Colorado* (Springfield, MA: Samuel Bowles and Company, 1867), p. 18.

7. Herman S. Davis, ed., *Reminiscences of General William Larimer and of his Son William H. H. Larimer* (Lancaster, PA: New Era Printing Company, 1918), pp. 78, 91.

8. An Act Establishing and Organizing the Counties of Montana, El Paso, Oro, Broderick, and Frémont. MSS 11-24, Steven Hart Library, Colorado Historical Society, Denver.

9. LeRoy R. Hafen, "Steps to Statehood in Colorado," *Colorado Magazine* 3 (3) (August 1926): 97.

10. J. L. Frazier, "Prologue to Colorado Territory," *Colorado Magazine* 38 (3) (July 1961): 163.

11. Smiley, *Semi-Centennial History*, vol. 1, p. 298.

12. *Rocky Mountain News*, April 23, 1859.

13. Ibid.

14. *Rocky Mountain News*, May 7, 1859.

15. Ibid., June 7, 1859.

16. Ibid.

17. *Missouri Republican*, May 25, 1859, quoted in Le Roy Hafen, ed., *Colorado Gold Rush: Contemporary Letters and Reports, 1858–1859*, vol. 10, Southwest Historical Series (Glendale, CA: Arthur H. Clark, 1942), p. 286.

18. *Rocky Mountain News*, August 1–4, 1859.

19. Ibid., August 6, 1859.

20. Ibid., September 17, 1859.

21. Ibid., October 20, 1859.

22. Ibid., November 10, 1859.

23. Hafen, *Colorado and Its People*, p. 209.

24. *Rocky Mountain News*, December 23, 1859.

25. Ibid., October 7, 1860.

26. Smiley, *Semi-Centennial History*, pp. 300–301.

27. Ibid., p. 302.

28. Ibid.

29. *Congressional Globe*, 36th Cong., 1st Sess., January 5, 1860, p. 342.

30. Charles J. Klapper, ed., *Indian Affairs: Laws and Treaties* (Washington, DC: Government Printing Office, 1904), pp. 807–809.

31. *Congressional Globe*, 36th Cong., 2nd Sess., February 4, 1861, p. 729.

32. Ibid., pp. 1003, 1205, 1274.

33. *Rocky Mountain News*, July 10, 1861.

34. Ibid., August 24, 1861.

35. Duane A. Smith, *The Birth of Colorado* (Norman: University of Oklahoma Press, 1989), pp. 18–19.

36. Military rosters and tables of ranks are taken from W. C. Whitford, *Colorado Volunteers in the Civil War: The New Mexico Campaign in 1862* (Denver: State Historical and Natural History Society, 1906; reprint ed., Boulder: Pruett Press, 1963).

37. Smith, *Birth of Colorado*, pp. 20–21.

38. Ibid., p. 22.

39. Smiley, *Semi-Centennial History*, vol. 1, p. 383.

40. Smith, *Birth of Colorado*, p. 25.

41. Ibid., pp. 26–27, 112–113.

42. Personal information about Colorado governors available: www.archives.state.co.us/gov.

43. Information about Indian activity and Evans response taken from "Interview with ex-Governor Evans," mss. P-L329, P-L123, Bancroft Library, Berkeley, California.

44. *Rocky Mountain News*, July 18, 1864.

45. Ibid., August 1, 1864.

46. Ibid., August 11, 1864.

47. Hafen, *Colorado and Its People*, p. 312.

48. Details of the march, the attack, and the aftermath are taken from U.S. Congress, Senate, "Massacre of Cheyenne Indians," Report of the Joint Commission on the Conduct of the War, 38th Cong., 2nd Sess., 1865.

49. *Rocky Mountain News*, December 7, 8, 13, 21.

50. Evans, *Reply of the Governor*, pp. 2, 15.

51. *Congressional Globe*, 38th Cong., 1st Sess., February 24, March 22, June 20, 1864, pp. 788, 1227, 1228, 3087. A supplemental law changed the date to the second Tuesday of September.

52. *Daily Miner's Register*, July 8, 14, 15, 19, 312; August 3, 4, 1864.

53. *Rocky Mountain News*, August 1, 2, 4, 6, 12, 17, 20; September 1, 1864.

54. Ibid., September 13, 1865.

55. U.S. Congress, Senate, 39th Cong., 1st Sess., 1866, Executive Document No. 10.

56. U.S. Congress, Senate, 39th Cong., 1st Sess., 1866, Executive Document No. 45.

57. U.S. Congress, Senate, 39th Cong., 2nd Sess., 1867, Miscellaneous Document No. 3.

58. U.S. Congress, Senate, 39th Cong., 2nd Sess., 1867, Executive Document No. 7.

59. Works Progress Administration, *Nebraska: A Guide to the Cornhusker State* (New York: Viking Press, 1939), pp. 55–56.

60. *Congressional Globe*, 39th Cong., 1st Sess., March 12, 1866, p. 1328.

61. Elmer Ellis, "Colorado's First Fight for Statehood, 1865–1869," *Colorado Magazine* 8 (1) (January 1931): 29.

62. U.S. Congress, Senate, 40th Cong., 2nd Sess., 1868, Miscellaneous Document No. 31.

63. U.S. Congress, Senate, 40th Cong., 2nd Sess., 1868, Miscellaneous Document No. 40.

64. "Alexander Cummings," available: www.archives.state.co.us/gov.

65. Smiley, *Semi-Centennial History*, p. 374.

66. U.S. Congress, House of Representatives, 40th Cong., 1st Sess., Committee on Elections, 1867, Report No. 3.

67. "Alexander Cameron Hunt," available: www.archives.state.co.us/govs.

68. "Edward Moody McCook," available: www.archives.state.co.us.govs.

69. Smiley, *Semi-Centennial History*, pp. 376–377.

70. "Samuel Hitt Elbert," available: www.archives.state.co.us/govs; see also Smiley, *Semi-Centennial History*, pp. 379–380.

71. *Greeley Tribune*, November 1875.

72. *Rocky Mountain News*, February 4, 10, 23; March 21, 23; April 1, 1875.

73. J. D. Richardson, ed., *A Compilation of the Messages and Papers of the Presidents, 1789–1899*, 10 vols. (Washington, DC: Government Printing Office, 1896–1899), 2: 268–287.

74. Frank Hall, *History of the State of Colorado*, 4 vols. (Chicago: Blakely Printing Company, 1890) vol. 2, pp. 268–287.

75. Thomas Patterson, Washington, D.C., to Katherine M. Patterson, Denver, Colorado, February 16, 1875. Thomas M. Patterson Family Papers, Western History Collection, University of Colorado, Boulder.

76. *Congressional Record*, 43rd Cong., 1st Sess., December 8, 1873, January 6, 12, 19, 26, February 20, March 18, 19, June 8, 1874, pp. 89, 431, 602, 770, 938, 1692, 2239, 2275, 4691.

77. Proceedings of the Constitutional Convention Held in Denver, December 20, 1875, p. 19.

78. C. B. Goodykoontz, "Some Controversial Questions before the Colorado Constitutional Convention of 1876," *Colorado Magazine* 17 (3) (July 1940): 6. See also the Colorado Constitution: Preamble.

79. Colorado Constitution, Article 7, "Suffrage and Elections."

80. Colorado Constitution, Schedule, Sections 19, 20.

81. *Rocky Mountain News*, July 2, 1876.

82. Frank Hall, *History of Colorado*, p. 357.

BIBLIOGRAPHY

Colorado Division of State Archives and Public Records. *Colorado Territorial Officers and Members and Officers of the Legislative Assemblies under Territorial Government*. Denver: Colorado State Archives, 1959.

Ellis, Elmer. "Colorado's First Fight for Statehood, 1865–1868." *Colorado Magazine* 8 (1931): 23–30.

Frazier, J. L. "Prologue to Colorado Territory." *Colorado Magazine* 37 (1961): 161–173.

Goodykoontz, C. B. "Some Controversial Questions Before the Colorado Constitutional Convention of 1876." *Colorado Magazine* 17 (1940): 1–17.

Hafen, LeRoy R. "Steps to Statehood in Colorado." *Colorado Magazine* 3 (1926): 97–110.

_____. *The Colorado Gold Rush: Contemporary Letters and Reports, 1858–59*. Glendale, CA: Arthur H. Clark, 1941.

_____, ed. *Colorado and Its People: A Narrative and Topical History of the Centennial State*. Vol. 1. New York: Lewis Historical Publishing, 1948.

Hall, Frank. *History of the State of Colorado*. Vol. 2. Chicago: Blakely Printing, 1890.

Kelsey, Harry E., Jr. *Frontier Capitalist: The Life of John Evans*. Boulder: Pruett Publishing, 1969.

Lohse, Joyce B. *First Governor, First Lady: John and Eliza Routt of Colorado*. Palmer Lake, CO: Filter Press, 2002.

Smiley, Jerome C. *Semi-Centennial History of Colorado*. Vol. 1. Chicago: Lewis Publishing Company, 1913.

Smith, Duane A. *The Birth of Colorado: A Civil War Perspective*. Norman: University of Oklahoma Press, 1989.

Smith, Robert E. "Thomas M. Patterson, Colorado Statehood, and the Election of 1876." *Colorado Magazine* 53 (1976): 153–162.

Stone, Wilbur F., ed. *History of Colorado*. Vol. 2. Chicago: S. J. Clarke, 1918.

Ubbelohde, Carl, Maxine Benson, and Duane A. Smith. *A Colorado History*. 8th ed. Boulder, CO: Pruett Publishing, 2001.

THE STATE OF CONNECTICUT

Ratified the Constitution of the United States: January 9, 1788

Ellen Holmes Pearson

INTRODUCTION

The thirteen North American colonies shared the common experience of revolution and nation building, but they each approached independence, confederation, and nationhood in very distinctive ways. Connecticut, the fifth colony to receive a charter from England and the fifth state to ratify the U.S. Constitution, helped to shape America's identity from the earliest decades of England's North American settlement. Its leaders helped to set the standards by which all subsequent applicants for statehood were admitted. Connecticut's colonial distinctions included its Puritan background, which created a special kinship with Massachusetts, the first Puritan colony. It eventually acquired a charter-based government, which gave that colony more autonomy than royal or proprietary colonies. This charter served the colony so well that the General Assembly chose to retain it after independence. Connecticut's charter-sanctioned possession of territory in the western reaches of North America—and its stubborn desire to cling to those lands—gave the state a key role in the ratification controversy surrounding the Articles of Confederation and in determining the success or failure of the Articles. Finally, Constitutional Convention delegate Roger Sherman helped to save the convention with his compromise proposal during the contentious debates over representation. This essay will address those issues as they pertain to Connecticut's role in the founding and early development of the United States.

COLONIAL DEVELOPMENT AND GOVERNMENT

Connecticut was distinguished from most other English colonies by its Puritan roots and its generous charter. The colony's first settlers were Puritans, a

Connecticut

Territorial Development:

- King Charles II granted Connecticut a royal charter, 1662
- Continental Congress approved Declaration of Independence from Great Britain, July 4, 1776
- Great Britain formally recognized American independence through the Treaty of Paris, September 3, 1783
- Connecticut became the fifth state to ratify the U.S. Constitution, January 9, 1788

Capitals Prior to Statehood:

- New Haven and Hartford, twin capitals from 1701–1788

State Capitals:

- New Haven and Hartford, twin capitals, 1788–1875
- Hartford, independent of New Haven, 1875–present

Origin of State Name: "Connecticut" comes from a Mohican and Algonquin word, "Quinnehtukqut," which means "beside the long tidal river."

First Governor: Samuel Huntington
Governmental Organization: Bicameral
Population at Statehood: 237,655
Geographical Size: 4,845 square miles

Calvinist community of English Protestants. They believed in predestination, which denied that people could earn salvation through good works. Instead, they believed their fates were predetermined by God. The Puritans emphasized the Bible in worship, and they were determined to simplify the Church of England by abandoning all remaining vestiges of Catholicism, such as saints, indulgences, and most of the sacraments. Their colony's existence was affirmed with a royal charter in which they were given considerable autonomy, compared to most other colonies. This freedom allowed Connecticut to grow and develop with relatively little interference from England, and the charter gave the colony's freemen considerable control over their political and social destinies.

Migrations from Massachusetts and *The Fundamental Orders*

Connecticut was settled by migrants from the Massachusetts Bay Colony. One of the most prominent founders of the new colony was Thomas Hooker, a Puritan minister who arrived in Boston in 1634. Hooker first settled in Newtown (now Cambridge), but his contingent soon began to agitate for more land or emigration to a place where they could procure more land. In September 1634, they submitted a petition to the Massachusetts General Court asking permission to immigrate to the Connecticut River Valley west of Boston. Their motivations were primarily economic. They wanted the abundant fertile land that lay to the south and west of the Massachusetts colony, but they also pointed out that their presence in the area would discourage Dutch claims to the territory, which, left unchecked, would most certainly encroach on English territory. In 1635, the general court approved their petition to emigrate, provided they remain under Massachusetts' governance.[1]

At first, Connecticut Valley settlers had to compete with Native Americans who inhabited the area and considered the valley their territory as well as Dutch traders who considered the English settlers intruders on their own commercial claims. These troubles among the Native Americans, English, and Dutch escalated into the Pequot War in 1637, during which the Pequot Indians were virtually exterminated. Throughout the seventeenth century, Connecticut's inhabitants still experienced sporadic conflict with the declining Indian population, and though they had driven the Dutch out of most of Connecticut, the English settlers continued to worry about the Dutch presence to the west of their settlements.

The first English settlers in Connecticut organized their colony around a religious covenant, but they soon found a need to create a civil form of government. In 1639, the freemen of three Connecticut towns, Windsor, Hartford, and Wethersfield, adopted a basic frame of government called *The Fundamental Orders*. Under the new government, only "admitted inhabitants," meaning adult males who usually belonged to the local Puritan church, could vote for deputies from each town. Women, children, apprentices, indentured servants, Negroes, and Indians were excluded from the franchise. The governing body was called the General Court and consisted of a governor and at least six men elected for a one-year term by the "admitted inhabitants" of each town. The governor had to belong to an approved congregation, though he did not have to be a Puritan, and he had to have experience as a magistrate. So that no one man could gain too much power, the governor could not succeed himself in office.

The General Court's powers included making and repealing laws, levying taxes, admitting freemen, granting unassigned lands to towns or individuals, hearing misdemeanor complaints, and dealing "in any other matter that concerns the good of this common welth excepte election of Magestrats." Towns were required to obey all laws passed by the General Court. The magistrates of the General Court, along with the governor, composed a court of justice. There were clearly delineated checks and balances in the government that *The Fundamental Orders* framed. For example, according to *The Fundamental Orders*, the governor convened the General Court, but only the court itself could adjourn the session. Additionally, if the governor or a majority of the magistrates failed to convene the court annually, the freemen could demand a meeting of the General Court. Some historians call this basic frame of government "the first written constitution." Whether or not one agrees with this designation, the document was an important contribution to American political development and it certainly fulfilled Reverend Hooker's vision of a government in which "the foundation of authority is laid in the free consent of the people."[2]

Connecticut Government and Society under the Charter of 1662

In 1649, England's King Charles I was deposed and executed during a civil war that placed Oliver Cromwell and his Puritan associates in power. Under the Puritan government, Connecticut had been allowed to grow without interference from Parliament or Whitehall. Connecticut Colony continued to function and grow under *The Fundamental Orders*, and other migrants founded the New Haven Colony south and west of Connecticut Colony. In 1660, Puritan rule ended with the Stuarts' restoration to the English throne, and enemies of Puritan New England came to power in London. Connecticut's leaders realized that, in the eyes of King Charles II's government, it had no legal foundation to exist as a separate colony because it lacked a charter. In the winter of 1660–1661, Connecticut's legislature appointed Governor John Winthrop, Jr., and eight others to prepare a petition to the king for confirmation of their privileges. Winthrop traveled to London to deliver the petition himself. After considerable lobbying effort and two revisions of Connecticut's petition, Winthrop succeeded in convincing the king in council to approve the petition.

The charter was a very generous document. The king gave Connecticut clear title to the colony and fixed its boundaries as Narragansett Bay to the east, Massachusetts to the north, the Long Island Sound and the Atlantic to the South, and the "South Sea," meaning the Pacific Ocean, to the west. These liberal boundaries would provoke lengthy and contentious disputes with Massachusetts, Rhode Island, New York, and Pennsylvania for years to come. The charter also granted Connecticut considerable political autonomy. It constituted a corporate body known as the "Governour and Company of the English colony of Connecticut in New England and America." Under the charter, freemen held all the "liberties and Immunities" of natural-born Englishmen and they were required to take the oath of supremacy, declaring their loyalty to England and its monarch before they could vote. The charter called for a governor, deputy governor, and twelve assistants, whom the colony's eligible voters, called freemen, elected annually. This group comprised the upper house, which would meet with a lower house of two representatives from each town to conduct colonial business as the General Assembly. The legislature had the power to enact all laws necessary for the colony's operation as long as they did not conflict with English law. The charter declared that the legislature or the governor or deputy governor and six assistants exercised the judicial powers in the colony.[3]

With the implementation of the charter, Connecticut gained political strength, while at the same time it gained strength in numbers. By 1664, Connecticut had annexed the colony of New Haven, and in 1701, the assembly made New Haven a joint capital with Hartford. During the last decades of the seventeenth century, Connecticut's population expanded at an unprecedented rate, primarily because of migration from Massachusetts. The oldest and most populous towns were in the eastern part of the colony, and because the election system favored seniority, the east remained stronger politically even as western towns grew in size.

Economically, Connecticut was not terribly strong. The colony produced livestock, lumber, flour, and New England rum for export to Britain and its holdings. There was no prominent port in Connecticut, so most of Connecticut's imports and exports traveled through New York, Newport, and Boston. Connecticut depended economically on several of its sister colonies, but common religious roots kept Connecticut tied most closely to Massachusetts throughout the colonial period. These ties would become more important during the conflicts leading up to the American Revolution.

Pre-Revolutionary Politics

From 1662, when the king granted a charter to Connecticut, until the French and Indian War in the 1750s, the colony had little contact, economically or politically, with London. Unlike royal or proprietary colonies, whose governors were appointed by either the Crown or the proprietor, Connecticut's charter allowed its freemen to choose their own political officers. Through the late seventeenth and eighteenth centuries, Connecticut governed itself with little interference from London. The General Assembly made law, levied taxes, oversaw land distribution, and generally managed the colony on its own. London had the authority to review the General Assembly's legislation, but except for a brief period (1686–1689) when Connecticut was incorporated into the Dominion of New England, the colony was generally left alone because of the uncoordinated nature of colonial management. In the 1760s, London began to tighten control over all the North American colonies. These control measures led to changes in Connecticut's internal political dynamics. By 1769, those in opposition to Britain's taxation and control measures had come to dominate Connecticut's politics, while those "Tories" who supported Parliament's decisions had been marginalized.

Early Debates over Parliamentary Control: Tories versus Patriots in the 1760s

In the mid-eighteenth century, Connecticut's inhabitants considered themselves loyal Englishmen, and they proved their allegiance during the Seven Years' War, also known as the French and Indian War. This war, fought on both sides of the Atlantic from 1754 to 1763, pitted English and colonial forces against the French and their Native American allies in a war for empire in North America. Connecticut had made a major contribution to the British victory in the French and Indian War. One in five Connecticut males between sixteen and forty-five years of age served in the British army. A few years after the war, however, postwar debt and depression were taking their toll on Connecticut's economy. Across the Atlantic, the British government sought ways to pay off its enormous war debt. Parliament settled on a series of imposts to be levied in the colonies as a way to generate revenue that would help to retire the war debt.

In 1763, the king and Parliament strengthened the enforcement of the Navigation Acts, and in 1764, the British passed the Sugar Act, which placed a steep tax on foreign sugar imports to mainland colonies. Connecticut governor Thomas Fitch drafted a protest entitled *Reasons why the British Colonies in America, should not be charged with internal taxes*. The arguments set forth in this pamphlet concentrated on the idea that parliamentary taxation would take away the colonists' traditional privileges to consent to internal taxes. Fitch, like other North American colonial officials, feared that the Sugar Act would cut off trade with the French sugar islands, which was much more profitable for merchants than the trade with the British sugar islands. The governor complained to London that it was unfair to satisfy the demands of the British

West Indian planters for greater profit at the expense of Connecticut's economic health.

The Stamp Act of 1765 caused even greater outcry. When Governor Fitch heard that Parliament was considering such a measure, he summoned a committee to draft objections to the legislation. These objections contained the popular complaint that the Stamp Act was taxation without consent, because Connecticut residents were not represented in Parliament. The committee also asserted that, by the Charter of 1662, Connecticut's General Assembly was to be responsible for all necessary internal legislative enactments and that responsibility could not be usurped, even by Parliament.

Despite colonial objections to the Stamp Act, Parliament passed the bill. Once the act was passed, Governor Fitch believed that all protest against the measure should cease. He explained that if Parliament, "in their Superior Wisdom," should judge the act expedient, then it was the colonists' duty to obey it. Fitch then chose to do his constitutional duty and take a Parliament-mandated oath to uphold the Stamp Act. With that act, Fitch sealed his political fate. He defended his actions in a pamphlet, claiming that he had taken the oath to safeguard Connecticut's charter privilege of electing magistrates. He and his constituency in the western part of the state were particularly afraid that if they raised the king's ire over the Stamp Act, he might revoke Connecticut's charter and neighboring New York could then lay claim to lands west of the Connecticut River.

Many Connecticut residents did not agree with Governor Fitch's assessment of the situation. A group of men led by Eliphalet Dyer of Windham and Jonathan Trumbull of Lebanon had already followed Boston's lead and formed the "Sons of Liberty," an organization that directed protests, boycotts, and non-importation agreements in response to Parliament's taxation measures. Connecticut's Sons of Liberty set out to convince Connecticut's freemen that their liberties could only be secured if the colony's "Tory" leaders, who primarily hailed from western Connecticut and were largely Anglican, were rejected and "patriotic" leaders from the heavily Congregationalist eastern part of the state were elected. After Fitch opted to take the oath, the Sons of Liberty embarked on a campaign to defeat the governor in the 1766 election. They argued that with Fitch at the helm, the colony's economic problems would only worsen, because Fitch's support of the tax undermined the economic well-being of the colony.[4]

Another Connecticut political leader whose career was cut short by his stance regarding the Stamp Act was Jared Ingersoll, a New Haven lawyer. He had been in London when the Stamp bill was proposed and Connecticut's General Assembly had asked him to speak against it on their behalf. Like Governor Fitch, however, Ingersoll believed that once the Stamp Act had been approved by Parliament, colonists should obey and enforce it. He even agreed to be a stamp distributor before he departed for Connecticut, a decision for which he was roundly criticized. The Connecticut *Gazette* ridiculed Ingersoll's new position and characterized him as a hypocrite for opposing the measure at first and then jumping on the bandwagon when opposition failed.[5] During a speech in New London, Dr. Benjamin Church, a Boston activist, called Ingersoll an enemy to American liberty. After Church's speech, Ingersoll was hanged in effigy from a tree. Soon thereafter, the Connecticut *Gazette* and the Connecticut *Courant* both reported an incident in which Ingersoll encountered about five hundred "Sons of Liberty" while he traveled to Hartford for a General Assembly meeting. The mob intimidated him into reading a letter of resignation that the Sons had prepared for him, and they forced him to offer three cheers for "liberty and property." Ingersoll was then escorted into Hartford and forced to repeat his resignation and three cheers. The assembly condemned the mob as rioters just before it appointed delegates to the Stamp Act Congress.[6]

The Sons of Liberty's gubernatorial ticket for 1766 included Hartford merchant William Pitkin for governor and Lebanon's Jonathan Trumbull for deputy governor. Despite Parliament's withdrawal of the Stamp Act in February 1766, the easterners maintained their campaign, and Pitkin and Trumbull won the election. Pitkin served as governor until his death in 1769. Trumbull then became governor and served from 1769 to 1784. In elections after 1766, the westerners' attempts to regain their power failed because the Sons of Liberty had already made an alliance with a westerner named William S. Johnson. In return for a seat in the upper house, Johnson delivered considerable support from the western Anglicans.[7] After the 1766 election, Patriot sympathizers remained in power and helped deliver Connecticut to the Patriot cause as conflicts surrounding taxation escalated in the 1760s and 1770s.

Connecticut's Political Stance: Supporting Massachusetts against the Coercive Acts

Any hope that Parliament's offenses against Britain's colonies had been unintentional was dashed when Britain passed the Townshend duties in 1767. It became obvious to the colonists that Parliament intended to exploit the colonies as sources of revenue. In Connecticut, the Sons of Liberty, led by Governor Pitkin, again went into action, organizing nonimportation and non-consumption agreements and boycotting British goods. Colonists began to form intercolonial communication networks, and in places like Boston and Newport, citizens held vocal demonstrations. Connecticut, however, played a largely passive role. The assembly petitioned Parliament in 1768 to drop the new duties, but beyond these legislative measures, there was little action. Part of the reason for this passive stance was that Connecticut imported very few British goods. Because they had no major harbors, they left the active protests to those colonies that boasted large ports. However, Connecticut was close enough to Massachusetts, the center of many of these more vigorous protests, to observe the consequences of their neighbor's bolder actions.

The nonimportation agreements and public demonstrations eventually forced Parliament to rescind all of the Townshend Acts except for the tax on tea, but a series of acts in the early 1770s gave Connecticut leaders more cause for concern. In 1772, Parliament revoked Massachusetts' control over its judicial system by decreeing that members of the Massachusetts Superior Court would receive their salaries from the Crown rather than from the provincial assembly. Next, the Tea Act of 1773 singled out Boston for harsh treatment and demonstrated to Connecticut's citizens just how far the British would go to try to control unruly Bostonians' protests. When Bostonians retaliated with the Tea Party, the Coercive Acts, particularly the Boston Port Act, which closed the port of Boston until the town paid for the tea, provoked hostility among Connecticut's citizens. The Connecticut General Assembly denounced the Port Act and asserted the right of all colonies to be governed by their general assemblies with regard to internal affairs. Many towns pledged to support Bostonians with supplies. Farmington residents burned the Boston Port Act in front of a liberty pole on their town green.

In May 1773, the Connecticut legislature resolved to support the Virginia Resolutions, a series of assertions authored by Patrick Henry. The published form of the Virginia Resolutions argued that colonists had a natural right to enjoy all of the rights and privileges of Englishmen, that taxation by consent was one of those rights, and that the colonial assemblies had an exclusive right to legislate all internal matters. The Connecticut General Assembly also created a standing Committee of Correspondence and Enquiry to "keep up and maintain a correspondence and communication with our sister Colonies, respecting the important considerations mentioned and expressed" in the Virginia Resolutions. The Committees of Correspondence represented the first coordinated effort among the North American colonies to unite and act in concert with one another.

In addition to these acts of unity with the other colonies, the Connecticut assembly sent a petition in response to Parliament's measures. Although the members emphasized their loyalty to King George and their desire to remain his faithful subjects, they called these acts of Parliament "a precedent justly alarming to every British Colony in America." They thought it "expedient and their duty at this time, to renew their claim to the rights, privileges, and immunities of Freeborn Englishmen," to which they believed they were entitled "by the laws of nature, by the royal grant and charter of his late Majesty King Charles the second, and by long and uninterrupted possession" of the colony. The legislators reiterated their belief that, as Englishmen, they had a right to be taxed only by their own consent, "given in person or by their representatives," that they had the right to elect their representatives and to expect that only these representatives would govern the internal workings of their colonies. They also emphasized their concern over the closure of Boston's port, asserting that only an act of the provincial legislature could close a harbor or port in a particular colony, because that was an internal matter. Finally, they expressed their fear of parliamentary acts that could remove those citizens accused of crimes from the place in which the crime allegedly took place and subject them to a summary trial without benefit of a jury of their peers. They called these new measures "unconstitutional and subversive of the liberties and rights of the free subjects of this Colony." This expression of solidarity with Massachusetts and concern for their own welfare sent a loud message to the king in Parliament that Connecticut stood with its sister colonies on these controversial subjects.

Uniting the Colonies under a Continental Congress

In June 1774, the Connecticut General Assembly empowered the Committee of Correspondence to appoint representatives to a Congress of Commissioners, set to convene in Philadelphia the following September. The committee appointed Roger Sherman, Eliphalet Dyer, and Silas Deane to represent the colony at that First Continental Congress. While the First Continental Congress sat in Philadelphia, the Hartford Committee of Correspondence called for a meeting of delegates from all Connecticut towns. All towns except Fairfield sent delegates. The representatives voted to supplement any nonimportation agreement proposed by the Continental Congress with a pledge not to purchase or consume British goods. The Congregationalist clergy was also involved in this effort. They were drawn to the Patriot cause by the fear that more British control in the colony would mean more power for the Anglican Church at the expense of their own church. They used the colony's fast day, August 31, to deliver political sermons against the Coercive Acts. These sermons identified civil liberty and religious liberty as one cause.

By early 1775, Connecticut towns were participating more vigorously in nonimportation of British goods and boycotts on exports of American products to Britain and its other colonies. In March 1775, Connecticut's representatives passed a resolution supporting citizens of the town of Boston, whom they claimed were suffering "under the hand of oppression, grievous and unparalleled hardships and distresses, in consequence of their resolution to support the great principles of constitutional liberty." As it had twice in 1774, the House asked the towns of Connecticut to contribute financially to Boston's relief. Two western Connecticut towns, Newtown and Ridgefield, rejected the nonimportation agreements, and there were significant pockets of resistance to Patriot efforts in Danbury, Redding, and New Milford in the western part of the colony, but even in those areas, loyalists were not numerous enough to wield much influence.[8]

Governor Trumbull attempted a diplomatic solution to the escalating conflict when he appealed to the Earl of Dartmouth, one of the king's "Principal Secretaries of State," to intervene on the colonies' behalf. Trumbull's letter made it clear that Connecticut's leaders considered English and colonial interests to be one, and they were "shocked at the idea of any disunion between them." He assured the earl that they wished "for nothing so much as a speedy and happy settlement upon constitutional grounds" and that the citizens of Connecticut could not "apprehend why it might not be effected if proper steps were taken." Trumbull assured the earl that Connecticut's leaders did not want to impair the authority of Parliament with regard to imperial affairs. However, he asserted their duty to claim and defend the "constitutional rights and liberties derived to us as men and Englishmen; as the descendants of Britons and members of an Empire whose fundamental principle is the liberty and security of the subject." He again expressed Connecticut citizens' loyalty to the king, and he reminded the earl that Connecticut, in the French and Indian War, had spent more than £400,000 sterling for which they had not yet received compensation. Finally, Trumbull expressed his support of Boston, "where we behold many thousands of his Majesty's virtuous and loyal subjects reduced to the utmost distress by the operation of the Port Act," and by Parliament's attempts to deprive Massachusetts citizens of what Trumbull called their "charter-rights." There is no record that the earl replied to Trumbull's letter.

One month after Trumbull's appeal to the Earl of Dartmouth, word of the battle of Lexington and Concord spread through Connecticut. About 3,600 Connecticut Sons of Liberty and militiamen immediately took up arms and joined the Patriots who were gathering at Cambridge. Upon hearing about the conflict at Lexington and Concord, Governor Trumbull again tried to use diplomatic means to relieve the tension. He sent a letter to General Thomas Gage, whom the king had appointed governor of Massachusetts. In the letter, Trumbull reminded Gage of the close ties between Connecticut and Massachusetts. He expressed alarm at Gage's military occupation of Boston "for the declared purpose of carrying into execution certain acts of Parliament," which, in Connecticut's eyes, were "unconstitutional and oppressive." Trumbull informed Gage that he had heard about "such outrages...as would disgrace even barbarians" being committed against Bostonians. "Why," Trumbull asked Gage, was "the town of Boston now shut up?" He assured General Gage that "the people of this Colony...abhor the idea of taking up arms against the troops of their sovereign, and dread nothing so much as the horrors of a civil war." But at the same time, Trumbull promised his Massachusetts counterpart that Connecticut's citizens were "most firmly resolved to defend their rights and privileges to the last extremity; nor will they be restrained from giving aid to their brethren if any unjustifiable attack is made upon them." He ended his letter with a challenge to Gage to defend himself as soon as possible.

Five days later, General Gage penned his reply. He acknowledged the alarming situation and the ties between Massachusetts and Connecticut. He, too, expressed the desire for a peaceful end to the conflicts. However, Gage believed that the only way a peaceful solution could be found was for Connecticut's citizens and those of other colonies to convince Massachusetts' inhabitants "of the impropriety of their past conduct, and to persuade them to return to their allegiance." He defended the decision to fortify Boston, explaining that he had to take this measure to defend imperial magistrates against threats on their lives. He refuted the accusation that his troops had acting barbarously, though he admitted that it was "very possible that in firing into houses from whence they were fired upon, that old people, women, or children, may have suffered: but if any such thing has happened, it was in their defence, and undesigned." He further explained that the "shutting up" of Boston was also an act of self-defense and was necessary "for the defence of those under my command."

With both sides claiming self-defense, the General Assembly in May 1775 published a call to arms that justified the move toward military hostility by pointing out that all of their "dutifull and loyal petitions to the throne for redress of grievances" had been ignored by the king, who instead had characterized colonists' "refusal to surrender our just rights, liberties and immunities" as rebellion. They speculated that Britain's show of force was a way "to force or terrify" them into submitting to Parliament's will. Therefore, the assembly, because of what they considered an imminent threat, appointed nine men as a committee to assist the governor in coordinating and supplying the Connecticut militia when the assembly was not in session. This group, known as the Council of Safety, immediately ordered three companies to march to Boston and join the Connecticut forces that were already there. This was the first wave in many subsequent deployments of militia troops and supplies to Boston. In October 1775, the assembly appointed Roger Sherman, Oliver Wolcott, and Samuel Huntington as delegates to represent Connecticut at the General Congress of the United Colonies in America for the following year.

Political Separation from Great Britain Begins

The acts of the December 1775 session of the General Assembly were the last to be published under the royal coat of arms, signifying the first steps in moving from colony to independent state. Other important changes in the language that assemblymen used to refer to themselves and to their polity followed in the May 1776 session. The assembly repealed "An Act against High Treason," an important move because, under this law, any act against the British monarch or government was considered a capital crime and by this time Connecticut's representatives were not merely contemplating but were acting on ideas of separation. They also removed the king's name and any reference to a monarch from all oaths. For example, under the new law, the oath for freemen read thus:

> "You, A.B. being by the providence of God an inhabitant within this Colony of Connecticut, and now to be made free of the same, do swear by the ever

living God to be true and faithfull to the Governor and Company of said Colony and the government thereof as now established and as expressed by the Charter."

Similar acts over the next few assembly sessions expunged references to the king and to British government. These changes in legal language testified to the changes in political attitudes toward Great Britain. No longer did Connecticut's leaders talk about reconciliation with the parent country. Instead, they prepared for separation. Through legislative acts, treason had become loyalty and these changes in language and law signified a change in the direction of their loyalties.

The spring 1776 assembly sessions saw even more decisive changes. Connecticut was no longer merely flirting with language, but along with the other colonies began to move away from England and toward a solid alliance with one another. In May 1776, the assembly issued a call to arms in which the representatives stated that the United Colonies were "being threatned [sic] with the whole force of Great Britain." Therefore, the representatives advised "all persons of every rank and denomination, to furnish themselves...with good sufficient fire-arms, and other warlike accoutrements" and for all able-bodied men to "equip themselves so as to be in readiness for mutual defence against our common enemy." In this call to arms, the assembly hearkened back to its Puritan heritage by cautioning Connecticut's citizens that their attempts to preserve their liberty would "prove vain and abortive unless attended with the blessing of Heaven." This blessing, however, would not be forthcoming unless the colonists showed "sincere repentance and reformation." To that end, the assembly members asked the inhabitants of Connecticut "to promote and cultivate charity and benevolence one towards another, to abstain from every species of extortion and oppression, sincerely to repent and break off from every sin, folly, and vice." If they looked to heaven for their deliverance and attended to the welfare of their neighbors, they would, according to the assembly, succeed. In the colonial period, the pulpit was one of the most efficient disseminators of information. The assembly therefore ordered that the call to arms be printed and read in "all the religious societies in this Colony."

Governor Trumbull followed this call to arms with a proclamation in June 1776. The language in this document represented a drastic departure from the petitions Connecticut had generated only a short while before. Instead of professing loyalty to the monarch, Trumbull condemned King George as "an unnatural King" who had "violated his sacred Obligations, and by the Advice of evil Counselors, attempted to wrest from us, their Children, the sacred Rights we justly claim, and which have been ratified and established by solemn Compact with, and recognized by, his Predecessors and Fathers." Trumbull asserted that the United American Colonies had been forced "to take up Arms for the Defence of all that is sacred and dear to Freemen, and make their solemn Appeal to Heaven for the Justice of their Cause, and resist Force by Force." Therefore, he informed Connecticut's citizens, "the honorable CONGRESS of the *American Colonies*, united for mutual Defence" had asked the colonies to raise a number of men and militia to defend against "the soon expected Attack and Invasion of those who are our Enemies without a Cause." Connecticut's share of this force would be seven thousand men, and Trumbull proudly announced that the assembly had granted "large and liberal Pay" for those who volunteered for this duty.

Trumbull's own Congregationalist background and beliefs shone through in his proclamation. He reminded his fellow citizens that the migration of their Puritan forefathers to America was a result of "Injustice and Oppression," and they undertook the move "to secure a lasting Retreat from civil and religious Tyranny." Their predecessors had, according to Trumbull, been successful at building a society of which they could be proud. At the end of his proclamation, like the assembly had done in its call to arms, Trumbull pleaded with his fellow citizens to "come forth with the Help of the Lord" to "convince the unrelenting Tyrant of *Britain* that they are resolved to be FREE." He pointed out that God had already "shewn his Power in our Behalf, and for the Destruction of many of our Enemies. *Our Fathers trusted in him and were delivered.*" Therefore, Trumbull encouraged Connecticut's inhabitants to do the same, "and he will save us with temporal and eternal Salvation."

Also in June 1776, the assembly officially admitted that there seemed to be little hope that Great Britain would cease its tyranny and that "all hopes of a reconciliation upon just and equal terms are delusory and vain." The legislature acknowledged that there was no alternative but "total separation from the King of Great Britain and renunciation of all connection with that nation." Therefore, the legislators instructed their delegates to the Continental Congress "to declare the United American Colonies Free and Independent States, absolved from allegiance to the King of Great Britain." Additionally, they directed their delegates to promote "a regular and permanent Plan of Union and Confederation of the Colonies, for the security and preservation of their just rights and liberties and for mutual defence and security." They did, however, express the desire that within this plan, the regulation of all internal business be left to the respective colonial legislatures.

On July 12, 1776, the Council of Safety received letters from the Congress that contained a copy of the Declaration of Independence and a request that the Declaration be published. The council discussed the manner in which the Declaration should be published but eventually tabled the question of publication until the October meeting of the General Assembly. It was not until three months later that Connecticut's government officials published their approval of the Declaration.

THE REVOLUTION IN CONNECTICUT

In the spring of 1776, when the Second Continental Congress began to draft the Declaration of Independence, the Congress also advised each of the United Colonies to pass resolutions declaring their independence. Additionally, it recommended that each colony draw up a constitution that framed its new republic's government. Although Connecticut's legislature resolved to declare independence, it balked at drafting a new frame of government. In its October session, in the same resolution in which the Declaration of Independence was accepted, the legislature also made it official that it would retain the frame of government that had been established in the Charter of 1662, so far as it was consistent with independence from Great Britain. All officials were to continue in their offices and the laws of the former colony would remain in force in the newly established state. By the end of 1776, all legal procedures were done in the name of the "Governor and Company of the State of Connecticut."

The ease with which Connecticut made the political transition, coupled with other key social and military advantages, allowed Connecticut to make some significant contributions to the colonial war effort. Not only did Connecticut provide key support to the Continental Army in the form of men, munitions, and supplies, but it also furnished intellectual and practical assistance with the formation of the new government. But not all of Connecticut's efforts were directed toward the general good. Connecticut, like the other newly united states, pursued individual interests, primarily with regard to its attempts to protect claims to western lands. These pursuits of self-interest undermined efforts to cement the new union under the Articles of Confederation.

Factors Contributing to Connecticut's Wartime Stability and Wartime Contributions

Several factors contributed to the state's stability during the Revolution. First, because Connecticut had been a charter colony before independence, the amount of political reorganization it had to undergo was minimal compared to the royal and proprietary colonies. Government officials were all elected by the freemen before the Revolution, and they continued thus during and after the Revolution. Jonathan Trumbull served as governor throughout the war. Other officials, such as Deputy Governor Matthew Griswold and Speaker of the House of Representatives William Williams also enjoyed long tenures of office. The composition of the General Assembly changed little.

Another factor that contributed to Connecticut's wartime stability was that the state was never occupied by British troops during the war. British and Patriot forces fought some major battles in Connecticut, including an assault on Danbury in 1777 that destroyed considerable property and Continental Army supplies. There were also assaults on salt works in Greenwich and raids on several other towns, most notably a massacre at New London and the burning of Groton, both of which happened under Benedict Arnold's command after he turned to the British side. Despite these raids, Connecticut officials were able to concentrate on contributing men and supplies to the Continental Army and to their own militia. The state was able to establish an exceptionally efficient supply system that provided clothing for state militia and continental regiments and its ration schedule later served as a model for the Continental Army. Connecticut was one of the biggest suppliers of gunpowder during the war. Through Governor Trumbull's tireless efforts, the state provided key supplies in the form of clothing and provisions that saved General Washington's troops from frostbite and starvation while at Valley Forge in the winter of 1778.

A final contributor to Connecticut's wartime stability was the early silencing of Tory opposition. By the end of the 1760s, British sympathizers no longer held elective offices in Connecticut. Although Connecticut did not see the kind of Tory-Patriot conflict that places like Pennsylvania, the Carolinas, or Georgia did, there were some loyalists in Connecticut. Most of Connecticut's Tories were Anglican and lived in western towns like Norwalk, Stamford, Fairfield, Ridgefield, Newtown, and Danbury. Historians estimate that Loyalists composed about 6 percent of the adult male population, or 2,000–2,500 of the 38,000 adult males. A few western Tories were initially successful at blocking their towns' political and financial support of Boston, but they were quickly subdued. In its December 1775 session, the assembly passed an act to restrain and punish those who opposed actions taken against Britain. They made it a crime to supply the English army or navy with provisions or supplies, to give any intelligence to British officials, to take up arms against Connecticut's militia, or to aid the British in any way. Punishment included forfeiture of estate and three years' imprisonment. Immediately after its decision to retain the colonial form of government, the assembly passed a new treason law that made it a capital crime to commit treason against the state of Connecticut. It also passed new oaths of fidelity to the state, which all freemen had to take before they were allowed to vote. Because of these restrictions, some Tories left Connecticut for New York and the protection of British forces. Others simply kept quiet.[9]

The legislature, on occasion, did have to enforce these anti-Tory laws. For example, in 1775, the Connecticut legislature dealt with the cases of Benjamin Stiles and John R. Marshall. Stiles, of Woodbury, was accused of "publickly and contemptuously" speaking against three of Connecticut's delegates to the Continental Congress and questioning their abilities and integrity. Additionally, Stiles was accused of speaking against the anti-British measures that had been adopted in Connecticut and in Congress. Stiles was directed to appear before the assembly to answer these charges. Marshall received similar treatment for speaking out against the "doings of the General Assembly."[10]

The Tory threat was so completely subdued in Connecticut by 1777 that Governor Trumbull and the assembly were able to adopt a softer position toward the Loyalists. The General Assembly eventually offered pardons to those Connecticut inhabitants who, "from ill advice...from inadvertence and mistaken apprehensions," had sided with the British "but are now supposed to be convinced of their error." If these wayward citizens agreed to take the oath of allegiance to the state and declared that they had broken off all connections with the enemy, they would be freed from prosecution for any act they committed while assisting Connecticut's enemies.

THE ARTICLES OF CONFEDERATION AND
THE WESTERN LANDS CONTROVERSY

Politically, Connecticut's leaders were key participants in the construction of the Articles of Confederation, the nation's first attempt at framing a republican government. The Articles were not a priority of the Continental Congress. During the first several months of Congress's existence, the delegates were trying to finance and fight a war while working out procedures and responsibilities as they went along. Finally, a committee chaired by John Dickinson placed a draft of the Articles before Congress in the fall of 1776. It took over a year for Congress to agree on a final draft, and it took three more years for all states to ratify the document.

Connecticut was one of the states that delayed ratification of the Articles because it was not happy with some of the provisions included in the final draft. In February 1778, the assembly proposed an amendment that would prohibit the establishment of a peacetime standing army for the United States. Additionally, Connecticut's leaders were dissatisfied with Article 8, which dealt with the states' contribution to common defense expenses. It stated that all expenses incurred for common defense or general welfare would be defrayed out of a common treasury. The amount that each state was to contribute to that treasury was determined proportionally by the value of the land within each state that had been granted to or surveyed for any person. The value of that land and the buildings and other improvements on it would be assessed periodically. Connecticut's assembly proposed an amendment to that article that replaced land value with population as the determining factor in the proportion of each state's common expense. The authors of this proposal explained that population would be much easier to estimate than land value and would be a more accurate gauge of a state's wealth. Population counts took into consideration the significant pool of manpower used in trade and manufactures, which were sources of wealth in some parts of the nation, particularly in the northern states. Connecticut did not get its way with these amendments, however, and in April of 1779, it became the next-to-last state to ratify the Articles of Confederation and Perpetual Union.

The most important obstacle to the ratification of the Articles was the question of who would control the western lands. Six states, including Connecticut, claimed significant tracts of land lying to the west of the established states. These claims were based on their original grants from the Crown, which specified that the colonies' land claims extended to the "South Sea," now known as the Pacific Ocean. New York also made western claims based on treaties it had signed with the Iroquois. These extensive grants had caused conflict between colonies before the Revolution, and they continued to provoke disputes among settlers. Connecticut's involvement in these disputes began in 1753, when growing population and a shortage of fertile land motivated a few of Connecticut's citizens to form the Susquehannah Company. The company intended to exercise Connecticut's "sea-to-sea" clause in the Charter of 1662 to claim land in Pennsylvania along the Susquehanna River. Of course, this attempt to encroach on William Penn's claim aroused protest from the Penn family. The idea of migration westward into the Susquehanna claim was never terribly popular among potential settlers, but Connecticut reasserted control over its western lands in 1774, causing more enmity between the Penns and Connecticut's leaders in the months just before the Revolution.

The land at issue during the debates over the Articles of Confederation was even farther west, beyond Pennsylvania's western border. Six other states with defined western borders, including Pennsylvania, wanted the western lands to become common territory of the United States. They demanded that the six states with western claims cede their territory to the confederation government. Those states with western lands prevailed in the debates, and the final draft of the Articles read that "no State shall be deprived of territory for the benefit of the United States." Because of this clause, Maryland, one of the states with defined western borders, refused to ratify the Articles.

Because ratification of the Articles had to be unanimous, Maryland's stubbornness caused delay in implementing the new frame of government. Finally, in October 1780, the Connecticut General Assembly entertained a congressional recommendation that the states holding vacant, unappropriated lands in the west "remove the obstacle that prevents a Ratification of the Articles of Confederation" and cede the western lands that lay within the boundaries of their charter "for the benefit of the confederated United States." The assembly approved a qualified cession of lands. Based on promises from Connecticut and other states to cede their western lands, Maryland finally ratified the Articles and the new frame of government went into effect in 1781. Although these state resolutions on the part of Connecticut, Virginia, New York, and others began the process of ceding land to the United States, the western lands did not immediately change hands and the question was not completely settled until several years later.

With this gesture of ceding western lands, Connecticut helped to pave the way for ratification of the Articles of Confederation. In 1783, the Treaty of Paris that ended the war with Great Britain confirmed possession by the United States of territory east of the Mississippi River and south of the Canadian provinces. At that time, the Connecticut assembly again resolved to cede a parcel of the western land claims to the United States. After a third resolution in 1786, the transfer was complete. The 1786 act also included the cession of Connecticut's Pennsylvania claim. However, Connecticut's assembly reserved a specific portion of land west of Pennsylvania for the state's benefit. Congress approved this reservation. That portion of territory became known as the "Western Reserve." The area, which borders Lake Erie and includes the land around what is now Cleveland, Ohio, eventually attracted considerable numbers of Connecticut emigrants. A parcel on the western side of the reserve was set aside for the benefit of those Connecticut towns that suffered property losses in British raids during the Revolution. The remainder of the land was sold to speculators in 1795 for $1.2 million.[11]

THE U.S. CONSTITUTION

The long and painful ratification process and the equally drawn out cessions of western lands were just two examples of the inherent problems with the Articles of Confederation. There were many others. Connecticut and other states repeatedly met with frustration over the confederation's ineffectiveness. Congress's inability to control revenue measures or to coerce the states into donating their fair share of the revenues was one of the biggest challenges of the new nation. Almost immediately after the Articles' ratification, there were calls for revision. In October 1782, New York governor George Clinton wrote Governor Trumbull about the prospect of convening a meeting of the states authorized to revise and amend the confederation. Although the assembly had never been satisfied with the Articles as they stood, Connecticut's representatives decided that it was not expedient to propose such a meeting at that time. However, the suggestions for revision continued. Eventually, one of Connecticut's political leaders would have a hand in crafting a new frame of government for the nation, and he and his fellow Federalists would encounter little trouble convincing their colleagues at Connecticut's ratification convention to approve it.

One of the problems plaguing the Articles was the concept of unanimous consent. The Articles required the approval of all thirteen states' assemblies for amendments to the frame of government, so approval of any amendment was practically impossible. In 1778, Connecticut had not gotten its way with the proposed amendment to change the standards by which states would contribute to the common treasury from land value to population. But they, along with several other states, continued to push for this amendment. In April 1783, it was reintroduced in Congress and offered to the state legislatures.

In May of the same year, Connecticut's assembly approved this amendment, but as unanimous consent was required for the change, the amendment was never ratified. This amendment, incidentally, was the first to use a three-fifths clause to calculate slave populations. Under the amendment, population was to be calculated by conducting a census counting "the whole number of White and other free Citizens and Inhabitants of every Age Sex and Condition including those bound to Servitude for a Term of Years, and three fifths of all other Persons not Comprehended in the foregoing description."[12] Although the amendment did not become part of the Articles of Confederation, it would provide a useful compromise when negotiating the terms of representation within the Constitution.

Although Connecticut's assembly and delegates to Congress tried to help correct an inadequate form of national government, the state was also part of the problem. Its own financial troubles, combined with continued demands from the confederation government for men and supplies to defend the western frontier from hostile Native Americans, provoked Connecticut's legislature to beg Congress's forgiveness for its delinquent contributions to the common treasury. In October 1785, the assembly asked the governor to send a letter to the president of Congress informing him of "the Situation of this State labouring under Embarrassments by reason of Arrearages of former Taxes and other reasons inducing a NonCompliance with the Requisitions at this Time, and to assure him of the Hearty Attachment of the good People of this State to the Union." Connecticut was not the only state that fell behind in payments because of its own debt, and the financial troubles mounted until the confederation Congress was virtually impotent.

By 1785, it was apparent that the Articles of Confederation were in need of an overhaul. Shays's Rebellion in western Massachusetts added to Connecticut officials' concern. Daniel Shays and his followers were protesting high taxes, the perceived bias of the courts toward inhabitants of the eastern half of the state, and scarcity of money on the frontier. In 1786, Shays and his followers attacked the federal arsenal at Springfield, Massachusetts, not far from Hartford. Rumors that a similar attack was afoot in Sharon, a western Connecticut town not far from the Massachusetts border, prompted an investigation by the assembly. The alleged ringleader, William Mitchell, was held for questioning. News of the failure of Shays's Rebellion helped to dispel Connecticut officials' fears, and charges against Mitchell were dropped. But Shays's Rebellion had a significant effect on those already concerned about the stability of the confederation.[13]

Another prominent influence on Connecticut's position with regard to the Articles was a young Yale College graduate named Noah Webster, Jr. In 1785, Webster published his *Sketches of American Policy*. In that work, he asserted that Congress, as it existed then, was too weak. He explained that "there must be a supreme power at the head of the union, vested with authority to make laws that respect the states in general and to compel obedience to those laws." If Congress did not have the power to compel obedience to the law, he warned, the union would not last. After he published his *Sketches*, Webster embarked on a lecture tour in major cities from New Hampshire to South Carolina. He distributed his essays along the way, and he personally presented a copy of his *Sketches* to General George Washington. This copy found its way to James Madison, and thus, according to Webster himself, he had a hand in bringing about the Constitutional Convention. At the very least, Webster's voice joined a strengthening chorus calling for a convention to amend the Articles.[14]

THE CONSTITUTIONAL CONVENTION AND THE CONNECTICUT COMPROMISE

In September 1786, a convention of commissioners from Virginia, Delaware, Pennsylvania, New Jersey, and New York met at Annapolis to discuss commercial problems of mutual interest. As a result of the discussions, this group asked Congress to call a general convention to consider strengthening the central government. Congress approved this motion in early 1787, but with a caveat introduced by the Massachusetts congressional delegation that restricted the purpose of the convention to meeting "for the sole and express purpose of revising the Articles of Confederation." When the call came for the convention, many Connecticut citizens did not want to send a delegation. As in many other states, a significant number of inhabitants were content with the existing confederation and they feared the establishment of a stronger government. In the end, however, the assembly voted to send three delegates: Roger Sherman, William Samuel Johnson, and Oliver Ellsworth.

Connecticut delegate Roger Sherman became a leader at the convention. He spoke in sessions more than any other delegate except for Virginia's James Madison. At age sixty-six, Sherman was the second-oldest delegate at the convention after Benjamin Franklin. Sherman is best known for introducing the "Connecticut Compromise," also known as the "Great Compromise," that succeeded in breaking a potentially fatal deadlock in the debate over forms of representation. The delegates had already determined that the new legislature should have two houses. The question that remained was how these legislative representatives should be elected. States with large populations wanted representation in the legislature based on either population or wealth. States with smaller populations did not want to be overwhelmed by the larger states; they therefore proposed equal representation for each state. Northern states did not want slaves to be counted either as population or as wealth in property. If the delegates could not find a solution, the issue threatened to kill efforts to draft a more effective form of government.

Sherman's compromise solved part of the problem. It called for a lower house based on population or wealth, satisfying the large states' demands for recognition of their contributions to the Union, and an upper house with an equal number of senators for each state, fulfilling the small states' demands for equal representation. The only question that remained was what to do about counting the slaves in the population or wealth of a state. Southern states, of course, had the most to lose if slaves were not counted in the population, and they insisted that the institution be protected and recognized as a form of national wealth. After heated debate, the delegates reached a compromise. They borrowed language from the previously proposed amendment to the Articles of Confederation that representation in the House would be based on the entire free population, including women and children, plus three-fifths of the slaves. Native Americans, who did not pay taxes, were not included in the population count. This additional compromise allowed the Connecticut Compromise to be implemented.

RATIFICATION DEBATES IN CONNECTICUT

Once the Constitution was drafted and presented to the states for ratification, each state settled down to debate the merits of the new frame of government. Ratification debates in Connecticut were intense. The assembly voted to direct each town to choose delegates for a convention to consider the plan. The town representatives convened in Hartford in January 1788 and took five days to debate the proposal. Although no official records of the convention proceedings are known to exist, accounts from various Connecticut newspapers and reprinted speeches were collected and published in volume 6 of the *Public Records of Connecticut*. These records represent the most complete account of what transpired in this convention, though, unfortunately, they include little in the way of Anti-Federalist argument. This thin coverage of opposition to the Constitution was indicative of general sentiment among Connecticut's leaders, most of whom supported the Constitution. Yet some opposition did exist. The delegates to the Constitutional Convention—Sherman, Ellsworth, and Johnson—led the defense of the Constitution. General James Wadsworth of Durham led the opposition.

Oliver Ellsworth opened the first day of debates with a speech supporting the Constitution. Ellsworth's speech followed the lines of many Federalist arguments of the day: that a more energetic system, complete with coercive power, was necessary to the preservation of the union. He began by asserting that a strong union was necessary for national defense. While there was safety in numbers when it came to a call to arms, Ellsworth pointed out that numbers were also a deterrent and the most effective way to keep peace was to present a united front against those who might wish to overpower a weaker and less numerous alliance. Moreover, Ellsworth pointed out, unity would preserve peace among the states. "If we be divided," Ellsworth asked, "what is to prevent wars from breaking out among the states? States, as well as individuals, are subject to ambition, avarice, to those jarring passions which disturb the peace of society." He suggested that a "parental hand" in the form of a strong central government would help to check these impulses. In that same vein, union would also preserve justice among the states, providing a check to larger states that could overpower the smaller ones. He warned his fellow delegates that Connecticut itself could be in danger of succumbing to "the ambition and rapacity of New York." He saw in that larger and richer state "the seeds of an overbearing ambition." Moreover, on Connecticut's other side lay Massachusetts, another powerful state. He warned that Connecticut had already "begun to be tributaries" of these larger neighbors, and if the states did not unite, Connecticut would become "a strong ass crouching down between two burdens." He pointed out that New Jersey and Delaware had already recognized this potential danger and had unanimously adopted the Constitution.

Samuel Johnson appealed to the new nation's sense of pride when he pointed out that under the present government, the nation's "commerce is annihilated," and the nation's "honour, once in so high esteem, is no more." He supported Ellsworth's assertion that coercion was necessary if they were to have an effective union. The solemn promises behind the compact binding the states did not prevent some of them from becoming delinquent in their obligations to one another, and under the current form, the only coercion available was that of military force, which, according to Johnson, would simply cause more division and conflict. Under the Constitution, however, the legislature was vested with power to make laws in matters of national concern, to appoint judges to decide on those laws, and to appoint officers to enforce the law. Therefore, the power of law, instead of military might, would provide the coercive force that the federal government needed to function.

General Wadsworth offered the only recorded objection when he expressed fears that the legislature's control over taxes, imposts, and excises would give it too much power. According to Wadsworth, because Congress had the power of the purse *and* of the sword, its authority would be despotic. He also expressed concern that the operation of imposts and excises would favor the southern states. Ellsworth responded to these objections by explaining that in return for the power to collect monies through taxation, the United States would bear all financial burdens of war and would defend all states and their inhabitants from hostile attacks. Ellsworth pointed out that wars cost money, and if the nation did not have the means to fight a war, it would surely become the victim of a foreign power that recognized their weakness. Besides, he asked, has anyone ever heard of a government without the power of the sword and the purse? "[T]he sword without the purse," Ellsworth asserted, "is of no effect, it is a sword in the scabbard."

With regard to impost taxes giving favor to the southern states, Ellsworth stated that collecting impost taxes was the most lucrative way for a federal government to make money. Manufactures would not be the only items taxed. Imports would increase as the population increased, providing for a steady income for the government. All people needed clothing, regardless of where they lived, and since there was less manufacturing in the South, Southerners would have to import and pay impost for more items. Moreover, nothing was to be excluded. They would even pay impost on the slaves they imported. Ellsworth exploited stereotypes of Southerners as lazy spendthrifts when he explained that although Virginia's exports were valuable, primarily because of its tobacco trade, Virginians were "poor to a proverb in money. They anticipate their crop; they spend faster than they earn; they are ever in debt. Their rich exports return in eatables, in drinkables, in wearables." All of these items would also be subject to the impost.

After the debates ended, several delegates rose to give speeches supporting ratification. Several newspapers published the speeches of Samuel Huntington, Oliver Wolcott, and Richard Law, and they noted that others also stood to express their support. Richard Law provided a particularly practical response to the objections of some that the states could never be united under a republic, because a republic could not survive in such a large territory. Law dismissed the argument by implying that Americans were greater than that. Because they had God on their side, they could overcome the obstacle of size to create a unified republic. He scoffed that Americans were "not satisfied with this assertion" and that they wanted "to try experiment." He admitted that "the old articles of confederation were once the best that we should have been willing to adopt. We have been led on by imperceptible degrees to see that they are defective; and now, if it be the design of providence to make us a great and happy people," he prophesied that God would "induce the people of the United States to accept of a constitution, which is so well calculated to promote their national welfare."

On January 9, 1788, Connecticut became the fifth state to ratify the Constitution. The vote was overwhelmingly in favor of ratification: 128 to 40.

CONNECTICUT UNDER THE U.S. CONSTITUTION

At the time that Connecticut ratified the Constitution and for thirty years thereafter, the state's government still operated under the basic framework outlined in the royal charter of 1662. When it was first established, the form of government was a liberal one, representing one of the most democratic provincial governments in existence at the time. Even the governor was elected by the freemen, unlike most other colonies, whose governors were appointed by the king or the proprietor. Town meetings represented the democratic nature of New England government. Connecticut's legislature was powerful. The governor was prevented from dissolving or proroguing the legislature, and if he did not call the legislature as directed by the charter, the towns could meet to do so. The council—the upper house—consisted of a governor, lieutenant governor, and twelve elected assistants who represented the state at large. The governor, or the lieutenant governor in the governor's absence, presided over the sessions, but he only voted if there was a tie. No minutes of council meetings were kept. The assistants wielded considerable power. They were justices of the peace and could serve in the place of a superior court judge. Three council members could reprieve a criminal and in times of urgency, an assistant could call out the militia. Seven members of the council could veto a measure that the lower house had passed. Because this small group of men possessed legislative, judicial, and executive powers, this committee was the most influential governing body in the colony. It had a hand in passing all laws, directing state policy, and appointing all officials. After 1697, assistants were elected by the people, but those elected were almost exclusively local elites.

Many Connecticut citizens still took pride in their form of government and believed, as Yale College president Timothy Dwight did, that it "approache[d] as near to a pure democracy" as any other. Frequent elections and the potential for many men to hold office in their lifetimes gave it a democratic cast. Government officials' salaries were, according to Dwight, inadequate for "decent support of those who receive them," a situation that Dwight did not see as disadvantageous. On the contrary, low salaries discouraged "men of ambition, avarice, or pleasure" from seeking office and, instead, attracted men of virtue, willing to perform public service for the common good.[15]

But by the end of the eighteenth century, Connecticut's government was beginning to show some wear. Although elections were annual for the government and other administrative officials and semiannual for the legislators, turnover in offices was not so frequent. Certain families tended to dominate elections—the Wolcotts, the Trumbulls, and the Ellsworths, for example—and the electoral system favored incumbents by listing nominees in order of seniority when votes were taken in town meetings. The office of governor, to some, seemed to be monopolized by men from certain powerful towns. To be sure, the composition of Connecticut's government remained overwhelmingly Federalist and Congregationalist throughout the first decades of the nineteenth century and even through the "Revolution" of 1800, when Thomas Jefferson's Republican allies took control of many state legislatures. The Republicans made only minor inroads in Connecticut.[16]

DISCONTENT WITH THE CHARTER GOVERNMENT

There were other criticisms leveled at the branches of government. For example, the council was criticized for its secrecy. Its sessions were always closed except when the body was receiving petitions, and debates among the members, minutes, and individual members' voting patterns were never disclosed to the public. The council also held undue influence over the judiciary because it annually appointed all judges and justices of the peace. Until 1804, council members were able to practice trial law before any court, which meant that they were asking judges whom they had appointed to rule on cases in which they were involved. Council members also commonly held more than one position in the judiciary, which could cause conflict of interest. The final criticism of Connecticut's government was that in the face of legal separation of church and state in the federal Constitution, Connecticut still gave the Congregationalist Church special status and financial support.

The question of a constitution for Connecticut first arose in the 1780s. In assembly sessions and in pamphlets, proponents of a new form of government for the state argued that the charter was not a valid form of government because it had not been created or ratified by the people, but rather it had been imposed on them by a power that no longer existed in that state. In 1782, Dr. Benjamin Gale published a pamphlet that argued that the state abrogated the charter when it went to war with England and that the assembly's declaration reestablishing the charter was extra-legal and should be only temporary. He wrote that the state had no constitution because "a civil *constitution* is a *charter, a bill of rights*, or a *compact* made between the rulers and the ruled." This was not true of the charter, according to Gale, because it had never been submitted to the freemen for approval. Others criticized the royal language and elitist principles of the charter and agitated for a frame of government that had been established by the people. They claimed that a government that was subject to change at the hands of elected officials was an unstable institution.[17]

Others defended the charter as a legitimate frame of government. Connecticut jurist Zephaniah Swift argued that Connecticut citizens could have called a convention in 1776, but they did not think it was necessary, because their government was grounded on the will of the people. He argued that the tacit consent of the people since 1776, in the form of obeying the laws and following the customary forms of civil procedure, had amounted to approval of the assembly's choice to retain the charter. Swift insisted that "the constitution of this state is a representative republic. Some visionary theorists have pretended that we have no constitution, because it has not been reduced to writing, and ratified by the people." But, Swift argued, it could be proven that the people had accepted and approved it when one traced "the constitution of our government to its origin."[18]

THE FORMATION OF POLITICAL PARTIES AND CONNECTICUT'S FIRST CONSTITUTION

The debate over the U.S. Constitution had created two factions: Federalists, who favored ratification of the Constitution and Anti-Federalists, who opposed the new document. In many states, these factions quickly solidified into political parties. Connecticut, however, was slow to develop political parties. The population was still homogenous, mostly of English ancestry, and most of the state's citizens were farmers or merchants. Landownership was widespread, so most people had similar political interests. But after George Washington became president, political interests began to coalesce around Federalist and Republican sentiments. In Connecticut, Federalists quickly gained the upper hand. Even at the height of Thomas Jefferson's political power in other parts of the nation, his party—the Republican Party—was unable to make significant inroads against those in control of Connecticut politics.

Because the electoral process favored the Federalists who were in power, Republicans found political progress in Connecticut to be a challenge. They made the call for a constitutional convention part of their platform in 1804, but supporters of the Constitution managed to delay change until 1818, when the Republicans had finally made enough inroads to overthrow the Federalists in Connecticut. In 1816, an alliance of Republicans and Episcopalians who preached toleration formed a political party that was determined to end the Federalist domination in Connecticut. They eventually championed the cause of a constitutional convention. The Toleration Party's 1816 gubernatorial candidate, Oliver Wolcott, Jr., had the name and the professional prestige that the party needed to succeed. For years he had been a Federalist, he had served on John Adams's cabinet, and he was a Congregationalist. Although he did not win the 1816 election, the Tolerationists secured some political power, and in 1817 Wolcott won the governorship.[19]

In 1818, the Toleration Party changed its name to the Constitution and Reform Party, and it swept the elections. At the opening legislative session, Wolcott asked the assembly to call a constitutional convention. The assembly issued the call. Town meetings were held on July 4 to choose convention delegates, and in August they met to draft the constitution. Connecticut's new constitution cut the governor's ties to the council, giving him more autonomy. It also bestowed limited veto power on the office. The new frame of government provided for appointment of supreme court and superior court judges for life, or "during good behavior," which released judges from the assembly's control and created Connecticut's first independent judiciary. The legislature received a revised system of apportionment that resulted in severe inequities. The constitution provided that all towns in existence at the drafting of the constitution would have two representatives in the house, whereas towns created after the adoption of the constitution would be entitled to one representative. This inequity was not remedied until the 1960s, when the U.S. Supreme Court ruled on the "one man, one vote" concept.

Although there were some objectionable parts of Connecticut's first constitution from the twenty-first-century perspective, there were many merits. The 1818 constitution provided for virtual manhood suffrage, eliminating property qualifications and giving the vote to almost every white male twenty-one years or older. Finally, the Republicans achieved their goal of religious freedom in Connecticut through this constitution. With the disestablishment of the Congregational Church, the constitution removed favoritism toward any particular religion.

SUMMARY

With the ratification of its own state constitution in 1818, Connecticut joined its counterparts, at that time numbering twenty, in the distinctively American custom of written constitutions. Of course, Connecticut citizens argued then, and they still do, that they already possessed written constitutions with *The Fundamental Orders* and the Charter of 1662. Whether one believes that Connecticut originated the custom or was a little slow to catch up with its counterparts, its citizens' contributions to the formation of the United States were significant. Their loyalty to the United Colonies and to neighboring Massachusetts galvanized them before and during the Revolution. Their own political and economic stability during the Revolution allowed them to make significant military and political contributions to the new union. Their sacrifice of western land claims, however reluctant, allowed the nation to make a first attempt at unity, while at the same time these kinds of exhibitions of individual interest helped to ensure the downfall of the Articles of Confederation. Finally, Connecticut's Roger Sherman provided a key compromise that prevented failure of the Constitutional Convention. Connecticut's subsequent enthusiastic ratification of the new Constitution eventually led to a reconsideration of its own frame of government. These events show the economic, social, and political interdependence that joined Connecticut to the other North American republics.

NOTES

1. Albert E. Van Dusen, *Puritans Against the Wilderness: Connecticut History to 1763* (Chester, CT: Pequot Press, 1975), pp. 11–12.

2. *The Fundamental Orders of 1639*, available: www.constitution.org/bcp/fo_1639.htm, March 17, 2003.

3. Connecticut Colonial Charter, 1662, *Colonial Records of Connecticut, from April, 1636–April, 1665, Inclusive*, vol. 1, Charles J. Hoadly, comp. (Hartford, CT: 1887), p. 416. Unless otherwise noted, all Connecticut documents, resolutions, and Acts of Assembly from the colonial period are drawn from vols. 1–15 of the *Colonial Records of Connecticut*.

4. David M. Roth and Freeman Meyer, *From Revolution to Constitution: Connecticut 1763 to 1818* (Chester, CT: Pequot Press, 1975), pp. 12–13.

5. Connecticut *Gazette*, August 9, 1765.

6. Connecticut *Gazette*, September 27, 1765; Connecticut *Courant*, September 23, 1765.

7. Richard Buel, *Dear Liberty: Connecticut's Mobilization for the Revolutionary War* (Middletown, CT: Wesleyan University Press, 1980), p. 16.

8. Ibid., p. 31.

9. *The Public Records of the State of Connecticut, from October, 1776 to February, 1778, inclusive with the Journal of the Council of Safety from October 11, 1776 to May 6,*

1778, inclusive, and an Appendix, Charles Hoadly, comp. (Hartford, CT: Press of the Case, 1894), vols. 1, 4, 5. Unless otherwise noted, all Connecticut documents, resolutions, and Acts of Assembly from October of 1776 on are drawn from vols. 1–6 of the *Public Records of the State of Connecticut;* Roth and Meyer, *From Revolution to Constitution,* p. 23.

10. *Colonial Records,* vol. 15, 157. See also p. 203 for other cases.

11. Roth and Meyer, *From Revolution to Constitution,* p. 82.

12. *Journals of the Continental Congress,* 24: 257–261, available: http://memory.loc.gov/ammem/amlaw/lwjc.html.

13. Roth and Meyer, *From Revolution to Constitution,* p. 42.

14. Noah Webster, *Sketches of American Policy* (Hartford, CT: Hudson and Goodwin, 1785). Available: http://personal.pitnet.net/primarysources/Webster.html, May 25, 2003.

15. Timothy Dwight, *Travels in New England and New York,* Barbara Miller Solomon, ed. (Cambridge, MA: 1969), p. 212.

16. Richard J. Purcell, *Connecticut in Transition: 1775–1818* (originally published, 1918; new edition, with foreword by S. Hugh Brockunier [Middletown, CT: Wesleyan University Press, 1963]), pp. 118–133.

17. Ibid., pp. 115, 128.

18. Zephaniah Swift, *A System of the Laws of the State of Connecticut, in Six Books* (Windham, CT: n.p., 1795), vol. 1, pp. 55–56.

19. Roth and Meyer, *From Revolution to Constitution,* pp. 48, 64–67.

BIBLIOGRAPHY

Buel, Richard, Jr. *Dear Liberty: Connecticut's Mobilization for the Revolutionary War.* Middletown, CT: Wesleyan University Press, 1980.

Colonial Records of Connecticut, from April, 1636 to October, 1776, Inclusive. Vols. 1–15.

Dwight, Timothy. *Travels in New England and New York.* Edited by Barbara Miller Solomon. Vol. 1. Cambridge, MA: Belknap Press of Harvard University Press, 1969.

Hoadly, Charles J., and Leonard Labaree, comp. *The Public Records of the State of Connecticut.* Hartford, CT: Press of the Case, Lockwood and Brainard Co., 1887–1890.

Public Records of the State of Connecticut, vols. 1–6, October, 1776 to January, 1819, Inclusive. Leonard Labaree, comp. Hartford, CT: Press of the Case, 1894–1945.

Purcell, Richard J. *Connecticut in Transition: 1775–1818.* Originally published 1918; new edition, with foreword by S. Hugh Brockunier. Middletown, CT: Wesleyan University Press, 1963.

Roth, David M., and Freeman Meyer. *From Revolution to Constitution: Connecticut 1763 to 1818.* Chester, CT: Pequot Press, 1975.

Swift, Zephaniah. *A System of the Laws of the State of Connecticut, in Six Books.* Windham, CT: n.p., 1795.

Van Dusen, Albert E. *Puritans Against the Wilderness: Connecticut History to 1763.* Chester, CT: Pequot Press, 1975.

Webster, Noah. *Noah Webster: On Being American: Selected Writings, 1783–1828*. Edited by Homer Babbidge Jr. New York: Frederick A. Praeger, Publishers, 1967.

———. *Sketches of American Policy*. Hartford: Hudson and Goodwin, 1785. Available: http://personal.pitnet.net/primarysources/webster.html.

THE STATE OF DELAWARE

Ratified the Constitution of the United States:
December 7, 1787

Jonathan S. Russ

INTRODUCTION

As any visitor to modern Delaware can attest, the state heavily promotes its historic role as the first to have ratified the Constitution of the United States on December 7, 1787. Its motto, "The First State," adorns license plates, highway signs, statuary, and all manner of tourist literature, pamphlets, and advertisements. It is a slogan that is further applied to the names of businesses, Little League teams, media outlets, and public spaces. Beyond mere moniker, however, Delaware's distinction as the first of the United States is a source of pride to many Delawareans. Although the names Caesar Rodney, George Read, or John Dickinson might have limited recognition outside of the state, Delawareans are familiar with Rodney's eleventh-hour ride to Philadelphia to vote in favor of the Declaration of Independence and the roles of Read and Dickinson in establishing the nation.

Because of its small size and moderate politics, Delaware was somewhat overshadowed by other colonies in eighteenth-century America. It was not a hotbed of political debate or intrigue, nor was the colony of particular concern to royal authorities in England. Nevertheless, Delaware's significance in the revolutionary period and in the subsequent formation of the country was recognized by prominent observers at the time. According to legend, Thomas Jefferson referred to Delaware as the "Diamond State" because its strategic location on the eastern seaboard made it a jewel among the states.

That Delaware was even a colony, however, let alone the eventual first state to ratify the Constitution, was rather remarkable. The land that came to be Delaware was claimed first by the Netherlands, then by Sweden, and eventually by Great Britain. Even under English rule, Delaware's status was in dispute

Delaware

Territorial Development:

- Duke of York granted the colony of Delaware to William Penn, 1682
- Continental Congress approved Declaration of Independence from Great Britain, July 4, 1776
- Great Britain formally recognized American independence through the Treaty of Paris, September 3, 1783
- Delaware became the first state to ratify the U.S. Constitution, December 7, 1787

Capitals Prior to Statehood:

- New Castle, 1704–1777
- Dover, 1777–1787

State Capitals:

- Dover, 1787–present

Origin of State Name: The state name is taken from the Delaware River and Bay, the source of the Delaware Indians' name as well.

First Governor: Joshua Clayton
Governmental Organization: Bicameral
Population at Statehood: 59,096
Geographical Size: 1,954 square miles

for a time, as both William Penn and Lord Baltimore thought the territory to be rightfully theirs. And even when that matter was eventually resolved, Delaware's independence as a colony did not happen until the eve of the Revolution. Thus, for the state that played a pivotal role in the birth of the nation, Delaware's existence had long been an uncertain one.

EARLY SETTLEMENT: THE DUTCH AND THE SWEDISH

Delaware's earliest recorded history stretches back to 1609, when English explorer Henry Hudson discovered what became known as the Delaware River on his journey to find passage to China. In the following year, English sailor Samuel Argall, who encountered the waterways when seeking shelter from a storm, named the river's adjacent bay after Lord de la Warr, then governor of Virginia.[1] Although English cartographers soon thereafter affixed the name Delaware to the river and bay, the land itself remained unsettled by Europeans for another two decades. The Native Americans who populated the area were known as the Leni-Lenape. They lived by a combination of fishing, hunting, and farming.

In the spring of 1631, a small Dutch settlement called Swanendael was established in southern Delaware near what is known today as Lewes Creek, marking the first time in which a European power staked a claim to the territory. At the southern boundary of New Netherland, Swanendael was short-lived. The settlement utterly failed, as a Dutch whaling expedition discovered in 1632 when it found Swanendael abandoned and its inhabitants mysteriously missing or dead. In light of Swanendael's demise, the Dutch concentrated their imperial efforts further to the north in the Hudson River Valley, although in the following decades they would once again lay claim to land in Delaware.

In March 1638, Swedish colonists successfully established a permanent settlement on the banks of a tributary to the Delaware River, near modern-day Wilmington. Arriving on the ships the *Kalmar Nyckel* and the *Vogel Grip*, both of which had Dutch captains, the twenty-five men called their settlement Fort Christina, in honor of the Swedish queen, Christina, and gave the same name to the river upon which it was located. The male settlers were joined by women and children in 1640, and in 1641, the settlement was officially established as a venture of the New Sweden Company. In 1643, Johan Printz was installed as the governor of New Sweden, thereby lending a quasi-governmental status to the settlement.

Although the population of New Sweden never exceeded one thousand inhabitants, it was a successful colony composed of farmers.[2] Lutheran ministers had accompanied the settlers, and apparently there was little difficulty in adapting to the land or the climate. New Sweden was quite independent of the motherland, and there was very little correspondence between the two.

Indeed, between 1648 and 1654 not a single ship came from Sweden to its North American colony.[3] Although this situation was of little consequence at first, by the mid-1650s the very survival of the colony was at stake and Governor Printz was frustrated at the lack of support he received from his superiors.

Without question, the Dutch territorial claim based on the early settlement of Swanendael posed the greatest threat to New Sweden. The colonial governor of New Netherlands, Peter Stuyvesant, long believed that the Swedish had unjustly usurped Dutch land, and he was determined to reassert control over the territory by whatever means necessary. To that end, in 1651 Stuyvesant ordered the construction of an outpost at a place called Sandhook, which would later be renamed New Castle by the English. Called Fort Casimir, the Dutch garrison was strategically located near the mouth of the Delaware River, south of New Sweden's Fort Christina and the rest of the Swedish settlement. Fort Casimir effectively gave the Dutch control of the Delaware River and, by extension, the Christina River as well. With its superior naval forces, therefore, the Dutch could cut off New Sweden whenever they chose.

Recognizing the potential peril his colony faced, Printz was eager for his government in Europe to solve the tensions in colonial America. He knew that his meager forces were no match for those of Stuyvesant and thus saw as his only solution a political settlement between his government and the Dutch in Europe. In the meantime he did what he could to pacify the situation in America. Sensing that the urgency of his plea was not understood, however, Printz set sail for Sweden in 1653 to press his case. In a cruel twist of fate, Printz had to sail from the colonial Dutch capital of New Amsterdam (later renamed New York) aboard a Dutch ship, but despite the indignity, sail he did in order to preserve his colony.

At the very time that Printz was working to save New Sweden, his successor, Johan Rising, quickly undermined all of his efforts. Upon arriving to America in 1654, Rising sized up the situation at Fort Casimir and determined that his forces could overwhelm the small Dutch contingent stationed there. Indeed, he was correct in his assessment, but he had failed to appreciate the trap into which he had blundered. Once Fort Casimir had been captured by Swedish forces, Dutch governor Stuyvesant retaliated by sending a large contingent that easily recaptured not only Casimir but also took all of New Sweden as well. On September 15, 1655, Rising surrendered to the Dutch, who promised to respect private property claims and customs, including religion, of all who wished to remain. Those who did not want to stay would be given passage back to Europe with Rising.[4]

Despite the change in colonial administration, however, many of the Swedish settlers remained in the territory. They were joined by Dutch settlers seeking land and opportunities for trade, especially in tobacco, which Dutch merchants acquired in Maryland and then resold on the international market. The Dutch referred to the territory as New Netherland, the same name affixed to their holdings in the Hudson River Valley to the north, just as they had when founding Swanendael. Although life in Delaware did not change dramatically during the period of Dutch rule, there were a few important developments that would have a long-lasting impact.

One innovation that came with Dutch control was the election of minor officials, including people such as fence inspectors. In the election of 1656, the Dutch introduced a practice known as double nomination that continued in Delaware even after the American Revolution. In this system, two people were elected for every post. After the election, the colonial administrator would then appoint either of the two candidates who had the highest number of votes.[5]

In addition, another practice that the Dutch introduced was that of using enslaved Africans as laborers. Although the first African slave was recorded to have come to the colony in 1639, it was during the period of Dutch rule that the slave population rose to 125 individuals, or 20 percent of the colony's total population.[6] Since the Dutch had gained experience with African slaves in their Caribbean colonies, where Stuyvesant himself had been a governor before taking up his post in North America, the use of slave labor was a familiar solution to labor shortages. In time, of course, this development would have a dramatic impact on Delaware's history.

Although their governance thus had a far-reaching impact upon Delaware, the duration of Dutch control was relatively brief. As part of the larger international struggle for trade, Britain and Holland had long been arch rivals, fighting three wars during the mid-seventeenth century. It was in this broader context that Britain attacked the New Netherland colony to expand its territorial holdings as well as to disrupt Dutch commercial activity in North America. The larger prize that Britain sought was the territory in the Hudson River Valley, but England also dispatched ships to Delaware in order to cut off Dutch access to the south. In August 1664, the English captured New Amsterdam without a battle and renamed the city New York. In the following month, it captured what was to become Delaware as well.

BRITISH RULE

In capturing the Dutch colonial possessions, Great Britain vastly expanded its claims in North America. At the very time that its empire was expanding geographically, England also took pains to ensure that its possessions were remunerative as well. With the creation of the Navigation Acts during the mid-seventeenth century, it was clear that the colonies were to play an important economic role in the well-being of the realm. Likewise, with additional territory at his disposal, King Charles II had new means by which he could bestow favor. It was thus that Charles granted his brother and heir, the Duke of York, the land that would be Delaware.

By granting Delaware to the Duke of York, however, King Charles irritated another of his subjects, Lord Baltimore. Baltimore had been granted Maryland in 1632, and he believed that his grant included territory that encompassed Delaware. He had long believed that the Swedish and the Dutch had encroached upon his land and was, therefore, disappointed when it was liberated, only to be given then to the Duke of York. Baltimore was cautious in pressing his claim against the Crown, but he did make his displeasure known.

If Baltimore had issue with royal claims, however, he was to be even more incensed when much of the territory in question was granted to William Penn. In 1681, Penn was granted the territory that became known as Pennsylvania. Sensitive about the grant already made to the Duke of York, Charles II was careful that Penn's grant did not infringe upon the earlier one made to his brother. Thus, Charles ordered that a semicircular arc be drawn twelve miles north of New Castle town, the largest and most important settlement in Delaware and the site of the original Fort Casimir, in order to create the boundary between Penn's land and that belonging to the Duke of York. Forever thereafter, it was this line that separated Pennsylvania from Delaware.

Although Penn's grant was of course a sizable one, he nevertheless was dissatisfied because it did not give him direct access to the Atlantic Ocean. In order to rectify this situation, Penn appealed to the royal family. Although it may appear rather bold for him to have done so, Charles II and the Duke of York were indebted to the Penn family for their help in securing the throne, so they were favorably inclined to honor Penn's request. Therefore, in 1682, William Penn was granted the Delaware holdings, thereby providing the ocean access he sought. Since the land was not part of his original Pennsylvania grant of 1681, however, the Delaware holdings were regularly referred to as the Lower Counties on the Delaware.

Then, as now, the territory that eventually came to be known as Delaware was composed of three counties: New Castle in the northern one-third of the state, Kent in the center, and Sussex in the south. The territory was rarely referred to collectively as Delaware. Indeed, it was not until 1776 that Delaware became its official name. Still, the Lower Counties on the Delaware had a distinct identity. Penn extended political representation to its inhabitants that mirrored the system enjoyed by residents of Pennsylvania.

From the beginning in 1682, the residents of Delaware were represented by delegates who were elected in each county to sit in assembly in Pennsylvania. That assembly first met in Chester but eventually convened in Philadelphia. Among the assembly's first acts was to adopt a "frame of government," or written constitution, that Penn had prepared in England. The result was the creation of a government where, in Penn's words, "God may have His due, Caesar his due, and the people their due."[7]

Although Penn was quick to draw Delaware into Pennsylvania's political orbit, he still had to contend with Lord Baltimore. Now that the land had passed from the Duke of York to Penn, Baltimore pressed his claim with authorities in England. Since the matter had to be sorted out before final title to the land could be granted, English authorities subsequently required both Penn and Baltimore to return to Britain to argue their cases.

In the autumn of 1685, the king's Privy Council issued a ruling in the case after having heard from both proprietors. The Delaware counties, it said, were not part of Maryland because Lord Baltimore's grant was only to land hitherto uncultivated. Since the Dutch had previously cultivated the land at Swanendael one year prior to Baltimore's grant in Maryland, Delaware was excluded from Maryland.[8] Rough boundaries were established between the Delaware counties and Maryland, but here, too, the precise borders remained in dispute until Mason and Dixon completed their survey nearly one hundred years later, long after both Penn and Baltimore had died.

By the time Penn returned to America fifteen years later in 1699, both Pennsylvania and the Delaware counties had developed considerably. Pennsylvania's population had swelled, and Philadelphia emerged as a vital colonial city. Although Delaware's growth was modest by comparison, it too became more populous. Kent and Sussex counties added migrants from Maryland and the Eastern Shore of Virginia, while New Castle County grew with people from Pennsylvania. In addition, Delaware also became a destination for Scotch-Irish immigrants pouring out of Ireland. Although Philadelphia was the favored destination of the Scotch-Irish, a number of them landed in New Castle, where vessels coming up the Delaware River usually stopped to take on water and disembark travelers and cargo intended for the Chesapeake.[9] The Scotch-Irish added diversity to the Dutch and Swedish populations already living in Delaware, in addition to a sizable Welsh settlement that was in the northwestern section of the colony near Maryland.

Politically, much had changed in Penn's absence as well. Despite giving Pennsylvania and the Lower Counties equal representation, neither party was particularly satisfied. For their part, the inhabitants of Pennsylvania were dissatisfied because they believed that the Delaware representatives wielded too much power. The three counties of Pennsylvania had the same number of representatives as did the three counties of Delaware, despite the considerably larger population residing in Pennsylvania. Nonetheless, Delaware residents believed that the Pennsylvania Quakers were unduly influential and overshadowed affairs of government. The friction between the two sides mounted until, in protest, the residents of the Lower Counties stopped sending elected delegates to the assembly in 1702.

Barbs were traded back and forth until 1704, when the Lower Counties established their own assembly, which met in the town of New Castle. Penn had pledged to the Pennsylvania and Delaware delegates that they could sit in separate assembly if either side wished to do so, and in 1703, the Pennsylvania contingent indicated that its members would certainly prefer to assemble without representatives from the Lower Counties. At the same time, the Pennsylvania delegates opted to increase their ranks in order to better represent their growing constituency.

Interestingly, the Delaware delegates elected in 1704 had initially expressed their willingness to assemble in Pennsylvania. However, upon learning that they would no longer sit in equal numbers with the Pennsylvania delegates, they chose to assemble in New Castle amongst themselves. It was a peculiar political situation indeed, since the Lower Counties on the Delaware continued to share a governor with neighboring Pennsylvania but now had their own independent representative government.[10]

Despite Penn's desire to combine both Pennsylvania and the Lower Counties into a single entity, by the early eighteenth century the two were drifting further apart. This was but one of a string of disappointments for Penn, who questioned whether his territories were worth the trouble or the money. In fact, Penn ultimately decided to sell his colonial grants to the Crown, but before he could do so, he suffered a severe stroke in 1712. As a result, the territories remained proprietorships and did not become royal colonies, as eight of the others were. The governors of Pennsylvania and the Lower Counties were therefore chosen by Penn's heirs and were in place both to govern and manage the Penn family interests.

Not surprisingly, the governor lived in Philadelphia, but he did journey to New Castle when the assembly met annually in November, as well as when special meetings were called on other occasions. This arm's-length arrangement apparently suited Delaware residents just fine. Although the governor could veto any legislation passed in the assembly, it was a power wielded infrequently since the assembly also controlled his salary. Once the governor approved a bill, it became law without further submission anywhere. Legislation was not sent to England for approval or review, either by the proprietors or by the Crown. In this respect, Delaware had rather unique powers of self-government, second only to Connecticut and Rhode Island, both of which elected their own governors. Even Pennsylvania had to forward all of its legislation to England for approval by the Privy Council, so the Lower Counties undoubtedly enjoyed an enviable measure of autonomy.[11]

In addition to having its own assembly, Delaware also had numerous elected offices at the county level, including sheriff and coroner. Each town elected officials such as tax assessors and election inspectors, whose function was to determine voter eligibility. The franchise in Delaware was fairly widespread. It required that voters own fifty acres of land, of which twelve had to be cleared, and have other tangible assets worth at least £40. Given the accessibility of land, the result was that many white males were eligible to vote. Neither women nor blacks were specifically disfranchised in Delaware law, but with few exceptions they did not vote, although by the end of the colonial era, some widows and free blacks could have met the property requirements.[12]

Delawareans were apparently satisfied with their political situation and enjoyed the growing autonomy afforded by the eighteenth century. Suspicion of Pennsylvania and its Quaker politicians that had arisen in the 1690s did not diminish over time, and perhaps even increased. According to Provincial

Secretary Thomas Logan, Delaware assemblymen used "the same language in reference to Pennsylvania that the Scots do in reference to England." As evidence of his observation, in 1757 the Delaware assembly issued a statement that read, in part, "We are independent of them (which we esteem no small part of our Happiness) and will ever assert and support that Independency."[13] Rapprochement between the neighboring territories seemed unlikely indeed.

DELAWARE'S EIGHTEENTH-CENTURY ECONOMY

Of course, Delaware's political independence from Pennsylvania was but one concern of average Delawareans in the first half of the eighteenth century. People focused on their daily routines of work and family, which, for the vast majority, revolved around agriculture. As the eighteenth century unfolded, Delaware farms produced fruits, vegetables, and livestock, most of which were consumed locally, although the neighboring markets of Philadelphia and Baltimore absorbed some of the output. Tobacco was grown to some extent in southern Delaware's Sussex County, but it was not nearly as important a crop as it was in Virginia or colonies further south. Tobacco cultivation was popular in the seventeenth century, but because of its labor intensity and the toll it exacted on soil, by the eighteenth century it was not a widely grown cash crop. By the mid-eighteenth century, it was clear to most Delaware farmers that wheat and corn were more profitable to grow.[14]

Wheat and corn were vital commodity crops and enjoyed a market well beyond the borders of the three counties. Although corn was grown in all three counties, wheat was especially prominent in Kent and New Castle counties. Some of the crops were used for feed, but much was processed into meals and flour. The processed grains found a ready market throughout the region, particularly in Philadelphia. Moreover, Delaware-produced flours and meals were exported to English colonies in the Caribbean, where planters found it more profitable to import foodstuffs while devoting their lands to the production of more exotic crops bound for England.[15]

With the commencement of the Seven Years' War in 1756, Delaware flour was shipped to England and elsewhere to be used in the British military effort. As a result, Delaware was drawn into a larger colonial orbit, from which it had largely been isolated. Suddenly the affairs of empire were not wholly remote but instead had an economic impact upon Delaware's farmers, millers, and shippers. Flour thus became something of a celebrated product, with mills located along the banks of waterways throughout Delaware.

It was near the city of Wilmington, however, that flour mills were particularly prominent. Chartered in 1739, Wilmington soon overshadowed the older and more established New Castle in the size of its population and economy, in part because of the mills that were developed along its rivers. By the end of the century, Wilmington's flour mills were not only the largest in the state but in fact were the largest in the country as a whole.[16] Among the mill owners were Joseph Tatnall and his son-in-law, Thomas Lea, both of whom would rise in political prominence during and after the Revolution. Their mills, in addition to other industries such as shipbuilding, tanning, iron production, and various small manufacturing ventures, formed the mainstay of the Wilmington economy.

Despite Wilmington's large flour mills and other industries, however, Delaware remained overwhelmingly agricultural and rural. Even though Wilmington was Delaware's largest city, its population on the eve of the Revolution was probably less than 1,300 people. The majority of Delaware's population instead toiled on farms, the most valuable of which were located near waterways. Because land was cheap and abundant, many lesser and middling farmers from Maryland and Pennsylvania left those colonies to try their luck in Delaware, as indeed some more prominent planters did as well. Landownership was widespread in Delaware, but rarely did it lead to the large fortunes that the elite planters enjoyed further south.[17]

Nevertheless, there were some sizable plantations in Delaware, where slaves performed much of the work. Just as Delaware's Caucasian population grew, so too did the number of enslaved blacks during the eighteenth century. Although the institution of slavery stemmed from the period of Dutch rule, it continued to expand steadily over the years. Prior to 1755, more than 55 percent of Delaware's slaves were African born, but subsequently the majority of slaves were born in either Delaware or elsewhere in colonial America. There was an active slave market in Wilmington that, while smaller than the one in nearby Philadelphia, had the added benefit that slaves could be bought and sold tax-free. Although precise census data do not exist, by the time of the Revolution, slaves accounted for roughly 20–25 percent of Delaware's total population.[18]

Despite the existence of plantation agriculture in Delaware, however, the wealthy elite in fact did not own most slaves. The use of slave labor peaked just prior to the Revolution, when perhaps as many as 30 percent of white households owned slaves.[19] That being the case, Delaware slaves and slaveholders most often lived and worked in close proximity to one another. While some 30 percent of whites may have owned slaves, typically they would only own a small number, unlike the larger labor units found in colonies such as Virginia or South Carolina.

By the eve of the Revolution, Delaware's social and economic structure thus presented a microcosm of colonial America. Northern New Castle County, which included the communities of New Castle and Wilmington, slowly became focused on commerce and industry. Although it would be an exaggeration to call either settlement urban, they nevertheless had characteristics in common with the larger cities to the north. Industry was growing in importance and greater numbers of New Castle County's residents were wage earners dwelling in town. The southern part of the state, by contrast, more closely resembled southern colonial conditions with plantation-style agriculture and the more widespread use of slave labor. Here, too, Delaware's plantations were more modest than their southern counterparts, yet nevertheless there were similarities. And so, with its differences north and south, urban and rural, commercial and agricultural, Delaware reflected colonial America's image, writ small.

THE REVOLUTION

Perhaps because of its proximity to Philadelphia and the whirlwind that unfolded there, the role of Delaware and its political leaders was somewhat over-shadowed during the war for independence. By all accounts, Delaware was not a hotbed of political activity, nor were its inhabitants particularly zealous as rebels or loyalists. Nevertheless, Delaware, like the rest of the colonies, was swept into the current of events, beginning with the Seven Years' War and British legislative action thereafter.

Because Delaware had its unique quasi-independent status, it enjoyed tremendous autonomy during the first half of the eighteenth century. As noted above, legislation passed in the assembly needed only gubernatorial approval and was not subject to review in England. While all of the American colonies grew accustomed to the period of "salutary neglect" that began in the 1730s as England left the colonies essentially to govern themselves, British authorities especially overlooked Delaware. It was thus all the more jarring to Delawareans when Parliament took renewed interest in colonial America during the Seven Years' War.

With British victory over the French in 1763, First Lord of the Treasury Grenville looked to the colonies to share in the financial burden of war. From the English perspective, this was entirely justified. After all, the colonists were English, and since the war had been fought in North America to extend and protect English interests, it was reasonable that the colonists should contribute to the effort. Thus began a series of new revenue measures including the Sugar Act of 1764 and the Stamp Act of 1765. Unwittingly, Grenville and Parliament set into motion a series of events that united the colonies like nothing before.

In October 1765, what became known as the Stamp Act Congress convened in New York to protest the new taxes. Since the Delaware assembly was not yet in session, the assemblymen in each county signed a letter appointing three delegates to the congress to represent Delaware and its interests.[20] Although one of the delegates opted not to travel to New York, the two others that did came to be among Delaware's leading voices during the Revolution. From New Castle County came attorney Thomas McKean, and from Kent County came Caesar Rodney, a prominent planter.

After the arduous journey to New York, McKean and Rodney joined with delegates from the other colonies in drafting a document to protest the new

English tax policies. It was there that the complaint of "taxation without representation" first gained popularity. Although the king and Parliament did not directly reply to that charge, the taxes were nevertheless repealed in the following year, much to the delight of the colonists. They had come together, protested what they viewed as an injustice, and had their grievances addressed. Along with their cohorts, McKean and Rodney undoubtedly felt a sense of accomplishment at their efforts.

A sense of satisfaction, however, was short-lived, for in 1767, Parliament once again enacted a new set of taxes aimed at raising revenue from the colonies. Known as the Townshend Acts, after Chancellor of the Exchequer Charles Townshend, they were tariffs levied on items such as glass, lead, paper, paint, and tea. Seeing that the Stamp Act Congress only had a short-term impact, colonial activists, led by John Dickinson, opted for a different strategy in battling the Townshend duties. Instead of convening a meeting and issuing a formal complaint, a committee of correspondence was created so that direct action could be planned and executed. It was in this way that a boycott of the taxed items was decided upon.

During this episode, Dickinson rose to national prominence. Born in Maryland, Dickinson had spent most of his life in Pennsylvania and Delaware. After studying law in Philadelphia and London, he became a highly successful attorney in Philadelphia but maintained close ties to the Lower Counties. In 1760, he was elected speaker of the Delaware assembly but left that position in 1762, whereupon he became a representative in the Pennsylvania legislature. To promote his views on the Townshend Acts, Dickinson published *Letters from a Pennsylvania Farmer*, which appeared in serial form in 1767 and 1768. He argued that the laws were inconsistent with English constitutional rights and thus promoted the concept of boycott, while at the same time opposing any sort of violent revolt.

Since few British goods were directly imported into Delaware, local merchants adhered to the boycott by working in conjunction with their Philadelphia suppliers, through whom most imported items came to Delaware. To ensure that the embargo was sustained in New Castle County, inspection committees were established for each town and instructed to monitor sales of embargoed goods and report any violations to a general committee, of which George Read, a New Castle attorney and assemblyman, was chairman. Should Read's committee uncover embargo violations, it seized the embargoed goods and sold them for the benefit of the county's poor.[21] Like McKean and Rodney before him, Read's involvement in this protest was later to catapult him into prominence during the Revolutionary era that soon followed.

Once again, the colonists' protests were successful, and the Townshend duties were repealed in 1770, save for the tax on tea. At this juncture, the boycott ended in Delaware and for the next three years there was general tranquillity. Protests began anew, however, in 1773, when the British Parliament granted a monopoly in the American tea trade to the East India Company.

The colonists resurrected their committees of correspondence to address this perceived injustice and again settled on a boycott as a means to undermine the monopoly. Given the hostile mood in the region, a ship bound for Philadelphia laden with tea was turned back as it approached the Delaware River in the late autumn of 1773. While noteworthy, the Boston Tea Party in December eclipsed any notoriety that might have resulted from the event on the Delaware.

Because of the Boston Tea Party in December 1773, British authorities acted decisively against Massachusetts by closing Boston's port and suspending the colony's government. As events unfolded rapidly in the northern colony, Delaware's counties each passed resolutions supporting Massachusetts and made preparations to send delegates to the Continental Congress that was to convene in August 1774. When the Delaware assembly met for this purpose, it selected the three men who had been active in earlier protests: Caesar Rodney, George Read, and Thomas McKean.

In assembling the Continental Congress, the colonists turned to the two methods that had yielded results during their protests against the Stamp Act and the Townshend duties. Despite the colonists' complaint to the king and Parliament and yet another boycott of English goods, the British refused to yield in their punishment of Massachusetts. When hostilities broke out in April 1775, it was clear that events had taken a turn for the worse and that broader hostilities may await on the horizon.

When the Second Continental Congress met in Philadelphia the next month, there was a greater sense of urgency among the delegates. Once again, Rodney, Read, and McKean represented Delaware and the three supported the creation of the Continental army to be commanded by George Washington. Meanwhile, in New Castle, a revolutionary committee was created to prepare Delaware for the likely hostilities to come. Committees of observation and inspection supervised the enforcement of the new boycott, while local commit-tees of safety gathered weapons and began providing basic military training. In September 1775, Delaware established a Council of Safety, to be responsible for coordinating all military matters. It was under the auspices of the council that the first Delaware regiment, commanded by Colonel John Haslet, was sent to join Washington in 1776 at the Battle of Long Island.[22]

As the Continental Congress continued to meet in Philadelphia, Delaware's three delegates remained the same. Their instructions from the Delaware assembly were rather ambiguous, which indeed reflected the mixed sentiment of Delaware residents. On the one hand, they were instructed to seek and support reconciliation with England if at all possible. On the other hand, though, Rodney, Read, and McKean were also instructed to support military measures if they saw fit. This seemingly contradictory position offered something to both radical and conservative assemblymen and underscored Delaware's tempered stance in the months leading up to the Declaration of Independence.

By June 1776, however, Delaware had more decisively moved against recon-ciliation with the Crown. With war having been waged for a year, hopes for a peaceful settlement to colonial complaints dimmed. On June 15, the assembly approved a resolution proposed by McKean to sever official ties with England and suspend royal authority. As a result, the Delaware legislature assumed all responsibilities formerly held by Pennsylvania governor John Penn. In practical terms, little had changed in Delaware's day-to-day governance, but of course the vote moved Delaware on a decisive path toward confrontation.

As if to emphasize the resolve with which Delaware severed ties with British officialdom, the assembly also wrote new instructions to the three congressional delegates. In the revised language, all reference to reconciliation was stricken. Although the assembly was too conservative to call specifically for independence, it did instruct the delegates to support whatever measures promoted liberty. By deliberately leaving the instructions somewhat vague, the assembly enabled the delegates to vote their conscience. As a result, Rodney, Read, and McKean were given wide power when they voted on behalf of Delaware, but the stage was also set for tension among them.

In addition, the June vote also meant that Delaware was truly independent of Pennsylvania and thus could assume a position as an autonomous entity. Although Delaware had been nominally independent of Pennsylvania since 1704, the assembly's action in June 1776 severed the one remaining political link between the two. If Delaware no longer recognized the authority of the Pennsylvania governor, with the Delaware assembly assuming all of his former powers, then by definition it was a distinct colony. It was at this juncture that Delaware became the thirteenth colony, ceasing to be an awkward appendage of the Penn proprietorship.

Of course, regardless of this technicality, Delaware's congressional delegation continued its work as it had done for the previous year, albeit under revised instructions. On June 7, 1776, Virginia's Richard Henry Lee had first introduced a motion seeking independence from Great Britain, and on July 1 debate on his proposal began. Delaware's complete contingent was not present, however, since Caesar Rodney was busy attending to his duties as a brigadier general in the state militia, therefore leaving only McKean and Read as participants in the debate.

Rodney's absence from the Philadelphia meeting proved to be significant, since McKean and Read did not agree on the issue of independence. McKean supported the measure, while Read did not. Since each state had one vote at the Congress, however, their deadlock effectively meant that Delaware could not vote. A preliminary poll of the delegates showed that a supermajority of nine states supported independence, so in theory Delaware's participation was unnecessary since the measure would have passed in any event. Nevertheless, before the final vote was taken on July 2, McKean was determined that Delaware should be among the supporters of independence and, believing that Rodney supported independence, therefore dispatched word for him to come to Philadelphia to break the deadlock.

In what became one of the most celebrated events in Delaware history, Caesar Rodney rushed to Philadelphia on horseback to side with McKean and put Delaware on the side of independence. That he rode to Philadelphia on a stormy summer night with his face bandaged because of an ongoing battle with facial skin cancer only added to the drama of the event. When the Continental Congress voted on July 2, 1776, the support for independence was carried unanimously. In addition to Delaware joining the previous day's majority, so too did South Carolina and Pennsylvania. New York's delegates had been instructed to seek reconciliation and thus could not vote for independence, but they agreed not to vote at all so that the resolution could be announced as carried by the unanimous vote of those states present and voting. Two days later, the decision of July 2 was embodied in the memorable words of Thomas Jefferson's Declaration of Independence, which was adopted without a recorded vote.[23]

Of course, by declaring their intention for freedom, the congressional delegates set the course for war, taking on the world's most formidable armed forces in the process. Delawareans remained fairly moderate throughout the summer of 1776 and, though generally supportive of independence, were circumspect as events unfolded. In August 1776, delegates assembled in New Castle to write a new state constitution. George Read, despite his opposition to independence in Philadelphia, was chosen to preside over the convention.

In choosing Read as its president, the Delaware Constitutional Convention was signaling the generally moderate stance of Delawareans. Although voting against independence in Philadelphia, Read was nevertheless unquestionably a patriot. He served as the president of the Delaware Council of Safety, which coordinated military matters within the state, and he had led resistance to British coercion since the 1760s. Moreover, when the Declaration of Independence was adopted and written in final form, Read joined McKean and Rodney and signed it. The moderate course Read followed—as an opponent to British mistreatment, as a skeptic of armed rebellion, and yet as a man willing to join the majority in the final analysis—was well suited to the spirit of Delaware.[24]

When the Delaware Constitutional Convention opened on August 27, 1776, the task before it was fairly straightforward. A new system of government had to replace the colonial structure, but as a moderate lot, Delawareans did not seek radical change. The most objectionable feature of colonial government had been the English governor, so with that position eliminated, the new constitution created an executive position to assume some of his responsibilities. Given the title of president, the new executive did not have the sweeping powers once vested in the governor. He could not veto legislation. Any appointments that he made had to be approved by a four-member Privy Council. The assembly appointed the members of that council as well as the president himself.

It took the convention only one month to draft a new constitution for Delaware, and by January 1777, it went into effect. The most noteworthy feature of the new government was the concentration of power in the legislature. In addition to selecting the president and his governing council, it also appointed judges. Moreover, the legislature itself changed in that it became bicameral. The upper chamber, called the Legislative Council, consisted of nine members elected to three-year terms. The lower chamber, known as the House of Assembly, had twenty-one members elected to one-year terms. As such, the two bodies served as a check on each other, since the executive branch lacked veto power.[25]

As for the broader populace, there were no changes in the qualifications for the franchise and only minor changes in the courts. Justices of the peace dominated local government, but they were now to be chosen by the president and his council from among a list of candidates nominated by the assembly. People were guaranteed a free press and freedom of religion, but only Christians were promised the right to participate in politics.[26] And, of great symbolic importance, the name "The Delaware State" was given to the land. Not only would Delaware officially be known as such for the first time, but also it could do so by proudly proclaiming itself to be a state.

In addition to structuring a new government, the state constitution also included a provision that banned the importation of slaves into Delaware. Although this ban later would evolve into further measures restricting the slave trade in Delaware, it was a noteworthy first step. In subsequent years, the export of slaves from Delaware to Georgia, the Carolinas, Maryland, and Virginia was specifically banned, but the 1776 constitution still enabled slaveholders to sell slaves out of state. The percentage of slaves living in Delaware peaked at about this very time, thereafter declining.

The first president of Delaware was John McKinly, a political leader and physician from Wilmington. McKinly was a strong supporter of the Revolution and, as such, a high-profile rebel. Like many a fellow Scotch-Irish immigrant, McKinly had a long distrust and dislike of the British. He was deeply devoted to unseating them. As the chief burgess of Wilmington, McKinly proved to be a competent administrator, which was all that the assembly sought. As the state's first president, the assembly intended that he do just that—preside over Delaware State, and not govern it.

As for the war itself, Delaware saw little military conflict, save for one notable skirmish on September 3, 1777, at a location known as Cooch's Bridge. The battle was a prelude to the Battle of the Brandywine and the British occupation of Wilmington. Since the British commanding general, William Howe, had been unsuccessful in capturing Philadelphia through New Jersey, he opted to bring his forces via the Chesapeake and through Maryland and Delaware in order to attack from the south. In so doing, thousands of British troops convened upon a place near the Aiken Tavern (where today the town of Glasgow, Delaware, is located) in preparation for their major assault.

As the English and their Hessian mercenaries assembled in Delaware, they encountered an American force of some 720 soldiers under the command of William Maxwell. Maxwell had been ordered by George Washington to disrupt the British advance as best he could and thus, despite the lopsided numbers, led his men into battle. The land upon which much of the fighting took place was owned by the Cooch family, hence the name given to the battle. At times pitched, the engagement was impossible for the Americans to sustain for long, and ultimately they withdrew. Although precise records do not exist, the Americans probably suffered thirty killed in the clash, with the British losing a total of thirty dead and wounded.[27] After encamping at Cooch's Bridge for three nights, the British ultimately resumed their march through Newark, Delaware, on their way to Kennett Square, Pennsylvania. The maneuver caught Washington by surprise, and in the encounter known as the Battle of the Brandywine, American and British forces clashed on September 11, 1777, ultimately resulting in a major British victory.

As a result of their victory, British forces easily captured Wilmington, during which time they seized Delaware president John McKinly, as well as the state treasury and many public records.[28] Wilmington was subsequently occupied for over a month, until which time British forces withdrew as they pressed on for Philadelphia. From that point on, most military activity moved outside of the state, though of course heavy fighting was nearby.

Fortunately for Delaware lawmakers, the occupation of Wilmington and the naval blockade of New Castle were not as dangerous as they might have been since the assemblymen had earlier fled New Castle County and moved the assembly to Dover in Kent County. Although New Castle was not under siege when the move occurred, assemblymen feared that danger was imminent and thus chose to meet downstate. At the time, the move was seen as a temporary measure, and for the next several years Delaware's assembly convened at various points around the state. Since Dover was centrally located, however, by 1781 it became the permanent site of the Delaware assembly.

THE FOUNDING OF A NATION

Perhaps one of the greatest challenges facing the former colonists during the Revolution was the creation of a country and a national identity. After all, many of the adults at one point in their lives had considered themselves British subjects, and they were now in the process of reorienting themselves socially and politically. Although the congresses and committees of correspondence had facilitated colonial communication, they were not intended to bind the states together legally. Recognizing future governance needs, the Second Continental Congress established a committee to draft the Articles of Confederation in the spring of 1776, well before the Declaration of Independence was issued in July. The Articles were to provide a legal alliance of the thirteen states represented in Philadelphia and the basic framework of a government binding them together.

First and foremost, the Articles created a national entity in order for the states to fight their common enemy, Britain. In addition, though, the Articles of Confederation also furnished a basis upon which the future of the United States would rest. Before the Articles of Confederation went into effect, all thirteen state assemblies had to approve the document. This did not occur until 1781. Interestingly, although Delaware was the first state to ratify the U.S. Constitution of 1787, it was the second-to-last state to ratify the Articles. The chief concern of Delaware lawmakers in regard to the Articles had to do with future national expansion. Since Delaware's boundaries were firmly established and it had no claims on western lands, there was fear in the assembly that states like Virginia, which had extensive land claims, would have overwhelming influence in the new government. Some would have preferred that unsettled lands belong to the Union as a whole, but obviously Virginians and others with claims disagreed. Although the Articles of Confederation were not changed to suit the objections raised by Delawareans regarding western lands, the states with significant western claims began making cessions to the federal government, as Virginia did in 1784. If these cessions had not been made, the system of admitting new states on equal terms into an enlarging Union might not have developed as it later did.[29]

Under the Articles of Confederation, the United States achieved several notable successes, among them winning the Revolution and establishing a system of land survey and government for the West that provided for future states. But the Confederation government was severely hampered because it could not raise taxes, nor could it regulate commerce.[30] Furthermore, the country's currency system was dismal and showed no signs for improvement. Understandably, the states feared strong central government, but it was equally clear that the Articles were insufficient to meet the challenges posed to the newly victorious country.

When a new Constitutional Convention was called to meet in Philadelphia in 1787, Delaware was eager to send delegates. Monetary conditions had worsened since the war's end, and Delaware merchants felt that some sort of national regulation of commerce had to occur. The Delaware assembly therefore sent five delegates to Philadelphia: John Dickinson, George Read, Gunning Bedford, Richard Bassett, and Jacob Broom. Each was chosen because of the different constituency he symbolized or the influence he could wield among delegates from other states. In what turned out to be a long, hot summer of debate, Delaware indeed would need all of the influence it could muster.

Of the five delegates, John Dickinson was certainly the best known throughout the new country. Although he had represented Pennsylvania during the debate over independence, he had since returned to Delaware. Dickinson was not without controversy, however, since he had voted against independence in 1776. Most who knew him understood that Dickinson's 1776 vote reflected his wish that perhaps reconciliation was still possible but that once the decision for independence had been made, he was a supporter of the American cause. Indeed, it was Dickinson who drafted the first version of the Articles of Confederation, though subsequently his version was rejected because many felt that it made the national government too powerful. Since Delawareans had come to believe that the Confederation was too weak, however, Dickinson became an obvious choice for one who would promote strong national government.

If Dickinson enjoyed a national standing, it was George Read who probably was the most politically important man in Delaware. As detailed above, he was a tireless public servant who had served in numerous capacities and a man who understood Delaware's needs in whatever new government would emerge from the Convention. Chief among those needs was equal representation in the new government. Undoubtedly the larger states would push for proportional representation, but given Delaware's modest size, equal representation was the key goal.

The remaining delegates were perhaps lesser known but were nevertheless influential and prominent. Gunning Bedford, a graduate of Princeton College, was Delaware's attorney general, and therefore a natural delegate for the General Assembly to select. He was read in the law and possessed a keen eye for detail. Richard Bassett was likewise an attorney, but also a large landowner with considerable wealth. He was among those Delawareans who looked for stronger national regulation of commerce, and in fact he had earlier been selected as a delegate to a convention on that very matter, although in the end the meeting yielded no results. Lastly, Jacob Broom, a manufacturer and entrepreneur from Wilmington, was also a man with commercial interests. Whereas Bassett was a planter rooted in more traditional economic pursuits, Broom symbolized an upcoming generation whose power and influence stemmed from industry.

As the five journeyed to Philadelphia, they had strict instructions from the General Assembly insisting that Delaware have an equal voice with other states in any new Congress that would be created. Aside from that charge, however, the delegates were given broad authority to vote their conscience. This flexibility was important, since neither the General Assembly nor the delegates themselves could predict the precise issues that would arise, but undoubtedly they would confront everything from matters of national defense to commerce to governmental structure. Despite their instructions, however, none of the five really needed a reminder in regard to equal representation. As Delawareans they all concurred on the matter, but the instructions were helpful as a bargaining tool. They enabled the five to remain steadfast in their negotiations with other states because of their orders and provided them with a ready excuse if pressed by delegates seeking proportional representation.

On May 29, just days after the Constitutional Convention had begun, James Madison introduced what became known as the "Virginia Plan" as a model by which the United States could be fashioned. His vision included many of the checks and balances that later were to become key components of the new government, but his plan also called for proportional representation of the states in Congress, precisely what Delaware wanted to avoid. Although the Constitutional Convention was held in strict secrecy lest the delegates be influenced by outside elements, it has since become clear that the less populous states, Delaware among them, were unhappy with the Virginia Plan and let their disquiet be known. It was at that juncture that Connecticut's Roger Sherman introduced a compromise that moved the convention forward.

Known as the "Connecticut Compromise" or the "Great Compromise," Sherman's concept adopted Madison's vision of a bicameral legislature, but provided for proportional representation in the House and equal representation in the Senate. His Republican vision suited the competing interests and, like most compromises, had a bit of something for everybody. The more populous states would have their proportional representation in the House and, of course, states like Delaware could be satisfied with an equal voice in the Senate. It was a compromise with which the delegates, including Delaware's five, could live.

Strictly speaking, the Connecticut Compromise did not precisely fulfill the instructions the Delaware delegates were given. Although equal representation was part of the measure, so too was proportional representation. Regardless, the Delawareans knew that this was the best they could accomplish at the convention and so embraced Sherman's plan. There would be some explaining to do once the five returned to Delaware's General Assembly, but Read in particular was confident that he could explain their position. Since he was the chairman of the committee that drafted the instructions in the first place, he knew his fellow assemblymen well and was hopeful that in the final analysis he could persuade them that Delaware could have done no better.

And so it was that the Constitutional Convention concluded its business in September 1787 and all of the delegates returned to their states. By agreement, nine of the states would have to approve the language of the proposed constitution before it could be ratified. Each of the states was to convene special sessions of their legislative bodies to consider the matter and vote in a timely fashion. Pennsylvania was the first to assemble such a convention, but when a special convention of the Delaware General Assembly met on Monday, December 3, 1787, it moved quickly. Since the proceedings of the Delaware convention no longer exist, the precise discussions and debates regarding the Constitution remain unknown. Nevertheless, by week's end, on December 7, the measure passed by a unanimous vote, making Delaware the first state to ratify the U.S. Constitution and, therefore, the first in the new Union.

Known as the Form of Ratification, the document the Delaware lawmakers signed read as follows:

> We the Deputies of the People of the Delaware State, in Convention met, having taken into serious consideration the Foederal [sic] Constitution proposed and agreed upon by the Deputies of the United States in a General Convention held at the City of Philadelphia on the seventeenth day of September in the year of our Lord one thousand seven hundred and eighty seven, Have approved,

assented to, ratified, and confirmed, and by these Presents, Do, in virtue of the Power and Authority to us given for that purpose, for and in behalf of ourselves and our Constituents, fully freely, and entirely approve of, assent to, ratify and confirm the said Constitution.[31]

Awkward as the language may have been, it was upon signing their names to this declaration that all thirty delegates to the state convention made Delaware the First State.

Delaware celebrated its place as the First State, but it should be noted that the unanimous vote to ratify was significant in itself. Delaware was by no means free from partisanship. By 1787, Delaware was in fact a rather divided state, with competing interests and socioeconomic structures. New Castle County, in the northern part of the state, had long been more closely aligned to the commercial and social sensibilities of its northern neighbors, particularly Pennsylvania. The southern counties, on the other hand, had long been more agriculturally oriented and were characterized by patterns predominant in the South, particularly in the development of plantations and the use of slave labor. While this north-south divide had long characterized the state, it was particularly pronounced by the end of the eighteenth century. That representatives from both regions, despite the divide between them, could come together on the issue of the Constitution was telling.

In coming together to support the Constitution, the Delaware assemblymen saw past their regional differences and recognized the benefits that the new United States would provide. In addition to guaranteeing equal representation with the other states in the Senate, the new government would have the ability to raise revenue and regulate commerce, two notable weakness of the government under the Articles of Confederation. Although the Revolution was a recent event, sufficient time had passed for lawmakers to accept a more powerful national government as a means of promoting the common good. Having cast their votes in favor of the Constitution, Delawareans now had to wait to see if other states agreed.

CONCLUSION

With New Hampshire ratifying the Constitution on June 21, 1788, the necessary two-thirds of the states had voted in favor of its adoption, and thus the United States was born. Still, it was not until the influential states of Virginia and New York ratified it on June 25 and July 26, respectively, that confidence in the new government prevailed. Three years afterward, the Bill of Rights was ratified, thus addressing several reservations and concerns that might have lingered. Throughout the new country, broadsides, pamphlets, and editorials cheered its successes and promoted the notion of Republican virtue.

As for Delaware, the state benefited from joining the new Union much as the assemblymen in December 1787 had hoped. The state constitution was revised in 1792 to reflect the U.S. Constitution and its initial amendments, and Delawareans were seemingly content with political affairs to the extent that they thought about them. For the most part, people focused upon their daily routines and their work in farming or commerce. That they were able to do so, however, testified to the stability of the country after years of colonial protest, war, and nation building.

Delaware had developed considerably since the Stamp Act crisis and the events leading to war. With independence first from Pennsylvania and then Great Britain, its political institutions had matured, and a new generation of leaders emerged to replace those who had led Delaware through so much. A growing population helped to spur economic activity throughout the state, particularly in northern Delaware with its manufacturing sector. The southern agricultural economy continued to prosper, although over time the number of slaves working on plantations began a long and steady decline.

If Delaware was different by the late 1780s than it had been twenty-five years earlier, however, the changes that had taken place were characterized by evolution and not revolution. For most of its history, Delaware had been stable and eased into changing circumstances. Even when colonial rulers changed, Delaware did not experience paradigmatic shifts. For example, as rule moved from the Swedish to the Dutch and finally to the English during the seventeenth century, life for ordinary Delawareans changed little. Property rights had been respected and, if anything, each shift in power brought a bit more political freedom and participatory governance. Likewise, when Delaware formed its own assembly in 1704, it did so not to craft an entirely new form of government but rather to better represent people of the Lower Counties closer to home. Although significant and important changes thus occurred early in Delaware's history, they did so with relatively smooth transitions and little disruption to ordinary affairs.

Even as Delaware declared independence from the Crown, it did so with some hesitancy and moderation on the part of its delegates. The division between Read, Rodney, and McKean was neither bitter nor deep. Theirs were honest differences of opinion among educated and circumspect men, reflective of Delaware as a whole. Delawareans were concerned that their rights had been violated, but they did not seek a completely new way of life. That they eventually chose rather drastic measures to secure those rights was in keeping with the sentiments found in their neighboring colonies and was not an expression of radical departure.

And so it was that Delaware took its place in the new nation. As the first to ratify the Constitution, Delaware sought to secure its hard-won gains with the best available option. It was a political system carved out of compromise, but it was a compromise with which Delawareans could live and ultimately prosper. Just as changes in colonial rule during the seventeenth century secured increasingly better rights for their ancestors, Delawareans at the end of the eighteenth century embraced the new Constitution as the best means for just and fair government in the future. As the first of the uniting states, Delaware looked toward the future with characteristically well-founded and considered optimism.

NOTES

1. John A. Munroe, *History of Delaware* (Newark: University of Delaware Press, 2001), p. 17.
2. Ibid., p. 23.
3. Ibid., p. 24.
4. Ibid., p. 26.
5. Ibid., p. 27.
6. William H. Williams, *Slavery and Freedom in Delaware, 1639–1865* (Wilmington, DE: Scholarly Resources, 1999), p. xii.
7. Munroe, *History of Delaware*, p. 37.
8. Ibid., p. 38.
9. Ibid., p. 55.
10. Ibid., p. 44.
11. Ibid., pp. 47–48.
12. Ibid., p. 49.
13. Ibid., p. 51.
14. Paul G.E. Clemens, *The Atlantic Economy and Colonial Maryland's Eastern Shore: From Tobacco to Grain* (Ithaca: Cornell University Press, 1980), p. 196.
15. Munroe, *History of Delaware*, p. 58.
16. Ibid.
17. Ibid., p. 59.
18. Williams, *Slavery and Freedom in Delaware*, p. 41, xv.
19. Ibid., p. 37.
20. Munroe, *History of Delaware*, p. 63.
21. Ibid., p. 64.
22. Ibid., p. 66.
23. Ibid., p. 69.
24. Ibid., p. 70.
25. Ibid., p. 72.
26. Ibid.
27. Christopher L. Ward, *The Delaware Continentals: 1776–1783* (Wilmington: Historical Society of Delaware, 1941), p. 192.
28. Munroe, *History of Delaware*, p. 74.
29. Ibid., pp. 77–78.
30. Ibid., p. 78.
31. Merrill Jensen, ed., *The Documentary History of the Ratification of the Constitution: Volume 3, Ratification of the Constitution by the States Delaware, New Jersey, Georgia, Connecticut* (Madison: State Historical Society of Wisconsin, 1978), p. 110.

BIBLIOGRAPHY

Clemens, Paul G.E. *The Atlantic Economy and Colonial Maryland's Eastern Shore: From Tobacco to Grain.* Ithaca: Cornell University Press, 1980.

Jensen, Merrill, ed. *The Documentary History of the Ratification of the Constitution: Volume 3, Ratification of the Constitution by the States Delaware, New Jersey, Georgia, Connecticut.* Madison: State Historical Society of Wisconsin, 1978.

Munroe, John A. *The History of Delaware.* Newark: University of Delaware Press, 2001.

Ward, Christopher L. *The Delaware Continentals: 1776–1783.* Wilmington: Historical Society of Delaware, 1941.

Williams, William H. *Slavery and Freedom in Delaware, 1639–1865.* Wilmington: Scholarly Resources, 1999.

☆☆☆

THE STATE OF FLORIDA

Admitted to the Union as a State: March 3, 1845

Andrew K. Frank

INTRODUCTION

From its independence, the United States viewed East Florida and West Florida as inevitable places for territorial expansion. In addition to the untapped, agriculturally rich terrain in the middle of its panhandle, Florida also offered to improve the nation's infrastructure with several ports on the Gulf of Mexico and Atlantic Ocean. Settlements in and around St. Augustine to the east and Pensacola to the west had economic and social ties to neighboring American communities, and many of Florida's residents desired annexation by the United States. Just as significant, many Americans believed that incorporating Florida would put an end to the long-resented role that the region played as a refuge for runaway criminals, slaves, and Indians.

In the aftermath of the 1820 Missouri Compromise, few Americans believed that they had eliminated the most contentious issue from the state-making process. The compromise created a short-term congressional solution to soothe the sectional strife. It incorporated the free state of Maine and the slave state of Missouri as the twenty-third and twenty-fourth states and established 36°30' as the future barrier between free and slave territory. Thomas Jefferson eloquently explained this preset dividing line: "I considered it [the Missouri Compromise] at once as the knell of the Union. It is hushed, indeed, for the moment. But this is a reprieve only, not a final sentence."[1] The premise behind and promise of the compromise continued in 1836–1837, when Congress simultaneously extended statehood to Arkansas and Michigan. For the time being, at least, the nation maintained its sectional balance of power.

Florida

Territorial Development:

- Spain ceded future Floridian territory to the United States through the Adams-Onís Treaty, February 22, 1819
- Florida organized as a U.S. territory, March 30, 1821
- Florida admitted into the Union as the twenty-seventh state, March 3, 1845

Capitals Prior to Statehood:

- St. Augustine and Pensacola endured as the capitals of East and West Florida, respectively, 1763–1824
- Tallahassee, 1824–1845

State Capitals:

- Tallahassee, 1845–present

Origin of State Name: "Florida" comes from the Spanish for "feast of flowers," the feast of Easter, the day on which the Spanish explorer Ponce de Leon discovered it.

First Governor: William D. Moseley
Governmental Organization: Bicameral
Population at Statehood: 87,445
Geographical Size: 53,927 square miles

The incorporation of Missouri and Arkansas as the twelfth and thirteenth slave states did little to resolve the exploding demand for arable land caused by the cotton boom in the American South. Southern planters continued to covet the arable lands to their south and west. There, the sovereignty of various Native and European nations slowed the spread of American settlement, even as many residents dreamed that their national borders would inevitably expand. Native American, Spanish, French, and English neighbors did not permanently stall America's "manifest destiny." Late eighteenth and early nineteenth-century Americans steadily moved into the southern interior onto lands incrementally ceded by the Creek, Cherokee, Choctaw, and Chickasaw Indians. The United States obtained 830,000 miles of French land through the unprecedented Louisiana Purchase in 1803, and the federal government slowly chipped away at the Spanish hold on its territory in the southeast.

National politics complicated the desire for expansion. On the one hand, the federal government encouraged expansion. Through the Northwest Ordinance of 1787, Congress established a precedent for acquired territories that determined they would become states as soon as they could be stable and self-sufficient entities. In addition to pledging that Congress would accept the right of territories to become states, the ordinance declared that statehood was a "sacred" and an "inviolable" right. Encouragement for expansion also came from Americans who saw it as a means to control strategic ports and waterways and otherwise protect their borders from the imperial designs of Britain, France, and Spain. On the other hand, sectional tensions about slavery brought some caution into the state-making process. The emergence of an organized and politically oriented abolitionist movement in the North brought a newfound urgency to fighting the spread of slavery. Limiting the spread of slavery or ensuring the rights of slaveholders led politicians throughout the nation to see territorial expansion as either the cause or solution to their problems.

TERRITORIAL (COLONIAL) GOVERNMENT

When Spain regained control of East Florida and West Florida from Great Britain in the 1783 Treaty of Paris, the territories immediately faced economic and military pressures from the north. There, the young United States looked to expand its agricultural empire into the Spanish territory. This expansion primarily occurred in West Florida, where a combination of diplomatic maneuvers, military invasions, and economic transactions allowed the United States to weaken Spanish control. In these endeavors, the United States frequently had the support of hundreds of English-speaking Protestant residents who came to the Floridas during British rule and had little loyalty to the Spanish Crown.[2]

The United States began its acquisition of Spanish lands by negotiating territory that the Treaty of Paris left in dispute. Pinckney's Treaty (also known as the Treaty of San Lorenzo del Escorial) in 1795 established the 31st parallel as Florida's northern boundary. This resulted in several western districts on Florida's northern border, most notably the Natchez District in Mississippi, coming under American dominion. The incorporation of Florida territory continued through the 1803 Louisiana Purchase. The United States insisted that France include the Spanish territory west of the Perdido River, and while it maintained a legal position in public, it covertly maneuvered to annex this territory. On September 23, 1810, local insurgents, with the private support of President James Madison, staged a rebellion that captured Baton Rouge and overthrew Spanish rule in the westernmost region of Spanish Florida. The residents of the region declared their independence from Spain and formally asked to be incorporated by the United States. President James Madison publicly rejected the calls for annexation and instead he repeated American claims that the territory was American soil as a result of the Louisiana Purchase. He ordered the U.S. military to occupy the lands. The West Florida Rebellion, as it is called, resulted in these lands becoming part of the Mississippi Territory and the state of Louisiana.[3]

The U.S. military further eroded the Spanish hold on Florida during the War of 1812. Although the United States was not at war with Spain, General Andrew Jackson found just cause to march through Alabama, enter Spanish West Florida, engage British forces who had retreated to Pensacola, and destroy the Spanish strongholds at Fort San Carlos de Barrancas and Saint Rosa Island. Jackson, who became an American war hero for his actions during the War of 1812, returned to Spanish Florida in 1818, when warfare with Red Stick Creeks and Seminoles intensified. Jackson did not fully subdue the "hostile" Indians, whom he blamed for attracting runaway slaves out of the lower South, but he did reveal Spain's weak grip on the region. While invading Spanish Florida, Jackson executed two British soldiers and two Red Stick chiefs for their hostility to the United States. He then marched to Pensacola and attacked the Spanish forces he blamed for supplying Indians who attacked frontier settlements in Alabama. Jackson destroyed the reconstructed Fort San Carlos de Barrancas and took the surrender of its Spanish troops. The United States controlled Pensacola for nine months before it allowed Spain to regain control in February 1819.[4]

Spain would only hold onto Pensacola and the entirety of East and West Florida for two more years. Jackson's invasions had effectively demonstrated that Spain had lost control of the territory, while fiscal problems at home convinced Spanish authorities that it could not afford to defend its Florida colonies. As a result, Spanish Minister Luis de Onís and U.S. Secretary of State John Quincy Adams negotiated the transfer of Florida's sovereignty. The resulting Adams-Onís Treaty, which was signed on February 22, 1819, and ratified on July 17, 1821, formally defined the claims of the United States and Spain to lands in North America. In addition to ceding East and West Florida to the United States, Spain also renounced its claims to the Oregon Territory. In return, the United States recognized Spain's control over Texas.

As much as it settled the territorial claims of Spain and the United States, the Adams-Onís Treaty did not clarify the future of Florida. Instead, the treaty promised that the current residents of East Florida and West Florida would be "incorporated in the Union of the United-States, as soon as may be consistent with the principles of the Federal Constitution." In other words, the provision allowed the citizens and territories to be welcomed into the preexisting states of Alabama or Georgia, but it did not declare American intentions to impose statehood. If statehood was to be the fate of the Florida territories, the treaty did not indicate whether they would become one or two states.[5]

General Jackson returned to Florida for a third time when President James Monroe appointed him U.S. commissioner and governor of the territories of East and West Florida. Although he was a controversial nominee, Monroe used the appointment to acknowledge Jackson's integral role in pressuring Spain to cede control of the territory and to vindicate the general's earlier invasions of the Spanish lands. Monroe gave Jackson three tasks—to receive and occupy the ceded lands, govern the territory, and establish a territorial government. Jackson began these tasks when he entered West Florida on June 14, only days before Spanish officials formally transferred their sovereignty over the territory and nearly 10,000 residents on June 17. Colonel Adjutant General Robert Butler, acting on Jackson's behalf, accepted the transfer of East Florida.[6]

Jackson quickly discovered that his new post in humid Pensacola was not to his liking. Monroe had appointed most of the territory's important officials without Jackson's consultation, and Jackson disliked dealing with Spanish officials who lagged behind to complete the transfer of power. Governing Florida proved equally difficult, as geographic distance and social networks separated the territory into distinct eastern and western parts. This division forced Jackson to employ two secretaries, one to reside in St. Augustine and the other in Pensacola. On October 5, 1821, after Jackson proclaimed that he had established an effective and stable government, Old Hickory resigned and returned to his home in Tennessee.[7]

While Jackson worked to stabilize Florida's territorial government, legislators in Alabama and Georgia maneuvered to annex the newly acquired territory and incorporate its citizens. Alabama sent a resolution to both houses of Congress indicating its desire to incorporate West Florida, and the citizens of West Florida added their support with a memorial to Congress.[8] Georgia wrote up its own resolution for East Florida, which had been economically and socially connected to Georgia long before 1821, but apparently never delivered it to Washington.[9] Perhaps this design was stalled by opposition in East Florida, where its citizens petitioned Congress to reject annexation by Georgia. These East Floridians were not opposed to becoming part of the United States but preferred to wait until they could become the state of East Florida. The U.S. Senate, largely because of a desire to see Florida become viable for statehood sooner rather than later, rejected Alabama's attempt to annex West Florida.[10]

On March 30, 1822, only months after Jackson resigned as governor, Congress brought the provisional structure of Florida's government to an end and placed East Florida and West Florida under a unified government. Virginian William Pope DuVal, who had served as a U.S. judge at Pensacola before succeeding Jackson, became governor of Florida. The new territorial government followed the principle established by the Northwest Ordinance that encouraged self-rule for acquired territories and statehood when territorial populations met the population ratios used to determine representation in the House of Representatives. By unifying the Floridas as a single territory, Congress increased the likelihood of obtaining the necessary population required to make Florida a state.

The new territorial government Florida obtained was a single government, with a governor, secretary, judiciary, and Legislative Council with thirteen members who were appointed by the president. In addition, Floridians now elected a nonvoting delegate to represent the territory in the U.S. Congress. To appease the geographic tensions within the territory, Congress ordered the Legislative Council to alternate its annual meetings between Pensacola and St. Augustine. East and West Florida became the territory's two counties—Escambia and Saint Johns. This division initially resulted in the state having two administrative parts and competing sections. Middle Florida and additional counties would not be formed until 1824, when the Territorial Council created a third court in the region between the Apalachicola and Suwannee rivers. In 1826, a congressional act turned the Legislative Council into an elective body, and twelve years later Congress made the council a bicameral body. Voting rights were extended to all white men over the age of twenty-one who had resided in the territory for at least three months.

The Legislative Council met in Pensacola for the first time on July 22, 1822. The meeting had been delayed for nearly two months because storms, shipwrecks, and yellow fever prevented the council members from reaching the westernmost part of Florida. Delays were magnified by the death of Council Chairman James C. Bronaugh. When the council finally achieved a quorum, it established a court structure, civil offices, militia, and revenue structure. The following year, the council met four hundred miles to the east in St. Augustine. After travel difficulties hindered the arrival of the delegates, it became clear that neither Pensacola nor St. Augustine was a suitable meeting place for members from the entire territory. Governor DuVal authorized the search for a permanent and centrally located site, and in November 1824, the council met at the new capital of the territory, Tallahassee.[11]

The establishment of a centrally located capital and the reality of living under a single territorial government convinced many residents that it would be best if Florida worked toward becoming a unified state. Even in East Florida, where sentiments in favor of creating two separate states continued up through the writing of the state constitution, sentiments gradually shifted. During the meeting of the 1826–1827 Legislative Council, delegates unanimously rejected the annexation of West Florida by Alabama on the grounds that dividing the territory would "destroy that which is their best hopes, that of becoming a state government."[12] Although historically East and West Florida were distinct social and economic entities, the councilmen recognized that at least for the time being, their best interests required unity.

THE DEBATE OVER STATEHOOD

In the years that followed, several individuals emerged as central players in the struggle over statehood. Six stand out in particular. David Levy, Robert R. Reid, and James D. Westcott became the three most prominent voices against the power of the bank. David Levy, who took the name of David Levy Yulee when he became the first senator from Florida, came to the center of territorial politics when he fought to unify Floridians around the idea of a single state. Reid would serve as the chairman of the Constitutional Convention in 1838–1839, and former Governor Westcott would chair the Committee on Banking and Other Incorporations.[13] On the other side of the aisle were pro-banking politicians Richard Keith Call and William Pope DuVal. Call, a lawyer who dabbled in land speculation, oversaw and led the movement for statehood as territorial governor.[14] DuVal, who also served as territorial governor, narrowly lost a bid to become the convention chair but became the leading pro-banking voice at the convention.[15] Finally, Charles Downing was the nonvoting member to Congress during Florida's final years as a territory, and at times, he became the most vocal supporter of the creation of a separate state of East Florida.

Several local issues shaped the path to statehood. Tensions among the eastern, middle, and western parts of the state proved to be the most enduring of the issues. Regional interests shaped how residents understood demographic growth, Indian relations, internal improvements, fiscal issues, and, most important, the contentious issue of banking. These issues shaped the debates that led up to the Constitutional Convention in 1838 and the ultimate content of the document.

Precedent established that territories could only become states when their populations met the current ratio used to determine representation in the U.S. Congress. The census of 1830 frustrated Florida's quest for statehood. It determined that Florida had a population of only 34,730, far below the existing ratio of representation. As a result, in 1832, acting Governor Westcott concluded that Florida should refrain from applying for statehood and advised the council that it might be wise to delay making application for a decade. At the same time, though, Westcott pointed to a possible solution to Florida's population woes—revolving the territory's disputed border with Georgia and annexing several southernmost counties of Georgia.[16] Discussions about annexing southern Georgia counties and thus increasing Florida's population lasted for a few years, especially as Southerners became increasingly anxious about the tenuous balance of power between slave states and free states.[17]

In 1834, the Committee on the State of the Territory determined that Florida's financial problems limited the desirability of statehood just as much as the territory's lagging population did. The committee, though, established a logic that would allow Florida to organize a state government despite its inability to meet the congressional ratio of representatives in the recent census. The committee determined that Florida could apply for statehood by pointing to the population increase it had presumably experienced since 1830 and the anticipated growth that the removal of the Seminole Indians would initiate. The committee also found the means to demonstrate how Florida could support a state government with a "moderate system of taxation."

The optimism of the Committee on the State of the Territory aside, fiscal problems plagued Florida and convinced the 1834 council to reject the committee's recommendation that the issue of statehood be presented to the people. Members of the council recognized that resistance to taxes was widespread in Florida and tax collection had always occurred haphazardly. Tax collection was the least consistent in East Florida, but throughout the territory, payments occurred irregularly. In most years, one-third to one-half of all Florida counties failed to turn over their annual taxes to the territorial government. Rather than support statehood, the council members decided that in their next session they would explore how to collect taxes in a more efficient manner.[18]

Difficulties with the Seminoles in 1835 also hindered Florida's territorial development and quest for statehood. These difficulties were rooted in tensions that had magnified since the 1820s, when Floridians and Georgians increasingly claimed that the Indians killed settlers, harbored runaway slaves, and stole their cattle. For their part, the Seminoles claimed that the settlers initiated the unrest, enslaved their black residents, and stole their cattle. The federal government saw only one solution to the problem: the forced removal of the Seminoles from northern Florida. In 1823, James Gadsden met with Seminole leaders and offered to trade southern lands for their rights to their homelands in the north. The resulting Treaty of Moultrie Creek exchanged 24 million acres of tribal lands in northern Florida for 4 million acres between the Peace and Withlacoochee rivers to the south. In addition, the United States would also compensate the Seminoles by paying them for the improvements they had to leave behind, by providing a $5,000 annuity for twenty years, moving expenses, a year's worth of food, a school, a blacksmith and gunsmith, tools, and livestock. Seventy-one chiefs and headmen attended the negotiations, but in the end, only thirty-two chiefs signed the treaty. Although most of the leaders rejected the terms of the treaty, the majority of the Seminole people moved south into the Florida interior by the end of 1824.[19]

Within a few years, a series of droughts and poor harvests convinced some Seminoles to return to their former homes in northern Florida. At the same time, American designs on Seminole lands to the south intensified. In April 1828, an exasperated Chief Jumper declared that

> it seems that the white people will not rest, or suffer us to do so, till they have got all the property belonging to us, and made us poor. The laws of the whites appear to be made altogether for their own benefit, and against the Indians, who can never under them get back any of *their* property.

The resulting conflicts resulted in silence on the discussions of statehood and renewed calls for the removal of the Seminoles from Florida entirely. Once again, Gadsden attempted to coax the Seminoles into an agreement. Negotiations resulted in the Treaty of Payne's Landing in 1832. Fifteen chiefs, none of whom could read or write English, placed their marks on a treaty, but Gadsden and the Seminoles disagreed about what exactly they had agreed upon. Gadsden pointed to a document that stated that the Seminoles pledged to move west en masse, but the Seminole delegates protested that they had only promised to send chiefs to inspect the western lands. Only a vote of the entire nation, the Seminoles insisted, could lead to the mass evacuation of Florida. When the delegates went west, they signed the equally controversial Treaty of Fort Gibson. This treaty declared that the Seminoles found the lands to be acceptable to their needs, even through the Creek Indians controlled these lands. The Seminoles objected and claimed that they would never find submission to the Creek Indians to be an acceptable solution. Furthermore, they argued that they signed the Treaty of Fort Gibson only because John Phagan, the U.S. agent in charge of the journey, refused to transport them home to Florida unless they signed.[20]

Despite the controversy about the treaties, President Jackson ordered their implementation. When soldiers arrived to implement the treaty, Seminole warriors resisted. The result was the Second Seminole War, a bloody conflict that lasted from 1835 to 1842. Not surprisingly, as war broke out with the Seminoles, discussions of statehood waned. The issue of statehood was not even discussed during the 1835 meeting of the Legislative Council. Instead, especially in East Florida, which bore the brunt of the destruction, residents looked to the federal government to help fund and provide protection. East Florida's economy was devastated by the constant raids, and its resources were drained in self-defense. In addition, the population suffered as newcomers stopped moving to the region and many settlers left their homes. As a result, the population of East Florida stagnated, increasing by fewer than sixty individuals between 1830 and 1838.[21]

The population of Florida as a whole did not suffer from the outbreak of war. While East Florida stagnated, Middle Florida flourished. Between 1830 and 1838, West Florida grew from 9,478 to 14,562, and Middle Florida grew from 15,779 to 22,532. Even sparsely settled South Florida doubled its population to 1,027 during this span. Population growth and the expansion of settlement continued when the Seminole War ended in a stalemate. Congress encouraged settlers to move into South Florida and further dispossess the Indians. The Armed Occupation Act in 1842 allowed any adult man capable of "armed defense" to claim 160 acres of land south of Gainesville and north of the Peace River. In response, nearly 6,000 people moved to the region. The end of hostilities also allowed the military garrison in Jacksonville to disperse into the northeastern interior.[22]

In 1836, abolitionist attacks on the institution of slavery brought the issue of statehood back to the Legislative Council. In the preceding months, Floridians held meetings in Leon and Jackson counties to address their fears of "the Fanatics of the North," who were trying to eliminate slavery from the territory of Washington, D.C., and otherwise orchestrate the immediate abolition of slavery.[23] The council entered the discussion by stating that even as a territory, Florida must have the right to regulate its internal affairs. The council proclaimed that it was "unwilling to acknowledge that the fundamental principles of rights and securities guaranteed under the constitution...were forfeited by a migration to a country, the domain of which is in the government of the confederation."[24] During this discussion, the councilmen acknowledged that statehood would limit the power of the federal government to regulate the internal affairs of Florida and called for a referendum on statehood. The urgency that the council felt was not shared by Governor John E. Eaton, who refused to sign the referendum.[25]

A change in governors resulted in renewed momentum for statehood. The following year, Governor Richard Keith Call initiated a resolution for statehood. Call supported the statehood movement largely because of the benefits of home rule. He and other proponents believed that statehood would allow Florida to appoint and elect effective leaders rather than be a place for distant leaders to extend patronage. Residents from non-slave states often held prominent territorial positions, and they would often go home after the legislative session even as local problems went unresolved. Governor DuVal, for example, was frequently chastised for returning to his home in Kentucky for months at a time, even as Indian depredations plagued the territory. Call made this complaint explicit when he explained that the court of appeals, whose members were appointed by the Congress, had not met for the past three years because of the lack of a quorum. Call believed that Floridians were ready for statehood and only this step would resolve the issue. "I am persuaded that the intelligence, the wealth and number, of our inhabitants, is now sufficient to enable us to assume a State Government...*responsible to the people*." In addition, the expense involved in funding the courts, Call declared, was "a trifling consideration when compared with the sacrifice of Independence. And the rights and privileges incident to a state government."[26] The Legislative Council voted in favor of the resolution and called for a referendum on statehood, even as East Floridians hoped that the issue could be postponed long enough for the territory's population to grow large enough to enter the Union as two states—East Florida and West Florida.[27]

The referendum on statehood, held in May 1837, revealed that 64 percent of voters in Florida supported statehood. In Middle Florida, supporters of political parties. Governor Richard K. Call led the Nucleus, a coalition of elite Middle Florida planters who controlled the Florida Land Office and held many of the territory's judicial posts. The Nucleus, in large part because of a desire to take advantage of rising cotton and land prices in Middle Florida, advocated internal improvements and supported liberal bank charters. The Nucleus's support of the bank and control of the lucrative land policies aroused the opposition and resentment of many Floridians. The Locofocos group was formed by David Levy, Robert R. Reid, and James D. Westcott. Floridians, the Locofocos declared, should not be responsible for paying off the "faith bonds" that the banks had issued with the guarantee of the territorial government.[32]

Neither political parties nor the governor dictated the subsequent path to statehood. Instead, the momentum toward statehood was aided by the Select Committee of the Legislative Council, which asserted that the Adams-Onís Treaty guaranteed that Florida had a right to become a state as soon as it could survive financially. The committee explained that in the preceding years, the state's financial position had improved. Florida was no longer in debt and thus could now meet the demands of a state budget. Although some counties still failed to turn over their taxes, the Committee on Finance determined that there were plenty of revenue-raising options, specifically the implementation of taxes on banks, railroads, and even "Faro Banks and other Gaming tables."[33] As a result, the committee reported a bill to hold a convention.

As it considered the bill to hold a convention, the council turned its attention to several procedural issues. The most serious debate concerned whether the territory should apply as one or two states. Pressure came from both the east and west. Once again, the Alabama legislature proposed annexing West Florida.[34] Residents in East Florida responded by supporting this action. On January 6, 1838, the *Florida Herald* declared that "perhaps it would suit all parties better to divide the Territory at the Suwanee and let that part west of the river 'set up for herself.'"[35] A month later, 289 residents of East Florida put these words into motion and met at a public meeting in St. Augustine to declare their desire for the creation of two separate states. With Dr. Andrew Anderson as their chairman, the residents of East Florida sent Congress a memorial to indicate their desires. A distinct East Florida was important, they declared, because the state was too big and geographically divided to allow for business ties to unite the east with the west and for government business to be conducted efficiently. The population east of the Suwannee River, it declared, would soon blossom because of "recent interesting discoveries of immense tracts of the finest soil…and…the natural elements for a state." Once the removal of the Seminoles was complete, the committee proclaimed, "our numerous harbours and rivers, the climate, produces and other advantages, will present too many inducements for this region to remain desolate. No doubt remains among the intelligent, that in three years our population would entitle us to a place in the Union." Until then, the memorial declared that they would patiently await statehood as the territory of East Florida.[36]

Not everyone agreed to the desirability of dividing Florida. Governor Call, for example, emphatically called for unity, stating that the annexation of West Florida would have "most fatal consequences" for the territory.[37] Florida's delegate to Congress, Charles Downing, declared that "Congress would laugh at the proposition" of creating a separate East Florida territory with a population of merely 5,000. Even if Congress agreed, Downing was convinced that its small population would allow Northern politicians to target East Florida for various abolitionist designs.[38] Downing submitted the memorial to the deaf ears of Congress and then arranged the introduction of a new bill about statehood. The bill authorized Governor Call to call a constitutional convention after the territory could meet the existing ratio or representation, which at that time meant that Florida had to demonstrate that it had a population of 47,700. In addition, the bill declared that the first order of business of the convention had to be a discussion and vote to determine "whether it is or [is] not expedient to form a constitution and State Government." Two-thirds of the delegates had to approve this measure before the convention could continue. The two measures served to dampen hopes for both statehood and the division of the territory. Division would prevent either territory from reaching the mandated population, and by requiring a two-thirds vote at the convention, Congress provided East Florida with the power to reject statehood. Fortunately, the bill was presented to Congress too late in the session, and it was never passed.[39]

At home, discussions about statehood turned to apportionment at the convention, an issue that aroused fears about the overwhelming power and population of Middle Florida. The solution was to give East and West Florida a disproportionately large number of representatives to the convention. Although the more populous Middle districts received twenty delegates, Eastern and Western districts both received sixteen delegates, enough to control the results of the convention.[40] The power of Middle Florida's cotton planters was further weakened by a decision to hold the convention at the Gulf Coast port town of St. Joseph, which was, according to newspaper editor Cosam Emir Bartlett of the *Apalachicola Gazette*, a case of "scratch my back and I'll tickle your elbow."[41]

The campaign to elect delegates immediately turned into a heated debate about banking. Animosity was widespread in the territory, in large part because of general Jacksonian-era resentment against banking that was exacerbated by the Panic of 1837 and the collapse in cotton prices. This had particular ramifications in Florida, where five commercial banks fueled the animosity of East and West Floridians. These banks, which came to Florida as early as 1823, fueled the explosive growth in the Middle Florida cotton belt. The Union Bank, the largest of the banks, catered exclusively to Middle Florida. Planters used inflated estimates of their land and slaves as collateral to obtain loans that enabled them to purchase more land and slaves. Making matters worse, the Nucleus had the territorial government use the Legislative Council to back nearly $4 million dollars worth of bonds. In 1838, when the convention met,

Chairman Reid carefully appointed all of the delegates to serve on appropriate committees. DuVal was made chairman of the influential Committee on the Executive Department. Thomas Brown became chair of the Committee on the Legislative Department, and he was joined on this committee by former president of the Legislative Council Abram Bellamy. R. C. Allen headed up the Committee on the Judicial Department. The Committee on Banking and Other Incorporations was evenly divided between pro- and anti-bank supporters, with anti-bank James Westcott serving as chair.[44]

The convention adjourned for the weekend. When it reconvened, the delegates had determined that the constitution of Alabama and those of other southern frontier states like Texas and Kentucky would serve as the blueprint for Florida. Almost immediately, several committees presented articles for consideration that were copied directly from Alabama's constitution. Other committees made small modifications before bringing the articles up for consideration by the Committee of the Whole. While discussions about more contentious issues lasted until the end of the week, a committee, composed of chairmen of other committees, served to consolidate the various articles into an appropriate format. The convention would consider the articles in the order they were to appear in the constitution.[45]

Committees frequently used the current territorial government as the framework for the new state government. An attorney general needed to be added to the executive department, but otherwise the territorial positions of governor, secretary of state, treasurer, and controller easily became state offices. The judiciary still contained a supreme court, courts of chancery, and justices of the peace. Circuit courts would simply replace the territorial superior courts. By mimicking the structure of territorial government and the constitution of Alabama, many delegates hoped that they could quickly write the constitution. The convention determined that most power would rest in the hands of the state assembly. Although voters would elect the governor by a plurality, a joint vote of the two houses would choose the rest of the executive officers, judges, solicitors, and clerk of the supreme court.

Fiscal issues slowed matters down, especially as delegates from East and West Florida sought to alleviate their tax concerns. Three of the five members of the Committee on Taxation and Revenue were from East Florida and another was from a poor section of West Florida. Their anti-planter interests shaped their motions. The committee charged with determining issues of taxation and revenue first considered an ad valorem method of assessment for all forms of property. Under territorial law, ad valorem taxes were levied only on town lots, with land and slaves subject to separate taxes. This change would have increased the burden on Middle Florida planters and as a result, the convention rejected the proposal, 32-18. A compromise was almost achieved when the committee revamped its recommendation to include land in the ad valorem tax, but still exclude slaves. Protests from Middle Florida delegates and some apparent vote swapping resulted in this section ultimately being stricken.[46]

Considerations of suffrage and the qualifications of officers brought a host of issues to bear. The convention lengthened the time voters had to reside in the state prior to an election from three months to two years. It also disfranchised qualified men who failed to enroll in the militia and prohibited ministers from holding the governorship or serving in either of the houses of the state legislature. Other proposals, such as an attempt to disqualify from public office individuals who did not believe in God, failed. Finally, the convention determined that anyone who participated in a duel would be prohibited from holding office.

When the bank question was finally considered by the convention on December 28, all hope for a quick constitutional convention had dissipated. Two weeks earlier, the Committee on Banking and Other Incorporations presented a report with proposals to restrict severely the future incorporation of banking institutions. Although a majority of the delegates came to the convention intent on limiting the power of banks and corporations, the committee did not include proposals to limit the power of existing banking institutions or deal with the outstanding bonds. Instead, it recommended the establishment of state banks with capital raised by the issuance of bonds guaranteed by the mortgages of borrowers. Westcott and Levy tried to bring up procedures for dealing with the Union Bank and the Bank of Pensacola. They urged the convention to order these banks to submit their charters to the first session of the General Assembly, which could choose to assume the obligations of the territorial bonds. If not, the banks could substitute their own bonds for those of the territory. The General Assembly would also have the ability to modify the charters of the smaller banks within the territory.[47]

The following day, several resolutions tried to push Florida's constitution toward the most extreme views of the pro-bank and anti-bank forces. Anti-bank leaders, like Westcott, Thompson, Levy, and Abram Bellamy, claimed that the charters were illegal forms of power and declared that the law should always outweigh the power of a contract. Bellamy called for the convention to repudiate the faith bond, forbid the General Assembly to raise revenue to pay them, and prohibit the pledge of the state's credit to aid any corporation. Pro-bank leaders, like Fitzpatrick, DuVal, Thomas Brown, Ward, and Thomas M. Blount, insisted on the validity of bonds and fiscal soundness of the bonds. Fitzpatrick proposed making the Union Bank the state bank of Florida and increasing its capital by $10 million.[48]

Thomas Baltzell changed the nature of the debate when he asked the convention to appoint a new committee specifically designed to ask Congress to revoke the ability of the territorial banks to issue additional bonds. Whereas most of the rest of the assembly worked with the assumption that the convention had the authority to address the issue of banking, Baltzell claimed this was a federal issue. He argued that because the territorial government was the creation of the general government, Congress had an obligation to protect the interest of the people of Florida.[49]

At one point during the debate, William Wyatt compared the logic of anti-banking to that of anti-slavery. Anti-banking doctrine "assumed all the grounds contended for by the abolitionists of the North, in relation to the powers of congress over Territories, and their right to abolish slavery in the Territory of Florida—Slaves are property, and like that acquired under acts of incorporation, is [sic] held by virtue of the [laws] of the Territorial Government." This comparison outraged many delegates and forced Wyatt to clarify, if not change, his meaning. Wyatt declared that he "did not mean to say...that those gentlemen were abolitionists.... In using the word treason, I meant to say, that if an avowed abolitionist was to entertain such doctrines in this place, it would be denounced by every southerner as treason." Wyatt's response served to remind the delegates that their actions took place on a national stage where slavery cast a shadow on the actions and arguments of all the delegates.[50]

While the committee accepted Baltzell's resolutions to call upon Congress to deal with the banking issue rather than leave it to the convention, delegates worked to insure that none of this was meant to "impair the obligations of contract or to weaken the credit, or, affect injuriously the character and honor of the people of Florida."[51] This did not satisfy the pro-bank delegates, and on January 3, Thomas Brown introduced resolutions that stated the convention had exceeded its mandate by interfering with territorial institutions and laws and by calling for the popular ratification of the constitution. Parliamentary procedure prevented the consideration of Brown's resolutions, while Baltzell's resolutions were supported by a 38-18 vote.[52]

The resulting restrictions on the future incorporation of banks were quite severe. The delegates, through Article 13, determined that the General Assembly could not pass any acts of incorporation without three months' public notice and the support of two-thirds of both houses of Congress. Banking corporations needed to have at least twenty persons and a majority of them had to be Florida residents. Other corporations needed to have at least ten persons, five of whom had to be Florida residents. Furthermore, the delegates ensured that banks would be short-term entities by declaring that bank charters could not be granted for more than twenty years and they could never be renewed. Banks could not deal in real estate, insurance, manufacturing, or imports or exports. Other restrictions declared that banks must have at least $100,000 in capital stock and that this amount had to be paid with specie. Bank liabilities could never exceed twice the amount of capital. Dividends were limited to 10 percent. Banks had to be annually examined, and the charters could be revoked for violations. They also ensured that banknotes would not serve as currency by limiting their ability to produce notes for less than $5. Bank officers could not be legislators or governors unless they left the bank for a year before entering public service. Finally, the General Assembly could not help corporations raise money by extending faith or credit. All of these regulations would be tightly enforced by state inspectors.[53]

Even after these provisions were adopted, the problem of banking remained on the table. The issue of the territorial banks and their relation to the General Assembly needed to be resolved. Pro-bank leaders hoped to turn the Union Bank into the state bank of Florida. Anti-bank men wanted the assembly to assume supreme power over the territorial banks. Deadlocks, absenteeism, and strong differences of opinion prevented any resolution until January 5, when E. Carrington Cabell made a motion to submit the constitution to the people for ratification, in part to resolve the acrimony that the banking discussion had engendered. Sending the constitution out for a public vote might allow the convention to finish its work quickly and before it was scheduled to be dissolved. In addition, the convention considered and rejected Brown's earlier resolution that declared that it was beyond the convention's mandate to limit the existing banking institutions and Baltzell's earlier motion for the popular ratification of the convention. In a narrow 29-26 vote, the convention decided to send Baltzell's language to Congress and to authorize the General Assembly to regulate territorial corporations in the interest of the people. The convention passed the articles on banking on January 9, even as pro-banking forces used various last-minute measures to void the votes.[54]

With the issue of banking seemingly resolved, matters turned to the last divisive issue: the apportionment of representatives in the new government. The issue revolved around whether territory or population would determine representation. East Florida hoped that territory would be the deciding factor. Although it only had 24 percent of the territory's population, it had nine of the twenty territorial counties and three-fourths of Florida's total territory. Middle and West Florida hoped that their populations would outweigh their relatively small geographic size. A compromise was easily achieved. Each county would receive at least one representative, and further representation would be based on the white population and three-fifths of the slave population, as determined by the decennial state census. Although most southern states did not include slaves in their considerations of representation, the Nucleus convinced the rest of the delegates to follow the lead of Georgia and North Carolina and included the federal government's three-fifths clause in the new constitution. The House would have no more than sixty members.[55]

After the articles related to apportionment and the census passed a third reading on January 5, the final issues were quickly handled. The convention hastily dealt with schooling, internal improvements, the location of the capital, and the possibility of constitutional amendments. In each case, the delegates set up a structure for dealing with future issues but left the particulars unclear. The delegates, for example, declared that Tallahassee would remain the capital for five years but left the possibility for change open for ten years. Only after a decade would the site become permanent.

The issue of slavery was the only substantive issue to be dealt with in the final days. The planters of Middle Florida, who had been soundly defeated in the banking debates, found their desire to support the institution of slavery a much easier task. Unified in their pro-slavery leanings, delegates wrote into the constitution support for slavery not evident in Alabama's constitution. The delegates rejected provisions that guaranteed humane treatment of slaves and allowed the legislature to limit the importation of slaves. At the same time, a majority of the delegates supported clauses that prohibited the General Assembly from passing laws that emancipated slaves or prohibited settlers from bringing slaves into the state. Delegates also empowered the General Assembly to pass laws that would prevent the immigration of free blacks.[56]

Finally, Florida needed to deal with its right to be admitted to the Union in spite of its population deficit. In its report, Florida pointed to the sixth article of the treaty of cession, which declared that Florida's statehood could be implemented as soon as the territory was competent. The Constitutional Convention, despite the population, was offered as that proof. In addition, the Committee on Federal Relations determined that the controlling constitutional provisions for statehood proclaimed that Congress could admit new states as long as the number of representatives could not exceed one for every 30,000 residents. Even if Congress insisted that Florida must meet the ratio of population, Florida's population exceeded 35,000, the number that would meet the ratio demanded of territories when Spain ceded the Florida territories.[57]

The report of the committee did not make provisions for submitting the constitution to Congress for ratification. Delegates from Middle and West Florida urged the convention to organize the state government in the hope that if a northern territory applied for statehood, Florida would become a state as a matter of political expediency. A new committee was organized to consider proposals designed to prepare the territory for statehood. Westcott and Ward wanted to form a state government proactively and await congressional approval, but the committee determined that a state government should be organized after the passage of an act of admission. Rather than adjourn, however, the committee determined that the members could vote to meet again at Tallahassee if Congress were to refuse to grant statehood to Florida. The convention adjourned on January 11, when all but one delegate, Richard Fitzpatrick of Dade County, voted in favor of the constitution. Fitzpatrick objected to the article on banking.

FEDERAL APPROVAL

While Florida voters and councilmen debated the merits of statehood, the newly written constitution, as well as a memorial that stated the rationale for Florida's admission as a state, reached Congress in February. Despite the rush, the quest for statehood would become mired in national politics and the rehashing of local issues for the next five years. During these years, Floridians split into three courses of action. Some maneuvered to arrange for immediate statehood, others sought to postpone any action, and many in East Florida continued to pursue the ultimate division of the state into two separate territories and states.

For his part, Charles Downing chose not to press the issue of statehood in Washington, D.C. Instead, in January he presented the St. Augustine memorial for division to Congress to the delight of several southern congressmen who welcomed the idea of creating two slave states, especially considering the imminent applications of Iowa and Wisconsin for statehood. In 1839, William P. DuVal presented an additional petition to Congress on behalf of ten East Florida council members, requesting the division of Florida. Other Floridians entered the fray, including Governor Reid, who referred to the idea of separation as a "suicidal" policy. Congress agreed, and when it adjourned, it had not brought the matter to a vote.

The Legislative Council, for its part, turned its attention to the Constitutional Convention's conclusions regarding the bank. Councilman S. L. Burritt led an assault on Baltzell's resolutions. The House agreed, and by a 20-8 vote, concluded that Baltzell had gone beyond the convention's mandate. As Baltzell and Westcott feared that their efforts of the convention might go for naught, they asked in vain if they could defend their actions at the council. The House then passed a bill, sponsored by Richard Fitzpatrick, to nullify the entirety of the convention. Both matters were sent to the Senate, which prevented the House from derailing the path to statehood by narrowly defeating both bills.[58]

Dissension was equally heated among Florida voters, who debated the bank, taxation, representation, and the desirability of statehood itself. Although some newspaper editors reminded readers that the constitution represented compromises between competing interests, critics could be found throughout the state. In East Florida and West Florida, critics pointed to the undue sway given to the state's plantation interests. By incorporating the three-fifths principle into the democratic structure, the St. Augustine *News* declared "If...East and West Florida should be forced into State Government under this Constitution, they will go in manacles, shacked, and disfranchised, to be the bondsmen and slaves of Union Bank nabobs, or of the representation by the Constitution unjustly extended to their slaves."[59] The *Florida Herald* in East Florida equated support for the constitution with the "the most odious taxation."[60] In Middle Florida, critics pointed to the inequity of all counties receiving a representative, especially when the counties of "Dade, without freeholders enough to form a Jury, and Musquito, without people enough, men and women included, to create a riot, are each entitled forever to one Representative."[61] Others in Middle Florida chastised the restrictions placed on the bank and declared their intention to "do all they can to defeat its adoption."[62]

In the same May 6, 1839, election in which the public voted on the merits of Florida's statehood, Floridians also went to the polls to choose between Downing and Baltzell as their non-voting representative to Congress. The two elections revealed the divisiveness within the state. Downing solidified his support for reelection by declaring that he would vote against the constitution.

Baltzell, the author of several well-known resolutions at the convention, ran as the pro-state and pro-planter candidate. Downing won the election easily, largely owing to widespread support in the eastern and western districts.[63] At the same time, the voters of Florida narrowly approved the constitution, by 2,065 to 1,961. Three of four voters from the populous Middle Florida supported it. Only 39 percent of voters in West Florida and 27 percent in East Florida supported it, and in the southern districts, 76 percent of the 284 voters supported it.[64]

While the votes for statehood were still being tallied in October 1839, Floridians elected delegates to the Legislative Council. Although the issue of statehood had not yet been resolved, banking reemerged as the central political issue in Florida. Anti-banking Locofocos members, who had increasingly attached themselves to the Democratic Party, called for an end to faith bonds and pointed to potential problems caused by the recent issuance of $274,000 worth of bonds by the Southern Life Insurance and Trust Company and the Union Bank's failure to resume specie payments. Whig candidates from Middle Florida supported an end to the faith bonds but spent most of their energies attacking the attempts to create a separate state of East Florida. By decrying the calls for division as part of an abolitionist design to create a free state in East Florida, the Whigs maintained the support of the state's slaveholding planters. Not surprisingly, the Locofocos nearly swept the support of Middle Florida, while anti-bank Democrats enjoyed most of their success in East and West Florida.

President Van Buren, by mentioning it in his 1840 annual message to Congress, brought Florida's debate over bonds to the forefront of national affairs. The Senate responded by asking Van Buren to arrange for gathering all relevant information on the banks and bonds. At the same time, newly elected Governor Reid asked for an investigation of the banks as well. The resulting reports by the House supported the Locofoco contentions: one chastised the banks for mismanagement, and the other recommended the repudiation of the questionable faith bonds. The Senate, controlled by the pro-banking Whigs, disagreed strongly and condemned the House for "destroy[ing] all confidence in the honor, integrity and good faith of the people of Florida."[65]

The heated debates over the bank were matched by the divisiveness throughout the territory on statehood. Calls for a separate East Florida remained, and once again Downing presented a bill to Congress to this end.[66] Downing proclaimed that his bill gave all sections what they wanted. Statehood would come to the western and middle districts, while East Floridians would not have to live under a constitution they had widely rejected. In this context, David Levy came to the forefront of Florida and national politics. Levy worked to solidify support for a unified state of Florida. He made the issue clear: "Indefinite postponement or prompt assumption of the rights and privileges of independence, is the issue now upon us."[67] Through letters, speeches, and a widely distributed pamphlet, Levy convinced a majority of voters that division would lead to a delay in the quest for statehood and that statehood would enable

Florida to obtain federal grants for railroad production and other internal improvements. In addition, statehood would allow Florida to achieve economic prosperity and obtain national prominence. Levy's arguments for statehood convinced enough Floridians to elect a council that would support Florida's application for statehood.[68]

Levy understood that national politics and debates in Iowa, not local debates at home, would determine Florida's bid for statehood. As the *Pensacola Gazette* explained: "Florida and Iowa are Siamese twins—one cannot go without the other."[69] In 1840, Iowa voters overwhelmingly rejected calls for a constitutional convention and rejected it again in 1842. When Iowa finally decided to hold a convention in April 1844, Congress turned its attention to Florida. The U.S. House and Senate made it clear that they would reject any proposal to make Florida into two territories, but the House Committee on the Territories reported a bill to admit Florida as a state that allowed for the possibility of a future division once the populations of East and West Florida both exceeded 35,000. Rather than voting on the bill, the committee recommended postponing any action until Iowa presented its application for statehood.[70]

Before the council renewed its application for statehood, Congress took action. On January 7, 1845, the Committee on the Territories began to consider a bill for the admission of Iowa and Florida. The bill allowed for the future division of Florida. While Congress considered the admission of the two states, Florida's Legislative Council confirmed its desire for statehood. There, a resolution for statehood passed the Senate by a vote of 9-6 on January 23 and the House by a vote of 24-6 on January 25.[71]

In the House of Representatives, discussion focused on the ability of Florida to be divided in the future and articles within Florida's constitution that prohibited the General Assembly from emancipating slaves and allowed it to prohibit free blacks from entering the state. At first, anti-slavery representatives pushed for the deletion of these clauses. When these efforts failed, they unsuccessfully tried to prevent the admission of Florida entirely by proposing that both states must meet the federal ratio of representation before statehood could be granted, a demand that would not have affected the more populous Iowa but would have stalled the admission of Florida. A substitution bill called for the admission of Iowa by itself, but it too failed. A solution to the issue was achieved by eliminating the provision that allowed the future division of Florida. With this modification, on February 13, 1845, the House passed the bill, 144-48. The Senate Committee on the Territories raised many of the same issues discussed in the House. Discussion about Florida's population was settled by Levy, who convinced the committee that Florida's population was at least 90,000. Debate ended after anti-slavery senators failed to delete the constitutional clauses that affected the emancipation of slaves and immigration of free blacks. On March 1, the Senate passed the bill to grant statehood to Florida and Iowa by a 36-9 vote.[72] On March 3, 1845, President John Tyler signed the bill.[73]

All that remained for statehood was the election of state officials. In the 1845 election, Democrats nominated William Moseley for governor and Levy for congressman, while the Whigs chose Call for governor and Benjamin A. Putnam for Congress. Banking policies as well as an economic turndown and the Second Seminole War were the central topics of debate. In the first statewide election, held on May 26, 1845, both Democratic candidates won. William D. Moseley became the first governor, even though he had lived in Florida for a mere six years. David Levy was elected to Congress, but before he departed for Washington, he was chosen to serve with James D. Westcott in the U.S. Senate. On June 25, just days after the death of Andrew Jackson, Florida inaugurated its officials and celebrated with cannon fire, a procession, a twenty-eight-gun salute, an inauguration speech by Moseley, and the unfurling of the new flag of the United States.[74]

SUMMARY

By simultaneously granting statehood to Florida and Iowa, the U.S. Congress successfully maintained a balance of power between free and slave states that would last only fifteen more years. The state's reliance on slavery and its social connections to Alabama, Georgia, and the rest of the southern states became more pronounced in the years after statehood. National political parties dominated local concerns, with most Locofocos becoming members of the Democratic Party, while the pro-banking Nucleus primarily turned to the Whig and various short-lived parties. Tensions among the regions became even more pronounced, especially as Middle Florida planters dominated the political structure and the state's economy. As a result, Florida's first constitution would only last until 1861, when Florida seceded from the Union and joined the Confederacy.

NOTES

1. Thomas Jefferson to John Holmes, April 22, 1820, in *The Writings of Thomas Jefferson*, ed. Andrew A. Lipscomb, 20 vols. (Washington, DC: Memorial Society of Thomas Jefferson, 1904), vol. 15, p. 249.

2. William S. Coker and Susan R. Parker, "The Second Spanish Period in the Two Floridas," in *New History of Florida*, ed. Michael Gannon (Gainesville: University Press of Florida, 1996), p. 150.

3. Charlton W. Tebeau, *A History of Florida* (Coral Gables: University of Miami Press, 1971), p. 103; Manjoni Waciuma, *Intervention in Spanish Florida, 1810–1813: A Study in Jeffersonian Foreign Policy* (Boston: Branden Press, 1976).

4. Robert V. Remini, *Andrew Jackson and the Course of American Empire, 1767–1821* (New York: Harper and Row, 1977), pp. 236–243, 351–367.

5. Treaty of Amity, Settlement, and Limits, February 22, 1819, in *Treaties and Other International Acts of the United States of America*, ed. Hunt Miller (Washington, DC: U.S. State Department, 1931), vol. 3, p. 8.

6. Daniel L. Schafer, "U.S. Territory and State," in Gannon, *New Florida History*, pp. 207–208.

7. Remini, *Andrew Jackson and the Course of American Empire*, pp. 406–408; Schafer, "U.S. Territory and State," pp. 208–209.

8. *Annals of Congress*, 17th Cong., 1st Sess., 1821–1822, pp. 142, 595, 826.

9. *Niles Weekly Register*, December 29, 1821; Paul E. Hoffman, *Florida Frontiers* (Bloomington: University of Indiana Press, 2002), p. 284.

10. *Annals of Congress*, 17th Cong., 1st Sess., 1822, p. 803.

11. Schafer, "U.S. Territory and State," pp. 209–211.

12. H. Doc. 19, 17th Cong., 2d Sess. (76), 1823, p. 3.

13. Arthur W. Thompson, "David Yulee: A Study of Nineteenth-Century Thought and Enterprise" (Ph.D. diss., Columbia University, 1954); Arthur W. Thompson, *Jacksonian Democracy on the Florida Frontier* (Gainesville: University of Florida Press, 1961).

14. Herbert J. Doherty, *Richard Keith Call, Southern Unionist* (Gainesville: University of Florida Press, 1961), pp. 70–83, 93–117.

15. James Owen Knauss, "William Pope DuVal, Pioneer and State Builder," *Florida Historical Quarterly* 11 (January 1933): 95–139.

16. Extract from a Message of Acting Governor Westcott, January 3, 1832, reprinted in Dorothy Dodd, *Florida Becomes a State* (Tallahassee: Florida Centennial Commission, 1945), pp. 100–101.

17. James Owen Knauss, *Territorial Florida Journalism* (DeLand: Florida State Historical Society, 1926), p. 80.

18. Territorial Legislative Council Journal, 1834, Florida State Library, Tallahassee, pp. 108–109, 126.

19. James W. Covington, *The Seminoles of Florida* (Gainesville: University Press of Florida, 1993), pp. 56–71; Hoffman, *Florida Frontiers*, p. 288.

20. Covington, *The Seminoles*, pp. 62, 63–76.

21. Tebeau, *A History of Florida*, p. 134.

22. Hoffman, *Florida Frontiers*, p. 309.

23. *Floridian*, August 22, 1835.

24. Territorial Legislative Council Journal, 1836, p. 47.

25. Dodd, *Florida Becomes a State*, p. 34.

26. Extract from a Message of Governor Call, January 3, 1837, reprinted in Dodd, *Florida Becomes a State*, p. 107, emphasis added.

27. Dodd, *Florida Becomes a State*, p. 35.

28. Extract from a Message of Governor Call, January 2, 1838, reprinted in Dodd, *Florida Becomes a State*, p. 113; F. W. Hoskins, "The St. Joseph Convention: The Making of Florida's First Constitution," *Florida Historical Quarterly* 16 (October 1937): 107.

29. Schafer, "U.S. Territory and State," p. 220; Arthur W. Thompson, *Jacksonian Democracy on the Florida Frontier* (Gainesville: University of Florida Press, 1961); Arthur W. Thompson, *The Whigs of Florida, 1845–1854* (Gainesville: University of Florida Press, 1959).

30. Herbert J. Doherty, Jr., "Political Factions in Territorial Florida," *Florida Historical Quarterly* 28 (October 1949): 131–155.

31. Cited in "Reports of Convention," December 21, 1838, in Knauss, *Territorial Florida Journalism*, p. 188.

32. Schafer, "U.S. Territory and State," p. 220.

33. Territorial Legislative Council Records, 1822–1838, February 3, 1838, Florida State Library.

34. Territorial Legislative Council Journal, 1838, p. 73.

35. *Florida Herald*, January 6, 1838.

36. Memorial to Congress of Inhabitants of St. Augustine, February 5, 1838, reprinted in Dodd, *Florida Becomes a State*, pp. 122–126.

37. Territorial Legislative Council Journal, 1838, p. 73.

38. *Florida Herald*, April 9, 1841.

39. House Resolution 780, 25th Cong., 2nd Sess., May 11, 1838.

40. "Journal of the Proceedings of a Convention of Delegates to Form a Constitution for the People of Florida, Held at St. Joseph, December 1838," reprinted in Dodd, *Florida Becomes a State*, pp. 133–134.

41. *Apalachicola Gazette*, February 19, 1838, cited in Knauss, *Territorial Florida Journalism*, p. 30.

42. Edward E. Baptist, *Creating an Old South: Middle Florida's Plantation Frontier Before the Civil War* (Chapel Hill: University of North Carolina Press, 2002), pp. 159–165; Hoffman, *Florida Frontiers*, p. 300.

43. Cited in Baptist, *Creating an Old South*, p. 165. See also Dodd, *Florida Becomes a State*, pp. 45–46.

44. Reports of Convention, December 7, 1838, reprinted in Knauss, *Territorial Florida Journalism*, pp. 133–135, 138–139.

45. Dodd, *Florida Becomes a State*, p. 51; Stephanie D. Moussalli, "Florida's Frontier Constitution: The Statehood, Banking and Slavery Controversies," *Florida Historical Quarterly* (Spring 1996): 423.

46. Dodd, *Florida Becomes a State*, pp. 52–53, 54.

47. Reports of the Several Committees of the Constitutional Convention, reprinted in Knauss, *Territorial Florida Journalism*, pp. 157–158, 168–170.

48. Convention Journal, reprinted in Dodd, *Florida Becomes a State*, pp. 177–180.

49. Convention Journal, December 14, 1838, reprinted in Dodd, *Florida Becomes a State*, pp. 185–186; Mr. Baltzell's Resolutions, reprinted in Knauss, *Territorial Florida Journalism*, p. 224.

50. Proceedings of the Convention, reprinted in Knauss, *Territorial Florida Journalism*, 192–193.

51. Mr. Baltzell's Resolutions, reprinted in Knauss, *Territorial Florida Journalism*, p. 224.

52. Convention Journal, January 2, 1839–January 3, 1839, reprinted in Dodd, *Florida Becomes a State*, pp. 230–236.

53. Reports of the Several Committees of the Constitutional Convention, reprinted in Knauss, *Territorial Florida Journalism*, pp. 154–157; Moussalli, "Florida's Frontier Constitution," p. 428.

54. Convention Journal, January 5, 11, 1839, reprinted in Dodd, *Florida Becomes a State*, pp. 253, 296–299.

55. Convention Journal, January 8, 1839, reprinted in Dodd, *Florida Becomes a State*, pp. 276–278; "Reports of the Several Committees of the Constitutional Convention," reprinted in Knauss, *Territorial Florida Journalism*, pp. 158–160; Moussalli, "Florida's Frontier Constitution," p. 435.

56. Convention Journal, January 8, 1839, reprinted in Dodd, *Florida Becomes a State*, pp. 272–276.

57. "Reports of the Several Committees of the Constitutional Convention," reprinted in Knauss, *Territorial Florida Journalism*, pp. 160–161.

58. Dodd, *Florida Becomes a State*, pp. 64, 75, 68.

59. St. Augustine *News*, February 8, 1845.

60. *Florida Herald*, April 11, 1839.

61. Tallahassee, *Floridian*, February 2, 1839, reprinted in Knauss, *Territorial Florida Journalism*, p. 221.

62. *Florida Herald*, February 7, 1839.

63. Dodd, *Florida Becomes a State*, p. 69.

64. Tebeau, *History of Florida*, pp. 125–126.

65. Dodd, *Florida Becomes a State*, pp. 70–71, 72.

66. *Address of Charles Downing, of Florida, to His Constituents* (Washington, DC: n.p., 1840).

67. *Florida Herald*, October 22, 1844.

68. Emily Porter, "The Reception of the St. Joseph Constitution," *Florida Historical Quarterly* 17 (October 1938): 122–123.

69. *Pensacola Gazette*, December 12, 1840.

70. Dodd, *Florida Becomes a State*, pp. 79, 83.

71. Resolutions of the Governor and Legislative Council, January 27, 1845, in Dodd, *Florida Becomes a State*, pp. 425–426.

72. An Act for the Admission of Iowa and Florida, March 3, 1845, reprinted in Dodd, *Florida Becomes a State*, pp. 426–428.

73. An Act Supplementary to the Act for the Admission of Iowa and Florida, reprinted in Dodd, *Florida Becomes a State*, pp. 428–430.

74. J. E. Dovell, *Florida: Historic, Dramatic, Contemporary*, 2 vols. (New York: Lewis Historical Publishing Company, 1952), vol. 1, pp. 286–288.

BIBLIOGRAPHY

Baptist, Edward E. *Creating an Old South: Middle Florida's Plantation Frontier Before the Civil War*. Chapel Hill: University of North Carolina Press, 2002.

Dodd, Dorothy. *Florida Becomes a State*. Tallahassee: Florida Centennial Commission, 1945.

Gannon, Michael, ed. *New History of Florida*. Gainesville: University Press of Florida, 1996.

Hoffman, Paul E. *Florida Frontiers*. Bloomington: University of Indiana Press, 2002.

Knauss, James Owen. *Territorial Florida Journalism*. DeLand: Florida State Historical Society, 1926.

Tebeau, Charlton W. *A History of Florida*. Coral Gables, FL: University of Miami Press, 1971.

THE STATE OF GEORGIA

Ratified the Constitution of the United States: January 2, 1788

Nicole Mitchell

INTRODUCTION

In 1788, Georgia became the fourth state to ratify the new Constitution of the United States of America. The youngest of the thirteen colonies, Georgia had just begun to develop when the thirteen colonies declared their independence from England. Most of the basic causes for the American Revolution had little immediate effect in Georgia. Yes, Georgians opposed the additional taxes imposed by England, but who would not? In the early 1770s, most Georgians feared revolt from the neighboring and warlike Creek Indians. The colony appealed to England for help in defending against the Indians, but the British government refused to aid its youngest colony. The British refusal to defend the colony against the Indians likely pushed Georgia forward and helped bring about the eventual break with the mother country. However, the fact that Georgia almost always acted after the other colonies did and in almost the exact same manner lends credence to the view that most Georgians would not have rebelled had they been left to their own devices.

Once the fighting began, though, Georgia responded the way one might expect. There was no way Georgia could defend itself on its own, yet the colony was originally intended to be a protector to the Northern colonies. The battles and skirmishes that occurred in Georgia were no worse than those in other states. Georgians also overthrew their colonial government and set up a state government along the same lines as the other colonies.

Georgia was founded in 1733, the last of the thirteen colonies to be established. This new colony was defined as the land between the Savannah River and the Altamaha River and from the Atlantic to the Pacific. Twenty-one

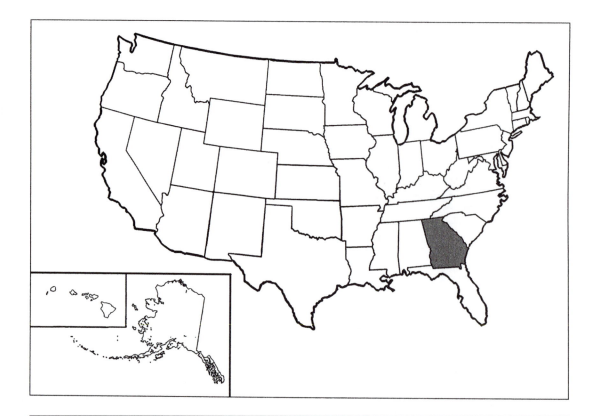

Georgia

Territorial Development:
- King George II granted the colony of Georgia to a private company, 1732
- Continental Congress approved Declaration of Independence from Great Britain, July 4, 1776
- Great Britain formally recognized American independence through the Treaty of Paris, September 3, 1783
- Georgia became the fourth state to ratify the U.S. Constitution, January 2, 1788

Capitals Prior to Statehood:
- Savannah, 1743–1779
- Augusta, 1779–1780
- Heard's Fort, and miscellaneous sites in Wilkes County, 1780–1781
- Augusta, 1781–1782; Ebenezer, 1782; Savannah, 1782
- Augusta, 1783
- Savannah, 1784; Augusta, 1784
- Savannah, 1785
- Augusta, 1786–1788

State Capitals:
- Augusta (1788–1796)
- Louisville (1796–1806)
- Milledgeville (1807–1864)
- Macon (1864–1865)
- Milledgeville (1865–1868)
- Atlanta (1868–present)

Origin of State Name: Georgia was named for George II, who granted James Oglethorpe a charter to found a colony under the king's name.

First Governor: George Mathews
Governmental Organization: Unicameral 1777–1789; bicameral 1789–present.
Population at Statehood: 82,548
Geographical Size: 57,906 square miles

men known as trustees petitioned for a royal charter in 1730. After two years of delays, the request was finally granted in the summer of 1732 and it was declared that the trustees of the colony would have full governing rights. The settlement of Georgia enlisted the interest and aid of a larger number of people than any other English settlement. Control of the new colony was given to the trustees for a period of twenty-one years. After twenty-one years, the colony of Georgia would revert to the Crown. Other restrictions prohibited trustees from holding office or owning land in Georgia. One of the provisions in the charter for Georgia was without precedent. None of the trustees was allowed to receive any salary, fee, or profit whatsoever. Land grants to individual settlers could not exceed five hundred acres, in order to prevent Georgia from becoming a colony of large plantations. Full religious freedom was promised to all except Catholics. Those in charge had great expectations for England's future with the founding of yet another colony. The trustees envisioned tremendous increases in the trade and wealth of the British Empire. Long before the charter was issued, the trustees were convinced that Georgia would be the new Eden.

James Edward Oglethorpe, resident trustee, and John Percival, the Earl of Egmont, were the principal trustees of the new colony. From its inception, Georgia was not meant to be just another British colony. The trustees intended for Georgia to be "something new and exciting—a kind of Holy Experiment." No trustee was allowed to own land, hold office, or receive a salary or income because of his efforts for the new colony. These stipulations set Georgia apart from any other British colony.

Since the establishment of Pennsylvania in 1681, there had been marked efforts on behalf of the British government to increase its control in America. There was also a strong inclination to substitute royal provinces for those of a proprietary or corporate nature. The Georgia charter showed several tendencies in this direction. All officers had to be appointed by the king and all laws submitted to him for approval. However, regulations and orders to fit special situations could be given without the king's approval. The most remarkable provision in the colony's charter was limiting the powers of government bestowed on the founders of Georgia to a period of twenty-one years. The person appointed to be governor of the colony had to take oaths and obey the acts of Parliament relating to trade and navigation. An annual account of all money received and expended was to be presented in writing to two officials of the English government.[1]

When Georgia was settled in 1733, it had been more than fifty years since a colony had been established by the English in America. All the motives that had inspired the founding of the other colonies—dreams of untold wealth, religious persecution—were absent when the Georgia charter was granted in 1732. What, then, were the causes leading to the establishment of Georgia, the last of the thirteen colonies?

In the early 1730s, England had four primary reasons for the establishment of another colony. First, on their frontiers, all of the colonies faced the claims of other European nations. South Carolina, the southern border of the twelve existing colonies, lay unprotected against raids from both the Indians and the hostile Spanish. With its southern border exposed, a constant flow of slaves escaped from South Carolina into Florida. A haven awaited them there offered by the Spanish. There had been wars with the Spanish in 1686 and again in 1703–1706, as well as the Yamassee Indian war in 1715. Grievances against the English kept adding up until the Indians finally attacked the South Carolina frontier. Caught off guard, the colony reeled from the unexpected Yamassee attack. The Yamassees once again threatened war in 1727. This particularly terrified the Carolinians because their principal defense, Fort King George, which was located on the Altamaha River, had been burned the year before. Therefore, South Carolina had no adequate defense from that direction. Indians, encouraged and probably aided by the French, who had moved into territory that is now Alabama, frequently came in from the west to wreak havoc on South Carolina. Consequently, South Carolina launched a campaign in England to expose the danger along its southern border and to encourage settlement there. Militarily, Georgia would serve as a buffer between the Carolinas, Spanish Florida, and the French, who were settling in the west. In addition to defending the "debatable land" between the Carolina settlements and St. Augustine, the Georgia colony was also intended to secure from the Spanish and French the trade of the Indians living between the Atlantic and the Mississippi. Whoever controlled the Indian trade profited economically and developed friendly relations with the Indians as well.[2]

Second, Georgia was intended to be a refuge for persecuted European Protestants and Jews. Roman Catholics, however, were exempt from this refuge. Within a year of Georgia's founding, a group of Salzburg Lutherans journeyed to the colony from Austria to escape religious persecution there. The first group of forty-six people arrived in Savannah in March 1734 and was led by two Lutheran pastors, one of whom was John Martin Bolzius. Over the years, four different groups of Salzburgers had settled in Georgia. Oglethorpe personally helped the new arrivals with their settlement, which they named Ebenezer, meaning Rock of Help. The original settlement of Old Ebenezer lay on an unnavigable creek. Two years after it was established, the town was moved six miles to the banks of the Savannah River in order to obtain better land, a healthier location, and more reliable water transportation. The Salzburgers ultimately became the most prosperous colonists in Georgia during the trusteeship period and came closest to fulfilling what the trustees desired of all colonists.

By 1752, there were 1,500 Salzburgers in Georgia. Their greatest contribution to the development of the colony was in their agricultural achievements. The Salzburgers were by far the most successful farmers in the colony, and their crops were greatly diverse. They grew everything from corn, peas, and potatoes to cabbages, pumpkins, wheat, and barley. The stereotypical view of Georgia brings cotton farming to mind, so it is ironic that the Salzburgers attempted to grow cotton but were discouraged from this endeavor by the trustees.[3]

Third, the colony was supposed to yield products that could not be produced in England. The trustees had grandiose visions that Georgia would become the major producer of goods such as silk, flax, hemp, wine, potash, and lumber. Much stress was placed on the possibility of Georgia for increasing the trade and wealth of England. Through Georgia, the mother country hoped to cease its reliance and dependence on others for those goods. Silk production was especially important to the English. The trustees even put silkworms on the common seal, and Italians were brought in to instruct the colonists in silk culture. It was hoped that Georgia would enable England to become an exporter of silk, because both land and mulberry trees would be free in the new colony and production would be cheaper than in competing countries. Each colonist was required to plant a certain number of mulberry trees to furnish food for the silkworms, and a filature was set up in Savannah to unwind the silk from the cocoons. Silk production had been tried with little success in Virginia and the Carolinas, yet the trustees still wanted to attempt the endeavor in Georgia.

Producing flax, hemp, and potash was also especially important to England. Great Britain annually imported from Russia more than 150,000 pounds worth of these goods. All of this could be saved in the balance of trade by importing raw materials from the new colony rather than importing manufactured goods from other countries like Russia. Despite the trustees' dreams of success, plans to make Georgia a major producer of goods unavailable in England were destined to fail. Georgia simply lacked the experience, climate, and assets necessary.[4]

Finally, central to the philanthropic vision of the trustees, the colony was intended to be a refuge for the working poor. Unemployment was a major problem in England in the early eighteenth century. Thousands of men were out of work. According to contemporary sources, four thousand people were committed to prison each year for debt in the city of London alone. The trustees hoped that sending families to live in Georgia would help alleviate the problem of unemployment in England. It was estimated that twenty thousand men could be employed in the Georgia silk industry alone.[5] Georgia was intended to provide relief for those deserving and working poor in England, not to make wealthy men even richer.

One legend about Georgia refuses to perish: that Georgia was colonized by debtors. Contrary to popular belief, Georgia was not settled as a colony of debtors recently released from British prisons. Much has been written about the debtors who formed the colony; all of it, however, is false. It is true that several of the trustees, including Oglethorpe, had served on a committee in 1729 to investigate the condition of British jails. Many expressed concern for England's imprisoned debtors. Yet the trustees actually set up a screening committee to interview prospective settlers. Any released debtors were eliminated during the initial screening process. Never had a colony's settlers been so meticulously selected. No evidence has been found to confirm the belief that any discharged debtors were ever sent to the fledgling colony. Oglethorpe and several of the original trustees for the colony had intended that Georgia serve as a haven for English debtors to be funded by the general public. Months of compromise, however, shaped the Georgia charter into a refuge for the working poor. The trustees believed that the standard of living for those deserving poor and unemployed was bound to improve once they had been removed from England and settled in Georgia.

Rather than debtors, the trustees wanted to send charity colonists, or "the worthy poor," to Georgia. The families selected to be Georgia colonists were by no means destitute. Most of these people were small tradesmen or artisans. The trustees emphasized the fact that because their settlers were not productive in England, their going to the new colony would not drain their homeland of needed workers. The trustees genuinely believed that they would aid the poor who were sent to Georgia by giving them a new chance to prosper there. The trustees chose potential colonists carefully since they would ulti-mately receive free passage to America along with supplies and food for one year, seeds and agricultural tools, and land on which to farm. Between 1732 and 1741, the trustees sent nearly two thousand people to Georgia at the trustees' expense. This figure included many Englishmen and more than eight hundred Protestants from Germany, Switzerland, and Austria. During the same period, over one thousand people also immigrated to Georgia at their own expense.[6]

SETTLEMENT AND LIFE IN TRUSTEESHIP GEORGIA

The trustees immediately began an extensive campaign to promote and advertise their new colony. They attempted to appeal to every motive that would stir an Englishman—religion, philanthropy, imperial defense, and national wealth. More than one hundred clergymen and churches in England set out to raise money for Georgia. Numerous promotional pamphlets were distrib-uted throughout England. The trustees themselves never donated more than £900 during Georgia's establishment.

The first group to make the journey to America was made up of small businessmen, tradesmen, and unemployed workers from London. One noted Georgia scholar wrote that the colonist screening process proved to be the most selective and discriminating of all the British colonies in America. Early writers of Georgia history drew their evidence for the debtor thesis mainly from the wording of the colony's charter and from superficial records.[7]

James Edward Oglethorpe, resident trustee of Georgia, was born in 1696 and had been a member of Parliament since 1722 as a representative from Haslemere. During his tenure in Parliament, Oglethorpe had frequently shown an interest in imperial and colonial affairs. He was eager to attempt founding a colony. Oglethorpe made the decision to journey to Georgia with full knowledge that even though he represented the trustees, he would not have the title or authority of a colonial governor. It was already clear that the trustees who remained at home in England would keep for themselves the power to make all decisions regarding the colony.

Once the Georgia charter had been granted, colonial governors wrote to various trustees discouraging them from acting too quickly. Governor Jonathan Belcher of Massachusetts wrote that the South had only succeeded in causing the deaths of the English who had tried to settle there. Governor Robert Johnson of South Carolina also urged the trustees to proceed with caution, citing the recent fever that had plagued his colony and taken his son and three servants. Nevertheless, Oglethorpe continued with his plans to found a new colony.[8]

When preparations for the first voyage of colonists to Georgia were being made, James Edward Oglethorpe decided to accompany the new settlers in person to ensure that they were safely settled in the new colony. Oglethorpe and approximately 120 settlers set sail for Georgia on November 17, 1732, on board the *Anne*. After a relatively easy journey, the ship carrying Oglethorpe and his colonists arrived off Charles Town on January 13, 1733. Except for the death of two children who were buried at sea, the venture had proved uneventful. On board the *Anne*, Oglethorpe took great pains to see that all of the colonists were comfortable. If any of the passengers became seasick, he made certain that they received everything they needed. Oglethorpe seemed to care genuinely about the Georgia settlers. He was much beloved by the people, and they bestowed upon him the title of "Father." Oglethorpe even acted as godfather to a child born aboard the ship. The colonists remained on the ship in Charles Town for several days while Oglethorpe found a spot on which to settle. The colonists brought with them four large tents to provide temporary shelter, tools, firearms, gunpowder, and food supplies, including 3,700 gallons of beer and wine.

Leaving the colonists on board the ship in Charles Town, Oglethorpe set out to meet with the local Indian tribe and find a location on which to settle. There had been a treaty between the Indians and South Carolina that no white settlements were to be made south of the Savannah River without the consent of the natives. Oglethorpe immediately sought to form a relationship with the Indians and arranged to meet with Tomochichi, chief of the Yamacraw Indians. He was able to convince Tomochichi that it would be advantageous to the Indians to let the English settlers come. This initial meeting between Oglethorpe and Tomochichi was the beginning of a long friendship between the English and the Indians that lasted throughout the proprietary history of the colony. Tomochichi gave Oglethorpe his permission for a settlement to be located on Yamacraw Bluff. Oglethorpe selected this spot because it was on high ground, had a source of fresh water, and was defensible.

Yamacraw Bluff, named for the Indians who lived there, was the first high ground Oglethorpe came to as he traveled upriver from the mouth of the Savannah. The Yamacraws were a small band of Creek Indians, totaling slightly more than one hundred. Yamacraw Bluff was an area well known to South Carolina Indian traders, as it had sometimes been used as a sort of loading and unloading spot. The bluff was elevated enough to be free of swamps, surrounded by ample forests for firewood and lumber, and isolated from Indians except for the minor Yamacraw group. It was also convenient for settlers because it was just across the river from South Carolina, convenient for transportation and close to South Carolina, should war ever break out with the Spanish or French. The bluff also provided the colonists with a nice view and allowed them to track potential enemies with ease. The colonists named their new settlement Savannah. Oglethorpe also made friends with the Creek Indians, who signed a treaty recognizing the right of the English to settle on their land.[9]

Oglethorpe continued his relationship with Tomochichi, chief of the Yamacraw, over the years and even took the latter and a few other Indians back to England with him in 1734. He intended to sensationalize Georgia in England through the Indians and to impress upon the Indians the strength and greatness of England. The Indians' visit to England proved successful for Georgia. England received Oglethorpe as a great hero and empire builder. Parliament also appropriated £26,000 to help finance another exodus to Georgia, and within a short time, the trustees had over one thousand applications from people wanting to move to the colony. When Tomochichi died in October 1739, Oglethorpe ordered an English military funeral for the Indian with himself serving as a pallbearer.

In August 1739, Oglethorpe, with Tomochichi's influence and help, organized a full meeting of the Creek nation at Coweta. During this ten-day conference, the Georgia-Creek boundary was made clearer than it had been in the 1733 treaty. During this time, Oglethorpe worked with Mary Musgrove, a half-breed niece of a Creek leader who had been raised among both Indians and whites. Mary was born circa 1708 to a Tuckabatchee Creek woman and a South Carolina trader named Edward Griffin. In 1725, Mary married half-breed trader John Musgrove. Mary and John opened a trading post at Yamacraw Bluff around 1730, and John became one of the leading Carolina Indian traders. Mary essentially became Oglethorpe's agent and interpreter in dealing with the Creeks. Oglethorpe's successors continued to use Mary to secure Creek friendship and aid. Mary Musgrove is often credited with playing a vital role in preserving the peace between the Indians and the new Georgia colony.[10]

Satisfied with his selection of Yamacraw Bluff as the site for the new settlement, Oglethorpe went back to South Carolina and joined his colonists. They departed Carolina in eight large boats and were accompanied by a regiment of South Carolina soldiers. They arrived at Yamacraw Bluff, the future site of

Savannah, on February 1, 1733. The colonists had been at their new home for less than an hour when Tomochichi and other Indians came to welcome them formally, bearing gifts of buffalo skin. That evening Oglethorpe and the other settlers spent their first night on Georgia soil. In the first few weeks after the founding of Savannah, Georgia settlers immediately went to work creating a home. On February 7, the settlers began to dig trenches as fortifications for possible attacks by the Indians or Spanish. The next day, each family was given an iron pot, a frying pan, three wooden bowls, a Bible, and a copy of the Book of Common Prayer. Every able-bodied man was given a musket and bayonet in order to defend himself and his family.

Oglethorpe planned Savannah along distinctive lines, imagining the colony's first settlement as a town centered around four squares. Each of the four squares was surrounded by forty lots that were sixty by ninety feet. Four larger trust lots lay to the east and west and were reserved for public use. Each group of ten single-house lots was called a tithing. A tithing man was placed in charge. Tithings were then grouped into wards. Lots in Savannah were of uniform size, twenty by thirty yards, and houses were supposed to be twenty-four feet long and sixteen feet wide. Settlers immediately started working on establishing a garden designated for public use. A ten-acre tract of land between Savannah and the river was chosen as the site for the garden. Like the town of Savannah, the garden was laid out in squares as well. Thus, Savannah became America's first pre-planned city. Only two other cities in America have this distinction: Washington, D.C., and Milledgeville, Georgia.

The Georgia charter limited land grants to five hundred acres, but the trustees resolved to reduce the amount of land to fifty acres for the charity colonists. Each charity colonist received fifty acres, a five-acre house, a garden plot at the edge of town, and a forty-five acre farm plot in the country. White indentured servants, upon release from their contracts, were granted only twenty acres. Independent settlers who came to Georgia at their own expense were eligible to receive the full five hundred acres, provided they brought with them six servants. Landownership was granted for life to prevent loss of land through poor management. Since women were not expected to serve in the militia, only males could own land in order to ensure that there was a fighting man for each fifty acres. Women could not possess or inherit land in early Georgia. Under no circumstances could land be sold or mortgaged. Landowners were also prohibited from willing their property to anyone other than their eldest son.

The trustees felt that if the Georgia settlers were unable to make easy profits from their land, then they would not be at risk of losing it, either. The trustees intended Georgia to be a place of hardworking small farmers rather than a colony settled by a few large-plantation owners. In keeping with this idea, Georgia's founders were especially concerned with instilling a strong work ethic in the colonists. They believed that Georgia would benefit the most from a populace of farmers. The purpose of Georgia was not to make the rich even richer. Georgia was supposed to be a place of white yeoman farmers.

By the 1750s, Georgia settlers were able to take advantage of a new and generous land policy that allowed heads of families to claim "headrights" of one hundred acres for themselves and fifty additional acres for each family member, servant, or slave. This new land policy contributed greatly to the establishment of an aristocracy. The policy also attracted numerous small farmers as well. Between 1752 and 1776, Georgia's population expanded from fewer than 4,000 people to approximately 40,000.[11]

When he returned from England in 1736, Oglethorpe put into effect three new laws that no other American colony experienced. Consistent with the idea of Georgia as a buffer area, the trustees forbade the introduction of slavery or of blacks into the colony. One reason for this prohibition was the fact that charity colonists would not be able to afford to buy slaves to work their land. The trustees also wanted Georgia to develop into a colony dominated by white yeoman farmers. The crops the trustees wanted grown in Georgia were not those traditionally farmed by slave labor. White servants would be able to do the job just as well. The trustees believed that slaves would only weaken the military effectiveness of the colony, because slaves were liable to rebel at any time. Constant surveillance was required to keep down insurrection. In that case, the colonists would be too busy suppressing slave uprisings to defend the colony successfully against the Spanish.

Many Georgians became embittered over the fact that they were prohibited from owning slaves when, just across the river, South Carolinians were prospering with slave labor. Some of these dissatisfied colonists formed themselves into a group known as the Malcontents. The Malcontents rallied in Savannah before the colony was even ten years old and led a movement to leave Georgia. Many chose to live in South Carolina instead. The trustees eventually repealed the law prohibiting slavery and allowed it into the colony. By permitting Georgian colonists to own slaves, the trustees essentially eliminated the last significant trace of the philanthropic nature of the original trustees. However, the trustees did specify that one indentured white servant be brought into the colony for each group of four slaves. Owners were supposed to ensure that the slaves were taught Christianity and they were to permit no interracial marriages.[12]

The trustees also imposed regulations on the Indian trade. This act created a Georgia Indian commissioner and required annual licensing for anyone who desired to trade with the Indians. Traders could go into Indian territory after procuring a license and taking an oath before the bailiff in Savannah. A fee of 10 shillings and a bond of £100 were required before a permit was granted. Should a trader bring Indians with him into the settlement, he had to vouch for their good behavior. Oglethorpe initially acted as Indian commissioner and was succeeded by William Stephens. This law proved beneficial for Georgia, as it undoubtedly led to good Indian relations. However, it was troublesome to South Carolinians, who were accustomed to trading with the Indians west of the Savannah River under a license from their own colonial authorities. South Carolina traders broke the law by bringing goods across the border to trading marts and by carrying on trade without a license. In response to this, trade from that region was restricted. The provincial council of South Carolina vehemently protested, and although South Carolina appealed its case to the British government, Britain refused to have the Georgia law rescinded.[13]

The final act the trustees imposed on the colonists prohibited all rum or brandy. This law proved to be the most unrealistic of the three. Indian chiefs appealed to the trustees to pass the legislation, complaining that overindulgence of rum had a bad effect on their people. Oglethorpe agreed with the Indians and also believed that rum had been the cause of the fatal fevers in Savannah in 1733. Restricting Georgians to wines and beer from England would "build up the colony's strength, improve relations with the Indians, and teach the colonists lessons in frugality and virtue." In the long run, the rum prohibition made it harder for Georgia to develop strong economic ties with the Indians and by 1742, the Rum Act was openly ignored.[14]

The trustees as individuals brought support to the newly established colony in several ways. Some, because of their interest and experience in charitable work, provided an invaluable knowledge that aided the poor charity colonists who were selected to settle in Georgia. Others were able to give or solicit financial assistance from private citizens. When the Board of Trustees was set up in July 1732, its members went to work immediately to raise money to fund the venture. The trustees appealed to every possible source and, in turn, were flooded with contributions. Still others were members of the House of Commons. These members were especially important because Parliament supplied much of the money to establish and maintain Georgia. Of the twenty-one men who composed the original trustees, ten were members of the House of Commons. The trust was left open-ended, meaning that its membership could be expanded. During the twenty years that the trust governed Georgia, fifty additional trustees were added. Of this group, only a few devoted themselves to the business of Georgia on a daily basis. The colony was generally just a secondary concern to the majority of the trustees.

The trustees governed Georgia from both London and Savannah. They employed two men, Benjamin Martyn as secretary and Harman Verelst as accountant, who served for the entire life of the trust. Throughout its existence, the trust had seventy-one trustees. The most well known among these were James Vernon, Henry L'Apostre, Thomas Towers, and James Oglethorpe. During the twenty-year period of the trusteeship, Georgia never had an official governor. The Georgia charter specified that the king would have to approve all laws passed by the trustees. The king was also granted a veto over any governor who might be appointed. The trustees did not appoint a governor lest they lose some of their authority, and they refused to give elected officials sufficient power to control the colony. They preferred to govern the colony by decrees or ordinances rather than by passing laws. In fact, the trustees passed only three laws during the trust's entire existence. Neither ordinances nor decrees were subject to the king's scrutiny.

The trustees believed that if Oglethorpe accompanied the settlers and got the colony off to a good start, Georgia would be able to prosper without much government. Oglethorpe was essentially the only government in Georgia though he did not actually hold an official position. While Oglethorpe had no real executive authority, he never hesitated to act when he felt it necessary and the trustees never objected or tried to stop him. Rather than playing the role of governor of the colony, Oglethorpe was actually the resident trustee, delegated special powers by the board. These powers included licensing people for trading with the Indians, making land leases, training the militia, and administering the oath of office to officials appointed by the board.[15]

Before the colonists left England, the trustees created the "Town Court of Savannah and the Precincts thereof." This was the only government Oglethorpe established in Savannah on July 7, 1733. The "Town Court" consisted of three justices, or bailiffs, and a recorder. It was given complete criminal and civil jurisdiction. Assisting with the judicial functions were two constables, two tithing men, and eight conservators of the peace. Lawyers were considered to be "the pest and scourge of mankind," and none of that profession was allowed into the colony. Instead of appointing a chief executive, the trustees appointed a number of executive officers for a variety of functions as the need arose. Each was independent of the others and responsible only to the trustees in London. Among those appointed were a storekeeper, schoolmasters, clergymen, port officials, a register of land grants, an agent to the Cherokees, and a surveyor.[16]

In 1750, the trustees finally gave the colonists the privilege of electing a representative assembly. The first assembly met in Savannah on January 15, 1751, and was composed of sixteen men elected from their communities on the basis of population. Initially, the sixteen men were elected without any qualifications as to age, sex, education, or wealth. However, as time went on, occupational requirements were required for membership. The first Georgia Assembly had no power to make laws, appropriate money, or vote. The Georgia Assembly essentially only reported opinion within the colony and recommended courses of action. It also offered the Georgians an avenue through which they could participate in colonial affairs. Many of those elected to the assembly expressed the fear that that once the trustees gave up their charter, the Carolinians would take over the colony. They asked the trustees to ensure that the king would continue to keep Georgia as a separate province after control of the colony reverted to the Crown. Only after the royal government took effective control of the colony did the concept of a truly representative assembly, which would have the power to legislate, come to fruition.[17]

At first glance, one might assume that the trusteeship period was a failure. Crops that were to be grown in Georgia were never produced successfully, and Georgia did not become the Eden that many had anticipated. The trustees passed only three laws during their existence, and by 1752, all of these laws had been openly ignored or abandoned. By the time the trustees returned their charter to the king, only a reduced percentage remained of the population they had assembled in Georgia. However, there were several positive achievements. The trustees had supervised the settlement of over 5,500 colonists in Georgia, 3,500 of whom traveled at their own expense. The colony also successfully acted as a buffer against Spain and served as a haven to persecuted European Protestants.[18]

GEORGIA AS A ROYAL COLONY

In 1754, the trustees relinquished their control of Georgia and it was made into a royal colony. Under this system of government, Georgia had three royal governors: John Reynolds, Henry Ellis, and James Wright. As the first royal governor of Georgia, Reynolds had the opportunity to establish a full-fledged legislature and a set of courts, neither of which Georgia had possessed before. The governor was the cornerstone of royal control in Georgia and was more powerful in that colony than in any other royal colony. The royal governor was bestowed with broad powers. He was able to convene, dissolve, or adjourn the assembly, grant land, command the militia, and conduct Indian negotiations. However, Reynolds proved to be an ineffective leader. His military plans for Georgia's defense were impractical and expensive. He, along with his private secretary, William Little, tried to monopolize political power within the colony. After an investigation into Reynolds's underhanded dealings, the Board of Trade removed him from office. Henry Ellis, who arrived in Georgia in February 1757, succeeded Reynolds. Although he remained in office for only three years, Ellis was able to reverse Reynolds's failures and turn the colony around.

James Wright served longest of the three royal governors, lasting almost two decades. Under Wright, Georgia prospered and grew both in population and in territory. Wright saw the population triple during his tenure, in part because of his efforts to recruit new settlers and to help them get established. He had much to gain personally if Georgia prospered because he was one of the colony's largest landowners and planters. Wright, the best remembered of Georgia's royal governors, was one of the most able men to ever govern the colony. His father had been the royal chief justice of South Carolina. Wright had previously served as South Carolina's attorney general and brought with him to the job an administrative skill others lacked. Educated in England, Wright was well prepared for the public duties awaiting him in Georgia. His first concern was the defense of the colony. Settlements in Georgia were spread thinly down the Atlantic Coast, and there was no active fort or fleet to protect them from the Spanish. However, after the Treaty of Paris in 1763 concluding the French and Indian War, Wright had no further cause for worry after Spain ceded Florida to England.

Wright's next concern was Indian relations. He had tremendous success in persuading the Indians to surrender enormous amounts of land to the Georgians. While Oglethorpe was trustee of Georgia, the Indians had given up over 1 million acres of land. Wright proved to be more success-ful than even Oglethorpe. In 1763 alone, he was able to secure more than twice the amount Oglethorpe ever had. In the Treaty of Augusta, Wright was able to get significant land cessions from the Creeks. The Augusta conference provided the first clear-cut line between Georgia and the Creeks. Wright also secured important land cessions in 1773. He met with Cherokee and Creek representatives in Augusta, where the Indians ceded over 2 million acres of land to the colony. In return for the land cession, the government assumed the Indian debt with Georgia traders. When Wright arrived in Georgia in 1760, Georgia comprised about 1 million acres. At the end of his tenure as governor, Wright had added over 6 million additional acres of land.[19]

GEORGIA IN THE AMERICAN REVOLUTION

Georgia was only forty-three years old when the American Revolution broke out. Colonial protest against English rule hardly existed before the conclusion of the French and Indian War in 1763. This war pitted England against both France and Spain and culminated in ousting the Spanish from Florida and the French from Canada. As the British gained all this new territory, their attention was focused on the American colonies as never before. The French and Indian War had left England with a very heavy debt. Taxpayers in England were already paying heavily when Parliament decided to look to the colonies as new sources of revenue in order to be able to keep troops and officials in America. Parliament decided to tax the colonists, since the war had essentially been fought for them. Parliament, however, failed to ask the colonists, and the question of taxation without representation became one of several issues raised by disgruntled Americans.

The American colonists saw things differently. They felt that they had already paid their share by providing soldiers to fight against the French. Tensions built up in all the colonies, including Georgia. The biggest disputes arose out of the new British colonial policy, and most notably the Sugar and Stamp Acts, the Townshend Acts, and the Intolerable Acts. There was opposition to all of these acts in Georgia. These disputes helped to build up a climate of opinion against the British government that eventually led Georgia and the other colonies to revolt against the mother country. After the French and Indian War, England expected its American colonies to share some of the financial burden incurred because the war had been for the colonies' defense. England's "New Colonial Policy" set off a movement that led to the American Revolution.

In 1764, Parliament passed the Sugar Act, the first piece of legislation intended to raise revenue in America. Massachusetts took the lead in colonial opposition to the Sugar Act, because, if properly enforced, the law would severely hinder the distillation of rum in New England. The Massachusetts House of Representatives sent a letter to all colonial assemblies protesting the policy of imposing taxes on the colonists. The Georgia Assembly instructed the colony's agent in London, William Knox, to join the other colonial agents in protesting the Sugar Act. The Sugar Act caused little excitement in Georgia, though there were protests from New England. Georgians were more worried that the Sugar Act might jeopardize Georgia's lumber trade with the Caribbean Islands than with theories of taxation. Under the Sugar Act, Georgia lumber would have to be landed in British territory and exchanged for British rum, sugar, or molasses. It was more profitable for Georgia lumber to be exchanged for cheaper sugar products from the Spanish West Indies.

The Georgia Assembly also directed its agent in London to protest against the proposed Stamp Act. The assembly believed that the financial burden the act would impose on Georgia would be too much for the colony to bear. The Stamp Act controversy was the first major disagreement between the people and the British government in which Georgia joined the other colonies. The Stamp Act met with more resistance in Georgia than its predecessor. This act, which became law in March 1765 and was to go into effect in December of that year, required that every newspaper, pamphlet, license, and legal document be written or printed on stamped paper sold by public officials. All income from the sale of stamps was to be used for defending the colonies. Effigies of stamp masters were burned and hanged in Savannah, and the Sons of Liberty was organized to oppose the Stamp Act and force the resignations of stamp masters. Most opposition to the Stamp Act took place in Savannah and was mainly from the artisan and small-merchant class. Although there was some protest of the Stamp Act in Georgia, the majority of the people were willing to submit to Parliament's decisions.

Georgia's Commons House of Assembly joined the other colonies in petitioning Parliament to repeal the Stamp Act. However, the colony did not send a delegate to the Stamp Act Congress in New York in 1765, still clinging to the hope that England would listen to America's demands. When the Massachusetts Assembly invited the other colonies to send representatives to the Stamp Act Congress, the Georgia Assembly was not in session. Sixteen of the twenty-five members met in Savannah in September, but Governor Wright opposed sending delegates to the congress and refused to call the assembly into session to discuss the situation. In stark contrast with other colonial governors, Governor Wright managed throughout the controversy to maintain law and order in Georgia. Wright became the only governor in the colonies who actually collected any stamps. Wright worked diligently, both publicly and privately, to influence the more important people against such rebellious actions and to get their backing in enforcing the law once stamps and a distributor arrived in Georgia. There was an outcry against Georgia in some of the other colonies because Georgia had sent no delegates to the Stamp Act Congress and seemingly went along with Britain's new colonial policies.

In December 1765, the first stamps arrived in Georgia. They were unloaded from the ship and placed in the royal warehouse, where they would remain until a stamp master arrived to sell them. Two hundred members of the Sons of Liberty, whom Governor Wright referred to as the Sons of Licentiousness, assembled in Savannah, threatening to seize the stamps and destroy them. In response, Governor Wright sent forty soldiers to keep watch over the warehouse. South Carolina, however, was still not satisfied with the degree of Georgia's rebellion. Georgia's neighboring colony attempted to cut off all trade with Georgia, threatened to burn any ship coming from that "infamous colony," and declared that its would put to death any South Carolinian who traded with a Georgian.

The most important conflict between Georgia and the British government arose in 1767 with the passage of the Townshend Acts. Charles Townshend, chancellor of the exchequer, believed that since the colonies had only objected to internal taxes such as the Stamp Act, they should have no objections to external taxes. These external taxes consisted of import duties on glass, paper, tea, and lead. The Townshend Acts also created an American customs service to administer the laws of trade in the colonies. The revenue received from these taxes was to be used to pay the salaries of royal governors and judges in the colonies. The Georgia Assembly instructed its agent in London, Benjamin Franklin, to work for the repeal of the Townshend Acts. A group of Savannah merchants met in September to protest against the Townshend Acts, agreeing that they were unconstitutional and that Georgia did not have sufficient funds to pay the taxes. These merchants resolved that they would no longer purchase any items taxed by the Townshend Acts. While the rest of the colonies abided by the agreement that they would not import goods from England, Georgia and Rhode Island did not. By the time the Georgia Assembly met in October 1770 to discuss the circumstances, the Townshend Acts had been repealed except for the tax on tea.

After the Tea Act of 1773, Georgians met in Savannah to discuss the measures. The resolutions adopted there were far from the radical or extreme measures adopted by other colonies. A Council for Safety was created in July 1775 to oversee the enforcement of boycotts and seek possible solutions to the crisis between Georgia and Britain. In September 1774, delegates from all of the colonies, except for Georgia, due to disorganization and Indian problems at home, met at Philadelphia's Carpenters Hall and formed the First Continental Congress. Even though the youngest colony did not send representatives to the First Continental Congress, Georgia did promise to go along with the actions of the other twelve colonies, and a heated debate ensued in Georgia. Rather than advocating independence from England, the First Continental Congress aspired to remedy grievances and restore harmony between the colonies and the mother country. This idea gained even more support from the colonies after the British closed the Port of Boston. At the end of October 1774, the First Continental Congress had adopted the Declaration of Rights and Grievances and had also issued a petition to King George III.

Georgia lingered behind the rest of the rebellious colonies for several reasons. Georgians were reluctant to sever their beneficial relationship with the mother country. Gratitude alone might well have made Georgia the last stronghold of British loyalty in America. There were many arguments for why Georgia should have remained loyal to England. Until 1763, Georgia was the youngest and weakest of the British colonies. The Treaty of Paris, however, which ended the French and Indian War, also removed the Spanish threat from Georgia. By gaining the Florida territory, Georgia's military security was heightened. The colony's frontiers were safer than they had ever been before. The 1763 treaty also created for the first time a definitive southern boundary for the colony, St. Mary's River. When the Spanish were expelled from the area, Georgia more than doubled the land available for settlement. Because Georgia was younger and poorer than the other colonies, it was more in need of help from England to protect its frontiers. Because most of the colony was occupied by Indians, the whites saw English troops as protectors rather than as potential oppressors. Georgia had been settled only forty years earlier, and many of the people there still had family ties with people in England. Georgia had also received more financial help from England than any other colony. During Georgia's short history, Parliament had provided more than 1 million dollars for the colony's support.

At the beginning of the American Revolution, Georgia's population was small and sparse. There were only about 20,000 whites and 17,000 blacks in the entire colony. Georgia's population on the eve of the Revolution was diverse. The backbone was English, yet two large components included the Scotch-Irish and the Germans. In Georgia, the Germans had found the religious freedom they desired and had prospered economically. Many feared that they would lose their land and everything they had gained if they opposed the royal government. The varied groups that made up Georgia's population and the physical isolation of the different groups made it difficult for Georgians to cooperate fully and to agree upon a common policy in opposing England. Older men who had been born in England continued to be loyal to the king and Parliament. It was the younger men, those who had no sentiment about England, who were eager to separate from the mother country and go their own way.

There were few local grievances with the British government, and the majority of Georgia settlers were slow to join the revolutionary movement.

Georgia had few reasons to complain about royal rule because royal governor James Wright had worked to negotiate large amounts of land from the Indians and had also kept South Carolina from claiming coastal areas south of the Altamaha River. Georgians placed great faith in their petitions to the king. Most were reluctant to take sides. They continued to hope that some sort of compromise would be worked out. By the end of 1775, however, the radical party had acquired control of the colony. The tide had been turned.[20]

When word of the Battle of Lexington reached Georgia in early May 1775, the Georgia Sons of Liberty, led by Noble W. Jones, Joseph Habersham, and Edward Telfair, broke into the public powder magazine and stole five hundred pounds of gunpowder. Tradition holds that the gunpowder was concealed in a shipment of rice and money sent to Massachusetts and that it was used in the Battle of Bunker Hill. Governor Wright offered a reward of £150 for the arrest of the raiders. On June 2, the Sons of Liberty also spiked the colony's twenty-one cannons in order to prevent their use in celebrating the king's birthday two days later. By June 1775, Georgia's prominent Whigs were certain they would uphold American rights while still remaining a part of the British Empire. A group of thirty-four leading Savannah Whigs met in mid-June and suggested that a petition objecting to the recent parliamentary acts intended to produce revenue in the colonies should be addressed to the king. At this stage, however, the Georgia Whigs still believed that they could restore American liberties and heal the division between the colonies and the mother country. The first action against the British in Georgia occurred in July 1775, when the Provincial Congress gave Joseph Habersham and Oliver Brown orders to capture a British ship anchored off the coast. The Georgia navy was able to seize nine thousand pounds of gunpowder from the British vessel. They sent five hundred pounds of it to the Continental Congress.

In January 1776, the Council of Safety ordered the arrest of Governor Wright, along with members of the Royal Council. They were taken into custody while in session at the governor's residence. Wright was allowed to remain in his home, but a guard was stationed there to prevent his escape. This proved futile, for in mid-February, Wright managed to elude the guards posted outside his house and to escape by boat during the night. With his departure, the last vestige of royal government in Georgia came to an end. When Governor Wright left for England in 1776, the revolutionists, or Whigs, set up a temporary government on April 15, 1776, to function until a constitution could be adopted. This government became the basis for the Second Provincial Congress.

The Provincial Congress acted as the legislative body, and Archibald Bulloch was elected to the position of president and commander in chief of Georgia. New courts were established to take the place of royal courts, and judges were appointed by the Provincial Congress. The congress also appointed five delegates—John Houstoun, Archibald Bulloch, Reverend John J. Zubly,

Noble W. Jones, and Lyman Hall—to represent Georgia in the next Continental Congress meeting in Philadelphia. The first four delegates were also members of the Provincial Congress. Georgia promised the other colonies full cooperation with whatever the Continental Congress might decide to do. It was beyond doubt now that Georgia had gone all the way with the other colonies in opposition to British parliamentary action. There was no turning back.

The Second Continental Congress assembled in Philadelphia on May 10, 1775, just three weeks after the Battle of Lexington. Delegates remained in Philadelphia until May 1, 1781. Georgia was at first partially and then fully represented at this second meeting of the colonies. The Georgia Assembly elected Archibald Bulloch, Noble Wymberly Jones, and John Houstoun as delegates to the congress. The Second Continental Congress began to shape the direction of both domestic and foreign policies for the continuation of the war and the establishment of peace.

In July 1776, delegates of the Second Continental Congress signed the Declaration of Independence. Georgia delegates Button Gwinnett, George Walton, and Lyman Hall all voted for and signed the document. Georgia played no crucial part in the adoption of the Declaration of Independence but did not delay it, as did some other states. In April 1776, Georgia's Provincial Congress reminded the state's delegates that the American cause was continental rather than simply provincial and advised them to do what was best for the common good of all Americans. Independence was announced in Georgia in August when President Bulloch read a letter from John Hancock, president of the Continental Congress, to the Council of Safety. When news of the Declaration reached Savannah, a mock funeral of George III was staged and mobs filled the streets.

After the Declaration of Independence was signed, immediate steps were taken to provide a permanent government for Georgia. Bulloch requested that all parishes and districts elect representatives to the Constitutional Convention set to meet in Savannah in October 1776. South Carolina was the first of the thirteen colonies to draft a temporary state constitution in March 1776 and a permanent constitution two years later, in March 1778. Georgia followed South Carolina's example and penned a temporary state constitution in April 1776 and a permanent one in February 1777.

THE CONSTITUTION OF FEBRUARY 5, 1777

The convention delegates assembled in Savannah understood a clear mandate to create new rules and regulations for future government. The preamble to the 1777 Georgia Constitution noted that "the conduct of the legislature of Great Britain for many years has been so oppressive on the people of America" and "repugnant to the common rights of mankind." Americans, "as freemen," became obliged, therefore, "to oppose such oppressive measures, and to assert the rights and privileges they are entitled to by the laws of nature and reason." At the request of Congress that the states create new governments no longer bound to the British Crown, independence having been declared on July 4, 1776, the delegates set out to redefine Georgia constitutional law.

The first article of the 1777 constitution declared that "the legislative, executive, and judicial departments shall be separate and distinct." The second article provided for the annual election of representatives, who, on their first day in session, would elect from among themselves a governor and an Executive Council. The council would have two members from each county, with the governor presiding. The remaining members would constitute the House of Assembly. Representation was based on counties, ten representatives for each, with special provisions for larger and new counties based on population. The fourth article concerned itself with renaming and redefining the counties. So, for example, the parish of St. George became Burke County and the parishes of Saint John, Saint Andrew, and Saint James became Liberty County. Gone were the parishes named after saints for more "American" county names like Richmond, Effingham, Chatham, Glynn, Camden, and Wilkes.

Representatives were to be chosen from the residents of each county. To stand for election, candidates had to have resided in the state for twelve months and in the county for three months. Furthermore, candidates had to be "of the Protestant religion, and of the age of twenty-one years" and had to own 250 acres of land or some property that reached that amount. The right to vote for representatives or any other officers was given to "all male white inhabitants, of the age of twenty-one, and possessed in his own right of ten pounds value, and liable to pay tax in this State, or being of the mechanic trade, and shall have been resident six months in this State." Anyone claiming a title of nobility or holding a military commission other than in the militia was excluded from running for office and voting. Clergymen "of any denomination" were also forbidden from sitting in the legislature. Every person with the right to vote "shall vote by ballot personally" and exercise one vote only. Failure to exercise one's right to vote without a good excuse could result in a fine not to exceed £5.

Executive power resided in the office of governor and the Executive Council. The governor had to have been a state resident for three years. He was chosen by legislative ballot annually but was not "eligible to the said office for more than one year out of three." The governor, "for the time being," was made the commander in chief of the state's militia and other military and naval forces, but most of his power had to be exercised in tandem with the advice of the Executive Council. The governor was forbidden from granting pardons and reversing fines. Any reprieves of criminals or suspensions of fines had to await action by the assembly.

The annually elected Executive Council had the power to appoint its own officers from among its members and settle on its own procedural rules.

However, the councillors were not permitted to vote individually. They were bound to vote by counties. Yet any individual councillor was given the right to protest "any measures in council he has not consented to," if he did it within three days. The council was to attend sessions of the assembly, and the council, through a committee, had five days in which to comment on or amend any laws passed by the assembly.

Superior courts were set up for each county in Article 36. Local matters were to be adjudicated locally. Justices of the peace and registers of probate were to be appointed by the House of Assembly. Further provisions were made for trial by jury, the composition of grand juries, and keeping the cost of actions in superior court below £3. Courthouses and jails were to be erected at public expense in each county. Schools were also to be erected in each county and "supported at the general expense of the State."

The constitution also laid out some specific rights that would, in slightly altered form, later find their way into the U.S. Constitution. Freedom of religion was guaranteed: "All persons whatever shall have the free exercise of their religion; provided it not be repugnant to the peace and safety of the State; and shall not, unless by consent, support any teacher or teachers except those of their own profession." The principles of habeas corpus were made part of the constitution, and citizens were guarded from "excessive fines" and "excessive bail." Freedom of the press and trial by jury were "to remain inviolate forever." Finally, the constitution could be altered, but not easily. A majority of the counties had to petition the assembly for constitutional amendments, and the petitions from each county were to be "signed by a majority of the voters in each county" before the assembly could order a convention.[21]

Archibald Bulloch was elected as the state's first governor under the new constitution, but he died suddenly in February 1777. Button Gwinnett, a Georgia delegate who had signed the Declaration of Independence, then took his place. The 1777 constitution remained in place for twelve years. Georgia's Constitutional Convention also designed a state seal to replace that used by the royal government. Georgia was one of the last states to enact legislation against citizens who remained loyal to England. The loyalists were expelled in the fall of 1777. Late in 1776, the South Carolina Assembly proposed a union between Georgia and South Carolina and sent two representatives to Georgia to promote the idea. Georgians were decidedly against the union, with Button Gwinnett leading the opposition.[22]

GEORGIA UNDER THE ARTICLES OF CONFEDERATION

Georgia took little part in the debate or in writing and adopting the Articles of Confederation. There is no evidence that Button Gwinnett, the Georgia delegate elected to the thirteen-member committee to draft the Articles, exercised any influence at all during the process. Gwinnett and fellow Georgia representative George Walton did argue considerably that Congress should have complete control of Indian affairs and trade as specified in the Articles. The Georgia delegates also advocated equal representation from all states.

The Articles of Confederation were sent to the states in November 1777, with the request that they be ready to ratify in the following March. Edward Telfair arrived on July 13, declaring that he had been authorized to sign the document for Georgia. However, Georgia's authorization for ratification was not presented to Congress until John Walton arrived ten days later. Both Telfair and Walton signed the document the next day. The Georgia Assembly had actually approved the Articles of Confederation in late February 1778 but had failed to send notification to Congress until Telfair arrived in July. The Georgia Assembly proposed four minor amendments to the Articles. The delegates were instructed, however, to ratify the Articles as they were, in the event that Congress did not agree to the changes.

The Articles of Confederation were adopted in 1778 by Georgia and ten other states, but they did not go into effect until 1781, when Maryland, the last of the thirteen colonies, accepted them. In 1781, the thirteen colonies entered into a loose union under a constitution known as the Articles of Confederation. However, the states continued to have as much independence as if they had been separate nations. During the seven-year period from the end of the Revolution until 1789, Georgia had seven governors, each serving a term of one year.

The confederation ultimately proved to be a failure, so a constitutional convention was planned for Philadelphia in 1787 to strengthen or reconfigure the government. Georgia elected six delegates to go to the convention, but only four ever attended. Those four were William Few, Abraham Baldwin, William Pierce, and William Houstoun. Only Few and Baldwin signed the new Constitution. A copy of the new Constitution reached Georgia in October 1787, and a convention was called to meet in Augusta on Christmas day to consider the document. Three other states ratified the Constitution earlier, but Georgia was the first southern state to do so. The Georgia convention ratified the new Constitution with a unanimous vote on January 2, 1788. That day a cannon was fired for each of the thirteen states.

CONCLUSION

Although Georgia played little part in the American Revolution, it became the fourth state to ratify the new Constitution of the United States in 1788. Twenty-one trustees founded the colony of Georgia in 1733, forty-three years before the outbreak of the Revolution, for a number of reasons. Militarily, Georgia was intended to act as a buffer between South Carolina, Spanish Florida, and the French, who were settling in the west. Georgia would also be a refuge for both persecuted Protestants from Europe and the working poor in England. The colony was also supposed to yield foodstuffs and other items that could not be produced in England such as silk, wine, potash, and hemp. Three laws set Georgia apart from any other colony. The Indian trade in Georgia was strictly regulated, rum and brandy were forbidden, and colonists were prohibited from owning slaves. Georgia is unique among the colonies because, until 1754, there was no governor in charge. The trustees did not appoint a governor in hopes of keeping all of the power for themselves. It was not until Georgia became a royal colony in 1754 that the king appointed a governor.

When the Revolution began, Georgia hesitated before joining in the fracas. Georgia was reluctant to abandon its advantageous relationship with England. Throughout Georgia's brief history, Parliament had provided more than one million dollars for the colony's support. Most Georgians believed that matters could be reconciled with the king. This idea, however, proved futile, and Georgia eventually joined the other colonies in rebelling against England.

NOTES

1. Kenneth Coleman, *History of Georgia* (Athens: University of Georgia Press, 1977), p. 17; Kenneth Coleman, *Colonial Georgia: A History* (New York: Scribner, 1976), p. 17.

2. Kenneth Coleman, *Georgia History in Outline* (Athens: University of Georgia Press, 1978), p. 3.

3. Coleman, *History of Georgia*, p. 23; James C. Bonner, *Georgia Story* (Oklahoma City, OK: Harlow Publishing, 1958), pp. 33–34.

4. Coleman, *Georgia History in Outline*, pp. 8–9; Coleman, *History of Georgia*, p. 26.

5. Amanda Johnson, *Georgia as Colony and State* (Atlanta: Walter W. Brown Publishing, 1938), p. 44.

6. Coleman, *Colonial Georgia: A History*, pp. 22–23.

7. Coleman, *History of Georgia*, pp. 17–18; Bonner, *Georgia Story*, p. 32.

8. Phinzy Spalding, *Oglethorpe in America* (Chicago: University of Chicago Press, 1977).

9. Coleman, *History of Georgia*, pp. 18–19; Bonner, *Georgia Story*, p. 30; Coleman, *Colonial Georgia*, p. 25.

10. Coleman, *Colonial Georgia*, pp. 79–80, 82.

11. Coleman, *History of Georgia*, pp. 19–21; Coleman, *Georgia History in Outline*, p. 8; Bonner, *Georgia Story*, p. 53.

12. Coleman, *History of Georgia*, p. 26; Bonner, *Georgia Story*, p. 58.

13. Bonner, *Georgia Story*, pp. 52–53; Johnson, *Georgia as Colony and State*, pp. 62–63.

14. Coleman, *History of Georgia*, p. 26.

15. Coleman, *Colonial History*, p. 89, 93; Bonner, *Georgia Story*, pp. 49–50.

16. Coleman, *Colonial History*, p. 91; Bonner, *Georgia Story*, p. 50.

17. Bonner, *Georgia Story*, p. 59; Coleman, *History of Georgia*, p. 43.
18. Coleman, *History of Georgia*, p. 44.
19. Ibid., pp. 45–46.
20. Coleman, *History of Georgia*, pp. 57–58, 67; Bonner, *Georgia Story*, p. 95, 99.
21. The Avalon Project at Yale Law School, "Constitution of Georgia; February 5, 1777," available: www.yale.edu/lawweb/avalon/states/ga02.htm.
22. Bonner, *Georgia Story*, p. 106–107; Johnson, *Georgia as Colony and State*, p. 134.

BIBLIOGRAPHY

Bonner, James C. *Georgia Story*. Oklahoma City, OK: Harlow Publishing, 1958.
Coleman, Kenneth. *Colonial Georgia: A History*. New York: Scribner, 1976.
———. *History of Georgia*. Athens: University of Georgia Press, 1977.
———. *Georgia History in Outline*. Athens: University of Georgia Press, 1978.
Johnson, Amanda. *Georgia as Colony and State*. Atlanta: Walter W. Brown Publishing, 1938.
Spalding, Phinzy. *Oglethorpe in America*. Chicago: University of Chicago Press, 1977.

☆☆☆

THE STATE OF HAWAII

Admitted to the Union as a State: August 21, 1959

J. D. Bowers

INTRODUCTION

Hawaii's path to statehood is unique among the fifty states. As a noncontinental territory, populated by a majority of nonwhite citizens, and with a lengthy history as an independent nation, no other state presents as complex a set of factors for consideration in the pursuit of statehood. Hawaiian statehood was never universally supported within the islands or within the nation. In fact, no other territory ever appealed for statehood as many times, nor been turned down as often, as Hawaii. Racial, economic, labor, political, and historical factors led to the creation of statehood and anti-statehood associations, all built on alliances that crossed many of the traditional political, racial, and class boundaries. The peoples of the islands battled internally over their place in American society while the national interests debated issues that were colored by a century of imperialism and centered on matters that had little to do with Hawaii itself. The prospects for Hawaiian statehood languished for decades under these conditions. Finally, when a tenuous consensus was finally reached, the pro-statehood faction emerged victorious. But in the five decades since statehood, that consensus has been challenged. Making its case as a unique entity once more, only in Hawaii is there a modern-day, active, and partially successful movement seeking sovereignty and challenging the legality of statehood.

HAWAII, 1959

Hawaii became the fiftieth and most recent state to join the Union on August 21, 1959, five months after the legislation was approved by the Eighty-sixth Congress.[1] Statehood was the final act of a lengthy quest to join the

Hawaii

Territorial Development:

- The Republic of Hawaii ceded all of its holdings to the United States through the Newlands Joint Resolution, July 7, 1898
- Hawaii organized as a U.S. territory, April 30, 1900
- Hawaii admitted into the Union as the fiftieth state, August 21, 1959

Capitals Prior to Statehood:

- Honolulu, 1845–1959 (after being established as the permanent capital of the Kingdom of Hawaii in 1845, Honolulu was also the capital of the Republic of Hawaii from 1893 to 1898 and the American Territory of Hawaii)

State Capitals:

- Honolulu, 1959–present

Origin of State Name: The islands may have been named by Hawaii Loa, who is supposed to have discovered them, but it is also possible that the name means "small homeland" or "new homeland," resulting from a combination of the word *hawa* ("traditional homeland") and *ii* (meaning both "small" and "raging").

First Governor: William Francis Quinn
Governmental Organization: Bicameral
Population at Statehood: 632,772
Geographical Size: 6,423 square miles

Union that had stretched over a period of sixty years. Its achievement, long overdue, was a cause for celebration among a large portion of the islands' population. Proponents of statehood, who felt that both history and precedent were on their side, viewed the lengthy process as embarrassing, frustrating, and unnecessary. Thus, when it finally came, they marked Statehood Day with widespread celebrations, both planned and spontaneous. Various communities staged bonfires, neighbors held impromptu dances, drivers of cars honked their horns, and people walked the streets in celebration—all to show they were now full-fledged Americans. Final recognition came the following year when the fifty-star flag, the twenty-seventh in the nation's history, was flown for the first time on July 4, 1960.

The achievement of statehood and its celebrations were colored by deep divisions within the territory and uncertainty over the impact of the change in status from territory to state. Class conflict was among the most notable, as concerns over potential shifts in property issues and ownership as well as the peculiar trade advantages of a territory led many in the islands' economic and social elite to oppose statehood. Native Hawaiian opposition to statehood, though not yet numerically significant, was organized on the historical foundations of the events of the 1893 overthrow of the queen and the 1898 annexation by the United States that resulted in their disenfranchisement and the end of the native monarchy. The uncertainties also spanned the Pacific Ocean, as mainland perceptions of Hawaii were negatively shaped by recent labor strikes that had crippled the state's import-export economy and exacerbated fears that Hawaii was populated with radicals and Communists.

On the national level, the prospects for Hawaiian statehood meant contending with issues far beyond the immediate concerns of the islands. Alaskan statehood, which had seemed like a nonissue in the early years of Hawaii's quest to become the forty-ninth state, suddenly mired Hawaii's prospects in myriad national political and military issues. Not surprisingly, the national backlash against communism carried over into the islands, as did parallel national controversies over civil rights and racial issues.

There were also important international issues surrounding the status of Hawaii and its native peoples that the United States was forced to consider. The postwar declaration by the United Nations placing Hawaii on the list of the non-self-governing territories in the Pacific that merited independence left the United States in an awkward situation. To grant statehood, not only did the nation have to resolve the islands' status in light of the changing moral and philosophical views on colonialism, but it also had to do so in a way that was consistent with its actions toward other island possessions and not undermine the authority of the United Nations, at the time a nascent international organization.[2]

The relationship between Hawaii and the United States was encased in issues that transcended time and space. Statehood was, by necessity, conditioned by these larger forces. As one of only two states to enter the Union in the modern era, the principles of statehood were more keenly debated, the implications seemed more meaningful, and the prospects for adding such a unique land were more contentious. To understand the decision to grant statehood fully, one must understand the history that brought Hawaii into the American mind, under American control, and to the brink of union.

FROM KINGDOM TO TERRITORY

Hawaii first came to the attention of the European world in 1778 when Captain Cook landed in Kealakekua Bay during his third Pacific voyage. His personal fate, a violent death at the hands of the natives, did little to stifle outside interest in the islands. They quickly became known as a place of anchorage and resupply for shipping interests. Through the stories of the sailors and other early guests, Hawaii came to occupy a central place in the European imagination as paradise. Once the news spread about the Sandwich Islands (as Cook had named them), nations and peoples traveled the vast expanse of the Pacific Ocean to reach the islands, the most remote inhabited island chain in the world. Hawaii's climate, culture, and native peoples presented an almost boundless potential for European plans in the Pacific. But the paradisiacal image quickly began to wear thin, and it became evident that complexities and problems of the islands—those that were both present upon the arrival of Cook and those that were created by the presence of outsiders—intruded upon the land and culture of the Native Hawaiians.

Hawaii's association with the United States began not long after Cook's encounter. The first diplomatic engagement, in 1826, resulted in "an imperfected treaty" concerning commercial relationships and recognition of sovereign powers. But the treaty was never presented to the U.S. Senate for ratification, leading to the conclusion that the United States had no intention of promoting "permanent contacts with Hawaii."[3] Over the course of the next seven decades, the relationship between the two nations retained an element of uncertainty and a lack of clear commitment, yet it gradually shifted toward a more permanent and substantive engagement. The changing relationship eventually included full and complete diplomatic recognition of Hawaii by the United States as well as treaties promising protection from potential incursions by European and other Pacific nations.[4]

During this period of initial diplomatic uncertainty in the 1830s, the first overtures to bring Hawaii into a formal dependent relationship with the United States were put forth by the Hawaiian monarchy. Threatened by European ambitions in the Pacific, Kamehameha III sought protection by seeking to develop a strategic alliance with the United States. To preserve the integrity of the kingdom, the king was even willing to pursue annexation.[5] The United States was not yet ready or willing to commit itself in the Pacific to such a degree. Kamehameha's overture was vehemently opposed in Washington, and the United States declined to act upon the request. Although it failed to result in an established connection between the two lands, the reasons for its failure introduced the issue of Hawaiian statehood for the first time. Those who were against making Hawaii a protectorate of the United States cited the virtual guarantee of statehood that would result from formal annexation as the central reason for their opposition.[6] Yet the United States did negotiate a series of trade agreements, which solidified diplomatic recognition of the kingdom and warned other powers of its willingness to use force against those who challenged the kingdom's independence.

Like the earlier diplomatic ventures, the first trade agreements were marked by uncertainty on the part of both nations. Attempts to negotiate treaties of commerce in 1845, 1855, and 1867 mostly proved unsuccessful. The first meaningful trade agreement, known as the Reciprocity Treaty, was ratified in 1875 and put into effect the following year, with subsequent revisions in 1884 and 1887.[7] The cumulative effect of these treaties, including those that were focused on ensuring Hawaii's neutrality, was to make Hawaii "industrially and commercially a part of the United States" and further U.S. military and economic designs in the Pacific, noted Senator Jon Morgan of Alabama. In exchange, Hawaii and its infant but influential sugar industry, which relied on access to American markets, was given tariff concessions that allowed it to compete in mainland markets.[8]

As the nineteenth century wore on, calls for a stronger alliance, including the previously rejected options of annexation or statehood, were bolstered by these economic and political developments. The U.S. desire for a military presence in the Pacific only grew stronger as Hawaii's suitability as a foreword port for Pacific trade and defense was realized. The later revisions of the Reciprocity Treaty included concessions from the kingdom concerning military installations, and the revisions that came out of the renewed convention in 1887 gave the United States exclusive control over Pearl Harbor.[9]

The increasing interest of the United States in the islands coincided with internal Hawaiian political and economic change. These changes, most notably a wholesale revision of Hawaiian land laws and the implementation of a new constitution, altered the traditional Hawaiian social and economic fabric in ways that facilitated American interests. The 1848 "Great Division," or *mahele*, implemented public and private ownership of land. Previously, all land was owned solely by the royal family. The *mahele* divided the land between the king, the *ali'i* (nobles), the government, and the people who worked it. Intended as a democratic action to make land available to the masses, the *mahele* actually resulted in more land passing out of the control of the people and into the hands of American and European sugar planters. Within decades, the distribution of landownership in Hawaii was heavily skewed toward the foreign-born sugar planters and the Hawaiian monarchy. These and similar land issues would continue to play a very important and divisive role in the future of Hawaii leading up to statehood, and even into the present day.[10]

Another internal development with lasting consequences was the imposition of a new constitution for the kingdom in 1887. It was actually the kingdom's fourth constitution, replacing the previous document, which was proclaimed by monarchial edict in 1864. Known as the "Bayonet Constitution" because King Kalakaua was forced into accepting the revisions under threat of force, the reforms posited by this new document stripped the monarch of most of his ruling powers and vested them in the hands of his cabinet.[11] The leading force behind this constitutional coup was the Hawaiian League, a predominantly white and foreign-born group of men with heavily vested interests in the success of sugar, trade, Christianity, and a closer alliance with the United States. The cumulative effects of the *mahele* and the Bayonet Constitution led to a permanent subordinate status for Native Hawaiians and put the islands on a path toward political dependency.[12]

By the end of the century, the military and economic needs of the American nation and the *haole* (foreign, white) businessmen in Hawaii converged.[13] As a result, what was a gradual shift in power within the islands came to a swift end with the overthrow of the monarchy in 1893. With the questionable involvement of the U.S. military, Queen Lili'uokalani was deposed, and subsequent attempts at restoration were put down. A republic was established under the watchful eye of the United States, which sent a variety of commissioners and investigators to determine the appropriate course of action. Should the United States recognize the new republic, or should it advocate a restoration of the monarchy? Was the overthrow merely an internal matter, as many in the *haole* elite claimed, or was the United States culpable in the events? Perhaps the most important question, then as now, was the extent to which the events reflected the will of the Hawaiian people. The answer to these questions could in no way satisfy all parties. At first the United States claimed that the overthrow was illegal and violated international law. In the end, after a change in administrations from Cleveland to McKinley, the United States refused to intervene further in the internal affairs of Hawaii. The Native Hawaiian opposition was ignored and overtures seeking a restoration of the queen were rebuffed. Such a diplomatic stance amounted to a tacit acceptance of the overthrow and resulted in the recognition of the Republic of Hawaii.[14] The decisions made in 1893 and 1894 regarding these events would have important implications in the quest for statehood over the next sixty years.

While many notable events took place under the rule of the Republic of Hawaii, which governed the islands from 1893 until 1898, none was as important when considering Hawaiian statehood as its last act. In 1898, under the terms of the Newlands Resolution, the Republic of Hawaii ceded the independent nation, all of its lands, and its people to the United States.

The first attempt to make Hawaii an official territory of the United States came in 1897, when President McKinley signed a negotiated treaty of annexation. Demonstrating once again that the desire to unite the two peoples was more urgent among the economic interests in Hawaii than it was for the

of the public lands and placing them into the federal land reserves, as had happened in most of the admissions acts for the western states, the public lands—former crown and kingdom lands—were placed under the control of a Land Commission. The Organic Act went so far as to void all previous claims to the Crown lands in order to ensure this unique trust and to prohibit any future conflicts over their designation. This feature of the law was later clarified and amended under the Revised Laws of Hawaii in 1915 and in the Hawaiian Homes Commission Act of 1920.[21] But the basic premise remained intact— public lands in Hawaii were to be controlled by Hawaii, and the proceeds from those lands were to be used to benefit the people of Hawaii. Another unique provision established a territorial judiciary, which was distinct from, though subservient to, the federal courts. No other territory had ever been given the right to set up its own court system, including a territorial supreme court, circuit courts, and all necessary lower-level courts. Finally, by voiding all of the political offices of the republic, the Organic Act created a powerful territorial governorship. Although the governor was to be appointed by the U.S. president, as was the territorial secretary (similar to a lieutenant governor position), significant veto and legislative powers were conferred upon the governor.

These significant features of the Organic Act were clear indications of the extent to which Hawaii was unique among all previously designated territories. In no other territory had the predominant minority been given citizenship. In no other territory had the public lands ever been placed under the control of a governing body other than the federal government. These novel features of Hawaii's territorial legislation established precedents in the islands that would have significant ramifications in pursuit of statehood and in the subsequent debates over that status throughout the last forty years of the twentieth century.

The adoption of the Organic Act created a mixed message for the ruling powers in Hawaii. Happy to have achieved territorial status, many of them assumed that statehood was not far behind. The precedent throughout the nation's history was quite clear. Territorial status implied that statehood was the automatic next step. Two Supreme Court rulings clearly supported this view of the relationship between becoming a territory and eventual statehood. In *Ex Parte Morgan* (1913), the court had ruled that a territory was considered an "inchoate State."[22] In *O'Donoghue v. United States* (1933), the court reaffirmed the earlier ruling when the justices made clear that there was a substantive distinction between "a territory," which they viewed as synonymous with a colony or province, and the more generic term, "the territory," which merely was a reference to a geographical designation. The court ruling stated: "[I]t may properly be said that the outlying continental public domain, of which the United States was the proprietor, was, from the beginning, destined for admission as a state or states into the union."[23] Although these decisions were issued after the passage of the Organic Act, the congressional debates concerning the establishment of the territorial government revealed similar thinking. When several amendments were put forth during the debate, specifying that future promises of statehood should not be implied by congressional action, they were rejected.[24] As an incorporated territory, Hawaii, like the other existing territories of Alaska, New Mexico, and Arizona, was in line to become a state. Getting to that point, however, proved far more difficult and contentious than anyone might have imagined in 1900.

TERRITORIAL HISTORY

The Organic Act, which was approved by Congress and became effective on June 14, 1900, remained the governing legislation of the territory until statehood in 1959. Throughout the six decades of territorial status, it was clear that Hawaii met all the traditional and formal tests for statehood that had been used to govern the transformation of previous territories into states. The territory possessed a sufficient population and a sizable and lucrative economy, played a vital role in America's military and economic designs in the Pacific, and had proven itself attentive to the demands of the nation. These factors all warranted equal and speedy inclusion within the Union.

Despite the readiness of the islands, more pressing national concerns conspired to keep Hawaii in an unequal relationship for more than sixty years. The people and their ability to govern themselves suffered under the terms of its territorial relationship and remained politically dependent upon the national government. Hawaii had to ask permission from Congress to convene its legislative sessions; political vacancies went unfilled for long periods of time; and the people of the territory paid far more in taxes than they drew in federal aid. During the first fifty years of territorial status, the prospects for statehood lay mostly dormant—unexpectedly mired in the internal squabbles of the islands between the various racial and economic factions as well as being overshadowed by more pressing national concerns. Not to be ignored, however, those within Hawaii who advocated statehood remained active, though often well out of the public eye.

The first act of the Hawaiian Territorial Legislature in 1903 was to pass a resolution calling on Kuhio Kalaniana'ole, the territory's nonvoting delegate, to request that the national Congress consider "an Act enabling the people of this Territory...[to] adopt a State Constitution" so as to be "admitted as a State into the Union."[25] It was the first of many such resolutions. After 1919, the delegates to Congress from Hawaii introduced repeated and numerous resolutions calling for statehood, some of which became bills through the efforts of sympathetic supporters in Congress. Each and every one of these resolutions was met with a resounding silence, demonstrating the continued disparity between political leaders in the islands and the national political powers. Over the course of the next several decades, some of the disparities were addressed, but other impediments would appear or reappear.

Economic status, landownership, race, and labor emerged as the major issues in the territory's pursuit of statehood. The issue of land was highlighted in

303

1920 when the U.S. Congress created the Hawaiian Homes Commission. The following year, the Hawaiian Homes Commission Act was enacted, setting aside nearly 200,000 acres of former Crown lands in a trust for the Native Hawaiian people.[26] The lands and the proceeds from their use were officially transferred in title to the territory. These were the same lands that had passed to the United States from the Republic of Hawaii, that were assumed by the republic from the monarchy, and that were designated, in part, by the divisions spelled out in the *mahele*. The money was set to be used for myriad purposes, including construction of public works projects, but much of the profits were to be used to help revitalize Native Hawaiian society and traditions. In 1959, when the commission was reaffirmed by a provision in the state constitution, the consequences of these earlier actions became clear. Today, land division and distribution remains a unique element of Hawaiian statehood, as these acts (and later revisions) created a trust obligation on behalf of the state and a fiduciary responsibility to the native peoples.

The quest for statehood played out quietly between 1900 and 1945. Various politicians, including the appointed territorial governors, several presidents, and numerous political interest groups, more or less supported statehood but were reluctant to press the issue through public legislation. The time never seemed appropriate, and local and national events always seemed to intrude at the very moment when action appeared most likely. National racial perceptions and policies always stood in the way of Hawaii's potential rise to statehood.[27] Economic and labor issues kept support in the islands from rising to a fevered pitch. The "Big Five" sugar companies feared what statehood would do to their labor practices and also what might happen to their political dominance in the islands if nonwhites were elevated to equality. The Republicans, as the dominant political party in Hawaii (some might say the only political party in Hawaii), were also reluctant to push for statehood too hard for fear of undermining their relationship with the planters and upsetting the tacit racial practices then in existence.

World War II changed the outlook for Hawaiian statehood. The events and outcome of the war dramatically altered the perceptions and the realities of Hawaii's relationship with the nation. The attack on Pearl Harbor was not viewed as an attack on a territory, but a direct attack on the nation. Japanese Americans living in Hawaii proved their devotion to the nation through their military and civilian roles, effectively answering charges of disloyalty and their perceived inability to be part of a democratic society. Finally, the need to be a permanent and powerful presence in the Pacific was confirmed. Thus, the role of the islands in the war made them more visible and necessary to the nation, and efforts to attain statehood began in earnest.

Unfortunately, the immediate postwar years did not result in the desired changes that many in the islands sought with regard to statehood. An unexpected impediment to statehood arose in 1945 with the formation of the United Nations, when the territory was placed under the jurisdiction of Article 73 of the UN Charter as a "Non-Self-Governing Territory."[28] The article called for self-governance of territories under colonial-style conditions. Neither the members of the United Nations responsible for governance nor the non-self-governing territories were specifically named until the following year, when the General Assembly adopted Resolution 66. As a result, when asked to report on the status of the named territories, the United States committed itself to establishing self-governance in the territories of Alaska, American Samoa, Guam, Hawaii, the Panama Canal Zone, Puerto Rico, and the Virgin Islands.[29] The UN declarations placed the status of Hawaii into a much larger international movement. The United Nations intended to end colonialism through its ideological stance but was not willing to exert absolute pressure or authority against member nations over such issues, especially against the United States. The United States thus continued and even extended its territorial control at the same time that many European nations were forced to give up control of their African and Pacific possessions. Left to its own devices, the United States simply tried to ignore the philosophical objectives of Article 73 in favor of its own practical needs. Although the nation was effectively able to ignore UN authority over such matters, the status of Hawaii played a role in the final days of statehood and in the late twentieth century as a central point of contention in the movement for Hawaiian sovereignty.

FROM TERRITORY TO STATE

From 1945 through 1959, despite repeated rejections and entrenched opposition to appeals for statehood, a sustained campaign was conducted to make Hawaii the forty-ninth state.[30] This campaign, which was eventually placed under the guidance of the Statehood Commission, was conducted on both the local and national levels, promoted in the press and through political lobbying, and directly confronted the fears of the opposition at the same time that it promoted the benefits of adding Hawaii to the Union. Hawaii dutifully sought to distance itself from communism, prove the "Americanness" of its mostly nonwhite population, and certify its readiness to assume equal status with the other states. Hawaiians went so far as to draft a constitution in 1950 as a demonstration of their democratic capabilities and principles. The goal of statehood advocates was simple: to show that Hawaii was ready for statehood and that the United States was ready for Hawaii.

Nevertheless, larger national issues and events continued to detract from these efforts, ensuring that any progress toward statehood was limited in scope. Throughout its final decade as a territory, Hawaii's prospects for statehood were mired in a political contest between the Republicans and Democrats, in efforts to conditionally link Hawaiian statehood with Alaskan statehood, and in the opposition of southern politicians who were leery of the civil rights implications should a racially diverse and tolerant Hawaii join their states on an equal footing. For more than a decade, these highly charged issues conspired to delay statehood. Only when Hawaii's delegates were willing to make substantial concessions, relinquish their quest in exchange for future promises, and a palatable compromise was reached on the social issues did Hawaii find itself in position to join the Union.

Party politics, both territorial and national, resulted in an endless cycle of conflicts over statehood that had to be resolved before any successful statehood bill could be achieved. Democrats and Republicans both played a role in the quest for Hawaiian statehood, yet neither party can be considered the sole champion of the cause. This was true for both the national and the state parties, with each unable to adopt a coherent and cohesive policy with regard to the issue.

As the prospects for Hawaiian statehood languished throughout the 1950s, the internal political dynamics of Hawaii were shifting away from the Republicans. Many people considered Hawaii a Republican stronghold, given its election history and the century-long dominance of the economic elites who controlled the Republican agenda from behind the scenes. There were Republican supporters of statehood, including the elected congressional delegate Joe Farrington and his wife, Elizabeth (who took over for him upon his death in 1954), who made significant efforts toward achieving statehood. But for the majority of island Republicans, ethnic equality and the resulting tempered political power that was sure to result in a broadened electorate was enough to drive them away from support for statehood. The "Big Five" feared the destruction of their labor practices as well as a shift away from the outer islands to Honolulu as the center of power.

The Democrats, who were only too willing to exploit the Republican inconsistencies on the issue, used statehood as a tool to develop their base among the politically and economically disenfranchised, driving a wedge between them and the *haole* community. The shift in political power toward the Democratic Party, under the grassroots and cross-cultural efforts of John Burns, brought unions, equal rights groups, and the ethnic minorities to the forefront of the political scene. The demographic forces of the islands, which had long favored the nonwhite population, caught up to the Republicans as Burns, a local-born white who had lived most of his life among the nonwhites and used his background as a means to catapult to political power, was able to cobble together a coalition that included Native Hawaiians, Americans of Japanese ancestry, Chinese Americans, and Filipinos, as well as liberal and sympathetic whites.[31] This collection of constituents heightened the fears of statehood obstructionists and forced new issues into the statehood debate.[32]

On the national level, party support for Hawaii statehood was just as inconsistent. Evidence of this can be seen in the congressional actions taken with respect to statehood between 1947 and 1954. During these eight years, the House of Representatives approved Hawaiian statehood three times and the Senate approved it once. But the actions never occurred simultaneously, and each approval was marked by support from different political quarters.[33]

President Truman and the Democrats were the first to strike on the national level following World War II. As part of Truman's larger civil rights plan, he actively promoted, though to little effect, the admission of Hawaii and Alaska as states. Truman argued for an end to their territorial status in response to international criticisms leveled by the United Nations and also as a means to address growing dissent over matters of unequal taxation and representation. As citizens of the United States, the people of the two territories sought relief from federal taxes on the grounds that they paid far more than what they received in return. Hawaii, in particular, felt the sting of federal control over its internal political affairs as a result of the presidential appointment of its governor. The shifting political winds in Hawaii meant that the national and state party dominance were never in sync. While Truman was in office, the Republicans, albeit tenuously, remained in control in Hawaii. By the time Eisenhower had become president and was able to appoint a governor, the Democrats had gained power. Thus, neither state party was able to hold the governor's office and control of the state legislature at the same time.

When President Eisenhower took office in 1953, he endorsed the admission of both territories as states, though he expressed a clear preference for Hawaii over Alaska. His position was hampered by a strong Democratic congressional caucus and dissent over the issue within his own party. The ambivalence of some congressional Republicans was driven by Democratic insistence that Hawaii be considered for admission in tandem with Alaska. While there was little question that Hawaii met the criteria for being a state, few shared similar opinions about Alaska's status, given its small population, the issues of federal landownership and control, and the vastness of the territory. Republicans also expressed concerns over several of the internal Hawaiian labor issues, citing the violent and costly dockworkers' strikes of the recent past. Northern Republicans, mostly from the industrial states, opposed admission on the grounds that it was unfair to their constituents. Hawaii, as a potential state with a relatively small population, also raised the issue of proportional representation. A Hawaiian senator would represent fewer than 620,000 people, whereas a senator from one of the industrialized states would represent more than ten times that population. Some Republican opposition was also driven by nascent signs of shifting political winds in Hawaii, leaving them uncertain of continued Republican supremacy in the territory.

Southern Democrats thwarted Eisenhower's efforts in the belief that the admission of Hawaii would sharpen the growing criticisms of the racial practices in their home states. Although racial issues were more muted in the 1950s than they were in earlier periods, there were still some politicians who openly expressed their fears that an Asian-born senator or congressman would be elected from Hawaii. Others cited the growing ethnic mixing among the people in Hawaii. Finally, proving themselves no better than the Republicans, some Democrats stalled consideration of statehood on the basis that Hawaii, which seemed staunchly Republican, would upset the balance of power and ensure the loss of the Democratic Party's slim majority in Congress.

Supporters of Hawaiian statehood refused to remain still even while their efforts seemed futile. On the heels of a 1950 referendum in which voters overwhelmingly supported immediate statehood for the territory, Hawaiians called a constitutional convention. Voter turnout for approval of the convention and the subsequent election of delegates was exceptionally high and served as a gauge of public and political opinion on the issue of statehood.[34] By drafting a constitution in advance of statehood, Hawaii was following a pattern set by fifteen other territories in the history of the nation. Supporters of statehood were also hoping that the action would pave the way toward statehood, or at least quell some of the opposition.[35] "An Act to provide for a constitutional convention, the adoption of a State constitution, and the forwarding of the same to the Congress of the United States, and appropriating money therefore," was approved by the Territorial Legislature on May 20, 1949. The constitutional convention, which began its work the following April, not only addressed external concerns about the islands' fitness to become a state but also internal issues that seemed to be dividing the people.

The delegates took their task seriously and drew upon several key resources in their efforts to craft a document acceptable to the people and flexible enough to meet the changing needs of one of the most dynamic and shifting societies in the U.S. sphere. In 1948, the Statehood Committee, in anticipation of such a convention, had created a committee empowered to give direct instruction to any future constitutional convention. This committee guided the convention on matters of constitutional principle as well as practical matters facing the Hawaiian people. The delegates also had previous examples upon which to base the new document. The convention that had drafted the document drew heavily from the founding documents of the United States, and, having solicited assistance from several states that had recently gone through their own constitutional revisions, the convention used the constitutions of other states to inform their discussions and document drafting.[36] The work of the delegates was slowed by lingering doubts about the suitability of statehood and the effects of both national and island political issues—most notably, labor conflicts and the ever-present fear of communism. After addressing these issues, the convention got down to business and ended up drafting an impressive governing document, notable for its political innovations.

The efforts of the convention were approved by a vote of the people in the November 1950 elections.[37] The constitution crafted then, which is still in effect as amended, was unique in several ways. First and foremost, it was succinct. The document's provisions were concise and left a great deal open to future interpretations and legislative decisions. The constitution also mandated that the people of Hawaii be presented with the option of having subsequent constitutional conventions (or "con cons," as they have come to be called in Hawaii) at least once every decade. The document also centralized many of the public services and responsibilities of government and, at the same time, promoted legislative behavior that was extremely responsive to the will of all voters, not just the prevailing majority.[38]

The constitution, as impressive as it was, was not enough to effect immediate statehood. It would take the remainder of the decade to achieve enough of a consensus to make Hawaiian statehood a reality. Racial issues continued to simmer under the surface, never emerging as the sole cause of delay but clearly shaping the view, actions, and even public pronouncements of opponents. Political issues also dominated the public discussion. Interparty politics and internal political rivalries were the major stumbling blocks, but so too were philosophical issues of representation and expansion.

From 1952 to 1957, another major national issue acted as an impediment to Hawaiian statehood because the quests for both Alaskan and Hawaiian statehood were inexorably linked. The major impetus behind a push for tandem consideration was political balance. Although both national political parties had adopted immediate Hawaiian statehood planks in their platforms, neither was willing to see the other party gain an advantage, should one territory be admitted without the other. The two territories were thus tied together in a manner reminiscent of the antebellum process of admitting two states together in order to achieve continued political balance (or at least prevent a further loss), allowing each party to claim victory.

Eisenhower's early position to delay the admission of Alaska and promote Hawaii on its own exacerbated the problem. Eisenhower's rationale was compelling and echoed the position adopted by various other political and civilian groups that had expressed reservations about Alaska's suitability for statehood. The prospect of Alaskan statehood entailed significant issues over the administration of defense installations and public lands. The Interior Department, eager to prolong federal jurisdiction over Alaska, also expressed the need for delay so that there would be time to open the region's land reserves for private development.

There was little that the supporters of statehood in Hawaii could do to counteract these national political maneuverings. Despite the formation of the Statehood Commission in 1946, with a budget that allowed it to lobby congressmen directly and print materials for public distribution, Hawaiian statehood remained elusive. The House of Representatives' vote in 1947 on H.R. 49, which was the first time either congressional body had approved statehood, was merely the first of several potential successes. The fact that the Senate failed to ratify the bill and that similar opportunities were ignored throughout the next decade gave rise to a growing sense of malaise among statehood supporters. Internal dissent grew in Hawaii, and Truman's original decision—to support joint admission or nothing—gained strength nationally. Even Eisenhower had to back away from his original position due to the uncertainty over political power in the islands.

In the face of such opposition, Hawaiian statehood supporters were forced to put a halt to their active efforts. Beginning in 1956, Hawaii stopped pushing for enabling legislation, and by 1958, statehood supporters had yielded to the Democratic congressional majority and stepped aside, publicly declaring their support for Alaskan statehood and disavowing their own pursuits. In truth this was a wise strategy that eventually aided Hawaii's cause, but at the time, the sting of being at the mercy of political maneuvering was hard to endure. As a result, Hawaii lost its bid to become the forty-ninth state—only to see that distinction awarded to Alaska in 1958. Yet with Alaskan statehood and its Democratic representation all but secured, Lyndon Johnson and other Democratic congressional leaders were willing and able to convince enough of their party members to support Hawaiian statehood. Civil rights issues still remained a potential bone of contention, but Johnson was able to sell enough of his fellow Southerners on the idea. Behind the scenes, but left out of the celebrations and public ceremonies, was John Burns, the man who had negotiated with Johnson to exchange Alaskan statehood for promises of Hawaiian statehood and achieve the dream for the many groups of Hawaiian citizens who felt abandoned by the traditional political system.

On March 18, 1959, President Eisenhower signed the bill granting Hawaii statehood, as passed by the Eighty-sixth Congress. The official admission date was set for later that year, on August 21. By the time Hawaii joined the Union, its "state" constitution was already nine years old. Not counting Alaska, it had been forty-eight years since the Arizona and New Mexico territories had been admitted, and at least until the present day, it has been forty-four more years since then. The Hawaii Enabling Act reflected the history of America's engagement with the island territory. Hawaiian statehood was built directly upon the foundations of the Organic Act and the 1950 constitution.[39] As such, the new state inherited the issues surrounding the ceded lands, the Hawaiian Homes Commission, and political enfranchisement of an extremely diverse society. Statehood saw a return of the ceded lands to the state in trust for the people, as outlined in the Organic Act. Although the federal government retained control of both military and national park lands, almost 40 percent of all the land in Hawaii was turned over to the state.[40] Given some of the singular aspects of Hawaiian statehood, the legislation delayed the official admission until the voters of Hawaii had a chance to ratify three referendums. These dealt with a congressionally mandated question concerning the state's boundaries, the inclusion of an article reaffirming the state's commitment to the Hawaiian Homes Commission, and the incumbent trust obligations, as well as affirming an immediate action on statehood.[41]

There were several shortcomings to the statehood legislation and the accompanying actions. One was the congressional mandate that Hawaii was permitted only one member to the House of Representatives until the results of the 1960 census were confirmed.[42] Another was the limitation of the statehood question. In its petition to have Hawaii removed from the list of non-self-governing territories by the United Nations, the United States cited the plebiscite in which the people of the islands voted for statehood as satisfactory evidence of their desire to join the Union. But the plebiscite clearly violated the terms established by the UN and did not permit the people of the islands a full range of options. The people of Hawaii were given a choice to affirm or reject statehood. According to the UN, however, three options were to be presented: full and equal association (statehood), the status quo (remaining a territory), or full and complete independence. This last option did not appear on the referendum.[43] Nor was commonwealth status ever seriously considered. This latter option enjoyed limited but notable support both nationally and locally. Proponents claimed that a Hawaiian commonwealth would provide statehood supporters most of what they desired, while not pushing the full impact of a statehood association on those who did not wish to strengthen the relationship between Hawaii and the United States mainland to that degree. Supporters of statehood viewed this as yet another way to prevent Hawaii from becoming a state and continuing to deny the territory the option of exercising any independent control.[44]

The Native Hawaiian community was split over the issue of statehood. A significant minority who favored political sovereignty and independence over political alliance with the United States was rarely heard from in the territorial and early statehood eras. Histories of statehood rarely include them. Their opposition was built on a historical foundation of the overthrow and annexation, during which several thousand Native Hawaiians submitted petitions to local and national legislators asking that the kingdom be restored. They saw themselves as excluded from the political and economic power of the territory and viewed statehood as a means of continued oppression. There was also a significant minority of Native Hawaiians who joined forces with the emerging Democratic Party. They believed that statehood would finally free the native peoples from oppression by establishing a more democratic system, enforceable by federal laws. But when the vote for statehood came, most Native Hawaiians refused to go to the polls, demonstrating their opposition through their silence. While many acknowledged that statehood held far more promise than territorial status, the events of history had already ensured their marginalization and the continued domination of non-Hawaiian values and culture.[45]

The most vocal opposition to statehood came from the Republican Party in Hawaii, the "Big Five" sugar interests, and the dominant *haole* community. The opposition was gathered under the umbrella of an organization known as Imua. With more than three thousand members, Imua, while never directly opposing any efforts toward statehood, marshaled its members and their associated citizens to take measures in open opposition to statehood.[46] Imua was against the elements of Hawaiian society that were leading the way toward change, establishing itself as a supremacist organization, in favor of continued marginalization of the lower classes, a continued economic imbalance, and sustained territorial status. It may seem ironic that the same people who now opposed statehood were the direct descendents (economically and politically, if not biologically) of those who fought to end the monarchy and have Hawaii annexed by the United States. Statehood, however, crossed their threshold of optimum association. They were more likely to thrive economically and remain in political and social domination under territorial status than they were under statehood. Statehood threatened to undermine the society that they had created.

Statehood came, in the end, because a majority of people in the islands saw the potential advantages of equality with other states, advantages that would assist the islands on a state level but also assist the people on an individual level. Under statehood, all of the people in the islands would have a vote and it was just a matter of time before they translated the franchise into political and economic power. Statehood also came when the United States finally acknowledged its permanent interests in the Pacific. Where World War II had failed to convince the nation, Korea succeeded. The United States could have easily continued its economic and military presence in the islands under territorial or even trusteeship status, but if the nation wished to have any political or moral standing in the Pacific, an alteration in Hawaii's status was necessary.

FROM STATEHOOD TO THE PRESENT

The matter of statehood in Hawaii is not just a historical memory. Hawaii's standing among the other forty-nine states, how Hawaii wishes to act as one of the states, and its very status as a state are all topics of current discussion and review. The implications of statehood, perhaps because they were so recently effected, run deep in Hawaiian society. Protecting the "host culture" of Hawaii has become an important legislative and cultural pursuit. Reviewing the statehood legislation and constitution has become a regular occurrence, happening at least once a decade by constitutional mandate. And most notably, the Native Hawaiian community, which was politicized in the 1970s through a cultural renaissance and the birth of the sovereignty movement, continues to challenge the legality and morality of past events that led to statehood.

Statehood brought a host of changes to the islands—politically, economically, and socially. With the adoption of the state constitution, political power shifted in the islands. What was once a system dominated by the "Big Five" sugar interests and the outer islands experienced a sudden shift in power. The first post-statehood election in 1959 reflected the fact that the political winds in Hawaii had not yet permanently shifted to the Democrats. The Republicans, under the leadership of William Quinn, won the governor's seat, gained control of the state Senate, and won one of two U.S. Senate seats. While these results can be attributed to the fact that Quinn was already the territorial governor, they still show that the people of Hawaii were not of one mind concerning their political future. In the 1962 elections, however, the Democrats completed a clean sweep of state and national offices, sending the state Republican Party into a tailspin from which it would not recover until the next century, making the Democratic Party the entrenched voting majority.[47]

An inter-island political shift also resulted from statehood. As with all states, legislative representation in Hawaii is based on districts that are created by drawing boundaries that reflect population density. In the pre-statehood era, the legislature did not reflect the population distribution of the territory but rather was based on a system that attempted to give weight to individual islands. This meant that Oahu, the home island of Honolulu, had been rated as only an equal player in Hawaiian politics. Under the terms of statehood, however, this distribution was altered, and Oahu became the dominant island, based on Honolulu's population, as that city contained some 70 percent of the total Hawaiian population. This altered not only internal state elections but also ended up being the determining factor in the allocation of House seats for Congress.[48]

There was also a corresponding shift in the economic structure of the state following its admission. Hawaii has always been a state that developed statehood plans (including the notable *Hawaii 2000* project) to determine the future of the state's land distribution, development, population growth, tourism promotion, Native Hawaiian issues, environmental concerns, and social matters.[49] To make the political shift in power caused by statehood more palatable to the people living outside of Oahu, island leaders determined that the outer islands should share in the wealth and economic future of tourism, and thus they actively sought to disperse the tourism away from Waikiki. The islands of Maui, Hawaii, and Kauai all experienced perceived gains in the tourist industry—including development of hotels, resorts, airports, and infrastructure—as a result. This planned shift not only promised new jobs to the people of the islands but also promoted the prospect of ending the hold of the "Big Five" on the economic life of the outer islands. Tourism provided an alternative to working in the cane fields and promoted the prospects for individual entrepreneurship and ownership that had been stifled by the land control of the sugar planters. By the 1970s, tourism was Maui's most important economic sector, with the island government's support.[50]

Nationally, Hawaii became an important state, wielding influence that transcended population statistics and economic output. As home to some of the most important military bases in the country, there are four major bases located in the state. Hawaii's role in federal planning and spending resulted in immediate political clout. So too did the growth in tourism, and a vocal, committed congressional delegation give Hawaii a national and international presence usually reserved for states that are far larger in size and population.[51]

The two main issues that have beset Hawaiian statehood are the trust relationship that the state assumed for Native Hawaiians—including matters of fiscal oversight, land distribution, political protection, and cultural preservation—and the growth of the sovereignty movement. These two issues are so interconnected that any history of the islands since statehood is best served by discussing them in tandem, as they relate to the larger story of the islands' development and maturity into statehood.

The trend in development and investment in the islands that received a boost from tourism has simultaneously displaced Native Hawaiians from the lands of their ancestors. Tourism, which became the single largest industry in Hawaii following statehood, pushed the native population to the economic and political margins by driving up costs, creating minimum wage jobs, stagnating wages, and allowing others to grab the political clout that went with the unionization of the workforce. The result was a systematic displacement not seen since the effects of the *mahele* in the previous century. As the rate of evictions increased, driven by the inability of Hawaiians to stave off the influx of foreign investment, the Hawaiians started to gather their strength and resist.[52]

Land issues, in conjunction with political developments, helped to bring about the creation of the modern sovereignty movement in Hawaii. The eviction of Native Hawaiians from the Kalama Valley in 1963, the birth of an ethnic Hawaiian studies program at the University of Hawaii, and the outrage over the military's use of Kaho'olawe as a bombing range all helped to draw the Native Hawaiian forces together and sparked their political activism. The bombing range issue was particularly galling to Native Hawaiians, who felt that the government's reaffirmation of federal control of the island under the Land Conveyance Act of 1963 continued the effrontery caused by federal land policy as passed down by the Organic Act and the Admissions Act.[53] In turn, Native Hawaiian activism, including a series of staged occupations of Kaho'olawe in the hopes that it would to end the military destruction of an island full of archeologically significant sites considered sacred to the people, led to further questions about the impact of statehood on the people.[54]

The 1970s witnessed the maturing of the sovereignty movement—through a cultural, linguistic, political, and economic revival. Two main thrusts fueled the movement. First was the uncontrollable development and tourism of the postwar era and the negative impacts of these two forces upon the native peoples. Second was the growth in ethnic pride that the culture of protest during the 1960s had created throughout the country, which had resonated with the Hawaiian people. All things truly and uniquely Hawaiian began to be seen in a positive light. One symbol that emerged was the rebirth of hula. Hula, which had been banned by the missionaries and degraded by the whites, was almost completely lost to the people. But it returned to the islands beginning in 1964 with the creation of the Merrie Monarch Festival, held each spring on the Big Island. The festival celebrated hula and honored King Kalakaua, who had included hula as a part of his coronation ceremony in 1883.[55] Such ethnic and cultural movements coincided with similar movements taking place in mainland America and captured the attention of Native Hawaiians, sympathetic residents, and tourists alike.

The same decade saw the emergence of a legal strategy to ensure the trust status of Native Hawaiians and challenge statehood as a legal action. By using the courts, through public action, in congressional resolutions, in international forums, and through social protest, the sovereignty activists were able to turn the American system against itself. The sovereignty movement leaders even began to espouse a new interpretation of the events of the past and challenge the traditionally accepted narratives of the overthrow, annexation, and even statehood. There emerged two competing versions of statehood: a predominantly American tale of justifiable expansion and cultural integration juxtaposed against an indigenous Hawaiian story of deception, oppression, and cultural destruction. The former narrative, focusing on the increasing need for America to expand both its economic and military presence in the Pacific, holds that the people of Hawaii were equal actors in this process, freely giving their consent and initiating the interaction between the islands and the United States, both asking for statehood and voting on the process. The United States was never a colonial or imperial power.

In stark contrast, the latter version holds that the incorporation of Hawaii into the United States was orchestrated by *haole* missionaries and imperialists as well as those who would benefit economically by the association. This narrative points to the marginalization of the Native Hawaiians, coupled to a lesser degree with the exclusion of the Chinese, Japanese, and Filipino residents, as a determinant force in the affairs of the islands. The monarchy was overthrown against the will of the people, the lands were stolen from their rightful owners, and integration was forced upon the people by an overwhelming military and political force. The United States went to great lengths to deny and obscure its imperialist behavior, creating a story of assimilation that was used as propaganda to promote its selfish designs. This, in turn, contributed to the growth of an indigenous movement to keep the islands separate from the United States in the early years and to challenge Hawaii's legal status as a state in the present.[56]

One of the most significant measures came during the 1978 Constitutional Convention, when the body of elected delegates presented the people with the creation of the Office of Hawaiian Affairs (OHA).[57] When the voters agreed to amend the state constitution in order to create the quasi-sovereign state agency, the organization came into being two years later and the agency was formally charged with its duties. Its official functions centered on the administration of services and programs to benefit the native peoples using the proceeds from the ceded lands, as stipulated in the 1959 statehood admission act. Intended to reverse the declines suffered by the native people, OHA extended its mandate by defending native activists from prosecution, stalling land evictions (Sand Island, Makua Valley, and Waimanolo), and generally pushing an agenda that was far different than the one envisioned by most people upon its creation.

OHA's creation and activities led to a strengthening and mainstreaming of native Hawaiian activism, but it also created the grounds for some enduring confusion surrounding the sovereignty movement and statehood issues. OHA was to receive state funds for the specific purpose of creating programs to benefit the native peoples. These funds, however, were separate from the homelands established by the Hawaiian Homes Commission Act of 1920. As a result, the state was forced to employ a complex and sophisticated allocation formula to determine the amount owed to the trust. This, in turn, led to conflicts over the state's payouts, with sovereignty activists concluding that there was a significant discrepancy between what the state owned and what the state paid, and eventually resulted in a court decision halting the use of the formula until the matter could be resolved by the courts.[58] A 1983 study, issued by President Reagan's appointed Native Hawaiian Study Commission (three of the eight members were from Hawaii), further exacerbated the land issues when they acknowledged that less than 20 percent of the land promised to the people under the Hawaiian Homes Commission Act of 1920 had been distributed. Although their primary objective was to assess the effectiveness of the land distribution program, and despite their conclusions on the paucity of distributions, they still voted 5-3 to deny further reparations or alterations in the program.

The international and national issues surrounding the events of the 1890s and 1950s have also been resurrected, bringing the status of Hawaii as a state into sharp relief. In 1988, the U.S. Justice Department agreed with the claims of sovereignty activists when they declared that the United States had acted extralegally in annexing the islands by virtue of a joint resolution. These findings provided the sovereignty movement and Hawaii's congressional caucus with substantial credibility in their efforts to get the government to act on some, if not all, of their demands. This was followed by the passage of Public Law 150-103, commonly known as the "Apology Resolution," in 1993.

In recognition of the 100th anniversary of the overthrow of Queen Lili'uokalani, President Clinton signed into law an official apology for the actions of the United States and subsequent deprivations suffered by the Native Hawaiian community. The apology, initially drafted by Davianna McGregor, a sovereignty activist and professor at the University of Hawaii, made its way through Congress under the efforts of the state's congressional delegation, eventually leading to Clinton's signature. For many, the resolution meant that the U.S. government was offering an official apology for the nation's actions surrounding the 1893 overthrow and subsequent 1898 annexation of the islands. In fact, the resolution reads like an apology, recognizing the social, cultural, religious, and economic systems destroyed by European and American actions and admitting U.S. culpability in illegal actions that led to the destruction of Hawaiian political sovereignty. The apology has led many to conclude that the federal government should seek to correct the mistakes of the past and help Native Hawaiians achieve contemporary control of their homelands.

Native Hawaiian sovereignty is not without its opponents. Those who argue against sovereignty in its many different forms argue that the Apology Resolution was merely a symbolic act, passed as a gesture of goodwill toward the host culture and that it holds little or no practical political value nor does it place any future obligations upon the federal government. They most commonly cite Section 3 of the resolution, which serves as a disclaimer, indicating that "nothing in this Joint Resolution is intended to serve as a settlement of any claims against the United States," which many activists have declared to be the restoration of land and political independence.[59]

Sovereignty activists, however, point to the fact that because Hawaii was admitted to the Union under the authority of a joint congressional resolution, removal can be achieved in the same manner, although they acknowledge that additional steps must be taken. According to the Apology Resolution, "the indigenous Hawaiian people never directly relinquished their claims to their inherent sovereignty as a people or over their national lands to the United States." The force of the apology comes in Section 1, Point 4, in which the government acknowledges "the ramifications of the overthrow…in order to provide a proper foundation for reconciliation." Sovereignty activists have been seeking to build upon those foundations ever since.[60]

More recent events have thrown Hawaiian statehood into a deeper morass of legality and conflict. In a 1999 Supreme Court decision, issued in *Rice v. Cayetano*, the Court ruled on a case involving a dispute over the legality of OHA and its exclusive Native Hawaiian membership and mission.[61] The Court overturned the decisions of the lower courts and held that under the Fifteenth Amendment, the existence of OHA violated the constitutional guarantees concerning racial discrimination. The Court decided, in a 7-2 vote, that the state's long-standing arrangement with Native Hawaiians and the previous U.S. federal agreements did not constitute sufficient evidence of a special relationship with Native Hawaiians that allowed for action similar to those of Native American Indian tribes. The trust relationship, ensured by the enabling legislation of statehood and reaffirmed by a plebiscite in 1959, was now undermined. The decision set forth in *Rice* had significant consequences. Not only were non-Hawaiians now allowed to vote for the trustees of OHA, but also the trustees no longer needed to be Native Hawaiian, a decision rendered in a district court decision subsequent to *Rice*.[62] In response, the entire body of trustees resigned their positions, causing a free-for-all election in November 2000. Hawaiians were about to lose control of the one institution, albeit a state institution, that was specifically designated to give them political standing and compensate for the years of oppression. There are still more challenges ahead. In mid-November 2003, a federal judge heard a legal challenge that sought a complete dismantling of the Office of Hawaiian Affairs and the Department of Hawaiian Home Lands. The challenge failed.

The United Nations interjected itself into Hawaiian affairs and brought its power to bear on the matter in contrast to the Supreme Court's ruling in the same year. After years of independent investigation, often at the behest of the Native Hawaiian community, the UN reviewed the 1959 plebiscite. Citing Article 73, Section B of the UN Charter, in which a member nation pledged to assist its dependent peoples to "develop self-government, to take due account of the political aspirations of the peoples, and to assist them in the progressive development of their free political institutions," the UN subsequently declared the Hawaiian statehood vote to be invalid. Given that Hawaii and Alaska are the only two states that joined the Union in the era of internationalism, the United Nations' role in the status of Hawaii bears consideration, given that it was the UN that bestowed the islands upon the United States and obtained from the government an official recognition of its trust obligation. That the United States was clearly allowing that trust relationship to be undermined was not lost on the UN delegates who reported their findings.[63]

In 2000, a report, "From Mauka to Makai: The River of Justice Must Flow Freely," was issued following several weeks of hearings held by the Departments of Interior and Justice. The report sought to build on the idea of reconciliation addressed in the Apology Resolution, address potential solutions to the *Rice* verdict, and set the government into action. These views were supported by earlier amicus briefs submitted on behalf of OHA in the *Rice* case. At the time, the U.S. solicitor general noted the United States had a continuing "trust obligation to indigenous Hawaiians because it bears a responsibility for the destruction of their government and the unconsented and uncompensated taking of their lands."[64] The report's recommendations became a central part of legislation introduced by the congressional delegation from Hawaii, which sought to do an end run around the Supreme Court ruling and provide Native Hawaiians with a substantive future.

The introduction of the Native Hawaiian Recognition bill (concurrent resolutions H.R. 4904 and S. 2899) in July 2000, known more commonly as the Akaka bill, seeks to codify some of the gains of the Native Hawaiian rights movement and also counter the potential negative consequences wrought by the *Rice* decision. The legislation seeks to "affirm and acknowledge the political relationship" between the U.S. government and the Native Hawaiian peoples, the latter to be represented by a duly elected delegation.[65] It also establishes recognition of Native Hawaiians as having "inherent rights as a distinct aboriginal, indigenous, native community," giving them an equal footing with Native Americans.[66] Simply put, Hawaiians are to be put on par with Native American Indians and be given their own internal government. The Akaka bill includes permitting only Native Hawaiians to elect the trustees or representatives to the government.[67] This would also give the new government a free hand in using the income from certain trust lands and state and federal monies, as well as allowing them to continue to seek additional measures of sovereignty, even at the expense of the non-Hawaiian population in the islands.

The National Congress of American Indians supported the measure. Through testimony given by Susan Masten, president of the organization, the NCAI cited over 150 previous legislative measures that recognized Native Hawaiians as a distinct group, but which failed to give them a formal, legalized government-to-government standing, similar to the standing held by Indian nations.[68] Masten argued that clarifying the political status of Native Hawaiians, as brought forth in both the Apology Resolution of 1993 and the *Rice* decision in 2000 would start Hawaiians down the path of self-governance.

Currently, H.R. 4904 and S. 2899 have been reintroduced and renumbered for consideration by the 108th Congress as H.R. 665 and S. 344, respectively. As of August 2003, the House legislation was "pending" in the Resources Committee, while the Senate bill was being held up over procedural matters. The legislation was given some urgency in 2001 and 2002 when the Hawaiian state legislature considered two resolutions petitioning the U.S. Congress, in light of previous international and national laws, to reconsider the status of Hawaiian statehood. Passage of the Akaka bill would forestall, most likely for a very long time, any discussion of the statehood issue.

THE ONCE AND FUTURE STATE?

The claim that "Hawaii after annexation was never anxious to win political sovereignty as an independent nation" has been overstated.[69] Assessments of island affairs based on such a belief have relied on traditional political and historical accounts, without taking into consideration the desires of the Native Hawaiians and by treating the process of absorption into the Union as a unilateral, unopposed quest. Will Hawaii ever cease to be a state of the Union? Given the lack of any precedent, it seems highly unlikely that any action will ever result in a complete reversal of the annexation and statehood actions. The possibility of an independent Hawaii is further undermined by sovereignty activists who remain sharply divided on their plans for a post-independence nation, with more than two dozen major and minor sovereignty groups, each with its own plan for the future, sapping the movement of much-needed unity. Those measures that are winning support among the broadest possible audience within the islands, the state legislature, Congress, the White House, and the international community, seem to be the more conservative attempts to carve out a niche in Hawaii for the Native Hawaiians while allowing the remaining 80 percent of the population to retain their rights and status.

While the Native Hawaiian Recognition bill would not remove Hawaii as a state of the union, it is bringing to light just how contentious issues arising out of Hawaiian statehood remain. Native Hawaiians, should they achieve federal recognition as a distinct, indigenous people, would constitute the single-largest native group in the United States. By setting aside Hawaiian-only lands, funds, and recognition, Hawaiian statehood would not end, but Hawaii's vision of itself would drastically change. Hawaiians of all stripes will continue to contest the history, legality, and current status of statehood. The very future of the state all depends on how the past is interpreted and how far America is willing to go to correct for prior injustices. Hawaiian statehood is not just a matter of history. Hawaiian statehood is an issue for the present.

NOTES

1. An Act to provide for the Admission of the State of Hawaii into the Union (Act of March 18, 1959, Pub. Law 86-3), 73 U.S. Statutes at Large 4.

2. Roger Bell, *Last Among Equals: Hawaiian Statehood and American Politics* (Honolulu: University of Hawaii Press, 1984), pp. 90–91, 278.

3. Sylvester Stevens, *American Expansion in Hawaii, 1842–1898* (Harrisburg: Archives Publishing Co. of Penna., 1945), pp. 1–2, ff. Accordingly, there is no record or mention of such a treaty in U.S. Statutes at Large. See also *House Report*, no. 92, 28th Cong., 2nd Sess., for the report on the ministerial visit to Hawaii that resulted in this nontreaty. For the text of the agreement, see Charles I. Bevans, *Treaties and Other International Agreements of the United States of America, 1776–1949* (Washington, DC: U.S. Government Printing Office, 1971), vol. 8, pp. 861–863.

4. The United States effectively extended the terms of the Monroe Doctrine to Hawaii in the December 1849 Treaty of Friendship, Commerce, and Navigation and a subsequent treaty reasserting the rights of neutral shipping in the Pacific, issues in 1855. See Bevans, *Treaties and Other International Agreements*, vol. 8, pp. 864–879.

5. *Papers Relating to the Foreign Relations of the United States, 1894: Affairs in Hawaii*, Appendix 2 (Washington, DC: U.S. Government Printing Office, 1895). Kamehameha sent representatives of the islands to Washington to discuss such matters in 1842.

6. U.S. Congress. Senate. Committee on Interior and Insular Affairs. *Statehood for Hawaii*. Hearings on H.R. 49, S. 51, H.R. 3575, 83rd Cong., 2nd Sess., June 29–30, July 1–11, 1953, and Jan. 7–8, 1954, p. 9. See also Charles H. Hunter, "Forty-Ninth State? For Fifty Years Hawaii Has Sought Admission to the Union," *American Heritage* 2 (Spring 1951): 10; Roger Bell, *Last Among Equals*, pp. 14–16; and Thurston Twigg-Smith, *Hawaiian Sovereignty: Do the Facts Matter?* (Honolulu: Goodale Publishing, 1998), pp. 19–22.

7. Convention between the United States of America and his Majesty the King of the Hawaiian Islands on Commercial Reciprocity, June 3, 1875. The terms of the agreement entered into force on September 9, 1876. 19 U.S. Statutes at Large 625.

8. Quoted in *The Native Hawaiian Study Commission* (Honolulu: privately printed, 1983), vol. 1, p. 267. Hawaii, between 1890 and 1897, was specifically exempted from the levies imposed by the McKinley, Wilson, and Dingley Tariff Acts.

9. Reciprocity Treaty of 1875 and Reciprocity Treaty of 1884. See Bevans, *Treaties and Other International Agreements*, vol. 8, pp. 874–879.

10. See Jon J. Chinen, *The Great Mahele: Hawaii's Land Division of 1848* (Honolulu: University of Hawaii Press, 1958).

11. Constitution of 1887, Kingdom of Hawaii. This constitution replaced the constitution of 1864, which was, itself, the third constitution in the kingdom's history, the other two having been issued in 1840 and 1852, both under the rule of Kamehameha III. See Anne Feder Lee, *The Hawaii State Constitution: A Reference Guide* (Westport, CT: Greenwood Press, 1993), pp. 2–5. The actual text of all Hawaii constitutions (kingdom, territory, and state) can be found on "Legal Foundation for Hawaiian Independence," available: www.hawaii-nation.org/legal.html (accessed Oct. 30, 2002). The Bayonet Constitution sought to restore several of the legislative and cabinet rights that had existed under the constitution of 1852.

12. Jonathan K.K. Osorio, *Dismembering Lahui: A History of the Hawaiian Nation to 1887* (Honolulu: University of Hawaii Press, 2002), pp. 238–249.

13. The term *haole* in its original form meant "foreigner." Today it is often used, erroneously but frequently, to refer to a white person.

14. Michael Kioni Dudley and Keoni Kealoha Agard, *A Call for Hawaiian Sovereignty* (Honolulu: Na Kane O Ka Malo, 1993), pp. 62–64.

15. Newlands Resolution, H.R. 259 and S.R. 127, *Congressional Record*, vol. 31, pts. 1–3, 55th Cong., 2nd Sess., p. 4600.

16. An Act to Admit Texas to the Union, 1845, 5 U.S. Statutes at Large 797.

17. U.S. Public Law 103-150 (S.J. Res. 19), 103rd Cong. Joint Resolution 19, November 23, 1993. See 107 U.S. Statutes at Large 1510.

18. President McKinley had officially approved the joint resolution of annexation on July 7, 1898. See 30 U.S. Statutes at Large 750.

19. An Act to Provide a Government for the Territory of Hawaii, 31 U.S. Statutes at Large 141.

20. The provisions granting citizenship and determining voting rights were very complex in practice. There were citizens of the republic who were Asian, and the republic, built upon the earlier efforts of the Hawaiian League and its Bayonet Constitution, had also placed significant property restrictions on voting, thus disenfranchising many Native Hawaiians. Likewise, all children born in the islands, pursuant to U.S. law, became citizens automatically. See Bell, *Last Among Equals*, pp. 36–37, and Tom Coffman, *The Island Edge of America: A Political History of Hawai'i* (Honolulu: University of Hawai'i Press, 2003), pp. 8–10.

21. Hawaiian Homes Commission Act of 1920, 42 U.S. Statutes at Large 108. The act, which did not go into effect until 1921, was one of the most notable territorial revisions in federal land policy in any territory.

22. *Ex Parte Morgan*, cited in 53 Supreme Court Reporter 745.

23. *O'Donoghue v. U.S.*, 53 S.Ct. 740, 289 U.S. 516, 77 L. Ed. 1356 (1933).

24. H.R. 305, February 12, 1900, W.S. Knox amend. H.R. 2972; *Congressional Record*, vol. 33, pts. 1–2, 56th Cong., 1st Sess.

25. Coffman, *Island Edge of America*, p. xi. See also *Laws of the Territory of Hawaii Passed by the Legislature*, vol. 3 (1903).

26. The groundwork for the Hawaiian Homes Commission was laid in an amendment to the Organic Act in 1910 (S.R. 3360, May 27, 1910) and then reaffirmed in a presidential proclamation issued by Wilson in 1920. See 36 U.S. Statutes at Large 443 and 41 Stat. 1786. For the act itself, see 42 U.S. Statutes at Large 108.

27. Bell, *Last Among Equals*, pp. 291–296.

28. Charter of the United Nations and Statutes of International Court of Justice, Article 73. *Yearbook of the United Nations*, vol. 54 (New York: Department of Public Information, United Nations, 2000), p. 1457.

29. Transmission of Information under Article 73e of the Charter. *United Nations Resolutions, Series I: Resolutions Adopted by the General Assembly*, vol. 1, *1946–1948* (Dobbs Ferry, NY: Oceana Publications, 1973), pp. 111–113.

30. Hawaii sought admission as the forty-ninth state for most of its territorial life. It was not until 1957–1958 that those in favor of statehood were forced to concede that honor to Alaska and pursue the fiftieth position.

31. Dan Boylan and T. Michael Holmes, *John Burns: The Man and His Times* (Honolulu: University of Hawaii Press, 2000), pp. 3, 7–17, 30–31.

32. Coffman, *Island Edge of America*, pp. 136–148. See also Boylan and Holmes, *John Burns*, pp. 141–154.

33. Bell, *Last Among Equals*, pp. 192–233.

34. This 1950 referendum was preceded by a 1940 plebiscite in which two-thirds of the voters expressed their support for statehood. The 1950 vote was even greater, with 79 percent of the electorate voting for the convention. See Lee, *The Hawaii State Constitution*, pp. 7–8.

35. Alaska would follow suit and draft its first "state" constitution in 1956.

36. *Manual on State Constitutional Provisions Prepared for the Constitutional Convention, Territory of Hawaii, 1950* (Honolulu: Legislative Reference Bureau, 1950). The manual, as subsequent manuals for the constitutional conventions of revision in 1968 and 1978 did, provided extensive information on the constitutions of other states and political entities.

37. Act 334, Session Law of Hawaii, *Laws of the Territory of Hawaii Passed by the Legislature*, vol. 24, 1949 (Honolulu: Territory of Hawaii, 1901–1959).

38. The single best source for a critical examination of Hawaii's state constitution, its various incarnations, and amendments is Lee, *The Hawaii State Constitution*, pp. 1–22.

39. An Act to provide for the Admission of the State of Hawaii into the Union (Act of March 18, 1959, Pub. Law 86-3), 73 U.S. Statutes at Large 4.

40. Coffman, *The Island Edge of America*, pp. 162–163.

41. Section 5(f) of the Admission Act, 73 U.S. Statutes at Large 5. See also Bell, *Last Among Equals*, p. 283.

42. While the population numbers warranted such caution, the decision is eerily similar to earlier attempts to amend the constitution so that Hawaii, should it become a state, would only be permitted one senator. See Bell, *Last Among Equals*, pp. 126–133.

43. These conditions are all derived from the language used in Resolution 66. *United Nations Resolutions, Series I: Resolutions Adopted by the General Assembly*, vol. 1, pp. 111–113.

44. Bell, *Last Among Equals*, pp. 258–260.

45. Hanani-Kay Trask, *From a Native Daughter: Colonialism and Sovereignty in Hawaii* (Honolulu: University of Hawaii Press, 1999, © 1993), pp. 67–74. See also Bell, *Last Among Equals*, p. 116.

46. Bell, *Last Among Equals*, p. 261.

47. Although Hawaii has voted almost consistently Democratic for both state and national offices in the era of statehood, Linda Lingle was elected in 2002 as the first Republican governor since William Quinn (1959–1962), who served as the last territorial governor under a presidential appointment and the first state governor. The state's Democratic governors have been: John Burns (1962–1974), George Ariyoshi (1974–1986), John Waihee III (1986–1994), and Benjamin Cayetano (1994–2002).

48. The constitutional convention of 1968, one of two such conventions since statehood, promoted protection of a split-districting formula that took into account both an island-by-island representation and population. See Lee, *The Hawaii State Constitution*, pp. 13–14. Today, the First District for Hawaii is made up of all of the islands except a section of Oahu, and the Second District is Honolulu and a large portion of Oahu. It should be noted that the Statehood Act allocated Hawaii only one seat in the House of Representatives. The allocation was set to change pending the results of the 1960 census, after which time (1962) the islands were given two seats.

49. *Hawaii for the Governor's Conference on the Year 2000.* George Chaplin and Glenn D. Paige, eds., *Hawaii 2000; Continuing Experiment in Anticipatory Democracy* (Honolulu: University Press of Hawaii, 1973).

50. Mansel Blackford, *Fragile Paradise: The Impact of Tourism on Maui, 1959–2000* (Lawrence: University Press of Kansas, 2001), pp. 6, 19–23.

51. The influential congressional leaders have included Walter Heen, John Burns, George Ariyoshi, John Waihee III (the first Native Hawaiian governor), Spark Matsunaga, Hiram Fong, Patsy Mink, and the current congressional delegates Daniel Akaka, Daniel Inouye, and Neil Abercrombie.

52. See Bob Krause, *A New Mahele? The Future of Hawaii's Leased Land* (Honolulu, HI: Honolulu Advertiser, 1976).

53. *United States v. Mowat,* 582 F.2d 1194 (9th Cir.), cert. denied, 439 U.S. 967, 99 S. Ct. 458, 58 L. Ed. 2d 436 (1978). Cited in 99 Supreme Court Reporter 458.

54. Kaho'olawwe is the smallest of the major islands. The United States began using it in 1941 as a military bombing range. In the 1970s, Native Hawaiians began their occupations as a protest against the military's use of the island as a larger symbol of cultural and historical destruction. The bombing was stopped in 1990 after two occupiers were killed. See Trask, From a *Native Daughter,* pp. 68, 81.

55. Helena G. Allen, *Kalakaua: Renaissance King* (Honolulu, HI: Mutual Publishing, 1994), pp. 137–138.

56. Trask, *From A Native Daughter,* pp. 4–19.

57. The Constitution of the State of Hawaii, as Amended and in Force November 7, 1978, Article 12. See also Lee, *The Hawaii State Constitution,* p. 19. Along with the creation of OHA, other significant measures included a mandate to teach Hawaiian history and culture in the public schools, recognize Hawaiian as an official language, and reaffirm the state's commitment to the Hawaiian Lands rehabilitation program.

58. In 1996, Circuit Judge Daniel Heely ruled in favor of OHA, noting that the back payments due from the state amounted to anywhere between $300 million and $1.5 billion. Robert D. Craig, *Historical Dictionary of Honolulu and Hawaii* (Lanham, MD: Scarecrow Press, 1998), pp. 152–153.

59. U.S. Public Law 103-150, 103rd Congress Joint Resolution 19, November 23, 1993, sec. 3. Disclaimer, 107 U.S. Statutes at Large 1510.

60. U.S. Public Law 103-150, 103rd Congress Joint Resolution 19, November 23, 1993, Preamble. Disclaimer, 107 U.S. Statutes at Large 1510.

61. *Rice v. Cayetano, Governor of Hawaii.* Certiorari to the U.S. Court of Appeals for the Ninth Circuit. No. 98-818. Argued October 6, 1999; decided, February 23, 2000. Cited in 120A Supreme Court Reporter, 1044.

62. *Arakai v. State of Hawaii,* Honolulu District Court, no. 17213, docket Civil no. 00-00514-HG, 2000.

63. Resolutions 54/90A and 54/90B. *Yearbook of the United Nations, 1999,* vol. 53 (New York: Department of Public Information, United Nations, 1999), pp. 540–547.

64. John G. Roberts, Jr., Washington, D.C., and Edwin S. Kneedler, Deputy Solicitor General, Department of Justice, Washington, D.C. (for United States, as amicus curiae), *Rice v. Cayetano, Governor of Hawaii.* October 6, 1999.

65. Executive Office of the President, *Statement of Administration Policy on H.R. 4904—To Express the Policy of the United States Regarding the United States Relationship with Native Hawaiians* (Washington, DC: Office of Management and Budget, September 26, 2000), n.p. Available: http://clinton4.nara.gov/OMB/legislative/sap/106-2/HR4904-h.html, accessed April 26, 2003.

66. H.R. 665, To express the policy of the United States regarding the United States relationship with Native Hawaiians and to provide a process for the recognition by the United States of the Native Hawaiian governing entity, and for other purposes, 3. Available: http://thomas.loc.gov/. Accessed July 23, 2003.

67. The legislation called for the establishment of the U.S. Office for Native Hawaiian Affairs, with a special trustee, within the Department of the Interior. It further called for a Native Hawaiian Interagency Task Force to address Hawaiian issues throughout the levels and agencies of government. Finally, it called for the creation of a nine-member Native Hawaiian Iterim Governing Council, the precursor to an elected Native Hawaiian Government. See Young, "Report [To accompany H.R. 4904]," sec. 7. September 26, 2000.

68. Susan Masten, "Testimony on S. 2899 and H.R. 4904, Native Hawaiian Recognition," August 30, 2000. Available: www.ncai.org/main/pages/issues/other_issues/documents/presmastestS2889.htm. Accessed April 29, 2002.

69. Bell, *Last Among Equals*, p. 2.

BIBLIOGRAPHY

Bell, Roger. *Last Among Equals: Hawaiian Statehood and American Politics*. Honolulu: University of Hawai'i Press, 1984.

Boylan, Dan, and T. Michael Homes. *John A. Burns: The Man and His Times*. Honolulu: University of Hawaii Press, 2000.

Budnick, Rich. *Stolen Kingdom: An American Conspiracy*. Honolulu: Aloha Press, 1992.

Coffman, Tom. *Nation Within: The Story of America's Annexation of the Nation of Hawai'i*. Honolulu: Epicenter, 1998.

———. *The Island Edge of America: A Political History of Hawai'i*. Honolulu: University of Hawai'i Press, 2003.

Dougherty, Michael. *To Steal a Kingdom: Probing Hawaiian History*. Waimanalo, HI: Island Style Press, 1992.

Dudley, Michael Kioni, and Keoni Kealoha Agard. *A Call for Hawaiian Sovereignty*. Honolulu: Na Kane O Ka Malo Press, 1993.

Hannum, Hurst. *Autonomy, Sovereignty, and Self-Determination: The Accommodation of Confliction Rights*. Philadelphia: University of Pennsylvania, 1990.

Lal, Brij V., and Kate Fortune, eds. *The Pacific Islands: An Encyclopedia*. Honolulu: University of Hawai'i Press, 2000.

Lee, Anne Feder. *The Hawaii State Constitution: A Reference Guide*. Westport, CT: Greenwood Press, 1993.

MacKenzie, Melody Kapilialoha, ed., *Native Hawaiian Rights Handbook*. Honolulu: Native Hawaiian Legal Corporation/Office of Hawaiian Affairs, 1991.

Osorio, Jonathan Kay Kamakawiwo'ole. *Dismembering Lahui: A History of the Hawaiian Nation to 1887*. Honolulu: University of Hawaii Press, 2002.

Trask, Hanani-Kay. *From a Native Daughter: Colonialism and Sovereignty in Hawaii*. Honolulu: University of Hawaii Press, 1999, © 1993.

Wright, Theon. *The Disenchanted Isles: The Story of the Second Revolution in Hawaii*. New York: Dial Press, 1972.

☆☆☆

THE STATE OF IDAHO

Admitted to the Union as a State: July 3, 1890

Katherine G. Aiken

INTRODUCTION

The Idaho state song proclaims, "And here we have Idaho…," as if it were a simple assumption.[1] However, Idaho's journey to territorial and then statehood status was a tortuous and complicated one. Following Colorado's admission in 1876, a decade passed before the flurry of admissions that eventually completed the map of the forty-eight contiguous states. As one of the last of the continental areas to become a state, Idaho was literally what was left over after other state boundaries had been drawn. As a result, Idaho geography is a study in contrasts. With its northern border following the 49th parallel and its southern border the 42nd parallel, only Texas and California, among the forty-eight contiguous states, have a longer distance between northern and southern boundaries. At its shortest distance, the Idaho Panhandle is only forty-eight miles from east to west, whereas the border with Nevada and Utah is 305 miles in length. The state includes 83,557 square miles of land. More than eighty mountain ranges dominate the Idaho landscape—it has the fifth-highest topography of any state in the Union. The result is a state whose shape has been variously described as a hatchet and a pork chop, and features a landscape with immense physical barriers that separate the north from the south.

There is even uncertainty as to the origin of the name "Idaho." According to one account, Colonel William Craig used the term "E-da-Ho" in the summer of 1861 as he traveled through Nez Perce Country and viewed a mountain range glistening in the sun. The Oregon Steam and Navigation Company had launched a steamer on the Columbia River in 1860 named *Idaho*. The company believed "Idaho" was a Columbia River Indian word that translated as "Gem

Idaho

Territorial Development:

- The United States and Great Britain signed a temporary treaty for joint tenancy of the Oregon Country, October 20, 1818
- The United States obtained formal title to all land in the Oregon territory south of the 49th parallel from Great Britain through the Oregon Treaty, June 15, 1846
- Idaho organized as a U.S. territory, March 3, 1863
- Idaho admitted into the Union as the forty-third state, July 3, 1890

Territorial Capitals:

- Lewiston, 1863–1865
- Boise, 1865–1890

State Capitals:

- Boise, 1890–present

Origin of State Name: Although popularly thought to be an Indian word, "Idaho" is a word invented by George M. Shilling, who at one point unsuccessfully pursued a position as delegate from the Territory of Colorado.

First Governor: George L. Shoup
Governmental Organization: Bicameral
Population at Statehood: 84,385
Geographical Size: 82,747 square miles

of the mountains," thus making Craig's usage a reasonable one. However, Idaho Springs, Colorado, was organized in June 1860, and the Washington Territorial Legislature created the original Idaho County in 1861. The origin of the name is murky, although all of these early uses claimed some association with Indian language. Despite considerable effort, no modern historian has been able to trace the roots of the word "Idaho" to any of the Indian dialects spoken in the region.[2]

Another explanation is that Dr. George M. Willing made the name up during a lobbying trip to the U.S. Congress on behalf of Pikes Peak, Colorado, residents. Some gentlemen approached Willing for a name. According to the story, he had just seen the young daughter of an acquaintance and had called to her, "Ida, ho—come and see me," prompting him to suggest the name Idaho. There is no substantiation for this derivation of the word, either. While many Idahoans cling to the notion that the state name must have Indian origins, the safest conclusion is that the word "Idaho" has no actual meaning other than that it sounds Indian and somewhat romantic.[3]

INDIAN CULTURES AND EARLY EXPLORATION

Most Idahoans view the Salmon River as the dividing line between northern and southern Idaho. It is no coincidence that this same geographic feature divided two distinct Indian cultures that anthropologists term Great Basin and Plateau. The Great Basin tribes, the Shoshone, Bannock, and Lemhi, inhabited the dry landscape of what is now southern Idaho, western Wyoming, and parts of Nevada and Utah and were the major political force there.

There are two groups of Indians in the northern part of the state (Plateau). In the Clearwater River Valley, the Nez Perce or the Nimíipuu (the people) occupied territory between the Bitterroot Range and the Blue Mountains and were one of the most influential Indian tribes in Idaho. The Kalispel, the Kutenais (Kootenai in some contexts), and the Coeur d'Alenes (named by French traders, but Schitsu'umsh in their own Salish language) occupied land in what is now the Idaho Panhandle. The Coeur d'Alenes lived on about 4 million acres with present-day Lake Coeur d'Alene as its center. The anthropologist Sven Liljebald has estimated that there were 3,000 Shoshone-Bannock, 3,000 Nez Perce, about 700 Coeur d'Alene, and about 300 Pend d'Oreille or Kalispel, and a few Kutenai in Idaho at the beginning of the nineteenth century.[4]

The expedition of Meriwether Lewis and William Clark marks the first direct contact that Euro-Americans had with the area we now know as Idaho. As we embark on the bicentennial of the Lewis and Clark expedition, Idaho Indian tribes are struggling to come to terms with these interlopers and their impact on Indian society and culture. The expedition journals that recount this remarkable journey of nearly eight thousand miles round trip from

St. Louis make it clear that what is now Idaho represented a daunting and intimidating barrier for the expedition.

The Lewis and Clark story is an oft-repeated one, beginning with how President Thomas Jefferson sent a secret message to Congress requesting funds for the exploration of the land between St. Louis and the Pacific Ocean. The Corps of Discovery began the official part of its work when it left St. Louis on May 14, 1804. The two captains and twenty-nine others, including twenty-seven young unmarried soldiers; George Drouillard a mixed-blood hunter; and York, an African American slave whom William Clark owned, embarked on the adventure.

During the winter of 1804–1805, the expedition camped with the Mandan Indians near present-day Bismarck, North Dakota. When the group continued its trek in the spring of 1805, Toussaint Charbonneau, an interpreter, and a young Lemhi-Shoshone woman, Sacagawea, accompanied them. Sacagawea's role remains a controversial one and certainly is the subject of much speculation. The fact that it is Sacagawea's countenance that appears on the face of U.S. dollar coins is illustrative of the place she has come to play in the American psyche. Exactly what her role was in a wider sense is open to debate, but it is clear that in the summer of 1805, she recognized some of the landscape and knew that the party had entered Shoshone territory. She certainly helped the men obtain packhorses from her relative Chief Cameawait. She was able to provide translating skills as well. The presence of Sacagawea and her child may have helped to convince local Indians that Lewis and Clark were not intent upon waging war.[5]

Most Americans recognize the name Sacagawea, but few are familiar with her Nez Perce counterpart, Wetxuuwíis (wet-k'hoo'wees). According to Nez Perce oral tradition, Wetxuuwíis (the person who returned home) had been captured as a young girl and spent time with the Mandans, where she had encountered whites and received good treatment from them. By the time the Lewis and Clark expedition reached the Nez Perce, Wetxuuwíis was a respected tribal elder and her positive words protected the Corps of Discovery from certain death. That one Indian woman has become something of an American icon and the other is virtually unknown perhaps illustrates the power of historical sources. The Lewis and Clark journal references to Sacagawea, the fact that she was a part of the white expedition, and the later life of her son, Jean Baptiste, among whites, brought her story to prominence.[6]

Lewis and Clark left their horses with the Nez Perce, and the Indians showed the whites how to build dugout canoes that allowed them to continue down the Clearwater, Snake, and Columbia rivers to the Pacific Ocean. The Nez Perce again played a pivotal role during the group's return trip, when snow in the Idaho mountains delayed the expedition, which then had to camp for twenty-seven days waiting for a thaw. After returning to St. Louis on September 23, 1806, the Lewis and Clark expedition reported that the area now known as Idaho had large numbers of beaver and other animals.

Soon, entrepreneurs engaged in the fur trade came to the area and relied upon the journals for information regarding the terrain, the wildlife, and the Indians.

THE FUR TRADE AND MISSIONARIES

While the fur trade is the stuff of legends, it was primarily a venture in capitalism that brought entrepreneurs to the region. Literally thousands of beaver pelts were needed to supply the men's hat-making industry. Fur trappers and mountain men were indeed the hearty individuals of folklore, but the fur trade itself depended upon large corporate entities. It also fostered a growing competition between Americans and the British behemoth, the Hudson's Bay Company. The fur trade in Idaho continued until the 1850s, when changing men's fashion and the influx of missionaries and settlers ended its economic viability.[7]

Along with fur traders, early Christian missionaries are noteworthy in Idaho's journey to territorial status. The relationship between missionaries and Indians has been the subject of considerable discussion in recent years, both on the part of historians and tribal members. Different Christian denominations were responsible for missionary efforts in each Idaho region. In 1836, the American Board of Commissioners for Foreign Missions sponsored two missionary couples, Marcus and Narcissa Whitman and Henry and Eliza Spalding. The Whitmans established a mission site near what is now Walla Walla in Washington state. The Spaldings built at Lapwai, about thirteen miles east of Lewiston, Idaho, where they hoped to convert the Nez Perce to Christianity and to a new way of life more in line with their own worldview. The mission soon boasted a church and a school, and the Spaldings started Idaho's first irrigated farm.

The Spaldings' efforts led to considerable disruption in Nez Perce culture. Since the Nez Perce had led a nomadic life, the idea of established farms was definitely a foreign one. Spalding added a gristmill and a water-powered sawmill to the establishment at Lapwai. He brought the first printing press to the Pacific Northwest and printed the Gospel of St. John in Nez Perce. His daughter, Eliza, was the first white child born in Idaho.

Sarah and Asa Bowen Smith operated a mission further up the Clearwater River at Kamiah, where Mr. Smith compiled a Nez Perce dictionary. Asa Bowen Smith believed that the Spaldings' attempts to induce the Nez Perce to take up farming were misguided. He constantly criticized those efforts in letters to the American Board of Commissioners for Foreign Missions (a body that included representatives from the Presbyterian, Dutch Reform, and Congregationalist churches). Tired of this controversy, the board recalled both the Smiths and the Spaldings and moved to have the Whitmans take over the missionary work in Idaho. Marcus Whitman braved the arduous trip East in the winter of 1842 to urge the board to reconsider, which it did. Upon his return in 1843, Whitman brought white settlers.

Although the main route to Oregon was south of the Whitman Mission, travelers who were ill found respite there. An epidemic of dysentery and measles killed half of the Cayuse people in the area, whereas most white children who contracted measles recovered. On November 29, 1847, tribal members attacked the mission and killed the Whitmans and eleven others. Following this incident, the Spaldings abandoned the Lapwai Mission, including forty-four acres under cultivation.[8]

Northern Idaho was the base for Roman Catholic missionaries. Pierre De Smet, a Belgian Jesuit, came to the Pacific Northwest in 1840. Along with Anthony Ravalli and Nicholas Point, De Smet established the Mission of the Sacred Heart on December 4, 1842. Located on the banks of what is now known as the St. Joe River, the mission site was subject to seasonal flooding, so work with the Coeur d'Alenes moved to a site on the Coeur d'Alene River. Using a Father Ravalli plan, members of the Coeur d'Alene tribe began construction work on a permanent church in 1846. Named for one of the priests who worked on the project, Joseph Cataldo, the Cataldo Mission (built between 1846 and 1877) is the oldest extant building in Idaho. During this period, the majority of Coeur d'Alenes were baptized into the Catholic Church, and the relationship between church and tribe continues to be a significant one.[9]

Under the direction of Prophet Brigham Young, the Church of Jesus Christ of Latter-day Saints constructed a mission post on a fork of the Salmon River in 1855, named in honor of King Limhi (later changed to Lemhi) of the Book of Mormon. Idaho's first white farming community was only a few miles from the first white campground—Lewis and Clark's Seventeen Mile Camp of 1805. The early mission was plagued with grasshoppers and other problems. Brigham Young and a group of church officials visited Fort Limhi in 1857, but the Mormons were not able to maintain the settlement, despite the fact that they succeeded in converting some of the Shoshone.[10]

WESTWARD TRAILS AND TERRITORIAL INCLUSION

In 1818, the United States and Great Britain agreed to a joint occupation of the Oregon Country. Following considerable diplomatic posturing, in 1846 the two powers divided the region at the 49th parallel, the present-day boundary between the United States and Canada. Congress established Oregon Territory in 1848, and it included the area now known as Idaho.[11]

The federal government renewed its interest in the area during the 1840s through a series of explorations historians call the Great Reconnaissance. Some of this activity started from the Pacific Coast and included river exploration as far inland as Lapwai, site of the Spalding Mission. John C. Frémont and others instigated expeditions that came overland from the east. Frémont was a member of the U.S. Army Corps of Topographical Engineers, and in May 1843, he and thirty-nine men left Independence, Missouri, charged with mapping the Oregon Trail. Charles Preuss, the group's cartographer, did in fact complete a map of the trail. Frémont presented the final report to Congress, and it attracted considerable attention from a variety of sources. Frémont was married to Jessie Benton, and her father, Senator Thomas Hart Benton from Missouri, became a vocal advocate for western expansion.[12]

Ten years later, Congress appropriated funds for a survey to determine the best railroad route to the Pacific Ocean. Washington governor Isaac Stevens led the northern survey team. Idaho was then a part of Washington Territory. George B. McClellan was part of this group, which surveyed several possible routes across the Panhandle. The Stevens survey, various maps, and lithographs by artists Gustavus Sohon and John Mix Stanley, were published together.[13]

John Mullan, a member of the party, continued the survey work and also supervised the construction of a military road from Fort Benton on the Missouri River to Fort Walla Walla. Constructed at a cost of $230,000, the road was 624 miles long. The rugged Bitterroot Mountains presented major challenges, and Mullan blazed a tree on what is now Fourth of July Canyon on July 4, 1861. By 1866, 20,000 people, 500 head of cattle and 6,000 mules had traveled across the Mullan road. The Mullan Tree is still visible just off the I-90 freeway, and that route follows much of the Mullan road path. Idaho towns all along the highway boast Mullan statues to commemorate his work.[14]

The famous Oregon Trail immigration route crossed the southern portion of what is now the state of Idaho. Travel across the Snake River Plain was arduous, to say the least. According to some estimates, between 1840 and 1860, about 53,000 immigrants traversed the Oregon Trail, and this route continued to be a major one until the completion of a railroad through southern Idaho in 1884. Most groups of potential Oregon settlers started their trip in Missouri in early spring in order to take advantage of plains grasses as feed for livestock. This meant that they confronted the Snake River Plain segment from Fort Hall to Fort Boise during the hot summer months. Although the travelers could see the Snake River, the trail passed high above on cliffs that were so steep that descent was not an option. Thus, the majority of the Oregon Trail immigrants viewed their trip across Idaho as a desert barrier to overcome and nothing more. Although most of the wagon trains did not stop in Idaho, they did have a lasting impact in that there are several locations in Idaho where a knowledgeable observer can still detect wagon wheel ruts.[15]

Thus, throughout the early history of white involvement in the area, the Idaho landscape was either an obstacle to overcome or part of the path to a final destination. It is not surprising, then, that in the several boundary revisions that Congress adopted between 1848 and 1868, what we now know as Idaho carried various designations. When Congress created Washington Territory in

1853, it divided Idaho between it and Oregon Territory. The state of Oregon was admitted to the Union in 1859, and the sparsely populated portion of the former territory outside of Oregon's borders was reattached to Washington Territory. This huge territory included all of the future states of Washington and Idaho and parts of what became Montana and Wyoming. Needless to say, governing this large territory was difficult.[16]

Incursions of Euro-Americans in increasing numbers only served to heighten tension with Indian tribes in the area. As part of Washington Territory (formed in 1853), Idaho was subject to Territorial Governor Isaac Stevens, who relentlessly worked to confine Indian tribes to reservations in an effort to facilitate white settlement. One of the earliest treaties guaranteed the Nez Perce the right to their ancestral lands in Idaho, Oregon, and Washington, which encompassed about 11,000 square miles.[17]

DISCOVERY OF GOLD AND MORMON SETTLEMENT

White perceptions of what is now Idaho and of the Nez Perce claim to their homeland changed dramatically with the discovery of gold. In 1860, Elias Davidson Pierce and about a dozen men illegally crossed the Nez Perce Reservation and found gold on Oro Fino Creek in the Clearwater drainage. A gold rush and everything that the term connotes was soon in full swing. Pierce City became the largest town in Washington Territory. Prospectors and gold seekers traveled up the Columbia River to the Snake and then to Lewiston. Miners then walked or rode horses or mules to Pierce or Oro Fino. Although the land still ostensibly belonged to the Nez Perce, the sheer number of prospectors made that ownership a moot point.

Many of the early gold seekers were farmers from the Willamette Valley, but soon fortune seekers from literally around the world joined them. Gold dust was valued at $16 an ounce, and during 1861, $3 million worth was shipped down the Columbia River. Soon, prospectors had made discoveries at Florence and Elk City, and eventually further south in the Boise Basin, where on August 2, 1862, they discovered gold on Grimes Creek. Miners had extracted $20 million worth of gold from the Boise Basin by 1866, and Idaho City boasted more population than Portland, Oregon. (Idaho City is now a ghost town and the focus of Idaho State Historical Society restoration and interpretive efforts.) Gold from the Idaho fields provided a needed infusion of the precious metal into the coffers of the U.S. government, then waging war against the Confederate States of America. Eventually the Boise Basin yielded perhaps as much as $66 million in gold. Fort Boise, a military post, was established on July 4, 1863. (There had been a Hudson's Bay Company post with the same name, but this new location represents the beginnings of Boise city). Although in July 1863, most American military attention was focused on Gettysburg,

Pennsylvania, and Vicksburg, Mississippi, Fort Boise boasted two thousand residents by the end of 1865.[18]

While fortune hunters streamed into the gold fields in the Clearwater and Boise basins, members of the Church of Jesus Christ of Latter-day Saints began to settle in what is now the southern part of Idaho. Thirteen Mormon colonists founded Idaho's first town, Franklin, on April 14, 1860. They were responsible for the beginning of agricultural production in southeastern Idaho. Three years later, General Charles C. Rich led a group of between thirty and fifty people to a site on Bear Lake they named Paris. Other Mormon settlements soon followed—Montpelier, St. Charles, Ovid, Bennington, Fish Haven, and Bloomington. The Organic Act for Utah Territory (1850) indicated the 42nd parallel as the northern boundary, but no one knew exactly where that was at the time. The early Franklin and Bear Lake settlers thought they were in Utah and paid taxes there until 1872, when an official survey publicized their error.[19]

Mormon livestock and crops threatened Indians. Unlike the situation in the Clearwater, the southern Idaho tensions between Mormon settlers and Indians ended in violence. The so-called Battle of Bear River, on January 29, 1863, resulted in the deaths of perhaps as many as 368 Shoshone tribal members, two-thirds of them women and children. (The more famous Battle of Wounded Knee, on December 29, 1890, resulted in 146 deaths.) The catastrophe virtually annihilated the Cache Valley Shoshone and ended the ability of Indians to oppose the expanding Church of Jesus Christ of Latter-day Saints' presence in the region.[20]

THE CREATION AND DIVISION OF IDAHO TERRITORY

Although the Mormon settlement in southern Idaho probably had more long-term impact on what became the state of Idaho, it was the mining boom that led to the creation of Idaho Territory. Oregon became a state in 1859, establishing the southeastern boundary of what is now Idaho and leaving an expanded Washington Territory that included present-day Idaho. Washington Territory officials in Olympia feared that the growing population in what were then called the eastern Washington gold fields (now Idaho) would jeopardize their power. Groups in Olympia, Walla Walla, Lewiston, Boise, and Virginia City (Montana) all jockeyed to have their town named as the territorial capital.

President Abraham Lincoln signed the organic act creating Idaho Territory on March 4, 1863. The new territory included 325,000 square miles—more than Texas—and was the last huge territory created. It incorporated all of what is now Idaho and Montana, along with most of the present state of Wyoming. Lewiston was the capital, primarily because it was actually possible to reach it via established transportation routes. Idaho City, in the gold mining area, had substantially more people but represented a travel nightmare. Ironically, Lewiston was still part of Nez Perce tribal holdings. Although a new treaty was negotiated on June 9, 1863, which reduced tribal lands to only about 1,100 square miles, the Senate did not ratify the agreement and Lewiston did not become an actual part of Idaho Territory until April 20, 1867.[21]

There were only 32,342 residents in the new territory—a geographic area larger than all of the New England states combined. Few people had any great loyalty for an entity named Idaho, since its creation had been so haphazard and only weeks before they had been residents of Washington Territory. As the First Territorial Legislature met in July 1863, national attention focused on the Battles of Gettysburg and Vicksburg, not on Lewiston, Idaho Territory. The legislators certainly recognized that the territory was just too large for any effective government, and they unanimously voted to petition Congress to divide it. Delegates from the Virginia City area demonstrated the efficacy of this request with their trip home following the session. They traveled down the Columbia River to Portland, took a ship to San Francisco, and then went cross-country to Salt Lake City, and finally on to Virginia City. In response, Congress created Montana Territory on May 26, 1864. This left an Idaho Territory with close to the current boundaries of the state and with the Salmon River effectively dividing south from north. Congress set the current border on July 25, 1868.[22]

TERRITORIAL GOVERNMENT

Transportation and communication difficulties made government a constant challenge. Most Idahoans did not trust officials appointed in Washington, D.C. Idaho's distance from the major Civil War battlefields made it an attractive destination for both Northerners and Southerners who sought to escape the conflict. They did not leave their sympathies in the East, however, so there were conflicts in Idaho. In addition, Idaho faced financial challenges. It was the custom for the federal government to provide funding for territorial governments, but conducting the Civil War stretched the government beyond its means as it was, and there was little left for Idaho. Sixteen men were confirmed as governor during the twenty-seven years of Idaho's territorial status. Six were in Idaho for less than a year, some of them for only a few months. Only eight served a year or more. Incompetence and economic irresponsibility marked the period, and the territorial governors received the pejorative "carpetbagger" label.

In fact, Idaho's territorial governors were, for the most part, a lackluster group. The president, with congressional confirmation, appointed the governor, but the $2,500 salary did not attract talented individuals to Idaho. William H. Wallace, the first territorial governor and a friend of Abraham Lincoln, arrived in Lewiston on July 10, 1863. He came to a position lacking in financial resources, because Idaho Territory was created at the end of the congressional session and Congress had neglected to appropriate any funds. Wallace viewed the territorial governorship as a political stepping-stone anyway and was delighted to leave for Washington, D.C., on December 6, following his election as Idaho delegate to the House of Representatives.

Wallace's replacement, Caleb Lyon, did not arrive until August 1864, and he soon found himself caught up in a battle over the location of the capital. As the mineral rush in the Clearwater diminished, fewer and fewer people lived in Florence, Elk City, Pierce, and Lewiston. Although the region had 10,000 residents in the summer of 1862, only about 1,000 remained by the time of Lyon's appearance on the scene. The Boise area had more that 16,000 inhabitants and the Virginia City region, close to 12,000.

In response to these population shifts, the Second Territorial Legislature voted on December 7, 1864, to move the capital to Boise. One of Caleb Lyon's first official acts was to approve this change. Lewiston boosters were enraged and went to court to prevent the move. They succeeded in getting a local judge to issue a temporary injunction forbidding the removal of the territorial seal and archives. While the governor escaped a subpoena by ostensibly going duck hunting in Washington, the Lewiston sheriff deputized local citizens to guard the seal and territorial documents in case of a Boise-based attempt to seize them (Boiseans did make such an attempt on December 31, 1864). Lyon returned to Washington, D.C., leaving Idaho without a territorial governor for two months. The acting governor, Clinton Dewitt Smith, succeeded in transferring the seal to Boise (or, according to the northern Idaho viewpoint, succeeded in stealing the seal), arriving there on April 14, 1864, the date of Abraham Lincoln's assassination. Five months later, Smith dropped dead during a chess game in Rocky Bar, and again Idaho had no governor. Much to most Idahoans' surprise, Caleb Lyon then returned to complete his term as governor. He stayed until 1866, then left amid accusations that he had taken $46,000 earmarked for Idaho Indians.

The Lincoln assassination and the ensuing Reconstruction Era were of course traumatic for the country as a whole, and no less so for Idaho Territory. It is probably not surprising that the same divisions that threatened to destroy the United States played a crucial role in early Idaho history. Although the first Idaho Territorial Legislature passed an anti-slavery resolution, there were a large number of Confederate sympathizers in the territory and the Democratic Party enjoyed a majority in Idaho. Some party members were out-and-out secessionists, but many more held views more in line with the antiwar Copperhead sentiment.

Although Idahoans were in both camps, the fourth Idaho Territorial Legislature refused to take the loyalty oath to the Union that was such a key part of Reconstruction in the South. In fact, it passed a law that only presidential appointees, not legislators, were required to take the oath. The Democratic majority was able to override the veto by Lincoln appointee Governor David Ballard. The governor countered with an order to the secretary of the treasury not to pay the legislators until they took the oath. Eventually, Territorial Secretary Solomon R. Howlett requested federal troops from Fort Boise to persuade the recalcitrant lawmakers, and twenty-two armed soldiers marched to the legislature in a show of force. Idaho Democrats believed they experienced a taste of what their southern colleagues lived with on a daily basis, but they signed the oath on January 14, 1867. Both sides were malicious in their rhetoric. Democrats said of Howlett that he was "atrociously corrupt, and totally unworthy of any position under the Government, save as a condemned felon in a Government prison." The Republican *Sacramento Daily Union* described the legislators as "true and actual representatives of second class hurdy-gurdy houses" and "Satanic."[23]

The well-documented friction between the Reconstruction Congress and President Andrew Johnson had ramifications in Idaho. Johnson fired Governor Ballard four times, but the same Tenure of Office Act that was so pivotal in the Johnson impeachment required congressional approval to replace Ballard. While the executive and legislative branches battled it out, the government withheld Johnson's salary. He continued to serve, and his Boise medical practice supported him. When Ballard did finally leave, it took a year to replace him, and Thomas Bowen served only from July to September 1871.

President Grant tried five times to appoint a successor before his sixth appointee, Thomas W. Bennett, accepted and remained for almost four years. Bennett wanted to hold the position as Idaho's delegate to Congress and ran for the seat as an Independent in 1874. Although he did not receive the most votes, Bennett, in his capacity as governor, declared himself the victor, resigned the governorship, and took up the territorial delegate duties in Washington, D.C. He completed most of the term before his opponent finally succeeded in unseating him. David P. Thompson was Idaho's territorial governor from April 6 to July 31, 1876. He resigned due to a conflict of interest with his transportation companies and actually was only in Idaho for a few weeks. Buffalo, New York, native Mason Brayman was another man with strong Republican credentials, having served as a general of the Illinois volunteers during the Civil War. He managed to antagonize just about everyone in the Idaho territorial bureaucracy during his tenure from August 1, 1876, to August 4, 1880.

Ohioan John Neil was Idaho's territorial governor from August 4, 1880, to April 24, 1883. He had been wounded at Shiloh and was a strong anti-Mormon. His successor, John Irwin, was governor only from April 24 to May 15, 1885. His position became untenable when Grover Cleveland won the first Democratic presidential victory since the Civil War. President Cleveland actually appointed an Idaho man to the governorship, Edward Stevenson, who served from October 10, 1885, to May 1, 1889. This marked not only the end of the "carpetbag" era for Republicans in Idaho, but it also signaled an end to outsider appointments. Stevenson came to the Boise Basin in 1863 and was embraced by both Democrats and Republicans as a true Idahoan. He and his successor, George L. Shoup (May 1, 1889, to July 3, 1890), who would also be Idaho's first state governor, played a vital role in regard to a number of issues that are discussed below. The Republican Shoup came to Idaho in 1866 and settled in Salmon in 1867, where he operated a general store.[24]

INDIANS, SECTIONALISM, AND MORMONS IN IDAHO TERRITORY

The territorial governors and legislators confronted three major issues. One was how to deal with the Indians in the face of growing white demands for land. The second was continuing north-south sectional conflict in Idaho that had been institutionalized when the final boundary was established. The third was the increasing influence of Jesus Christ of Latter-day Saints residents in southern Idaho who were supporters of the Democratic Party.

No Idaho Indian episode has received more attention than the Nez Perce War of 1877. When the Clearwater gold rush precipitated a renegotiation and eventually a reduction in Nez Perce land in 1863, about one-third of the Nez Perce refused to acknowledge it—the non-treaty Nez Perce. One group under Whitebird lived on the lower Salmon River south of the new reservation and another group led by Chief Joseph inhabited Oregon's Wallowa Valley. In 1871, young Chief Joseph became the leader. He insisted that his band of about four hundred Nez Perce were not bound by the 1863 treaty because his father had never signed it. At first the federal government recognized this position and in 1873 created a reservation in part of the Wallowa Valley. Whites in the area protested, and the government reversed its position two years later. The government directed Chief Joseph and his band to move to the Nez Perce Reservation on the Clearwater. In May 1877, General Oliver O. Howard ordered Joseph and his band to leave the Wallowa Valley within thirty days. They would have to cross Hell's Canyon and the Snake and Salmon rivers at high water. In the middle of June when the relocation was underway, three young warriors (local whites had murdered the father of one) killed four settlers and the peace ended.

Eight hundred Indian men, women, and children with a herd of more than two thousand horses, attempted to flee across the Bitterroot Mountains to Montana, where they hoped to find asylum with the Crows. If that did not work, their backup plan was to escape across the border into Canada. O. O. Howard and his soldiers followed the fleeing Nez Perce. At the Battle of the Big Hole River on August 9 and 10, the Nez Perce suffered seventy casualties and the army had twenty-one men killed and forty wounded. By September 30, the Nez Perce were only about forty miles from their destination when Colonel Nelson Miles and 383 troopers overtook them. The cavalry attacked, and following a day of fighting and five days of siege in extremely cold conditions, the soldiers emerged victorious. Joseph surrendered on October 5, and according to one of Howard's aides, made his famous declaration, "Hear me, my chiefs! I am tired. My heart is sick and sad. From where the sun now stands I will fight no more forever."

The Nez Perce odyssey had covered over 1,500 miles. The army took eighty-seven men, 184 women, and 147 children as captives and the federal government exiled these tribal members to Oklahoma, where they remained until 1885. There was so much ill feeling in the Clearwater that Chief Joseph lived the remainder of his life on the Colville Reservation in north-central Washington. The conflict of 1877 cost the federal government $930,000 and 180 lives. One hundred tribal members, including fifty-five women and children, died. General Howard moved on to fight the Bannocks and Paiutes in southern Idaho in 1878, driving them back to their reservation. Shortly thereafter, the Fort Hall Reservation's size was reduced to one-fourth its former area to open land for white settlement.[25]

Mining discoveries again dominated the Idaho economy. The Wood River boom was a lead-silver rush that centered around Hailey (near the present-day Sun Valley resort). Two thousand mining claims were filed in 1880, and Wood River Mines yielded $6 million between 1884 and 1887. The 1893 depression ended the Wood River rush.[26]

The story of the Coeur d'Alene mining district is much different, since the district continues to produce precious metals. A. J. Pritchard had been doing some panning in a location later known as Murray. Word got out, and in 1882 other prospectors came. Soon the Northern Pacific Railroad was advertising that "[n]uggets have been found which weigh $50, $100, $166, and $200" and a rush was underway. About ten thousand people came to the North Fork of the Coeur d'Alene River from 1883 to 1885. Then, Noah S. Kellogg, an aging itinerant prospector, needed a grubstake and he approached Murray general store proprietors O. O. Peck (a small contractor) and Dr. J. T. Cooper (a former surgeon) for the money. Cooper and Peck, at least according to one story, agreed to the loan if Kellogg would take with him a jackass that had been disrupting the peace of the Murray community with its braying. Sometime in August 1885, Kellogg traveled to Milo Gulch on the South Fork of the Coeur d'Alene River. Following a nap, Kellogg awoke to find the donkey had run away. When he finally caught up with the beast, Kellogg looked down and found galena. In April 1886, First District judge Norman Buck ruled that the donkey had indeed discovered the fabulous Bunker Hill lode, so Cooper and Peck deserved part of the mine. The Bunker Hill became one of the country's most significant producers of lead, zinc, and silver and was northern Idaho's key economic enterprise throughout the nineteenth century. The Coeur d'Alenes became a population and production center just as the Idaho territorial period was ending. Northern Idaho mining interests played an important role in Idaho statehood.[27]

The Republican Party platform of 1860 railed against the "twin evils of barbarism"—slavery and polygamy. Throughout the Idaho territorial period, anti-Mormonism was a recurring theme. In fact, tension between members of the Church of Jesus Christ of Latter-day Saints and nonmembers was perhaps the most significant conflict in the Idaho transition from territory to statehood. There were many levels to the discord. Mormons lived together in tightly knit, hierarchically organized communities. Church leaders were also political leaders. This, coupled with the cooperative economic initiatives the Latter-day Saints pursued, resulted in suspicion among gentiles or non-church members. The Idaho Mormon communities had cooperative general stores with profits distributed "in kind" to residents. Zion's Cooperative Mercantile Institution (ZCMI) is still a retail force in the region. Water was and is the most valuable commodity in the West, and Mormons even controlled water through the church's communal structure. These practices appeared to violate the basic tenets of free enterprise and capitalism that other Americans held dear, which led to suspicion. At the same time, the success of the Church of Jesus Christ of Latter-day Saints in both commerce and agriculture fostered jealousy.

Political factionalism compounded the situation. Given the church's high level of organization, it is not surprising that Mormons tended to vote in blocks for Democratic candidates during the late territorial period. Since Democrats were victorious in Idaho elections until the 1880s, this did not upset the political scene to any great degree, although unsuccessful candidates often blamed their defeats on powers in Salt Lake City who ostensibly had little interest in actual Idaho issues. As the number of Mormon residents increased, their power at the polls did also.

Although many historians have argued that this political clout and the Mormons' economic unity and success actually threatened gentiles' conceptions of Americanism, there is no doubt that the Mormon practice of plural marriage fostered the most potent animosity among non-Mormons. Most estimates show that only about 3 percent of Idaho Mormons actually practiced plural marriage, but outsiders focused on what they termed as polygamy to indict the Church of Jesus Christ of Latter-day Saints and its individual members. Cartoons in the popular press portrayed lecherous, bearded Mormon men taking advantage of bevies of young women in seeming disregard of Victorian America's family values.

By the 1872 election, the Mormons in southern Idaho recognized that they were in fact Idaho residents and their Democratic votes controlled elections in that area. Mormon bishop Lorenzo Hill Hatch of Franklin served as a representative for Oneida County and temporary speaker of the territorial House. Alexander Stalker, another Mormon church member, served as chaplain. Republicans realized they would never get Mormons to vote for their party. As a result, the so-called Mormon question became related to another key territorial period issue—boundary readjustment. Whereas mining interests in the Idaho Panhandle believed they shared more of a community of interest with both eastern Washington and Montana than with southern Idaho, non-Mormons there were opposed to any contemplation of a separation because it would give the Mormons a decided voting majority. A coalition of anti-Mormons, which included more settlers attracted by railroads and the Wood River mining rush, annexationists in the north, and federal officials in Boise, joined together in 1882 to elect Idaho's first Republican Territorial Legislature.

Fred T. Dubois, a U.S. marshal, was the catalyst for converting general anti-Mormon sentiment into a full-blown political movement. Idaho was not the only area where individuals found plural marriage to be inimical to community standards. In response, Congress passed the Edmunds Act in 1882. The act made it illegal for polygamists to vote, hold public office, or serve on juries in litigation involving plural marriage. Marshal Dubois was determined to enforce the law in Idaho.

The Mormons closed ranks to protect themselves. They systematically organized to hide male practitioners of plural marriage from authorities. Despite the fact that Fred Dubois had no difficulty in obtaining warrants for the arrest of Mormon polygamists, he found it almost impossible to apprehend them. A U.S. marshal and his deputies stood out in Mormon communities, and an established warning system allowed polygamists to hide before authorities could locate them. Fred Dubois certainly sought to make it difficult for Mormon polygamists to live openly. However, his major goal was to link the Democratic Party to the practice of plural marriage and thereby discredit it. Dubois hoped that he and other Republicans would benefit politically.[28]

Arguments against polygamy were powerful. On December 22, 1884, the Territorial Legislature fashioned a new county, called Bingham County, from the northern 80 percent of predominantly Mormon Oneida County. This isolated Mormons in Oneida and created a counterbalance to their political power. In 1885, the Idaho legislature adopted the Test Oath, which required people to swear under oath as to whether they were members of the Church of Jesus Christ of Latter-day Saints and believed in its doctrines. The Test Oath, therefore, impacted not just those who practiced plural marriage, but all Mormons. Church of Jesus Christ of Latter-day Saints membership was enough to bar a man from voting, holding office, or serving on a jury—in other words, the established rights of citizenship.[29]

Four sessions of the Idaho Territorial Legislature petitioned Congress to annex the Idaho Panhandle to either Washington or Montana. In early 1887, both houses of Congress actually approved moving the northern portion of Idaho to Washington. This plan would have had the added advantage of allowing the southern portion of Idaho to join Nevada, where the end of the mining rush was creating economic difficulties and actually a decline in population. Senator William M. Stewart of Nevada saw the annexation of southern Idaho as a solution with a proposed capital at Winnemucca. Then the Panhandle could join with Washington, or in light of the Coeur d'Alene mining boom, perhaps with Montana. Many residents of the Panhandle rejoiced at this development— a reflection of tensions between the northern and southern parts of the state that continue to the present. Edward Stevenson, the territorial governor, objected to the change in Idaho boundaries and helped to convince President Grover Cleveland to pocket veto the legislation.[30]

In an attempt to assuage the continuing hard feelings in the northern part of the state, Territorial Council Bill No. 20 stipulated that Idaho's Morrill Act/land grant university would be located in Moscow. Introduced in January 1889, the bill had virtually no opposition and created the unusual situation that the University of Idaho is located only nine miles from the state of Washington's land grant college, Washington State University in Pullman. Latah County voters stopped supporting annexation movements once the site was designated.[31]

THE CONSTITUTIONAL CONVENTION

While Idahoans struggled with their regional differences, developments on the national scene complicated statehood. Along with several other territories, Idaho experienced difficulty in gaining congressional approval for statehood because Democrats in the national body did not wish to admit states that would vote Republican. Republicans gained control of the White House and both houses of Congress in the election of 1888. Before the newly elected members of Congress could take office, Democrats voted in favor of statehood, perhaps in an attempt to gain some political advantage from the act. An omnibus bill began the process of admitting Washington, Montana, North Dakota, and South Dakota to statehood. Idaho and Wyoming were conspicuously absent from the legislation.[32]

Oregon senator John Mitchell introduced a bill authorizing an Idaho constitutional convention in 1888. The bill was referred to committee and no action was taken before the Senate adjourned. The last session of the Idaho Territorial Legislature also had before it a bill calling for a constitutional convention, but a controversy involving the boundaries of Alturas County proved more critical.[33]

Territorial governor Edward A. Stevenson issued a call for the convention on April 2, 1889. When President William H. Harrison, a Republican, took office, he appointed a new territorial governor, George L. Shoup. On May 11, Governor Shoup reiterated the call for a convention. Idaho residents were determined to hold a special convention and draft a constitution, even though Congress had not made provisions for these actions. This explains why historians often consider Idaho one of the omnibus states, but this is, strictly speaking, not the case.

Electing the delegates represented the next challenge to the Idaho Constitutional Convention. The Republican and Democratic party central committees established the process. Idaho Territory had eighteen counties, and the plan was to elect seventy-two delegates. The number of votes cast in the 1888 general election would determine the apportionment of the delegates. However, only Custer and Owyhee counties held popular elections. Party central committees appointed delegates in ten counties, and local conventions chose delegates in six counties. The delegates met in Boise on July 4, 1899, to write a state constitution. Boise citizens paid for the convention in the hope that the new state legislature would reimburse them later.

There were thirty-eight Republican delegates, thirty-three Democrats, and one Labor Party member. Exactly half of the delegates (thirty-six) represented the five largest counties—Ada County, where Boise is located; Shoshone County, home of the Coeur d'Alene mining district; Bingham County (created in 1884 to counteract Mormon influence); Alturas County (the Wood River Mining District); and Latah County, home of Moscow and the University of Idaho. Historians have a complete transcription of the proceedings at their disposal. Published in 1912 by Idaho's venerable Caxton Press, the *Proceedings and Debates of the Constitutional Convention of Idaho 1889* (2 volumes) remains the key primary source for any discussion of the process that led to the Idaho state constitution.

Forty-two percent of the delegates were trained lawyers, thus providing a considerable pool of legal talent. At the same time, there was a danger that, as one delegate noted, "[a] large majority of the members are lawyers, and as quibbling and priddling is a part of their training, if not of their nature, the chances of an extended session are favorable." Two especially prominent lawyers were among this group. William Clagett represented Shoshone County. Clagett chaired the Constitutional Convention sessions and was probably the greatest orator among the delegates. Known as the "Silver-Tongued Orator of the West," Clagett had practiced law in Iowa and then enjoyed a career as a mining and criminal lawyer in Nevada and Colorado before coming to Idaho when gold was discovered in the Coeur d'Alenes in 1883. James Beatty from Alturas County was one of the best-known mining lawyers in the country. He came to Idaho during the Wood River Valley rush in 1882.[34]

The list of other delegates to the Idaho Constitutional Convention reads like a who's who of early Idaho history. Frank Steunenberg from Ada County became Idaho's fourth governor. His assassination in 1905 outside his Caldwell home led to one of the most colorful trials in Idaho history. Weldon B. Heyburn, a mining lawyer from Shoshone County who served as legal counsel for the influential Bunker Hill and Sullivan Mining and Smeltering Company, later served as U.S. senator from Idaho. Latah County delegate William McConnell was Idaho's third governor and his daughter, Mary, married William E. Borah. Another Latah delegate, Willis Sweet, was the first Idaho member of the House of Representatives. Many convention delegates became members of the Idaho state legislature and served as judges and in other positions.

Henrietta Skelton of the Women's Christian Temperance Union urged the convention delegates to include prohibition in the constitution. The convention delegates debated prohibition on July 15, and the section dealing with temperance was the first portion of the Idaho Constitution completed. The men on the convention floor tended to treat this issue with humor and declined to enact prohibition, instead approving language taken from the Republican Party national platform: "The first concern of all good government is the virtue and sobriety of the people and the purity of the home which all legislation should further by wise and well-directed efforts for the promotion of temperance and morality."[35]

As would be expected from a convention with so many lawyer-delegates, the Idaho Constitution includes sections that impact the court system. The territorial supreme court included three justices that the president appointed. Each of the supreme court justices presided as district judge in one of the three judicial districts and had to be a resident in that district. Thus, if someone appealed a district court ruling, the justice who had issued the ruling would sit on the appeals court. Many of the lawyers at the convention resented this, along with the fact that the presidential appointment of these judges had led to no judicial continuity in Idaho. There were eleven chief justices of the Idaho territorial supreme court between 1863 and 1889 and fifteen associate justices. The system was obviously politicized, and during the territorial period, the Democratic legislature often remonstrated against Republican judicial appointees. In response to their criticism of the territorial system, the Idaho delegates provided for the election of supreme court justices.[36]

William Clagett was a reformer in the area of juries. He thought that majority decisions as opposed to unanimous decisions would improve the judicial system. This was hotly debated, but eventually Clagett won. The Idaho Constitution provides for five-sixths verdicts in misdemeanor cases, and delegates approved that stipulation by a vote of 31-21. A three-fourths majority in civil cases required only a voice vote.[37]

While early commentators on the Idaho Constitution pointed to its reiteration of the sanctity of private property, recent observers see a more complicated story. Eminent domain—the government's right to take property for public use if compensation is paid, even if the property owner does not wish to sell—was an established principle. However, Section 14 of the Idaho Constitution provides for the taking of private property for private use in certain situations, especially when it would further the development goals of mining and irrigation.[38]

In the light of current discussions regarding the separation of church and state, the delegates' discussion of Bible reading is of interest. The proposal was that "[n]o sectarian or religious tenets or doctrines shall ever be taught in the public schools." This phrase was part of the territorial law. Just before the Idaho convention, the territorial superintendent of public instruction had decided that Bible reading in public schools violated this rule. William McConnell and others thought that local school officials should have the right to read the Bible if the community residents were so inclined. The debate over Bible reading crossed party lines and was contentious, to say the least. A motion to make it constitutional to read the Bible in schools was eventually defeated, 25 opposed and 23 in favor.[39]

No topic is of greater import in the arid West than water, and the delegates to the Idaho Constitutional Convention were acutely aware of the significance of their debates involving water rights. As Edgar Wilson from Ada pointed out, "But God does not sprinkle these plains, and so they are absolutely barren waste, and without water never can be used."[40]

Indians in the region knew that water was central to their culture. The Nez Perce had established fishing rights before the Euro-American incursions began and the Shoshone and Bannock tribes used the Snake River waters. As indicated above, the first irrigation use of Idaho water was by the missionary Henry Spalding, as part of his attempt to alter the basic lifestyle of the Nez Perce to match more closely white expectations. Mormons launched the second irrigation experience in Lemhi County, and irrigation was part of the permanent Church of Jesus Christ of Latter-day Saints settlement at Franklin. Mining required large amounts of water. Water was needed for sluice boxes and placer mining, as well as in more sophisticated hydraulic mining and hardrock mining operations. Therefore, in Mormon settlements and mining camps, systems did develop to resolve conflicts around water issues. Many Idaho miners came from California and brought with them practices established there. Based on the Spanish tradition, miners utilized the principle of prior appropriation. Mormon settlements followed the Utah practice of the community use of water and the ability of the local bishop to resolve any controversies.

The Idaho convention debated what remains an essential issue in water law: whether priority or prior appropriation—first in time, first in right—should be the defining consideration or if the common law idea of riparian rights (often used in the East) should define water rights. Under the riparian principle, those who own land through which a water source runs have rights to that water. Several delegates to the Idaho Constitutional Convention were already involved in a water rights case that was at the territorial supreme court at the time of the convention. The court had taken *Drake v. Earhart* under advisement. The case dealt with water in Quigley Gulch, near Hailey (close to the present-day Sun Valley ski resort). Plaintiffs based their claim on prior use, and the defendants argued a riparian right.

The committee that worked on water rights was named "Manufactures, Agriculture, and Irrigation," but there is no doubt that irrigation was the main topic. The committee members represented southern Idaho counties where irrigation was an issue. William McConnell of Latah County was the only delegate from north of the Salmon River. McConnell had himself dug one of the earliest ditches in Idaho Territory, and he became the major spokesperson for the water rights segment of the constitution. The committee proposed the priority principle—first in time, first in right. However, it went on to suggest a hierarchy of preferred uses: first domestic use, then agricultural, then manufacturing. Isaac Coston of Ada County argued for the agricultural preference, "If the water power of this country can be used to prevent irrigation of the country, if it can be held by virtue of a prior right, good-bye to all the prosperity that we expect to come from the use of the water in irrigating our plains and developing this country."[41] Conversely, James Beatty attempted to make a case that manufacturing should not be excluded. He said, "Here you will give the farmer, we claim, more preference right to all the water of that stream, and shut down a manufacturing establishment that may employ a hundred families in carrying on its business. You will destroy the interests and rights of a hundred families in order to benefit one agriculturalist."[42] Agricultural priority won out over pure priority, in a vote of 26-16. Article 14, Section 3, of the Idaho Constitution reads:

> [W]hen the waters of any natural stream are not sufficient for the service of all those desiring the use of the same, those using the water for domestic purposes shall (subject to such limitations as may be prescribed by law) have the preference over those claiming for any other purpose; and those using the water for agricultural purposes shall have preference over those using the same for manufacturing purposes.

However, the convention delegates then diluted the agricultural preference when they added that agricultural preference could not be exercised without due process and without compensation.[43]

Mining interests were powerful at the Idaho Constitutional Convention and they worked to make certain that the agricultural preference water section of the constitution would not inhibit their activities. Most delegates believed that mining and agricultural uses were not in competition because of the geographic location of each pursuit. They therefore added: "And in any organized mining district those using the water for mining purposes or for milling purposes connected with mining, shall have preference over those using the same for manufacturing and agricultural purposes."[44]

Along with water issues, determining who would be allowed to vote in the new state was one of the most important topics the delegates considered. They discussed whether women should receive the suffrage, a topic the Idaho Territorial Legislature had also explored. Dr. Joseph Williams Morgan introduced a suffrage bill in the House of Representatives in 1871. The bill was defeated in a roll call vote when the House deadlocked, 11-11. The Territorial Legislature did allow unmarried female taxpayers to vote in school taxation elections in 1879. Six years later, women's voting expanded to include school board elections, and women were allowed to hold elected school office.

In a remarkable set of events, the Idaho Constitutional Convention delegates heard addresses from two proponents of women's suffrage with very different viewpoints. Henrietta Skelton was president of the Idaho branch of the Women's Christian Temperance Union, which had formed in Boise in 1883. By 1889, the group was well established and was holding its own annual convention in Boise at the same time as the constitutional convention. In her short speech to the delegates, Skelton explained that temperance was her major concern, but that she and other WCTU members believed that votes for women would facilitate their prohibition activities. She said, "We come to you with a new voice today of the motherhood, of the sisterhood, of the womanhood, asking you to place in that constitution something which shall be a weapon to the dear women of the land to protect our homes … ." Henrietta Skelton appealed to the higher nature of the delegates and concluded her address with a presentation of a bouquet to the convention. Another member of the WCTU invited the delegates to an ice cream social.[45]

Abigail Scott Duniway also petitioned the convention to include a women's suffrage plank, but that is where any similarity between the Duniway and Skelton appeals ended. It would not have occurred to Abigail Scott Duniway either to present the delegates with flowers or to invite them for ice cream. Duniway had been working for women's suffrage in the Pacific Northwest for twenty years. She had edited the *New Northwest,* a suffrage paper; she was active in the National American Woman Suffrage Association; and she had been a frequent speaker on the suffrage circuit. Abigail Scott Duniway was a forceful orator, and her speech expressed her firm conviction that women's suffrage was a matter of natural rights, not a boon the convention delegates could bestow. She reminded the convention that "governments derive their just powers from the consent of the governed." She disagreed stridently with Henrietta Skelton's position that temperance and women's suffrage were connected. Duniway had a long record of opposing the combination of suffrage and temperance. Washington's experience provided support for her position, since Washington women received the vote, only to have it rescinded after women had worked to pass a prohibition law. The delegates voted against the women's suffrage plank, 36-20.[46]

The Idaho Constitution also denied suffrage to "Chinese and persons of Mongolian descent" who were not born in the United States and to Indians who were "not taxed [and] who have not severed their tribal relations and adopted the habits of civilization." Idaho had a considerable Chinese population, first attracted to the southern Idaho mining booms (northern Idaho miners kept Chinese out of the Coeur d'Alenes). The 1870 census reported 4,272 Chinese residents; only California had a larger Chinese population. The Chinese Exclusion Act of 1882 made the Idaho constitutional ban on non-native Chinese unnecessary until it was repealed in 1943. The Idaho Constitution stipulations regarding Indian citizenship did not follow the pattern of the U.S. government. The Dawes Act conferred citizenship on Indians who received allotments. The allotment process was underway on the Nez Perce Reservation when the constitutional convention deliberated. Clearly, the Idaho delegates did not want Indians to vote under any circumstances.[47]

Delegates from both political parties agreed that the Church of Jesus Christ of Latter-day Saints posed a threat in Idaho. Delegates considered language to guarantee freedom of religion, but not to the point of excusing "acts of licentiousness or justify[ing] polygamous or other pernicious practices, inconsistent with morality or the peace or safety of the State." Anti-Mormon sentiment was strong. On a voice vote, the delegates approved language to outlaw bigamy and polygamy. Weldon B. Heyburn (R–Shoshone) sought to have the Test Oath be part of the constitution. The Idaho territorial supreme court had ruled on two occasions that the Test Oath did not violate the First Amendment—in two cases, *Innis v. Bolton* and *Wooley v. Watkins*.[48]

The suffrage committee included four Republicans and three Democrats. Only two of them came from Mormon areas, F. W. Beane from Bingham County and Beatty from Alturas. Beane represented railroad interests, and Beatty, mining interests. Both groups were anti-Mormon. The entire issue became a political one, with Democrats claiming that the Republicans wanted to disenfranchise Mormons only because the Mormon church members were staunchly Democratic. One of the convention delegates, John Lewis of Oneida County, was a Josephite Mormon (later, the Reorganized Church of Jesus Christ of Latter-day Saints). The Josephites remained loyal to Joseph Smith, did not follow Brigham Young to Utah, and did not accept the doctrine of plural marriage. Another delegate, John Morgan from Bingham County, had served as chief justice of the territorial supreme court and had presided over prosecutions of Mormons under the Edmunds Act. He described the Church of Jesus Christ of Latter-day Saints as a theocracy seeking to overthrow the government of the United States. He warned the delegates, "And if we adopt a constitution here that will permit these Mormons by any hook or crook to come into this territory to vote, we can be overwhelmed and voted down within six months." Democrats did not defend the Mormons, since they had learned through ten years of territorial politics that this damaged their party's chances for electoral success. The committee report that included the ban on Mormon voting passed the convention, 42-10.[49]

Republicans indeed benefited from the oath, and Fred Dubois became the Idaho territorial delegate to Congress. In fact, the Mormon issue had larger ramifications. Mormon disenfranchisement allowed Idaho Republicans to take power from Democrats. If Idaho had been a Democratically controlled state, the Republican U.S. Congress might not have acted so quickly to grant statehood. Clearly, both political expediency and prejudice against Mormons informed the convention's actions.

Delegates to the constitutional convention appointed a committee to prepare an address to the people of Idaho to explain to them why they should ratify the constitution. The first half of the address enumerated the complaints Idahoans had against the territorial system. A primary one was the lack of say in the appointment of officials. The report particularly pointed out that governors who owed their appointments to Washington, D.C., often vetoed bills the territorial legislature had passed. The other area of concern was the turnover and Washington, D.C., control of the judiciary. The second part of the address turned to worries that state government would be more expensive than territorial government. The committee estimated that the state government would cost $138,125 (actual first year's expenses amounted to $196,449), in contrast to territorial government expenses of $84,365. The convention delegates claimed that this increase would be offset through the use of fees to pay local officials and a decline in educational costs because the federal government would provide lands to support public education.

The address noted that the constitutional convention had for the most part avoided partisanship. It reminded Idahoans that every county had delegates from both political parties. "This happy combination of political forces was reflected in the spirit which at every stage of its deliberations animated the convention." A major argument for statehood was that until Idaho became a member of the Union, its residents were not full citizens of the United States.[50]

Despite this address, the convention did not provide a mechanism for ratification. Governor Shoup issued a proclamation calling for a ratification election on October 2, 1889, with county commissioners conducting the election and providing funds for the said election. Wrangling over the funding and organizational aspects of the election continued.

THE RATIFICATION OF THE CONSTITUTION

Greater economic development opportunities were a significant inducement for statehood. If Idaho became a state, it would no longer be under the Alien Land Act that banned foreign investment in the territories. As a state, Idaho would be entitled to two senators and a member of the House of Representatives who could give voice to Idaho issues in Washington, D.C. Idahoans who favored development believed that the federal government could assist in three direct ways. Idaho silver producers and silver miners hoped that the government would issue paper money backed by silver. (Idaho had a significant People's Party or Populist contingent in 1892 and 1896.) Idaho lead producers, especially in the Coeur d'Alene Mining District, wanted tariffs on the importation of Mexican lead. Finally, Idaho farming interests hoped that the federal government would sponsor irrigation projects in the state.

Although there was no formal anti-statehood organization, there were geographic areas where opposition to statehood was noticeable. Mormons were one group. A significant number of people in the northern part of the state still hoped that annexation to Washington would be possible. Democrats tended to be less supportive of statehood because they feared that Republicans would dominate the new state government. Anti-statehood people claimed that Idaho's population was not large enough to support a state government. In fact, there was considerable disagreement as to what the actual population of Idaho Territory was. The 1880 census counted 32,610. Governor Shoup claimed that there were 113,777 residents in Idaho Territory as part of his argument for statehood to the U.S. Congress. The 1890 census found 84,385 residents, many more than the 60,000 required under the terms of the Northwest Ordinance of 1787.[51]

Idaho voters ratified the constitution on November 5, 1889, by a vote of 12,398 to 1,775. The election itself had many irregularities. One observer noted, "The system of conducting the polls was of such an informal character that anything wearing hide, hair, feathers or boots could vote, and the result is such that no one believes half the returns sent in."[52] While some northern counties boasted support in the ninetieth percentile, only eighty-three voters cast ballots in Bear Lake County, a Mormon Center, and of those, only 53 percent voted yes. Annexation sentiment remained strong in Nez Perce County, still smarting over the "theft" of the capital from Lewiston in 1864. Two hundred and fifteen voters participated and slightly more than half favored ratification. In total, 14,190 votes were cast, 1,944 fewer ballots than in the 1888 territorial election.

FEDERAL ACTION ON STATEHOOD

Fred Dubois was the major player in terms of the work in the federal Congress on behalf of Idaho statehood. He was elected territorial representative to Congress in 1886 and reelected in 1888. A strident anti-Mormon, he achieved political notoriety through the prosecution of Mormon Edmunds Act violators. Dubois thought that if Congress approved Idaho statehood, he would receive the appointment as Idaho senator. Dubois realized that Idaho statehood would receive its greatest scrutiny in the Democratic House of Representatives. Dubois orchestrated the Senate to consider Idaho statehood first, where he believed support to be more likely.

Dubois himself garnered an appointment to the House Committee on Territories so that he would be well positioned to put forward Idaho's case. Everything seemed to be in order, but then there was trouble. Idaho was not the only territory seeking statehood in the Fifty-first Congress. North Dakota, South Dakota, Montana, and Washington had all held constitutional conventions during the summer of 1889. However, Congress had authorized these conventions in the Omnibus Act. Wyoming was also seeking statehood and it had held an unauthorized convention. Democrats, in the House especially, were worried about the large number of Republican states being admitted to the Union. Their strategy was to admit Republican Idaho and Wyoming only if Democratic New Mexico and Arizona were admitted at the same time.

The delay of Idaho admission was the result of the U.S. Supreme Court hearing *Davis v. Beason*. A member of the Church of Jesus Christ of Latter-day Saints, Samuel D. Davis, had taken the Test Oath and voted in the 1888 general election. He was subsequently indicted for perjury and convicted. Davis appealed unsuccessfully to the territorial supreme court and then to the U.S. Supreme Court claiming that the Test Oath represented a violation of the

First Amendment to the U.S. Constitution. This clearly had ramifications for the Idaho Constitution, because if the Supreme Court sided with Davis, the anti-Mormon sections of the Idaho Constitution would not meet the constitutionality test. Dubois wrote to Aaron F. Parker, "If their decision is adverse, of course we are done. If not, it ends all objection on that score. I shall not ask for statehood unless we can keep the Mormons out of our politics. In fact I would oppose it."[53]

Republican Senator Orville H. Platt from Connecticut introduced Idaho's first admission bill on December 8, 1889. It was referred to the Committee on Territories, and Dubois testified in favor of statehood. His testimony included glowing reports on the status of Idaho's economy and people and a unanimously supported memorial from the Idaho legislature urging admission. The legislators did note, "the only drawback to the statement of our high prosperity and great future promise, we confess with mortification, is the settlement within the Territory of colonies of ignorant and fanatical Mormons, anti-American in precept and practice." The Idahoans assured the Congress that Mormons would not control the state.[54] Dubois also introduced an Idaho statehood bill in the House of Representatives on December 18.

The Senate territorial committee postponed its January hearings regarding Idaho statehood in the hopes that the Supreme Court would issue a decision in *Davis v. Beason*. Governor Shoup and former governor Stevenson spoke on behalf of statehood. William Budge, a Mormon bishop, addressed the committee on both January 13 and 14 and argued against Idaho statehood. Dubois rebutted Mormon claims that Idaho should not be admitted on the grounds of insufficient population, extravagant salaries for state officials, and Mormon disenfranchisement. The U.S. Supreme Court affirmed Davis's conviction on February 3, 1890. This made Mormon arguments that the Idaho State Constitution violated their First Amendment Rights moot. The Senate Committee on Territories gave the Idaho statehood bill a favorable report on February 18.

The Wyoming bill passed the House on March 26 by a vote of 139 to 127. The House considered Idaho statehood on April 2 and 3. The Mormon question was significant in the federal congressional debate as well with Democratic representatives Charles H. Mansur (Missouri), J. Logan Chipman (Michigan), and William C. Oates (Alabama), claiming that the Idaho Constitution denied citizens the natural right of suffrage. The final vote was 129 to 1 in favor of admitting Idaho, but fifty-seven of the Democrats present abstained from voting. The House bill reached the Senate on April 5 but was tabled. Ironically, the Senate's time was taken up with debate over the silver question, an issue dear to the heart of Idahoans. Finally on June 27, the Senate approved the Wyoming bill, 29-18. Although senators voiced arguments similar to those presented in the house, Idaho admission was granted without a roll call vote.[55]

Fred Dubois thought it would be appropriate for President Harrison to sign the Idaho statehood bill on July 4. However, stars were added to the flag only once a year on July 4. Consequently, the president signed the Idaho bill on July 3, and Dubois telegraphed to Idaho: "Turn the Eagle Loose."[56]

CONCLUSION: THE NEW STATE OF IDAHO

Voters went to the polls to elect state officers on October 1, 1890, and Republicans emerged victorious. The new state legislature met in Boise from December 8, 1890, to March 14, 1891. George L. Shoup became Idaho's first state governor and Willis Sweet, who had successfully bargained for the university to be established in Moscow, was elected to the U.S. House of Representatives. Sectional differences continued, and the legislature could not decide on the requisite two senators. In fact, the first Idaho legislature chose four senators, three of whom actually served. Both political parties had promised northern Idaho residents that one senator would be from that part of the state. Fred Dubois, who assumed he would be one of Idaho's first senators, asked the Senate Judiciary Committee if Idaho could elect three senators—one for a full term and then two who would split a term. Dubois received one of the senate seats, and George L. Shoup and William McConnell were to split the other. Upon their arrival in Washington, the two drew lots. When McConnell drew the first, abbreviated term, northerners concluded that they had again come out on the short end. The Idaho legislature then elected William Clagett to Dubois' seat. Clagett went to Washington, D.C., but was not able to convince the Senate to unseat Dubois. Shoup, who resigned the governorship after having successfully presided over the transition from territory to state, ended up serving from 1890 to 1900. His is one of the two statues in Statuary Hall, along with the one of Idaho senator William E. Borah, that commemorate prominent Idahoans.[57]

The first state legislators further recognized the continued sectional animosity through other attempts to ameliorate it. They confirmed that Boise would serve as the Idaho state capital and that Moscow would be the site of the state university. The University of Idaho opened on October 3, 1892. The legislature mandated that the Idaho state supreme court hold some of its sessions in Lewiston as well as in Boise.

Although Mormons challenged the Test Oath all the way to the U.S. Supreme Court, on February 3, 1890, the Court ruled in *Davis v. Beason* that the oath was constitutional. Wilford Woodruff, president of the Church of Jesus Christ of Latter-day Saints, ordered all Mormons to comply with civil law regarding marriage in September 1890, thus ostensibly eliminating a major roadblock to Idaho citizenship for Mormons. Nonetheless, Idaho's first legislature barred church members from the polls. Although the Idaho legislature did end most restrictions on Mormon civic activity and repealed the Test Oath on February 3, 1893, the Idaho Constitution was not changed to reflect this until 1982. Even then, some counties voted in opposition to this constitutional change.[58]

After a relatively low-key campaign, residents of every Idaho county except Custer voted in favor of women's suffrage in November 1896. Idaho joined Wyoming, Colorado, and Utah as suffrage states. Washington women received the vote in 1910, and Oregon women, in 1912. Historians are divided as to how to explain this. In part, the Mormon Church, with its large number of women, was anxious to extend the franchise to them. Regionalism also reared its head. Southern Idaho farmers and families believed that the male miners in northern Idaho represented an unsavory interest in Idaho politics. Idaho's constitution was not amended to allow foreign-born Chinese to vote until 1962.[59]

At about the time that white Idahoans were contemplating statehood, the U.S. Congress passed the General Allotment Act (Dawes Severalty Act) in 1887. Ostensibly designed to encourage Indians to assimilate into the majority culture, the Dawes Act sought to facilitate the transformation of the Indian lifestyle to an agrarian one. The Dawes Act reduced the size of reservation lands, thus allowing whites access to even more property. In the case of the Coeur d'Alenes, the 638 remaining tribal members each received 160 acres of land, but about three-fourths of the former reservation became available for white settlement. An Oklahoma-like land grab was staged on the Nez Perce Reservation on November 18, 1895. The government compensated the Nez Perce with five installment payments, for a total of $1.6 million. The U.S. government passed the Indian Citizenship Act in 1924. However, Idaho did not amend its constitution to end Indian disenfranchisement until 1950.[60]

In 1916, Idahoans voted 90,576 to 35,456 in favor of a prohibition amendment to the Idaho Constitution, and Idaho remained dry even after the repeal of the Eighteenth amendment. Although the framers of the Idaho Constitution had taken steps to prohibit Bible reading in public schools, in 1925 the Idaho legislature passed a law that required the practice of Bible reading each morning and no one challenged it until 1963.[61]

Following the Idaho Constitutional Convention, James Beatty was named to the Idaho supreme court and wrote the opinion in *Drake v. Earhart*. The case is a landmark one in Idaho water law, and it was most certainly informed by the discussion at the convention and Beatty's position there. Beatty had favored pure prior appropriation at the convention and did so in the opinion as well. He held that "the maxim, 'first in time, first in right'" was the law in Idaho. Of course, the Idaho Constitution included exceptions to this notion.

Since the ratification of the Idaho Constitution, the biggest controversy involving water has been how to view hydroelectric power development within the context of the constitution. This is even more complex because often Idaho state agencies are pitted against federal government agencies over water rights tied to hydroelectric development. The adjudication of all water rights in the Snake River drainage began in 1984. The Idaho Constitution continues to be the touchstone in one of the largest debates in Idaho in the twenty-first century.[62]

There was a movement for a revised Idaho Constitution in 1965 in line with efforts in several states to modernize their constitutions. Voters considered this new constitution on November 3, 1970. They voted overwhelming in opposition to the changes, 220,204 (66 percent) to 75,138 (34 percent). Even after eighty years, Idahoans continued to support their original constitution.[63]

NOTES

1. Dorothy Dutton and Caryl Humphries, *A Rendezvous with Idaho History* (Boise, ID: Sterling Ties Publications, 2000), p. 20.
2. *Boise Daily Statesman,* July 16, 1889.
3. *New York Daily Tribune,* December 11, 1875.
4. "Idaho's Indian Population in 1800," *Idaho Historical Society Reference Series* 29 (December 1964); Deward E. Walker Junior, *Indians of Idaho* (Moscow: University of Idaho Press, 1978), p. 1357.
5. Gary E. Moulton, ed., *The Definitive Journals of Lewis and Clark*, Vol. 5, *Through the Rockies to the Cascades* (Lincoln: University of Nebraska Press, 1988, paperback, 2002), pp. 109, 114, 122, 144, 196–230.
6. Nimíipuu (Nez Perce)—Lifelong Learning on line in Collaboration with Nimíipuu, an e-publication, Nez Perce Tribe, University of Idaho, the National Aeronautics and Space Administration, 2002; available at www.13-lewisandclark.com.
7. See, for example, Hiram M. Chittendon, *The American Fur Trade of the Far West*, 2 vols. (Stanford: Academic Reprints, 1954).
8. Henry H. Spalding and Asa Bowen Smith, *The Diaries and Letters of Henry H. Spalding and Asa Bowen Smith Relating to the Nez Perce Mission, 1838–1842*, Clifford M. Drury, ed. (Glendale, CA: Arthur H. Clark, 1958).
9. Schitsu'umsh (Coeur d'Alenes)—Lifelong Learning on line in Collaboration with Schitsu'umsh, an e-publication, Coeur d'Alene Tribe, University of Idaho, the National Aeronautics and Space Administration, 2002; *Wilderness Kingdom: The Journals and Painting of Father Nicholas Point* (New York: Holt, Rinehart, and Winston, 1967); *Life, Letters and Travels of Father Pierre-Jean DeSmet, S.J., 1801–1873*, 4 vols. (New York: Francis P. Harper, 1905; reprint, New York: Kraus Reprint Company, 1969).
10. John D. Nash, "The Salmon River Mission of 1855," *Idaho Yesterdays* 11 (Spring 1967): 22–31.
11. 9 Stat. 869.
12. John C. Frémont, *The Exploring Expedition to the Rocky Mountains* (Washington, DC: Smithsonian Institution Press, 1945; reprint, 1988).
13. U.S. War Department, *Reports of Explorations and Surveys to Ascertain the Most Practicable and Economic Route for a Railroad from the Mississippi River to the Pacific Ocean*, 12 vols. (Washington, DC: U.S. Government Printing Office, 1855–1860).
14. John Mullan, *Miners' and Travelers' Guide to Oregon, Washington, Idaho, Montana, Wyoming, and Colorado* (New York: William M. Franklin, 1865).
15. See, for example, John Mack Faragher, *Women and Men on the Oregon Trail* (New Haven: Yale University Press, 1979).
16. 10 Stat. 172; 11 Stat. 383.

17. Treaty with the Nez Perces, 1855, *Indian Affairs: Laws and Treaties*, vol. 2, *Treaties*, Charles J. Kappler, comp. and ed. (Washington, DC: Government Printing Office, 1904), pp. 702–706.

18. E. D. Pierce, *The Pierce Chronicle: Personal Reminiscences of E.D. Pierce as transcribed by Lou A. Larrick*, J. Gary Williams and Ronald W. Stark, eds. (Moscow: Idaho Research Foundation, n.d.), and Merle W. Wells, *Gold Camps and Silver Cities: Nineteenth Century Mining in Central and Southern Idaho* (Moscow: Idaho Department of Lands/Bureau of Mines and Geology, 1983).

19. *Idaho Statesman*, September 17, 1870.

20. Larry Jones, "Battle of Bear River, January 29, 1863," *Idaho State Historical Society Reference Series* 235; available at www.idahohistory.net.

21. Treaty with the Nez Perces, 1863, *Indian Affairs: Laws and Treaties*, vol. 2, *Treaties*, Charles J. Kappler, comp. and ed. (Washington, DC: Government Printing Office, 1904), pp. 843–848. A remarkable set of documents is Dennis Baird, Diane Mallickan, and W. R. Swagerty, eds., *The Nez Perce Nation Divided: Firsthand Accounts of Events Leading to the 1863 Treaty* (Moscow: University of Idaho Press, 2002); *Congressional Globe*, 37th Cong., 3rd Sess., 1863, p. 1542.

22. *Congressional Globe*, 38th Cong., 1st Sess., December 14, 1863–May 27, 1864, p. 1168; Merle W. Wells, "The Creation of the Territory of Idaho," *Pacific Northwest Quarterly* 40 (April 1940): 106–123.

23. Quoted in Merrill D. Beal and Merle W. Wells, *History of Idaho* (New York: Lewis Historical Publishing, 1959), vol. 1, p. 378.

24. Ronald H. Limbaugh, *Rocky Mountain Carpetbaggers: Idaho's Territorial Governors, 1863–1890* (Moscow: University of Idaho Press, 1982); and Robert C. Sims and Hope A. Benedict, *Idaho Governors: Historical Essays on Their Administrations* (Boise: College of Social Science and Public Affairs, Boise State University, 1992), pp. 211–222.

25. Quoted in L. V. McWhorter, *Hear Me, My Chiefs: Nez Perce History and Legend* (Caldwell, ID: Caxton Printers, 1983), p. 498; Joseph, Nez Perce Chief, *Chief Joseph's Own Story*, 1879 (reprint, Fairfield, WA: Ye Galleon Press, 1972).

26. See Clark D. Spence, *For Wood River or Bust: Idaho's Silver Boom of the 1880s* (Moscow: University of Idaho Press, 1999).

27. Dallas E. Livingston-Little, *Economic History of North Idaho, 1800–1900* (Los Angeles: Journal of the West, 1965), pp. 86–88; William Stoll, *Silver Strike: A True Story of Silver Mining in the Coeur d'Alenes* (reprint, Moscow: University of Idaho Press, 1991); Richard Magnuson, *Coeur d'Alene Diary* (Portland: Binford and Mort, 1968).

28. Merle Wells, *Anti-Mormonism in Idaho, 1872–92* (Provo, UT: Brigham Young University Press, 1978).

29. General Laws of the Territory of Idaho, Thirteenth Session.

30. *Salt Lake Tribune*, November 28, December 19, 1888.

31. Fourteenth Territorial Legislature, *Journal of the Council*, p. 18.

32. *Congressional Record*, 50th Cong., 2nd Sess., 1888–1889, pp. 121, 223, 1253, 1909.

33. I. W. Hart, ed., *Proceedings and Debates of the Constitutional Convention of Idaho, 1889* (Caldwell, ID: Caxton Printers, 1912), pp. 2097–3011.

34. "The Spirit of State," *Caldwell Tribune*, July 13, 1889; Dennis Colson, *Idaho's Constitution: The Tie That Binds* (Moscow: University of Idaho Press, 1991), pp. 6–14.

35. *Proceedings*, p. 118.

36. Ibid., pp. 1519–1520, 2092.

37. Ibid., pp. 259–260.

38. Ibid., pp. 1596–1633.

39. Ibid., pp. 688, 1443.

40. Ibid., p. 1359.

41. Ibid., p. 1123.

42. Ibid., p. 1117.

43. Ibid., p. 1364.

44. Ibid., p. 1156.

45. Ibid., p. 89.

46. Ibid., pp. 164–165; 913.

47. Ibid., p. 914.

48. *Innis v. Bolton*, 2 Idaho 442, 17 Pac. 264 (1888); *Wooley v. Watkins*, 2 Idaho 590, 22 Pac.102 (1889).

49. *Proceedings*, p. 1041.

50. Ibid., p. 2095.

51. *Statistics of Population of the United States at the Tenth Census (June 1, 1880)* (Washington, DC: Government Printing Office); *Compendium of the Eleventh Census: 1890*, 52 Cong., 1 Sess., House Misc. Doc. no. 340, pt. 6 (Washington, DC: Government Printing Office, 1892), p. 2.

52. *News-Miner*, November 15, 1889, quoted in Colson, *Idaho's Constitution*, p. 219.

53. Quoted in *Ketchum Keystone*, December 28, 1889.

54. *Admission of Idaho, Arizona, and Wyoming into the Union*, Report no. 4053, February 13, 1889, 50th Cong., 2nd Sess., House of Representatives, Committee on Territories, Dubois testimony, pp. 54–57.

55. *Congressional Record*, 50th Cong., 2nd Sess., 1889–1890, pp. 2927–2952; 6832–6834.

56. *Idaho Statesman*, July 3–4, 1890; Merle W. Wells, "The Admission of the State of Idaho," *Secretary of State Twenty-Seventh Biennial Report*, 1944.

57. Margaret Lauterbach, "A Plentitude of Senators," *Idaho Yesterdays* 21 (Fall 1977): 2–8.

58. 1895 Idaho Sess. Laws, pp. 37–39.

59. 1895 Idaho Sess. Laws 232, SJR, no. 2, ratified November 1896; 1961 Idaho Sess. Laws 1073, S.J.R., no. 1, ratified November 6, 1962.

60. 1949 Idaho Sess. Laws 597, H.J.R., no. 2, ratified November 1950.

61. 1925 Idaho Sess. Laws, pp. 48–49.

62. *Drake v. Earhart*, 2 Idaho 750, 23 P. 541 (1890).

63. Colson, *Idaho's Constitution*, p. 229.

BIBLIOGRAPHY

Arrington, Leonard J. *History of Idaho*. 2 vols. Moscow: University of Idaho Press, 1994.

Beal, Merrill D., and Merle W. Wells. *History of Idaho*. 3 vols. New York: Lewis Historical Publishing Company, 1959.

Colson, Dennis G. *Idaho's Constitution: The Tie That Binds*. Moscow: University of Idaho Press, 1991.

Limbaugh, Ronald H. *Rocky Mountain Carpetbaggers: Idaho's Territorial Governors, 1863–1890*. Moscow: University Press of Idaho, 1982.

Peterson, F. Ross. *Idaho: A Bicentennial History*. New York: Norton, 1976.

Schwantes, Carlos. *In Mountain Shadows: A History of Idaho*. Lincoln: University of Nebraska Press, 1991.

Sims, Robert C., and Hope A. Benedict, eds. *Idaho's Governors: Historical Essays on Their Administrations*. Boise: Boise State University College of Social Sciences and Public Affairs, 1992.

Walker, Deward E., Jr. *Indians of Idaho*. Moscow: University of Idaho Press, 1978.

Wells, Merle W. "The Creation of the Territory of Idaho." *Pacific Northwest Quarterly* 40 (April 1940): 106–123.

———. *Anti-Mormonism in Idaho, 1872–92*. Provo, UT: Brigham Young University, 1978.

THE STATE OF ILLINOIS

Admitted to the Union as a State: December 3, 1818

Michael E. Meagher

INTRODUCTION

France held title to what is now Illinois until 1763. In that year, Great Britain assumed sovereignty over the area. With British rule came the establishment of the future Missouri city of St. Louis in 1763 by Pierre Laclede. However, a French community remained in what was now British territory. By the time the British Parliament adopted legislation providing for autonomy for the French settlers of Illinois, the American Revolution had begun. Under the terms of the Treaty of Paris in 1783, sovereignty over Illinois was assumed by the United States. Unofficially, prior to the Treaty of Paris, Virginia had been claiming control over this region.

In its acquisition of Illinois, the United States assumed responsibility for an area of ethnic diversity. French settlers, Native Americans, African Americans, and white settlers from the South were part of this small community. Although it was in decline, the French culture in the 1780s had established a climate of toleration of other ethnic groups that was not typical of the newly organized United States of America.

The French influence on early Illinois was substantial. Settled by individuals from Quebec and France, Illinois, before the arrival of large numbers of Americans, was noted for its excellent relations with Native Americans and fair treatment of slaves. Particularly noteworthy was the French community's relations with Native Americans, in which not only economic ties were formed but also bonds of marriage. Marriage between settlers and Native Americans was quite common. In a general sense, the French community had a more tolerant and accepting attitude toward other ethnic groups. Although the French

Illinois

Territorial Development:

- Great Britain ceded future territory of Illinois to the United States through the Treaty of Paris, September 3, 1783
- The United States passed the Northwest Ordinance: territorial claims inherited from colonial charters ceded to the public domain; future Illinois Territory organized as part of the Northwest Territory, July 13, 1787
- Reorganized as a part of the Indiana Territory, 1800
- Reorganized as the Illinois Territory, February 3, 1809
- Illinois admitted into the Union as the twenty-first state, December 3, 1818

Territorial Capitals:

- Kaskasia, 1809–1818

State Capitals:

- Kaskasia, 1818–1820
- Vandalia, 1820–1839
- Springfield, 1839–present

Origin of State Name: "Illinois" is the French spelling of an Indian word, *ilini*, which means "man" or "warrior."

First Governor: Edward Coles
Governmental Organization: Bicameral
Population at Statehood: 55,211
Geographical Size: 55,584 square miles

did have slaves, French treatment of slaves was much more humane than that of the Americans.

The French community's manner of living did cause conflict with the American settlers. Not only did intermarriage and treatment of slaves cause tension between the Americans and the French, but the Roman Catholicism of the French settlers was also an issue. The Catholic faith of the French clashed with the frontier faith traditions of the American settlers. Eventually, French influence in Illinois faded. However, many small towns in present-day southern Illinois have French origins. Columbia, Illinois, was Grand Ruisseau while nearby Waterloo was known as Bellefontaine.

Because of Virginia's prior claim, Illinois, under the United States, became part of Virginia. When Virginia extended its political control over Illinois, it was respectful of the area's French heritage. The government of Virginia allowed the newly created County of Illinois to retain the French legal code and several of the offices that had existed prior to Virginia's assumption of sovereignty. One change that did spark some dissension among the French was new regulations to deal with slavery. The Americans viewed the French as too lax in their treatment of the slaves of Illinois. Virginia was determined to change that condition. Its efforts only hastened the movement of the French settlers out of Illinois. Eventually, because of challenges created by extending its control over such a long distance, Virginia transferred its political control over Illinois to the national government.

With the disappearance of the French influence, conditions in Illinois changed dramatically. While conflicts remained in Illinois life and politics, the nature of the disputes reflected the inherent tensions of the newly created United States. Slavery in the South and the proper relationship between the states and the national government became prominent issues. The tolerance that was evident during the period of large-scale French settlement gave way to the realities of a territory and later a state with southern values regarding politics and in some measure, slavery.

Although geographically a northern state, Illinois, at statehood, was in sentiment a southern state with southern aristocrats holding the new state's political offices. In fact, from its days as a territory under American sovereignty, Illinois looked to the South for settlers as well as leaders. With the northern section of the state remote and difficult to populate, southern Illinois was the center of decision-making involving the new state's future. At this early date, Chicago was unsettled and not necessarily seen as part of Illinois, while the old French village of Kaskaskia, near St. Louis, was the area's largest city.

Politically and socially, southern attitudes regarding slavery and national issues were dominant in Illinois. Very few individuals from New England settled in territorial Illinois. Kentucky and Virginia provided the largest number of settlers for Illinois. In political terms, this meant that Illinois residents and politicians, though favorably minded toward the South, could not advocate slavery for the territory. As long as the territory dreamed of admission to the Union it could not contemplate slavery, for this would harm Illinois' chances in the federal Congress. This conundrum notwithstanding, slavery was an undercurrent of Illinois politics, and following statehood there would be a movement to amend the Illinois Constitution to provide for the ownership of slaves.

Nationally, the southern influence was restricted by the terms established when the area was acquired by the United States following the Revolutionary War. While Virginia had political jurisdiction over Illinois, Virginia's Act of Cession transferred authority to the national government. Understandably, debate ensued over how to govern this large area. Although Thomas Jefferson had elaborate plans for the territory within which Illinois was to exist, even envisioning the creation of ten new states, the blueprint for the newly acquired territories was set with the enactment of the Northwest Ordinance. Becoming law on July 13, 1787, the Northwest Ordinance defined the requirement for territorial status, statehood, and organization of the areas of the Northwest. The ordinance declared that "there shall be formed in the said territory, not less than three nor more than five states," protected the basic rights of residents, prohibiting the suspension of habeas corpus, defining a right to trial by jury, and prohibiting "cruel and unusual punishments." Freedom of religion was established as a fundamental right. James Monroe is often mentioned as the author of the document, but this is not certain. He did, however, make a fact-finding trip to the new territories before the ordinance was penned. Of northern Illinois and its massive prairie, Monroe would say that the area had unpromising prospects for future development.[1] Although history would prove him wrong on this point, Monroe enhanced northern Illinois' development prospects by prohibiting slavery in the Old Northwest. The ordinance's ban on slavery would be crucial in Illinois' march to statehood and beyond.

It would take several years before the Northwest Ordinance had an impact on Illinois. Conditions in the Northwest were chaotic. Conditions in Illinois, on the edge of the Northwest, were even more severe. Although adopted by Congress in 1787, it would take another three years before the rudimentary elements of a civil administration could be established. On March 5, 1790, Arthur St. Clair was named governor of the Northwest Territories by the president, George Washington. St. Clair, who had served as a member and president of the Continental Congress, went to his new assignment with great aspirations. One of his first actions was to visit Kaskaskia and Cahokia, and then establish the first county in Illinois. Modestly, he named the county St. Clair and appointed his brother, William, as county clerk.[2]

The Northwest Ordinance established three levels of political maturity for the eventual states: first stage, second stage, and statehood. Initially, the Northwest Territory operated under conditions of first-stage government, with limited opportunities for political involvement by citizens. Officeholders consisted of a governor, secretary, and three judges. In preparing legislation for the area, the officeholders were limited to the range of laws currently on the books in the existing states. Moreover, their actions had to be transmitted to the federal Congress, where modifications or outright rejection could take place. In time, the territory was eligible for second-stage governance, which provided for greater opportunities for self-government. To attain this level, an area needed "five-thousand male residents of full age."[3]

Providing for more opportunities for political involvement, the second level most notably authorized a legislative branch for the territory. A House of Representatives, elected by the white male population, and a Legislative Council, selected on the basis of property requirements, formed the legislative bodies of the new territories. To achieve statehood, each state "shall have 60,000 free inhabitants" and adopt a constitution that "shall be republican and in conformity to these articles."[4] A major step for statehood was taken in 1800, when second-stage government was adopted for Indiana, which at that time included Illinois.[5]

William Henry Harrison played a central role in the development of the present-day states of Indiana and Illinois. With its capital in Vincennes, Indiana was recognized by the federal Congress in Washington in 1800 as having reached territorial status. Harrison, in his capacity as delegate to Congress for the Northwest Territory, worked behind the scenes to build support for a new territorial government. Achieving victory, Harrison returned to the territory to become its governor. Although the territory carried the name of Indiana, it was a substantial piece of territory, containing the present-day states of Illinois, Indiana, Wisconsin, and parts of Michigan. Harrison's job of governor was very difficult, as residents of Illinois objected to the faraway new territorial capital, Vincennes. In addition, some members of the Illinois community called for legalization of slavery within Illinois, while others agitated against Harrison, calling him indifferent to the needs of Illinois. Shortly after the acquisition of the Louisiana Territory from France in 1803, some Illinois residents publicly advocated separating from Indiana and becoming part of the newly acquired Louisiana Purchase.[6]

Unhappiness with the Indiana territorial government, a long-term complaint in Illinois, made union with the territories of the Louisiana Purchase attractive. In 1803, Illinois residents called for Illinois to separate from the lands of the Old Northwest Territory. Without question, the Northwest Ordinance itself was a leading cause of this agitation. To be sure, dissatisfaction with Indiana was part of the equation. However, removing Illinois from Indiana and attaching it to the Louisiana Purchase would have removed the Northwest Ordinance's prohibition against slavery. As always, slavery was a constant undercurrent in early Illinois politics.[7]

The anti-slavery restriction in the Northwest Ordinance caused controversy during the territorial years. With French residents and their slaves living in the area between Kaskaskia and St. Louis, Illinois public figures were certain to focus on this issue. Many French residents, in fact, left Illinois, settling instead in the Louisiana Territory in what would become Missouri. In 1796, residents of Kaskaskia, the old French settlement on the Mississippi, called on Congress to reconsider the slavery component of the Northwest Ordinance. Four years later, in 1800, French residents, noting the migration of French settlers out of Illinois, asked for a revision. In 1805, under pressure from representatives from Illinois, the Indiana Territorial Legislature again asked Congress to amend the Northwest Ordinance. Two years later, over the signature of Jesse Burgess Thomas, another request was sent to Washington. Once again, the effort to amend the Northwest Ordinance failed.[8]

The loss of the French population had ramifications for the Native American residents of Illinois. Long accustomed to an active fur trade with the French communities of southern Illinois, the Native Americans of Illinois felt increasingly isolated. Unlike the French, white settlers in Illinois did not accept the various tribes of Illinois, nor were they willing to cooperate with them. The vulnerability of Native American tribes would lead to conflict in the territorial years and beyond.

TERRITORIAL STATUS

The movement to become a territorial government was difficult. Indiana opposed the creation of a separate Illinois, fearing this action would weaken Indiana's standing as a political unit. At the same time, these were years in which the early political elites would emerge in Illinois politics. Gaining territorial status placed Illinois on a path to statehood much faster than anyone at the time could have imagined. Despite this, the territorial years witnessed much conflict and turmoil.

Indiana's opposition to territorial status for Illinois was intense. Asserting that Illinois was part of the Indiana Territory and that separate status would be harmful to the interests of Indiana, Indiana's political leaders made their case in Washington, D.C. Local issues involving the status of the territorial capital in Vincennes was instrumental in creating and maintaining the opposition. Backroom political bargaining over the election of the territorial representative to Washington played a significant role in the process of giving territorial status to Illinois.

Residents of Vincennes, capital of the Indiana Territory, were mindful that a grant of territorial status to Illinois would threaten that city's hold as capital. With Illinois as a territory, many Indiana residents and political leaders would favor moving the capital to a more central location. Interestingly, the geographic location of Vincennes, near the Wabash River, was a factor in convincing Illinois political figures to press for territory status for Illinois. At this time, most Illinois residents lived along the Mississippi River, with concentrations in St. Clair County and the old French settlement of Kaskaskia. Travel from these areas in Illinois to Vincennes was exceedingly difficult. Civic figures in

Vincennes were aware of the stakes involved in separating Illinois from Indiana.[9]

A resident of Vincennes, Jesse Burgess Thomas, would play a major role in making Illinois a territory. Thomas, originally from Maryland and a former resident of Kentucky, became active in Indiana politics shortly after his arrival. Representing Dearborn County, Indiana, in the Territorial Legislature beginning in 1805, he gradually moved to political office. He was elected speaker of the legislature and formed a close friendship with the territorial governor, William Henry Harrison, who named him captain of the territorial militia. By 1808, residents of Illinois were making known their interest in separation. At the same time, Indiana residents were vocal in opposition to a division of the territory. Benjamin Parke, the representative for Indiana in Congress, reflected the wishes of many of his constituents in opposing the movement for Illinois territorial status.[10]

In 1809, Parke resigned as representative to Congress and an election to fill the vacancy was necessary. Thomas, despite his residency in Vincennes, desired to be elected to the post. Although he had served as speaker of the Territorial Assembly and as a member and officer of the militia, he could not win the office without the support of Illinois voters. However, Illinois political figures refused to support Thomas without securing a promise from him that he would support territorial status when elected to the office. Eventually, he gave a pledge in writing, and on the basis of support from Illinois, he was elected territorial representative to Congress. Thomas was now in the ironic position of living in Vincennes and serving as Indiana representative in Congress, but working on behalf of separating Illinois from the Indiana territory.[11]

On March 7, 1809, Congress approved the Enabling Act establishing the Territory of Illinois and Thomas was named as one of the new territorial judges of Illinois. Obviously, his political future in Indiana was over, so he settled near the new territorial capital of Illinois, Kaskaskia. In Indiana, Thomas was indeed unpopular. Governor Harrison faced constitutional challenges as a result of his delegate's behavior in Congress. The birth of the Illinois Territory reduced the size of the legislative bodies of Indiana, thus requiring some artful actions by Harrison to continue government. Illinois had now acquired its own identity legally, and the movement, though slow and challenging, was to statehood.

The constitutional challenges in Indiana following the creation of the Illinois Territory were extraordinary. The loss of representatives from Illinois meant that Indiana's legislative body was without its constitutionally mandated number of members. Governor Harrison tried to remedy the situation but only made the matter worse.

On April 3, 1809, as required by law, the eligible voters of Indiana elected members to serve in the legislative body of their truncated territory. With the loss of Illinois, however, only four members could be elected. Indiana law required at least nine members of the Territorial Assembly. To rectify this,

Harrison issued an emergency decree creating a new county and increasing the number of representatives from the remaining Indiana counties. While this seemed to satisfy the constitutional dilemma, it only made matters worse. Harrison's actions created only eight representatives, one short of the constitutional requirement. Harrison was bound by the Indiana Constitution, which provided for representation by counties. When Illinois became its own territory, Harrison was able to appoint only members from the remaining counties in Indiana, a number below the constitutional requirements. Therefore, when the special election to fill these offices was held on May 22, 1809, the legality of the Territorial Assembly was in doubt.[12]

In the fall of 1809, Indiana's Territorial Assembly met under a cloud of suspicion. Many members claimed they had no legal right to enact laws for the Indiana Territory, given the failure to reach the constitutionally specified number of nine members. To correct the trauma to Indiana's government caused by Illinois' territorial status, the Indiana legislators asked the U.S. Congress for authorization to create a new district and for approval of the actions of the governor, William Henry Harrison. The Congress responded by passing the required legislation, and once again an election was specified for the Territorial Assembly. In April 1810, elections were held in Indiana, and this time the results were regarded as valid.[13]

Family intrigue defined early Illinois politics, as many leading officials were related. Kentucky senator John Pope lobbied for the appointment of Ninian Edwards of Kentucky as the new governor. When Edwards became governor of the Illinois Territory, his cousin, Nathaniel Pope, nephew of Senator Pope of Kentucky, was already serving as territorial secretary of Illinois. A decade later, Daniel Pope Cook, the nephew of Nathaniel Pope and son-in-law of Ninian Edwards, would play a major role in achieving statehood for Illinois.

It was far from certain that Edwards would accept the office of territorial governor. His early career was spent in Kentucky. Endeavoring to build a political career in that state as well as enjoying himself socially, Edwards secured positions in the Kentucky government. In 1806, he became a judge in the Kentucky court of appeals. In 1808, Edwards was named chief justice of that state. Earlier, he had served as a Kentucky elector in the presidential election of 1804. Ironically, one of his colleagues from the Kentucky court, John Boyle, was named territorial governor of Illinois in 1809. When Boyle refused to take the less than attractive post of territorial governor of a wilderness area, Henry Clay lobbied President Madison to nominate Edwards. On April 24, 1809, Edwards was officially appointed territorial governor of Illinois. He became a fixture in that office, securing reappointment in 1812 and 1815.[14]

Ninian Edwards was the central figure in Illinois territorial politics. Born in 1775 in Maryland, he moved to Kentucky as a young man. A member of a prominent family from the East, he stayed in the new state of Kentucky until summoned by President James Madison to be governor of Illinois. As a wealthy individual and slave owner, Edwards was unable to immediately assume his duties as governor. Instead, he left his cousin, Territorial Secretary Nathaniel Pope, in charge of the territorial government until his slaves and family relocated to Illinois. As the new governor, Edwards was given one thousand acres in the American Bottom, an area of farmland near Kaskaskia and St. Louis. Edwards would be active in Illinois politics as late as 1830, when his aristocratic ways no longer fit the frontier conditions of a rapidly changing state. Under the territory and the state, he would serve as governor and senator and as the leader of a political faction opposed to the influence of Jesse Burgess Thomas.[15]

As territorial governor, Edwards presided over a major enhancement to Illinois government. In March 1812, he proposed an election on whether to move to second-stage government, an action to give the territory its own legislative bodies. The elections were held October 8–10, 1812. This was an inevitable move along the path of political development outlined by the Northwest Ordinance.

As the territory struggled to develop, some in Illinois felt that the territorial government should aim at statehood status. However, this objective was not viable. Illinois had difficulty attracting settlers. It was truly a wilderness area waiting to be developed. Yet at this early time, few believed Illinois would develop into a large and significant state. Much of the land was unavailable for settlement, the prairie lands of Illinois intimidated many potential settlers, and the northern part of the territory was largely untouched. Although the prairie would become a great agricultural region for the nation, at this time it was seen as impossible to tame. The prairie lands, with hard sod, could not be broken, and this convinced most farmers to avoid it. It would take international developments to nudge Illinois slowly in the direction of statehood.

Between 1810 and 1820, Illinois experienced a rapid increase in population. According to the 1810 census, Illinois contained 12,282 white residents. By 1820, the census results indicated that 55,211 whites resided in the state.[16] In large measure, the disruption caused by the War of 1812 influenced settlement patterns. During this conflict, the British, seeking to use the Native American communities as weapons against the United States, pledged to protect them from the United States and even promised a semi-independent nation-state. Naturally, these developments caused alarm in Illinois, with Governor Edwards calling for military action against the tribes of the territory. Illinois organized military forces to challenge the Native American residents in northern Illinois. A fort was established north of present-day Edwardsville (named for the governor), and the military forces were charged with guarding the areas with the highest levels of settlement. Battles were fought near Springfield and Peoria under his command. In 1813, he lost command of the military organization as William Henry Harrison was given a commission to command a military district including the Illinois Territory. Harrison, in turn, named the Missouri governor as commander of the military forces in Illinois. In response, Edwards left Illinois and named Nathaniel Pope as acting governor during his absence.

Edwards returned to the territory, of course, as many political battles would be fought in the coming years, most notably the effort for statehood.

During the territorial years, the first political divisions began to form. Although the nation's first political parties, the Federalists and Democratic-Republicans, differed on matters of public policy, Illinois' political groupings revolved around personalities and political expediency. Strictly speaking, Illinois did not develop political parties. Instead, factions developed around the two dominant personalities of Illinois government, Ninian Edwards and Jesse Burgess Thomas. Although supporters of Thomas were likely to be more steadfast in support of slavery than the followers of Edwards, Edwards himself was a slave owner. Indeed, in later years Edwards would support the presidential ambitions of South Carolina's John C. Calhoun. Edwards and Thomas would remain active in Illinois politics until roughly 1830. Political parties did not become a fixture of Illinois politics until the 1830s.

The war made it easier for former soldiers to settle in the territory. The territory experienced an increase in population after 1814. The Indian tribes ceded large areas of central and northern Illinois to the United States during the conflict. During and after the war, governmental authority was strengthened and British influence removed. New laws to encourage settlement were enacted. In 1816, a land office opened in Edwardsville. In 1817, Congress offered former soldiers who settled in Illinois 160 acres of land. For those seeking to purchase land, the minimum purchase was reduced from 160 acres to 80 acres, and financing was made available to those seeking to settle in the territory.[17]

Following the defeats inflicted by the Americans on the Native American communities of Illinois during the war and its aftermath, the tribes of the territory and state were unable to challenge American supremacy. Especially without British support, the remaining tribes were weak and without means of resistance. The last attempt to use force against the then state of Illinois happened in 1830, when an effort was made under the leadership of Black Hawk. Unsuccessful, the Black Hawk War marks the end of the Native American presence in the state. An autobiography, purportedly that of Black Hawk, was published. It marks the final statement of principles and ideas of the Native American cause in Illinois.

Settlement in early Illinois involved several efforts to create distinct ethnic settlements. One of the most unique was the project of George Flower and Morris Birkbeck to set up an English colony in southeastern Illinois, near Albion in Edwards County. Exploring the territories of the Old Northwest, Flower and Birkbeck were impressed by the prairie land that moved eastward from the Wabash River. The area attracted English settlers, who joined religious organizations decidedly different from other regions of the state. Episcopalian and Unitarian churches appeared in this section of southern Illinois. In time, the efforts of the English to form their own community would cause tension with southern settlers near Mt. Carmel.

In Albion, colony organizers "settled in Edwards County after the War of 1812, when memory of the war was fresh, and perpetuated certain English traits."[18] Tensions between the English community of Edwards County and southern settlers persisted. According to Davis, "efforts at Albion to replicate English deference and class arrangements affronted republican Americans."[19] In 1821, angry residents of present-day Wabash County were so frustrated that they marched with their arms on Albion, the county seat.[20]

As historian Daniel Boorstin has noted, the American frontier made attempts to import European-style hierarchical arrangements to the United States unworkable and unsustainable. Although English settlement at Albion continued, it too faced the realities of American frontier life. English hierarchical structures gave way and the influx of other ethnic groups, notably the Germans, watered down the uniqueness of Edwards County's experiment with creating an English society in Illinois.

THE STATEHOOD DEBATE

The entry of Illinois into the Union as a state came as a great surprise to many. Only through some clever political maneuvering was statehood achieved. Even then, there was no guarantee Illinois would succeed in its quest for statehood. The main problem concerned Illinois' abysmally low population.

Despite the population increase following the war, Illinois was still a sparsely populated area. Whether the territory could reach the minimum population required for statehood was problematic. Despite this, statehood was widely supported throughout Illinois. Political leaders were united in securing this status for the Illinois Territory. Despite this, political figures were acutely aware of the shortcomings of Illinois that might derail statehood. In this regard, they expressed grave concern over the low population level of the territory. In 1818, 12,000 residents lived along the Wabash River, with the business settlement of Shawneetown serving as its hub. Another 12,000 residents were scattered throughout the territory in sparsely populated areas, while 15,000 lived in a 2,000-square-mile area beginning at Kaskaskia and extending northward to Saint Louis. Although the population of Illinois had increased steadily since 1787, it still failed to reach the number for admission set by Congress in the Northwest Ordinance of 1787.

Daniel Pope Cook, nephew of Nathaniel Pope and future son-in-law of Ninian Edwards, was twenty-one years old when the territory started the process of applying for statehood. Indeed, Cook was pivotal in convincing territorial leaders to initiate the process. A native of Kentucky, Cook, like many other Illinois leaders, moved to the territory for the chance to gain political success and notoriety. In 1815, Cook became an attorney in Illinois and was made publisher of the territory's only newspaper, the *Illinois Herald*.[21] He had served President James Monroe in a diplomatic mission to London in 1817 and hoped that this effort would lead to a federal position in Washington City, as the U.S. capital was then known. When Monroe did not name him to a post, he returned to Illinois and became an outspoken advocate of statehood.

Although Daniel Pope Cook's role in statehood was substantial, his ambitions caught many leading Illinois public figures by surprise. Nathaniel Pope, the Illinois delegate in Congress, did not expect his territorial government to ask Congress for statehood. Realizing the territory's weaknesses, Pope was amazed that he was to present the territorial legislature's call for statehood to Congress. According to one scholar, "Pope was taken aback when he received the statehood petition in mid-January 1818."[22]

In print, Cook used the name "A republican," calling for greater accountability in government. Claiming that the territorial governor's absolute veto was too much power in the hands of one man, he said that statehood would rectify that constitutional problem. Speaking practically, Cook maintained that statehood held the prospect of attracting more settlers and transforming the frontier into a prosperous society. In this way, he was able to challenge one of the key objections to statehood, namely, its high cost. The financial burden of funding the various offices of a state government would be higher than the cost of operating a territorial government. Yet without statehood, Cook maintained, the territory would continue to show low levels of growth and, thus, lower levels of prosperity. While Cook's newspaper was calling for statehood, Cook himself became involved with the territorial government. In December 1817, Cook was named clerk of the Territorial Assembly. On December 2, 1817, Governor Edwards proposed a census. On December 6, 1817, Illinois formally asked Congress for admission to the Union.

Illinois' first newspaper was the *Illinois Herald*, established in 1816. It would play a major role in the statehood movement, especially after Daniel Pope Cook purchased an ownership in the publishing firm. Following Cook's investment in the paper, the *Herald* changed its name to the *Western Intelligencer*. Given its political connections among the ruling families of Illinois, the paper did have an important say in the debate over statehood. Cook published pro-statehood writings in the paper, and this certainly impacted political feelings in the territory.[23] Following statehood, the *Western Intelligencer* continued its role in Illinois politics. In fact, the paper later went through several editorial changes following the territory's admission to the Union. With the move of the state capital from Kaskaskia to Vandalia, the *Intelligencer* followed the new state's political elites to the interior of the state.[24]

Although Daniel Pope Cook, a member of the Edwards faction, ran an anti-slavery platform, his former newspaper struggled, as did the state, over the meaning and significance of slavery. While in Vandalia, the paper at first declared an anti-slavery position. This, however, was followed by a rather dramatic reversal of editorial policy as the paper suddenly announced a pro-slavery position. In Vandalia, the paper again changed its name to the *Illinois Intelligencer*.[25]

In response to the call from Illinois, a House Select Committee was established consisting of Nathaniel Pope, Richard M. Johnson of Kentucky, John C. Spencer of New York, Ezekial Whitman of Maine-Massachusetts, and Thomas Claiborne of Tennessee. Nathaniel Pope's connections with Johnson of Kentucky would prove instrumental. In addition to the close connections between the Kentucky and Illinois political figures such as Ninian Edwards and Nathaniel Pope, Pope was on friendly terms with Johnson. Earlier, when Illinois applied for second-stage government under the Northwest Ordinance, Johnson had provided much help to achieving that victory in Congress. Although Daniel Pope Cook may have applied some youthful pressure on behalf of statehood in Kaskaskia, it was the veteran politician, Pope, who steered the matter through a difficult congressional process.[26]

On April 18, 1818, Congress passed the Enabling Act for Illinois. Nathaniel Pope, Illinois delegate to Congress, played an instrumental role in writing the provisions of the enabling legislation. His political skills were on display in the provisions of the act. Pope was able to secure territory in the North for Illinois that was legitimately considered part of Wisconsin. Realizing that a canal linking Lake Michigan with the Mississippi via the Illinois River was being proposed, Pope's efforts secured the land that would eventually contain most of the state's population. In this matter, Pope was guided by the Indiana Enabling Act of 1816, which moved that state's border ten miles north, giving it an extensive connection with Lake Michigan. Pope moved the Illinois border beyond the ten miles, however. With help from his colleagues in Congress, the Enabling Act specified that Illinois's boundary should extend to 42°30' north latitude, giving Illinois eight thousand additional square miles of territory. In comparison, while Indiana's boundary jutted north ten miles, Illinois' new border extended forty-one miles north of its original mark. The Enabling Act thus claimed for Illinois an area that would become home to Chicago, the Chicago northern, western, and southern suburbs, Rockford, eventually the state's second-largest city, and Galena, a small community in northwestern Illinois that would in time emerge as a historic town. Moreover, he was able to reduce the entry requirements for admission to the Union. Accordingly, Illinois was required to establish a republican form of government, hold a constitutional convention, and conduct a census to determine whether the state would contain at least 40,000 residents.[27] This last item is noteworthy, for under the Northwest Ordinance states were required to have at least 60,000 residents.

The validity of the Illinois census has been the topic of much debate and analysis. Illinois probably did not reach the population level specified in the Enabling Act and certainly did not satisfy the stricter requirements of the Northwest Ordinance. In negotiating with other members of Congress over the wording of the Enabling Act, Nathaniel Pope secured language that permitted Illinois to name is own census takers. In this way, the federal role in the census was minimized. In another tactical decision, the Illinois Territorial

Assembly moved the conclusion date of the census from June to December 1818. This action allowed territorial authorities to count settlers up to the deadline established by the Enabling Act. Yet despite these actions, Illinois barely met the minimum requirement. The census showed a population of 40,258. As one writer puts it, "with a wink and a nod, Illinois slipped into Union with perhaps 36,000 bona fide residents, making it the smallest state ever admitted."[28]

The Enabling Act also included stipulations designed to encourage settlement. For three years following admission, the military's bounty lands were to be tax abated. The opening of these lands to settlers without a tax burden was seen as a method of attracting new residents to an underpopulated state. To discourage land speculators, the tax rate for nonresidents was set at the same rate as for Illinois residents.[29] Ironically, the Edwards political faction, of whom Nathaniel Pope was a part, was noted for its own land speculation in Illinois. Indeed, individuals associated with Ninian Edwards were involved in land speculations associated with the selection of a new state capital for Illinois.

To encourage the development of education, the Enabling Act specified that 60 percent of Illinois' share of land sales would go to the establishment of schools. Illinois was to receive 5 percent of the proceeds from land sales. Moreover, some of the profits from the salt mines, concentrated in southeastern Illinois near Shawneetown, were to be used for education. Moreover, some of the funds were earmarked for a public university, although it took the state many decades to establish an institution of higher learning.[30]

THE ILLINOIS CONSTITUTIONAL CONVENTION

Given the backgrounds of the new political leadership of Illinois, it is perhaps not surprising that the constitutional convention would deal with subjects usually associated with slave-owning states. Although slavery was an issue, other concerns were on the agenda as well. Most notably, would Kaskaskia remain the capital of the new state?

When elections were held in July 1818 for delegates to the Illinois constitutional convention, the major issue was slavery. Of all the areas of the Northwest Territory, Illinois had the most slaves. Illinois voters elected thirty-three delegates to the convention. Of these, five were attorneys, with the remainder consisting of farmers. Two delegates would assume leadership responsibilities at the convention: Jesse Burgess Thomas and Elias Kent Kane. Politically experienced, they both knew that Illinois' chances of statehood would diminish if the convention voted in favor of slavery.[31]

The constitutional convention was held on July 6–8, 1818, at Kaskaskia. Jesse Burgess Thomas, who played a central role in securing territorial status, was named president of the convention. Thomas and his followers played a key role at the constitutional convention. The political faction of Ninian Edwards was at a serious disadvantage in terms of delegates to the convention. The convention produced a constitution that met the Enabling Act's requirement for a republican form of government, and it reflected the tendency of this era to base most of the political power in the hands of the legislative branch. The governor was given the power of veto, although that power could be exercised only through a Council of Revision, consisting of the governor and the members of the state supreme court. Interestingly, although early Illinois was settled primarily by individuals of southern descent, the constitution contained a prohibition against slavery: "Neither slavery nor involuntary servitude shall hereafter be introduced into this state." This constitutional prohibition was in conformity with the requirements of the Northwest Ordinance. A notable exception to this was the constitution's grandfather clause for slave-owning individuals of French descent. "Each and every person who has been bound to service by contract or indenture shall be held to" their obligations.[32]

Although the 1818 constitution provided for universal white male suffrage, it imposed a property requirement for members of the General Assembly. "In all elections, all white male inhabitants above the age of twenty one years, having resided in the state for six months next preceding the election, shall enjoy the right of an elector; but no person shall be entitled to vote except in the county or district in which he shall actually reside at the time of the election." However, the constitution's standard for the House of Representatives and Senate was higher. Individuals were eligible for election to the House of Representatives at age twenty-one, if they had lived in their district or county for one year and had "paid a state or county tax." Senators were expected to be at least twenty-five, to have lived in the district or county for one year, and to have also "paid a state or county tax." In this way, property owners were the only residents of Illinois who could serve in the General Assembly. Clearly, then, another tradition of the eastern states was imported into the constitution of this frontier state.

Although the delegates to the constitutional convention favored relocating the capital from Kaskaskia to an interior location, this issue was the cause of much controversy during the debates. The obvious question was where to locate the new capital. As early as 1817, rumors circulated among land speculators that the new state capital would be in the area of present-day Vandalia, Illinois.[33] This was by no means a foregone conclusion, as delegates had their individual preferences. Finally, the convention reached agreement and the Schedule of the Constitution, Thirteenth Section, declared, "the seat of government of the state shall be Kaskaskia, until the General Assembly shall otherwise provide. The general assembly, at their first session holden [sic] under the authority of this constitution, shall petition the Congress of the United States to grant to this state a quantity of land." The section goes on to say that the new capital should be "situated on the Kaskaskia river." In constitutional language that would plague the state for many years, the constitution said that this new capital "shall be the seat of government for the term of twenty years."[34] Although Vandalia became the state capital, it never developed into a significant city, in part because this provision of the 1818 constitution made Vandalia seem like a temporary location. In future years, Illinois governors would ask for funds to construct permanent buildings for the state. These proposals were rejected every time they were presented. As the end of the constitutionally mandated twenty-year period approached, most political and business leaders anticipated the movement of the capital to central Illinois. With the movement of the state's population into central and even northern areas of Illinois, there was a desire to locate the capital in a more convenient location. Led by influential members of the legislature from central Illinois, the state legislature decided to locate Illinois' capital in Springfield. A young representative, Abraham Lincoln of Sangamon County, supported the move. Interestingly, Lincoln and Stephen A. Douglas both served together as legislators when Vandalia was the capital.

In retrospect, the issue about where to locate the capital seems quite unimportant when compared with the debate over slavery. Most delegates to the constitutional convention were favorably minded toward slavery. However, they were realistic about the chances of getting a pro-slavery constitution through Congress.

Although the constitution did identify Illinois as a slave state, it also contained provisions specifying the nature of the slavery that existed within the state's boundaries. Article 6, Section 1 begins with a clear statement of public policy: "Neither slavery nor involuntary servitude shall hereafter be introduced into this state other than for the punishment of crimes whereof the party shall have been duly convicted." Although this appeared to classify Illinois as a free state, other provisions of Article 6 made the issue less straightforward. Section 3 said that "[e]ach and every person who has been bound to service by contract or indenture in virtue of the laws of the Illinois Territory heretofore existing, shall be held to a specific performance of their contracts or indentures."[35] When presented to Congress for approval, some members from northern states objected to the proposed constitution, saying it provided protection to slavery in violation of the Northwest Ordinance.

According to the constitution, the executive, legislative, and judicial powers were to be exercised separately and in accordance with the doctrine of checks and balances. Still, the framers of the Illinois Constitution provided that the legislative branch would be dominant among the three branches. In this regard, the establishment of a Council of Revision, closely paralleling that of the New York Constitution, would hamper the ability of the Illinois governor to exercise independent judgment. While the Council of Revision blurred the separation of powers between the executive, legislative, and judicial branches, it was consistent with the standards set for Congress for admission to the Union. The same statement could not be said about the provisions relating to slavery.

In addition to Illinois' low population numbers, this was the other obstacle to admission.

Members of Congress from northern states raised concerns about the Illinois Constitution. With its provisions protecting existing slavery and maintaining the system of indentured servants, anti-slavery forces in the Congress questioned whether the constitution was compatible with the requirements of the Northwest Ordinance. Led by Representative James Tallmadge of New York, the charge was made that the anti-slavery clause of the ordinance had been violated. Illinois' member of Congress, John McLean, was prevented from taking his seat in the lower chamber by the anti-slavery opposition. On November 19, 1818, he was told the House would not seat him until it had reviewed the Illinois application for statehood, including the compatibility of the Illinois Constitution with the Northwest Ordinance. In this matter, however, representatives favoring Illinois admission made the claim, to be repeated in coming years, that Virginia's decision to transfer sovereignty over the Northwest Territory to the United States took precedence over the Northwest Ordinance. Specifically, Virginia's transfer included a clause protecting existing slavery in the Northwest. Eventually, of course, opposition to seating the Illinois representative and approving Illinois statehood came to an end. By a vote of 151-34, the House of Representatives approved Illinois' admission to the Union. Strategically, the Illinois constitutional convention made a wise choice in not writing slavery into the constitutional law of the new state. Kane's leadership during the constitutional convention proved crucial in the final analysis, for he convinced the pro-slavery forces not to press the issue of slavery to its fullest extent. Illinois joined the United States on December 3, 1818.

THE PERSISTENCE OF PRE-STATEHOOD ISSUES

The slavery controversy plagued Illinois state politics following admission to the Union. Although the 1818 constitution declared Illinois a free state, this status had been obtained for reasons of political expediency by the constitutional convention. Most delegates, led by Jesse Thomas, were sympathetic to pro-slavery factions in Illinois. Yet they realized that a pro-slavery constitution would have imperiled the territory's prospects for statehood. In many respects, the admission of Illinois marked the beginning of the fissures that would eventually divide the country between North and South and ultimately challenge the concept of Union.

Ironically, the number of slaves in Illinois was low. In 1810, slave owners in the Illinois territory held 168 slaves. In 1820, two years after statehood, 917 slaves were in the state. Of the 928 slaves in Illinois in 1820, Ninian Edwards owned twenty-two, and 500 were working in the salt mines of southern Illinois.[36] The numbers are in stark contrast with the numbers from Missouri. Whereas 3,000 slaves were held in Missouri in 1810, by 1820 over

10,200 were in the territory. Interestingly, Illinois' population of free blacks actually declined from 600 in 1810 to 450 in 1820. In neighboring Indiana, the population of free blacks increased from 400 to 1,200.[37] Undoubtedly, the hostile climate in Illinois, exemplified by the black codes, kept free blacks from settling in the territory and state.

Ninian Edwards and Jesse Burgess Thomas were elected as the first two U.S. senators from Illinois. In going to the nation's capital, they carried with them the political battles of the new state. Edwards, the undisputed leader of his faction, was determined to stymie Thomas in his endeavors. Thomas, who, along with Kane, was the leader of the anti-Edwards faction, struggled with Edwards in Washington over the federal appointments in Illinois. Soon the two senators became embroiled in presidential politics, with Edwards supporting John C. Calhoun and Thomas backing the secretary of the treasury, William Crawford in the 1820 campaign. Moreover, the Edwards and Thomas division spilled over into Missouri politics, with Edwards supporting the senatorial candidacy of John Cook, the brother of Daniel Pope Cook. This action caused difficulties for Edwards, as the winner, Thomas Hart Benton, allied himself with Edward's implacable foe, Jesse Burgess Thomas. In early Illinois, this was the nature of politics—often personal, based on family grouping and factions, but never in the form of political parties.[38]

Following admission, Illinois enacted a "black code." Although nominally a free state, Illinois enacted regulations for slaves and freed blacks more stringent than found in most southern states. One scholar has written that "from the beginning Illinois had a savage black code."[39] The first General Assembly of Illinois in 1819 mandated strict registration requirements for slaves and freed slaves. Among other items, bond of $1,000 was required for each slave freed by a slave owner. The intent of this regulation was to make it financially difficult for slave owners to free slaves. The enactment of "black codes" by the first state legislature demonstrated the political strength of the pro-slavery movement in Illinois.[40]

On the national level, politicians in Washington City faced the prospect of two slave states joining the Union. Although nominally a free state, Illinois' admission was followed by that of Alabama, a territory admitted to the Union as a slaveholding state. While Alabama was petitioning the Congress for admission, Missouri, geographically a northern state but in sympathy a southern state, applied for admission as well. Missouri's application touched off a national debate about the extension of slavery into the new territories, for Missouri's admission would tilt the balance of power in the Senate away from the non-slaveholding North to the states of the American Southland. Would Illinois remain a "free" state?

Unfortunately for opponents of slavery, internal conditions in Illinois strengthened the position of slavery advocates. Illinois' economy declined immediately after the territory won statehood. This caused many pro-slavery advocates to claim that slavery could help Illinois regain its prosperity and develop into a great state. Arguments were advanced that slavery would encourage settlers from the South to move to Illinois. In addition to increasing the population, the new residents would bring money and other resources to the state. Because settlement would increase, the demand for land, and hence land prices, would rise.

In political terms, pro-slavery supporters were emboldened by the controversy surrounding Missouri's admission to the Union. During congressional debate over Missouri, several members of Congress objected to the claim that the Northwest Ordinance could force a state in perpetuity to prohibit slavery. Former Indiana territorial governor and now Ohio senator William Henry Harrison claimed that Ohio, though a free state, could amend its constitution to provide for slavery. The Northwest Ordinance could not prohibit the new states from taking actions deemed to be in the public interest. Moreover, many members of Congress asserted that the Northwest Ordinance and proposed restrictions on Missouri regarding slavery would transform new states, like Illinois and Missouri, into second-rank states. That is, while the old states of the original Union were free to amend their constitutions on the matter of slavery, the new states would be prohibited from doing so. When Missouri gained admittance as a slave state, this only increased pressure within Illinois for the introduction of slavery.

In the biography written by his son, Ninian Edwards is portrayed as a friend of northern interests. The biography notes that Edwards supported admission of Missouri on its own terms, meaning that Missouri would be entitled to prepare a constitution enshrining slavery as a matter of constitutional law. Edwards is also portrayed as an opponent of slavery and a reluctant supporter of its extension into Missouri. This, however, ignores Edward's own southern heritage, his ownership of slaves, and his friendship with southern political leaders, most notably his friendship with John C. Calhoun. According to the biography, he was opposed to "its introduction in his own state," but on the Missouri question, he felt that it was "the right of the people of each state to have such a constitution and institutions as they might adopt for themselves." Edwards's son, trying to present his father as a supporter of northern causes, notes that "Northern and Eastern inhabitants were the friends of Governor Edwards" and this lost him the support of southern elements in the state.[41]

Illinois congressman Daniel Pope Cook voted against the Missouri Compromise. Far from representing the views of his father-in-law's political faction, Cook's vote reflected the division within Illinois over slavery. Many public figures in the Edwards political faction were pro-slavery, and many were anti-slavery. However, Cook assumed the anti-slavery position, believing it to be helpful to his political career. In 1819, he defeated Illinois' first member of the U.S. House of Representatives, John McLean, by waging an anti-slavery campaign against him. Claiming that McLean favored slavery in Illinois, he forced his opponent to publicly express opposition to pro-slavery forces in the state. In Cook's 1820 reelection campaign, he continued this strategy against his opponent, the chief writer of the 1818 constitution, Elias Kent Kane. During the 1820 campaign, Cook's supporters claimed that Kane supported the importation of slavery from Missouri and that should he win, it would mean the opening of an offensive on behalf of the extension of slavery to Illinois. Although Kane lost his campaign against Cook, pro-slavery forces were determined to act against the 1818 constitution and replace it with a new one.

Following his defeat of John McLean, Daniel Pope Cook became a fixture in the post of U.S. representative to Congress. He handily defeated his opponents. In the congressional election on August 7, 1820, he defeated Elias Kent Kane, 4,493 to 2,445. Two years later, in a rematch with McLean when the question of slavery was becoming more critical, he still won reelection, 4,620 to 3,646. Yet the election returns showed a division between northern and southern regions of the state, a division that would become even more evident during the years of the nineteenth and twentieth centuries. In the counties of the American Bottom, especially in the counties of St. Clair and Madison, Cook won by large margins. In 1819, 86 percent of St. Clair County supported his candidacy, while in Madison County, 85 percent voted for him. In the southern counties, it was a different story. In Gallatin County, home to the salt mines using slave labor, only 6 percent supported Cook. In another southern county, 21 percent supported the candidacy of Cook.[42] Clearly, at this early date the divisions over slavery were evident in the Illinois electorate.

On the state level, Illinois elected Shadrach Bond, a pro-southern politician, as its first governor. Although Governor Bond was politically weak, his election was symbolic of the potent energies of the pro-slavery elements in the state. In 1819, some Illinois residents discussed the possibility of amending the state's constitution to legalize slavery. While no action was taken at that time, it was a harbinger of things to come. Serving only four years, Illinois in 1822 elected Edward Coles, a political figure hostile to slavery and generally progressive in political outlook. Although Governor Coles was elected governor, he won the office with a plurality, not a majority, vote. He immediately moved to urge the state to remove all vestiges of slavery from Illinois life.

It is indicative of the politics of the new state that its first governor, Shadrach Bond, a political independent, was forced by the political currents to align with one of the two factions in Illinois politics. Bond, like many public figures, lived in the American Bottom between Kaskaskia and St. Louis. His independence was the basis for his election in 1818, though such flexibility was regarded as an obstacle to public success in early state politics. Although Bond eventually joined the Thomas faction, he served only one term in office. His successor, Edward Coles, was, like Bond, a politician without a political base in either the Edwards or Thomas factions. As such, Coles's administration can be termed an accidental governorship.

In the election of 1822, the Ninian Edwards faction was unable to agree on a candidate for governor. The result was a wide open field for the state's executive office, and given Coles's record on slavery, he was regarded as a weak candidate. As always, early political discourse in Illinois revolved around the question of slavery. When the votes had been counted, Illinois had a new governor, though it was someone who was above the political fray of Illinois politics. This aloofness would not help him through the difficult years of his administration.

Coles was an unusual figure in Illinois politics. Although a Southerner and slave owner, he was an abolitionist. Well connected to prominent families in Virginia, Coles interacted with Madison and Monroe on a personal and professional basis. As private secretary to President Madison for six years, Coles was principled and intelligent. Attending the Illinois constitutional convention in 1818, Coles made the question of slavery the deciding factor in whether he should settle in Illinois. When the convention voted to make Illinois a "free state," Coles moved his household from Virginia to Illinois and freed his slaves. Although an aristocrat like Ninian Edwards, Coles lacked the political skills of Edwards. Elected governor with one-third of the votes and by only 170 votes over his opponents, Coles entered office in a weakened position politically. It was a close race. Coles received 2,854 votes to Joseph Phillips's 2,687, Thomas Browne's 2,224, and James B. Moore's 622.[43] Moreover, since he did not belong to either the Thomas or Edwards faction, Coles lacked a political base to pursue his ambitious goal of ending slavery in the state.

Within Illinois, Governor Coles's action caused the pro-southern elements to call for an amendment to the Illinois Constitution declaring Illinois a slave state. Pro-slavery politicians expressed contempt for Governor Coles. Using the black codes, they embarrassed the governor by filing charges against him for freeing his slaves without paying the required funds with Madison County officials. With the support of leading public figures, the effort was successful in getting the pro-slavery issue before the voters. Opponents of the amendment claimed that it would violate the Northwest Ordinance, which declared the territory of the Old Northwest free from slavery. In response, pro-slavery advocates said that Virginia's original title to Illinois took precedence over the Northwest Ordinance.[44] Under the laws of Virginia, slavery was legal and the residents of Illinois could amend their constitution, if desired, to legalize the institution of slavery.

The advocates of a new pro-slavery constitution stated their case in economic terms. Simply put, slavery would spur the development of Illinois. This argument was used with great effect in far southern Illinois near Shawneetown. Here, a small community, settled by individuals of southern heritage, depended on the salt mines of Gallatin County. Under the 1818 constitution, no new contracts for indentured servants were to be written after 1825.[45] Many saw this date as an approaching storm for Shawneetown. Yet Illinois was not a state of the deep South and slavery was never institutionalized in Illinois as it was in parts of the American South. In fact, the number of slaves in Illinois was never large. Given the state's ambivalence over the slavery issue, most supporters of the proposed constitution said that slavery, if more widely introduced in Illinois, would be temporary and would gradually disappear.[46]

The political battle over the 1818 constitution was intense. Pro-slavery forces successfully challenged the credentials of a member of the legislature who had opposed the call for a new constitution. Charges were filed against Governor Coles for violating the black code. Accusations of favoritism were levied against the governor when those charges were set aside. In fact, the charges facing Governor Coles were reinstated and would not disappear until 1826. Both sides used newspapers to sway public opinion. Although it seems that the pro-slavery side enjoyed an advantage in the newspapers, the governor and his allies resorted to strong tactics as well. A newspaper in Edwardsville was established to publish the views of supporters of the 1818 constitution. After a period of great intensity, the supporters of a new constitution were handed a defeat. Illinois voters rejected a new constitution by a strong majority, 6,640 against a constitutional convention and 4,972 in favor.[47]

In the end, Coles was successful in defeating the measure. Illinois voters rejected the slavery measure. However, this victory did not represent a long-term defeat for the Illinois political factions with pro-southern leanings. On the contrary, these elements would hold most of the political power in the state until the Civil War. As for Edward Coles, after serving as Illinois governor, he eventually left the state and settled in Philadelphia. His son would die fighting for the Confederacy.

In the long term, the battle over whether to maintain Illinois' first constitution pointed to future trends that were to typify Illinois elections in the nineteenth and twentieth centuries. Northern counties sided with the anti-slavery position more heavily than the southern counties. This division between north and south became a hallmark of Illinois politics. It was a sign that the southern influence in the state was bound to decline as northern Illinois gained population throughout the nineteenth century.

As a southern state culturally and politically, Illinois was not the typical "northern" state during its early history. Although northern Illinois would eventually dominate the politics of the state, in its early years the northern counties were even more sparsely settled than the rest of the state. Moreover, given the prominent role of Southerners in the politics of early Illinois, the settlers of northern Illinois, many from New England, were ill suited for statewide politics. Then too, the state government tended to ignore the concerns of its northern regions. These factors made the unity of Illinois problematic. Just as the North-South division was evident in national politics, so too was this separation obvious in Illinois. Practically, how would the northern counties interact with the state government? In this regard, Nathaniel Pope's victory in detaching the northern counties from Wisconsin had never been accepted in that territory. As Wisconsin was preparing to apply for admission to the Union, political figures in Wisconsin and northern Illinois considered the possibility of detaching the area from Illinois and joining it with Wisconsin.

Former Illinois governor Thomas Ford, whose political history of Illinois provides a synoptic overview of political life in Illinois, wrote that the era of political factions began to fade in 1826. In that year, Daniel Pope Cook, close ally and family member of Ninian Edwards, was defeated in his reelection race for the U.S. House of Representatives. Ford, close personally and politically to Cook, claimed that Cook's defeat "is a new era in our elections, and marks the origin, though not completion, of a great revolution in men's motives for political action."[48] While noting the new dynamics of the emerging Jacksonian era in American politics, Ford goes on to note that its passing meant the fading away of the old family-patron style of politics characteristic of the territorial and early statehood years. In Illinois as elsewhere, the nature of the Jacksonian style of politics was its focus on the energies of political parties. Aristocrats like Ninian Edwards were outdated politically by this time. A long era of dominance by Jacksonian Democrats was on the horizon.

SUMMARY

The Illinois Territory was slow to develop economically and in population levels. Only with political skill and some questionable tactics with regard to meeting population requirements for entry into the Union were early Illinois leaders successful in transforming a territory into a state. Even with statehood, Illinois grew slowly. Challenged in its early years by pro-slavery forces, the early state government confronted the divisive question of slavery that would inflame northern and southern passions until the decisive decision in the Civil War. Initially a territory with a substantial French community, this element of diversity was lost as French settlers gradually left for Missouri and the French-controlled Louisiana Territory. Contemporary evidence of the state's French heritage may be found in small towns in southern Illinois that continue to have French names, such as Menard, Prairie du Rocher, and Renault. This loss of the French weakened the Native American communities of Illinois as well. Here too, however, the remnants of an ancient Native American civilization may be found at the Cahokia Mounds, located in the Illinois section of the St. Louis metropolitan area.

Despite its modest beginnings, Illinois emerged as a prosperous state in the mid- and late nineteenth century. Chicago gradually emerged as a major business, financial, manufacturing, and transportation center for the Midwest. Chicago replaced St. Louis, Missouri, as the business center of the Midwest. Although some predicted a prosperous future for Chicago in the 1820s, no one could have imagined the extent of the development that occurred. Many early Illinois business and political leaders realized that eventually Lake Michigan would be connected through the Illinois River to the Mississippi River. However, these individuals thought the connection would be of most benefit to southern Illinois and the region now referred to as the St. Louis area.

In fact, some enterprising figures developed Alton, Illinois, as an Illinois rival to the city of St. Louis. Chicago became a great inland port, as it not only had connection with the Mississippi through the Illinois River but, more important, to the Atlantic through the St. Lawrence Seaway in the twentieth century. In agriculture, great improvements were made as well. The Illinois prairie, so difficult to tame in earlier years, provided the basis for the state to emerge as a great farming area. With fertile soil, the small towns of Illinois became a major agricultural region for the nation.

When Abraham Lincoln was born in 1809, Illinois was a struggling territory with its leaders uncertain as to when it might become a state. By 1858, Lincoln, by then a successful attorney in Springfield, Illinois, engaged in a statewide debate with the Illinois senator Stephen A. Douglas over the issues challenging the unity of the nation. Two years later, Lincoln won election to the presidency and immediately faced a secession crisis as southern states left the United States and formed the Confederate States of America. From its origins as a southern territory and state, Illinois, by the time of Lincoln's election to the presidency, had moved away from its southern heritage and had become a Midwestern state with loyalties to the Union, despite some southern sympathies in the southern part of Illinois. However, by this time, southern Illinois was no longer the center of politics in the state.

NOTES

1. James E. Davis, *Frontier Illinois* (Bloomington and Indianapolis: Indiana University Press, 1998), p. 94.

2. Robert P. Howard, *Illinois: A History of the Prairie State* (Grand Rapids, MI: William B. Eerdmans, 1972), p. 65.

3. An Ordinance for the Government of the Territory of the United States North-West, July 13, 1787.

4. Ibid.

5. Howard, *Illinois*, p. 69.

6. Ibid., pp. 69–70. See also Arthur Clinton Boggess, *The Settlement of Illinois, 1778–1830* (Chicago: Chicago Historical Society, 1908; reprint, Freeport, NY: Books for Libraries Press, 1970), p. 85.

7. *The Laws of the Indiana Territory, 1801–1809* (Springfield: Illinois State Historical Library, 1930), vol. 2, p. xxiii.

8. Boggess, *The Settlement of Illinois*, pp. 177–178.

9. See J. F. Snyder, *Transactions of the Illinois State Historical Society for the Year 1904* (Springfield, IL: Phillips Brothers, State Printers, 1904).

10. Ibid.

11. Howard, *Illinois*, p. 72.

12. Louis B. Ewbank and Dorothy L. Riker, eds., *The Laws of Indiana Territory, 1809–1816* (Indianapolis: Indiana Historical Bureau, 1934), pp. 8–9.

13. Ibid.

14. Ninian Wirth Edwards, *History of Illinois, from 1778–1838: and Life and Times of Ninian Edwards* (Springfield: Illinois State Journal Company, 1870), p. 66.

15. Howard, *Illinois*, pp. 76–77.

16. Davis, *Frontier Illinois*, p. 156.

17. Ibid.

18. Ibid., p. 263.

19. Ibid., p. 307.

20. Thomas J. Wood, "Blood in the Moon: The War for the Seat of Edwards County, 1821–1824," *Illinois Historical Journal* (Autumn 1992): 143.

21. Franklin William Scott, *Newspapers and Periodicals of Illinois, 1814–1879* (Springfield: Illinois State Historical Library, 1910), p. 211.

22. James A. Edstrom, "With…Candour and Good Faith: Nathaniel Pope and the Admission Enabling Act," *Illinois Historical Journal* (Winter 1995): 243.

23. Scott, *Newspapers and Periodicals of Illinois*, p. 211.

24. Ibid., p. 211.

25. Ibid., p. 211–212.

26. See Edstrom, "With…Candour and Good Faith."

27. Fifteenth Congress of the United States, *The Enabling Act for Illinois Statehood*, April 18, 1818.

28. Davis, *Frontier State*, p. 161.

29. Fifteenth Congress of the United States, *Enabling Act for Illinois Statehood*, April 18, 1818.

30. Ibid.

31. Davis, *Frontier State*, p. 163.

32. *Constitution of the State of Illinois*, 1818.

33. Paul E. Stroble, *High on the Okaw's Western Bank: Vandalia, Illinois 1818–39* (Urbana and Chicago: University of Illinois Press, 1992), p. 9.

34. *Constitution of the State of Illinois*, 1818, Schedule, Section 13.

35. *Constitution of the State of Illinois*, 1818, Article 6.

36. Howard, *Illinois*, p. 131.

37. Boggess, *The Settlement of Illinois*, pp. 177–179.

38. See Thomas Ford, *A History of Illinois: From Its Commencement as a State in 1818 to 1847* (Chicago: S. C. Griggs, and New York: Ivison and Phinney, 1854; reprint, Urbana and Chicago: University of Illinois Press, 1995).

39. Theodore Calvin Pease, *The Frontier State, 1818–1848* (Urbana and Chicago: University of Illinois Press, 1967), p. 48.

40. Howard, *Illinois*, p. 131.

41. Edwards, *History of Illinois*, p. 101.

42. Theodore Calvin Pease, ed., *Illinois Election Returns, 1818–1848* (Springfield: Illinois State Historical Library, 1923), pp. 1–2.

43. Ibid., p. 15.

44. Davis, *Frontier Illinois*, p. 165.

45. *Constitution of the State of Illinois*, 1818.

46. Pease, *The Frontier State*, p. 85.

47. Pease, *Illinois Election Returns*, pp. 27–29.

48. Ford, *A History of Illinois*, p. 47.

BIBLIOGRAPHY

Alvord, Clarence Walworth. *The Illinois Country, 1673–1818*. Chicago: Loyola University Press, 1965.

Boggess, Arthur Clinton. *The Settlement of Illinois, 1778–1830*. Chicago: Chicago Historical Society, 1908; reprint, Freeport, NY: Books for Libraries Press, 1970.

Carr, Kay J. *Belleville, Ottawa, and Galesburg: Community and Democracy on the Illinois Frontier*. Carbondale: Southern Illinois University Press, 1996.

Davis, James E. *Frontier Illinois*. Bloomington and Indianapolis: Indiana University Press, 1998.

Duitsman, Janet. *Constitution Making in Illinois, 1818–1970*. Urbana: University of Illinois Press, 1972.

Dunne, Edward Fitzsimmons. *Illinois, the Heart of the Nation*. Chicago: Lewis Publishing Company, 1933.

Federal Writers Project of the Work Projects Administration for the State of Illinois. *Illinois: A Descriptive and Historical Guide*. Compiled and written by the Federal Writers Project of the Work Projects Administration for the State of Illinois. Chicago: A. C. McClurg and Company, 1939.

Ford, Thomas. *A History of Illinois From Its Commencement as a State in 1818 to 1847*. Chicago: S. C. Griggs, and New York: Ivison and Phinney, 1854; reprint, Urbana and Chicago: University of Illinois Press, 1995.

Harris, Norman Dwight. *The History of Negro Servitude in Illinois: And of the Slavery Agitation in that State, 1719–1864*. New York: Haskell House, 1969.

Havighurst, Walter. *Land of Promise: The Story of the Northwest Territory*. New York: Macmillan, 1947.

Howard, Robert P. *Illinois: A History of the Prairie State*. Grand Rapids, MI: William B. Eeerdmans, 1972.

Jensen, Richard J. *Illinois: A Bicentennial History*. New York: Norton, 1978.

Kenney, David, and Barbara L. Brown. *Basic Illinois Government: A Systematic Explanation*. Carbondale: Southern Illinois University Press, 1993.

Pease, Theodore Calvin. *The Story of Illinois*. Chicago: University of Chicago Press, 1949.

Reynolds, John. *The Pioneer History of Illinois, Containing the Discovery, 1673, and the History of the Country to the Year 1818, When the State Government Was Organized*. Chicago: Fergus Printing Company, 1887.

Simon, Paul. *Freedom's Champion: Elijah Lovejoy*. Carbondale: Southern Illinois University Press, 1994.

Stroble, Paul E. *High on the Okaw's Western Bank: Vandalia, Illinois, 1819–1839*. Urbana and Chicago: University of Illinois Press, 1992.

THE STATE OF INDIANA

Admitted to the Union as a State: December 11, 1816

John P. Hundley

INTRODUCTION

Indiana statehood was virtually a foregone conclusion from the moment Congress passed the Northwest Ordinance in 1787. The ordinance "for the government of the territory of the United States north west of the River Ohio" laid the groundwork and provided the blueprint for organizing the territory running from the Ohio Valley in the south to the Mississippi River in the west to the Canadian border in the north. It specifically stipulated statehood, in some form, for the lands therein. By whatever name, in whatever year, and whatever its boundaries, there would be an Indiana.

In sum, the ordinance of 1787 called for a three-step road to statehood for the lands encompassed. The national government appointed major officials, including a territorial governor, minor officials, and the judiciary, who in turn appointed lesser offices. Upon reaching a population base of five thousand free, white, male residents over twenty-one years of age, delegates could be nominated to form a territorial legislature, though the territorial governors were given the power to both choose from the nominees and veto absolutely any legislation they might care to pass. Finally, when the population reached 60,000, the territory could apply for statehood, draft a constitution, and form a state government.

The ordinance was passed against a backdrop of sectional division and constitutional crisis. The question of slavery was a wedge creating an ever-widening gap in the nascent United States. The Congress was broke and hard pressed to pay or even feed an army fresh off the Revolution. This same army suddenly, with the territory acquired in the aftermath of the Revolution, had

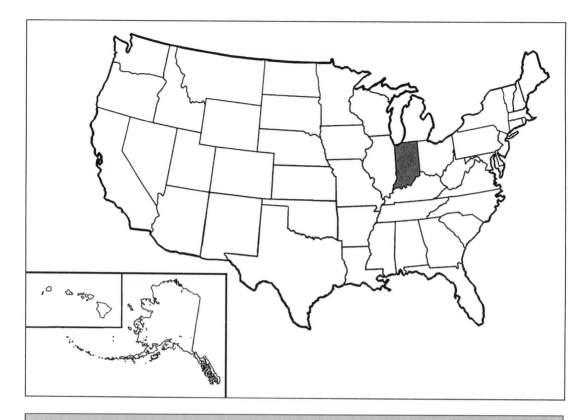

Indiana

Territorial Development:

- Great Britain ceded future Indiana Territory to the United States through the Treaty of Paris, September 3, 1783
- United States passed the Northwest Ordinance: territorial claims inherited from colonial charters ceded to the public domain; future Indiana Territory organized as part of the Northwest Territory, July 13, 1787
- Reorganized as the Indiana Territory, May 7, 1800
- Indiana admitted into the Union as the nineteenth state, December 11, 1816

Territorial Capitals:

- Vincennes, 1800–1813
- Corydon, 1813–1816

State Capitals:

- Corydon, 1816–1821
- Indianapolis, 1821–present

Origin of State Name: "Indiana" is a word created by the U.S. Congress that is intended to mean "land of the Indians."

First Governor: Jonathan Jennings
Governmental Organization: Bicameral
Population at Statehood: 147,178
Geographical Size: 35,867 square miles

nearly double the holdings to protect. The "Indian Problem," by now essentially moot in the newly minted states in the East, was another matter entirely along this new, western frontier.

The land had been technically off-limits to the Americans under the British following the Treaty of Paris. By the outbreak of the Revolution, the colony of Virginia had laid claim to much of the area and the new state of Virginia would maintain the claim. Nevertheless, the Proclamation of 1763 forbade settlement west of the Alleghenies, and the land was home to numerous tribal groups of natives. White presence was limited to a scattering of trappers, traders, and soldiers. The military was concentrated in Fort Ouiatanon (near present-day Lafayette) and Fort Miami (later Ft. Wayne) and the longtime French settlement, and later British fort, at Vincennes.

After the war, however, white settlers began rapidly moving into these previously forbidden lands. Some of these were war veterans claiming lands granted to them for their service to the new nation. Some were younger sons of eastern gentry, unfortunate in being lower in order of birth and thereby inheritance, looking for estates of their own. Many were simply poor pioneers seeking land on which to start new lives. In all cases, Congress fretted over these "semisavage banditti squatters" spreading unchecked over the frontier.[1]

"A PROPER MIXTURE OF CITIZENS": THE INDIANA TERRITORY

From the beginning, the prime motivation of the ordinance of 1787 and most of the following legislation and debate surrounding the Northwest Territory was the attraction of permanent settlers. The nascent nation recognized how precarious its economy and security were. The development of the new territories would provide room to grow, but it would also create a buffer against foreign powers and hostile natives, new markets for eastern goods, and a safety valve for increasing populations. At the same time, the orderly selling of the lands would bring much-needed income into the national treasury at a time when there was still a revolution for which to pay. The agriculture and manufacturing sure to follow permanent settlement would supply eastern markets with inexpensive, homegrown goods that would ease reliance on importation. The successive presidencies of Washington, Adams, Jefferson, and Madison all recognized the importance of the new American frontier to the success of the Union.

At the same time, the government also feared that uncontrolled growth and settlement could create a society independent of its reach. There was a very real fear that a new western nation could be forged if the territory was not properly governed and regulated. Such a new nation might well look beyond the United States both for markets and military alliances. In such circumstances, Washington predicted the west could become a "formidable and dangerous neighbor."[2] Jefferson, too, realized that should the new western citizens choose independence, "we are incapable of a single effort to retain them." Counter-arguments citing familial, brotherly bonds between new settlers and the East holding the sections together struck Jefferson as even more reason why a push for separation would succeed. "Our citizens," he wrote, "can never be induced...to cut the throats of their own brothers and sons."[3]

The land ordinances of the late eighteenth century were designed to create and cement East-West connections and create a national market for the western lands. In that way, the attractions of an independent frontier would be minimized. The challenge was twofold. First, new settlers had to be assured that the lands they were to buy would have free and clear title. Already, squatters and speculators were moving wholesale into the territory and staking out the best lands. The shoddiness of most national surveys had created situations in which competing land claims could take years to untangle. In Kentucky, the situation became so muddled that as many as six or eight different surveys might exist for the same lands, and it seemed that every land purchase came complete with its own lawsuit. It was this situation in Kentucky that led settlers like Thomas Lincoln to move his family north across the river to the Indiana Territory.

The second challenge was to attract what Jefferson referred to as the "proper mixture of citizens" to the new lands to the west.[4] Those in the stream of squatters and speculators who had begun moving into the territories were vilified by those in the East as "savages," "bandits," "wild animals," and "malcontents." Such characterizations were at least in part self-serving. It was important to the U.S. government that the lands in the west be made productive and profitable. Squatters and speculators were attempting to circumvent governmental controls. However, they also had tremendous potential to create problems with issuing unencumbered title to good lands to settlers following the rules. Speculators were the greater problem, as they threatened to overthrow the fine balance between the public and private interests necessary to maintain a capitalistic republic, as the government was finding out.

What the government wanted was to attract industrious, market-oriented settlers. The squatters were primarily subsistence farmers not much interested in creating surpluses to ship to hungry markets back East. The lands in the new territories were extraordinarily rich and fertile. Correspondent after correspondent commented, upon visiting the territories, on the natural beauty and fecundity of the land. A reader back East could be forgiven for thinking that the West was a near Eden, with nature's bounty springing forth from the ground at every turn. The Congress was concerned that the land was so productive and would provide such an easy living that settlers would become lazy and indolent.

The Indiana the settlers were coming to did not really encourage indolence. The soil was uncommonly rich, which had resulted in two-thirds of the state being covered with exceptionally dense forest. One early traveler to the area joked that a squirrel could traverse the whole of the territory and never set foot on the ground. In 1800, the territory had almost no routes of travel that could really be called proper roads. Most newcomers followed old buffalo and Indian game traces. As late as 1816, the year of statehood, citizens were still required to work on road building and improvement as part of their taxation, and legislation limiting the height of stumps in the road to one foot was still in effect. Much of the territory was inaccessible in the spring and fall, as the rains made the roads impassable. Just getting to their new land was hard work for the settlers. Most came by water, most often along the Ohio River, and then headed north through the tangle of undergrowth among trees in the forest.

Once the settlers arrived, shelter had to be built and land had to be cleared for planting. After a couple of years, enough land could have been cleared and producing enough to consider planting surplus for the eastern markets. Of course, not all newcomers were farmers. Some were merchants and traders, and eventually manufacturers. They settled in the little river towns along the Ohio (Jeffersonville, Vevy, Corydon, Madison) and the Wabash (Vincennes, Lafayette, Logansport). As this land was gobbled up, they moved farther to the north and east. Indiana, unlike most states, was by necessity settled from south to north.

Most of the early settlers came from the middle and upper South. The territory's population moved in from the Carolinas, Virginia, and Kentucky. One of the reasons slavery became such a heated issue in Indiana was that so many early citizens had previously lived with it. A smaller stream of settlers came from Pennsylvania and New York. A thin trickle, too, came in from New England, but mostly after statehood.

As a whole, the settlers were of modest means and background. Most were farmers looking for larger areas of land to till. They were overwhelmingly, but not exclusively, white. They were young, most in their twenties and thirties, and tended to come in family groups rather than alone. They had little education, but recognized its value. They were hardworking, as they had to be, and conservative.

The settlers' relations with the natives ran the gamut. Most were not overtly hostile or antagonistic, but very few, coming from a European background and ethic, could understand the Indian conception of the land as natural provider incapable of being "owned," anymore than the natives could grasp white concepts of ownership and "higher use" through agriculture and development. Such fundamental differences were bound to create tension and conflict. They did. Whites saw the Indians as "lazy" and "unproductive," while the natives saw the Americans as what poet Joseph Payne Brennan called "the swarming breed." Sporadic violence periodically erupted on both sides, and treaties and land cessions did little to resolve these conflicts.

WHO WAS WHO, AND WHY

There was no particular indispensable man or woman on the road to Indiana statehood. There was no Hoosier Washington, Bolívar, or Gandhi. What became the state of Indiana did not, and does not, bear the stamp of any one, overpowering individual's influence, and there is no person who can be said to have in any real sense shaped or defined the state's character.

Arguably the single most significant figure in Indiana's road to statehood was also its most well known. William Henry Harrison was appointed the territory's first governor in 1800 by then President John Adams. Prior to this he had served as secretary of the Northwest Territory and later became a territorial delegate to Congress. Politics ran in his blood. Harrison was born in 1773 to Benjamin Harrison III, a wealthy Virginia planter, soon to become a delegate to the Continental Congress, a signer of the Declaration of Independence and eventual governor of the new state of Virginia. Young William attended Hampden-Sydney College in his home state and later studied medicine in Richmond and Philadelphia.

Shortly after achieving his majority, Harrison tired of medicine and joined the military, seeking adventure and advancement. He served as aide-de-camp to Anthony Wayne on the campaign that culminated in the Battle of Fallen Timbers and the negotiations for the Treaty of Greenville in 1795. His military training and background would serve him well even after his transition to politics, as would the patrician manners learned at his father's knee in Virginia society. His exploits against Tecumseh's Indian confederacy in the War of 1812 later provided the form and basis of his campaign for the presidency. His easy way with men and society helped him govern with, and over, other territorial politicians of greater age and experience.

Adams also appointed the men directly under Governor Harrison, including Territorial Secretary John Gibson and Judges Henry Vanderberg, John Griffin, and William Clarke (d. 1802, replaced by Thomas T. Davis). Together, these men laid the blueprint of law in the Indiana Territory in its nonrepresentative phase, nonrepresentation being a carryover from the Northwest Territory. Griffin and Clarke are the only two white men mentioned thus far who do not have Indiana counties named for them.

Gibson was from Pennsylvania, making him a rarity among the Virginians and Kentuckians who dominated early Indiana political life. He was sixty years old as he began his appointment and a veteran of both the Revolution and the Pennsylvania state constitutional convention. As a youth, he had been captured and adopted by Indians, and his wife was an Indian. This did not seem to play any role in his dealings with the natives in the Indiana Territory. He served as territorial secretary, becoming acting governor when Harrison resigned to take a military commission in the War of 1812. He served several months until Thomas Posey was officially appointed to replace Harrison.

Thomas Posey served as governor between his appointment in 1813 and statehood in 1816. At the time of his appointment, Posey was serving an appointed term in the U.S. Senate representing Louisiana. Like Harrison, he was born and raised in Virginia and had lived for a time in Kentucky prior to moving to Louisiana. He claimed not to have sought his appointment as territorial governor or even to have known he was under consideration prior to his selection. Sensitive to Indiana's volatility on the slavery question, Posey acknowledged that he was a former slave owner but had emancipated his slaves several years before. He promised his new constituents that he would not support any legislation attempting to overturn the territory's ban on slavery.

Posey proved to be an able public servant. While openly opposed to statehood on economic grounds (coincidentally, the territorial legislature's memorial to Congress requesting progression to statehood happened to coincide with his solicitation of reappointment to the governorship), he fought for improvements to the territorial system. He attempted to force the national government to reorganize the chaotic and inefficient territorial court system, and when unsuccessful, he called a special session of the legislature and pushed through local reorganization. He worked for improvements to the roads, revised the state militia organization, and argued in favor of public schools. With statehood looming as a certainty in 1816, he ran a spirited campaign to become the new state's first governor but lost the general election to Jonathan Jennings.

Jennings came to prominence during the first election for the territory's congressional delegate in 1809. Fairly new to Indiana, the twenty-five-year-old had grown up in western Pennsylvania, studied the law, and had only recently been admitted to practice in Vincennes in 1807. The next year he moved east to Clark County, seeking political opportunities among the more anti-slavery element residing there. He made himself available as a candidate for delegate specifically as an anti-slavery and anti-Harrison alternative. His election was one of the signs of Harrison's waning influence and power.

Jennings was reelected as territorial delegate in 1812, and he became increasingly influential in Indiana politics in the final years before statehood. He was elected as a delegate to the first constitutional convention and once there was selected as president of the convention. Jennings supported Posey's efforts at judicial reform and used his position in Congress to lobby for them, though to no avail. His work in the convention assured that the reforms Posey had helped push through the territorial legislature were given proper attention in the new constitution.

One of the men responsible for the drafting of the judicial section of the constitution was Jennings's associate and fellow anti-Harrison man, James Noble. In addition, Noble chaired the committees on the legislature and banking. Noble was a lawyer and militia officer originally from Virginia. Moving to Indiana, he was elected to the Territorial Assembly in 1812 as a representative from Franklin County. He was quickly recognized for his bright and able legal mind and served also as the county's prosecuting attorney. At the conclusion of the constitutional convention, Noble was elected as one of Indiana's two rookie senators. Ironically, once in Washington, he found himself living in a boarding house with a newly elected representative from Ohio, William Henry Harrison.

The final two figures of importance in the formation of Indiana were not politicians in the traditional sense, but they played major roles in creating the political and social weave of the new state. Tecumseh and his younger brother, best known as the Prophet, were born in what would become Ohio, both around 1770. These two Shawnee men created the last, largest, and most successful native opposition to white settlement in the eastern United States. Tecumseh, recognizing the relative weakness of any individual tribe in the face of the U.S. military, worked tirelessly to create a pan-Indian confederacy to stand up to further encroachment onto Indian lands. Viewing the interests of any native peoples as being in common with all native peoples, he was able to bring a previously unknown level of cohesion to the inherently fractionated relations of different tribes. The Prophet, as a result of a visionary experience, provided a spiritual base for the differing tribes to find common ground in the repudiation of white ways.

Although the brothers' confederation and native spiritual renewal were ultimately unsuccessful in stemming the tide of white settlement and U.S. expansion, they altered the face of that expansion and briefly held the territory, and expanding nation, at bay.

POLITICS

Although there were clashing personalities, political rivalries, philosophical differences, and a few genuine obstacles to be overcome, it must be acknowledged that there was no serious, coherent objection to Indiana statehood. The few who protested or warned against it objected only to its timing, not its substance. Likewise, the constitutional and boundary controversies that surrounded Ohio statehood were absent in Indiana. Missing too was the party fighting that accompanied Ohio's birthing process. Political friction in Indiana had little to do with party affiliations and nearly everything to do with personalities. The grandest of these personalities was, as would be expected, William Henry Harrison.

When Harrison was appointed territorial governor in 1800, his primary focus was opening up Indian land to white settlement, and he pursued this with great zeal. Another of his duties, however, was the administration of a government over a population that continued to both grow, and grow restless, over the course of his twelve years in office. Throughout his tenure, Harrison was accused of elitism, favoritism, aristocratic arrogance, and self-serving behavior. He was also praised as an able, inspiring leader, a man of unimpeachable integrity, and a selfless public servant. Even after leaving office in Indiana in 1812 to take a military appointment and leaving the territory for good after the war, Harrison was such a touchstone that the constitutional convention in 1816 was still painted as a showdown between pro- and anti-Harrison men.

Although there was grumbling about Harrison throughout his tenure, there was really no anti-Harrison movement in the early days. Indiana's nonrepresentational phase of government did not allow for much anti-Harrison activity. The governor had full appointment power and created whatever legislation he thought was needed. The second, semi-representative phase was instituted in 1804 after Harrison, responding to public sentiment, petitioned for the territory to advance. He was, of course, criticized by those who felt he was moving too quickly as well as by those who felt he was moving too slowly.

With this new phase came the first legislative body, the elected General Assembly and an appointed upper house, the Territorial Council. Ostensibly, the governor was to send a slate of nominees for the council chosen by the assembly to the president, who would select from among them. Harrison sent such a list along to Thomas Jefferson, who sent back a confirmation letter with the names left blank and a letter suggesting that Harrison make the choices, remembering to reject "dishonest men [and] those called Federalists, even the honest among them...."[5] Harrison did appoint one Federalist out of five total. Another Harrison crony, Benjamin Parke, became Indiana's first delegate to Congress.

The territorial legislature served as little more than Harrison's rubber stamp in its first few years. For his part, the governor had thrown his weight behind pro-slavery candidates, and they returned the favor by throwing their weight behind him. It was in this period, for example, that legislation was repeatedly passed attempting to circumvent the ban on slavery called for by the Northwest Ordinance.

As the population of Indiana grew, it diversified and moved north and east, out of the direct sphere of influence of the governor in Vincennes and Knox County. The settlers, the poor, and the farmers coming in ever greater numbers, were less inclined to look favorably on slavery and what was increasingly seen as an aristocratic rule. Harrison began to face agitation from the west too, where residents were lobbying for the separation of the Illinois Territory, which finally took place in 1809.

The year 1809 proved to be a watershed in territorial politics. The office of delegate to Congress was again up for election. Harrison's handpicked candidate was Thomas Randolph, recently appointed attorney general. At thirty-eight years old and a cousin of Thomas Jefferson, Randolph was from Virginia and had served in the assembly of that state. In many ways, he was just like Harrison and the voters found him so: aristocratic and pro-slavery.

Randolph's principal opponent was Jonathan Jennings, only two years in the territory but already known as a vehement critic of Harrison. Jennings virtually ignored Knox County and Vincennes in his campaign, choosing instead to tour the central, east, and southeast sections of the territory. Seen as a "man of the people," Jennings won a very tightly contested race. Randolph alleged voting irregularities and contested the election. He also challenged a

Quaker who had criticized him in a newspaper to a duel. The Quaker declined.[6] Lastly, Randolph traveled to Washington for the opening of Congress along with Jennings. A congressional committee reported its opinion that the entire election had been illegal, but the House as a whole refused to accept the report, allowed Jennings to be seated, and sent Randolph home.[7]

The door to legislative dissension was open. The 1810 General Assembly repealed previous Harrison-backed legislation from 1803 and 1805 allowing for the holding of "servants" and "indentured servants," circumventing the laws against slavery in the territory. The same body began plans to move the capital from Vincennes to a more central location. Publicly, they cited the growth of population in the eastern and central parts of Indiana, but this was also an unveiled insult to Harrison, who had built an extravagant home in Vincennes. Additionally, the legislature petitioned Congress, asking it to remove the landownership qualification for voting in territorial elections. Congress did them one better, removing the qualification and also making ineligible for membership to the General Assembly anyone already holding an office appointed by the governor, save justices of the peace or militia officers. The insults, it must have seemed, were coming from all sides.

Harrison's resignation to accept a military commission in 1812 was certainly one of the best decisions of his political life. Rather than stay in office and watch his power and reputation diminish, as they surely would have, he went on to military acclaim that he was able to use to rekindle his political career in Ohio after the war. He even returned to Indiana, symbolically at least, for his successful run for the presidency in 1840. John Gibson, the aging territorial secretary who replaced Harrison on an interim basis, did yeoman's work in holding the territory together during the war but was not a factor politically beyond rallying popular support for the militia and vetoing a bill that would have barred blacks from settling in Indiana.

Thomas Posey, appointed as Harrison's permanent replacement, must have seemed almost a copy. He was born in Virginia, had an upper-class background, and was a former slave owner, but he did not generate the same disdain and hostility that plagued Harrison in his last years in office. Jennings worked with him, or at least alongside him, for judicial reforms, and there is no record of serious animosity toward him on the part of the citizens or the legislatures that met under his watch. His loss to Jennings in the first state gubernatorial race appears to have been based upon issues and not personalities, per se.

The men who drafted the state constitution were a mixed bag, but still, four years after he left office, they were broken into pro- and anti-Harrison camps rather than split by party affiliations. Even at that, they worked together in relative harmony for what they saw as the good of the state and their fellow citizens. The constitutional convention did not keep a record of debate and discussion, but if its members argued for selfish ends, those arguments did not make it into the finished document.

TO STATEHOOD: THE INDIAN, THE NEGRO, AND CASH FLOW PROBLEMS

The Indian Problem

Initially, the greatest obstacle to Indiana statehood was its native population. From the creation of the Indiana Territory until 1813, the Indian problem was the most vexing one for white settlers and their governors alike. At the time of the establishment of the new territorial boundaries in 1800, the white population of the Indiana Territory (including what would become the Illinois Territory and much of the future Michigan) was 5,641. Accurate figures for the native population are impossible to ascertain, but would have been at least two to three times as many. A number of tribal groups called the land home at least part of the year, including the Miami, Potawotami, Sauk, Fox, Delaware, Shawnee, Piankashaw, and Wea.

Native relations under the French in the eighteenth century were, as a rule, calm, pleasant, and beneficial to both sides. The French had no aspirations to mass settlement. What forts and settlements they established were intended primarily as trading centers, and the natives were nearly always happy to trade. They exchanged furs for manufactured goods and readily adapted everything from woven cloth to silver jewelry to cooking utensils to their established ways of life. The French were happy to acquire furs for the ever hungry European markets. Both sides saw the other as first and foremost trading partners, and while there were sporadic incidents of misunderstanding and violence, these were far outstripped by peaceful and productive interactions. There was a good deal of intermarriage, virtually always between native women and French men. Such personal alliances generally strengthened group and trading bonds.

Once the future territory came under British control even before the 1763 Treaty of Paris, native-white relations were altered. The British, too, carried on an active trade with the Indians but saw them first as subjects of the empire, an attitude that rankled native sensibilities. In addition, the French habit of greeting the Indians with gifts and goodwill offerings was seen by the British as bribery and was discontinued. Lastly, the French traders treated the natives as friends and business partners, whereas the British treated them as employees or, at best, suppliers. Especially arms and ammunition, provided in goodwill by the French and upon which the Indians had become dependent for hunting, were treated by the British as just another trade good and routinely denied to the natives. Resentment of the British by the natives inevitably followed, and in 1763, a confederation of tribes under the Ottawa leader Pontiac plotted to run the British from the territory.

Pontiac had fought for the French in the Seven Years' War and continued to view them as allies, noting that the French had lived among the Indians as tenants, that is, on Indian land, and therefore the British had no right to claim the land as spoils of war. The Pontiac confederacy could not hold together. Despite several victories in the field, the disruption of British trade, and settlement in the territory, the fractional nature of the tribes within the coalition led to a lack of concerted and coordinated efforts, and, coupled with the capitulation of the remaining French resistance, the confederacy collapsed in late 1765. Regardless of its ultimate failure, Pontiac's pan-Indian confederacy served as a blueprint for later coalitions under both Little Turtle and Tecumseh.

The Northwest Ordinance clearly called for the western expansion of the new United States. The British Proclamation of 1763, forbidding American settlement in the west, had slowed the onslaught of white pioneers, but not stopped it. The American victory in the Revolution reopened the gates. As could have been expected, the more settlement, the more conflict followed. In 1879, faced with increasing hostility and depredations on both sides, President Washington wrote to then Northwest Territory governor Arthur St. Clair that if "a peace can be established...the interests of the United States dictate that it should be effected as soon as possible."[8]

Laboring under pessimistic reports from his agents and his own inclinations, St. Clair felt that such a peace could not be effected, and a number of military forays were conducted against the Indians in the territory. St. Clair himself led a force into the field in the autumn of 1791, only to see it decimated by a pan-Indian coalition under Little Turtle. The number of killed, wounded, and missing Americans ran to over nine hundred, making it the greatest defeat the U.S. Army would ever suffer at the hands of the native population.

The defeat of St. Clair briefly halted white settlement in the territory and served to bolster Indian resistance. It also sent a message to Washington and the Congress as to the weakness of their frontier fighting forces. They responded by providing a complete reorganization of the western army, which came to be known as the Legion of the United States. To command this new force they chose General Anthony Wayne.

Wayne took the better part of two years to collect and train his troops, drilling them relentlessly and teaching them methods of Indian warfare. To his men he was known as "Mad Anthony," a nickname he had earned in the Revolution. The Indians came to call him the Chief Who Never Sleeps.

During this time a number of efforts were made to find a peaceful end to the white-Indian conflict. Suspicion and bad faith on both sides rendered most of these efforts moot. The Indians, emboldened by the defeat of St. Clair, believed they could hold American encroachment at bay. The Americans believed that the doctrine of "higher use" entitled them to the lands. Finally, in the summer of 1794, Wayne's troops were ready to advance, and on August 20 they met a large force of Wyandot, Delaware, Shawnee, Miami, and Ottawa Indians on the banks of the Maumee River at a place known as Fallen Timbers, named for the scattering of trees previously uprooted by a tornado. Wayne's well-ordered and disciplined men overwhelmed the natives and set them to full retreat.

Demoralized and disorganized after the defeat at Fallen Timbers, many of the tribes began making overtures for peace and accepted, somewhat hesitantly, the Treaty of Greenville, which established new northern and western boundaries to Indian lands and effectively forced the tribes living in the Ohio Valley westward into Indiana. The era of treaties came to the Northwest, and later Indiana, Territory. It brought with it a period of relative peace, but one that would be short-lived.

The most significant native figure in Indiana history was Tecumseh, a Shawnee born in Ohio around 1768. The son of a minor Shawnee chief, Tecumseh, along with his brother Tenskwatawa, better known as the Prophet, led a pan-Indian confederacy that hindered and disrupted settlement in and governance of the Indiana Territory in the years between 1805 and 1813. Soured on the U.S. government and whites in general after his father's death at the Battle of Point Pleasant (Ohio) in 1774, Tecumseh spent his formative years moving from settlement to settlement as the Shawnee were driven farther and farther north and west by white settlement and treaty boundaries. He distinguished himself for personal bravery and leadership in a series of raids on white settlements in Ohio, Indiana, and Kentucky.

During this same time, his younger brother had fallen into a life of drunkenness and dissipation before having a religious awakening in the autumn of 1805. Convinced he had been visited by the "Good Spirit," he underwent a profound personality change and began preaching that the salvation of his people (initially the Shawnee, but later to encompass all native groups) lay in rejecting the ways of the whites, including clothing, religion, and his own personal demon, alcohol. His message found a ready audience in an oppressed people, and the Prophet's new religion gained a strong following both inside and outside of his tribe.

This also provided an entry point for the political views of Tecumseh. Certain that white encroachment would not stop until the Indian was completely removed or eradicated, Tecumseh began attempting to organize disparate native tribes into a confederation that would stand together to resist further white settlement. He insisted that all Indian lands belonged to all Indian people as a whole and that previous treaties, often negotiated with tribes that had no claim to the lands they were selling to the United States, were invalid. William Henry Harrison, governor of the Indiana Territory and hence the chief negotiator of many of these treaties, added fuel to the fire by not inviting representatives of many tribes, including the Shawnee, to the councils at which they were negotiated.

Tecumseh's travels took him not only all around the territory but also to the northeast, south, and west in search of allies. Word of his efforts caused great unease among settlers all along the frontier, and incidents of violence against both whites and Indians increased. Settlers in Indiana formed militia and built blockhouses for security in case of raids or attacks. Harrison initially chose to respond by attacking the Prophet, writing to the Shawnee and Delaware that he was a charlatan who "speaks not the words of the Great Spirit, but those of the devil...."[9] Learning of a large council meeting of tribal representatives, President Jefferson also wrote to natives in the Detroit area, warning them against breaking the established peace.

Matters between Tecumseh and Harrison, and effectively between whites and natives, came to a head in August 1810. Attending a council at Vincennes, Tecumseh put forth the new, and to Harrison alarming, proposition that all Indian land was held in common by all tribes and could not be sold or ceded without the consent of all. As a result, he, and by extension all natives, viewed all previous treaties as invalid. Harrison considered this nonsense, and the two men came perilously to blows. No violence broke out, but the council ended there. Tecumseh set out to bolster his confederacy, and Harrison, convinced that open warfare could not be averted, petitioned the federal government for additional troops.

Nearly two years before, the Prophet had relocated his village of followers to an area just north of present-day Lafayette, Indiana. Known as "Prophets-town," the village became a hub of intertribal activity and the center of the new Indian religion. In September 1810, with Tecumseh still away, Harrison and the Fourth Regiment of the U.S. Army, along with units of local militia, headed north to force the Prophet out of the territory. Tecumseh, anticipating such an action, explicitly ordered his younger brother to avoid armed confrontation, but the Prophet, aware of Harrison's presence and fearing imminent hostilities, mounted a surprise attack on the morning of November 7. The battle that followed went badly for both sides, and after two hours, the natives broke off and abandoned Prophetstown. Harrison marched his battered troops back to Vincennes. The Battle of Tippecanoe was a military draw, but Harrison achieved his primary objective. The Prophet was never again a serious threat to the Indiana Territory or its (white) inhabitants.

It took war with England, however, to completely settle the Indian problem. Frustrated over repeated acts of aggression both military and economic, the U.S. Congress declared war in June 1812. (The territorial delegates were not permitted to vote, despite having a major stake in the action.) Native groups in the Indiana Territory were split in their allegiance. Tecumseh, who would have allied with any power that seemed to promise the natives autonomy, sided with the British.

Harrison was initially bypassed for military assignment, but his own protests and those of his political allies eventually led him to a brevetted rank of major general with the Kentucky militia and later to command of the Northwestern Army, charged with retaking Detroit and the invasion of Canada. Unable to hold Detroit, the British evacuated the fort in the autumn of 1813 and fled east, pursued by Harrison's forces. Tecumseh led his warriors into Canada to aid the British and had met up with them before Harrison overtook both on October 5, on the banks of the Thames River. In the battle that followed, the British were routed and Tecumseh killed. Again, Harrison achieved his objectives. With their defeat, the British ceased any further engagement in the West. When Tecumseh died, all serious native resistance in the Old Northwest died with him.

The Negro Problem

The "Negro problem" was solved with much less drama, and little bloodshed, but it was not so much to Harrison's liking. The Ordinance of 1787 prohibited slavery in the Northwest Territory in Article 6, and the laws of the Indiana Territory followed suit. This did not necessarily keep slavery out of Indiana. Blacks of African descent had been in the area nearly as early as whites, often accompanying them. The French brought their slaves into the territory with them, and free blacks trapped and traded. As early as 1746, five blacks were living at the trading post at Vincennes, along with forty Frenchmen. The first permanent trading post at what would become Chicago was founded by Jean Baptiste Pointe du Sable, a free black man, in about 1775, at least ten years prior to the Northwest Ordinance. Although no accurate figures are available until the census of 1810, in that year there were 630 black residents, of whom 237 were listed as slaves.[10] Of the rest, some were almost certainly held under indentures, but others were, equally certainly, free.

Early territorial debate viewed the question of slavery as of secondary importance. As has been seen, the primary concern was the rapid but orderly settling of the region in such a way as to maintain economic links with the established states. The prohibition on slavery as laid out in the Northwest Ordinance was not so much an ideological reaction against human bondage as it was an attempt, on the one hand, to encourage settlers from the north and northeast and, on the other, to discourage these new settlers from competing with the southern states in large-scale agriculture, especially in tobacco and indigo. (The rise of King Cotton was still a few years off.)

In addition to limiting competition, the southern states supported the anti-slavery article in the ordinance as an expedient to its passage, which would allow the sales of land to pay off state and national debts. Virginia, in particular, saw the new territory as a buffer for the extended and exposed Kentucky frontier. Besides, the nature of travel to and from the new territories, by river and proposed water-transportation improvements, virtually guaranteed that the fruits of the new settlers would arrive first in Virginia.

Once established and functioning, however, the Indiana Territory struggled anew with the question of slavery and the status of blacks. Despite the wording of Article 6 of the ordinance, "There shall be neither Slavery nor Involuntary Servitude in said territory," it was rarely interpreted retroactively. That is, persons held in slavery prior to 1787 were consistently found to continue as slaves regardless of their residency in the territory. Arthur St. Clair, the first governor of the Northwest Territory, repeatedly asserted that the prohibition applied only to slaves brought into the territory after 1787.

In addition to its passive supporters, slavery had its active boosters as well. Many of the men administering the territory's government were themselves slaveholders or otherwise in possession of blacks as "servants" under long-term indentures. In 1802, William Henry Harrison, claiming that the majority of the people in the territory favored slavery in one from or another, called for a convention to be held in Vincennes. On Christmas Day, twelve delegates adopted a resolution to be sent to the U.S. Congress asking for a ten-year suspension of Article 6 of the ordinance. Congress refused. Regardless, Harrison continued to keep a number of "servants" whether they were "slaves for life or only serve a term of years."[11] Harrison was the most notable of territorial slave owners, but he was not alone.

At the first meeting of the new General Assembly in the second, semi-representational phase of territorial government in 1805, the assembly passed a bill allowing any person owning or purchasing slaves outside the territory to bring them into Indiana lawfully. Such slaves would be bound in the territory. If the slaves were over fifteen years of age, they could be "signed" to an indenture for any number of years. Many indentures were for the fixed term of ninety years. The most common were for periods from twenty to forty years. Hence, once the physically vigorous period of life was past, the "servant" could be discarded without further financial commitment. Should the slave be reluctant to sign, the owner was given sixty days to remove him or her from the state without losing title. This, of course, would allow for selling the reluctant slave to an owner in a state or territory without such restrictive laws. Slaves under fifteen were to be registered with the county of residence and required to serve their masters until age thirty-five, if male, or thirty-two, if female. Children born to slaves in the territory were to serve their parents' master until age thirty (male) or twenty-eight (female). They too could be signed to indentures by their parents.

This same assembly also authored a memorial to Congress asking that Article 6 be revoked, but it ultimately failed because riders were attached protesting the separation of the Illinois Territory and seeking immediate admission to statehood. The memorial was sent along to Washington, over some members' protest, where the committee to which it was assigned supported it but took no further action.

The next year, a second session of the assembly expanded upon its previous bill by passing legislation allowing blacks and "mulattoes" bound under the 1805 bill to be sold as part of personal estates. Again, and this time with full support, the ruling body sent a memorial asking for the revocation of Article 6. And again, the committee responded favorably but took no more action.

Finally, an anti-slavery movement began to form. A mass meeting was held following the second session on October 10, 1807, in Clark County. The intent was to take action against the bill passed in the previous years. The meeting drafted its own memorial to Congress and took the bold step of asking Congress to withhold any further legislation on the matter until Indiana should have the opportunity eventually to settle the question itself in a state constitution. The residents of Dearborn County had sent a petition opposing slavery in the territory in 1805. Now they took the even bolder step of asking to be annexed into Ohio, which entered the Union as a free state in 1803. The Senate committee that received these decided it imprudent to alter Article 6 and took no action on severing Dearborn County from the territory.

With the Second General Assembly, in 1808, Harrison and his supporters began to lose their hold on the politics of slavery, and in general, of the territory. Population and its attendant representation had been growing in the eastern portion of the state, far away from Vincennes and the governor's sphere of influence. A report was read in session calling the violations of Article 6 and the admission of slavery into the territory a "retrograde step into barbarism." The report was accompanied by a bill to repeal the 1805 indenture act. The bill passed the House immediately, but it did not pass second reading in the Legislative Council.[12] The tide, though, had begun to turn.

It is important to remember that anti-slavery was not synonymous with pro-black. As in the rest of the young country, many early residents of Indiana sought to exclude slavery from the territory without having the slightest desire to extend rights, citizenship, or even freedom to the blacks held under it. Many opposed slavery on purely economic bases. The introduction of large-scale slavery into the territory could have created a planter class, as it had in the South, in which a small, wealthy elite controlled the bulk of agriculture, the economy, and political power while small farmers struggled and failed. Most of the settlers in Indiana who had come from the South were victims of this very system and fought vehemently against its introduction in their new homeland. Many, regardless of which column they came down in, were simply racist.

Still others objected to the inequalities in representation that had come into existence with the three-fifths compromise in the U.S. Constitution, which gave the southern states disproportionate representation in Congress. Even among those who objected to slavery on moral or philosophical grounds, most did not suggest opening society to blacks. That was left to the small but growing population of Quakers within the state.

Quakers began moving into the Indiana Territory shortly after the turn of the century. Most came from the Upper South, predominantly North Carolina, as local slave laws and sanctions became increasingly intolerable to them. They were mostly small-scale farmers, and Indiana offered them inexpensive, fertile land in a free territory. By around 1815, they had established communities in eastern and southeastern Indiana and had encouraged a number of free blacks and escaped slaves to relocate in Indiana. Settlements like Roberts and Lick Creek, founded by blacks near existing Quaker communities, would eventually thrive throughout most of the nineteenth century.

Little was accomplished legally by the anti-slavery factions until the constitutional convention of 1816, but their growing numbers eliminated any further serious challenge to Article 6. With the adoption of the first state constitution, the matter was settled for good, except perhaps for the 190 persons still listed as slaves in the 1820 Indiana census. It would be 1840, in fact, before Indiana became "slave-free."[13]

The Cash Flow Problem

The third and final significant obstacle to statehood was economic. By 1816, the federal government was still bearing over half of the cost of the territorial government. Although the total cost of running the Indiana Territory from its establishment in 1800 until statehood just shy of sixteen years later "would have been less than $100,000," little of that came from the territory itself.[14] In the early years, the federal government bore the entire salaries of the governor and other territorial officials, as well as most of the costs of such necessities as postage, housing, and printing for the government. On top of these were sums spent on treaty negotiations, Indian annuities, and the wages, housing, and feeding of federal troops protecting the settlers. While the territory bore a greater share of expenses over time, it never did come near meeting its own costs. Most estimates regarding expenditures under statehood projected that they would increase by as much as four times.

Of course, the federal government was making a little money on the territory as well. The sale of public lands through Indiana land offices exceeded $2,000,000 during the territorial period, not counting lands sold through the Cincinnati Land Office. In the last years of territorial status, taxes on such items as liquor and stills, along with the licenses to sell them, netted the federal government still more income, though nothing to compare with land sales. The new state, once established, would be restricted from taxing federal lands for the first five years of its existence.

The War of 1812, however, took a major economic toll on both the nation and the territory. With the war and Tecumseh's Indian confederacy combined, land sales slowed to a trickle, and many settlers were unable to make their payments, defaulting on their loans and losing their lands back to the government. The territory was unable to collect taxes from many citizens, and at one point in 1813, the territorial treasury fell to a balance of $2.42.[15]

The territorial legislature slowly but steadily increased taxes in the postwar years, but they were not enough to offset the expenses that would come with statehood. The economic objections to statehood were never fully addressed or overcome, they were simply drowned out. While the constitutional convention was meeting in June of 1816, Territorial Governor Thomas Posey was sending letters to the U.S. Congress asking it to deny statehood due to the poor state of Indiana's financial situation. Congress did not comply.

CONSTITUTION MAKING: BECOMING "INDIANA"

Although they didn't know it at the time, members of the Indiana Territory General Assembly met for the final time in December 1815, including a session on Christmas Day. For the first time, Governor Posey did not appear, having his message read in his absence. He congratulated the members on the end of the war, the termination of which initiated a new wave of immigration into the territory. With military action no longer requiring attention, he suggested legislators now focus on roads and education.[16]

The assembly did pay attention to roads, passing an act raising taxes to pay for them but reducing the period of compulsory work to two days per year, except in the case of new roads being built, which called for an extra two days. Road taxes could be worked off as well. The town of Vincennes was allowed to levy new taxes, including a $15 tax for billiard tables, a 50 cent tax for hogs allowed to run free in the streets, and a $1 tax per dog. The counties of Jackson and Orange were organized at this session, bringing the total of territorial counties to fifteen. And the assembly asked Congress to allow the territory to form a convention for the drafting of a state constitution. Governor Posey immediately wrote his letter to Washington recommending against the idea.

Congress passed the Enabling Act on April 19, 1816, and stipulated that election of delegates to the constitutional convention be held by May 13. Word of the passage did not reach Vincennes until May 2, creating a scramble for nominees. Since, however, the passage was viewed by most as a certainty, a number of those interested in becoming delegates had already made that desire known. Jonathan Jennings, serving in Washington as a territorial representative, had written as early as February that he would be "gratified" to be part of the convention.[17] Another near certainty was that Jennings would be chosen president of the convention when it met on June 10, in Corydon.

Like most of the territory's early settlers, the majority of the delegates to the convention originally came from the Upper and Middle South. Only nine of the forty-three delegates had not lived at least part of their lives below the Mason-Dixon Line. Twenty-seven had lived in Kentucky. Six were born in Europe. At least twenty-six had served in the territorial government, eleven as legislators. Five had served under Harrison on the Tippecanoe campaign. Five would have Indiana counties named for them. James Dill, a delegate from Dearborn County, a staunch Harrison man and frequent appointee, wrote of his fellows as a whole, "Talents are most damnably lacking here—and he who has but a moderate share is looked upon as a great man."[18] Dill himself must have posed a curious figure in his own right. Born in Ireland, he still, in 1816 wore a queue and appeared in court in knee britches with silver buckles. A kinder student of the convention considered the group "clear-minded, unpretending men of common sense...sufficient, when combined."[19]

As in the territorial period as a whole, the delegates broke into two major camps, the anti-Harrison men, led as ever by Jennings, and the pro-Harrison camp, represented by Benjamin Parke and other friends of the former governor, who played no direct role in the convention himself, by this time running for Congress in Ohio. The group led by Jennings was in the clear majority, but a number of delegates voted independently. Parke and Jennings were the two most experienced and able politicians in Corydon in the summer of 1816. The factions were still divided, in general, geographically, with the Jennings group coming from the eastern and southeastern section of the territory, the pro-Harrison faction, from the west.

The journals of the convention did not record discussion, speeches, or debate, so it is impossible to know how heated the proceedings may have become. In any event, the assembled delegation seems to have gone about its work in a businesslike fashion, even stipulating in the adopted rules, "Every member shall particularly forebear personal reflections, nor shall any member name another in argument or debate" (Rule 17) and insisting that no article or section could be approved without having been read for three days unless a two-thirds majority voted to dispense with the rule (Rule 22). On the third day of the convention, fourteen (later expanded to sixteen) committees were named to prepare specific sections of the proposed constitution, and they quickly got down to work.

Most of Indiana's first state constitution is taken wholesale from previous state and territorial documents, most notably those of Ohio and Kentucky. Less than 10 percent of the final document consists of wholly original material. It was not, however, a simple cut-and-paste work, but the "borrowed" sections taken from elsewhere were selected carefully and altered as the committees, and finally full convention, saw fit.

The Preamble and Article 1 were largely modeled on those of Ohio, written thirteen years before, with minor revisions. The Preamble asserts the right of the state of Indiana to be formed and admitted to the United States on equal footing with the existing states as set forth under the Ordinance of 1787.

Article 1, also adapted closely from Ohio, and with an eye at the U.S. Constitution, lays out a bill of rights for the citizens of the new state. In twenty-four sections, it addresses "certain natural, inherent, and unalienable rights, among which are the enjoying and defending life and liberty, and of acquiring, possessing and protecting property, and pursuing and obtaining happiness and safety." It sets forth provisions for free and equal elections of a government of and for the people and the right to alter that government "in such manner as they may think proper."

Further, it creates freedoms of religious practice, the press, and assembly, and establishes trial by jury. It forbids illegal search and seizure, or "unnecessary rigour" in the treatment of those under arrest. Article 1 continues by laying out further rights of individuals under the law and solidifies these rights by declaring "that every thing in this article, is excepted out of the general powers of Government, and shall forever remain inviolable."

Article 2 deals with the division of the state's powers into three branches that are, in turn, covered in Articles 3, 4, and 5. The third article was taken largely from similar passages in Ohio's constitution, but it lowers the age requirements for holding office to twenty-one for representatives and twenty-five for senators.

As well, it lowers the residential requirement of two years in Ohio to one year in Indiana. The committee attempted to do away with any requirement that representatives must have previously paid state or county taxes, but this was vetoed by the main body. Section 20 stipulates that no one holding elected or appointed office could simultaneously run for or accept another office, but this was amended to allow then current territorial office holders to accept positions in the new state government. Representation is apportioned by the population of adult, white males, which was determined by a census every five years.

The office of governor is addressed in Article 4, which, mirroring a number of state constitutions, sought to limit executive powers. In the years immediately after the Revolution, most of the new states were leery of creating a system of government that allowed too much power to fall into the hands of any one man or office. Indiana, drawing mainly from the Kentucky constitution, did not limit the executive to quite the same extent as the earlier states. The governor and his next in command, the lieutenant governor, are to be elected to three-year terms. They are allowed to run for reelection but can serve no more than six out of any nine years. The governor is required to be at least thirty years of age and to have been a resident of the territory (or henceforth, the state) for a minimum of five years. He is to be the commander in chief of the state army, navy, and militia but cannot himself take the field unless granted permission, or by the request of the state legislature. Nonetheless, while the governor can veto legislative action, overriding his veto requires only a simple majority of both houses. This severely limits his ability to thwart the will of the people as expressed by their representatives.

A committee made up primarily of lawyers drafted Article 5, addressing the judicial branch. The territorial court system had been heavily criticized, and the committee sought to rectify what it considered its defects. The committee members drew upon both the Ohio and Kentucky constitutions for their recommendations, but their original draft was rejected by the convention, and a new committee, with some of the same members, was appointed to redraft the article. The original, which created judges' terms as lasting "during good behavior," was rewritten to appoint them for terms of a better-defined seven years. Presiding judges would not be appointed by the governor but rather elected by a joint ballot of the two legislative houses. Only two of the three state supreme court justices are required to form a quorum, rather than the original draft's requirement of a full court. Circuit courts were created and the terms of their officers set out.

The boundaries of the franchise followed in Article 6. A residency require-ment of one year was adopted for potential voters. As in territorial days, there was a good deal of consideration given to whether the method of voting should be by ballot or voice ("*viva voce*"). The former was chosen, but with the provision that the question would be readdressed by the General Assembly in its 1821 session, after which its decision would be unalterable.

The "all men," who in the Preamble were vested with inalienable rights, was interpreted literally in regard to extending the franchise to women but was viewed more in the abstract when it came to blacks and Indians, many of whom lived within the state. None was given the vote, nor was any person decided by the legislature to have committed an "infamous" crime. Voters in Indiana, as in virtually every other state at that time, were white males over twenty-one.

The American victory in the War of 1812 effectively ended Indian resistance to settlement and expansion within the proposed state, but that was not yet readily apparent to the constitutional convention. Article 7 covers the formation and maintenance of a state militia. "All free able bodied male persons" could be called by the state to serve. As with voting, "Negroes, Mulattoes and Indians" are excepted. Conscientious objectors would not be forced to serve, but they would be assessed an annual fee. Officers were to be elected by their troops at the level of rank below them and commissioned by the governor, who would appoint only adjutant and quartermaster generals. All commissioned officers would hold their commissions subject to "good behavior" until the age of sixty.

The question of amending the new constitution proved a daunting one and the provisions made for such are in the curious Article 8. Seemingly at odds over how to approach the subject, the convention passed a vague process. The article allows for a vote to be held every twelve years at the time of the regular gubernatorial election, letting the people decide whether they are in favor of holding a convention to "revise, amend or change" the current constitution. The process is laid out in one long, syntax-challenged sentence. It is unclear as to whether it was intended that such a vote should occur only every twelve years or at least every twelve years. The General Assembly of 1822–1823 seemed to accept the latter interpretation, as it passed the first referendum, to be held the following August. The next were held in 1828 and 1840, adhering to the twelve-year schedule. The 1846 and 1849 referendums were held by special legislation.

What is clear is the intent of the convention to settle the question of slavery once and for all. Added to the original draft of the article was a second sentence instructing that "no alteration of this constitution shall ever take place so as to introduce slavery or involuntary servitude in the State." With that, the status of slavery and its indentured proxy was decided for good in the state of Indiana. The status of blacks themselves would continue to be in question until the end of the Civil War fifty years later.

As noted earlier, the specific eradication of slavery in the new constitution did not indicate that its framers were enlightened men, but the bold Article 9 does display a certain amount of progressive thinking. Unusual for their day, they acknowledged and codified the education of the populace as "being essential to the preservation of a free Government." This article requires that the state provide "for a general system of education, ascending in a regular graduation, from township schools to a state university, wherein tuition shall be gratis, and equally open to all." It goes on to instruct the legislature to "pass such laws as shall be calculated to encourage intellectual, Scientifical, and agricultural improvement…of arts, sciences, commerce, manufactures, and natural history…." The fines assessed from conscientious objectors and those collected for "any breach of the penal laws" were to be applied to educational facilities within the counties where they were assessed. Public libraries were to receive 10 percent of the proceeds from the sale of lots in county seats. Even allowing for the "all" to exclude women, blacks and Indians, none of whom are specifically mentioned one way or another, this was a forward-thinking stipulation for 1816. Unfortunately, a qualifier early in the article, "[a]s soon as circumstances will permit," enabled the state's legislatures virtually to ignore education until a new constitution was adopted in 1851. The remainder of the article requires the establishment of the penal code and lays the framework for founding homes and asylums for the aged and physically and mentally ill. In all, it provided recognition of social responsibility unusual for the frontier.

At the time of the convention, the Indiana Territory had several functioning banks that were issuing their own credit, and a committee was appointed to create some form of regulation within the new state. The committee, headed by James Noble, provided in Article 10 that there should be no establishment of a state bank but did not prevent the future legislatures from doing so. The currently functioning banks at Vincennes and Madison were allowed to continue as they were. Either might be adopted as the state bank at some future point, with the other then becoming a branch.

Article 11 is something of a hodgepodge of sections dealing with items as diverse as the definition of treason against the state ("levying war against it, in adhering to its enemies, or giving them aid and comfort"), to an additional section (Section 7) prohibiting slavery. Section 11 codifies Corydon as the state capital "until the year eighteen hundred and twenty-five, and until removed by law." Other sections set up requirements for serving in government positions, Section 13 stating that no persons could hold "more than one lucrative office at the same time," without defining "lucrative." Finally, Section 17 establishes the geographical boundaries of the new state. (As late as the previous spring, the town of Ft. Wayne was not certain as to whether it was part of Indiana or Ohio.[20])

Finally, Article 12 addresses the transition from territorial to state government. It confirmed that all contracts, debts, legal agreements, and claims would continue to be binding so long as not specifically forbidden by the new constitution. Officeholders would continue to serve until provisions could be made for new elections. All territorial laws not directly addressed in the constitution would continue to be in force. The delegates signed the final draft on June 29, 1816. It was not submitted to the electorate for ratification but became operative upon signing. Thus did Indiana, not yet a state, acquire a state government.

The work of the convention lasted nineteen days and was completed at a total cost of just over $3,000. Each member was paid $2 per day plus a travel stipend that varied based upon the mileage traveled to Corydon. The costs included payments to a printer in Louisville for printing and stitching copies of the finished document as well as the journal of the proceedings. A bargain, the first constitution of the state of Indiana would serve for thirty-six years, outliving nearly all of its authors.

THE SEAL OF APPROVAL

The convention mandated elections, to be held under territorial law, for August 15, a scant six weeks away. Printing presses were available in a number of Indiana towns, and Fourth of July gatherings provided ideal settings for both readings of the new constitution and political stump speeches. The campaign for the governorship of the not-yet-new state quickly emerged as a race between Thomas Posey and Jonathan Jennings. As in the convention itself, Jennings had the lion's share of support, and on November 7, he was inaugurated as the first governor of the state of Indiana, a state that still did not technically exist. Christopher Harrison (no relation to William Henry) was sworn in as lieutenant governor. William Hendricks was elected as Indiana's first representative to Congress. On the following day, the General Assembly elected James Noble and Waller Taylor to the U.S. Senate.

The final word on the question of statehood had to come from Washington. Although the Ordinance of 1787 made the process of statehood clear, the Indiana Territory certainly qualified under all of the required steps, and Congress was quick to accept the memorial of the previous spring, but the state would not exist until signed into law.

This "in between" status would not last long, but it would provide a couple of interesting situations for newly elected officials. Congress had made no allowance for Indiana in the presidential elections of 1816. Regardless, the General Assembly selected three state electors on November 16. The three met briefly and delivered their votes for James Monroe. The status of their votes was in limbo until February 1817. Likewise, while Hendricks was sworn into the U.S. House and seated with his fellows on December 2, the Senate questioned the status of Noble and Taylor and refused to allow them to be seated until December 12.

The timing for their admission logically followed, as on December 11, 1816, Congress resolved "[t]hat the State of Indiana shall be one, and is hereby declared to be one, of the United States of America, and admitted into the Union on an equal footing with the original States, in all respects whatever," including having its senators seated. James Madison approved the resolution the same day.

Technically, federal law was not formally extended to the new commonwealth until March 3, 1817, but the December 11, 1816, date has since been held as Indiana's "birthday," and 1816 is used on the state seal and all official documents and histories.

BEING INDIANA

In 1816, the new state was still a frontier. Most historians extend Indiana's pioneer era until 1830–1840. Simply getting there was still a hard row to hoe. Once one got there, it was still primarily a forest with a few little towns scattered about, mostly in the south, along the Ohio River. The capital would remain in Corydon, the "central location" intended to frustrate Harrison, until the ever-growing population pushed far enough north to require another central location and the swamp that was Indianapolis was drained and platted.

The congressional Enabling Act of 1816 provided that 3 percent of the sale of public lands would go to improving roads and transportation. Recognizing its inadequacy, later state legislatures passed grand public-spending bills to build roads and canals. So grand were they that they bankrupted the state in the 1840s, and the men who wrote the next constitution, in 1850–1851, included an article forbidding the state to go into debt ever again. Ultimately, though, the big spending worked. Although the canals would never actually be completed, the improvements connected the state to the east along with its markets and populations headed west. You could finally get here from there.

New indentures were a thing of the past with statehood, but the fact of slavery would remain until the 1840s, when the last registered slave in the state died. Its legacy lasted longer. Thousands of blacks settled in Indiana between statehood and the Civil War, mostly in all-black settlements, but also in urban areas like Indianapolis and Ft. Wayne. The 1850–1851 constitution also forbade blacks from settling in Indiana, but they did anyway, welcome or not. There was relatively little violence shown them and the law against their settling was little enforced.

Political parties eventually caught on with a vengeance during the Jacksonian era and partisan wrangling became an entertaining fixture of Hoosier town life. This was epitomized in the invention in 1840 of the modern political campaign by none other than William Henry Harrison, who succeeded in convincing a majority of voters that he was both a humble Hoosier frontiersman and vigorous Indian fighter, despite his pedigree, mansion in Ohio, and advanced age. By that time, too, nearly all of the Indian population had been forced into removal to the "Indian Country" that became Oklahoma. At mid-century, the "Land of the Indians" was home to a few scattered Miami who either ignored the removal order or simply turned around and walked back from Oklahoma once the soldiers dispersed.

As a whole, though, Indiana thrived after statehood. Settlers continued to pour into the state, clearing forests, creating farms, towns, and what might even pass for cities in the East. By 1840, the frontier that Harrison's campaign romanticized had retreated to the far side of the Mississippi, and the Hoosier state was fully settled and a vital part of the Union. Residents of the towns along the new National Road could sit on their front porches watching the covered wagons taking the next generation of pioneers "out west" to a newer frontier.

NOTES

1. Peter S. Onuf, *Statehood and Union: A History of the Northwest Ordinance* (Bloomington and Indianapolis: Indiana University Press, 1987), p. 1.
2. Ibid., p. 4.
3. Ibid., p. 7.
4. Ibid., p. 36.
5. Freeman Cleaves, *Old Tippecanoe: William Henry Harrison and His Time* (New York and London: Charles Scribner's Sons, 1939; reprint, Newtown, CT: American Political Biography Press, 1990), p. 47.
6. John D. Barnhart and Dorothy L. Riker, *Indiana to 1816: The Colonial Period* (Indianapolis: Indiana Historical Bureau and Indiana Historical Society, 1971), p. 359.
7. Ibid.
8. William Henry Smith, *The St. Clair Papers: The Life and Public Services of Arthur St. Clair* (Cincinnati: R. Clarke, 1882), vol. 2, p. 125.
9. Logan Easery, ed., *Messages and Letters of William Henry Harrison* (Indianapolis: Indiana Historical Collections, 1922), vol. 1, p. 250.
10. U.S. Bureau of the Census, 1811.
11. Harrison to James Henry, May 10, 1806, quoted in Emma Lou Thornbrough, *The Negro in Indiana Before 1900: A Study of a Minority* (Indianapolis: Indiana Historical Bureau, 1957; reprint, Bloomington and Indianapolis: Indiana University Press, 1993), p. 12.
12. *Journals of the General Assembly*, pp. 232–238.
13. U.S. Bureau of the Census, 1820, 1840.
14. Barnhart and Riker, *Indiana to 1816*, p. 432.
15. Ibid., p. 414.
16. *Journals of the General Assembly*, December 1815, pp. 839–841.
17. Jennings to John F. Ross, February 7, 1816, quoted in *Indiana Magazine of History* 39 (1943): 290–291.
18. Dill to Samuel Vance, June 16, 1816, quoted in Barnhart and Riker, *Indiana to 1816*, p. 446.
19. John B. Dillon, *A History of Indiana from Its Earliest Exploration by Europeans to 1816* (Indianapolis: Bingham and Doughty, 1859), p. 559.
20. Gayle Thornbrough, ed., *Letter Book of the Indian Agency at Fort Wayne, 1809–1815* (Indianapolis: Indiana Historical Society, 1961), p. 228.

BIBLIOGRAPHY

Barnhart, John D., and Dorothy L. Riker. *Indiana to 1816: The Colonial Period.* Indianapolis: Indiana Historical Bureau and Indiana Historical Society, 1971.

Cleaves, Freeman. *Old Tippecanoe: William Henry Harrison and His Time*. New York and London: Scribner's Sons, 1939; reprint, Newtown, CT: American Political Biography Press, 1990.

Dillon, John B. *A History of Indiana from Its Earliest Exploration by Europeans to... 1816....* Indianapolis: Bingham and Doughty, 1859.

Easery, Logan, ed. *Messages and Letters of William Henry Harrison*. 2 vols. Indianapolis: Indiana Historical Collections, 1922.

Madison, James H. *The Indiana Way: A State History*. Bloomington and Indianapolis: Indiana University Press and Indiana Historical Society, 1986.

Onuf, Peter S. *Statehood and Union: A History of the Northwest Ordinance*. Bloomington and Indianapolis: Indiana University Press, 1987.

Richardson, James D., comp. *A Compilation of the Messages and Papers of the Presidents*. 20 vols. New York: Bureau of National Literature, 1897.

Smith, William Henry. *The St. Clair Papers: The Life and Public Services of Arthur St. Clair*. 2 vols. Cincinnati: R. Clarke, 1882.

Sugden, John. *Tecumseh: A Life*. New York: Henry Holt and Company, 1997.

Thornbrough, Emma Lou. *The Negro in Indiana Before 1900: A Study of a Minority*. Indianapolis: Indiana Historical Bureau, 1957; reprint, Bloomington and Indianapolis: Indiana University Press, 1993.

Thornbrough, Gayle, ed. *Letter Book of the Indian Agency at Fort Wayne, 1809–1815*. Indianapolis: Indiana Historical Society, 1961.

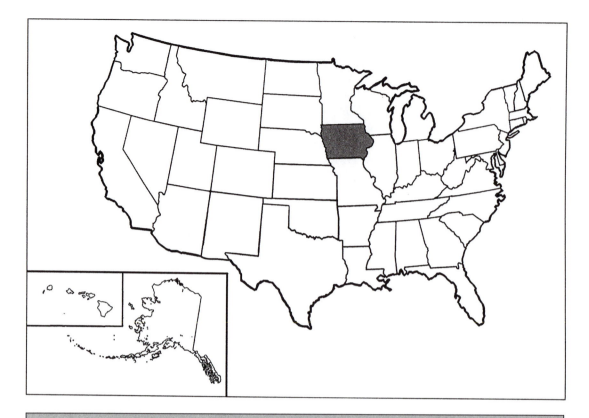

Iowa

Territorial Development:

- The United States obtained future Iowa territory from France through the Louisiana Purchase, April 30, 1803
- Future Iowa territory organized as part of the Indiana Territory, 1804
- Reorganized as part of the Territory of Louisiana, 1805
- Reorganized as part of the Missouri Territory, 1812
- Became an unorganized territory, 1821
- Organized as part of the Michigan Territory, 1834
- Reorganized as part of the Wisconsin Territory, 1836
- Reorganized as the Iowa Territory, June 12, 1838
- Iowa admitted into the Union as the twenty-ninth state, December 28, 1846

Territorial Capitals:

- Burlington, 1838–1840
- Iowa City, 1840–1846

State Capitals:

- Iowa City, 1846–1852
- Des Moines, 1852–present

Origin of State Name: "Iowa" is taken from the name for the tribal Indians of the area, "Ayuxwa," which became "Iowa" and "Ayoua" in French, and "Ioway" in English.

First Governor: Ansel Briggs
Governmental Organization: Bicameral
Population at Statehood: 192,214
Geographical Size: 55,869 square miles

THE STATE OF IOWA

Admitted to the Union as a State: December 28, 1846

William Roba

INTRODUCTION

Iowa was paired with Texas for entry into the Union in 1846. When Texas became the fourth postcolonial republic to join America in February, the newly elected governor, General Henderson, pointedly referred in his inaugural address to the "free consent of the people of the two Republics," represented by Texas and the United States of America.[1]

The public perception of these two states could not vary more, with the dry grasslands of Texas contrasting to the forested Iowa Territory. Early on, the artist and explorer George Catlin remarked on the bluffs and timber, grandeur and beauty of the Mississippi River valley north of St. Louis. As he headed toward the mouth of the Wisconsin River, six hundred miles upriver, he commented on how a traveler "will see but little of picturesque beauty in the landscape, until he reaches Rock Island, and from that point he will find it growing gradually more interesting, until he reaches Prairie du Chien...."[2] He also speculated on the future American character. He viewed the region as having the potential to change the New England personality that was the American stereotype of the time, expanding it into a national version through exposure to the river valley where "the true character of the *American* is to be formed...."[3]

By the mid-1840s, a generation of settlers north of St. Louis had experienced the full implementation of President Jackson's vision of the rise of the common man. This strong belief in socioeconomic mobility and competition underpinned many of the deliberations over Iowa's statehood. In short, Iowa was represented by the twenty-ninth star of the American flag as the first non-slave state created out of the Louisiana Purchase.

Taking a longer view, between 1804 and 1838, the territorial area of what later became Iowa had been administered by six different jurisdictions because it lacked geographical integrity. It had no natural boundaries to the north and the west. In the late 1820s, to the east was Illinois, half the size of what it would become, and to the south, Missouri, with a poorly surveyed boundary line.

The beauty of the area remained unique and rewarding in every season. In the midst of winter in the 1830s, Father Samuel Mazuchelli recorded his impressions of one of the dominant land forms.

> In the great prairies, however, the tracks do not remain clear and well-defined as in the woods because of the wind which blows there as it does over the sea and carries with it the frozen snow like dust, obliterating tracks as soon as they are made. The inexperienced traveler must overcome many difficulties: there are unbridged streams with high banks, whose waters, fed by nearby springs, do not freeze; the ice is not always solid on the lakes and is very treacherous on certain rivers, in the hollows of the undulating prairies the snow is often heaped by the winds in drifts of six or seven feet.[4]

The bluffs along the Mississippi River dramatically contrasted with the prairies in the summer. Caleb Atwater wrote in the late 1820s about its beauty aboard a steamboat, where "the beautiful country on the west side of the river opened to view, and from the first moment we saw it, all eyes were turned towards it.... We could hardly persuade ourselves, many times, when we first saw any one of these beautiful spots, that all the art that man possessed, and wealth could employ, had not been used to fit the place...."[5]

Soon after the territorial process began, public relations followed. Probably the most powerful concept appeared in the early 1830s nickname, "the hawk's eye," evoking precision and accuracy unsurpassed among the raptors. It was first printed by James G. Edwards, formerly a member of the editorial staff of James Gordon Bennett's New York *Herald*. Edwards moved to Fort Madison and started publishing the first Whig newspaper, the *Patriot*. "If a partition of the territory (i.e., Wisconsin) is proposed, we suggest that the Iowans adopt the nickname of Hawk Eyes. The derivation would have more meaning than that of the Wolverines, Suckers, Gophers among others [commonly used to refer to Michigan, Illinois and the Minnesota frontier]...."[6]

Until the early 1820s, the area north of St. Louis remained either under the control of indigenous cultures north of the new state of Illinois or part of Upper Louisiana until the Territory of Missouri became a state. With the introduction of steam boating on the Upper Mississippi in the 1820s, the area began to attract some civilians to settle around the three major forts (Armstrong, Crawford, and Snelling). They took advantage of the indigenous cultures, and some managed to create profitable incomes from their major economic activities of fur trading and lead mining. No one could have predicted that the three forts would eventually develop into three new states by 1860: Iowa, Wisconsin, and Minnesota.

The first type of governance was the creation of the so-called Half-Breed Tract in 1824. This quaint Victorian term applied to "mixed race" children of whites having "Indian marriages" for good tribal relations as traders. It consisted of 120,000 acres on a peninsula formed by the confluence of the Des Moines and Mississippi rivers. It had been set aside for thirty-eight civilized offspring of the Sauk-Fox tribe who would not receive any of the annuities announced in 1816.[7] By the 1820s, Euro-Americans had moved to the area and had overrun the tract, declaring ownership based upon "squatters rights."

At the same time, the federal government began leasing land in an area around Fort Crawford near Prairie du Chien. The French trader Julien Dubuque (1762–1810) had been given sole rights by the Spanish government to mine the area, but years after his death, this land, which was reserved for various indigenous cultures, had been leased by congressional legislation. The area thus represented an almost 5,000-square-mile diamond.[8] The key economic ingredient was twenty-five public mines east of Prairie du Chien, continuing along the Wisconsin River with the Military Road going north of the town of Mineral Point. Over the next two decades, more than 800 million pounds of lead were mined and exported to St. Louis with a value of $33 million.[9] The lead region extended through 225 square miles of land legally owned by three indigenous cultures. The Ottawa, Chippewa, and Potawotami tribes were gradually induced to abandon their traditional hunting grounds. This wedge between the Wisconsin and Rock rivers was a strip forty miles wide, parallel to the Mississippi River.[10] In addition, a treaty was negotiated with the Winnebago, who sold their lands east of the Mississippi River in 1829.

This became a federal district, separate from the state of Illinois to the south. Besides the creation of the district, the river link to St. Louis appeared in 1822 when the town of Galena was established. The name was designed to combat the public relations problem of being on the banks of the Fever River (an American corruption of the French word for beans), at least for those potential settlers familiar with the classical physician Galen. Primarily a group of unsold town sites, the erection of the Federal Customs Building in 1825 and a few other permanent buildings began to create the image of a real settlement. Only ten miles away, the settlement of Dubuque provided competition in the keelboat trade of lead. The governmental difference emerged when Dubuque was included in the first territorial mechanism, the Michigan Territory in 1827. By the 1830s, Dubuque had become a town of two hundred houses. The possibility of a new territory, broken off from the Wisconsin Territory, remained a lively vision with the Wisconsin territorial government issuing charters of incorporation for mining companies and Illinois banks providing charters for branch banks in the settlements.

For the next five years, a very fluid situation existed in terms of settlement patterns upriver from St. Louis. A variety of land speculation was possible, due to very loose legal bases and working relationships with one of the major indigenous culture groups, the Sauk-Fox tribe. The only coordinated tribe in

North America, they were Algonquian-speaking cultivators of the soil who worked easily with the agents of John Jacob Astor's American Fur Company. The level of socialization for this tribal grouping was near enough to Euro-American communities to ensure that there would be "smoother" relations between the two settlement groups.

In October 1829, the legislators of the Michigan Territory created a large Iowa County between the Mississippi and Wisconsin rivers around the principal city of Mineral Point. Generally known as the Wisconsin District, the surrounding boundaries included the area south of the Wisconsin River, west of Lake Michigan, north of the middle border of Illinois, and east of the Mississippi River. Following the sad spectacle of a remnant of the Sauk-Fox tribal organization becoming involved in the Black Hawk War of 1832, new lands were added to this political entity.

The Black Hawk Purchase was added to its jurisdiction in 1833, which consisted of more than 6 million acres following a fifty-mile edge west of the Mississippi River. The treaty, supervised by General Winfield Scott, provided thirty years of annuities valued at $20,000, or about ten cents an acre. On June 28, 1834, the purchase was legally recognized after more than a year of settlement by the Michigan Territory. The Michigan Territory created two counties divided by an imaginary line due west of Fort Armstrong on the large Rock Island. The northern county of Dubuque had one township, Julien, and the southern county of Des Moines had one township, Flint Hills, but these political arrangements remained theoretical.

Due south of this was the Keokuk Reserve, which contained the majority of the Sauk-Fox tribal members, who had not followed the leadership of Black Hawk but rather moved eighteen miles south of Fort Armstrong and were not involved in the violence of the 1832 Black Hawk War. This area around the Iowa River remained under the control of the indigenous culture for another three years. It was relatively undeveloped, consisting of 400 sections of land, or almost 250,000 acres.

The southernmost area was the Half-Breed Tract of 120,000 acres. In 1834, Congress vested title to this land, which should have only been the property of the offspring of the original thirty-eight children, but in twenty years there had been a dangerous policy of inbreeding, along with informal proof of landownership. The result was the enormous problem of 200–300 claimants, with little guidance as to which claims were genuine.[11] In September 1836, on the well-known Rock Island near Fort Armstrong, more than 500 Sauk family leaders gathered, including Black Hawk, Keokuk, Poweshiek, and Wapello. They met with the most powerful capitalists in the emerging territory: George Davenport, Antoine LeClaire, and their publicist, William Patterson. The indigenous culture leaders sought to sell most of the Half-Breed Tract land. By representing thirty of the rightful owners, the tribal members wanted to sell "half-breed shares," which equaled about three thousand acres, or about five sections each. The shares had a market value in the newly founded village of

Davenport of about $250–$300. Davenport and LeClaire bought "120,000 acres of choice land in the south part of Lee County, lying on the fork of the Mississippi and Des Moines Rivers."[12] Some of the owners sold their parcels two or three times, with the resulting number of at least 300 titles, which meant a golden opportunity for lawyers, who indeed kept the litigation going until the 1860s.

The key town site here was the village of Keokuk, north of the Half-Breed Tract, where log buildings called "Rat Row" sheltered a tavern, the American Fur Company store, twenty Sauk families, and forty-two half-breeds. It had been surveyed in 1833 and was a "company town," controlled by the American Fur Company and Russell Farnham, associated with George Davenport to the north.[13] The importance was its location on the mouth of the Des Moines River, which was navigable for 170 miles during part of the year and thus a major artery of settlement. The town was described with a verbal sniff by the British traveler Charles Augustus Murray as consisting "chiefly of watermen who assist in loading and unloading the keel-boats in towing them up when the rapids are too strong for the steam-engines....Their chief occupation seems to consist in drinking, fighting and gambling."[14]

When the Territory of Wisconsin was organized in 1836, about one-half of the 10,531 settlers lived in the Iowa District, about one-half of the territory's white population. Thus, the appointed governor, Henry Dodge, gave the Iowa District six of the thirteen Territorial Council members, and eleven of the twenty-five Territorial House members. The actual functioning of the two counties and two townships remained theoretical. A close reading of the Territorial Statutes shows that the wording for counties and townships had actually been adopted from Ohio statutes in a hybrid form of local government that superimposed the county commissioner form of the Wisconsin Territory upon the county-township split.[15]

Soon there was a second Black Hawk Purchase in 1837, which made an additional 1,250,000 acres available for settlement to the west of the first purchase. An interesting estimate of the population of indigenous cultures at this time gave a total of about 11,000: 5,000 followers of Poweshiek were living on the banks of the Cedar River and the Keokuk Preserve, and another 6,000 Potawotami were living on the eastern bank of the Missouri River, which was technically included in the Wisconsin Territory.

With the creation of the Territory of Iowa in 1838, the census revealed that the population in that area had doubled to 23,242 in sixteen counties. The land mass consisted of about 160,000 square miles, including the modern state of Minnesota west of the Mississippi River, and west of the Missouri River, North Dakota and South Dakota. The newly formed territory had almost 80 percent of the Iowa land mass owned by the Sauk-Fox tribe in 1838. During the next seven years, the population rose from 22,859 to about 90,000. Willard Barrows, an early settler, recalled that "this narrow belt of river settlement was constantly broadening westward, and with all the crude and novel conveyances that had been used from the days of [Daniel] Boone...."[16] By the 1840s, about 90 percent of the settlers had stayed in the twenty-one eastern counties, with 80 percent of the land in the hands of Euro-American settlers.

During the next two years, the Mississippi River towns acted as urban corridors channeling settlers into the western lands. Many of the river towns showed great diversity. In 1843, Burlington's special enumeration of its 1,831 inhabitants showed that almost half (779) were born in Europe, with the largest ethnic groups being Germans with 175, and British (English and Irish) with 99. An analysis of the 1840 U.S. Census showed that 17,816 (40 percent) lived in the southeastern triangle of Lee, Van Buren, and Des Moines counties. Another 4,328 (about 10 percent) lived in the northeastern corner of Dubuque, Clayton, and Allamakee counties.

In 1843, more land became available with the cession of the eastern half of the Sauk-Fox lands in the Des Moines River Valley. An unknown correspondent of the New Haven, Connecticut *Palladium* predicted its probable development. "It is a valuable purchase, having an excellent soil, well watered, and abounding in timber conveniently interspersed throughout the prairie. The Indians are to yield possession on the 1st of May. Now comes a rush and a scramble for town sites, mule privileges, county seats, and spring tracts such as no one but an eye-witness can have any idea of."[17] In the early 1840s, an estimated 90 percent of the population was involved in farming. Some of the more interesting crops in this earlier and more experimental period were hemp, which was grown for local rope production, and grapes, for wine production.

The growth of newspapers in this period indicates the literacy level of the Territory of Iowa. John King's Dubuque *Visitor* appeared first on May 11, 1836, followed by Dr. Isaac Galland's *Western Adventurer* in Lee County on June 28, 1837. Burlington followed with James G. Edwards publishing the *Iowa Patriot* on March 24, 1838, and Andrew Logan printing Davenport's *Iowa Sun* on August 5, 1838. In these frontier newspapers, the success of territorial status appeared with stories about the mapping of the Upper and Lower Rapids in 1837 by Lieutenant Robert E. Lee; the building of military roads, bridges and culverts by the Topographical Corps; the near doubling of the population to 75,000 by midsummer 1844 and the triumphs of Congressional Delegate Augustus Dodge, who secured more than $50,000 for internal improvements.[18]

In later reminiscences, this was the early idyllic period of Iowa history. It remains arguable that without state government, much was accomplished. With a vital, urban frontier along the Mississippi River, towns became associated with professions: Dubuque was the miner's town; Burlington, the lawyer's town; Iowa City, the politician's town; and Davenport, the businessman's town.[19]

TERRITORIAL LEADERS

The intertwining of frontier leadership and the success of territorial status forestalled the development of a movement for statehood until the 1840s.

This was partially due to the rise of six very different leaders in the emerging regional area. Using the nineteenth-century fascination with types, the Victorian typology focuses on the Immigrant, the Half-Breed, the Chief, the Family, the Politician, and the Intellectual.

George Davenport

The first leader to appear in the Upper Mississippi region was significant for the indigenous cultural group known as the Sauk-Fox. The retail supplier to the army was stationed near Fort Armstrong, and to civilians nearby or passing through, he became a figure of influence. In this way, George Davenport developed patterns of trade with the indigenous cultures in order to secure fur and to sell products.

The thirty-year-old Davenport had apparently changed his name from John King after migrating from England in 1806. He may have served under Colonel Lawrence, who supervised the Eighth Regiment in building the fort on Rock Island, in transporting Aaron Burr to Virginia after Burr's expedition toward New Orleans in 1807. His success in trade with the Sauk-Fox came from his fair dealing and British accent, which the tribal leaders recalled from their British allies during the War of 1812. They called him "Saganosh," the Sauk word for Englishman, and his Cockney accent worked wonders. It was reported that "these words operated like magic—they loosed holds, and commenced to shake him by the hands...."[20] By 1819, he began his yearly trips to St. Louis on the keelboat named the *Flying Betsy*. He established trading posts downstream from Fort Armstrong on nearby Credit Island and farther afield near the Flint Hills. Northward, he built posts at the mouth of the Wapsipinicon and Maquoketa rivers.

During the next decade, Davenport traveled over the prairies in winter to the hunting camps. In the early spring, furs and skins were carefully packed and he then personally supervised transporting the cargo to St. Louis. After 1822, he became an agent for the American Fur Company, becoming the first trader to ship a flatboat cargo of lead from the Fever River to St. Louis and established himself as the preferred retailer of alum, whisky, port, combs, calico, flannel shirts, cream of tartar, silk, shoes, carpeting, gun locks, frying pans, teacups, plates, woolen socks, and quills.[21] He continued to be a consultant for the U.S. government, useful in the signing of treaties, disbursing credit, and developing the various land holdings. He worked to maintain the territorial status that had meant special charters, ease of landownership, and connections with officials in St. Louis and Washington City. His financial capital increased immeasurably when the 1832 treaty rewarded his partnership with Russell Farnham with $40,000 for alleged credit losses during the 1820s. When his partner died in the cholera epidemic, Davenport was able to use the entire amount in shrewd investments.

Antoine LeClaire

The second regional leader was a key partner to Davenport. Antoine LeClaire's father was French and his mother was a Potawotami Indian princess. The result was his ability to speak eighteen different languages as a "Half-Breed." He worked steadily for Davenport and was awarded land southeast of Fort Armstrong in Illinois. With the successful negotiations of 1832, he received two sections of land opposite the fort on what would become the Iowa Territory. He remained a land developer and partner with Davenport. LeClaire was the publicly known businessman who was accessible. George Davenport remained private in his dealings and unavailable to most settlers. A prospective settler, Stephen H. Hayes, made inquiries in 1845 and calculated that both of them were millionaires in terms of influence. Davenport was probably worth $200,000, with two sons in the business. LeClaire was worth $100,000 but had no children.[22] This partnership came to an abrupt end on July 4, 1845, when late at night, the dying George Davenport was found on the floor of his mansion on Rock Island.

Keokuk

Keokuk, or Running Fox, was the third regional leader. Acknowledged by General Scott as the leader of his tribe, he was a powerful orator who had decisively followed advice given to him by Davenport and went along with the land squeeze of the Black Hawk War. General Scott, unusual in his neutrality in dealing with indigenous cultures, was impressed by Keokuk's tribe. Three decades after the ending of the Black Hawk War, Scott used a triplet by Dryden to remind him of the Sauk:

Free as nature first made man,
Ere the base loss of servitude began,
When wild in woods the noble savage ran.[23]

Instead of joining in the war plans of other Sauk leaders, Keokuk had moved most of the tribe southward to Muscatine Island and later lived in a village on the Des Moines River. He was a proud man who naturally owned the best horses available. George Catlin noted the fine-blooded horse he owned, which cost him $300 and also remarked that the chief disbursed more than $50,000 yearly in annuities and could easily afford such a fine horse.[24] Moreover, the proceeds from the 1832 treaty amounted to $192,000, or seventy-five cents per acre.

Catlin found Keokuk to be "a very subtle and dignified man, and well fitted to wield the destinies of his nation."[25] He led the removal of his tribe to the west, where he had gained a tract of four hundred square miles for not joining in war against the United States. This Keokuk reserve extended along both banks of the Iowa River to within a few miles of the Mississippi River. In 1837, the second purchase, west of the original tract, was secured by the United States. Finally, after the failure to sign a treaty in 1841, Governor Chambers agreed to allow some of Keokuk's advisors to move, and during the week of October 4–11, 1842, the tribe assembled a few miles east of Ottumwa. It was here that the landscape was dotted for the last time with innumerable wickiups, the homes of the Sauk-Fox. Keokuk used Antoine LeClaire as interpreter and sought the advice of George Davenport, both of whom were trusted business advisers.

As it turned out, the practices of frontier credit worked against the indigenous cultures. The Sauk-Fox had debts of $250,000 to traders such as George Davenport, so they sold their lands to pay off their debts, also paying off one-third of the eventual interest on $800,000 yearly. This meant they ended up selling their land for twelve cents an acre.[26] Keokuk made this decision after due consultation with George Davenport, whom he and the other leaders had trusted since 1819 when he was a humble sutler on the island. Davenport later gave up the fur trade and withdrew from the American Fur Company after this final tribal treaty. Thus, Keokuk became the first influential leader of the Iowa frontier in deciding to cooperate with the U.S. Army and the territorial governor and led the Sauk-Fox away from their ancestral lands to go to the trans-Mississippi frontier west of the Missouri River.

The Langworthy Brothers

The fourth influential leadership actually came from the family of Langworthy brothers, who gained prominence in business in Dubuque by the 1830s. James, Lucius, Edward, James L., and Solon moved by the 1830s to the town of Galena. Edward Langworthy, then nineteen years old, recalled leaving Warsaw, Illinois, in June 1827 and having to use a pirogue or "large skiff and for the next ten days literally worked our passage up as far as Rock Island, rowing, poling, cordelling and bushwhacking along in the broiling sun of June."[27] It is fascinating to read Langworthy's alternative version of this emerging trans-Mississippi frontier region, in which he makes his major orientation the various mines and rivers: Hardscrabble near Hazel Green in the Wisconsin Territory, the Drummond Lode, the Langworthy Cave, Menominee Diggs, Detandebaratz's Furnace, British Hollow, Langworthy Hollow, Ewing Range, Snake Hollow, Snake Diggings and Zollicoffer Lake; and the Fever, Maquoketa, and Timber rivers. The Langworthy brothers were involved in the Miner's Committee of June 17, 1830, which pertained to arbitration but was viewed as an indigenous form of democratic agreement, like the seventeenth-century Mayflower Compact in Massachusetts Bay Colony. Some of the boys became interested in the profits of steamboating, and between 1833 and 1842 invested in the *Heroine*, *Olive Branch*, and *Jo Davies*. The *Brazil* sank after hitting a snag near the upper rapids by Fort Armstrong.

Robert Lucas

The fifth frontier leader was the first territorial governor, Robert Lucas. His Democratic appointment meant that he shared in the vision of economic growth on the moving edge of settlement. He also dealt with an interesting and early skirmish on boundaries, which became the biggest issue in the entire debate over statehood. The basic difficulty was a poorly defined boundary with the state of Missouri. In 1837, a new survey was established on the basis of the rapids of the Des Moines River, not the Mississippi. It was a line about nine miles north of the traditional line on the east and thirteen miles on the west end, encompassing an area of more than 2,600 square miles. Furthermore, ownership of hollow trees used by bees for honey in the "big bend" of the Des Moines River led to attempted taxation of Iowa bees by Missouri law enforcement.

Governor Lucas prepared a Thanksgiving address in 1839 that strongly recommended Iowan statehood, and he suggested boundaries as a warning to the Missourians. By the winter of 1839, actual militia was called out for both disputants. The crisis was averted with cold weather, but the newspapers had used it as a method of increasing circulation. A popular song arose that was sung to the tune of "Yankee Doodle":

Ye freeman of the happy land,
Which flows with milk and honey
Arise! To arms! Your ponies mount!
Regard not blood or money.
Old Governor Lucas, tiger-like
Is prowling 'round our borders.
But Governor Briggs is wide awake—
Just listen to his orders.[28]

It may have appeared amusing to some at the time. One of the more picturesque vignettes was the raising of local troops. Captain S. C. Hastings took command of almost 1,200 Iowa militia members on December 7, 1839. He thought that he was adequately prepared with five wagon loads hastily brought along to the staging area near the mouth of the Des Moines River. Many of the local militia had questionable firearms. The Scott County troops, representing Davenport and the river towns, brought flintlocks, ancestral swords, and "one loyal soul arrived with a sausage stuffer." One of the commanding officers stopped a very drunk volunteer who was banging on the top of a huge but dead old log. When asked what he thought he was doing, he replied that he was "killing a Missouri boy." The Missouri contingent consisted of more than two thousand battle-hardened troops who had recently been engaged in the Mormon War, and they posed a definite threat, which only cold weather could seasonally stop.

Governor Lucas persevered and decided to develop some strategy in the annoying but potentially damaging dispute with Missouri. He called an extra session of the territorial legislature into session on July 13, 1840. At this session, the governor called for an August vote on statehood that helped create a benchmark for future discussion on the idea of statehood. On election day, the major voter attention was on the congressional delegate race, with 7,595 votes cast. Less than half of the voters, or 3,844, voted on the statehood issue. In the fourteen existing counties, the opposition was decisive, winning by 76 percent of the vote (2,907 to 937).[29]

Theodore S. Parvin

The last type of frontier leader who played a prominent role in the movement for Iowa statehood was Theodore S. Parvin. He had graduated from both Cincinnati College and Woodward College and completed his legal studies before meeting the former governor of Ohio, Robert Lucas. The twenty-two-year-old lawyer met with Lucas in Cincinnati in the summer of 1838 and accepted the offer to become his private secretary. Parvin had already established a library in Cincinnati and was soon appointed Parvin territorial librarian, because he was probably "then the best read man in Iowa...with orders to prepare a catalogue for the ready use of legislators."[30] Although young, he was versatile and quickly became a district attorney for the middle district, secretary to the territory, and a Johnson County judge, a position similar to the Missouri office, which was really closer to the later concept of county supervisor.

His first significant action was to break with his former mentor, George Lucas, and oppose the adoption of the 1844 constitution. The boundaries had been revised downward and the territorial delegate, Augustus Dodge, was openly defeatist in accepting the national will of Congress. The prominent leaders of the Democratic Party urged its adoption, but Parvin and several other Democrats such as Enoch W. Eastman and Frederick D. Mills joined the minority Whig Party in canvassing the territory. Parvin used his Masonic membership as a way of meeting influential leaders in the various counties and argued not against statehood but against congressionally mandated smaller boundaries. It was a courageous stand based upon his own convictions and the rationale of the original intention of Lucas.

His second significant contribution was in a nearly forty-year association with the Iowa Historical Society, not only collecting early Iowa documents and archiving them with the society but editing the *Annals of Iowa* for many years. His view of the territorial period influenced the writing of its history for more than a century. He is specifically mentioned in the footnotes to the two articles written by James A. James, professor of history at Northwestern University, in 1897 and 1900, which influenced the interpretation of Iowa's earliest history.

These seven types of leaders are important in revealing the shifting coalitions that helped to define the direction of Iowa in gaining statehood. One group was opposed to rushing toward statehood. Their economic success was based upon near monopolistic control of land and speculation in new developments. Thus, Davenport and LeClaire were supported by the dominant indigenous culture, the Sauk-Fox tribe and the leadership of Keokuk, for the first decade of territorial status. They were also mutually supportive of the Langworthy brothers and their support for the Territory of Huron, with Dubuque as the largest city and capital of an area extending into southeastern Wisconsin. In this analysis, it is important to realize that this group's influence waned in the early 1840s with the sheer volume of Euro-American settlers and their interest in a more open economy. With the judicious control of newspaper coverage and "holding down" the vote, they successfully used their influence in Washington City and throughout the territory.

The opposing side consisted of Governor Lucas and his successors, who all took an intellectual view of the future. With the growing population, there was a need for more types of governmental service, not only for settlers on the prairie but also for the cities. By 1841, the Territory of Iowa was larger than the state of Arkansas. It was estimated that by the summer of 1844, the population would reach 100,000 to 150,000 people, thereby making the population of Iowa Territory larger than each of the states of Tennessee, Illinois, Missouri, Indiana, and Mississippi. The new Whig territorial governor, John Chambers, called for a referendum in August 1842. One thousand fourteen Iowans voted, but 62 percent of them as well as every county opposed the plan.

What were the recurring issues brought up by the coalition and skillfully interwoven into the public discussion? The earliest one had to do with the economy. In 1837, a major recession hit the Eastern cities, and the downturn in the economy and land sales spread into the frontier. In the early 1840s, the coalition began to attack taxation. As a territory, Congress paid for basic projects, opened several federal land offices, and theoretically offered protection against the indigenous cultures. Locally, law enforcement, land title registration, and political elections were about the only basic services offered. The recurring theme was the lack of any need for increased services and taxation. In a letter from Jon Brown to Dr. Gideon Bailey in the village of Bedford, the case of Indiana was referred to as an example of heavy indebtedness because of a rush to statehood.[31] These arguments changed yearly but stayed close to this rationale for letting things remain the same.

TERRITORIAL POLITICS

In the late 1830s, it was very difficult to pinpoint the political affinities of Iowa settlers. The territorial election day of October 2, 1836, provided a modicum of practical experience in presidential elections. George Davenport and his sons were originally Democrats. A special charter for the city of Davenport allowed partisan elections, and both Democrats and Whigs won alderman positions.

It was the appointment of fifty-eight-year-old Robert Lucas, former U.S. Congressman and Democratic governor from Ohio, that coincided with the appearance of territorial partisan politics. He used his considerable experience to the best advantage, responding to Missouri's territorial intrusions with a statement on July 29, 1839, modeled after a Michigan Territorial Legislature act against Ohio while he was still governor. By 1840, statehood was strongly favored by many rank-and-file Democrats. The Whig press accurately analyzed this as a strong desire for increased patronage.[32] Lucas left office with the election of a Whig president in 1841.

Lucas's replacement, sixty-one-year-old John Chambers, former Whig congressman from Kentucky, faced an antagonistic majority of Democrats in the territorial legislature. In a message to the assembly on December 6, 1841, Chambers angered many Democratic leaders when he spoke for temperance supporters and strongly came out against whisky sales to "Indians," which he claimed worsened the problems settlers had with the Sauk-Fox. In particular, he singled out licensed traders, such as George Davenport, as irresponsible businessmen who took advantage of the Indian propensity for liquor. And of course, these licensed traders were, incidentally, leading Democratic leaders, albeit privately. The question of statehood generated many partisan arguments, which remained in place until 1846.[33] Chambers continued to work toward statehood, but on August 1, 1842, a majority of the voters in the seventeen counties voted against having a constitutional convention. The only close vote was in Lee County, where voters supported the idea, 705-663.[34]

CONSTITUTIONAL CONVENTIONS

With the population of the territory having now risen to an estimated 80,000 people, the April 1, 1844, vote on statehood brought a new result in sentiment. Almost 63 percent of the voters (6,976) favored a convention, while 27 percent opposed it (4,181), meaning a majority of 2,795 voters in favor of a constitutional convention. In Lee County, there was a dramatic shift with 1,343 in favor and only 353 against. The five river counties (Clinton, Louisa, Muscatine, Scott, and Dubuque) combined for a slim margin of 52 percent disapproval: 994 for and 1,102 opposed. The vote in April engendered a hardening of partisan views, which appeared in newspaper editorials and letters to the editor throughout the territory. The Whig press had continued its campaign against statehood, broadening it to include corporations. "These soulless monsters have tyrannized enough; and we rejoice that Iowa in the outset bound the hydra, hand and foot."[35]

Amended by an act of the territorial legislature, the general election of August 1844 decided on constitutional convention delegates. The Democratic Party controlled the constitutional process, and on November 1, 1844, shortly before the presidential election, the convention reported to the U.S.

congressional Committee on Territories that a constitution had been created. Eventually, on March 3, 1845, Congress agreed to a constitution, but the new state would have truncated boundaries, based on boundaries that had been recommended by J. N. Nicollet, a French geographer. He had toured the Upper Mississippi River Valley with Lieutenant John C. Frémont and Charles Geyer, a botanist, in 1843. The proposal stated that this plan would provide "sufficient space for five new states of large size, compact in their forms, and having a good portion of fertile soil; most of them possessing convenient navigable streams, with a fair prospect of mineral resources."[36] When voters realized what the reduced boundaries meant, there was widespread opposition to the vote. The congressional proposal was to eliminate the western boundary of the Missouri River slope (where thirty-one counties were later organized) and to extend the northern boundary west to replace the angled boundary. The result would have been a state 180 miles long and 250 miles wide, with the northern edge of the Des Moines River as the capital of the new state because of its geographical center, all of which would change the property value of thousands of speculative landowners. However, the resulting state size of approximately 40,000 square miles would have made it a big state from the perspective of Washington City politicians, the size of Ohio or New York.

The Iowa City *Capitol Reporter* agreed with "the necessity of carving Iowa up into potato patches, as it were, to secure an equilibrium of representation in the U. S. Senate...."[37] In other words, that was the way to get it accepted by Congress. The real opposition continued to come from the Whigs, who "kept up an active campaign against the constitution because of their hostility to the election of judges and state offices by the people; too low salaries; to internal improvements secured by direct taxation and the method of amendment [which was only by convention]."[38]

The Nicollet-boundary constitution was voted down twice that year. On April 7, 1845, 54 percent were opposed, and on August 4, 1845, 53 percent were opposed. The margin of votes had declined from 1,004 to 421. With the appointment of James Clarke as governor by the Democratic president, James K. Polk, a new plan began to take shape. Clarke was an excellent choice because he had lived in the territory for seven years, serving as territorial secretary from 1839 to 1841 and editing a newspaper in Burlington. In the spring of 1846, the proponents of statehood laid out their plans and called for a new constitutional convention. On May 4, 1846, the Iowa Constitutional Convention convened with thirty-two delegates, twenty-two Democrats, and ten Whigs. Interestingly, the delegates did not represent counties, but rather districts roughly equivalent to population size, with Lee, Des Moines, and Van Buren counties each getting three delegates; Cedar, Scott, Clinton, and Johnson each getting one delegate; and Dubuque and four other counties together getting two delegates. The Whigs tried to use the "no party" designation, but voting by political party was used in the balloting.

One of the new objections raised by the Whig Party in the Iowa Territory was over the location of the state university. William Penn Clarke was a twenty-seven-year-old lawyer in Iowa City who supported the local interests in wanting his town to be the permanent capital of the new state. But the new boundaries seemed to threaten that because Johnson County would no longer be the approximate center of the new state. He inferred that Augustus Dodge's solution to the boundary problem would be moving the state capital to an area around the fork of the Raccoon River in the center of the enlarged state. Clarke prophesized that "to quiet the center, we shall probably be promised a state university or something of that character, and then be cheated in the end; for the state will not locate such an institution in the same place where there are already one or two chartered institutions of learning in operation."[39]

Since the territory operated as a de facto single-party political entity, subregional concerns often pitted Democrats against other Democrats, with the river counties divided into a Dubuque faction advocating separatism. In the election of August 1845, the counties along the Mississippi River were still opposed to statehood by a 54 to 46 percent margin, whereas with all twenty-four counties voting, the same as the territory as a whole, there was only a majority of 996 votes against statehood.[40] The population continued to rise, with twenty-eight counties voting a year later. The river counties remained opposed, but only with 51 percent of the voters. One significant change was Scott County, where the death of George Davenport may have removed a major leader against statehood. In that county, the statehood issue passed, with 296 for and 245 against. The conclusion of one editor was that "it is strictly a party constitution.... The Locofocos [Democratic faction], while professing love for the people, have bound them hand and foot."[41]

One related problem politically was a classic example of particularism. The Langworthy brothers of Dubuque represented the true thinking of the lead mining district. Although the river town of Dubuque had the wealth of mining, there were lingering questions about the original Spanish land grants in what had been Upper Louisiana and continuing rivalry from the city of Galena, only ten miles away. This had been going on for a long period of time. Already in the 1820s there were petitions and memorials to Congress for an independent territory. At the first session of the Wisconsin Assembly in the fall of 1836, the representatives from the lead mining district voted against a proposed territorial capital of Madison, which was in Des Moines County, but to their dismay, sixteen other towns received votes for the temporary location, further upsetting the Dubuque delegates. Eventually, the largest number of representatives compromised on Burlington. The resulting perspective against a large territory remained constant thereafter. "Having failed in her attempt to become the capital of Iowa, Dubuque aspired to become the capital of a new state which would be created north of a line drawn westward from the Mississippi" down to the Wapsipinicon River, which created the northern border of Scott County.[42]

This became the dream of the state of Huron, amalgamating the lead district portions of what became the state portions of northeastern Iowa, southwestern Wisconsin, and southeastern Minnesota. Galena had developed on the northern frontier of an expanded Illinois and was no longer located in a federal district. There was a solid voice for this view with the selection of Stephen Hemstead of Dubuque in the voting of the second legislative assembly. It is not surprising that this regional view found expression in the newspapers. The *Miner's Express*, a Democratic paper, approved the idea that having more, smaller states in the Mississippi River Valley would be an advantage, and the congressional response was an indirect endorsement of the Huron Territory idea. Documentation appears in an April 1846 petition to the U.S. House of Representatives. It called for northern boundaries for Iowa at the 42nd parallel, which would have cut the boundaries in half and left out Dubuque. This proposed Territory of Huron was not a mystical chimera but a practical political gambit that had to be dealt with. Illinois Congressman Stephen A. Douglas suggested in the House of Representatives that those Dubuquers wanted "Dubuque to be the largest town in a little State" or "the central town of a large state."[43] In all of the voting, the county was adamantly opposed to Iowa statehood from 1842 until 1846. In April 1844, the vote against statehood in Dubuque was 293 to 282 (51 percent); in April 1845, a much more solid 542 to 191 (74 percent); in August 1845, a closer vote of 502 to 278 (64 percent); in the last vote, the vote dropped further, 597 to 395 (60 percent). The changes probably came from population growth. The population density quickly rivaled Eastern states, with settlement following the interior river system. In 1840, the five river counties had the highest density: Des Moines at 13.3; Lee at 11.9; Dubuque at 5.1; Scott at 4.7; and Muscatine at 4.4. By 1850, these had surged ahead, with Des Moines at 31.1; Lee at 36.8; Dubuque at 18.0; Scott at 13.2; and Muscatine at 13.1.[44] The population acceleration in the southeastern portion of the state in Lee and Des Moines counties meant an even larger number of votes in favor of statehood, which had occurred in each of the four votes in these two counties.

THE CONSTITUTION

In the summer of 1844, the actual process of state constitutionalism had started. The Democrats named fifty-one delegates to the twenty-one Whigs, almost two-thirds of the seventy-three delegates for this third attempt at statehood.[45] At the constitutional convention in Iowa City, the delegates spent twenty-six days debating and adopting a document for statehood. The delegates did not represent counties but rather districts roughly equivalent to population size with Lee, Des Moines, and Van Buren counties each getting three delegates; Cedar, Scott, Clinton, and Johnson each getting one delegate; Dubuque and four other counties together had two delegates.[46]

The 6,000-word document, which had thirteen articles and 108 sections, started out by restating the Bill of Rights and other lofty Enlightenment thoughts and sentiments. One early issue came up on October 7, when the discussion focused upon opening every session with a prayer. A Keokuk farmer, Richard Quinton, was heard to say that it would "force men to hear prayers."[47] After much speechifying, a majority of the sixty-three delegates assembled decided that it was not necessary and also agreed to give atheists the right to give testimony in state courts.[48] A second decision was to adopt the original boundaries of Robert Lucas. The third issue was over the location of the new state capital. After some desultory argumentation, it was decided that the capital of the new state would remain in Iowa City until 1865.

Three additional items were smoothed over, with eventual consensus among the dominant Democratic majority. The fourth issue was captured in Article 9, where major restrictions were placed upon banking and other business corporations, requiring legislative action. The fifth issue was in Article 11, which outlined local government as it had been implemented in parts of the territory. Counties and townships were summarily described. The fifth issue was in Article 12, which allowed for revision of the constitution by the General Assembly. Although rambling in places, it was an accurate portrayal of territorial concepts.

The second constitutional convention in Iowa City convened on May 4. The thirty-two delegates were elected at township meetings in April, with the Democrats gaining twenty-two seats and controlling the sessions as before. They were initially presided over by James Grant, a Scott County delegate who had served on the first convention, but officers were quickly elected. Indeed, the delegates wrapped up their business in two weeks. This version was more carefully edited and shorter than the earlier version, with some notable changes. The boundary specifications were a compromise between the Lucas and Nicollet versions. Individuals who dueled were not permitted to hold office. The office of lieutenant governor and the specifics of local government were omitted. The General Assembly was forbidden to create corporations by special laws (banks were outlawed), and finally, the constitution could only be changed by a constitutional convention.[49]

FEDERAL APPROVAL OF STATEHOOD

In creating the territorial basis for Iowa, the initial response from the federal government concerned the issue of basic governmental services. By the end of 1833, the Black Hawk Purchase had been put under the jurisdiction of the Michigan Territory. Unfortunately, there was very little government offered its far-flung areas. With continuing incidents of illegal behavior, the demand for extended territorial services periodically surfaced. One of the more infamous events occurred on May 19, 1834, when a Dubuque miner, Patrick O'Connor, had illustrated this deficiency by killing his partner. A de facto jury was assembled, since there was no available judge, his guilt ascertained, and on

June 20, he was hanged. In April 1836, Congressman Patton of Virginia remarked on the "peculiar situation of the inhabitants" of this area, who are "without government and without laws."[50] When Michigan became a state, Congress followed up by creating the Wisconsin Territory in 1836.

Two years later, the issues of squatter sovereignty and free labor resurfaced on the national level. In a short debate in the House of Representatives, Waddy Thompson of South Carolina spoke at length about the issue of slavery and how this would relate to possibly annexing the newly independent Republic of Texas. After some questioning, the vote in the House on June 5, 1838, was 118 for a Territory of Iowa and 51 against. The next day, the Senate convened and some fancy maneuvering cleared the way for a positive vote. Senator John C. Calhoun was expected to oppose the bill forcefully, so a young Iowan had been selected to try to influence his vote. He managed to strike up a conversation with Senator Calhoun's niece, Anna Calhoun, who was talented and beautiful. Anna sent her uncle a message, and Senator Calhoun left the chambers shortly before the vote came up. It passed by a vote of 33 to 6. The six senators voting against the bill all represented slave states: Georgia, South Carolina, Arkansas, Maryland, North Carolina, and Tennessee. Less than a week later, President Martin Van Buren signed a congressional act that created the territorial government after July 3, 1838. That government would last for eight and a half years.

The form of Iowa's territorial government followed earlier precedents. The president appointed a territorial governor who maintained legislative functions himself. This territorial governor could make law, but only with the support of a two-tiered legislative assembly. This consisted of a council formed by thirteen members elected every two years and a House of Representatives with its twenty-six members elected annually. Although dominated by the Democrats, the assembly disagreed with the governor on many issues and as early as December 28, 1839, the House created a select committee for the removal of the governor because of his unpopular vetoes. It was actually the Whig presidential landslide in 1840 that turned Governor Lucas out of office.

His replacement, John Chambers, faced a Democratic-controlled assembly but followed much the same course as his predecessor. He requested a legislative referendum in December messages in 1841 and 1843. It was the 1844 proposal that first gathered serious consideration in the U.S. Congress. Samuel F. Vinton, a Whig congressman from Ohio, was a veteran with twenty-one years of political experience, and he opposed the idea of statehood on a rather complex basis. His argument was that the power of western states was necessary in order to counter centrifugal forces such as the issue of free or slave labor.[51] Congressman Belsen of Alabama favored the pairing of Florida and Iowa in entering the Union. There were many objectives to Florida's entrance, which had been held up for many years.[52] The abolitionist minority in the House strongly condemned the "Florida Compromise." One of the most outspoken was John Quincy Adams, who called the paired-states bill a "slave-monger trick." The eventual compromise was twofold: omit any reference to the festering issue over the boundary line with Missouri and plan on Iowa as a smaller state so as to insure a future balance of power between slave and free-worker status. This meant, however, that the size of the state had been reduced by two-thirds from the original 60,000 acres of the Lucas boundaries. It eliminated the Minnesota River Valley that had been settled by families related to those migrating to the territorial districts southeast of Mankato.

The truncated demarcation purportedly followed the recommendations of Nicollet, who had surveyed the territory. The compromise idea gathered consensus with floor leadership from Stephen A. Douglas, who publicly said that although he disapproved of several parts in Florida and Iowa's proposed constitutions, he would vote for admission.[53] The compromise passed by a 3 to 1 margin, 145 to 46. After this process of argumentation, the Senate debate on the bill pairing the two territories centered on Florida, but it also passed easily, 36 to 9.[54]

Iowa's territorial delegate, August C. Dodge, urged Iowan voters to accept the reduced size. His explanation was that free-soil Whigs were appalled by the prospect of annexing the gigantic Republic of Texas and in order to maintain their congressional power, "had urged the creation of several, albeit smaller northern states," which would allow them to continue influencing the Congress.[55] This strategy took into account the population potential of the Territory of Iowa, but as a vision of anti-slavery senators, it ignored the sentiments of Iowan voters, who voted against the revision twice.

In general, Dodge's behavior reflected his own concept of the territorial delegate representing the wishes of the majority of territorial inhabitants, not necessarily his own beliefs. His ability to maneuver in Congress while accepting the wishes of a majority in the territory of Iowa "shows faithfulness to his constituents, prompt compliance with his instructions, and for the second time and in the face of opposing forces, a strong defense to prevent the dismemberment of the Territory."[56] He was an able negotiator who could work with both political parties in Congress. With the compromise over boundaries and popular support by Iowan voters, the stage was set for a successful conclusion. Congressman Samuel F. Vinton had offered an amendment that would have further decreased the size of the State of Iowa, but it failed on a regionally based vote of 68 to 54. James B. Brolin of Missouri, in a show of good intentions, moved a different amendment that led to the adoption of the revised Iowa Constitution on August 3, 1846, to be completed by the end of the year.[57]

CONCLUSION

By December 1846, the Iowa territorial newspapers started referencing the upcoming change over to statehood and the myriad political changes it would entail. The power of myth began to spread over the Hawk's Eye view of the land. August C. Dodge was widely quoted about his work in developing the compromise idea and his sanguine predictions for political debate in 1847. The larger papers devised doggerel verse such as a "Paper Carrier's New Year's Poem" in the eastern river towns of Iowa. With the death of George Davenport on the previous July 4 celebration in Davenport, one of the leading territorial influences of public opinion had been silenced. The stage was set for the new realm of statehood.

NOTES

1. John W. Monette, *History of the Discovery and Settlement of the Valley of the Mississippi*, vol. 2 (New York: Harper, 1846), p. 595.

2. George Catlin, *Letters and Notes on the Manners, Customs, and Condition of the North American Indians*, vol. 2 (London: Tasswell and Myers, 1841), p. 129.

3. Ibid., p. 159.

4. Samuel Mazuchelli, *The Memoirs* (Chicago: Priory Press, 1967), pp. 168–169.

5. Caleb Atwater, *Remarks Made on a Tour to Prairie du Chien* (Columbus, OH: Isaac N. Whitney, 1831), p. 63.

6. Quoted by August Richter, *Geschichte der Stadt Davenport und des County Scott* (Davenport, IA: 1917), p. 299.

7. Statutes at Large, 229.

8. *Galena City Directory* (Galena, IL: W. W. Huntington, 1858), p. 135.

9. Ibid., pp. 138–139.

10. Ronald Rayman, "Confrontation at the Fever River Lead Mining District: Joseph Montfort Street vs. Henry Dodge, 1827–1828," *Annals of Iowa* 44 (4) (Spring 1978): 278–295; see also George Catlin, *Letters and Notes*, vol. 2, p. 149.

11. Hawkins Taylor, "Before and After the Territorial Organization of Iowa," *Annals of Iowa* 9 (1) (January 1871): 353; Michael A. Ross, "Cases of Shattered Dreams: Justice Freeman Miller and the Rise and Fall of a River Town," *Annals of Iowa* 57 (3) (Summer 1998): 201–239; William J. Petersen, "Iowa in 1835," *Palimpsest* 16 (3) (March 1935): 89.

12. Suel Foster, "Origin of Our Missouri War (1839) in a Land Grab," *Annals of Iowa* 11 (3) (July 1873): 540.

13. Jacob Van der Zee, "The Opening of the Des Moines Valley," *Iowa Journal of History and Politics* 14 (4) (October 1916): 483.

14. Charles August Murray, *Travels in North America* (New York: Harper, 1839), p. 73.

15. Taylor, "Before and After," p. 450; Jesse Macy, "Institutional Beginnings in a Western State," *Johns Hopkins University Studies in History and Political Science* 7 (July 1884): 365–367; Tom Schmedeler, "Frontier Forms of Iowa's County Seats," *Annals of Iowa* 57 (1) (Winter 1998): 10.

16. Willard Barrows, "Pioneers, Once and Now, in the United States," *Magazine of Western History* 5 (3) (January 1889): 547.

17. "Westward," *Nile's National Register* 64 (April 22, 1843): 120–121.

18. W. Turrentine Jackson, "The Army Engineers as Road Builders in Territorial Iowa," *Iowa Journal of History and Politics* 47 (1) (January 1949): 15–33; Emory H. English, "As Iowa Approaches Statehood," *Palimpsest* 26 (12) (December 1945): 360.

19. John C. Parish, "Iowa in the Days of Lucas," *Palimpsest* 3 (8) (August 1922): 247. He mentions the first three with Davenport added.

20. *Collections of the Illinois Historical Society* 36 (Springfield: Illinois Historical Society, 1973): 248, n. 2; Franc B. Wilkie, *Davenport, Past and Present* (Davenport: Luse, Lane & Co., 1858), p. 152.

21. William Roba, *The River and the Prairie* (Quad-Cities, IA-IL: Hesperian Press, 1986), pp. 18–19.

22. Stephen H. Hayes, "Letters from the West in 1845," *Iowa Journal of History and Politics* 20 (1) (January 1922): 42.

23. Winfield Scott, *Memoirs* (New York: Sheldon and Company, 1864), p. 221.

24. George Catlin, *Letters and Notes*, p. 212.

25. Ibid., p. 217.

26. Edith Rule and William J. Petersen, *True Tales of Iowa* (Mason City, IA: Yelland and Hanes, 1932), p. 132.

27. Edward Langworthy, "[1893] Sketches," *Iowa Journal of Politics and History* 10 (3) (July 1910): 345.

28. "Boundary Line Bees Cause Honey War," *Iowa Conservationist* 3 (6) (June 15, 1944): 45; Irma Barkes Bennett, "The Sweetest Little War," *American Mercury* 90 (May 1960): 129–131; Rex Gogerty, "Iowa Fights Missouri—1939," *College Spokesman* 44 (1) (November 1946–January 1947): 75; Pauline Cook, "Scott Co. Militia," *Indiana Folklore* 9 (1950): 107–111.

29. Jack T. Johnson, "No Convention in 1840," *Palimpsest* 21 (10) (October 1940): 315.

30. Luella Wright, "Iowa's Oldest Library," *Iowa Journal of History and Politics* 38 (4) (October 1940): 408–428.

31. *Annals of Iowa* 8 (2) (July 1907): 146–147; for an exhaustive summary, see "Sundry Tax Payers," *Iowa Capitol Reporter* (July 23, 1842) in *Iowa Journal of History and Politics* (July 1916): 397–437.

32. *Davenport Gazette*, July 28, 1842.

33. Stephen McCarthy, "Governmental Administration and Political Developments in Iowa, 1836–1846," M.S. thesis, Drake University, 1972, pp. 76–78.

34. *Iowa City Standard*, September 10, 1842.

35. *Burlington Herald*, May 10, 1844; *Iowa Capitol Reporter*, April 3, 1844.

36. Jean Nicholas Nicollet, "The Nicollet Boundaries," *Palimpsest* 3 (5) (May 1928): 175.

37. *Iowa Capital Reporter*, October 22, 1845.

38. James A. James, "National Politics and the Admission of Iowa into the Union," *Annual Report of the American Historical Association* (1897): 172–173.

39. Benjamin F. Shambaugh, *Documentary Material Relating to the History of Iowa*, vol. 1 (Iowa City: State Historical Society, 1897), p. 209.

40. *Bloomington Herald*, September 20, 1845.

41. Shambaugh, *Documentary Material*, p. 214; *Iowa Capital Reporter*, June 3, 1846.

42. William J. Peterson, "Prologue to Statehood," *Palimpsest* 26 (12) (December 1945): 355.

43. John Ely Briggs, "Ripe for Statehood," *Palimpsest* 27 (5) (May 1946): 136.

44. Rayman, "Confrontation at Fever River," p. 146.

45. Benjamin F. Shambaugh, *History of the Constitutions of Iowa* (Des Moines: Historical Department of Iowa, 1902), p. 193.

46. Jacob Swisher, "Three 'No Men,'" *Palimpsest* 27 (2) (November 1945): 322.

47. Shambaugh, *Documentary Material*, p. 185.

48. Ibid., p. 196.

49. Ibid., pp. 299–304.

50. Shambaugh, *History of the Constitutions of Iowa*, p. 74.

51. James A. James, "National Politics and the Admission of Iowa Into the Union," *Annual Report of the American Historical Association* (1897): 166.

52. Franklin A. Doty, "Florida, Iowa, and the National 'Balance of Power,' 1845," *Florida Historical Quarterly* 35 (1) (1956): 43.

53. *Congressional Globe*, 28th Cong., 2d Sess., 1844–1845, vol. 14, p. 284.

54. Ibid., p. 383.

55. Doty, "Florida, Iowa, and the National 'Balance of Power,'" p. 58.

56. Louis Pelzer, *Augustus Caesar Dodge* (Iowa City: Iowa State Historical Society, 1908), p. 127.

57. Ibid., p. 126.

BIBLIOGRAPHY

Briggs, John Ely. "The Birth of the Territory." *Palimpsest* 9 (1) (January 1928): 8–29.

_____. "Ripe for Statehood." *Palimpsest* 27 (5) (May 1946): 129–141.

Catlin, George. *Letters and Notes on the Manners, Custom and Condition of the North American Indians*. London: Tasswell and Myers, 1841.

Doty, Franklin A. "Florida, Iowa, and the National 'Balance of Power,' 1845." *Florida Historical Quarterly* 35 (1956): 30–59.

English, Emory H. "As Iowa Approached Statehood." *Annals of Iowa* 27 (3) (January 1946): 207–216.

Hawkins, Taylor. "Before and After the Territorial Organization of Iowa." *Annals of Iowa* 9 (1) (January 1871): 450–457.

James, James Alton. "Constitution and Admission of Iowa Into the Union." *Johns Hopkins University Studies in Historical and Political Science* 18 (7) (July 1900): 7–54.

Mazuchelli, Samuel. *The Memoirs*. Chicago: Priory Press, 1967.

Monette, John W. *History of the Discovery and Settlement of the Valley of the Mississippi*. New York: Harper, 1846.

Murray, Charles August. *Travels in North America During the Years 1834, 1835 and 1836*. New York: Harper, 1839.

Nicollet, Jean Nicholas. "The Nicollet Boundaries." *Palimpsest* 9 (5) (May 1928): 170–175.

Parish, John C. "Iowa in the Days of Lucas." *Palimpsest* 3 (8) (August 1922): 244–249.

Petersen, William J. "Beginnings in Iowa." *Iowa Journal of History and Politics* 28 (1) (January 1930): 3–54.

_____. "Iowa in 1835." *Palimpsest* 16 (3) (March 1935): 87–103.

_____. "Town and Countryside in 1843." *Palimpsest* 10 (October 1943): 323–332.

_____. "Prologue to Statehood." *Palimpsest* 26 (12) (December 1945): 353–369.

Roba, William H. *The River and the Prairie*. Quad-Cities, IA-IL: Hesperian Press, 1986.

Rule, Edith, and William J. Petersen. *True Tales of Iowa*. Mason City, IA: Yelland, 1932.

Scott, Winfield. *Memoirs*. New York: Sheldon and Co., 1864.

Shambaugh, Benjamin F. *Documentary Material Relating to the History of Iowa*. Iowa City: State Historical Society, 1897.

_____. *History of the Constitutions of Iowa*. Des Moines: Historical Department of Iowa, 1902.

Swisher, Jacob A. "Large State or Small" *Palimpsest* 26 (4) (April 1945): 97–109.

_____. "Three 'No Men.'" *Palimpsest* 26 (11) (November 1945): 321–331.

_____. "Selecting Convention Delegates." *Palimpsest* 27 (2) (February 1946): 49–60.

Taylor, Hawkins. "Before and After the Territorial Organization of Iowa." *Annals of Iowa* 9 (1) (January 1871): 450–457.

Kansas

Territorial Development:

- The United States obtained portions of the future Territory of Kansas from France through the Louisiana Purchase, April 30, 1803
- Lands obtained through the Louisiana Purchase resolved into the Territory of Orleans (Louisiana) and the District of Louisiana; Kansas became an unorganized territory, 1804
- The United States obtained additional lands expanding the future Territory of Kansas through the annexation of Texas, December 29, 1845
- Kansas organized as a U.S. territory, May 30, 1854
- Kansas admitted into the Union as the thirty-fourth state, January 29, 1861

Territorial Capitals:

- Pawnee, 1855–1856
- Lecompton, 1856–1858
- No definite capital, 1858–1861

State Capitals:

- Topeka, 1861–present

Origin of State Name: "Kanze," which became "Kansas" in the French spelling, is a Sioux word that means "people of the south wind."

First Governor: Charles Lawrence Robinson
Governmental Organization: Bicameral
Population at Statehood: 107,206 (figure taken from the 1860 census)
Geographical Size: 81,815 square miles

THE STATE OF KANSAS

Admitted to the Union as a State: January 29, 1861

M. H. Hoeflich

INTRODUCTION

Kansas today is a peaceful, mostly rural state. There is very little strife, and violence is mainly confined to the football field. Yet one need only spend a few minutes walking through any of the major towns of northeastern Kansas to see traces of its turbulent history. Walk down Massachusetts Street in Lawrence past the Eldridge Hotel and a plaque on the wall details its destruction at the hands of "Border Ruffians." Drive on Route 1029 toward Lecompton and you will see a marker pointing you to the "Constitution Hall" built by pro-slavery forces to be the capitol of a slave state, a capitol that was never built. Drive outside Lawrence and you will see the remains of the site of the Battle of Black Jack, where John Brown defeated a pro-slavery force and took twenty-nine prisoners.

The state of Kansas was born in blood and passion. What had been a peaceful territory with few white settlers and to which many Native American tribes had been sent by the U.S. government became the center of a national crisis.[1] In just a few short years, from 1854, when the Kansas-Nebraska Act was passed by Congress and signed into law, until 1861, when a Congress relieved of its southern members passed the legislation admitting Kansas into the Union, Kansas was the scene of terrific political and military struggles.

FIRST STEPS TOWARD THE CREATION OF KANSAS TERRITORY

The history of the creation of Kansas Territory begins with the acquisition by the United States of the Louisiana Territory in 1803 and the Lewis and

Clark expedition of 1804. The Louisiana Purchase brought vast new lands into the United States, and the Lewis and Clark expedition to the Pacific Ocean convinced Americans that this territory could eventually be settled and become a vital part of the Union. In fact, Kansas was at the outermost western boundary of the new territory and was, therefore, of much less immediate interest to white settlers than those parts of the Purchase farther to the east. But in spite of its remote location, what was to become Kansas played an important role in American politics from early days. Although the Louisiana Purchase provided the land and resources that would eventually fuel the westward drive known as "Manifest Destiny," it also posed a major political problem. By 1820, it was becoming increasingly clear that the great political issue of the nineteenth century was to be slavery. Further, as new states were created and entered the Union, it became still clearer that some system to regulate slavery in these new states was necessary. The answer given by Congress in 1820 was the Missouri Compromise.

The Missouri Compromise of 1820 was a brilliant solution to a vexing problem. In 1820, the United States consisted of twenty-four states, equally divided on the issue of slavery.[2] The last two states to have been admitted were Louisiana, a slave state, and Maine, a free state. But in 1820, Missouri petitioned to become the twenty-fifth state. The difficulty was that Missouri would be a slave state and there was no other new free state ready for admission at this time. This meant that the balance between slave and free states would be disrupted and the potential that this imbalance might become permanent was unacceptable to those members of Congress for whom slavery was an abomination. The Missouri Compromise solved this problem by establishing that from 1820 onward, slavery would be impermissible in all states and territories west of the Mississippi and north of 36°30′, the northern boundary of the new state of Missouri.

The Compromise of 1820 was not universally praised by any means, and most politicians realized that it was a temporary solution at best. By 1836, when the western boundary of Missouri was extended to the Missouri River in the northwest as part of the Platte Purchase, the principle was violated. While this measure of 1836 did not signal a deathblow to the compromise, the later Compromise of 1850, which admitted California as a free state but left the possibility that the new territories of Utah and New Mexico might become slave states, certainly did so. The Compromise of 1850 made it clear that the Missouri Compromise was no longer a living law and that some new agreement on the admission of new states and territories had to be hammered out.

It was within this context that Senator Stephen A. Douglas of Illinois introduced the notion of popular sovereignty (also known as "squatter sovereignty"). Douglas began a campaign to convince his fellow members of Congress that this was the best solution to the problem posed by the breakdown of the Missouri Compromise. Douglas believed that Congress should not decide the question on its own. He believed, rather, that the best way to determine whether a new state should be free or slave should rest with the people (i.e., the white males) who lived in these newly created states. Thus, in 1854, Douglas introduced the bill that has come to be known as the Kansas-Nebraska Bill. This bill specified that the territories petitioning for statehood, namely Kansas and Nebraska, should vote as to whether they wished to be either free states or slave states. Since this territory was within the "perpetually" free area established by the Missouri Compromise, passage of the Kansas-Nebraska Act was an annulment of that 1820 compromise. Thus, the battle over slavery in the West was now fully joined.[3]

Douglas's promotion of popular sovereignty was strongly opposed by members of Congress from the North, including such notables as Charles Sumner of Massachusetts and William Seward of New York. It also provided the basis for the meteoric rise of one of Douglas's colleagues from Illinois, Abraham Lincoln, and for the political turmoil and bloodshed that would mark the territorial years of Kansas, beginning in 1854.

When Kansas became a territory in 1854, there were few whites living there. One estimate of the white population at this time put the total at about seven hundred. For decades before passage of the Kansas-Nebraska Act, Kansas had been viewed as unfit for permanent white settlement.[4] Indeed, in the immediately preceding decades, many Native American tribes had been resettled from the East to Kansas, whose rolling prairies and arid conditions were deemed better suited to a nomadic hunting existence than to whites' agricultural economy. As a result of the treaties that led to this resettlement, one of the immediate obstacles to white emigration to Kansas was the need to obtain the permission of these tribes. Such permission was obtained, but was often done so by fraud and coercion.[5] Indeed, one of the great historical ironies of the struggle over Kansas is that both sides, pro-slavery and free state, found no difficulty in violating valid treaties and displacing the Native American tribes that lawfully inhabited Kansas.

Kansas became a battleground neither because of the inherent worth of the land nor because of the strategic location of Kansas on the trails to California and the West.[6] Instead, Kansas Territory became the focus of national attention simply because it was the first territory to have to decide its own fate as to slavery and freedom. The anti-slavery forces of the Northeast saw the Kansas-Nebraska Act as a free pass to the slave forces in Missouri to move into the new territory and ensure that supporters of slavery would dominate its population. In retaliation, these anti-slavery forces adopted the unique strategy of immigration. The notion was simple: provide the resources to assist anti-slavery groups to move into Kansas and settle there. In short, the first phase of the battle for Kansas was to be fought through immigration. The Missouri pro-slavery forces had the advantage of proximity. It was but a short ride over the border. The northeastern anti-slavery forces had the advantage of resources. Some of the greatest industrialists of the antebellum period, such as Amos Lawrence, the

Massachusetts textile magnate, were prepared to dedicate substantial sums to the cause.[7]

It is necessary, before beginning any detailed discussion of the battle for territorial Kansas, to make it clear that not all "Free Staters" held the same beliefs. Whereas the pro-slavery forces generally all supported the same political credo—that slavery be legal—the various anti-slavery forces were by no means of a similar unanimity. Some of the supporters of the cause were abolitionists who favored the national prohibition of slavery. Others simply wanted to keep slavery out of the new states. Very few, if any, were in favor of granting civil rights in the modern sense to freed slaves or believed that blacks were the equals of whites. And, as will become apparent, some favored the use of violence, while others preferred more peaceful means to achieve their goals.

There was one characteristic, however, common to both the pro-slavery and anti-slavery forces. This was their zealousness in pursuit of their causes. During the first years of the battle for Kansas, both sides engaged in what today would be called a war of propaganda, perhaps the first such in national history.[8] They used the press, they used political debate and oratory, and they used literature. Both sides understood the power of words in a way reminiscent of the great debates of the revolutionary period. For instance, the Lawrence *Herald of Freedom*, a free-state newspaper, published the "Song of the Kansas Emigrant" in its issue of October 21, 1854:

> We cross the prairies as of old
> The Pilgrims crossed the sea
> To make the West as they the East
> The homestead of the free.
>
> The homestead of the free, my boys,
> The homestead of the free,
> To make the West as they the East,
> The homestead of the free.[9]

To these and other verses, hundreds of believers left behind their comfortable homes in Massachusetts, New York, and other eastern states and set out on their journey to make a new life in the free state of Kansas.

The pro-slavery forces were no less enthusiastic, if somewhat less poetic. On June 10, 1854, a group of pro-slavery Missourians met at Salt Creek Valley in Kansas, near Fort Leavenworth. There they organized the Squatter's Claim Association and adopted a series of twelve "resolutions," including the following:

> (1) That we are in favor of a *bona fide* Squatter Sovereignty, and acknowledge the right of any citizen of the United States to make a claim in Kansas Territory, ultimately with the view of occupying it...

(8) That we recognize the institution of slavery *as always existing in this Territory*, and recommend slaveholders to introduce their property as early as possible....[10]

The pro-slavery opinion on the eastern immigration movement was also simply expressed, as in the following statement printed on June 8, 1854, by *Democratic Platform*, a newspaper published in Liberty, Missouri: "Shall we allow cut-throats and murderers, as the people of Massachusetts are, to settle in the territory adjoining our own state? No! If popular opinion will not keep them back, we should see what virtue there is in the force of arms."[11]

The rhetoric was backed up on both sides. Even before passage of the Kansas-Nebraska Act, both sides had begun preparations for moving supporters into the new territory to gain a voting majority. In the East, this took the form of "emigrant aid societies," the best organized and most successful of which was the Massachusetts Emigrant Aid Society, funded by Massachusetts abolitionists like Amos Lawrence of Boston and Eli Thayer of Worcester.[12] During the summer and fall of 1854, the first two parties of emigrants sponsored by the Massachusetts Emigrant Aid Society made their way to Lawrence, Kansas, where they formed a town association and began the task of organizing their lives and their political forces.[13] At the same time that Lawrence began its life as the center of the free-state movement, President Franklin Pierce, no friend to the free-state movement, appointed Andrew H. Reeder of Pennsylvania as the first territorial governor.[14] He also appointed other federal officials, the most important of whom for the troubled history of the territory was Samuel Lecompte of Maryland, who was appointed as the chief justice of the Kansas territorial supreme court. These officials arrived in Kansas in the fall of 1854. At this point, as fall turned into winter and 1854 segued into 1855, the ground was set for what came to be called "Bleeding Kansas" and one of the most turbulent periods in the history of the state. The next few years would see the proliferation of political parties, an increase in violent acts against both people and property culminating in the "Wakarusa War," a succession of five more territorial governors after Governor Reeder gave up the office, and, eventually, the crystallization of those social and political forces that would eventually lead to the Civil War.

BLEEDING KANSAS: 1855–1857

Andrew Reeder remained as territorial governor for less than a year. During that year he achieved a great deal. In November 1854, the first election for a territorial delegate to Congress was held. John Whitfield, the pro-slavery candidate, was elected. In early 1855, Reeder ordered the first census of the territory, and in March 1855, he ordered the first election for the new territorial legislature. This first election was held on March 30, 1855. Missourians in large numbers crossed into Kansas, often under arms, camped out prior to the election, and, when the polls opened, made sure to dominate the voting. The result was a clear victory for the pro-slavery party. As soon as the election returns were in, however, the Free Staters raised a hue and cry claiming fraud and intimidation. Governor Reeder, much to the surprise of those who believed that as a Pierce appointee, he would be sympathetic to the pro-slavery victory, set aside the election results and called for a re-vote in a number of election districts. This began a wave of violence. One newspaper office, that of the *Parkville Luminary*, which had published articles in favor of Reeder's action, was destroyed by pro-slavery forces.[15] On April 30, 1855, a Free Stater shot and killed a pro-slavery leader. This, in turn, led to mob violence and the tarring and feathering of a lawyer who was accused of instigating the shooting.[16] By the time the re-vote was held in May 1855, the pro-slavery forces had gained so much power that they decided simply to boycott these elections.

In July 1855, the territorial legislature met for the first time in Pawnee. One of the first acts of this legislature, still dominated by pro-slavery candidates, was to call for the removal of all of the Free State members elected at the May election and to unseat them. Following this, the legislature voted to move from Pawnee, the site chosen by Governor Reeder, to Shawnee Mission. Once there, the legislature quickly moved to pass a memorial asking the U.S. Congress to remove Governor Reeder from office. Reeder, already under a cloud because of allegations of dishonesty, was dismissed as governor on July 28.[17]

The Shawnee legislature began its work in earnest once it had removed the Free State candidates and sent its memorial to Washington. Its most important task was the organization of the apparatus of government in Kansas and the establishment of a Kansas legal system. The legislators chose to model the Kansas laws on those of Missouri, thus ensuring that the legal system would provide for the legality of slavery and protect slaveholders' property rights. The new laws also included a so-called Black Code, a series of laws designed to criminalize any acts by whites to aid slaves and to punish any slaves acting in rebellion against their masters. The penalties were death. In fact, the Black Code adopted by the Shawnee legislature has been characterized as going far beyond even the Missouri laws in their severity.[18]

Spring 1855 also saw a number of other extremely important developments. The disputed elections and convening of the Pawnee legislature led to the first Free State meetings at Lawrence. It also saw the first involvement of a number of men who were to play major roles in the coming years. James H. Lane, a Democrat who was to become a leader of the most violent faction of the Free State forces, came to Lawrence in July.[19] On July 11, the first Free State convention was held at Lawrence. Lane, once a Democrat and supporter of the Kansas-Nebraska Act, now announced himself a Free Stater. The convention adopted, as well, a number of resolutions including a condemnation of the Missourians' attempts to subvert the elections. A second convention was held at Lawrence the next month and again condemned the pro-slavery party and its tactics and called for Free State candidates elected in May to take their rightful seats in the legislature. These two meetings also called for a September convention to be held at Big Springs. It was here that the Free State Party was formally organized, candidates were nominated for various offices, and a platform was adopted.

Between October 23 and November 11, 1855, a constitutional convention was held at Topeka. Free Staters elected this convention's delegates in October in an election not recognized by the pro-slavery party. The result, of course, was that the Topeka convention was, in essence, a Free State convention. The Topeka constitution that was produced by this convention, therefore, represented the beliefs of the Free State Party and prohibited slavery in Kansas.[20] Several months later, it was presented to Congress, but never approved. At the same election in October, the Free State Party elected former Governor Reeder to be the Kansas territorial delegate to Congress. Just a week earlier, at a separate election, the pro-slavery forces had elected John Whitfield as territorial delegate. Congress refused to seat either delegate.

By late fall of 1855, further developments had taken place. Wilson Shannon had arrived in Kansas as the new governor, and what has come to be called the "Wakarusa War" had begun. Just as Governor Shannon arrived, the violence between the opposing political parties escalated. In late November, a land claim dispute between a Free Stater, Charles Dow, and a pro-slavery advocate, Frank Coleman, resulted in the shooting death of Dow. This led to the burning of several pro-slavery homes, allegedly by Free State Party members. This, in turn, led to a call to arms issued by Sheriff Samuel Jones, a pro-slavery appointee, who arrested Jacob Branson, a Free State leader.[21] At the news of the arrest, a party of armed men left Lawrence to confront Jones and his posse. They forced the release of Branson at gunpoint.

Jones responded to the capture and release of his prisoner by writing to Governor Shannon for help. Shannon called out the territorial militia. A request was also made to call out the federal troops stationed at Fort Leavenworth, but the officer in charge refused to send out his men without explicit orders from the government in Washington. As the territorial militia, strengthened by pro-slavery irregulars from Missouri, encamped near Lawrence, the Free State forces turned Lawrence into an armed camp. The Free Staters were well equipped with the deadly Sharps rifles they had acquired from their eastern supporters. Charles Robinson led the forces. James Lane was second in command. Tensions continued to increase. Armed patrols roamed the countryside. A Free Stater, Tom Barber, was shot to death by pro-slavery forces, but his two companions escaped. A major battle seemed inevitable. Governor Shannon, hoping to avoid further bloodshed, came to Lawrence and attempted to mediate. Miraculously, and with the aid of a Kansas ice storm, he succeeded. The pro-slavery forces gradually abandoned their positions and returned home. Unfortunately for Shannon, his mediation also led eventually to his political downfall. Although the "Wakarusa War" took few lives, it did bring James Lane further into the center of the Free State Party. Great loss of life was avoided, but this reprieve was only temporary.

The beginning of 1856 saw further developments on the Free State side. In January, pursuant to the Topeka constitution, Free Staters elected a slate of state officers that included Charles Robinson as governor. In March, legislators who had been elected at the January elections attempted to hold a legislative session at Topeka. At this point, even though the Free State government at Topeka had done virtually nothing, the political situation in Kansas was chaotic. There were now two legislatures, the Shawnee Mission legislature, referred to by the Free State forces as the "bogus legislature," and the Topeka legislature, deemed illegitimate by the pro-slavery forces. Charles Robinson, a Lawrence Free State leader, was now the governor according to the Free State Party, but Wilson Shannon continued to hold his presidential appointment as territorial governor. Charges flew back and forth, and the propaganda was nonstop. More significant, the presidential appointees to the Territorial Legislature, led by Samuel Lecompte, remained firmly in control of the territorial judiciary. This had fateful consequences.

In April 1856, Congress sent an investigating committee to discover and report on the true conditions in the Kansas Territory.[22] Within days of the arrival of the congressional party, Sheriff Jones obtained writs for the arrest of the men who had taken away his prisoners several times before. He came to Lawrence on several consecutive days, but each time he was turned away without the men he sought. Finally, Jones was assigned a small detachment of federal troops who marched with him into Lawrence on April 23 and succeeded in arresting a group of Free State leaders. These he took into custody and brought back to his camp to be guarded by federal soldiers. Late that night, a solitary sniper shot Jones in the back. Jones was taken to Lawrence for care. Wounded, but assured of survival, he was removed to pro-slavery territory the next day by his supporters.

The shooting of Jones brought a further escalation in the war of words. Justice Lecompte, sitting in his court in Lecompton, finally convened a grand jury in early May that immediately brought in indictments for treason against several of the Free State leaders, including James Lane, Charles Robinson, and Andrew Reeder, who was back in the territory as part of the congressional investigating committee. Robinson was taken prisoner. Lane escaped from the territory. Over the next several weeks, the possibility of mass violence grew. Pro-slavery forces, many from Missouri, massed near Lawrence. The U.S. marshal had a warrant for the arrest of those indicted. The Free State forces in Lawrence prepared themselves for battle. Finally, on May 21, Lawrence was attacked.[23] The offices of the two Free State newspapers were destroyed, as was the Free State Hotel, long the headquarters of the party. Interestingly, loss of life was minimal: two Free Staters and one pro-slavery fighter. The success of the raid, however, was great, for the financial damage to the Free State Party was substantial and the party's leaders were under arrest.[24]

The "Sack of Lawrence" in May 1856 began several years of the bloodiest fighting in the history of the state. Truly "the dogs of war [had] been loosed," and a new figure emerged on the scene. John Brown and his four sons had come to Kansas, ostensibly to farm. In truth, however, Brown and his sons had come as radical abolitionists determined to ensure that Kansas would be free. Whether Brown was a madman or divinely inspired no one will ever know, but he was a charismatic leader perfectly willing to use unrestrained violence to achieve his ends.[25] When news of the Lawrence attack reached Brown, he began his war on both pro-slavery and federal forces in earnest, a war that was to last until he was finally caught, tried, and hanged. Within days of the Lawrence attack, Brown and his men attacked and burned the homesteads of several pro-slavery men and then killed them. At Black Jack, near Lawrence, Brown met a force of more than one hundred men under Colonel Pate, defeated them, and took them prisoner. This was just the beginning.[26] Meanwhile, the spring and summer of 1856 was also a time of turmoil over Kansas in Congress. Bitter debates were held over the submission of the Topeka constitution and the report of the investigating committee. It was during one of these debates that Senator Brooks of South Carolina, an ardent pro-slavery man, attacked and seriously wounded Senator Charles Sumner of Massachusetts after Sumner's "Crime Against Kansas" speech.[27]

Meanwhile, on July 4, the Topeka legislature attempted to reconvene and continue its work. It was prevented from doing so by the intervention of U.S. troops, under orders to force the legislature to disband. Events began to move more rapidly from this point on. Lawrence continued to be harassed by pro-slavery forces. The Free State men under the command of James Lane struck back. Several battles, including those at Fort Titus and at Franklin, were fought and won by the Free State forces.[28] Then, in mid-August, Governor Shannon, exhausted by the continuing violence, resigned. Soon thereafter, U.S. soldiers struck a return blow at John Brown and his men and attacked his stronghold at Osawatomie. One of Brown's sons was killed and their encampment was burned.

The violence in Kansas had reached new heights by late August 1856. John Brown was leading his zealots on violent raids against the federal troops and the pro-slavery residents. The federal troops were opposed to the Free State men, the worst of whom would soon be called "Jayhawkers." The Missouri "Border Ruffians" were now openly attacking the Free State men, and the Free State men were also on the warpath.

The extent of the violence that plagued Kansas in 1856 has long been debated. Contemporary newspaper accounts, none of which is objective, paint a picture of a territory wracked by constant acts of partisan violence. And yet we also know that the number of lives lost during this period was quite small compared to what would become the norm only a few short years later during the Civil War.

Although the loss of life was relatively small, however, we certainly can say that there was a sense of insecurity among the residents of Kansas during 1855–1856. In large part, this insecurity was over property. The Sack of Lawrence destroyed only selected targets—the hotel and the newspapers—but this was only one incident that attracted national attention. There were so many different warring groups of pro- and anti-slavery forces, federal troops and state militias, as well as roving bands of what can only be classified as simple thieves and bandits, that the residents of the Kansas Territory at this time must have recognized that they could not be secure in their businesses and their homes.

The insecurity of so many of the new emigrants to Kansas was made considerably worse by the circumstances of their coming to Kansas in the first place. Kansas was then at the frontier. The trip was long and arduous and required many sacrifices. Those who came to Kansas were forced to give up their homes in the East and to leave behind most of their property and their former occupations. They came not only to serve their individual political causes but also to make new lives for themselves. Thus, to be at risk of losing what they had brought with them or earned in the new territory was especially hard.

In February 1857, after the worst of the violence in the northeastern portions of the territory was over, the Territorial Legislature passed a bill creating a "Commissioner for Auditing Claims" who was charged with taking testimony from the residents of the northeastern counties of the territory to determine what their property losses had been during the previous several years. The hope was that these claims might eventually be recognized by the federal government in Washington and lead to restitution for those who had suffered. H. J. Strickler was appointed as commissioner. Strickler took testimony from nearly five hundred residents and their witnesses. This testimony was compiled and printed in 1859 and provides an unparalleled credible contemporary account of these losses. It also permits us, more than a century and a half later, to hear the actual voices of the men and women who suffered through these years.

Samuel N. Simpson's home was vandalized by unknown members of the territorial militia on May 21, the day of the Sack of Lawrence. He lost several articles of clothing, a gold watch, books, and five thousand feet of pine and walnut lumber worth $275. His total losses were $573. He lost, interestingly, two weapons, a "sporting rifle" and a Sharps rifle. It is easy to understand why the militia might have disarmed Simpson, particularly of the deadly Sharps rifle, but it is less easy to imagine any "official" purpose to taking his lumber, clothing, and gold watch. This would seem to have been simple brigandage.

According to his testimony, on September 1, 1856, John Wakefield, a farmer in Douglas County, was also visited by members of the territorial militia. In his case, property was not stolen but destroyed. Both his house and his barn were burned, as were the contents thereof. He lost tools, furniture, clothing, even his stove. Eight bedsteads were destroyed along with bedding. The militia also destroyed his food stocks, including a barn filled with grain. They set fire to his garden and destroyed his corn and potatoes. They even damaged his well. Wakefield was not an ignorant man. He possessed a substantial library by contemporary standards: one hundred books. These were all burned. Even sadder, he apparently was an author and had written a book himself. This, too, was destroyed in seven hundred manuscript pages and, thus, was irrecoverably lost to the fires. Although he placed a value of $500 on the lost text, we can be certain that no amount of money could have made up for the wanton destruction of so much literary labor.

The massive property loss suffered by Wakefield at the hands of the militia illustrates one crucial aspect of the violence that took place during 1855 and 1856. Although few men and women were killed or even injured, the purpose of the violence was not to seize property. Its primary purpose was to frighten the settlers and to convince them to leave the territory. It was, thus, to a large extent, motivated by a strategy of intimidation, one designed to convince the victims that they would be better off leaving Kansas for a safer place.

In pursuit of this strategy of intimidation, the violence was not limited to homes and farms but extended also to places of business. The idea, no doubt, was to make it impossible for the settlers to maintain a normal lifestyle by making it impossible for them to make their livings. Thus, in Wakefield's case, not only did he lose his home and furnishings, he lost his crops, his seeds, his farm tools, even his garden and well.

It was not only the territorial militia, a pro-slavery force, which brought havoc to the residents of the territory. The Free State forces, under James Lane, were as lawless as their opponents. In September 1856, Lane and his men staged a series of raids in Shawnee County. D. B. Castleman, a merchant there, explained to Commissioner Strickler what had happened to him and to his property:

> I have resided in the town, county and Territory since the first day of June, A.D. 1856, and I settled there in good faith to become a Citizen of the same, and still reside there, desirous of living in a country where personal security and the rights of property are regarded by the inhabitants, and guaranteed by the federal arm in its protection to infant territories.... I was engaged in the business of a merchant, and had acquired a considerable run of trade, and had on hand a considerable stock of assorted goods suitable to the market....

Unfortunately for Mr. Castleman, Lane's men were not inclined to permit him to carry on his business. According to Castleman, a group of about fifty of Lane's men, "armed with Sharp's rifles, Colt's revolvers, pistols, bowie knives, and other deadly weapons, mounted on horses," attacked his store. They returned with reinforcements the day after and took whatever had been overlooked the day before. He lost, all told, over $3,800 worth of goods. During this same period, Lane and his men attacked the homes and businesses of other pro-slavery residents, taking anything they could, including horses, weapons, food, and liquor.

The picture that emerges from the testimony given before Commissioner Strickler is one of a territory under siege, where both sides were using violence to achieve their political ends. The goal was not, as in a true war, to kill the enemy. Rather, what both sides wanted was to frighten their enemies into abandoning their homes and businesses and leaving the territory. Killings were, for the most part, either the result of passion or accident during this period. Later, in 1858 in southeastern Kansas, John Brown and his men changed the situation. Far more radical than the forces that plagued northeastern Kansas earlier, they were much more interested in killing the enemy.

As the violence among the various parties increased, the war of words also reached new heights. Now the Kansas Free State men and women doubled their efforts to gain northern support. They needed money for printing presses and for weapons. They were greatly assisted in this effort by the publication of a book by Charles Robinson's wife, Sara, *Kansas—Its Interior and Exterior Life*, which pled the Free State cause.[29] This book helped to raise thousands of dollars in the sympathetic North, money that would prove crucial to the final phases of the struggle for a free Kansas.

THE FINAL PHASES

By the fall of 1856 the struggles in Kansas had become a national political crisis. The president appointed a new territorial governor, John W. Geary.[30] Geary, an experienced soldier and former mayor of San Francisco, was charged with bringing the violence to an end. This was a formidable task. James Lane had been active on the lecture circuit raising arms and men back East and had made the northern route through Iowa the lifeline for supplying the Free State.[31] The pro-slavery forces under Samuel Jones and David Atchison, a former vice president of the United States, were massing for what seemed to many to be a final all-out assault designed to "exterminate" the Free State forces. During the period following Shannon's resignation and Geary's arrival, the acting territorial governor, Daniel Woodson, had permitted chaos to take over. Indeed, the day after Geary arrived at Fort Leavenworth, a band of Free State partisans defeated a pro-slavery force at Slough Creek, and they were, in turn, defeated and taken prisoner by U.S. forces and held for trial for murder. Recognizing the immensity of his task, Geary immediately set about to disband the "volunteer militia," convince the Missourians to return across the border, and bring peace to the territory. His efforts reached a high point when he arrived in Lawrence to discover an armed force in excess of 2,500 men camped nearby ready to attack. He successfully took command of these forces and convinced them to disband, although stragglers continued to wreak havoc on their route home.[32] By the end of 1856 and the beginning of the new year, Geary had brought a stop to the worst of the violence. According to George W. Martin, "by the spring of 1857 marauding, except in Southeastern Kansas, had practically ceased."[33] Yet as the internal violence wound down in 1857, the political battles over creating a permanent constitution and seeking statehood grew in intensity.

of the pro-slavery party.[38] At this first session, little was done other than to establish an organization and officers for the convention. The delegates chose to delay further business until after the October election for the territorial legislature.[39] This election took place on October 5.[40] All sides took part, and in spite of accusations of voting fraud leveled against the pro-slavery forces, the Free State Party took a clear majority of the votes. One precinct, in particular, was troublesome. There were over 1,600 votes cast in a community that had only eleven permanent residents.[41] Governor Walker and Secretary of State Stanton disallowed these votes, thereby ensuring a Free State majority in both houses of the new legislature and in the election of the territorial delegate to Congress. The pro-slavery forces were both enraged at Walker and Stanton and also made aware of how precarious their cause had become.

On October 19, the constitutional convention reconvened at Lecompton and began its work in earnest.[42] The purpose of the convention was clear: to draft a constitution that would guarantee the continuance of slavery in the territory and that could be submitted to Congress as the basis for statehood. The problem that the delegates faced was that the recent elections made it absolutely clear that such a constitution would not be ratified by a popular vote, which was required. The delegates to the Lecompton convention found a way to achieve their ends in spite of this legal difficulty. The provisions calling for the ratification of the Lecompton constitution were drafted in a clever manner.[43] As drafted, it guaranteed the rights of all slaveholders in the territory to retain their slaves and their slave offspring as their property. Further, it prohibited any territorial or state government from emancipating slaves without the consent of their owners and, in the case of gaining such consent, without paying full compensation to their owners. The constitution also provided that new immigrants to Kansas could bring their slaves with them and that the government could not prevent them from maintaining them as their property once in Kansas. Finally, the constitution's Bill of Rights made it illegal for "any free Negroes…to live in the state under any circumstances."[44]

As already noted, the big problem for the Lecompton delegates was ratification by the people. How could ratification be attained when the Free State forces might well have a majority of votes? To solve this dilemma, the delegates voted to submit the constitution to a popular vote for ratification, but they proposed that the vote be for the constitution "with or without slavery." A vote for the constitution "with slavery" was a vote for the constitution as drafted by the convention. A vote for the constitution "without slavery," however, did not mean that slavery would be prohibited in Kansas, only that the provision permitting new immigrants to bring in and maintain slaves would be dropped. Either way, residents of Kansas at the time of adoption would be permitted to retain their slaves and all the slave offspring of their slaves (the "increase"). Thus, there was no option to make Kansas a free state.[45]

The actions of the Lecompton constitutional convention brought swift reactions. Governor Walker, unhappy at the result, left for Washington and was soon removed by the president. Among the Free State forces, the legal sleight of hand effected by the Lecompton convention brought both an increase in factionalism and a sense of desperation. The radical wing, led by James Lane, seemed inclined to open warfare. The more moderate wing, led by Charles Robinson, continued to seek a political, nonviolent solution.[46]

The Free State forces gathered at Lawrence in early December to hold a convention at which they denounced the Lecompton constitution, rejected the right of the convention to produce such a document, and challenged the validity of the vote proposed on the Lecompton constitution. The Lawrence convention also endorsed the Topeka constitution and urged its submission to Congress in lieu of the Lecompton constitution. Several days later, the newly elected territorial legislature, dominated by Free Staters, met and again repudiated the Lecompton constitution and demanded that no constitution be submitted to Congress except one that had been voted upon in a true election. On December 21, an election was held under the auspices of the pro-slavery forces on the Lecompton constitution. Since this election was boycotted by Free State voters, the vote was overwhelmingly in favor of adoption of the constitution with slavery.[47]

Immediately after this vote took place, the Free State supporters held an emergency convention to decide whether to participate in the upcoming January elections for a new state government, as prescribed by the Lecompton constitution, elections that would choose state officers, legislators, and a member of Congress as well as decide on whether the constitution would be submitted to Congress.[48] The Free State supporters were split on the question, and many decided to boycott these elections as well. In spite of this partial boycott, the elections went forward on January 4, 1858. In the elections for state officers and others, both the pro-slavery advocates and a majority of Free State supporters voted. The Free State candidates won all of the officer elections and a majority of the legislative seats. The pro-slavery forces boycotted the election on the Lecompton constitution on the grounds that this had already been decided on December 21. Naturally, therefore, the vote was against the constitution. At the same time these elections were being held, the territorial legislature, now firmly under the control of elected Free State members, met for the third time. Among the business carried on was a vote calling for a constitutional convention to counter the pro-slavery Lecompton convention. An election for delegates to this convention was held on March 9 and, of course, was dominated by the Free State forces.

The constitutional convention met first at Minneola, Kansas, on March 23 and reconvened at Leavenworth on March 25. This convention produced a draft constitution quite similar to the Topeka constitution. Among the differences, however, was a provision that permitted all free males [including blacks] to vote. The convention adjourned on April 3, and the constitution was put to a vote on May 18. The turnout at this election was extremely small. It was boycotted not only by pro-slavery forces but also by many Free State supporters who disliked parts of the document or who questioned the legality of the convention itself, often on factional grounds.[49] Regardless of this vote, however, other events in Washington soon rendered it of little importance. As things stood in the spring of 1858, Kansas had three proposed constitutions: the Topeka constitution, the Lecompton constitution, and the Leavenworth constitution and, to make matters worse, President Buchanan and the Congress in Washington decided to get more involved in the process.

KANSAS IN WASHINGTON

During the winter and spring of 1858, the Thirty-fifth Congress considered the Lecompton constitution that had been submitted to them with the backing of President Buchanan. Buchanan and his cabinet were clearly in favor of acceptance of the Lecompton constitution and admission of Kansas to the Union as a slave state. The debates in Congress lasted weeks and centered not only on the slavery question but also on the issue of whether the people of Kansas had been able to exercise true sovereignty in the election as called for under the Kansas-Nebraska Act.[50] Stephen A. Douglas opposed acceptance of the Lecompton constitution because he feared that the elections on the constitution had been fraudulent. The Senate, after heated debate, voted 32–25 to accept the constitution. The House, however, passed a substitute bill that required the Lecompton constitution to be resubmitted to a "fair" vote in Kansas. This, the Senate refused. Finally, a Senate-House committee, chaired by Mr. English of Indiana, reported out a compromise bill, known as the "English Bill," which was passed by both houses of Congress.[51]

The English Bill, like the Lecompton constitution itself, was a brilliantly drafted document. It provided for the Lecompton constitution to be resubmitted for a popular vote of rejection or acceptance. If the people of Kansas accepted the Lecompton constitution, then it also provided that the United States would provide substantial land grants to Kansas for building schools, roads, public buildings, a state university, and salt springs. On the other hand, if the Lecompton constitution were to be rejected, then not only would Kansas not be given these lands, but Kansas also would not be permitted to apply for statehood until its population had reached 93,500, a population far greater than had been required of other applicants.

The debates and political machinations that took place in Congress and in the White House over the Lecompton constitution in the spring of 1858 led to national indignation and calls for investigation. Two years later, another congressional investigating committee, the Covode Committee, was appointed and reported in 1860 that widespread bribery and the use of improper influence had accompanied the votes on these bills.[52] This was, however, of little relevance. When the Lecompton constitution was put to another vote in Kansas in early August 1858, at the order of then governor Denver, who had been appointed acting governor after Walker left for Washington, it was defeated by a nearly ten to one majority. With the August defeat of the Lecompton constitution, the political battle over whether the new state would be free or slave was effectively over. It was obvious that a pro-slavery constitution could not win popular ratification. Now the question was what concessions the pro-slavery forces could exact. Violence, particularly in southeast Kansas, where John Brown was operating, continued, but the political future of Kansas was finally becoming clear. In October 1858, Governor Walker resigned and the sixth and last territorial governor, Samuel Medary, was appointed.[53] It was left to his administration to oversee the final drafting of a constitution, the Wyandotte constitution, and to eventually lead Kansas to statehood.

THE WYANDOTTE CONSTITUTION

Soon after Governor Medary arrived in Kansas in late December 1858, he made his intentions clear. On January 3, he asked whether Kansans were desirous of entering the Union or whether they wished to continue as they were. Just a few days later, the territorial legislature answered his question by beginning discussions on a law that would call a new constitutional convention.[54] The debate on this bill lasted several weeks and highlighted the issues that would face such a convention. One of the most important issues was that of apportionment of representation at a constitutional convention. Much other than slavery was at stake. At this time a number of railroad companies had their eyes on Kansas and wanted to make sure that representatives were chosen who would favor their petitions for rights-of-way and other benefits. After tortuous debates and parliamentary maneuvers, the apportionment issues were settled.[55] Where to hold the convention was another issue of great contention. Both Lawrence and Manhattan wanted to be the site of the convention, but both failed in their attempts to get a majority. Wyandotte succeeded as a compromise candidate. Finally, the territorial legislature agreed to permit the people to vote on whether they wanted to have another constitutional convention on March 4. They further provided that if the vote were favorable, which it was, then a second election for delegates would be held in June and that the convention itself should meet in July.

During the late winter and early spring, the wisdom of having another convention was debated. During that period the old parties that had dominated Kansas politics since 1854 began to lose strength. It was clear that Kansas politics were now a vital part of national politics. The old pro-slavery groups were now fully aligned with the national Democratic Party. On the other side, Horace Greeley, a leader of the national Republican Party, visited Kansas in May. Soon thereafter, the old Free State Party held its last convention and a new Kansas Republican Party was formed, ensuring that the two national parties would be the parties that would preside at the upcoming Wyandotte constitutional convention.[56]

The delegates who began their deliberations at Wyandotte on July 5 were divided; there were thirty-five Republicans and seventeen Democrats. Sixteen listed themselves as farmers, eighteen as lawyers, six as merchants, three as doctors, and the rest represented varying professions. Thirteen listed Ohio as their place of origin; seven listed Indiana; six listed Pennsylvania; two listed Massachusetts; and the rest listed other states, plus one each from Scotland, Ireland, and Germany. They ranged in age from twenty-five to fifty.[57] All were agreed that their task was to draft a new constitution for Kansas that would be acceptable to Congress and lead to the admission of Kansas to the Union.

The work on the convention was done, in the first instance, by sixteen committees, each of which had a Republican as chair and each of which contained a Republican majority. This ensured that the Republicans would dominate the convention and its work.[58] The convention began its debate and drafting with discussion of what to use as a model. The decision taken, not surprising given the backgrounds of the delegates, was to use the Ohio constitution of 1850 as the primary model.[59] In spite of this, there are many differences between the two, and subsequent research has shown that other state constitutions as well as earlier Kansas constitutions were also consulted for language and ideas.[60] Among the basic issues that roused much debate were the executive power of the governor and the apportionment of representation in both the proposed new house and senate.

One of the great issues before the convention was suffrage—who would have the vote in the new state of Kansas? Mrs. Clarinda Nichols, on behalf of the women of Kansas, made a presentation to the convention asking for suffrage for women, who had struggled alongside the men in years past.[61] The convention, however, declined to grant such suffrage generally, although it did vote to permit women to vote in school elections. Even more debate was occupied on the question of black suffrage. The Democratic delegates were opposed. Indeed, there were motions presented to keep blacks entirely out of the new state.

On July 18, the Committee on Elections and Suffrage presented to the convention for debate the question of whether blacks and people of mixed race (mulattos) would be permitted to vote. The proposed provision before the committee would have limited suffrage to "whites." An amendment to strike the word "white" was proposed and voted down. There ensued a long discussion of what the word "white" meant and whether various people of mixed race or foreign heritage would be deemed white. After a number of "clarifying" amendments were proposed and defeated, the convention at last voted to retain the word "white" in the constitution by an overwhelming majority.

It may seem rather strange that by the time of the drafting of the Wyandotte constitution, a time when the Free State Party had clearly won the day, that a debate over black suffrage would take place, let alone result in blacks being denied the vote. But here it is necessary to remember that the Free State movement was not, by and large, a movement that favored the expansion of civil rights for blacks. On the contrary, the unifying policy of the Free State movement throughout the territorial period was opposition to slavery and no more. Indeed, expanded civil rights were also not the policy of the majority of the national Republicans, soon to be led by Abraham Lincoln. Thus, the debates at the Wyandotte constitutional convention represented a broad range of opinions on this and related questions.

W. Hutchinson, a farmer of Douglas County and a former resident of Vermont, argued against including the requirement that only whites could vote. His opinion was unequivocal:

> If the operation of the elective franchise is beneficial—if you And I are made better by being allowed the right to vote—then we should extend that benefit to every class of men. We ought not to say one class should be made less intelligent than we. No, Sir. But why do we pretend to do it? We have the laws, the strength, the government.... We are not here to make a Constitution for one class—for class legislation—but to make a Constitution for the whole people of the State of Kansas.... We have no right to erect separate standards as to the right of the elective franchise. No right to say that a person who has eyes of a particular color, or wears clothes of a particular color, shall exercise the right of the ballot box.[62]

Hutchinson's moral fervor did not extend to the majority of his colleagues in the convention. Robert Graham, a merchant from Atchison, who had emigrated from Ireland, argued that the extension of suffrage would be politically unwise:

> I am opposed to striking out the word "white." I came from a state where I resided forty-eight or forty-nine years. My first vote was cast side-by-side with the colored man. In 1836, we changed that; and we believed the change of Constitution was made as much for that purpose as any other. I am opposed to striking out the word "white," for I believe we have the right to say who shall have the right to vote. I am opposed to it from past experience. And another thing, I am not positive, but I think those men always voted the Democratic ticket.[63]

When the roll call was taken on this section of the constitution, only three of the forty delegates to the convention voted to strike out the qualifier "white" and extend suffrage to blacks. They were Hutchinson, formerly of Vermont, Ritchey, a farmer formerly of Ohio, and Stokes, a manufacturer formerly of Pennsylvania. All three were then residents of Douglas County. The other thirty-seven delegates voted to retain the qualifier "white," thereby depriving black Kansans of the right to vote. Among those who voted against black suffrage were several of the leaders of the former Free State Party, including John James Ingalls and Solon Thacher, both of whom would go on to successful political careers during statehood.[64]

The convention had, at that moment, lost its opportunity to make Kansas a harbinger of civil rights, and though the convention did vote to end slavery in Kansas, it did not take the next step and give universal suffrage to Kansans. Another issue involving the rights of blacks, which was debated hotly, was whether blacks would be permitted to go to school in the new state. A number of Democratic delegates opposed giving this right. The proposal was defeated.[65]

Two other issues embroiled the convention delegates in passionate debate. The first concerned the question of boundaries. The great question was whether the region to the north of the Platte River would be annexed to Kansas or would be left to Nebraska. Democrats favored annexation because they believed that the voters of this region would be loyal to their party. Republicans feared such an annexation for obvious reasons. The question of the northern boundary vexed the convention throughout its tenure, but the Republican majority ensured that the region would be left out of the new state.[66]

The other contentious issue was where the new state capital would be located.[67] Lecompton, of course, was out of the question as the former center of the pro-slavery forces. Lawrence, however, the great Free State redoubt, desperately wanted the honor. There was far more involved than honor. Whichever town received the designation of the state capital was guaranteed a substantial economic boost. The location of the capital was also of great importance to the various railway companies vying for rights-of-way. For a time, Lawrence seemed the likely winner, but then charges of bribery and corruption surfaced involving members of the convention and Lawrence was displaced by Topeka, which became and remains the state capital.

When the convention's work was finished and the new "Wyandotte Constitution" was adopted on July 29, 1859, an era closed. By no means were all Kansans happy with what the convention produced. In fact, the Democrats, angry at their inability to win more concessions, refused to sign. It was left to the people of Kansas to decide in a ratification vote whether the Wyandotte constitution would be the constitution by which Kansas would seek admission to the Union.

RATIFICATION AND ADMISSION

A ratification election was called for October 4, 1859.[68] This left both parties only two months to win support for their respective positions. Both made maximum use of their leaders and of their newspaper allies. The attacks on each side were vicious, and no charge was too wild or base to be rejected. In the end, however, the election was a massive victory for the Republicans.

Of the almost 16,000 votes cast, over 10,000 were in favor of ratification of the Wyandotte constitution. At this point, the battle for the constitution was over and the Republican and Democratic parties shifted their attention away from constitution making and toward winning control of the soon to be admitted new state and its governmental organization. Passions over slavery and suffrage gave way to the normal jostling for preferment and patronage.

In December 1859, W. F. N. Arny arrived in Washington to present the Wyandotte constitution to the Congress.[69] On February 15, 1860, Representative Grow of Pennsylvania introduced legislation to the House to admit Kansas to the Union under the Wyandotte constitution.[70] Two days later, Senator Seward of New York introduced a similar bill to the Senate. The bills were eventually sent to committee, where they languished for months. Attempts to have the bill passed were defeated. By this point, the Congress was caught up in the partisan fights and sectionalism that marked its efforts in the year leading up to the outbreak of hostilities between the North and the South. Congress also knew that there was a presidential election on the horizon, an election that would have potentially far-reaching effect. Thus, it was not until mid-December 1860, after Lincoln had been elected president, that the bill for the admission of Kansas finally saw the light of the Senate chamber and began to wend its way to passage. Still, a vote on admission was delayed until January 21, 1861, when the senators from the states of Mississippi, Alabama, and Florida followed the lead of those of South Carolina and formally withdrew from the Senate because of their states' withdrawal from the Union. After their withdrawal, the bill to admit Kansas was put to a vote, and a weary, now reduced Senate passed it by a vote of 36-16. One week later the bill was passed by the House, and on January 29, 1861, President Lincoln signed the law admitting Kansas to the Union.[71] The Kansas legislature ratified the Act of Admission on January 23, 1862, and Governor Robinson signed the Ratification Bill into law immediately.[72] After eight long and wearying years of struggle, Kansas became a state.

CONCLUSION

Although the territorial period of Kansas lasted only eight years, so much occurred during those years that its history is still a subject of open debate. One scholar has characterized the political and legal history of this period as the most "confusing and confused" in American history.[73] There is a wealth of information on this period in Kansas history because the battles that determined the fate of the territory were fought as much in newspapers and books and on the speaker's rostrum and the stump as they were on the battlefields. Modern scholars often wonder at the passion of the two sides and the overstating of cases that so marked the period. The Sack of Lawrence in 1856 is a case in point. The national newspapers were filled with accounts of this incident, and if one were to judge only by the reports in the pro–free state papers, one would be under the impression that hundreds or thousands of innocent settlers were brutally murdered. Yet in reality, very few people lost their lives during this period. Indeed, one might argue that compared to the loss of life common just a few years later during the Civil War, the total number of men and women killed during the period of "Bleeding Kansas" was remarkably small. But passion tends to make even minor events seem great and small losses major. The battle for Kansas was far more than a simple battle for control of a territory. Ultimately, the battle for Kansas and the road to statehood was a battle for the soul of the nation, to determine whether the nation could live as one that tolerated, if not exalted, the institution of slavery. And, thus, the territorial period of Kansas and its history remains one of the most crucial periods in the history of the United States.

NOTES

1. On the "removal" of the Indian tribes to Kansas, see William Unrau, *The Emigrant Indians of Kansas: A Critical Bibliography* (Bloomington: Indiana University Press, 1979); see also the essays contained in Rita Napier, ed., *Kansas and the West* (Lawrence: University Press of Kansas, 2003).

2. The political and social history recounted in this essay is heavily dependent upon several seminal works and collections. Most important is the first volume of A. T. Andreas, *History of the State of Kansas* (Chicago: Andreas, 1883; reprint, Atchison, KS: Atchison County Historical Society, 1976). Andreas's volume contains both the standard, pro-free state account of the territorial period and selections from key documents, any of which are otherwise inaccessible. Another useful, older history of this period also drawn from substantially is Noble Prentis, *A History of Kansas*, ed. Henrietta Race (Topeka, KS: Caroline Prentis, 1909). A number of general histories of Kansas have also been useful, particularly the masterful recent volume by Professor Craig Minor, *Kansas; The History of the Sunflower State, 1854–2000* (Lawrence: University Press of Kansas, 2002). When recounting matters of fact, Andreas and other works listed above have not been noted. Notes have been added only when the text contains either a particularly important fact, one of the above authors' interpretations, or when another work is involved.

3. By far the best source for the history of the Kansas-Nebraska Act in its relation to the creation of the state of Kansas is James C. Malin, *The Nebraska Question, 1852–1854* (Lawrence, KS: James C. Malin, 1953).

4. Andreas, *History of Kansas*, p. 82.

5. Ibid., p. 83.

6. Both the Santa Fe and the Oregon Trails ran through Kansas. Traces of these trails can still be seen today throughout much of the state.

7. On Lawrence, see William R. Lawrence, ed., *Extracts from the Diary and Correspondence of the Late Amos Lawrence...* (Boston: John Wilson for the Author, 1855).

8. On Kansas newspapers of the territorial period, see Kansas State Historical Society, *History of Kansas Newspapers* (Topeka, KS: State Printer, 1916).

9. Printed in Prentis, pp. 77–78.

10. Andreas, *History of Kansas*, p. 83.

11. Ibid.

12. Ibid., pp. 84–85; Ralph V. Harlow, "The Rise and Fall of the Kansas Aid Movement," *American Historical Review* 41 (1935): 1–25; Samuel Johnson, "The Emigrant Aid Company in Kansas," *Kansas Historical Quarterly* 1 (1932): 429–441. One of the most important propaganda tracts for this movement was Edward Everett Hale, *Kansas and Nebraska* ... (Boston: Phillips, Sampson, 1854).

13. The best source for the early history of Lawrence is Reverend Richard Cordley, *A History of Lawrence, Kansas from the First Settlement to the Close of the Rebellion* (Lawrence, KS: Journal Press, 1899).

14. On Reeder, see "Biography of Governor Andrew H. Reeder," *Publications of the Kansas State Historical Society* 1 (1886): 5–86.

15. Andreas, *History of Kansas*, p. 98.

16. Ibid., p. 99.

17. Ibid., pp. 104–105.

18. Ibid., p. 105.

19. On Lane, one of the most fascinating and controversial figures of the time, see Wendell H. Stephenson, "The Political Career of General James H. Lane," *Publications of the Kansas State Historical Society* 3 (1930); William H. Conneley, *James Henry Lane: "The Grim Chieftain" of Kansas* (Topeka, KS: Crane, 1899).

20. Andreas, *History of Kansas*, pp. 107–110.

21. Ibid., pp. 116–120.

22. Ibid., p. 122. The report of this committee was published; see *Report of the Special Committee Appointed to Investigate the Troubles in Kansas* ..., Report No. 200, 34th Cong., 1st Sess. (1856).

23. Andreas, *History of Kansas*, pp. 130–131.

24. These great losses were national news; see, for instance, the *Daily News* of Philadelphia for June 9, 1856, which lists the losses. For instance, George Brown, one of the newspaper owners, is listed as having $30,000 in losses, and the Eldridge brothers, owners of the hotel, are listed as having lost $40,000.

25. There is a wealth of literature on John Brown. See, particularly, W. E. Connelley, *John Brown* (Topeka, KS: Crane and Co., 1900); Stephen B. Oates, *To Purge This Land with Blood: A Biography of John Brown* (New York: Harper and Row, 1970). See also, Merrill D. Peterson, *The Legend Revisited: John Brown* (Charlottesville: University of Virginia Press, 2002).

26. See G.W.E. Griffith, "The Battle of Black Jack," *Kansas Historical Collections* 16 (1923–1925): 524–528.

27. Andreas, *History of Kansas*, pp. 122–123.

28. Ibid., pp. 140–145.

29. Sara Robinson, *Kansas: Its Exterior and Interior Life* (Boston: Crosby, Nichols, 1856). This book went through eight editions.

30. On Geary, see John H. Gihon, *Geary and Kansas* (Philadelphia: J.H.C. Whiting, 1857).

31. Andreas, *History of Kansas*, pp. 149, 153.

32. Ibid., pp. 149–152.

33. George W. Martin, "The First Two Years of Kansas," *Kansas State Historical Collections* 10 (1907–1908): 142.

34. Andreas, *History of Kansas*, p. 155.

35. On Walker, see George W. Brown, *Reminiscences of Gov. R.J. Walker; with the True Story of the Rescue of Kansas from Slavery* (Rockford, IL: printed by the author, 1902); Andreas, *History of Kansas*, pp. 158–159.

36. Andreas, *History of Kansas*, p. 160.

37. See Thomas Goodrich, *War to the Knife* (Mechanicsburg, PA: Stackpole, 1998), pp. 213–253.

38. Andreas, *History of Kansas*, p. 156.

39. Ibid., pp. 156–157.

40. Ibid., pp. 162–163.

41. Ibid., p. 163; Prentis, p. 111.

42. Andreas, *History of Kansas*, pp. 162–163; see also Robert W. Johannsen, "The Lecompton Constitutional Convention: An Analysis of Its Membership," *Kansas Historical Quarterly* 23 (1957): 225–243.

43. For these and the following clauses, see Andreas, *History of Kansas*, pp. 163–164.

44. Ibid., p. 163, section 23.

45. Ibid., pp. 163–164.

46. Ibid., p. 164.

47. Ibid., p. 165.

48. Ibid., pp. 166–169.

49. On all of these political maneuvers, see ibid., pp. 166–169.

50. Ibid., p. 170.

51. Ibid.; see also Leverett W. Spring, *Kansas; The Prelude to the War for the Union* (Boston: Houghton, Mifflin, 1888), pp. 231–236.

52. *Report of the Covode Committee*, House of Representatives, 36th Cong., 1st Sess., Report No. 648 (June 16, 1860), pp. 59–325.

53. Andreas, *History of Kansas*, p. 171; William E. Connelley, *History of Kansas. State and People*, vol. 1 (Chicago: American Historical Society, 1928), pp. 593–606.

54. The most important and thorough study of the Wyandotte constitution is G. Raymond Gaeddart, *The Birth of Kansas* (Lawrence: University of Kansas Press, 1940; reprint, Philadelphia: Porcupine Press, 1974), which has been heavily relied upon in the following discussion. The constitution, along with the legislative history of the proceedings is published in *Kansas Constitutional Convention* (Topeka, KS: State Printer, 1920). See also Gary L. Cheatham, "'Slavery All the Time or Not at All': The Wyandotte Constitution Debate, 1859–1861," *Kansas History* 21 (1998): 168–187; Francis Heller, *The Kansas State Constitution* (Westport, CT: Greenwood Press, 1992), pp. 3–9.

55. Gaeddart, *Birth of Kansas*, pp. 47–49.

56. Andreas, *History of Kansas*, p. 172.

57. Ibid., p. 173; Gaeddart, *Birth of Kansas*, p. 39.

58. Gaeddart, *Birth of Kansas*, p. 39, n. 37.

59. Ibid., p. 44; see also Rosa Perdue, "The Sources of the Constitution of Kansas," *Kansas Constitutional Convention*, pp. 676–696.

60. Gaeddart, *Birth of Kansas*, pp. 65–71.

61. *Kansas Constitutional Convention*, pp. 72–76; Gaeddart, *Birth of Kansas*, pp. 50–51.

62. *Kansas Constitutional Convention*, pp. 298–335.

63. Ibid., p. 300.
64. Ibid., p. 301.
65. On suffrage and school rights, see also Gaeddart, *Birth of Kansas*, pp. 55–57.
66. Ibid., pp. 58–59.
67. Ibid., pp. 60–64.
68. On the debates over ratification, see ibid., pp. 72–84.
69. Ibid., p. 85.
70. *Congressional Globe* (1859–1860), p. 795; Gaeddart, *Birth of Kansas*, p. 85.
71. Gaeddart, *Birth of Kansas*, p. 91.
72. Ibid., p. 93.
73. See Minor, *History of the Sunflower State*, pp. 1–17.

BIBLIOGRAPHY

Andreas, A.T. *History of the State of Kansas*. Chicago: Andreas, 1883; reprint, Atchison, KS: Atchison County Historical Society, 1976.

Connelly, William E. *History of Kansas. State and People*. Vol. 1. Chicago: American Historical Society, 1928.

Gaeddart, G. Raymond. *The Birth of Kansas*. Lawrence: University of Kansas Press, 1040; reprint, Philadelphia: Porcupine Press, 1974.

Goodrich, Thomas. *War to the Knife*. Mechanicsburg, PA: Stackpole, 1998.

Kansas Constitutional Convention. Topeka, KS: State Printer, 1920.

Malin, James C. *The Nebraska Question, 1852–1854*. Lawrence, KS: James C. Malin, 1953.

Minor, Craig. *Kansas; The History of the Sunflower State, 1854–2000*. Lawrence: University Press of Kansas, 2002.

Napier, Rita, ed. *Kansas and the West*. Lawrence: University Press of Kansas, 2003.

Prentis, Noble. *A History of Kansas*. Edited by Henrietta Race. Topeka, KS: Caroline Prentis, 1909.

Report of the Special Committee Appointed to Investigate the Troubles in Kansas. Report No. 200, 34th Cong., 1st Sess. (1856).

Kentucky

Territorial Development:

- Great Britain cedes future Indianan territory to the United States through the Treaty of Paris, September 3, 1783
- The United States passes the Northwest Ordinance: territorial claims inherited from colonial charters ceded to the public domain, July 13, 1787
- Future territory of Kentucky organized along with the future state of Tennessee as part of the Southwest Territory, May 26, 1790
- President Washington signs a federal Enabling Act for the potential state of Kentucky, February 4, 1791
- Kentucky admitted into the Union as the fifteenth state, June 1, 1792

Capitals Prior to Statehood:

- Lexington, 1780–1792

State Capitals:

- Frankfort, 1792–present

Origin of State Name: "Kentucky" is a Wyandot word meaning "plain," referring to the state's central plains.

First Governor: Isaac Shelby
Governmental Organization: Bicameral
Population at Statehood: 73,677 (according to the 1790 census)
Geographical Size: 39,728 square miles

THE COMMONWEALTH OF KENTUCKY

Admitted to the Union as a State: June 1, 1792

Stephen Asperheim

INTRODUCTION

The satisfaction felt by Vermonters on the occasion of entering the Union as an independent state was not shared by their fellow Americans in Kentucky, who were less than enthusiastic at the news. Kentuckians had been concurrently struggling to achieve statehood and were dismayed at what they perceived as Vermont's relatively easy accession. "Vermont was brought forward with Kentucky, admitted at the same session, and was entitled to a representation in Congress one year sooner than Kentucky was," statehood advocates grumbled. Moreover, while Kentucky had displayed "submissive patience" and "undeviating moderation and respect" in the quest for statehood, "[Vermont's] separation [from New York] was arbitrary, violent and insolent." Favoritism for Vermont could only be "the result of Eastern policy and jealousy."[1]

The bitterness was perhaps understandable. The statehood movement for Kentucky had been long and complicated. Ten statehood conventions over seven years had been necessary to achieve the desired goal in June 1792. Unlike most states, Kentucky needed authorization not only from Congress but also from its "parent state" Virginia, out of which Kentucky was carved. Before Virginia could accede to Kentucky's wishes, the Old Dominion first had to solidify its claim to the District of Kentucky against those of the regional Native American tribes and powerful land speculation companies. Shifting political factions within Kentucky, including one that sought to detach Kentucky from the Union as well as Virginia, jockeyed to control the statehood process. The national transition from the Articles of Confederation to the federal Constitution imposed further delay. For Vermont to be admitted before Kentucky was the last in a long train of insults.

Despite the length of the process, the establishment of the Commonwealth of Kentucky set some important precedents. Kentucky was the first western state. Statehood for Kentucky was a triumph for partisans of the new federal government who were keen to extend its authority beyond the Appalachians and so counteract the claims of Spanish agents who were challenging expansion by the United States into the region. Statehood was also a major setback for regional separatists who were toying with the idea of an independent western confederacy. In the face of rampant Anti-Federalism in the district, the Washington administration had succeeded, for the time being, in winning the confidence of Kentuckians, who indicated a willingness to give the experiment in constitutionalism the benefit of the doubt. The new state constitution of Kentucky also showed that the West, although it would be American, would be a land of slavery. The paired admission of Vermont and Kentucky served as a model for sectional compromise, which would reverberate through the antebellum period.

ESTABLISHING SOVEREIGNTY

Unlike most states, Kentucky never experienced the luxury of a period of self-government either as a colony or as a territory before entering the Union as a state. The District of Kentucky remained part of Virginia until the first state legislature was elected. Before Congress could accept an independent Kentucky into the Union, Virginia needed to pass an Enabling Act permitting Kentucky's separation. Virginia's claim to govern Kentucky and control the statehood process for its western frontier did not go unchallenged, however. For much of the 1770s and 1780s, it was not at all clear that Virginia would be able to control the destiny of Kentucky. The trans-Appalachian West of the Revolutionary era was a borderland where sovereignty was contested from many quarters. Ultimately, Virginia's claim of jurisdiction over Kentucky and its demand for full authority over the statehood process prevailed, but Virginia first needed to defend its title against pressing challenges.

The Old Dominion's claim to Kentucky ultimately lay in its colonial charter. The 1609 charter issued by the British Crown granting the London Company a domain called "Virginia" included vague but extremely broad boundaries, usually interpreted to comprise much of North America. After the Seven Years' War set the western border of British America at the Mississippi River, Virginia continued to assert that its charter included all land between the Appalachian Mountains and the Mississippi River. On this basis, Virginian colonial officials negotiated with the Indians and sold land in the trans-Appalachian West.[2]

The British Crown, however, had its own plans for the West. In the wake of the imperial struggle against France, and especially after Pontiac's rebellion, royal officials were skeptical of the ability of colonial legislatures to handle western security issues. They envisioned as a solution a strict separation between British and Native American communities. The Proclamation Line of 1763, drawn along the spine of the mountains, set aside the West as a Native American reservation. Apart from scattered military garrisons, there would be no white settlement in the West, and Virginia colonial leaders would have no control over its disposition.

Virginia colonists did not passively accept this decree and almost immediately put pressure on the British government to move the Proclamation Line and open portions of the West to colonial speculation and settlement. One particular grievance of Virginian officials was that the sizable grants they had already made beyond the Line were now nullified. Speculators, including George Washington, considered the Line as temporary and petitioned royal officials to readjust it. There were also a number of Native American communities east of the Line, and certain tribes were also calling for a revision. Emboldened after the victory over France, many settlers ignored the proclamation and moved into Native American territories. Neither the British army nor colonial governments were able to check their movements. In spring 1765, royal negotiators began discussing boundary adjustments with tribal leaders. With the Treaties of Fort Stanwix (1768) and Lochaber (1770), most of the area that is now West Virginia was opened to colonial settlement. In 1771 Virginia unilaterally purchased and surveyed territory extending to the Kentucky River. Agents of land speculation companies, drawn by accounts of the fertility of the Bluegrass country, swarmed into the region. British officials were unhappy with the chaotic situation on the frontier, but the incipient Revolution along the seaboard was a more pressing concern.[3]

Although the Crown may not have given western issues especially high priority, settlers' encroachments were of great consternation to the regional Native Americans. The Treaty of Fort Stanwix had been made with the Iroquois, but only because the British recognized Iroquois hegemony by right of conquest. In the 1680s the Iroquois had swept into the Ohio Valley and had driven out the local tribes, the predominant one having been the Shawnee. By the mid-1700s, however, after a long period of migration and ethnic mixing, the Shawnee had returned to their traditional homeland and were successful in maintaining their autonomy over the Iroquois, whose regional power was on the wane. Although no Native American villages were located within Kentucky, the Shawnee, who resided north of the Ohio River, claimed the region as a hunting ground and were incensed when the Iroquois ceded the territory without consulting them. The Shawnee did not recognize the Treaty of Fort Stanwix. In the early 1770s they called for an intertribal confederation to oppose the cession and prevent settlement by the "Long Knives," as the Virginians were known. Dunmore's War broke out in 1774, and after a short but decisive contest, certain Shawnee representatives agreed to give up claims to land south of the Ohio.[4]

The Shawnee tribe was a decentralized polity whose leaders were far from united on this decision. A number of factions chose to continue the struggle for Kentucky. Cornstalk, an important chief, expressed dissatisfaction in 1776 at seeing "your people seated on our Lands.... All our Lands are covered by the white people, & we are jealous that you still intend to make larger strides.... That was our hunting Country & you have taken it from us."[5] During the American Revolution, the Indians in Ohio launched an all-out struggle to wrest Kentucky from Virginia. With British assistance, they kept the situation at a stalemate throughout the period. With the end of the Revolutionary War and the Treaty of Paris (1783), however, the British abandoned the Native American cause, and the Indians' ability to resist American settlement was broken. Shawnee and other Indians in Ohio carried out sporadic guerrilla attacks into the 1790s, but never again did they pose a serious challenge to Virginia's possession of Kentucky. After 1783, Virginia was independent of Britain and free from Shawnee claims to Kentucky.[6]

THE STATEHOOD MOVEMENT

Phase One: The Congressional Claim

Virginia was not yet free to impose its will on the West. The Shawnee were not the only challengers to Virginia's claim to Kentucky. Virginia's authority to govern the District was seriously disputed by other Americans, and swirling out of these debates emerged the first calls for statehood. While Virginia was embroiled in the military challenge of the Shawnee, it also faced a legal challenge from a coterie of land speculators with connections in the royal government. The shifting Native American boundaries and the waning of British imperial power in the early 1770s led to a scramble for the leverage to buy and sell land in the rich Ohio Valley. Land speculators from Pennsylvania, in particular, posed a threat to Virginia's claim. Unlike Virginia, Pennsylvania's charter did not give it access to land in the West. The only way that these private Philadelphia companies could profit from western lands would be by supplanting Virginia's claim. In 1773, the Board of Trade, under the influence of the Vandalia Company, the most important of these ventures, proposed a new western colony in what is now West Virginia and eastern Kentucky. The company's financial resources and political connections, coupled with Virginia's indecision, seemed for a time to guarantee the colony's success. Because the company was closely associated with the British government, it lost influence during the Revolution, and the Vandalia project collapsed. Its near success, however, alerted Virginia officials that they would need to construct a sound legal defense of their claim to the West if they wanted to retain control of the region in these tumultuous years.[7]

Virginia was, therefore, better prepared when a similar and more serious challenge to its claim emerged a few years later from a group of North Carolina speculators. In March 1775, the Transylvania Company, led by Richard Henderson, an associate judge who had decided to pursue a more lucrative career, scored an audacious coup by signing the Treaty of Sycamore Shoals with the Cherokees. In violation of both royal and colonial edicts forbidding private citizens from making treaties with Indians, Judge Henderson acquired the Cumberland River valley and all of western Kentucky, which the Cherokees claimed as their hunting ground. Henderson proceeded to establish the colony of Transylvania and sell land warrants, setting up a capital in Boonesborough. Even in the fluid political environment of the West, this action was highly controversial and provoked outrage in Virginia. With the coming of the Revolution, Transylvania was rhetorically transformed from a colony into a state, a legislature was seated, and its leaders petitioned the Continental Congress to be admitted into the Union. Virginia had already issued warrants for land in the region, and the holders of these warrants protested vigorously. Petitioners to the Virginia legislature complained of Henderson and his associates: "They stile themselves the true and absolute Proprietors of the new Independent Province (as they call Transylvania).... Virginia, we conceive, can claim this country with the greatest justice and propriety, its within the Limits of their Charter, They Fought and bled for it."[8] Even settlers who were initially tolerant of the company turned against it. Henderson received no sympathy from Congress. On December 7, 1776, Virginia created Kentucky County specifically to delegitimize Transylvania, and two years later the legislature voided the Treaty of Sycamore Shoals. In 1779 Virginia passed major land laws regulating the sale of land in the region and subsequently created the District of Kentucky, setting the pattern by which Virginia aggressively defended its claim. The familiar argument over the coming years was that Congress had no authority to recognize independent western states because the entire region fell within the boundaries of Virginia.[9]

Despite this strategy, Virginia recognized the impracticality of maintaining perpetual jurisdiction over the West. Its 1776 constitution opened the possibility that "one or more Territories shall hereafter be laid off, and Governments established Westward of the *Allegheny* Mountains."[10] The challenge of governing Kentucky became apparent with the huge influx of settlers into the region at the close of the Revolutionary War. Whereas in 1776 only a few hundred white settlers lived in Kentucky, by 1785 the population had reached 30,000. People arrived there from Virginia as well as from Maryland, Pennsylvania, and North Carolina. Some were ordinary farmers coming to achieve freeholder status; others were wealthy planters and merchants trying to establish substantial plantations. The diversity of the population in class and place of origin could be a source of tension. There was a perceived distinction between wealthier "lowland old Virginians" and "Backwoods Virginians and Northward men, Scotch, Irish, etc., which seems, In some measure, to make Distinctions and Particions amongst us."[11]

These divisions within the community were sharpened by Virginia's policy of selling land. The anarchic state of affairs in the Ohio Valley in the previous two decades had resulted in different speculation companies selling the same tracts to different people. Virginia's own method of selling land was inaccurate and confusing. In 1777 Virginia proffered settlement grants to anyone who would improve a plot but two years later rescinded this offer, opening a land office and offering millions of acres for sale, encouraging speculation and large purchases. The wave of settlers who arrived in 1778 and 1779, therefore, found that the promise of free land had ended and that even purchasing good land was out of the question, because most had been immediately snatched up in large parcels. Added to this confusion was the endemic inaccuracy of frontier surveying; a situation emerged in which "almost every square inch of Kentucky land was disputed." The result was a great deal of anxiety, bewilderment, and anger, much of it directed at Virginia.[12]

> Because many settlers considered Virginia's land laws to be unfair and others possessed titles that Virginia did not recognize, there was a resurrection of the challenge to Virginia's claim to Kentucky in the early 1780s. Opponents of Virginia's policies wanted control over Kentucky to revert to Congress. Kentucky could then petition Congress for statehood and for a thorough redistribution of land from those with Virginia title to those without. The Kentuckians who made this argument were known as "partisans." The main argument of the partisans was that those who actually occupied the land, improved it, and risked their lives to defend it were those who had the right to it, as opposed to absentee landholders in Virginia. Male settlers from plebeian backgrounds defined personal independence in terms of owning enough land to support a family and distribute to their children. As the possibility of local political autonomy and land redistribution became real, personal independence was conflated with state independence. The linking of the homestead ethic to the statehood movement was expressed by pioneer Daniel Boone in his "autobiographical" sketch written by John Filson in 1784. Since the Indian war has ended, Boone said, I now live in peace and safety, enjoying the sweets of liberty, and the bounties of Providence, with my once fellow-sufferers, in this delightful country, which I have seen purchased with a vast expense of blood and treasure, delighting in the prospect of its being, in a short time, one of the most opulent and powerful states on the continent of North-America, which, with the love and gratitude of my country-men, I esteem a sufficient reward for all my toil and danger.[13]

The idea that those who had worked to win the land were the rightful possessors was at the heart of the partisan argument for statehood.[14]

For all the appeals by actual settlers for fair and equal land distribution, the partisan drive was led by the Pennsylvania speculators who were selling the warrants that Virginia's claim jeopardized. Other dynamics also influenced the congressional statehood movement. The land companies were joined in their cause by those states that lacked western prerogatives in their charters and were eager to pare down Virginia's territorial claims. Maryland, for example, did not recognize Virginia's claim and was refusing to ratify the Articles of Confederation as long as the Old Dominion retained a stranglehold on the West. There were also Americans who saw the logic in turning the West over to Congress for the sake of national power. Creating a national domain would give the new government an ample source of funds through land sales.[15]

Agents of the land companies began to circulate the theory within Kentucky that Congress was legally entitled to the district. To support their cause, they hired Thomas Paine, the famous Revolutionary pamphleteer and author of *Common Sense*. Influenced by their arguments and by the company shares granted him, Paine produced a new pamphlet, *Public Good*, in which he clearly and succinctly made the case that Virginia had no legal stake to the West. The 1609 charter, Paine argued, was vaguely worded. "In short, there is not a boundary in this grant that is clear, fixt and defined." Furthermore, the charter was between the Virginia Company and the Crown, and because the company was long defunct, the charter no longer applied. More relevant than the charter was the Proclamation of 1763, which, Paine claimed, had set a boundary between white and Native American settlements and also established a new colonial border for Virginia at the crest of the Appalachians. "And all lands exterior to these bounds as well of Virginia as the rest of the states, devolve, in the order of succession to the sovereignty of the United States for the benefit of all." Virginia's continued grip on the region would only cause hardship, Paine wrote. "The situation which the settlers on these lands will be in, under the assumed right of Virginia, will be hazardous and distressing, and they will feel themselves at last like aliens to the commonwealth of Israel, their habitations unsafe and their title precarious." The solution was for Congress to form a new state, which Paine set as the borders of, roughly, modern Kentucky. Correctly recognizing that "the laying out of new states will some time or other be the business of the country," Paine proposed speculative ground rules for the statehood process, with an emphasis on gradualism and eventual equality with the original states.[16]

Public Good became the showpiece of the partisan effort. Two leaders of the cause, John Campbell and George Pomeroy, both Pennsylvania speculators, traveled throughout Kentucky in 1782 disseminating Paine's pamphlet and claiming that Congress had already taken possession of Kentucky and promised to make it a state. Pro-Virginia settlers in Kentucky notified the General Assembly about "an Inflamatary Pamphlet intitled publick Good."[17] Virginia leaders like James Madison vociferously attacked Paine's claims. The partisan cause was further energized by the efforts of Arthur Campbell (no relation to John Campbell), another speculator who opposed Virginia's claim. He had already been involved in establishing a state in western North Carolina and now sought to do the same in Kentucky. He circulated a petition in 1779 blaming Virginia for the confused land situation. The year 1780 saw the first formal appeal, signed by more than 600 people, asking Congress to grant Kentucky statehood. The partisan cause hit a roadblock in 1784, however, when Pomeroy and an associate were convicted of spreading lies, fined, and compelled to leave the state.[18]

More significant in ending the partisan drive for statehood were the actions of Congress. After three years of contention, Virginia finally ceded most of its western territory to Congress in March 1784. It retained Kentucky, however. Given the amount of land Virginia had sold there, it had a vested interest in retaining the district. Many politically connected men were involved in western speculation, and others wished to move to the district to build new fortunes. The Northwest Territory, on the other hand, was largely under the control of Native American tribes and beyond the state's real control. In return for the national domain, Congress recognized Virginia's claim to Kentucky. It refused to acknowledge the appeals of the partisans and appropriate the district. With Congress having made its decision, the partisan cause was largely deflated.[19]

Hope still remained that Virginia might make further western cessions, and some perplexity existed as to whether it already had done so. Thomas Jefferson, as leader of the congressional committee drafting the Ordinance of 1784 to set up a temporary plan for dealing with the new western territories, exceeded his mandate and proposed a map that partitioned the region both north and south of the Ohio into states with new names. Kentucky disappeared and was replaced by "Pelisipia" in the east and by "Polypotamia" in the west. Jefferson knew that such a grid would depend on Virginia's ceding Kentucky, but his map was evidence of his hopeful expectation that this might soon come to pass. Jefferson was afraid that the statehood process for Kentucky, if controlled by his native state, would be disorderly and fractious. He would have much preferred congressional management, as would eventually be the case in the Old Northwest. For Kentucky, however, Jefferson's geographical plan was significantly altered by the committee, Virginia never made further cessions, and the Northwest Ordinance of 1787 superseded that of 1784. Jefferson's draft map was leaked, however, and maps were published in almanacs erroneously depicting the West, including the area formerly known as Kentucky, as already sectioned into fancifully named states. Jefferson's proposals and cartographic fantasies added further confusion to the issue of Kentucky's status.[20]

The first statehood convention within Kentucky was also the last time the partisans played a dominant role in the statehood movement. Spurred by a renewed wave of Native American attacks from north of the Ohio River, militia groups from across the district elected delegates to meet to discuss defense and other issues stemming from frustration at Virginia's ineptitude. The delegates wanted to launch reprisals, but their hands were tied by the need to obtain permission of the General Assembly, all the way in Richmond. In December 1784 the delegates gathered in Danville and discussed a wide range of complaints, among them surveying problems and land taxes. There was also evidence of support for the freehold ideal, because the delegates approved a protest that grants of land should be no larger than needed to support a family. They also agreed that some grievances could be solved only by a separation from Virginia, but although the tenor of the meeting ran toward calling for separation, doing so was beyond what the delegates' authority. They decided to call for a second convention to meet in May 1785 to deal specifically with separation. The partisans seemed to be on the verge of getting what they wanted, but the convention issued no statements or petitions to Congress or Virginia, and there was no clear statement as to how this separation was to be achieved. The partisan movement had been seriously weakened by events, and now the statehood movement was taken over by a different faction within Kentucky.[21]

Phase Two: Seeking Virginia's Approval

Partisans had been largely those settlers without land or with specious titles. While the partisans agitated for congressional separation, those with Virginia titles opposed statehood and appealed to Virginia to defend its claim. Now that Congress had recognized that claim, and the partisan movement was moribund, it now began to appear worthwhile to some wealthy Virginia claimants to call for statehood. Through the 1780s Kentucky had drawn growing numbers of well-to-do men. Typically Virginians, they held land warrants from their home state and had the money and influence to defend them. Many had legal training and political skills, and state leadership would emerge from their ranks. However, although the gentry of Kentucky were united in opposing the partisan cause, they were divided among themselves on the statehood question in 1784.

One faction within the gentry, known as the "country party," opposed statehood. These men were the early surveyors and speculators who had quickly claimed tracts of the best Bluegrass land. Having relocated, they set about establishing themselves as planters and merchants on the Tidewater model. They still felt close personal connections with Virginia and believed that, although Kentucky had its problems, they could be dealt with successfully by the parent state. The second faction within the gentry, the "court party," believed that statehood was necessary. These men were largely lawyers associated with the District Court, which had been established in 1782. Like the country party, court party members owned land under Virginia title but, having arrived somewhat later, typically did not own as much or as good land. They envisioned a future for Kentucky focused on local manufacturing and commerce and were more enthusiastic about the idea of an independent state, provided, of course, that they would be its leaders. With Virginia's claim secure, the court party took control of the statehood movement. Meanwhile, the partisans, their hopes for a congressional separation dashed, shifted to opposition to statehood, because a separation on Virginia's terms would not serve their interests and, they feared, would result in higher taxes.[22]

Although the call for a second statehood convention had been issued by the partisan-led convention of December 1784, the court party controlled it. Delegates at the May 1785 convention resolved unanimously "That a petition be presented to the Assembly, praying that the said district may be established into a state, separate from Virginia," and afterward that it "ought to be taken into union with the United States of America, and enjoy equal privileges in common with the said states."[23] Statehood would take place with the cooperation of Virginia. The delegates drafted a petition but chose to delay sending it, apparently because they wanted further assurances of local popular endorsement. Instead, they called for a third convention to meet in three months. The second convention did issue an address to the people of Kentucky explaining its actions to build support for statehood. Modeled after the Declaration of Independence, it began with a declaration of rights and proceeded to list complaints against Virginia, including its lax efforts at defense against Native American attacks, its insistence that residents appeal court decisions in Richmond, and its failure to promote the economic welfare of the district.[24]

The third convention, meeting in August 1785, went more smoothly. Again the delegates voted unanimously to petition the General Assembly for statehood, and two delegates were chosen to travel to Richmond to present it. The Virginia leadership had become resigned to statehood. The assembly agreed that "the interjacent natural impediments to a convenient and regular communication" made statehood for Kentucky inevitable.[25] An Enabling Act was passed in January 1786. To the chagrin of those who had hoped for quick results, however, the act stipulated important conditions that Kentucky would have to meet. There would be no immediate constitutional convention. The new state of Kentucky would need to guarantee Virginia's land claims, shoulder a portion of Virginia's public debt, and protect the rights of absentee landholders. The act required Kentuckians to hold yet another preliminary convention. Its members would be elected in accordance with Virginia law—by county, not population, as the last two conventions had been elected. Only delegates elected in the appropriate way could be said truly to represent the people. If the fourth convention agreed to these terms, and Congress approved the separation, statehood would go into effect.[26]

Many members of the court faction were upset by these conditions. A number of them began calling for an immediate separation without Virginia's approval. Adding to their frustration, the fourth convention, which met in September 1786, was a failure. Many delegates were absent because of expeditions against Native Americans, and there was no quorum. In January 1787 a quorum was achieved, and the convention agreed to the requirements of the Enabling Act, but the four-month delay had caused the convention to miss the deadline set by the Enabling Act, and their decisions were invalidated. Virginia needed to pass a second Enabling Act, which called for another convention to go through the same steps.[27]

The fifth convention met in September 1787, unanimously approved the second Enabling Act, and set a date for the election of delegates to a constitutional convention. The delegates chose John Brown, a leading lawyer and member of the Virginia Senate, to represent the district in a state delegation to push the separation through Congress. When the delegation arrived in New York City in December, however, it encountered further delays. The petition from the fifth convention was placed before Congress in February 1788, and the Virginians motioned that Congress approve the separation. In June a committee was established with one member from each state to draw up an act to grant statehood "in a mode conformable to the Articles of Confederation." In the midst of these discussions about Kentucky, however, the much more serious business of ratifying the new federal Constitution was underway. In July Congress decided that because nine states, including Virginia, had ratified the Constitution, it would be "manifestly improper" for the present Congress to take up such a significant matter. Nevertheless, it expressed the hope that the new Congress would act "as soon after proceedings shall commence under the said constitution as circumstances shall permit," so that "no impediment may be in the way of the speedy accomplishment of this important business."[28]

Growing numbers of Kentuckians saw nothing but impediments. Court party members were increasingly convinced that Virginian and congressional delays were deliberate and that Easterners were blocking statehood because they did not respect western rights. There was a new round of calls to ignore Virginia's Enabling Act and to declare independence unilaterally. These threats received a boost from a new issue in the statehood movement, which by this time was more significant than all others—foreign relations with Spain. The calls for immediate separation became tied to international intrigue, and the statehood process entered its most dramatic stage.

Phase Three: A Spanish Conspiracy

The United States might claim to possess territory to the banks of the Mississippi River, but Spanish officials in New Orleans controlled access to the river itself. Anyone wishing to bring goods down the river had to pay duties. Kentuckians who wished to export their produce had no other realistic option, because travel over the Appalachians was so difficult. Court party members, interested in developing the district's commercial prosperity, were extremely interested in securing stable access to the river. Therefore, they became alarmed when the Spanish Crown, in an effort to rein in American expansion, ordered the river closed in June 1784. For its part, Congress attempted to persuade Spain to open the river. Negotiations were undertaken between John Jay, secretary of foreign affairs, and Don Diego de Gardoqui, the Spanish plenipotentiary. Jay favored opening the river immediately but needed to devise a treaty proposal that would win adequate support in Congress. Many, especially in New England, openly opposed western settlement and the creation of western states, fearing that the interests and habits of the settlers would put them at odds with Easterners. In May 1786, Jay came from his talks with Gardoqui with a proposal to allow the river to remain closed for twenty-five to thirty years, in return for concessions. Jay's rationale was that western settlement was currently so sparse that such a plan would have little deleterious impact on the country.[29]

Jay acutely misread western and southern feelings. In late 1786, when news of Jay's proposal hit the West, it provoked immediate and widespread outrage. Westerners sent a flurry of petitions and letters to Congress protesting the proposed treaty. Kentuckians, already upset by eastern foot-dragging, threatened to secede from the Union if the treaty were approved. Court party member Caleb Wallace wrote to James Madison, "I fear if Congress cannot adjust this affair to the satisfaction of the western people, that their attachment to the American Union will be weakened."[30] John Campbell, a land speculator with an interest in a unilateral separation, similarly warned Madison that if Jay's proposals should go into effect, Westerners "will look upon themselves relieved from all Federal Obligations and fully at Liberty to exact alliances & Connections wherever they find them."[31]

Southerners, especially Virginians, were concerned about where such sentiments might lead. Many in Congress sympathized with Westerners and wanted to see prosperous western states. Madison recognized that if Jay's proposals were approved, they would "not fail to alienate the Western Country & confirm the animosity & jealousy already subsisting between the Atlantic States."[32] Similarly, Jefferson's survey of the situation gave him "serious apprehensions of the severance of the Eastern & Western parts of our confederacy.... [T]he moment we sacrifice their interests to our own, they will see it better to govern themselves."[33] The Virginia House of Delegates, responding to Kentuckians' cries, sought to appease them with a resolution to Congress opposing Jay's proposals, referring to "the just resentments and reproaches of our Western Brethren, whose essential rights and interests would be thereby sacraficed and sold."[34]

Despite such eastern support, many in Kentucky were not sure if these voices of reason would prevail in Congress. Some members of the court party became convinced that a future within the Union would never be satisfactory and began to explore other geopolitical alternatives for the West.

In spring 1787, James Wilkinson, a dominant figure within the court party, decided to take radical action to shape Kentucky's future. Wilkinson was a merchant and speculator with a strong personal interest in resolving the Mississippi question. He had been active in the statehood conventions but now embarked on a different route to solve Kentucky's problems. He loaded a flatboat with agricultural goods and took it down the river. Upon his arrival in New Orleans in June, he managed to talk and bribe his way into a meeting with Louisiana Governor Esteban Rodriguez Miro. Portraying himself as a man with considerable influence over the Kentucky political scene, Wilkinson convinced Miro that he could encourage Kentuckian leaders to approve a plan to make Kentucky a Spanish province. He successfully recommended that Kentuckians under Spanish authority be guaranteed religious freedom and local self-government. Wilkinson took an oath of allegiance to the Spanish crown. In return, he was granted a permit to ship goods to New Orleans. He returned to Kentucky in February 1788 and was greeted as a hero for his success in opening the river. He had a shipping monopoly, but he would be able to transport others' produce.

Historians will probably never know exactly what Wilkinson's plan was. He may have been simply playing on the dreams of Spanish officials for personal economic and political gain. He was forthcoming only to a few close associates in Kentucky and told different stories about how he had won his franchise depending on how he gauged their sentiments. Wilkinson knew that most Kentuckians were hardly interested in becoming Spanish subjects. He told most that he was only seeking Spanish military protection of an independent Kentucky or trade concessions. Regardless of the eventual outcome they envisioned, a small circle of Kentucky politicians was now committed to separating Kentucky from both Virginia and the Union.[35]

This cabal received additional endorsement from another location. Independently of the Wilkinson-Miro scheme, Spanish envoy Gardoqui approached John Brown, still in New York City, in summer 1788. Gardoqui made a similar proposal: that if Kentucky were to leave the Union, they could reach an accommodation on the Mississippi question. Brown believed that the best plan of action would be for Kentucky to declare independence unilaterally and then, if it seemed advantageous, to petition for admission into the federal Union. Brown's court party associates in Kentucky were encouraged when he informed them of his talks with Gardoqui.[36]

Wilkinson and his friends then decided to try to influence the statehood process in their favor. If they could persuade the other delegates to turn their backs on Virginia's mode for achieving statehood, they could declare independence immediately and proceed to develop some type of relationship with Spain. The sixth convention, which met in July 1788, had been intended by the delegates of the fifth convention to draft a constitution, but because Congress had chosen not to act on Kentucky statehood, the deadline set by the second Enabling Act had expired, and the delegates were legally prohibited from acting until Virginia passed yet another Enabling Act with a new timetable. Nevertheless, the delegates unilaterally made plans to hold a new convention that would have sweeping powers to create a new independent state, work out a solution to the Mississippi issue, and draft a state constitution. To acquire broad support for the expansive program, the right to vote for delegates was extended to all free men, in violation of Virginia's property qualification laws.

This extralegal statehood convention, the seventh, was held in November 1788. Wilkinson was elected chairman, and he openly proposed that Kentucky declare immediate independence so that it might make favorable terms with Spain regarding the Mississippi. Kentucky would then have the option of joining the Union if doing so seemed advantageous. It soon became clear that the court party could muster little support for this plan. An ambiguously worded resolution to make Kentucky independent from Virginia was rejected. Petitions opposing immediate separation, signed by hundreds of people, were presented for the convention's consideration. In the end, all the convention could do was issue addresses to Congress and the General Assembly. The latter accepted the legal framework Virginia had authorized. The delegates agreed to reconvene in August 1789, and in the meantime Virginia passed its third Enabling Act, putting the statehood process back on course. Most Kentuckians had decided to keep their faith in Virginia and Congress to meet their needs.

National events had shifted in Kentucky's favor. It had become clear in early 1787 that Jay's treaty proposals were dead, blocked by the southern states. By 1789, lawyer George Nicholas could assure Madison that most Kentuckians were not in favor of "a total separation from the union." Those who once had "remained silent in the Convention and have continued so since."[37] Negotiations between Spanish officials and the Kentucky conspirators faltered. Wilkinson left Kentucky in 1791.[38]

Having totally failed to achieve popular support for an immediate separation, the court party's influence on the statehood movement waned. Its image was tarnished by rumors of the secret negotiations with Spain, which would continue to dog these politicians well into the nineteenth century. Into the power vacuum stepped the country party. Now that Virginia was favorably inclined toward granting Kentucky independence, the country party, which had initially opposed separation, now supported it. Unlike the court party, however, its members had remained committed to working within the framework established by the General Assembly and were mostly uninvolved in the Spanish gambit. They were also Federalists and looked forward to Kentucky's participation within the new government. Now the road was clear for the admission of Kentucky into the Union through normal channels, with the security of Virginia's claim guaranteed. The country party took control of the statehood process and moved it to its conclusion.

Phase Four: The Virginia Compact

All was not smooth sailing, however, because yet another impediment to statehood presented itself. Because of congressional delays, Virginia needed to pass a third Enabling Act in December 1788 allowing for the election of delegates to an eighth statehood convention. This act was different from the previous two in that it had more stringent rules concerning the debt burden Kentucky would shoulder and Virginia's control over military lands. A wave of protests greeted this act, including new threats to secede. In spite of these objections, because the country party was now in charge, no obstructive action was taken. Nevertheless, Kentuckians were able to play on eastern fears of disunion to persuade Virginia to change its decision. A series of letters published in the *Virginia Gazette* in spring 1789 called this act a "wretched political decision" and suggested that Kentucky make a separate treaty with Spain to open the Mississippi.[39] George Nicholas warned Madison, "No people will remain long under a Government which does not afford protection.... [T]he people here have been taught to believe that they are to expect nothing but oppression and a sacrifice of their dearest rights from the new Government."[40] At the same time, Levi Todd reassured the governor that in truth, "a great majority of the District wish for a separation on amicable principles and an admission into the Federal Government."[41] The threat of actual secession had passed. The eighth convention did nothing more than petition the Assembly to remove the offending clauses from the third Enabling Act.

In December 1789 the Assembly passed the fourth (and final) Enabling Act, which reversed much of what the Kentuckians had found offensive about the third act. The ninth convention met in July 1790 and called for statehood, accepting the terms of the fourth Enabling Act, which would become known as the Virginia Compact, or Separation Agreement. There was some dissension. Although previous votes for statehood had been unanimous, the vote by this convention was 24–18. The partisans, who had opposed statehood since 1784, made a political comeback and put in a strong showing at this convention. They were still afraid that statehood would result in ruinous taxes. The policies would, as one petition put it, "devour our liberty" and provide "no security to our property."[42] Despite the strong partisan showing, the country party prevailed, and statehood was secured. June 1, 1792, was agreed on as the date for the separation to take effect. Besides final approval from Congress and the president, all that remained was for the tenth and last convention to draft a constitution.[43]

THE CONSTITUTION

Kentuckians wrote their constitution in the midst of a great deal of discussion of and experimentation with creative constitutionalism. The men in the convention had watched the original states write their constitutions in 1776 and then in many cases revise them in the 1780s. They had paid close attention to the drafting and ratification of both the Articles of Confederation and the United States Constitution. The latter document had been printed in the *Kentucky Gazette*, and fourteen Kentuckians had been members of the state ratification convention in Richmond. Kentuckians were also aware of the shift in thinking about constitutionalism that had taken place in the country. Whereas the original state constitutions had been more radical and put most power in the hands of the legislature, the newer ones were more concerned with a balance of power among the branches of government. The delegates were now working within a political culture steeped in constitution making, and they had many different models from which to choose.[44]

Despite this stimulating milieu, there was some concern about the caliber of leadership within the district. Was there sufficient collective talent to write a constitution? Appeals to eastern leaders like Madison and Jefferson for assistance were politely declined. The professionals who would have been most adept at writing a constitution, namely lawyers, had largely withdrawn from the political scene because of their embarrassing involvement in the Spanish conspiracy. Although in 1786 court party members had founded an informal debating organization, the Danville Political Club, to discuss the issues surrounding constitution making, only one actual member of the club served in the convention. Many Kentuckians were nervous about how the constitution would turn out, especially given the degree of factionalism apparent in the district.

Into the gap strode George Nicholas, who had arrived in Kentucky only in 1789, but who quickly became one of its most prominent citizens. Recognized as an excellent lawyer, he had been a member of the Virginia House of Delegates. He was a committed Federalist who had been a member of the ratifying convention and was friends with Madison and the future Republican Party establishment. Upon arriving in Kentucky, he had initially kept a low profile and so avoided damage to his reputation in the intense political atmosphere of the district. Now, as plans for the constitutional convention got underway, Nicholas assumed an active role. More than anyone else, his words and ideas shaped the final document.

The ninth convention set the ground rules for how delegates to the constitutional convention would be chosen. Free, white, adult males who had lived in Kentucky for one year could vote. Of the forty-five delegates chosen, representatives were almost equally divided between the partisan faction and the gentry. The court party was notably absent—only two lawyers had been elected. Given the dearth of delegates with solid legal or political experience, Nicholas was clearly the leading member. The most striking difference from the composition of previous conventions was the presence of seven ministers. No ministers had served on any of the statehood conventions. As events would show, their presence indicated the strength of the anti-slavery movement.

Through 1791 there was a flurry of interest in constitutional issues. The first newspaper in the district, the *Kentucky Gazette*, had been founded in 1787. Its pages were full of heated debate over the contours of the new constitution. Now that the new state was a fait accompli, the partisans decided to throw their weight into the constitution-drafting process to influence it in their favor. They formed several county committees to write proposals and instruct delegates. The Bourbon County committee put forward a strikingly democratic draft, including a one-house legislature and predominantly elective, rather than appointive, offices. In this model, county committees would retain an ongoing power to instruct the legislature, thereby retaining democratic control over the government and weakening the influence of lawyers and their ilk. The gentry expressed fears about the partisan influence on the convention and the potential for an inordinately populist constitution. They wanted the constitution-writing process to remain in their hands and questioned the legality of these committees. There was, therefore, a great deal of public discussion about how democratic the new constitution should be.

Besides democracy, slavery emerged as a key issue. By 1792, 23 percent of households in Kentucky owned slaves. The population of the area was diverse and growing rapidly, and there was a wide range of opinions on the "peculiar institution." Many wanted the state to protect slavery so that wealthy and respectable planters would be drawn to Kentucky and so boost its reputation. Although many ordinary white farmers looked forward to some day owning slaves themselves, others were opposed to the institution on moral, political, and economic grounds. Free blacks were a minuscule portion of the district's inhabitants, but their presence allowed them to serve as case studies of what emancipation would produce on a larger scale. A casual survey of the American political scene might have led one to assume that slavery was a dying institution. Gradual emancipation was being introduced in the New England states, and slavery had already been banned altogether in the Northwest Territory. When the convention opened, it was by no means clear if Kentucky would follow in the footsteps of its parent state.

The tenth convention got underway on April 2, 1792. Extant documents provide an incomplete record of the debates, but Nicholas emerged as the leader, and many of his initial proposals found a place in the final draft. One important way he maintained authority in the politically divided convention was by co-opting the partisans. Nicholas was by no means a democrat himself, but he was a pragmatist with ambitions to lead a state with a history of popular protest. He put forward democratic proposals like a one-house legislature, liberal suffrage laws, and direct election of the governor. Nicholas's astute political intuitions helped the process go more smoothly than it might otherwise have done. By April 13 the convention had come up with twenty-two resolutions that provided the framework for the document. A committee of ten, chaired by Nicholas, was appointed to draft an actual constitution. On April 17 the committee presented its draft, and two days later the draft was accepted by the convention. This was the end of the process. It was not deemed necessary to send the draft to the people for ratification. In a little over two weeks Kentucky had been furnished with its first constitution.

The final draft embodied a compromise between gentry and partisan demands. On the one hand there was an unusually strong governor and a comparatively weak lower house. The governor was not directly elected but was chosen by electors to serve a four-year term, the longest in the country, and without term limits. He had no elected committee or council to advise him. A strong governor, the gentry hoped, could serve as a check on dangerous democratic forces and deter a populist legislature from tinkering with land laws, as the partisans still hoped to do. On the other hand, the constitution also contained the most liberal suffrage requirements in the country. All free, adult men could vote, and election was by ballot, not voice. Nicholas justified these policies on the grounds that full manhood suffrage would actually guarantee the security of the propertied because it would inhibit corruption and make poor people more willing to accept the rule of the wealthy gentlemen who would, Nicholas was confident, be elected. Nicholas's curious blend of faith in and distrust of the people was perhaps typical of the shifting political landscape of the early Republic.

The framers took pains to codify how land disputes, the key source of political tension in the district, would be settled. The supreme court, known as the Court of Appeals, would "have original and final jurisdiction in all cases respecting the titles to land under the present land laws of Virginia…and in all cases concerning contracts for land, prior to the establishing of those titles." Complainants would need to produce their defenses in writing. Partisans had opposed giving the supreme court ultimate authorization for land cases, preferring to allow the legislature the final authority. Nicholas had succeeded in giving power to the courts, but, again, there were compromises. Land disputes required jury trials, and the legislature had the power to "pass an act or acts to regulate the mode of proceedings in such cases, or to take away entirely the original jurisdiction hereby given to the said court in such cases." The bill of rights also forbade debtors' prison, prohibited excessive bail and fines, and decreed "that all courts shall be open, and every person for an injury done him in his lands, goods, person or reputation, shall have remedy by the due course of law; and right and justice administered without sale, denial or delay."[45] These checks on the power of the court were enough to win the approval of the partisan delegates.

Compromise was also in evidence on the issue of slavery, but the victory for pro-slavery forces was clear. The constitution included an ironclad slavery defense in Article 9: "The Legislature shall have no power to pass laws for the emancipation of slaves without the consent of their owners, or without paying their owners" for the slaves.[46] The legislature also could not restrict slave owners from bringing their property into the state. Emancipation by individual owners was only possible if creditors were first paid their share of the slave's value and the freed men and women would not be a burden on the community. The bill of rights carefully stated, "[A]ll men, when they form a social compact, are equal."[47] The intent of this wording was to exclude slaves, who had not voted for representatives to the convention and so presumably were not included in the social compact. Following an eloquent appeal in the convention by David Rice, a Presbyterian minister, there had been a vote to keep the slavery article out of the constitution altogether, but it had been defeated sixteen to twenty-six, with slave ownership contributing to but not determining the voting pattern. All the ministers had voted against the article.[48] The constitution did allow the restriction of the slave trade and importation from abroad, and a slave code was authorized to protect the "humanity" of slaves. Nevertheless, this was the first state constitution explicitly to protect slavery.

For all its novelties, the first constitution of Kentucky was a rather derivative document. Its authors were practical men of the Enlightenment who were interested in conforming to English and American legal traditions. Precisely because of their long familiarity with its drawbacks, the Virginia state constitution was not their major influence. The partisans were most inspired by the radical 1776 Pennsylvania constitution, which provided a unicameral legislature, an elected executive council instead of a governor, annual elections, and vote by ballot. One of the members of the Kentucky convention had served on the 1776 Pennsylvania convention. The gentry, however, saw this model as one they needed to avoid. Pennsylvania had recently produced a new, more conservative constitution, and this constitution was the dominant influence on Nicholas and the final draft.[49]

FINAL CONGRESSIONAL AND PRESIDENTIAL ACTION

Each Enabling Act had specified that Congress must be consulted after Virginia and Kentucky approved the act and that it must give its consent for Kentucky to attain statehood. After the members of the ninth convention approved the Virginia Compact, they sent a message to the president and Congress informing them that an agreement had been reached. They attached a petition, similar to previous ones, declaring, "[T]he inhabitants of this country are warmly devoted to the American Union, and as firmly attached to the present happy establishment of the Federal Government, as any of the citizens of the United States." They explained that independence was necessary and that they had the numbers and wherewithal to deserve it:

> The inconveniences resulting from its local situation, as a part of Virginia, at first but little felt, have for some time been objects of their most serious attention.... It now remains with the President and the Congress of the United States to sanction these proceedings, by an act of their honorable Legislature... for the purpose of receiving into the Federal Union the people of Kentucky, by the name of the State of Kentucky.[50]

President Washington had long been familiar with events in the West and was keenly interested in making the region secure, strong, and connected to the East by commercial and political ties. In a sense, as a longtime land speculator with large holdings, he was a Westerner himself. Like most other members of the Virginia gentry, he had always supported his state's claim to the region against those of competing speculators and governments. He had been worried about the overtures made to Spanish officials by Kentucky politicos and had communicated in code with contacts in the region to keep up with the situation. Washington also favored statehood for Kentucky, provided it was obtained legally and peaceably. In his second annual Presidential address on December 8, 1790, he informed Congress of the separation agreement that had been made.

> The liberality and harmony with which it has been conducted will be found to do great honor to both the parties; and, the sentiments of warm attachment to the Union and its present Government, expressed by our fellow-citizens of Kentucky,

cannot fail to add an affectionate concern for their particular welfare to the great national impressions under which you will decide on the case submitted to you.[51]

The Senate replied to the president:

In confidence that every constitutional preliminary has been observed, we assure you of our disposition to concur, in giving the requisite sanction, to the admission of Kentucky as a distinct member of the Union; in doing which, we shall anticipate the happy effects to be expected from the sentiments of attachment towards the Union, and its present Government, which have been expressed by the patriotic inhabitants of that district.[52]

The House similarly responded that the conditions struck between Virginia and Kentucky "exhibit a liberality mutually honorable to the parties. We shall bestow upon this important subject the favorable consideration which it merits, brand, with the national policy which ought to govern our decision, shall not fail to mingle the affectionate sentiments which are awakened by those expressed on behalf of our fellow-citizens of Kentucky."[53] Given the years of rancor and the threats to American sovereignty in the region, it is not surprising that both Congress and the president wished to emphasize the themes of harmony, loyalty, and nationality.

A Senate committee was appointed to deal with the Kentucky issue. Upon reviewing the Virginia Compact, the committee concluded, "[I]t would be proper for Congress to consent that the said District should become an independent State and be admitted as a member of the United States of America." The Senate passed "[a]n act declaring the consent of Congress that a new State be formed within the jurisdiction of the Commonwealth of Virginia, and admitted into the Union, by the name of the State of Kentucky." The House of Representatives passed the act on February 4, 1791. The president then signed it.[54]

Two weeks later Congress passed the bill admitting Vermont. A sectional compromise had been made: a northern and a southern state would be admitted simultaneously. Initially, after the Revolution, Southerners had opposed the creation of new western states on the grounds that Westerners would hold ideas contrary to their own. Eventually, however, they judged that these new states would be southern first and western second, thereby augmenting southern power in Congress. James Monroe, for example, had at first opposed Kentucky statehood but eventually proposed "the admission of a few additional States into the Confederacy in the Southern Scale."[55] Northerners were arriving at the same conclusions. The paired admission helps explain why Kentucky's accession passed through Congress without much trouble.

CONCLUSION

The first set of elections in the new state went smoothly but quickly, to be ready in time for the June 4 deadline set in the Virginia Compact. Men voted for representatives and electors simultaneously. The electors subsequently selected the senators and governor. As first governor they chose Isaac Shelby, the popular Revolutionary War "hero of King's Mountain." Shelby had participated in the statehood conventions but had said little and emerged as a Washingtonian figure who transcended partisanship. The legislature proceeded to establish the court system and to look for a site for the state capitol.[56]

Nicholas's intent had been to create a strong government that could check democratic trends. Despite his diligence, it soon became apparent that real power in the new state was being channeled to forces not specified by the constitution. Because the state's population continued to expand rapidly through the 1790s, the central government could not maintain control over local affairs. Authority shifted downward to the county courts. Justices of the peace served life terms and were not elected but rather were chosen by other court members. Despite Nicholas's wish for a vigorous governor, Shelby chose not to engage the full scope of his powers. He rarely used the veto and left after one term. The plan of the convention delegates did not function as they expected it would.[57]

Perhaps aware of the potential for failure, the delegates had inserted into the constitution an important clause that in 1797 the voters could, if they so chose, elect representatives to a new constitutional convention to revise or replace the first constitution. This was a most significant constitutional compromise, because it allowed people the security of knowing that, if they were dissatisfied with the outcome, it might be only temporary. After seven years of loud calls for reform, a new convention was held. The second constitution, drafted in 1799, reflected the new realities in state government. It established a more pragmatic, less theoretical framework that recognized the power of the county courts, weakened the governor, and raised the profile of the General Assembly. Moreover, because slavery was even more entrenched and the emancipationists had lost potency, the delegates were free to add stronger defenses of the institution. Suffrage was specifically denied to free blacks, mulattos, and Indians. This second constitution remained in force until 1850.[58]

The political factions produced in the long statehood movement—the country party, the court party, and the partisans—played roles in state and national politics in the future, albeit in different guises. Party systems in both Kentucky and the United States were inchoate in the late eighteenth century but gradually achieved greater organization and firmer identity. Local groupings within the commonwealth became associated with the nascent national political parties. Members of the country party became members of the Federalist Party of Alexander Hamilton. The court party became aligned with the emergent Democratic Republican Party of Jefferson and Madison. The partisans remained a force in state politics, representing the interests of the small farmer and calling for a more democratic government than either of the two major parties was willing to contemplate. The statehood process had politicized Kentuckians and introduced them to the spectrum of political discourse.[59]

Kentucky was the first trans-Appalachian state, but despite regional leaders' hopes, western identity failed to override loyalties to the North and South. Kentucky was simultaneously a southern and a western state. The decision by Nicholas and other state leaders to racialize citizenship and to allow the perpetuation of slavery guaranteed that the Ohio River would become a sectional border. Other new states used the slavery clause in Kentucky's constitution as a model. An anti-slavery movement persisted well into the nineteenth century, and Kentuckians exhibited divided loyalties during the Civil War, but the fateful decision made in the first constitutional convention guaranteed that human bondage would be one of the American institutions to benefit from westward expansion.

In picking symbols for the new state, Governor Shelby stressed the theme of national and local unity. For the state motto, he chose the familiar slogan, "United We Stand, Divided We Fall." The state seal consisted of an image of "two friends embracing." Given the level of discord with national policies manifested in the 1780s, Shelby's wish to shore up relations with the federal government and Easterners metaphorically was logical. Statehood brought an end to the debate as to whether or not the West would be American. Spain episodically continued in its attempts to persuade Kentuckians to leave the Union, and some Kentuckians reopened discussions with Spanish officials in the 1790s, but never again was there a serious possibility of the region's falling into Spanish hands. The issue of sovereignty had been resolved. Statehood tied Kentuckians to the nation by giving them a direct role in policy-making and a stake in its success. The idea that the federal government did not represent western interests gradually faded, and, especially with the admission of new states like Tennessee and Ohio, the West would soon be coming into its own.

NOTES

1. William Littell, *Political Transactions in and Concerning Kentucky, From the First Settlement Thereof, Until it Became an Independent State, In June, 1792* (1806; reprint, Louisville: John P. Morton & Company, 1926), pp. 27, 37–38.

2. Lowell H. Harrison, *Kentucky's Road to Statehood* (Lexington: The University Press of Kentucky, 1992), p. 3; Peter S. Onuf, *The Origins of the Federal Republic: Jurisdictional Controversies in the United States, 1775–1787* (Philadelphia: University of Pennsylvania Press, 1983), pp. 78–79.

3. Jack M. Sosin, *Whitehall and Wilderness: The Middle West in British Colonial Policy, 1760–1775* (Lincoln: University of Nebraska Press, 1961), pp. 27–78, 99–180.

4. Richard White, *The Middle Ground: Indians, Empires, and Republics in the Great Lakes Region, 1650–1815* (Cambridge: Cambridge University Press, 1991), pp. 351–365. Colin G. Calloway, *The American Revolution in Indian Country: Crisis and Diversity in Native American Communities* (Cambridge: Cambridge University Press, 1995), pp. 158–163.

5. Quoted in Calloway, *American Revolution in Indian Country*, p. 166.

6. Ibid., pp. 163–181. Stephen Aron, *How the West Was Lost: The Transformation of Kentucky from Daniel Boone to Henry Clay* (Baltimore: The Johns Hopkins University Press, 1996), pp. 35–53.

7. Sosin, *Whitehall and Wilderness*, pp. 181–210.

8. Petition No. 2, dated June 7–15, 1776, in James Rood Robertson, ed., *Petitions of the Early Inhabitants of Kentucky to the General Assembly of Virginia, 1769 to 1792* (Louisville: John P. Morton & Company, 1914), pp. 36–37.

9. Onuf, *Origins of the Federal Republic*, pp. 84–85; Aron, *How the West Was Lost*, pp. 59–68.

10. Final draft of Virginia Constitution, in Julian P. Boyd, ed., *The Papers of Thomas Jefferson* (Princeton: Princeton University Press, 1950–present), 1:383.

11. Robert Johnson to Gov. [Patrick] Henry, December 5, 1786, *Calendar of Virginia State Papers and Other Manuscripts* (Richmond: Public Printer), 4:191.

12. Patricia Watlington, *The Partisan Spirit: Kentucky Politics, 1779–1792* (New York: Atheneum, 1972), pp. 3–27 (quotation on p. 16).

13. John Filson, *The Discovery and Settlement of Kentucke* (1784; reprint, Ann Arbor: University Microfilms, Inc., 1966), pp. 81–82.

14. Watlington, *Partisan Spirit*, pp. 44–53; Aron, *How the West Was Lost*, pp. 64–69.

15. Onuf, *Origins of the Federal Republic*, pp. 87–94.

16. Thomas Paine, *Public Good: Being an Examination into the Claim of Virginia...* (1780; reprint, Albany, 1793), pp. 11, 24, 34, 40–41.

17. Petition No. 15, endorsed 1782, in Robertson, *Petitions*, p. 64.

18. Watlington, *Partisan Spirit*, pp. 61–67. Harrison, *Kentucky's Road to Statehood*, pp. 13–14.

19. Watlington, *Partisan Spirit*, pp. 67–68; Onuf, *Origins of the Federal Republic*, pp. 94–102.

20. Editorial note, in Boyd, *Papers of Thomas Jefferson* 6:581–600. Robert F. Berkhofer, Jr., "Jefferson, the Ordinance of 1784, and the Origins of the American Territorial System," *William and Mary Quarterly* 3 (29) (April 1972): 231–262.

21. Thomas P. Abernethy, ed., "Journal of the First Kentucky Convention, Dec. 27, 1784–Jan. 5, 1785," *Journal of Southern History* 1 (1935): 67–78.

22. Watlington, *Partisan Spirit*, pp. 35–78, 109–113.

23. "Journal of May 1785 convention; extracts," in Littell, *Political Transactions*, p. 61.

24. Address reprinted in Thomas D. Clark, ed., *The Voice of the Frontier: John Bradford's Notes on Kentucky* (Lexington: The University Press of Kentucky, 1993), pp. 63–66.

25. "An act concerning the erection of the District of Kentucky into an independent State," in Littell, *Political Transactions*, pp. 72–73.

26. Harrison, *Kentucky's Road to Statehood*, pp. 34–42; Watlington, *Partisan Spirit*, pp. 103–06.

27. Harrison, *Kentucky's Road to Statehood*, pp. 42–46; Watlington, *Partisan Spirit*, pp. 107–108, 117–121.

28. W.C. Ford, et al., *Journals of the Continental Congress, 1774–1789* (Washington, DC: Government Printing Office, 1904–1937), 34:72–73, 194, 287–294.

29. Arthur Preston Whitaker, *The Spanish-American Frontier: 1783-1795* (Boston: Houghton Mifflin Company, 1927), pp. 63–77, 90–96.

30. Caleb Wallace to Madison, November 12, 1787, in William T. Hutchinson and William M.E. Rachal, ed., *The Papers of James Madison, Congressional Series* (Chicago: University of Chicago Press; Charlottesville: University Press of Virginia, 1962–1991) (hereafter cited as *PJM*) 10:249–250.

31. John Campbell to Madison, February 21, 1787, *PJM* 10:287.

32. Madison to James Madison, Sr., November 1, 1786, *PJM* 9:154.

33. Jefferson to Madison, December 16, 1786, *PJM* 9:211.

34. "Resolutions Reaffirming American Rights to Navigate the Mississippi," November 29, 1786, *PJM* 9:183.

35. On Wilkinson, see Harrison, "James Wilkinson: A Leader for Kentucky?" *Filson Club Historical Quarterly* 66 (July 1992): 334–368. Watlington, *Partisan Spirit*, pp. 139–147.

36. Watlington, *Partisan Spirit*, pp. 160–165.

37. George Nicholas to Madison, May 8, 1789, *PJM* 12:138.

38. Harrison, *Kentucky's Road to Statehood*, pp. 67–72; Watlington, *Partisan Spirit*, pp. 175–182.

39. Quoted in Hazel Dicken-Garcia, *To Western Woods: The Breckinridge Family Moves to Kentucky in 1793* (London: Associated University Presses, 1991), pp. 133–134.

40. George Nicholas to Madison, 8 May 1789, *PJM* 12:138–141.

41. Levi Todd to Gov. Beverly Randolph, May 27, 1789, in *Calendar of Virginia State Papers* 4:630.

42. Petition No. 58, summer 1789, in Robertson, ed., *Petitions*, pp. 121–122.

43. Harrison, *Kentucky's Road to Statehood*, pp. 81, 86–90.

44. On Nicholas, see Harrison, *Kentucky's Road to Statehood*, pp. 74–75, 96–97; Watlington, *Partisan Spirit*, pp. 200–203; Joan Wells Coward, *Kentucky in the New Republic: The Process of Constitution Making* (Lexington: University Press of Kentucky, 1979), pp. 12–15.

45. "The Kentucky Constitution of 1792," in Harrison, *Kentucky's Road to Statehood*, pp. 159–160, 166.

46. Ibid., pp. 162–163.

47. Ibid., p. 164.

48. Watlington, *Partisan Spirit*, pp. 220–221.

49. On Kentucky's first constitution, see Harrison, *Kentucky's Road to Statehood*, pp. 93–130. Watlington, *Partisan Spirit*, pp. 209–222. Coward, *Kentucky in the New Republic*, pp. 15–47.

50. *Debates and Proceedings in the Congress of the United States, 1789-1824*, 42 vols. (Washington, DC: Gales and Seaton, 1834–1856), 2:1731–1732.

51. Ibid., p. 1729.

52. Ibid., p. 1733.

53. Ibid., p. 1799.

54. Ibid., pp. 1742, 1745, 1862, 1885.

55. Quoted in Onuf, *Origins of the Federal Republic*, p. 154.

56. Harrison, *Kentucky's Road to Statehood*, pp. 131–148.

57. Coward, *Kentucky in the New Republic*, pp. 48–96.

58. Ibid., pp. 97–161.

59. Watlington, *Partisan Spirit*, pp. 225–234.

BIBLIOGRAPHY

Abernethy, Thomas P., ed. "Journal of the First Kentucky Convention, Dec. 27, 1784– Jan. 5, 1785." *Journal of Southern History* 1 (1935): 67–78.

Allen, Jeffrey Brooke. "The Origins of Proslavery Thought in Kentucky, 1792–1799." *Register of the Kentucky Historical Society* 77 (Spring 1979): 75–90.

Aron, Stephen. *How the West Was Lost: The Transformation of Kentucky from Daniel Boone to Henry Clay.* Baltimore: The Johns Hopkins University Press, 1996.

Asperheim, Stephen. "Double Characters: The Making of American Nationalism in Kentucky, 1792–1833." Ph.D. dissertation, University of Illinois at Urbana-Champaign, 2003.

Clark, Thomas D., ed. *The Voice of the Frontier: John Bradford's Notes on Kentucky.* Lexington: The University Press of Kentucky, 1993.

Coward, Joan Wells. *Kentucky in the New Republic: The Process of Constitution Making.* Lexington: The University Press of Kentucky, 1979.

Filson, John. *The Discovery and Settlement of Kentucke.* 1784. Reprint. Ann Arbor: University Microfilms, Inc., 1966.

Harrison, Lowell H. *The Antislavery Movement in Kentucky.* Lexington: The University Press of Kentucky, 1978.

———. *Kentucky's Road to Statehood.* Lexington: The University Press of Kentucky, 1992.

Onuf, Peter S. *The Origins of the Federal Republic: Jurisdictional Controversies in the United States, 1775–1787* . Philadelphia: University of Pennsylvania Press, 1983.

Robertson, James Rood, ed. *Petitions of the Early Inhabitants of Kentucky to the General Assembly of Virginia, 1769 to 1792.* Louisville: John P. Morton & Company, 1914.

Watlington, Patricia. *The Partisan Spirit: Kentucky Politics, 1779–1792* . New York: Atheneum, 1972.

Wrobel, Sylvia and George Grider. *Isaac Shelby: Kentucky's First Governor and Hero of Three Wars.* Danville, KY: The Cumberland Press, 1974.